CONTINUOUS-TIME FINANCE

Robert C. Merton

Foreword by

Paul A. Samuelson

BLACKWELL
Cambridge MA & Oxford UK

First published 1990
Revised and first published in paperback 1992
Reprinted 1993

Blackwell Publishers
238 Main Street
Cambridge, Massachusetts 02142, USA

108 Cowley Road, Oxford, OX4 1JF, UK

Library of Congress Cataloging in Publication Data

Merton, Robert C.
  Continuous-time finance/Robert C. Merton; foreword by Paul A.
    Samuelson
    p. cm.
  Includes bibliographical references.
  ISBN 0–631–15847–2
       0–631–18508–9 (Pbk)
    1. Finance—Mathematical models. 2. Investments—Mathematical
models. 3. Portfolio management—Mathematical models. 4. Options
(Finance)—Mathematical models. 5. Finance, Public—Mathematical
models. I. Title.
HG173.M44 1990   89–18169
332′.01′18—dc20   CIP

British Library Cataloguing in Publication Data
A CIP catalogue record for this book is available from the British Library.

Typeset in 10 on 12pt Times
by TecSet Ltd, Wallington, Surrey.
Printed in the USA

This book is printed on acid-free paper

Contents

Foreword

A great economist of an earlier generation said that, useful though economic theory is for understanding the world, no one would go to an economic theorist for advice on how to run a brewery or produce a mousetrap. Today that sage would have to change his tune: economic principles really do apply and woe to the accountant or marketer who runs counter to economic law. Paradoxically, one of our most elegant and complex sectors of economic analysis – the modern theory of finance – is confirmed daily by millions of statistical observations. When today's associate professor of security analysis is asked, "Young man, if you're so smart, why ain't you rich?", he replies by laughing all the way to the bank or to his appointment as a high-paid consultant to Wall Street.

Among connoisseurs, Robert C. Merton is known as an expert among experts, a giant who stands on the shoulders of such giants as Louis Bachelier, John Burr Williams, George Terborgh, Keynes, James Tobin and Harry Markowitz, Kenneth Arrow and Gerard Debreu, John Lintner and William Sharpe, Eugene Fama, Benoit Mandelbrot, and the ubiquitous Black–Scholes. (Benjamin Graham occupies another part of the forest.) The pole that propelled Merton to Byronic eminence was the mathematical tool of continuous probability à la Norbert Wiener and Kiyoshi Itô. Suddenly what had been complex approximation became beautifully simple truth.

The present book patiently explicates for readers with imperfect mathematical background the essentials of efficient-market asset pricing. Many of its chapters reproduce articles that have become classics in the literature. Several chapters are new to this book and break novel ground.

I am proud to have figured in the Mertonian march to fame. When a youngster, with an electrical engineering bachelor degree and beginning Cal Tech graduate work in applied mathematics, decided to be an economist, he applied to several graduate schools for admission in economics. All but one, he says, turned him down: MIT, *mirabile dictu*, offered him a fellowship! He worked with me and was a joy to work with. One of the great pleasures in academic life is to see a younger savant develop, evolving into a colleague and co-author – and then, best of all, is the rare sight of the companion at arms who forges ahead of you as you were able to do at the inflection point of your own career. Robert K.

Merton, anthropological observer of the zoo of scientists (and fond mentor of Robert C.), will want to add this saga to his case studies of how science actually evolves.

   To the reader I repeat:
Bon Appetit!

Paul A. Samuelson
MIT

Preface

This book develops the mathematics and economic theory of finance from the perspective of a model in which agents can revise their decisions continuously in time. Time and uncertainty are the central elements that influence financial economic behavior. It is the complexity of their interaction that provides intellectual challenge and excitement to the study of finance. To analyze the effects of this interaction properly often requires sophisticated analytical tools. Indeed, advanced mathematical training has become a prerequisite for researchers in the field. Yet, for all its mathematical complexity, finance theory has had a direct and significant influence on finance practice. A casual comparison of current practices with those of 20 years ago is enough to note the impact of efficient market theory, portfolio selection, risk analysis, and contingent-claim pricing theory on money management, financial intermediation, investment banking, and corporate financing and capital budgeting procedures. The effects of this theory have even been observed in legal proceedings such as appraisal cases, hearings on rates of return for regulated industries, and revisions of the "prudent person" laws governing behavior for fiduciaries. The role of finance theory in the current wave of financial innovations in capital markets has been often documented in the financial press. See especially the carefully researched book by Bernstein (1992). Evidence that this influence on practice will continue can be found in the curricula of the best-known schools of management, where the fundamental financial research papers (with their mathematics included) are routinely assigned to MBA students. Although not unique, this conjoining of intrinsic intellectual interest with extrinsic application is a distinctive and prevailing theme of research in finance.

It was not always thus. Finance was first treated as a separate field of study early in this century, and for the next 40 years it was almost entirely a descriptive discipline with a focus on institutional and legal matters. As recently as a generation ago, finance theory was still little more than a collection of anecdotes, rules of thumb, and manipulations of accounting data. The most sophisticated tool of analysis was discounted value and the central intellectual controversy centered on whether to use present value or internal rate of return to rank corporate investments. The subsequent evolution from this conceptual potpourri to a rigorous economic theory subjected to scientific empirical examination was, of course, the work of many, but most observers would agree that Arrow, Debreu, Lintner, Markowitz, Miller, Modigliani, Samuelson, Sharpe, and Tobin were the early pioneers in this transformation.

Since the continuous-time model is the mode of analysis used throughout the book, a few background remarks on the model as both synthesis and watershed of finance theory are perhaps in order. It was in 1900 at the Sorbonne that Louis Bachelier wrote his magnificent dissertation on the theory of speculation. This work marks the simultaneous births of both the continuous-time mathematics of stochastic processes and the continuous-time economics of option and derivative-security pricing. Although Bachelier's research was unknown in the economics and finance literature for more than a half-century and although from today's perspective his economics and mathematics are flawed, the lineage from Bachelier to modern continuous-time finance is direct and indisputable.

Over the past two decades, the continuous-time model has proved to be a versatile and productive tool in the development of finance. Although mathematically more complex, the continuous-time formulation often provides just enough additional specificity to produce both more precise theoretical solutions and more refined empirical hypotheses than can otherwise be derived from its discrete-time counterpart. As a case in point, we need only consider an early version of the continuous-time model of portfolio selection first published in 1969 and reprinted here as Chapter 4. In the late 1960s, the primary capital-market models in finance were the one-period mean–variance model of Markowitz and Tobin and its equilibrium version, the Sharpe–Lintner–Mossin Capital Asset Pricing Model. Although quite feasible for practical use and remarkably elegant in their simplicity, these models nevertheless received relatively limited application in the broader community of economic research. The main reason was a widespread belief that the mean–variance criterion is not consistent with the generally accepted von Neumann–Morgenstern axioms of choice unless either asset prices have Gaussian probability distributions or investor preferences are quadratic. In addition to being rather specialized conditions, normal distributions for prices violate the fundamental provision of limited liability for owners of financial assets. Furthermore, quadratic utility appears to be grossly inconsistent with observed behavior. However, by replacing the generic "one period" with a definite specification of the time interval between successive portfolio revisions, the continuous-time model with log-normally distributed asset prices (which do satisfy limited liability) produces optimal portfolio rules that are identical in form with those prescribed by the mean–variance model and the Capital Asset Pricing Model. Moreover, this result obtains for general von Neumann–Morgenstern preferences. Thus, somewhat paradoxically, introducing the greater realism of a dynamic intertemporal model served to make more plausible the optimal rules derived from these classic static models.

In this sense, the continuous-time model is a watershed between the static and dynamic models of finance. As we shall see in the chapters to follow, continuous-time analysis shows that those other classic pillars of finance theory – the Arrow–Debreu complete-markets model and the Modigliani–Miller theorems – are also far more robust than had been believed.

While reaffirming old insights, the continuous-time model also provides new ones. Perhaps no better example is the seminal contribution of Black and Scholes that, virtually on the day it was published, brought the field to closure on the subjects of option and corporate-liability pricing. As the Black–Scholes work was closing gates on fundamental research in these areas, it was simultaneously opening new gates: in applied and empirical study and in setting the foundation for a new branch of finance called contingent-claims analysis. As shown in Part IV, the applications of contingent-claims analysis range from the pricing of complex financial securities to the evaluation of corporate capital budgeting and strategic decisions. As we shall also see, it has an important place in the theory of financial intermediation.

As surely exemplified by the more than a thousand equations that appear in this volume, finance is a highly analytical subject, and nowhere more so than in continuous-time analysis. Indeed, the mathematics of the continuous-time finance model contains some of the most beautiful applications of probability and optimization theory. But, of course, not all that is beautiful in science need also be practical. And surely, not all that is practical in science is beautiful. Here we have both. With all its seemingly abstruse mathematics, the continuous-time model has nevertheless found its way into the mainstream of finance practice. Perhaps its most visible influence on practice has been in the pricing and hedging of financial instruments, an area that has experienced an explosion of real-world innovations over the last decade. In fact, much of the applied research on using the continuous-time model in this area now takes place within practicing financial institutions.

Any virtue can readily become a vice merely by being carried to excess, and just so with application of the continuous-time paradigm. Its powerful analytics are a temptation to excessive focus on mathematical rigor with the unhappy consequence of leaving the accompanying substantive economics inaccessible to all but a few. Attention to formal technique without equal attention to the underlying economics assumptions leads to misplaced concreteness by confusing rigor in the mathematical sense with rigor in the economic sense. In Chapter 3, the mathematics and basic economics assumptions of the continuous-time model are developed with this in mind. The focus is on those mathematical concepts such as the Itô calculus that are essential for applying continuous-time analysis in finance. By taking elementary probability theory and ordinary calculus as its only prerequisites, the chapter sacrifices some mathematical rigor and generality in return for greater accessibility and, I hope, clarity. In the same spirit, the derivation of stochastic dynamic programming in Chapter 4 also requires no more than these prerequisites. Ample mathematical references are, of course, provided for those who would prefer a broader and more formal treatment of the subject.

As in mathematics, emphasis on compactness of models and their presentation is a virtue highly prized in mathematical economics. But, when taken to an extreme, such emphasis has the surely unintended consequence of reducing the substantive richness of the analysis by deleting institutional settings and interpretations of the models that are seemingly redundant from the mathematical perspective but that are not at all redundant in the economics domain. It will be granted that the model development and analysis presented here are not immune to excessive austerity of this particular kind. Yet, especially but not exclusively in the chapters on financial intermediation and general equilibrium theory, I try my hand at correcting such omissions, by including considerably more institutional interpretation of the models than is the usual practice in neoclassical economics treatments of finance theory. Perhaps I will be forgiven if, in places, my attempts to avoid excessive laconism lead to sheer verbosity.

The core of the book is a collection of 15 previously published papers and a widely circulated working paper, written over the period spanning from 1969 to the present. These chapters are organized into six parts according to subject matter rather than date of original publication. In reprinting these articles, I have made minor revisions in language and have corrected misprints and technical errors without indicating changes from the original. An asterisk identifies added footnotes that describe either more extensive revisions or citations to subsequent research on the topic. Published references are substituted for original citations of unpublished manuscripts and working papers that have subsequently appeared in print. The original notation of each paper is preserved and notation is therefore not entirely uniform across the chapters. And since each chapter is largely self-contained, some repetition of analyses does occur. Perhaps some readers will find these repetitions a useful form of emphasis to underscore important concepts in the theory.

I need hardly say that when these papers were first written they were not intended as chapters of a single volume on the continuous-time theory of finance. It would be foolish therefore to suggest that this format of synthesis is an unconstrained optimal design. Temporal differences in the original publication of the papers would alone dictate a path of development for the subject that follows its historical evolution more closely than might otherwise be optimal. I nevertheless harbor the hope that a logical coherence will be found in the organization of the parts and the selection of papers. To facilitate the continuity and expand the scope of coverage, I have added five essays to the core of reprinted papers. Written expressly for the book, these essays include a short introductory chapter and four other chapters in the areas of optimal consumption and portfolio selection, option pricing, financial intermediation, and general equilibrium theory. To provide unity with the core, each of these chapters follows the same self-contained style of a separate journal article. Other new materials on intertemporal capital asset pricing and contingent-claims analysis have been added. These appear not as separate essays but, to preserve the continuity of subject matter further, have been placed in new sections added to the original papers on those topics reprinted as Chapters 13 and 15.

Many economists and mathematicians have contributed to the development of the continuous-time theory of finance. Whenever known, they are referenced in the text and in the numerous notes to the individual chapters. There are, undoubtedly, others whose contributions are not cited but should be, and to them, I offer both blanket apology and acknowledgment. But, even if the list of citations were complete, it would still be inadequate to trace all the sources of influence that over the years led me to the conceptions set forth in this book. Among those sources, there are a few to whom I owe special and long-standing debts that I want to acknowledge here.

The earliest of these debts, incurred before my ever studying economics, is to the Columbia School of Engineering and the California Institute of Technology. With its small and flexible program and fine faculty, Columbia was a great place for an undergraduate to explore mathematics and its applications. It was there that I first became intrigued with stochastic processes and optimal control theory. I remember with particular fondness John Chu's course on heat transfer that turned on the light for me regarding the power of advanced mathematics for solving real-world problems. A brief year of graduate study at Cal Tech added much to my stock of mathematics. Most valuable was the Cal Tech creed of immediately involving students in "playing" with the subject in a quasi-research mode rather than just passively absorbing information. I am grateful to Gerald Whitham (then department head) who, although he thought it was "crazy," supported my decision to leave Cal Tech (and mathematics) to study economics. Among other things, he allowed me to take economics courses with Alan Sweezy and Horace Gilbert (surely an interesting combination for one's introduction to the subject).

To members of the Economics Department at Massachusetts Institute of Technology in 1967, I am deeply indebted for their taking a flyer and admitting one with no background in economics, when departments elsewhere would not. I am especially thankful to Harold Freeman who (as I discovered only later) was instrumental in the Department's decision and who, on my arrival in Cambridge, advised me to eschew the standard first-term curriculum and to take Paul Samuelson's course in mathematical economics.

To that teacher, mentor, colleague, co-researcher, and long-time friend, Paul A. Samuelson, I have come to owe an incalculable debt. Again, as before (cf. Merton, 1983a), I cannot find the words to pay adequate tribute to him. Reiteration would only dull the insufficient thanks expressed on those occasions. Instead, I say only this: because of Paul, no one could have had a better introduction to the study of economics than mine. After taking that course of Paul's (which erased any lingering doubts that Whitham was wrong), I had the great good fortune to spend the rest of my graduate student years living in his office as both research assistant and tutee.

As readers of the following pages will soon recognize, I owe a great debt to a circle of brilliant colleagues in the Finance Group at MIT Sloan School of Management: Fischer Black, John Cox, Chi-fu Huang, Franco Modigliani, Stewart Myers, Myron Scholes, and – as always, gladly included as *ex officio* members of the Group – Stanley Fischer and Paul Samuelson. The tenure and tenor of this small collegium varied considerably during my 18 years at Sloan. Indeed, the entire finance faculty rarely numbered more than a half dozen. But, throughout those years, there were reliable constants among my colleagues: quality of mind, diversity of thought, and a genuine affection for one another. Sloan was not only a stimulating place in which to do research; it was also a happy place for research.

Added to this array of long-term debts, there are other, current debts. I am especially indebted to Peter Dougherty for proposing the book and for his unwavering confidence that a selected combination of my published papers, together with some new material, would have a value exceeding the sum of its parts. I trust only that the final result approximates his expectations. As acknowledged in later notes, I am grateful to various publishers for permission to reprint papers appearing in their journals and to Paul Samuelson for agreeing to have our joint paper reprinted as Chapter 7. Aid from the National Science Foundation, which supported the work reported in several of the chapters, is also gratefully acknowledged. I am thankful to the MIT Sloan School of Management for a reflective sabbatical year during which much of the book was written and to the Harvard Graduate School of Business Administration for providing research facilities and support that year and since.

I have been blessed by having a remarkable and still young applied mathematician serve as a research assistant on the book. With great skill and verve, Arnout Eikeboom checked each of the dozens of theorems and hundreds of equations. It was pure serendipity when he also showed an equal talent for uncovering and correcting poorly phrased text, confusing notation, and even mere errors of spelling. My special thanks to Deborah

Hannon for typing a difficult manuscript and for general administrative assistance in preparing the volume. To one of the six to whom this book is dedicated, I am deeply grateful for editorial suggestions, and so much more.

R. C. Merton
Harvard University

To

June

Samantha, Robert F., and Paul

Suzanne and Robert K.

with

unbounded love, admiration, and gratitude

Part I

Introduction to Finance and the Mathematics of Continuous-Time Models

1

Modern Finance

It is generally agreed that financial management of firms and households, intermediation, capital market and microinvestment theory, and much of the economics of uncertainty fall within the sphere of modern finance. As is evident from its influence on other branches of economics including public finance, industrial organization, and monetary theory, the boundaries of this sphere, like other specialties, are both permeable and flexible.[1] The theoretical and empirical literatures covering this large and imperfectly defined discipline are truly vast. Furthermore, the theme of extensive interplay between research and practical application is quite distinctive of the finance corpus. Thus, even with the "continuous-time" qualifier in its title, this book's promise of a general synthesis does not suffer from undue modesty of dimension.

We know that synthesis involves abstraction from the complex whole. Here, we must be severely selective in our abstractions, since the wide-ranging scope and seemingly unbounded volume of finance researches allows only a few aspects of the work to be developed. Moreover, the law of comparative disadvantage rules out my examining either empirical or applied matters in fitting detail. I therefore use annotated references and notes to only touch upon those important elements of the subject. But, even with this understandable focus on theory, further stringent abstraction remains necessary. It is surely better to abstract by concentrating in detail on a small subset of the theory than by attempting to summarize the whole of it: hence the notion of an anthology on finance theory from the perspective of the continuous-time model. And so by way of a general introduction, I survey the limited set of topics to be covered in this book.

The core of the theory is the study of how best to allocate and deploy resources across time in an uncertain environment and of the role of economic organizations in facilitating these allocations. The key organizations in finance are households, business firms, financial intermediaries, and capital markets. The tradition in neoclassical economics is to take the existence of households, their tastes, and their endowments as exogenous

Portions of this chapter draw heavily on Merton (1983a, 1989, 1990a).

1 Cf. Fischer and Merton (1984) for a discussion of topics in finance that intersect with macroeconomics.

to the theory. However, this tradition does not extend to other economic organizations and institutions. They are regarded as existing primarily because of the functions they serve and are therefore endogenous to the theory. Thus, optimal financial behavior of households is derived from individual and exogenously specified preference functions that rank-order alternative programs of lifetime consumption and bequests for each household. In contrast, optimal management decisions for business firms and financial intermediaries are derived from criteria determined by the functions of those organizations within the financial economic system.

In the models of this book, business firms serve the principal functions of owning the physical ("real") assets and operating the production technologies of the economy. The real assets held by firms include both tangible assets, such as machinery, factories, and land, and intangible assets, such as an ongoing organizational structure, trademarks, and patents. Purchases of these assets are financed by issuing financial securities, such as stocks and bonds, either to households or to financial intermediaries. The managers who make the capital budgeting and financing decisions for the firms are treated as agents of the owners who are the current stockholders.[2] It follows that the primary objective of management is to operate the firm in the best interests of the stockholders.[3]

In both theory and practice, financial intermediaries often act as agents of their household and business-firm customers to provide transactional services including money transfer. However, their main function in the

2 A stereotypical corporate structure in which ownership and active management of firms are generally separated is assumed throughout the book. Division of labor, comparative advantage, and economies of scale including reductions of redundant information processing provide the well-known arguments for gains in economic efficiency from such separations in large and diverse economies. However, this separation inevitably leads to conflicts between owners' and managers' interests that can also cause losses in efficiency. Jensen and Meckling (1976) discuss this basic "principal–agent" problem and present a theory of agency to analyze the rich set of alternative organizational forms, management incentive systems, and approaches to financial contracting that we observe in the real world. Williamson (1988) pursues a different line of inquiry to explain these same observations.

3 It is my understanding that, under US laws, managers are viewed as fiduciaries, which implies an even stronger legal obligation to shareholders than if they were simply the owners' agents. This stronger legal bonding does not, of course, obligate managers to benefit owners by violating other laws, nor does it prohibit managers from giving due consideration to other stakeholders of the firm. Common practice in finance theory is to translate this obligation to shareholders into the simple operating imperative: maximize the current value of the equity of the firm. Although in efficiency terms this rule works for entirely equity-financed firms in an environment with frictionless, competitive, and complete financial markets it does not apply in general. See Merton and Subrahmanyam (1974), Merton (1982a, Section 6) and Duffie (1988, Section 13) for references and a discussion of conditions under which value maximization produces efficient economic allocations.

analyses here is to act as principals and create financial instruments that, because of scale and specificity of terms, cannot be efficiently supported by direct trading in organized financial markets. Demand deposits, commercial loans, private placement of corporate securities, mortgages, mutual funds, annuities, and a wide range of insurance contracts are among the financial products offered by "real-world" intermediaries such as commercial banks, investment banks, thrift institutions, and insurance companies. Although some of these specific products and institutions are used for descriptive purposes in the text, the focus is on the economic function of financial intermediaries and their products rather than on their particular institutional forms.

Like business firms, financial intermediaries raise capital for operations by issuing stock and debt to investors. The theory therefore assumes that managers of intermediaries and business firms share the same primary objective of maximizing the interests of current stockholders. But, unlike business firms, intermediaries hold only financial assets and, more importantly, they create explicit new liabilities whenever they sell their products.[4] Indeed, we know that in the real world the vast bulk of insurance company and bank liabilities are held by their customers, not their investors. Arising from the specific economic function of intermediaries, this distinctive characteristic leads to a theory of managerial and regulatory behavior for intermediaries that differs from that derived for business firms.

The capital market is the collection of organized financial markets for trading standardized securities such as stocks, bonds, futures contracts, and options.[5] It provides the central external environment connecting the financial activities of households, business firms, and intermediaries. By transacting in the capital market, firms raise the funds necessary for investment and households deploy their savings to be used for future consumption. In the basic cash-flow cycle, firms sell securities to households and use the cash to purchase real assets for their production operations. Later, the firms make dividend and interest payments and undertake repurchases of their securities to return the cash generated by these operations to the household sector. A portion of these cash flows is used for current consumption and the balance is recycled through the

---

4 For a typical financial product, a customer pays cash to the intermediary now in return for a contract promising a stream of state-contingent cash payments in the future. Issuance of this contract thus creates a liability for the intermediary. Of course, business firms almost always incur some implicit liabilities whenever they sell their products, and these become explicit in the case of product warranties. However, the magnitude of these liabilities as a fraction of total product sales is considerably smaller for business firms than for intermediaries.

5 In places, we expand this definition to include financial intermediaries and their financial products.

capital market back to the business firms to support further investment. As with the products offered by financial intermediaries, the function of the often-elaborate menu of securities traded in the capital market is to provide households with risk-pooling and risk-sharing opportunities that facilitate the efficient allocation of resources.

In addition to these manifest functions, the capital market serves an important, perhaps more nearly latent, function as a key source of information that helps coordinate decentralized decision-making in the various sectors of the economy. Security prices and interest rates are used by households in making their consumption–saving decisions and in choosing the allocation of their wealth among the available assets. These same prices provide critical signals to managers of firms in their selection of investment projects and financings. Thus, even managers of firms with no anticipated need to transact in the capital market will nevertheless use that market to acquire information for decisions.[6] Efficient separation of financial functions among specialized organizations can obtain only if there is a corresponding separation of the information sets needed to perform each function. A common theme threaded throughout the chapters of this book, therefore, is the influence of information requirements on the design of financial instruments and organizations.

The exogenous–endogenous asymmetry of the treatment of households and other economic organizations makes examination of the optimal financial behavior of households a natural entry point for study of the financial economic system. Households are both consumers and investors, and their financial decisions reflect those dual roles. As consumer, the household chooses how much of its income and wealth to allocate to current consumption, and thereby how much to save for future consumption including bequests. As investor, the household solves the portfolio-selection problem to determine the fractional allocations of its savings among the available investment opportunities. In general, the optimal consumption–saving and portfolio-selection decisions cannot be made independently of each other. For that reason, the continuous-time model is applied first in Part II to solve the combined lifetime consumption and portfolio-selection problem for the individual household.

Two reference chapters precede the analyses in Part II. Designed to provide background on basic terminology, concepts, and theorems in capital-market theory, Chapter 2 formulates and solves the portfolio-selection problem in the classical static framework, taking as given the

---

6 The conscious motivation for creating a capital market is to provide the means for financial transactions. However, an objective consequence of this action is to produce a flow of information that is essential for all agents' decision-making, including that of those agents who only rarely transact in the market. The manifest and latent functions of social behavior and organizations as a general analytical idea is developed by R. K. Merton (1957, Ch. 1).

household's consumption decision. To help locate and connect the findings of the continuous-time model with those of the one-period models, emphasis is placed on derivations of spanning and mutual-fund theorems, the Ross Arbitrage Pricing Theory (APT) Model, and the Sharpe–Lintner–Mossin Capital Asset Pricing Model (CAPM). Chapter 3 contains an introduction to the mathematics of continuous-time processes including Itô's calculus and stochastic differential equations for mixtures of diffusion and Poisson-driven random variables.

In Chapter 4, the basic two-asset version of the lifetime consumption and portfolio-selection problem is solved by using stochastic dynamic programming. Since modeling ideas often originate in a discrete-time setting, the analysis begins with a discrete-time formulation of the intertemporal model and then derives the continuous-time formulation as a limiting case. This approach also permits a development of the optimality equations that requires no more mathematical background than Taylor's theorem and elementary probability theory. By assuming a risky asset with log-normally distributed returns and a riskless asset with a constant interest rate, we derive explicit optimal consumption and portfolio rules for households with preferences that exhibit either constant relative risk aversion or constant absolute risk aversion. The intertemporal age-dependent behavior of optimal consumption is shown to be consistent with the Modigliani –Brumberg Life-Cycle Hypothesis. The derived optimal portfolio rules have the same structure as those prescribed in the Markowitz–Tobin mean–variance model.

In Chapter 5, the model is expanded to include wage income, uncertain lifetimes, and several assets with more general probability distributions of returns. Itô's lemma is introduced as a tool for analyzing the dynamics of asset prices, wealth, and consumption. In the prototypal case of joint log-normally distributed asset returns, the derived structure of each household's optimal demands for assets is such that all optimal portfolios can be generated by simple combinations of just two portfolios. This mutual-fund theorem is identical in form with the well-known separation theorem of the static mean–variance model. Closed-form solutions for optimal consumption functions are found for members of the family of utility functions with hyperbolic absolute risk aversion. It is further shown that these are the only time-additive and independent preference orderings that lead to optimal consumption functions which are linear in wealth.

In the determination of these optimal policies, the analyses of Chapters 4 and 5 do not explicitly impose the feasibility constraints that neither consumption nor wealth can be negative. Moreover, the models posit a single consumption good and further assume that preferences are time additive with no intertemporal complementarity of consumption. Chapter 6 focuses on exploring the robustness of the derived results with respect to relaxation of these assumptions. It also provides the occasion to introduce the important Cox–Huang application of martingale theory to the solution of the lifetime consumption and portfolio problem. As an alternative to stochastic dynamic programming, the Cox–Huang technique is especially well suited for incorporating these particular nonnegativity constraints. Unlike the analyses in the unconstrained case, this analysis shows that with mild regularity conditions on preferences the optimal consumption and portfolio strategies of households never risk personal bankruptcy. Although the details of the optimal strategies are affected by these constraints, the fundamental spanning and mutual-fund theorems of the preceding unconstrained analyses are left unchanged. This same preservation of the essential structure of optimal portfolio demands is also shown to obtain for households with preferences that depend on other variables in addition to current consumption and age. Specific cases examined include multiple consumption goods, money-in-the-utility function, and preferences with nonzero intertemporal complementarity of consumption.

Having developed the optimal investment behavior of households, the analysis turns next to the pricing of financial instruments traded in the capital markets. Warrant and option pricing theory marks the earliest example of the application of continuous-time analysis.[7] During the last 15 years, these highly specialized securities have become increasingly more important in the real world with the creation and successful development of organized option markets. However, neither history nor commercial success is the reason for the extensive treatment of option pricing in Part III. Instead, the prominent role for options analysis evolves from the fact that option-like contracts are found in just about every sector of the economy. As a prototypal structure, options serve as the simplest examples of securities with nonlinear sharing rules.

Just as Chapter 2 provides a bridge between static and dynamic models of portfolio selection, so Chapter 7 serves to connect the one-period preference-based models of warrant and option pricing to the dynamic arbitrage-based pricing models. Development of modern option pricing theory begins in Chapter 8 with the derivation of price restrictions that are necessary to rule out arbitrage opportunities. Not surprisingly, these restrictions are insufficient to determine a unique set of option prices. However, conditional on the twin assumptions of continuous trading and a continuous-sample-path stochastic process for the underlying stock price dynamics, the seminal Black–Scholes model applies and a unique set of option prices can be derived from arbitrage considerations alone. The chapter concludes with application of this "conditional-arbitrage" model to the pricing of several types of options and warrants.

In Chapter 9, option pricing is examined for the case in which discontinuous changes or gaps in the underlying stock price are possible. With such

7   Cf. Bachelier (1900) and Samuelson (1965a).

jumps in prices a possibility, the conditional-arbitrage argument used to derive the Black–Scholes model is no longer valid. However, with the further assumption that the discontinuous components of stock-price· changes are diversifiable risks, an equilibrium model of option prices is derived.

Since the publication of the Black–Scholes model in 1973, there has been an explosion of theoretical, applied, and empirical research on option pricing. The impact of that explosion has even been felt beyond the borders of economics. In applied statistics, it created renewed interest in the estimation of variance rates for stochastic processes. In numerical methods, it stimulated extensive new research on numerical integration of the partial differential equations that must be solved to determine the Black–Scholes option prices. Hence, in Chapter 10 on further developments in option pricing analysis, we can do little more than give references to the many directions of expansions and extensions of the subject. There are three topics, however, without which even the most rudimentary presentation of modern option pricing theory would be conspicuously incomplete. Thus, Chapter 10 contains a more detailed development of the Cox–Ross "risk-neutral" pricing methodology, the binomial option pricing model, and the basic theory for pricing options on futures contracts.

Contingent-claims analysis (CCA) combines the dynamic portfolio theory of Part II with the Black–Scholes option pricing model of Part III to create one of the most powerful tools of analysis in modern finance. In Part IV, CCA is used to study a wide range of topics in the theory of corporate finance and financial intermediation. Continuing the study of financial instruments initiated in the preceding part, Chapters 11–13 develop a unified theory for the pricing of corporate liabilities. Like Chapter 7, Chapter 11 provides a transition from the one-period utility-based theory of pricing to an intertemporal theory based on conditional arbitrage. In the process, it also provides an introduction to the pricing of general capital assets and to the determination of the term structure of interest rates, topics which are developed more fully in Part V.

The most common division of a firm's capital structure is between debt and equity. Chapter 12 investigates the pricing of corporate debt and levered equity, beginning with the simplest, nontrivial capital structure of a single homogeneous zero-coupon bond issue and equity. The analysis shows that corporate debt can be represented functionally as a combination of default-free debt and unlevered equity. Just as the term structure uses maturity to distinguish among bond yields, so the risk structure of interest rates uses default risk to distinguish among promised yields. The derived pricing model for corporate bonds is used to define the risk structure and comparative statics are applied to demonstrate the effects of parameter changes on that structure. The analysis is extended to include corporate coupon bonds. The important Modigliani–Miller theorem that the value of the firm is invariant to its choice of debt–equity mix is shown to obtain even in the presence of bankruptcy possibilities.

In Chapter 13, a model for pricing general contingent claims or derivative securities[8] is developed using continuous-time dynamic portfolio theory. With frictionless markets and no taxes, the Modigliani–Miller theorem is proved for firms with general corporate-liability structures. It is well known that the Modigliani–Miller theorem generally fails in an environment of corporate taxes and deductibility of interest payments. Therefore, the chapter includes a discussion of modifications to the pricing model that are sufficient to accommodate the effects of taxes on financing choice. The analysis concludes with a survey of the applications of CCA to corporate finance issues that range from investment and financing decisions to the evaluation of corporate strategy.

The subject of Chapter 14 is the theory of financial intermediation with focus on the risk-pooling and risk-sharing services provided by intermediaries. The discussion is organized around three categories of contributions of continuous-time analysis to the theory and practice of financial intermediation: product identification, product implementation and pricing, and risk management and control for an intermediary's entire portfolio.

The theory holds that financial intermediaries and derivative-security markets are essentially redundant organizations in an idealized environment in which all investors pay neither transactions costs nor taxes, have the same information, and can trade continuously. To provide an important economic function for these activities in the theory, therefore, the posited environment must include some type of transaction or information cost structure in which financial intermediaries and market makers have a comparative advantage with respect to some investors and corporate issuers of securities. Thus, the formal analysis of Chapter 14 begins with a simple binomial model of derivative-security pricing in the presence of transactions costs. This analysis serves to demonstrate that bid–ask spreads in these prices can be substantial and that significant economic benefits can accrue from efficient intermediation. With this established in a simple model, we then explore the theory of intermediation using a continuous-time model in which many agents cannot trade without cost, but the lowest-cost transactors, financial intermediaries, can. This model both provides a *raison d'être* for derivative-security products and allows the use of standard CCA to determine the costs for intermediaries to produce them.

The theory of optimal consumption and portfolio choice is used to identify customer demands for a list of intermediary products ranging from

---

8 Derivative securities are securities with contractual payoff structures that are contingent on the prices of one or more traded securities.

generic multipurpose mutual funds to custom-designed financial contracts tailored to fit each investor's specific needs. The analysis also contributes to the theory of product implementation by specifying in detail the production technologies and costs for intermediaries to manufacture these products. The same CCA and dynamic portfolio-selection tools are used to examine the problem of overall risk management for an intermediary. In preparation for the equilibrium analysis in Part V, we discuss the role that an efficient financial intermediation system plays in justifying models that assume dichotomy between the real and financial sectors of the economy. The chapter concludes with a few observations on policy and strategy issues drawn from the continuous-time theory of intermediation.

The separate investigations of the main organizations comprising the financial economy are brought together in Part V to provide an equilibrium analysis of the entire system. Optimal financial behavior of individual agents and organizations is described by a set of contingent decisions or plans that depend on current prices and probability beliefs about the future evolution of the economy. The conditions satisfied by an equilibrium set of prices and beliefs are that all optimal plans can be implemented at each point in time ("market clearing") and that the resulting *ex post* time path of the economy is consistent with *ex ante* probability assessments ("rational expectations"). In the analyses, it is assumed that all agents and organizations are price-takers in the capital markets and that financial intermediation is a competitive industry. A standard Walrasian setting is posited as the mechanism to clear markets at each point in time.

The centerpiece of the classic CAPM is the Security Market Line, a linear equation that relates the equilibrium expected return on each asset (or portfolio of assets) to a single identifiable risk measure. Reduced-form equations of this genus are among the most widely and frequently used analytical tools in both applied and empirical finance. The focus of Chapter 15 is on establishing similar types of necessary conditions to be satisfied by intertemporal equilibrium prices of capital assets. We show that in the intertemporal Capital Asset Pricing Model, equilibrium expected returns are linearly related to a vector of risk measures. This reduced-form equation of the continuous-time model is called the Security Market Hyperplane. Under somewhat more restrictive conditions, the Breeden Consumption-Based Capital Asset Pricing Model (CCAPM) is shown to obtain. In this important version of the intertemporal model, equilibrium expected returns can again be expressed in terms of a single risk measure. That risk measure, however, is different from the one in the static CAPM.

Further results on investor hedging behavior and mutual-fund theorems derived in Chapter 15 add important detail to the product identification part of the financial intermediation theory in Chapter 14. However, the model itself does not explicitly include either derivative-security markets or much of the intermediation sector, a simplification justified by the quasi-dichotomy findings of that chapter. Moreover, as in the development of the original CAPM, the analysis emphasizes the demand side of the capital markets and thus treats as largely exogenous the dynamics of the supply curves for securities. Therefore the model does not provide all the structural equations of endogenous behavior required for a full equilibrium analysis of the system. Such is the subject matter of Chapter 16.

For this general equilibrium study of the financial economy, the continuous-time model is reformulated to fit the framework of the Arrow–Debreu model of complete markets. As we know, an Arrow–Debreu pure security provides a positive payoff at only one point in time and in only one state of the economy. In an Arrow–Debreu economy, pure securities are traded for each possible state of the economy at every future date. It follows that the continuous-time version of an Arrow–Debreu economy requires a continuum of such securities. However, as we shall see, financial intermediaries and other zero-cost transactors can synthetically create a complete set of pure securities by trading continuously in a finite number of securities. The continuous-time model thus provides a concrete demonstration of the Arrow and Radner observation that dynamic trading in securities can be a substitute for a full set of pure-security markets. Building on the theory of intermediation in Chapter 14, we derive explicit formulas for the trading technologies and production costs required to manufacture pure securities. The specificity of these theoretical findings suggests the possibility of feasible approximations in real-world financial markets to the seemingly unrealistic requirements of complete markets in an Arrow–Debreu world.

Having established the mechanism by which a complete set of pure securities is created, we then solve the lifetime consumption allocation problem for households, using static-optimization techniques as in the original Arrow–Debreu analysis. These state-contingent optimal demand functions are used to derive equilibrium allocations, prices, and rational expectations for the case of a pure-exchange economy. Production and optimal investment behavior of business firms are added in a second competitive equilibrium model. A third, more specific version shows that the prescriptions of the original CAPM can obtain in an intertemporal general equilibrium model with production.

The formal analyses of these 16 chapters can be used in the study of international finance and comparative financial systems. The posited structure of organizations and their functions, however, is modeled after the US system. Moreover, the institutional discussions surrounding those analyses abstract from the special issues that arise with intersystem transactions which cross sovereign borders. Happily, there is an extensive and accessible literature on applications of the continuous-time finance model that addresses the particular characteristics of an international setting.[9]

The general equilibrium analysis of Part V follows the traditional line of separation between macroeconomics and finance and excludes the public-sector component from its model of the financial system. That analysis, therefore, does not explicitly capture the effects of central bank and other government activities on the financial economy. However, the concluding part of the book contains five essays that apply continuous-time analysis to selected topics on the border between private and public finance.

In Chapter 17, a Ramsey–Solow macro model is developed to analyze the dynamics of long-run economic growth in an economy with uncertainty about either demographics or technological progress. The focus of the analysis is on the biases introduced in long-run forecasting and planning by neglecting uncertainty. Closed-form solutions for the steady-state proba-bility distributions of the relevant economic variables are derived for the case of a Cobb–Douglas production function and a constant proportional savings function. The analysis concludes with an examination of the stochastic Ramsey problem of central planning.

The subject of Chapter 18 is the design of public pension plans. Both academics and practitioners have often suggested that pension annuities be indexed to protect retirees against inflation. However, such annuities do not provide protection against real gains in the standard of living. A new type of plan that indexes benefits to aggregate per capita consumption is investigated as a possible solution for protecting pensioners against both of these risks. The analysis posits a simple model for mortality with the standard assumption that individual mortality risk is diversifiable across the population. The equilibrium prices of consumption-indexed annuities are derived by applying the competitive arbitrage techniques of Chapter 9. Under the condition that household preferences satisfy the Life-Cycle Hypothesis, the optimal consumption–saving model of Chapter 5 is used to determine the required contribution rate to the pension plan that ensures an optimal level of retirement benefits. The formal analysis is followed by a brief discussion of the feasibility of implementing such a plan.

An important topic in both private and public finance is the evaluation of loan guarantees. The next two chapters use CCA to develop generic models for pricing these guarantees and apply them to the analysis of deposit insurance. Third-party guarantees of financial perfor-

9 Adler and Dumas (1983) and Branson and Henderson (1984) provide excellent surveys on the application of the continuous-time model in international finance, an application pioneered by Solnik (1973, 1974). See also Kouri (1976, 1977), Kouri and de Macedo (1978), Stulz (1981, 1984), de Macedo, Goldstein and Meerschwam (1984), Eun (1985), Dumas (1988), Dixit (1989a), and Penati and Pennacchi (1989).

mance on loans and other debt-related contracts are widely used throughout the USA and other well-developed economies. Parent corporations often guarantee the debt obligations of their subsidiaries. In return for fees, commercial banks offer guarantees on a broad spectrum of financial instruments ranging from letters of credit to interest rate and currency swaps. More specialized firms sell guarantees of interest and principal payments on tax-exempt municipal bonds. However, the largest provider of financial guarantees is the federal government, either directly or through its agencies. In the corporate sector, it has guaranteed loans to small businesses and on occasion, as with Lockheed Aircraft and the Chrysler Corporation, it has done so for very large businesses. Established in 1980, the United States Synthetic Fuels Corporation was empowered to grant loan guarantees to assist the financing of commercial projects that involve the development of alternative fuel technologies. Through the Pension Benefit Guaranty Corporation, the government provides limited insurance of corporate pension-plan benefits. Residential mortgages and farm and student loans are examples of noncorporate obligations that the government has guaranteed. But perhaps the most important of its liability guarantees, both economically and politically, is deposit insurance.

The Federal Deposit Insurance Corporation (FDIC) and the Federal Savings and Loan Insurance Corporation (FSLIC) insure the deposits of commercial banks and thrift institutions up to a maximum of US $100,000 per account.[10] With such insurance, the economic responsibility for monitoring a bank's activities shifts from its depositors to the insurer. In a frictionless world with only liquid assets and no surveillance costs, the insurer would continuously monitor the value of those assets in relation to deposits. It could thereby avoid any losses by simply forcing liquidation of the assets before the insolvency point is reached. But, of course, most bank assets are not liquid and there are surveillance costs, and so our models for determining the cost of deposit insurance take account of both the potential losses from insolvency and the cost of monitoring. The evaluation of deposit insurance is further complicated in the real world because, unlike some private-sector guarantees, deposit insurance obligations are not traded in markets. The government, therefore, must estimate the actuarial cost of providing this insurance, without the benefit of market prices.[11] As we shall see, implementation of CCA generally does not

10   After passage of the Financial Institutions, Reform, Recovery and Enforcement Act in August 1989, FSLIC was replaced by the Savings Association Insurance Fund and the Resolution Trust Corporation.

11   Even if the government were not to charge for deposit insurance, it would still require such cost estimates to determine the amount of the subsidy given to banks and their depositors. The federal and provincial governments of Canada use loan guarantees to subsidize local corporations (cf. Baldwin, Lessard, and Mason, 1983). It is my understanding that they have built models using the CCA methodology to evaluate the costs of these subsidies.

require historical price data on the security to be priced. This evaluation technique of Chapters 19 and 20 is thus a well-suited appraisal tool for estimating the costs of deposit guarantees.

The concluding chapter of the book analyzes optimal portfolio and expenditure rules for university endowment funds. A common approach to the management of endowment is to treat it in isolation as if it were the only asset of the university. This approach leads to rather uniform prescriptions for optimal investment and expenditure policies. In contrast, the model in Chapter 21 follows a more integrative approach to endowment management that takes account of the university's overall objectives and total resources. Inclusion of other university assets (in addition to endowment) in the analysis leads to significantly different optimal portfolios and expenditure patterns among universities with similar objectives and similar sized endowments, but different non-endowment sources of cash flow. The model also takes account of the uncertainty surrounding the costs of the various activities such as education, research, and knowledge storage that define the purpose of the university. As a result, the analysis reveals a perhaps somewhat latent role for endowment: namely, hedging against unanticipated changes in those costs.

This completes the itinerary for our journey through the continuous-time theory of finance. I hope that, by journey's end, some readers find it a compact and codified method for organizing their understanding of financial activities and the interactions among them. But, before embarkation, I must add a word of caution against absolutizing the theory. As with much of neoclassical economics, the foundation of modern finance theory rests on the *perfect-market paradigm* of rational behavior and frictionless, competitive, and informationally efficient capital markets. With its further assumption of continuous trading, the base of our theory should perhaps be labeled the *super perfect-market paradigm*. The conditions of this paradigm are not, of course, literally satisfied in the real world. Furthermore, its accuracy as a useful approximation to that world varies considerably across time and place.[12] The practitioner should therefore apply the continuous-time theory only tentatively, assessing its limitations in each application. Just so, the researcher should treat it as a point of departure for both problem finding and problem solving.

---

12 A general discussion of the limits of the perfect-market paradigm can be found in Merton (1987a, b). Caveats on the specific assumptions of the continuous-time model are dispersed throughout the book. However, see the concluding sections of Chapters 14 and 16, especially. Information efficiency in the sense of the Efficient-Market Hypothesis of Samuelson (1965b, 1973) and Fama (1965a, 1970a, 1991) requires that the dynamics of speculative prices satisfy rational expectations. In the models here, we impose the rational expectations assumption only in the equilibrium analyses of Part V and Chapter 20.

2

Introduction to Portfolio Selection and Capital Market Theory: Static Analysis

2.1 INTRODUCTION

It is convenient to view the investment decision by households as having two parts: (a) the "consumption–saving" choice where the individual decides how much income and wealth to allocate to current consumption and how much to save for future consumption; and (b) the "portfolio-selection" choice where the investor decides how to allocate savings among the available investment opportunities. In general, the two decisions cannot be made independently. However, many of the important findings in portfolio theory can be more easily derived in a one-period environment where the consumption–savings allocation has little substantive impact on the results. Thus, we begin in Section 2.2 with the formulation and solution of the basic portfolio-selection problem in a static framework, taking as given the individual's consumption decision.

Using the analysis of Section 2.2, we derive necessary conditions for static financial equilibrium that are used to determine restrictions on equilibrium security prices and returns in Sections 2.3 and 2.4. In Section 2.4, these restrictions are used to derive spanning and mutual-fund theorems that provide a basis for an elementary theory of financial intermediation.[1]

Reproduced from *Handbook of Monetary Economics*, B. Friedman and F. Hahn, eds, 1990, Amsterdam: North-Holland. This chapter includes Sections 2–4 of Merton (1990a), which is a revised and expanded version of Merton (1982a).

1 Spanning and mutual-fund theorems for the intertemporal continuous-time model are developed in Chapters 5, 15, and 16. The role of financial intermediation in this model is discussed in Chapter 14.

2.2 ONE-PERIOD PORTFOLIO SELECTION

The basic investment-choice problem for an individual is to determine the optimal allocation of his or her wealth among the available investment opportunities. The solution to the general problem of choosing the best investment mix is called *portfolio-selection theory*. The study of portfolio-selection theory begins with its classic one-period or static formulation.

There are n different investment opportunities called *securities* and the random variable one-period return per dollar on security j is denoted Z_j ($j = 1,...,n$) where a "dollar" is the "unit of account." Any linear combination of these securities which has a positive market value is called a *portfolio*. It is assumed that the investor chooses at the beginning of a period that feasible portfolio allocation which maximizes the expected value of a von Neumann–Morgenstern utility function[2] for end-of-period wealth. Denote this utility function by $U(W)$, where W is the end-of-period value of the investor's wealth measured in dollars. It is further assumed that U is an increasing strictly concave function on the range of feasible values for W and that U is twice continuously differentiable.[3] Because the criterion function for choice depends only on the distribution of end-of-period wealth, the only information about the securities that is relevant to the investor's decision is his subjective joint probability distribution for $(Z_1,...,Z_n)$.

In addition, the following assumptions are made.

Assumption 1 Frictionless Markets

There are no transactions costs or taxes, and all securities are perfectly divisible.

Assumption 2 Price-Taker

The investor believes that his actions cannot affect the probability distribution of returns on the available securities. Hence, if w_j is the fraction of the

2   von Neumann and Morgenstern (1947). For an axiomatic description, see Herstein and Milnor (1953) and Machina (1982). Although the original axioms require that U be bounded, the continuity axiom can be extended to allow for unbounded functions. See Samuelson (1977) for a discussion of this and the St Petersburg paradox.

3   The strict concavity assumption implies that investors are everywhere risk averse. Although strictly convex or linear utility functions on the entire range imply behavior that is grossly at variance with observed behavior, the strict concavity assumption also rules out Friedman–Savage type utility functions whose behavioral implications are reasonable. The strict concavity also implies $U'(W) > 0$, which rules out individual satiation.

investor's initial wealth W_0 allocated to security j, then $\{w_1,...,w_n\}$ uniquely determines the probability distribution of his terminal wealth.

A *riskless security* is defined to be a security or feasible portfolio of securities whose return per dollar over the period is known with certainty.

Assumption 3   No-Arbitrage Opportunities

All riskless securities must have the same return per dollar. This common return will be denoted by R.

Assumption 4   No-Institutional Restrictions

Short-sales of all securities, with full use of proceeds, are allowed without restriction. If there exists a riskless security, then the borrowing rate equals the lending rate.[4]

Hence, the only restriction on the choice for the $\{w_j\}$ is the budget constraint that $\Sigma_1^n w_j = 1$.

Given these assumptions, the portfolio-selection problem can be formally stated as

$$\max_{\{w_1,...,w_n\}} E\left\{ U\left(\sum_1^n w_j Z_j W_0 \right) \right\} \tag{2.1}$$

subject to $\Sigma_1^n w_j = 1$, where E is the expectation operator for the subjective joint probability distribution. If $(w_1^*,...,w_n^*)$ is a solution to (2.1), then it will satisfy the first-order conditions

$$E\{U'(Z^* W_0) Z_j\} = \frac{\lambda}{W_0} \qquad j = 1,2,...,n \tag{2.2}$$

where the prime denotes derivative, $Z^* \equiv \Sigma_1^n w_j^* Z_j$ is the random variable return per dollar on the optimal portfolio, and λ is the Lagrange multiplier for the budget constraint. Together with the concavity assumptions on U, if

---

4   Borrowings and short-sales are demand loans collateralized by the investor's total portfolio. The "borrowing rate" is the rate on riskless-in-terms-of-default loans. Although virtually every individual loan involves some chance of default, the empirical "spread" in the rate on actual margin loans to investors suggests that this assumption is not a "bad approximation" for portfolio-selection analysis. However, explicit analyses of risky-loan evaluation are provided in Chapters 11–14 and Chapters 19 and 20. See also Merton (1990b, pp. 272–85).

the $n \times n$ variance–covariance matrix of the returns $(Z_1,\ldots,Z_n)$ is non-singular and an interior solution exists, then the solution is unique.[5] This nonsingularity condition on the returns distribution eliminates "redundant" securities (i.e. securities whose returns can be expressed as exact linear combinations of the returns on other available securities).[6] It also rules out that any one of the securities is a riskless security.

If a riskless security is added to the menu of available securities (call it the $(n + 1)$th security), then it is the convention to express (2.1) as the following unconstrained maximization problem:

$$\max_{\{w_1,\ldots,w_n\}} E\left\{U\left(\left[\sum_1^n w_j(Z_j - R) + R\right]W_0\right)\right\} \qquad (2.3)$$

where the portfolio allocations to the risky securities are unconstrained because the fraction allocated to the riskless security can always be chosen to satisfy the budget constraint (i.e. $w_{n+1}^* = 1 - \Sigma_1^n w_j^*$). The first-order conditions can be written as

$$E\{U'(Z^*W_0)(Z_j - R)\} = 0 \qquad j = 1,2,\ldots,n \qquad (2.4)$$

where Z^* can be rewritten as $\Sigma_1^n w_j^*(Z_j - R) + R$. Again, if it is assumed that the variance–covariance matrix of the returns on the risky securities is nonsingular and an interior solution exists, then the solution is unique.

As formulated, neither (2.1) nor (2.3) reflects the physical constraint that end-of-period wealth cannot be negative. That is, no explicit consideration is given to the treatment of bankruptcy. To rule out bankruptcy, the additional constraint that, with probability one, $Z^* \geq 0$ could be imposed on the choices for $(w_1^*,\ldots,w_n^*)$.[7] If, however, the purpose of this constraint is to reflect institutional restrictions designed to avoid individual bankruptcy, then it is too weak, because the probability assessments on the $\{Z_j\}$ are subjective. An alternative treatment is to forbid borrowing and short-

---

5   The existence of an interior solution is assumed throughout the analyses. For a discussion of necessary and sufficient conditions for the existence of an interior solution, see Leland (1972) and Bertsekas (1974).

6   For a trivial example, shares of IBM with odd serial numbers are distinguishable from ones with even serial numbers and are therefore technically different securities. However, because their returns are identical, they are perfect substitutes from the point of view of investors. In portfolio theory, securities are operationally defined by their return distributions, and therefore two securities with identical returns are indistinguishable.

7   If U is such that $U'(0) = \infty$ and, by extension, $U'(W) = \infty$, $W < 0$, then from (2.2) or (2.4) it is easy to show that the probability of $Z^* \leq 0$ is a set of measure zero. Mason (1981) has studied the effects of various bankruptcy rules on portfolio behavior. See also Chapter 6.

selling in conjunction with limited-liability securities where, by law, $Z_j \geq 0$. These rules can be formalized as restrictions on the allowable set of $\{w_j\}$, such that $w_j \geq 0, j = 1, 2,..., n + 1$, and (2.1) or (2.3) can be solved using the methods of Kuhn and Tucker (1951) for inequality constraints. In Chapters 6, 13, 14, and 16, we formally analyze portfolio behavior and the pricing of securities when both investors and security lenders recognize the prospect of default. Thus, until those chapters, it is simply assumed that there exists a bankruptcy law which allows for $U(W)$ to be defined for $W < 0$, and that this law is consistent with the continuity and concavity assumptions on U.

The optimal demand functions for risky securities, $\{w_j^* W_0\}$, and the resulting probability distribution for the optimal portfolio will, of course, depend on the risk preferences of the investor, his initial wealth, and the joint distribution for the securities' returns. It is well known that the von Neumann–Morgenstern utility function can only be determined up to a positive affine transformation. Hence the preference orderings of all choices available to the investor are completely specified by the Pratt–Arrow[8] *absolute risk-aversion function*, which can be written as

$$A(W) \equiv \frac{-U''(W)}{U'(W)} \tag{2.5}$$

and the change in absolute risk aversion with respect to a change in wealth is therefore given by

$$\frac{dA}{dW} = A'(W) = A(W)\left[A(W) + \frac{U'''(W)}{U''(W)} \right] \tag{2.6}$$

By the assumption that $U(W)$ is increasing and strictly concave, $A(W)$ is positive, and such investors are called *risk averse*. An alternative, but related, measure of risk aversion is the *relative risk-aversion function* defined by

$$R(W) \equiv -\frac{U''(W)W}{U'(W)} = A(W)W \tag{2.7}$$

and its change with respect to a change in wealth is given by

$$R'(W) = A'(W)W + A(W) \tag{2.8}$$

---

8   The behavior associated with the utility functions $V(W) \equiv aU(W) + b, a > 0$, is identical with that associated with $U(W)$. Note that $A(W)$ is invariant to any positive affine transformation of $U(W)$. See Pratt (1964).

The *certainty-equivalent end-of-period wealth* W_c, associated with a given portfolio for end-of-period wealth whose random variable value is denoted by W, is defined to be such that

$$U(W_c) = E\{U(W)\} \qquad (2.9)$$

i.e. W_c is the amount of money such that the investor is indifferent between having this amount of money for certain or the portfolio with random variable outcome W. The term "risk averse" as applied to investors with strictly concave utility functions is descriptive in the sense that the certainty-equivalent end-of-period wealth is always less than the expected value $E\{W\}$ of the associated portfolio for all such investors. The proof follows directly by Jensen's inequality: if U is strictly concave, then

$$U(W_c) = E\{U(W)\} < U(E\{W\})$$

whenever W has positive dispersion, and because U is an increasing function of W, $W_c < E\{W\}$.

The certainty equivalent can be used to compare the risk aversions of two investors. An investor is said to be *more risk averse* than a second investor if, for every portfolio, the certainty-equivalent end-of-period wealth for the first investor is less than or equal to the certainty-equivalent end-of-period wealth associated with the same portfolio for the second investor with strict inequality holding for at least one portfolio.

While the certainty equivalent provides a natural definition for comparing risk aversions across investors, Rothschild and Stiglitz[9] have in a corresponding fashion attempted to define the meaning of "increasing risk" for a security so that the "riskiness" of two securities or portfolios can be compared. In comparing two portfolios with the same expected values, the first portfolio with random variable outcome denoted by W_1 is said to be *less risky* than the second portfolio with random variable outcome denoted by W_2 if

$$E\{U(W_1)\} \geqslant E\{U(W_2)\} \qquad (2.10)$$

for all concave U with strict inequality holding for some concave U. They bolster their argument for this definition by showing its equivalence to the two following definitions:

---

9 Rothschild and Stiglitz (1970, 1971). There is an extensive literature, not discussed here, that uses this type of risk measure to determine when one portfolio "stochastically dominates" another. Cf. Hadar and Russell (1969, 1971), Hanoch and Levy (1969), and Bawa (1975).

There exists a random variable Z such that W_2 has the same distribution as $W_1 + Z$ where the conditional expectation of Z given the outcome of W_1 is zero (i.e. W_2 is equal in distribution to W_1 plus some "noise"). (2.11)

If the points of F and G, the distribution functions of W_1 and W_2, are confined to the closed interval $[a,b]$, and $T(y) \equiv \int_a^y [G(x) - F(x)]\, dx$, then $T(y) \geq 0$ and $T(b) = 0$ (i.e. W_2 has more "weight in its tails" than W_1). (2.12)

A feasible portfolio with return per dollar Z will be called an *efficient portfolio* if there exists an increasing strictly concave function V such that $E\{V'(Z)(Z_j - R)\} = 0, j = 1,2,\ldots,n$. Using the Rothschild–Stiglitz definition of "less risky," a feasible portfolio will be an efficient portfolio only if there does not exist another feasible portfolio which is less risky than it is. All portfolios that are not efficient are called *inefficient portfolios*.

From the definition of an efficient portfolio, it follows that no two portfolios in the efficient set can be ordered with respect to one another. From (2.10), it follows immediately that every efficient portfolio is a possible optimal portfolio, i.e. for each efficient portfolio there exists an increasing concave U and an initial wealth W_0 such that the efficient portfolio is a solution to (2.1) or (2.3). Furthermore, from (2.10), all risk-averse investors will be indifferent between selecting their optimal portfolios from the set of all feasible portfolios and selecting their optimal portfolios from the set of efficient portfolios. Hence, without loss of generality, assume that all optimal portfolios are efficient portfolios.

With these general definitions established, we now turn to the analysis of the optimal demand functions for risky assets and their implications for the distributional characteristics of the underlying securities. A note on notation: the symbol Z_e will be used to denote the random variable return per dollar on an efficient portfolio, and a bar over a random variable (e.g. $\bar{Z}$) will denote the expected value of that random variable.

Theorem 2.1

If Z denotes the random variable return per dollar on any feasible portfolio and if $Z_e - \bar{Z}_e$ is riskier than $Z - \bar{Z}$ in the Rothschild and Stiglitz sense, then $\bar{Z}_e > \bar{Z}$.

PROOF

By hypothesis, $E\{U[(Z - \bar{Z})W_0]\} > E\{U[(Z_e - \bar{Z}_e)W_0]\}$. If $\bar{Z} \geq \bar{Z}_e$, then trivially $E\{U(ZW_0)\} > E\{U(Z_eW_0)\}$. But Z is a feasible portfolio and Z_e is an efficient portfolio. Hence, by contradiction, $\bar{Z}_e > \bar{Z}$. QED

Corollary 2.1

If there exists a riskless security with return R, then $\bar{Z}_e \geqslant R$, with equality holding only if Z_e is a riskless security.

PROOF

The riskless security is a feasible portfolio with expected return R. If Z_e is riskless, then, by Assumption 3, $\bar{Z}_e = R$. If Z_e is not riskless, then $Z_e - \bar{Z}_e$ is riskier than $R - R$. Therefore, by Theorem 2.1, $\bar{Z}_e > R$.   QED

Theorem 2.2

The optimal portfolio for a nonsatiated risk-averse investor will be the riskless security (i.e. $w_{n+1}^* = 1$, $w_j^* = 0$, $j = 1,2,...,n$) if and only if $\bar{Z}_j = R$ for $j = 1,2,...,n$.

PROOF

From (2.4), $\{w_1^*,...,w_n^*\}$ will satisfy $E\{U'(Z^*W_0)(Z_j - R)\} = 0$. If $\bar{Z}_j = R$, $j = 1,2,...,n$, then $Z^* = R$ will satisfy these first-order conditions. By the strict concavity of U and the nonsingularity of the variance–covariance matrix of returns, this solution is unique. This proves the "if" part. If $Z^* = R$ is an optimal solution, then we can rewrite (2.4) as $U'(RW_0)E\{Z_j - R\} = 0$. By the nonsatiation assumption, $U'(RW_0) > 0$. Therefore, for $Z^* = R$ to be an optimal solution, $\bar{Z}_j = R$, $j = 1,2,...,n$. This proves the "only if" part.   QED

Hence, from Corollary 2.1 and Theorem 2.2, if a risk-averse investor chooses a risky portfolio, then the expected return on that portfolio exceeds the riskless rate, and a risk-averse investor will choose a risky portfolio if at least one available security has an expected return different from the riskless rate.

Define the notation $E\{Y|X_1,...,X_q\}$ to mean the *conditional expectation of the random variable* Y, conditional on knowing the realizations for the random variables $(X_1,...,X_q)$.

Theorem 2.3

Let Z_p denote the return on any portfolio p that does not contain security s. If there exists a portfolio p such that, for security s, $Z_s = Z_p + \epsilon_s$, where $E\{\epsilon_s\} = E\{\epsilon_s|Z_j, j = 1,...,n, j \neq s\} = 0$, then the fraction of every efficient portfolio allocated to security s is the same and equal to zero.

PROOF

The proof follows by contradiction. Suppose Z_e is the return on an efficient portfolio with fraction $\delta_s \neq 0$ allocated to security s. Let Z be the return on a portfolio with the same fractional holdings as Z_e except that, instead of security s, it holds the fraction δ_s in feasible portfolio Z_p. Hence, $Z_e = Z + \delta_s(Z_s - Z_p)$ or $Z_e = Z + \delta_s\epsilon_s$. By hypothesis, $\overline{Z}_e = \overline{Z}$, and because portfolio Z does not contain security s, by construction, $E\{\epsilon_s|Z\} = 0$. Therefore, for $\delta_s \neq 0$, Z_e is riskier than Z in the Rothschild–Stiglitz sense. But this contradicts the hypothesis that Z_e is an efficient portfolio. Hence, $\delta_s = 0$ for every efficient portfolio. 　　QED

Corollary 2.3

Let ψ denote the set of n securities with returns $(Z_1,...,Z_{s-1},Z_s,Z_{s+1},...,Z_n)$ and ψ' denote the same set of securities except that Z_s is replaced with $Z_{s'}$. If $Z_{s'} = Z_s + \epsilon_s$ and $E\{\epsilon_s\} = E\{\epsilon_s|Z_1,...,Z_{s-1},Z_s,Z_{s+1},...,Z_n\} = 0$, then all risk-averse investors would prefer to choose their optimal portfolios from ψ rather than ψ'.

The proof is essentially the same as the proof of Theorem 2.3, with Z_s replacing Z_p. Unless the holdings of Z_s in every efficient portfolio are zero, ψ will be strictly preferred to ψ'.

　　Theorem 2.3 and its corollary demonstrate that all risk-averse investors would prefer any "unnecessary" uncertainty or "noise" to be eliminated. In particular, by this theorem, the existence of lotteries is shown to be inconsistent with strict risk aversion on the part of all investors.[10] While the inconsistency of strict risk aversion with observed behavior such as betting on the numbers can be "explained" by treating lotteries as consumption goods, it is difficult to use this argument to explain other implicit lotteries such as callable sinking-fund bonds where the bonds to be redeemed are selected at random.

　　As illustrated by the partitioning of the feasible portfolio set into its efficient and inefficient parts and the derived theorems, the Rothschild–Stiglitz definition of increasing risk is quite useful for studying the properties of optimal portfolios. However, it is important to emphasize that these theorems apply only to efficient portfolios and not to individual securities or inefficient portfolios. For example, if $Z_j - \overline{Z}_j$ is riskier than $Z - \overline{Z}$ in the Rothschild–Stiglitz sense and if security j is held in positive amounts in an efficient or optimal portfolio (i.e. $w_j^* > 0$), then it *does not* follow that $\overline{Z}_j$ must equal or exceed $\overline{Z}$. In particular, if $w_j^* > 0$, it does not follow that $\overline{Z}_j$ must equal or exceed R. Hence, to know that one security is

----

10　I believe that Christian von Weizsäcker proved a similar theorem in unpublished notes some years ago. However, I do not have a reference.

riskier than a second security using the Rothschild–Stiglitz definition of increasing risk provides no normative restrictions on holdings of either security in an efficient portfolio. And because this definition of riskier imposes no restrictions on the optimal demands, it cannot be used to derive properties of individual securities' return distributions from observing their relative holdings in an efficient portfolio. To derive these properties, a second definition of risk is required. Development of this measure is the topic of Section 2.3.

2.3   RISK MEASURES FOR SECURITIES AND PORTFOLIOS IN THE ONE-PERIOD MODEL

In the previous section it was suggested that the Rothschild–Stiglitz measure is not a natural definition of risk for a security. In this section, a second definition of increasing risk is introduced, and it is argued that this second measure is a more appropriate definition for the risk of a security. Although this second measure will not in general provide the same orderings as the Rothschild–Stiglitz measure, it is further argued that the two measures are not in conflict and, indeed, are complementary.

If Z_e^K is the random variable return per dollar on an efficient portfolio K, then let $V_K(Z_e^K)$ denote an increasing strictly concave function such that, for $V_K' \equiv dV_K/dZ_e^K$,

$$E\{V_K'(Z_j - R)\} = 0 \qquad j = 1,2,\ldots,n$$

i.e. V_K is a concave utility function such that an investor with initial wealth $W_0 = 1$ and these preferences would select this efficient portfolio as his optimal portfolio. While such a function V_K will always exist, it will not be unique. If $\text{cov}(x_1,x_2)$ is the functional notation for the covariance between the random variables x_1 and x_2, then define the random variable Y_K by

$$Y_K \equiv \frac{V_K' - E\{V_K'\}}{\text{cov}(V_K',Z_e^K)} \tag{2.13}$$

Y_K is well defined as long as Z_e^K has positive dispersion because $\text{cov}(V_K',Z_e^K) < 0$.[11] It is understood that in the following discussion "efficient portfolio" will mean "efficient portfolio with positive dispersion." Let Z_p denote the random variable return per dollar on any feasible portfolio p.

---

11   For a proof, see Theorem 236 in Hardy, Littlewood, and Pólya (1959).

Definition

The measure of risk b_p^K of portfolio p relative to efficient portfolio K with random variable return Z_e^K is defined by

$$b_p^K \equiv \text{cov}(Y_K, Z_p)$$

and portfolio p is said to be *riskier than portfolio p' relative to efficient portfolio K if $b_p^K > b_{p'}^K$.*

Theorem 2.4

If Z_p is the return on a feasible portfolio p and Z_e^K is the return on efficient portfolio K, then $\overline{Z}_p - R = b_p^K(\overline{Z}_e^K - R)$.

PROOF

From the definition of V_K, $E\{V_K'(Z_j - R)\} = 0, j = 1, 2, \ldots, n$. Let δ_j be the fraction of portfolio p allocated to security j. Then,

$$Z_p = \sum_1^n \delta_j(Z_j - R) + R$$

and

$$\sum_1^n \delta_j E\{V_K'(Z_j - R)\} = E\{V_K'(Z_p - R)\} = 0$$

By a similar argument, $E\{V_K'(Z_e^K - R)\} = 0$. Hence,

$$\text{cov}(V_K', Z_e^K) = (R - \overline{Z}_e^K)E\{V_K'\}$$

and

$$\text{cov}(V_K', Z_p) = (R - \overline{Z}_p)E\{V_K'\}$$

By Corollary 2.1, $\overline{Z}_e^K > R$. Therefore, $\text{cov}(Y_K, Z_p) = (R - \overline{Z}_p)/(R - \overline{Z}_e^K)$.
QED

Hence, the expected excess return on portfolio p, $\overline{Z}_p - R$, is in direct proportion to its risk and, because $\overline{Z}_e^K > R$, the larger is its risk, the larger is its expected return. Thus, Theorem 2.4 provides the first argument why b_p^K is a natural measure of risk for individual securities.

A second argument goes as follows. Consider an investor with utility function U and initial wealth W_0 who solves the portfolio-selection problem

$$\max_{w} E\{U([wZ_j + (1 - w)Z]W_0)\}$$

where Z is the return on a portfolio of securities and Z_j is the return on security j. The optimal mix w^* will satisfy the first-order condition

$$E\{U'([w^*Z_j + (1 - w^*)Z]W_0)(Z_j - Z)\} = 0 \qquad (2.14)$$

If the original portfolio of securities chosen was this investor's optimal portfolio (i.e. $Z = Z^*$), then the solution to (2.14) is $w^* = 0$. However, an optimal portfolio is an efficient portfolio. Therefore, by Theorem 2.4, $\bar{Z}_j - R = b_j^*(\bar{Z}^* - R)$. Hence, the "risk-return tradeoff" provided in Theorem 2.4 is a condition for personal portfolio equilibrium. Indeed, because security j may be contained in the optimal portfolio, w^*W_0 is similar to an excess demand function. b_j^* measures the contribution of security j to the Rothschild–Stiglitz risk of the optimal portfolio in the sense that the investor is just indifferent to a marginal change in the holdings of security j provided that $\bar{Z}_j - R = b_j^*(\bar{Z}^* - R)$. Moreover, by the Implicit Function Theorem, we have from (2.14) that

$$\frac{\partial w^*}{\partial \bar{Z}_j} = \frac{w^*W_0E\{U''(Z - Z_j)\} - E\{U'\}}{W_0E\{U''(Z - Z_j)^2\}} > 0 \quad \text{at } w^* = 0 \quad (2.15)$$

Therefore, if $\bar{Z}_j$ lies above the "risk-return" line in the $(\bar{Z}, b^*)$ plane, then the investor would prefer to increase his holdings in security j, and if $\bar{Z}_j$ lies below the line, then he would prefer to reduce his holdings. If the risk of a security increases, then the risk-averse investor must be "compensated" by a corresponding increase in that security's expected return if his current holdings are to remain unchanged.

A third argument for why b_p^K is a natural measure of risk for individual securities is that the ordering of securities by their systematic risk relative to a given efficient portfolio will be identical with their ordering relative to any other efficient portfolio. That is, given the set of available securities, there is an unambiguous meaning to the statement "security j is riskier than security i." To show this equivalence along with other properties of the b_p^K measure, we first prove a lemma.

Lemma 2.1

  (i) $E\{Z_p|V'_K\} = E\{Z_p|Z^K_e\}$ for efficient portfolio K.
 (ii) If $E\{Z_p|Z^K_e\} = \bar{Z}_p$, then $\text{cov}(Z_p,V'_K) = 0$.
(iii) $\text{cov}(Z_p,V'_K) = 0$ for efficient portfolio K if and only if $\text{cov}(Z_p,V'_L) = 0$ for every efficient portfolio L.

PROOF

  (i) V'_K is a continuous monotonic function of Z^K_e and hence V'_K and Z^K_e are in one-to-one correspondence.
 (ii) $\text{cov}(Z_p,V'_K) = E\{V'_K(Z_p - \bar{Z}_p)\} = E\{V'_K E\{Z_p - \bar{Z}_p|Z^K_e\}\} = 0$.
(iii) By definition, $b^K_p = 0$ if and only if $\text{cov}(Z_p,V'_K) = 0$. From Theorem 2.4, if $b^K_p = 0$, then $\bar{Z}_p = R$. From Corollary 2.1, $\bar{Z}^L_e > R$ for every efficient portfolio L. Thus, from Theorem 2.4, $b^L_p = 0$ if and only if $\bar{Z}_p = R$.   QED

Properties of the b^K_p measure of risk are as follows.

Property 1

If L and K are efficient portfolios, then for any portfolio p, $b^K_p = b^K_L b^L_p$.
From Corollary 2.1, $\bar{Z}^K_e > R$ and $\bar{Z}^L_e > R$. From Theorem 2.4,

$$b^K_L = \frac{\bar{Z}^L_e - R}{\bar{Z}^K_e - R} \qquad b^K_p = \frac{\bar{Z}_p - R}{\bar{Z}^K_e - R} \qquad b^L_p = \frac{\bar{Z}_p - R}{\bar{Z}^L_e - R}$$

Hence, the b^K_p measure satisfies a type of "chain rule" with respect to different efficient portfolios.

Property 2

If L and K are efficient portfolios, then $b^K_K = 1$ and $b^L_K > 0$.

Property 2 follows from Theorem 2.4 and Corollary 2.1. Hence, all efficient portfolios have positive systematic risk, relative to any efficient portfolio.

Property 3

$\bar{Z}_p = R$ if and only if $b^K_p = 0$ for every efficient portfolio K.

Property 3 follows from Theorem 2.4 and Properties 1 and 2.

Property 4

Let p and q denote any two feasible portfolios and let K and L denote any two efficient portfolios. $b_p^K \gtreqless b_q^K$ if and only if $b_p^L \gtreqless b_q^L$.

Property 4 follows from Property 3 if $b_p^L = b_q^L = 0$. Suppose $b_p^L \neq 0$. Then Property 4 follows from Properties 1 and 2 because

$$b_q^L / b_p^L = b_K^L b_q^K / b_K^L b_p^K = b_q^K / b_p^K$$

Thus the b_p^K measure provides the same orderings of risk for any reference efficient portfolio.

Property 5

For each efficient portfolio K and any feasible portfolio p, $Z_p = R + b_p^K(Z_e^K - R) + \epsilon_p$ where $E\{\epsilon_p\} = 0$ and $E\{\epsilon_p V_L'(Z_e^L)\} = 0$ for every efficient portfolio L.

From Theorem 2.4, $E\{\epsilon_p\} = 0$. If portfolio q is constructed by holding one dollar in portfolio p, b_p^K dollars in the riskless security, and short-selling b_p^K dollars of efficient portfolio K, then $Z_q = R + \epsilon_p$. From Property 3, $\bar{Z}_q = R$ implies that $b_q^L = 0$ for every efficient portfolio L. But $b_q^L = 0$ implies $0 = \text{cov}(Z_q, V_L') = E\{\epsilon_p V_L'\}$ for every efficient portfolio L.

Property 6

If a feasible portfolio p has portfolio weights $(\delta_1, \dots, \delta_n)$, then $b_p^K = \Sigma_1^n \delta_j b_j^K$.

Property 6 follows directly from the linearity of the covariance operator with respect to either of its arguments. Hence, the systematic risk of a portfolio is the weighted sum of the systematic risks of its component securities.

The Rothschild–Stiglitz measure of risk is clearly different from the b_j^K measure here. The Rothschild–Stiglitz measure provides only for a partial ordering while the b_j^K measure provides a complete ordering. Moreover, they can give different rankings. For example, suppose the return on security j is independent of the return on efficient portfolio K, then $b_j^K = 0$ and $\bar{Z}_j = R$. Trivially, $b_R^K = 0$ for the riskless security. Therefore, by the b_j^K measure, security j and the riskless security have equal risk. However, if security j has positive variance, then by the Rothschild–Stiglitz measure, security j is more risky than the riskless security. Despite this, the two measures are not in conflict and, indeed, are complementary. The Rothschild–Stiglitz definition measures the "total risk" of a security in the sense that it compares the expected utility from holding a security *alone* with the expected utility from holding another security *alone*. Hence, it is the appropriate definition for identifying optimal portfolios and determining the efficient portfolio set. However, it is not useful for defining the risk of securities generally because it does not take into account that investors can mix securities together to form portfolios. The b_j^K measure does take this into account because it measures the only part of an individual security's risk which is relevant to an investor: namely, the part that contributes to the total risk of his optimal portfolio. In contrast with the Rothschild–Stiglitz measure of total risk, the b_j^K measures the "systematic risk" of a security (relative to efficient portfolio K). Of course, to determine the b_j^K, the efficient portfolio set must be determined. Because the Rothschild–Stiglitz measure does just that, the two measures are complementary.

Although the expected return of a security provides an equivalent ranking to its b_p^K measure, the b_p^K measure is not vacuous. There exist nontrivial information sets which allow b_p^K to be determined without knowledge of $\bar{Z}_p$. For example, consider a model in which all investors agree on the joint distribution of the returns on securities. Suppose we know the utility function U for some investor and the probability distribution of his optimal portfolio Z^*W_0. From (2.14) we therefore know the distribution of $Y(Z^*)$. For security j, define the random variable

$$\epsilon_j \equiv Z_j - \bar{Z}_j$$

Suppose, furthermore, that we have enough information about the joint distribution of $Y(Z^*)$ and ϵ_j to compute

$$\text{cov}[Y(Z^*),\epsilon_j] = \text{cov}[Y(Z^*),Z_j] = b_j^*$$

but do not know $\bar{Z}_j$.[12] However, Theorem 2.4 is a necessary condition for equilibrium in the securities market. Hence, we can deduce the equilibrium expected return on security j from $\bar{Z}_j = R + b_j^* (\bar{Z}^* - R)$. Analysis of the necessary information sets required to deduce the equilibrium structure of security returns is an important topic in portfolio theory and one that will be explored further in Section 2.4.

The manifest behavioral characteristic shared by all risk-averse utility maximizers is to diversify (i.e. to spread one's wealth among many investments). The benefits of diversification in reducing risk depend upon

12   A sufficient amount of information would be the joint distribution of Z^* and ϵ_j. What is necessary will depend on the functional form of U'. However, in no case will knowledge of $\bar{Z}_j$ be a necessary condition.

the degree of statistical interdependence among returns on the available investments. The greatest benefits in risk reduction come from adding a security to the portfolio whose realized return tends to be higher when the return on the rest of the portfolio is lower. Next to such "countercyclical" investments in terms of benefit are the noncyclic securities whose returns are orthogonal to the return on the portfolio. Least beneficial are the procyclical investments whose returns tend to be higher when the return on the portfolio is higher and lower when the return on the portfolio is lower. A natural summary statistic for this characteristic of a security's return distribution is its conditional expected-return function, conditional on the realized return of the portfolio. Because the risk of a security is measured by its marginal contribution to the risk of an optimal portfolio, it is perhaps not surprising that there is a direct relation between the risk measure b_p of portfolio p and the behavior of the conditional expected-return function $G_p(Z_e) \equiv E\{Z_p|Z_e\}$, where Z_e is the realized return on an efficient portfolio.

Theorem 2.5

If Z_p and Z_q denote the returns on portfolios p and q respectively and if, for each possible value of Z_e, $dG_p(Z_e)/dZ_e \geq dG_q(Z_e)/dZ_e$ with strict inequality holding over some finite probability measure of Z_e, then portfolio p is riskier than portfolio q and $\bar{Z}_p > \bar{Z}_q$.

PROOF

From (2.13) and the linearity of the covariance operator,

$$b_p - b_q = \text{cov}[Y(Z_e), Z_p - Z_q] = E\{Y(Z_e)(Z_p - Z_q)\}$$

because $E\{Y(Z_e)\} = 0$. By the property of conditional expectations,

$$E\{Y(Z_e)(Z_p - Z_q)\} = E\{Y(Z_e)[G_p(Z_e) - G_q(Z_e)]\}$$
$$= \text{cov}[Y(Z_e), G_p(Z_e) - G_q(Z_e)]$$

Thus

$$b_p - b_q = \text{cov}[Y(Z_e), G_p(Z_e) - G_q(Z_e)]$$

From (2.13), $Y(Z_e)$ is a strictly increasing function of Z_e and, by hypothesis, $G_p(Z_e) - G_q(Z_e)$ is a nondecreasing function of Z_e for all Z_e and a strictly increasing function of Z_e over some finite probability measure of Z_e. From Theorem 236 in Hardy, Littlewood, and Pölya (1959), it follows that $\mathrm{cov}[Y(Z_e), G_p(Z_e) - G_q(Z_e)] > 0$, and therefore $b_p > b_q$. From Theorem 2.4, it follows that $\bar{Z}_p > \bar{Z}_q$.   QED

Theorem 2.6

If Z_p and Z_q denote the returns on portfolios p and q respectively and if, for each possible value of Z_e, $dG_p(Z_e)/dZ_e - dG_q(Z_e)/dZ_e = a_{pq}$, a constant, then $b_p = b_q + a_{pq}$ and $\bar{Z}_p = \bar{Z}_q + a_{pq}(\bar{Z}_e - R)$.

PROOF

By hypothesis, $G_p(Z_e) - G_q(Z_e) = a_{pq}Z_e + h$ where h does not depend on Z_e. As in the proof of Theorem 2.5,

$$b_p - b_q = \mathrm{cov}[Y(Z_e), G_p(Z_e) - G_q(Z_e)] = \mathrm{cov}[Y(Z_e), a_{pq}Z_e + h]$$

Thus, $b_p - b_q = a_{pq}$ because $\mathrm{cov}[Y(Z_e), Z_e] = 1$ and $\mathrm{cov}[Y(Z_e), h] = 0$. From Theorem 2.4,

$$\bar{Z}_p = R + b_q(\bar{Z}_e - R) + a_{pq}(\bar{Z}_e - R) = \bar{Z}_q + a_{pq}(\bar{Z}_e - R)$$

QED

Theorem 2.7

If, for all possible values of Z_e,

(i) $dG_p(Z_e)/dZ_e > 1$, then $\bar{Z}_p > \bar{Z}_e$;

(ii) $0 < dG_p(Z_e)/dZ_e < 1$, then $R < \bar{Z}_p < \bar{Z}_e$;

(iii) $dG_p(Z_e)/dZ_e < 0$, then $\bar{Z}_p < R$;

(iv) $dG_p(Z_e)/dZ_e = a_p$, a constant, then $\bar{Z}_p = R + a_p(\bar{Z}_e - R)$.

The proof follows directly from Theorems 2.5 and 2.6 by substituting either Z_e or R for Z_q and noting that $dG_q(Z_e)/dZ_e = 1$ for $Z_q = Z_e$ and $dG_q(Z_e)/dZ_e = 0$ for $Z_q = R$.

As Theorems 2.5, 2.6, and 2.7 demonstrate, the conditional expected-return function provides considerable information about a security's risk and equilibrium expected return. It is common practice, moreover, for security analysts to provide conditioned forecasts of individual security returns, conditioned on the realized return of a broad-based stock portfolio such as the Standard & Poor's 500. As is evident from these theorems, the conditional expected-return function does not in general provide sufficient information to determine the exact risk of a security. As follows from Theorems 2.6 and 2.7(iv), the exception is the case where this function is linear in Z_e. Although surely a special case, it is a rather important one, as will be shown in Section 2.4.

2.4 SPANNING, SEPARATION, AND MUTUAL-FUND THEOREMS

Definition

A set of M feasible portfolios with random variable returns $(X_1,...,X_M)$ is said to *span* the space of portfolios contained in the set Ψ if and only if for any portfolio in Ψ with return denoted by Z_p there exist numbers $(\delta_1,...,\delta_M)$, $\Sigma_1^M \delta_j = 1$, such that $Z_p = \Sigma_1^M \delta_j X_j$. If N is the number of securities available to generate the portfolios in Ψ and if M^* denotes the smallest number of feasible portfolios that span the space of portfolios contained in Ψ, then $M^* \leq N$.

Fischer (1972) and Merton (1982a, pp. 611–4) use comparative statics analysis to show that little can be derived about the structure of optimal portfolio demand functions unless further restrictions are imposed on the class of investors' utility functions or the class of probability distributions for securities' returns. A particularly fruitful set of such restrictions is the one that provides for a nontrivial (i.e. $M^* < N$) spanning of either the feasible or efficient portfolio sets. Indeed, the spanning property leads to a collection of "mutual-fund" or "separation" theorems that are fundamental to modern financial theory.

A *mutual fund* is a financial intermediary that holds as its assets a portfolio of securities and issues as liabilities shares against this collection of assets. Unlike the optimal portfolio of an individual investor, the portfolio of securities held by a mutual fund need not be an efficient portfolio. The connection between mutual funds and the spanning property can be seen in the following theorem.

Theorem 2.8

If there exist M mutual funds whose portfolios span the portfolio set Ψ, then all investors will be indifferent between selecting their optimal portfolios from Ψ and selecting from portfolio combinations of just the M mutual funds.

The proof of the theorem follows directly from the definition of spanning. If Z^* denotes the return on an optimal portfolio selected from Ψ and if X_j

denotes the return on the jth mutual fund's portfolio, then there exist portfolio weights $(\delta_1^*,...,\delta_M^*)$ such that $Z^* = \Sigma_1^M \delta_j^* X_j$. Hence, any investor would be indifferent between the portfolio with return Z^* and the $(\delta_1^*,...,\delta_M^*)$ combination of the mutual-fund shares.

Although the theorem states "indifference," if there are information-gathering or other transactions costs and if there are economies of scale, then investors would prefer the mutual funds whenever $M < N$. By a similar argument, one would expect that investors would prefer to have the smallest number of funds necessary to span Ψ. Therefore the smallest number of such funds, M^*, is a particularly important spanning set. Hence, the spanning property can be used to derive an endogenous theory for the existence of financial intermediaries with the functional characteristics of a mutual fund. Moreover, from these functional characteristics a theory for their optimal management can be derived.

For the mutual-fund theorems to have serious empirical content, the minimum number M^* of funds required for spanning must be significantly smaller than the number N of available securities. When such spanning obtains, the investor's portfolio-selection problem can be separated into two steps: first, individual securities are mixed together to form the M^* mutual funds; second, the investor allocates his wealth among the M^* funds' shares. If the investor knows that the funds span the space of optimal portfolios, then he need only know the joint probability distribution of $(X_1,...,X_{M^*})$ to determine his optimal portfolio. It is for this reason that the mutual-fund theorems are also called "separation" theorems. However, if the M^* funds can be constructed only if the fund managers know the preferences, endowments, and probability beliefs of each investor, then the formal separation property will have little operational significance.

In addition to providing an endogenous theory for mutual funds, the existence of a nontrivial spanning set can be used to deduce equilibrium properties of individual securities' returns and to derive optimal rules for business firms making production and capital budgeting decisions. Moreover, in virtually every model of portfolio selection in which empirical implications beyond those presented in Sections 2.2 and 2.3 are derived, some nontrivial form of the spanning property obtains.

While the determination of conditions under which nontrivial spanning will obtain is, in a broad sense, a subset of the traditional economic theory of aggregation, the first rigorous contributions in portfolio theory were made by Arrow (1953, 1964), Markowitz (1952, 1959), and Tobin (1958). In each of these papers, and most subsequent papers, the spanning property is derived as an implication of the specific model examined, and therefore such derivations provide only sufficient conditions. In two notable exceptions, Cass and Stiglitz (1970) and Ross (1978) "reverse" the process by deriving necessary conditions for nontrivial spanning to obtain.

In this section necessary and sufficient conditions for spanning are presented along the lines developed by Cass and Stiglitz and Ross. Discussion of the specific models of Arrow, Markowitz, and Tobin can be found in Merton (1982a, 1990a).

Let Ψ^f denote the set of all feasible portfolios that can be constructed from a riskless security with return R and n risky securities with a given joint probability distribution for their random variable returns $(Z_1,...,Z_n)$. Let Ω denote the $n \times n$ variance–covariance matrix of the returns on the n risky assets.

Theorem 2.9

Necessary conditions for the M feasible portfolios with returns $(X_1,...,X_M)$ to span the portfolio set Ψ^f are (a) that the rank of $\Omega \leqslant M$ and (b) that there exist numbers $(\delta_1,...,\delta_M)$, $\sum_1^M \delta_j = 1$, such that the random variable $\sum_1^M \delta_j X_j$ has zero variance.

PROOF

(a) The set of portfolios Ψ^f defines an $(n + 1)$-dimensional vector space. By definition, if $(X_1,...,X_M)$ spans Ψ^f, then each risky security's return can be represented as a linear combination of $(X_1,...,X_M)$. Clearly, this is only possible if the rank of $\Omega \leqslant M$. (b) The riskless security is contained in Ψ^f. Therefore, if $(X_1,...,X_M)$ spans Ψ^f, then there must exist a portfolio combination of $(X_1,...,X_M)$ which is riskless. QED

Proposition 2.1

If $Z_p = \sum_1^n a_j Z_j + b$ is the return on some security or portfolio and if there are no "arbitrage opportunities" (Assumption 3), then

$$\text{(a)} \ b = (1 - \sum_1^n a_j)R \quad \text{and} \quad \text{(b)} \ Z_p = R + \sum_1^n a_j(Z_j - R)$$

PROOF

Let $Z^\dagger$ be the return on a portfolio with fraction $\delta_j^\dagger$ allocated to security j, $j = 1,...,n$; δ_p allocated to the security with return Z_p; and $1 - \delta_p - \sum_1^n \delta_j^\dagger$ allocated to the riskless security with return R. If $\delta_j^\dagger$ is chosen such that $\delta_j^\dagger = -\delta_p a_j$, then $Z^\dagger = R + \delta_p[b - R(1 - \sum_1^n a_j)]$. $Z^\dagger$ is a riskless security and therefore, by Assumption 3, $Z^\dagger = R$. But δ_p can be chosen arbitrarily. Therefore $b = (1 - \sum_1^n a_j)R$. Substituting for b, it follows directly that $Z_p = R + \sum_1^n a_j(Z_j - R)$. QED

As long as there are no arbitrage opportunities, from Theorem 2.9 and Proposition 2.1 it can be assumed without loss of generality that one of the portfolios in any candidate spanning set is the riskless security. If, by convention, $X_M = R$, then in all subsequent analyses the notation $(X_1,...,X_m,R)$ will be used to denote an M-portfolio spanning set where $m \equiv M - 1$ is the number of risky portfolios (together with the riskless security) that span Ψ^f.

Theorem 2.10

A necessary and sufficient condition for $(X_1,...,X_m,R)$ to span Ψ^f is that there exist numbers $\{a_{ij}\}$ such that $Z_j = R + \Sigma_1^m a_{ij}(X_i - R)$, $j = 1,2,...,n$.

PROOF

If $(X_1,...,X_m,R)$ span Ψ^j, then there exist portfolio weights $(\delta_{1j},...,\delta_{Mj})$, $\Sigma_1^M \delta_{ij} = 1$, such that $Z_j = \Sigma_1^M \delta_{ij} X_i$. Noting that $X_M = R$ and substituting $\delta_{Mj} = 1 - \Sigma_1^m \delta_{ij}$, we have that $Z_j = R + \Sigma_1^m \delta_{ij}(X_i - R)$. This proves necessity. If there exist numbers $\{a_{ij}\}$ such that $Z_j = R + \Sigma_1^m a_{ij}(X_i - R)$, then pick the portfolio weights $\delta_{ij} = a_{ij}$ for $i = 1,...,m$, and $\delta_{Mj} = 1 - \Sigma_1^m \delta_{ij}$, from which it follows that $Z_j = \Sigma_1^M \delta_{ij} X_i$. But every portfolio in Ψ^f can be written as a portfolio combination of $(Z_1,...,Z_n)$ and R. Hence, $(X_1,...,X_m,R)$ span Ψ^f and this proves sufficiency.   QED

Let Ω_X be the $m \times m$ variance–covariance matrix of the returns on the m portfolios with returns $(X_1,...,X_m)$.

Corollary 2.10

A necessary and sufficient condition for $(X_1,...,X_m,R)$ to be the smallest number of feasible portfolios that span (i.e. $M^* = m + 1$) is that the rank of Ω equals the rank of $\Omega_X = m$.

PROOF

If $(X_1,...,X_m,R)$ span Ψ^f and m is the smallest number of risky portfolios that does, then $(X_1,...,X_m)$ must be linearly independent and therefore, the rank of $\Omega_X = m$. Hence, $(X_1,...,X_m)$ form a basis for the vector space of security returns $(Z_1,...,Z_n)$. Therefore the rank of Ω must equal the rank of Ω_X. This proves necessity. If the rank of $\Omega_X = m$, then $(X_1,...,X_m)$ are linearly independent. Moreover, $(X_1,...,X_m) \in \Psi^f$. Hence, if the rank of $\Omega = m$, then there exist numbers $\{a_{ij}\}$ such that $Z_j - \bar{Z}_j = \Sigma_1^m a_{ij}(X_i - \bar{X}_i)$ for $j = 1,2,...,n$. Therefore, $Z_j = b_j + \Sigma_1^m a_{ij} X_i$, where $b_j \equiv \bar{Z}_j - \Sigma_1^m a_{ij} \bar{X}_i$. By the same argument as that used to prove Proposition 2.1, $b_j = (1 - $

$\Sigma_1^m a_{ij})R$. Therefore, $Z_j = R + \Sigma_1^m a_{ij}(X_i - R)$. By Theorem 2.10, $(X_1,...,X_m,R)$ span Ψ^f. QED

It follows from Corollary 2.10 that a necessary and sufficient condition for nontrivial spanning of Ψ^f is that some of the risky securities are redundant securities. Note, however, that this condition is sufficient only if securities are priced such that there are no arbitrage opportunities.

In all these derived theorems the only restriction on investors' preferences was that they prefer more to less. In particular, it was not assumed that investors are necessarily risk averse. Although Ψ^f was defined in terms of a known joint probability distribution for $(Z_1,...,Z_n)$, which implies homogeneous beliefs among investors, inspection of the proof of Theorem 2.10 shows that this condition can be weakened. If investors agree on a set of portfolios $(X_1,...,X_m,R)$ such that $Z_j = R + \Sigma_1^m a_{ij}(X_i - R)$, $j = 1,2,...,n$, and if they agree on the numbers $\{a_{ij}\}$, then by Theorem 2.10 $(X_1,...,X_m,R)$ span Ψ^f even if investors *do not* agree on the joint distribution of $(X_1,...,X_m)$. These appear to be the weakest restrictions on preferences and probability beliefs that can produce nontrivial spanning and the corresponding mutual-fund theorem. Hence, to derive additional theorems it is now further assumed that all investors are risk averse and that investors have homogeneous probability beliefs.

Define Ψ^e to be the set of all efficient portfolios contained in Ψ^f.

Proposition 2.2

If Z_e is the return on a portfolio contained in Ψ^e, then any portfolio that combines positive amounts of Z_e with the riskless security is also contained in Ψ^e.

PROOF

Let $Z = \delta(Z_e - R) + R$ be the return on a portfolio with positive fraction δ allocated to Z_e and fraction $1 - \delta$ allocated to the riskless security. Because Z_e is an efficient portfolio, there exists a strictly concave increasing function V such that $E\{V'(Z_e)(Z_j - R)\} = 0$, $j = 1,2,...,n$. Define $U(W) \equiv V(aW + b)$, where $a \equiv 1/\delta > 0$ and $b \equiv (\delta - 1)R/\delta$. Because $a > 0$, U is a strictly concave and increasing function. Moreover, $U'(Z) = aV'(Z_e)$. Hence, $E\{U'(Z)(Z_j - R)\} = 0$, $j = 1,2,...,n$. Therefore there exists a utility function such that Z is an optimal portfolio, and thus Z is an efficient portfolio. QED

It follows immediately from Proposition 2.2 that, for every number $\bar{Z}$ such that $\bar{Z} \geqslant R$, there exists at least one efficient portfolio with expected return equal to $\bar{Z}$. Moreover, we also have that, if $(X_1,...,X_m)$ are the returns on M candidate portfolios to span the space of efficient portfolios Ψ^e, then without loss of generality it can be assumed that one of the portfolios is the riskless security.

Theorem 2.11

Let $(X_1,\ldots,X_m)$ denote the returns on m feasible portfolios. If, for security j, there exist numbers $\{a_{ij}\}$ such that $Z_j = \overline{Z}_j + \Sigma_1^m a_{ij}(X_i - \overline{X}_i) + \epsilon_j$ where $E\{\epsilon_j V'_K(Z_e^K)\} = 0$ for some efficient portfolio K, then $\overline{Z}_j = R + \Sigma_1^m a_{ij}(\overline{X}_i - R)$.

PROOF

Let Z_p be the return on a portfolio with fraction δ allocated to security j; fraction $\delta_i = -\delta a_{ij}$ allocated to portfolio X_i, $i = 1,\ldots,m$; and $1 - \delta - \Sigma_1^m \delta_i$ allocated to the riskless security. By hypothesis, Z_p can be written as

$$Z_p = R + \delta\left[\overline{Z}_j - R - \sum_1^m a_{ij}(\overline{X}_i - R)\right] + \delta\epsilon_j$$

where

$$E\{\delta\epsilon_j V'_K\} = \delta E\{\epsilon_j V'_K\} = 0$$

By construction, $E\{\epsilon_j\} = 0$, and hence $\operatorname{cov}(Z_p, V'_K) = 0$. Therefore the systematic risk of portfolio p, b_p^K, is zero. From Theorem 2.4, $\overline{Z}_p = R$. But δ can be chosen arbitrarily. Therefore $\overline{Z}_j = R + \Sigma_1^m a_{ij}(\overline{X}_i - R)$.   QED

Hence, if the return on a security can be written in this linear form relative to the portfolios $(X_1,\ldots,X_m)$, then its expected excess return is completely determined by the expected excess returns on these portfolios and the weights $\{a_{ij}\}$.

Theorem 2.12

If, for every security j, there exist numbers $\{a_{ij}\}$ such that

$$Z_j = R + \sum_1^m a_{ij}(X_i - R) + \epsilon_j$$

where $E\{\epsilon_j | X_1,\ldots,X_m\} = 0$, then $(X_1,\ldots,X_m,R)$ span the set of efficient portfolios Ψ^e.

PROOF

Let w_j^K denote the fraction of efficient portfolio K allocated to security j, $j = 1,...,n$. By hypothesis, we can write

$$Z_e^K = R + \sum_1^m \delta_i^K(X_i - R) + \epsilon^K$$

where $\delta_i^K \equiv \Sigma_1^n w_j^K a_{ij}$ and $\epsilon^K \equiv \Sigma_1^n w_j^K \epsilon_j$ with

$$E\{\epsilon^K|X_1,...,X_m\} = \sum_1^n w_j^K E\{\epsilon_j|X_1,...,X_m\} = 0$$

Construct the portfolio with return Z by allocating fraction δ_i^K to portfolio X_i, $i = 1,...,m$, and fraction $1 - \Sigma_1^m \delta_i^K$ to the riskless security. By construction, $Z_e^K = Z + \epsilon^K$ where $E\{\epsilon^K|Z\} = E\{\epsilon^K|\Sigma_1^m \delta_i^K X_i\} = 0$ because $E\{\epsilon^K|X_1,...,X_m\} = 0$. Hence, for $\epsilon^K \not\equiv 0$, Z_e^K is riskier than Z in the Rothschild–Stiglitz sense, which contradicts that Z_e^K is an efficient portfolio. Thus, $\epsilon^K \equiv 0$ for every efficient portfolio K, and all efficient portfolios can be generated by a portfolio combination of $(X_1,...,X_m,R)$.
QED

Therefore, if we can find a set of portfolios $(X_1,...,X_m)$ such that every security's return can be expressed as a linear combination of the returns $(X_1,...,X_m,R)$ plus noise relative to these portfolios, then we have a set of portfolios that span Ψ^e. The following theorem, first proved by Ross (1978), shows that security returns can always be written in a linear form relative to a set of spanning portfolios.

Theorem 2.13

Let w_j^K denote the fraction of efficient portfolio K allocated to security j, $j = 1,...,n$. $(X_1,...,X_m,R)$ span Ψ^e if and only if there exist numbers $\{a_{ij}\}$ for every security j such that $Z_j = R + \Sigma_1^m a_{ij}(X_i - R) + \epsilon_j$, where $E\{\epsilon_j|\Sigma_1^m \delta_i^K X_i\} = 0$, $\delta_i^K \equiv \Sigma_1^n w_j^K a_{ij}$, for every efficient portfolio K.

PROOF

The "if" part follows directly from the proof of Theorem 2.12. In that proof, we only needed that $E\{\epsilon^K|\Sigma_1^m \delta_i^K X_i\} = 0$ for every efficient portfolio K to show that $(X_1,...,X_m,R)$ span Ψ^e. The proof of the "only if" part is long and requires the proof of four specialized lemmas (see Ross, 1978, Appendix). It is therefore not presented here.
QED

Corollary 2.13

(X,R) span Ψ^e if and only if there exists a number a_j for each security j, $j = 1,...,n$, such that $Z_j = R + a_j(X - R) + \epsilon_j$ where $E\{\epsilon_j|X\} = 0$.

PROOF

The "if" part follows directly from Theorem 2.12. The "only if" part is as follows. By hypothesis, $Z_e^K = \delta^K(X - R) + R$ for every efficient portfolio K. If $\overline{X} = R$, then from Corollary 2.1, $\delta^K = 0$ for every efficient portfolio K and R spans Ψ^e. Otherwise, from Theorem 2.2, $\delta^K \neq 0$ for every efficient portfolio. By Theorem 2.13, $E\{\epsilon_j|\delta^K X\} = 0$, for $j = 1,...,n$ and every efficient portfolio K. But, for $\delta^K \neq 0$, $E\{\epsilon_j|\delta^K X\} = 0$ if and only if $E\{\epsilon_j|X\} = 0$.   QED

In addition to that of Ross (1978), there have been a number of studies of the properties of efficient portfolios (cf. Chen and Ingersoll, 1983; Dybvig and Ross, 1982; Nielsen, 1986). However, there is still much to be determined. For example, from Theorem 2.13, a necessary condition for $(X_1,...,X_m,R)$ to span Ψ^e is that $E\{\epsilon_j|Z_e^K\} = 0$ for $j = 1,...,n$ and every efficient portfolio K. For $m > 1$, this condition is not sufficient to ensure that $(X_1,...,X_m,R)$ span Ψ^e. The condition that $E\{\epsilon_j|\Sigma_1^m\lambda_i X_i\} = 0$ for all numbers λ_i implies that $E\{\epsilon_j|X_1,...,X_m\} = 0$. If, however, the $\{\lambda_i\}$ are restricted to the class of optimal portfolio weights $\{\delta_i^K\}$ as in Theorem 2.13 and $m > 1$, it does not follow that $E\{\epsilon_j|X_1,...,X_m\} = 0$. Thus, $E\{\epsilon_j|X_1,...,X_m\} = 0$ is sufficient, but not necessary, for $(X_1,...,X_m,R)$ to span Ψ^e. It is not known whether any material cases of spanning are ruled out by imposing this stronger condition. Empirical applications of the spanning conditions generally assume that the condition $E\{\epsilon_j|X_1,...,X_m\} = 0$ obtains.

Since Ψ^e is contained in Ψ^f, any properties proved for portfolios that span Ψ^e must be properties of portfolios that span Ψ^f. From Theorems 2.10, 2.12, and 2.13, the essential difference is that to span the efficient portfolio set it is not necessary that linear combinations of the spanning portfolios exactly replicate the return on each available security. Hence, it is not necessary that there exist redundant securities for nontrivial spanning of Ψ^e to obtain. Of course, all three theorems are empty of any empirical content if the size M^* of the smallest spanning set is equal to $n + 1$.

As discussed in the introduction to this section, all the important models of portfolio selection exhibit the nontrivial spanning property for the efficient portfolio set. Therefore, for all such models that do not restrict the class of admissible utility functions beyond that of risk aversion, the distribution of individual security returns must be such that

$$Z_j = R + \sum_1^m a_{ij}(X_i - R) + \epsilon_j$$

where ϵ_j satisfies the conditions of Theorem 2.13 for $j = 1,...,n$. Moreover, given some knowledge of the joint distribution of a set of portfolios that span Ψ^e with $Z_j - \overline{Z}_j$, there exists a method for determining the a_{ij} and $\overline{Z}_j$.

Proposition 2.3

If, for every security j, $E\{\epsilon_j | X_1,...,X_m\} = 0$ with $(X_1,...,X_m)$ linearly independent with finite variances and if the return on security j, Z_j, has a finite variance, then the $\{a_{ij}\}$, $i = 1,2,...,m$, in Theorems 2.12 and 2.13 are given by

$$a_{ij} = \sum_1^m v_{ik} \operatorname{cov}(X_k, Z_j)$$

where v_{ik} is the ikth element of Ω_X^{-1}.

The proof of Proposition 2.3 follows directly from the condition that $E\{\epsilon_j | X_k\} = 0$, which implies that $\operatorname{cov}(\epsilon_j, X_k) = 0$, $k = 1,...,m$. The condition that $(X_1,...,X_m)$ be linearly independent is trivial in the sense that knowing the joint distribution of a spanning set one can always choose a linearly independent subset. The only properties of the joint distributions required to compute the a_{ij} are the variances and covariances of $X_1,...,X_m$ and the covariances between Z_j and $X_1,...,X_m$. In particular, knowledge of $\overline{Z}_j$ is not required because $\operatorname{cov}(X_k, Z_j) = \operatorname{cov}(X_k, Z_j - \overline{Z}_j)$. Hence, for $m < n$ (and especially so for $m \ll n$), there exists a nontrivial information set which allows the a_{ij} to be determined without knowledge of $\overline{Z}_j$. If $\overline{X}_1,...,\overline{X}_m$ are known, then $\overline{Z}_j$ can be computed by the formula in Theorem 2.11. By comparison with the example in Section 2.3, the information set required there to determine $\overline{Z}_j$ was a utility function and the joint distribution of its associated optimal portfolio with $Z_j - \overline{Z}_j$. Here, we must know a complete set of portfolios that span Ψ^e. However, here only the second-moment properties of the joint distribution need be known, and no utility function information other than risk aversion is required.

A special case of no little interest is when a single risky portfolio and the riskless security span the space of efficient portfolios and Corollary 2.13 applies. Indeed, the classic mean–variance model of Markowitz (1952, 1959) and Tobin (1958) exhibits this strong form of separation. Moreover, most macroeconomic models have highly aggregated financial sectors where investors' portfolio choices are limited to simple combinations of two securities: "bonds" and "stocks." The rigorous microeconomic foundation for such aggregation is precisely that Ψ^e is spanned by a single risky portfolio and the riskless security.

If X denotes the random variable return on a risky portfolio such that (X,R) spans Ψ^e, then the return on any efficient portfolio, Z_e, can be written as if it had been chosen by combining the risky portfolio with return X with the riskless security: namely, $Z_e = \delta(X - R) + R$, where δ is the fraction allocated to the risky portfolio and $1 - \delta$ is the fraction allocated to the riskless security. By Corollary 2.1, the sign of δ will be the same for every efficient portfolio, and therefore all efficient portfolios will be perfectly positively correlated. If $\overline{X} > R$, then by Proposition 2.2, X will be an efficient portfolio and $\delta > 0$ for every efficient portfolio.

Proposition 2.4

If $(Z_1,...,Z_n)$ contain no redundant securities, δ_j denotes the fraction of portfolio X allocated to security j, and w_j^* denotes the fraction of any risk-averse investor's optimal portfolio allocated to security j, $j = 1,...,n$, then for every such risk-averse investor

$$\frac{w_j^*}{w_k^*} = \frac{\delta_j}{\delta_k} \qquad j,k = 1,2,...,n$$

The proof follows immediately because every optimal portfolio is an efficient portfolio and the holdings of risky securities in every efficient portfolio are proportional to the holdings in X. Hence, the relative holdings of risky securities will be the same for all risk-averse investors. Whenever Proposition 2.4 holds and if there exist numbers δ_j^* where $\delta_j^*/\delta_k^* = \delta_j/\delta_k, j,k = 1,...,n$ and $\Sigma_1^n \delta_j^* = 1$, then the portfolio with proportions $(\delta_1^*,...,\delta_n^*)$ is called the *Optimal Combination of Risky Assets*. If such a portfolio exists, then without loss of generality it can always be assumed that $X = \Sigma_1^n \delta_j^* Z_j$.

Proposition 2.5

If (X,R) spans Ψ^e, then Ψ^e is a convex set.

PROOF

Let Z_e^1 and Z_e^2 denote the returns on two distinct efficient portfolios. Because (X,R) spans Ψ^e, $Z_e^1 = \delta_1(X - R) + R$ and $Z_e^2 = \delta_2(X - R) + R$. Because they are distinct, $\delta_1 \neq \delta_2$, and so assume $\delta_1 \neq 0$. Let $Z \equiv \lambda Z_e^1 + (1 - \lambda)Z_e^2$ denote the return on a portfolio which allocates fraction λ to Z_e^1 and $1 - \lambda$ to Z_e^2, where $0 \leqslant \lambda \leqslant 1$. By substitution, the expression for Z can be rewritten as $Z = \delta(Z_e^1 - R) + R$, where $\delta \equiv \lambda + (\delta_2/\delta_1)(1 - \lambda)$. Because Z_e^1 and Z_e^2 are efficient portfolios, the sign of δ_1 is the same as the sign of δ_2. Hence, $\delta \geqslant 0$. Therefore, by Proposition 2.2, Z is an efficient portfolio. It follows by induction that for any integer k and numbers λ_i such that $0 \leqslant \lambda_i \leqslant 1$, $i = 1,...,k$ and $\Sigma_1^k \lambda_i = 1$, $Z^k \equiv \Sigma_1^k \lambda_i Z_e^i$ is the return on an efficient portfolio. Hence, Ψ^e is a convex set.   QED

Definition

A *market portfolio* is defined as a portfolio that holds all available securities in proportion to their market values.

To avoid the problems of "double counting" caused by financial interme-diaries and inter-investor issues of securities, the equilibrium market value of a security for this purpose is defined to be the equilibrium value of the aggregate demand by individuals for the security. In models where all physical assets are held by business firms and business firms hold no financial assets, an equivalent definition is that the market value of a security equals the equilibrium value of the aggregate amount of that security issued by business firms. If V_j denotes the market value of security j and V_R denotes the value of the riskless security, then

$$\delta_j^M = \frac{V_j}{\Sigma_1^n V_j + V_R} \qquad j = 1,2,...,n$$

where δ_j^M is the fraction of security j held in a market portfolio.

Theorem 2.14

If Ψ^e is a convex set, and if the securities' market is in equilibrium, then a market portfolio is an efficient portfolio.

PROOF

Let there be K risk-averse investors in the economy with the initial wealth of investor k denoted by W_0^k. Define $Z^k \equiv R + \Sigma_1^n w_j^k(Z_j - R)$ to be the return per dollar on investor k's optimal portfolio, where w_j^k is the fraction allocated to security j. In equilibrium, $\Sigma_1^K w_j^k W_0^k = V_j$, $j = 1,2,...,n$, and $\Sigma_1^K W_0^k \equiv W_0 = \Sigma_1^n V_j + V_R$. Define $\lambda_k \equiv W_0^k/W_0$, $k = 1,...,K$. Clearly, $0 \leqslant \lambda_k \leqslant 1$ and $\Sigma_1^K \lambda_k = 1$. By definition of a market portfolio, $\Sigma_1^K w_j^k \lambda_k = \delta_j^M$, $j = 1,2,...,n$. Multiplying by $Z_j - R$ and summing over j, it follows that

$$\sum_1^K \lambda_k \sum_1^n w_j^k(Z_j - R) = \sum_1^K \lambda_k(Z^k - R) = \sum_1^n \delta_j^M(Z_j - R) = Z_M - R$$

where Z_M is defined to be the return per dollar on the market portfolio. Because $\Sigma_1^K \lambda_k = 1$, $Z_M = \Sigma_1^K \lambda_k Z^k$. But every optimal portfolio is an efficient portfolio. Hence, Z_M is a convex combination of the returns on K efficient portfolios. Therefore, if Ψ^e is convex, then the market portfolio is contained in Ψ^e.   QED

Because a market portfolio can be constructed without the knowledge of preferences, the distribution of wealth, or the joint probability distribution for the outstanding securities, models in which the market portfolio can be shown to be efficient are more likely to produce testable hypotheses. In addition, the efficiency of the market portfolio provides a rigorous microeconomic justification for the use of a "representative man" to derive equilibrium prices in aggregated economic models, i.e. the market portfolio is efficient if and only if there exists a concave utility function such that maximization of its expected value with initial wealth equal to national wealth would lead to the market portfolio as the optimal portfolio. Indeed, it is currently fashionable in the real world to advise "passive" investment strategies that simply mix the market portfolio with the riskless security. Provided that the market portfolio is efficient, by Proposition 2.2 no investor following such strategies could ever be convicted of "inefficiency." Moreover, the market portfolio will be efficient if markets are "complete" in the sense of Arrow (1953, 1964) and Debreu (1959) and investors have homogeneous beliefs. Unfortunately, general necessary and sufficient conditions for the market portfolio to be efficient have not as yet been derived.

However, even if the market portfolio were not efficient, it does have the following important property.

Proposition 2.6

In all portfolio models with homogeneous beliefs and risk-averse investors, the equilibrium expected return on the market portfolio exceeds the return on the riskless security.

The proof follows directly from the proof of Theorem 2.14 and Corollary 2.1. Clearly, $\bar{Z}_M - R = \Sigma_1^K \lambda_k(\bar{Z}^k - R)$. By Corollary 2.1, $\bar{Z}^k \geq R$ for $k = 1,...,K$, with strict inequality holding if Z^k is risky. But, $\lambda_k > 0$. Hence, $\bar{Z}_M > R$ if any risky securities are held by any investor. Note that using no information other than market prices and quantities of securities outstanding, the market portfolio (and combinations of the market portfolio and the riskless security) is the only risky portfolio where the sign of its equilibrium expected excess return can always be predicted.

Returning to the special case where Ψ^e is spanned by a single risky portfolio and the riskless security, it follows immediately from Proposition 2.5 and Theorem 2.14 that the market portfolio is efficient. Because all efficient portfolios are perfectly positively correlated, it follows that the risky spanning portfolio can always be chosen to be the market portfolio (i.e. $X = Z_M$). Therefore, every efficient portfolio (and hence every optimal portfolio) can be represented as a simple portfolio combination of the market portfolio and the riskless security with a positive fraction allocated to the market portfolio. If all investors want to hold risky securities in the same relative proportions, then the only way in which this is possible is if these relative proportions are identical with those in the market portfolio. Indeed, if there were one best investment strategy, and if this "best" strategy were widely known, then whatever the original statement of the strategy, it must lead to simply this imperative: "hold the market portfolio."

Because for every security $\delta_j^M \geqslant 0$, it follows from Proposition 2.4 that, in equilibrium, every investor will hold nonnegative quantities of risky securities, and therefore it is never optimal to short-sell risky securities. Hence, in models where $m = 1$, the introduction of restrictions against short-sales will not affect the equilibrium.

Theorem 2.15

If (Z_M, R) span Ψ^e, then the equilibrium expected return on security j can be written as

$$\bar{Z}_j = R + \beta_j(\bar{Z}_M - R)$$

where

$$\beta_j \equiv \frac{\text{cov}(Z_j, Z_M)}{\text{var}(Z_M)}$$

The proof follows directly from Corollary 2.13 and Proposition 2.3. This relation, called the *Security Market Line*, was first derived by Sharpe (1964) as a necessary condition for equilibrium in the mean–variance model of Markowitz and Tobin when investors have homogeneous beliefs. It has been central to most empirical studies of securities' returns published during the last two decades. Indeed, the switch in notation from a_{ij} to β_j in this special case reflects the almost universal adoption of the term "the 'beta' of a security" to mean the covariance of that security's return with the market portfolio divided by the variance of the return on the market portfolio.

In the special case of Theorem 2.15, β_j measures the systematic risk of security j relative to the efficient portfolio Z_M (i.e. $\beta_j = b_j^M$ as defined in Section 2.3), and therefore beta provides a complete ordering of the risk of individual securities. As is often the case in research, useful concepts are derived in a special model first. The term "systematic risk" was first coined by Sharpe and was measured by beta. The definition in Section 2.3 is a natural generalization. Moreover, unlike the general risk measure of Section 2.3, β_j can be computed from a simple covariance between Z_j and Z_M. Securities whose returns are positively correlated with the market are procyclical, and will be priced to have positive equilibrium expected excess returns. Securities whose returns are negatively correlated are countercyclical, and will have negative equilibrium expected excess returns.

In general, the sign of b_j^K cannot be determined by the sign of the correlation coefficient between Z_j and Z_e^K. However, as shown in Theorems 2.5–2.7, because $\partial Y(Z_e^K)/\partial Z_e^K > 0$ for each realization of Z_e^K, $b_j^K > 0$ does imply a generalized positive "association" between the returns on Z_j and Z_e^K. Similarly, $b_j^K < 0$ implies a negative "association."

Let $\Psi_{\min}$ denote the set of portfolios contained in Ψ^f such that there exists no other portfolio in Ψ^f with the same expected return and a smaller variance. Let $Z(\mu)$ denote the return on a portfolio contained in $\Psi_{\min}$ such that $\overline{Z}(\mu) = \mu$, and let δ_j^μ denote the fraction of this portfolio allocated to security j, $j = 1,...,n$.

Theorem 2.16

If $(Z_1,...,Z_n)$ contain no redundant securities, then (a) for each value μ, δ_j^μ, $j = 1,...,n$, are unique, (b) there exists a portfolio contained in $\Psi_{\min}$ with return X such that (X,R) span $\Psi_{\min}$, and (c) $\overline{Z}_j - R = a_j(\overline{X} - R)$, where $a_j \equiv \text{cov}(Z_j,X)/\text{var}(X)$, $j = 1,2,...,n$.

PROOF

Let σ_{ij} denote the ijth element of Ω and, because $(Z_1,...,Z_n)$ contain no redundant securities, Ω is nonsingular. Hence, let v_{ij} denote the ijth element of Ω^{-1}. All portfolios in $\Psi_{\min}$ with expected return μ must have portfolio weights that are solutions to the problem: minimize $\Sigma_1^n \Sigma_1^n \delta_i \delta_j \sigma_{ij}$ subject to the constraint $\overline{Z}(\mu) = \mu$. Trivially, if $\mu = R$, then $Z(R) = R$ and $\delta_j^R = 0$, $j = 1,2,...,n$. Consider the case when $\mu \neq R$. The n first-order conditions are

$$0 = \sum_{1}^{n} \delta_j^{\mu} \sigma_{ij} - \lambda_{\mu}(\bar{Z}_i - R) \qquad i = 1,2,\ldots,n$$

where λ_{μ} is the Lagrange multiplier for the constraint. Multiplying by δ_i^{μ} and summing, we have that $\lambda_{\mu} = \text{var}[Z(\mu)]/(\mu - R)$. By definition of $\Psi_{\min}$, λ_{μ} must be the same for all $Z(\mu)$. Because Ω is nonsingular, the set of linear equations has the unique solution

$$\delta_j^{\mu} = \lambda_{\mu} \sum_{1}^{n} v_{ij}(\bar{Z}_i - R) \qquad j = 1,2,\ldots,n$$

This proves (a). From this solution, $\delta_j^{\mu}/\delta_k^{\mu}, j,k = 1,2,\ldots,n$, are the same for every value of μ. Hence, all portfolios in $\Psi_{\min}$ with $\mu \neq R$ are perfectly correlated. Hence, pick any portfolio in $\Psi_{\min}$ with $\mu \neq R$ and call its return X. Then every $Z(\mu)$ can be written in the form $Z(\mu) = \delta_{\mu}(X - R) + R$. Hence, (X,R) span $\Psi_{\min}$ which proves (b), and from Corollary 2.13 and Proposition 2.3, (c) follows directly. QED

From Theorem 2.16, a_k will be equivalent to b_k^K as a measure of a security's systematic risk provided that the $Z(\mu)$ chosen for X is such that $\mu > R$. Like β_k, the only information required to compute a_k is the joint second moments of Z_k and X. Which of the two equivalent measures will be more useful obviously depends upon the information set that is available. However, as the following theorem demonstrates, the a_k measure is the natural choice in the case when there exists a spanning set for Ψ^{e} with $m = 1$.

Theorem 2.17

If (X,R) span Ψ^{e} and if X has a finite variance, then Ψ^{e} is contained in $\Psi_{\min}$.

PROOF

Let Z_{e} be the return on any efficient portfolio. By hypothesis, Z_{e} can be written as $Z_{\text{e}} = R + a_{\text{e}}(X - R)$. Let Z_p be the return on any portfolio in Ψ^f such that $\bar{Z}_{\text{e}} = \bar{Z}_p$. By Corollary 2.13, Z_p can be written as $Z_p = R + a_p(X - R) + \epsilon_p$, where $E\{\epsilon_p\} = E\{\epsilon_p|X\} = 0$. Therefore, $a_p = a_{\text{e}}$ if $\bar{Z}_p = \bar{Z}_{\text{e}}$; $\text{var}(Z_p) = a_p^2 \text{var}(X) + \text{var}(\epsilon_p) \geq a_p^2 \text{var}(X) = \text{var}(Z_{\text{e}})$. Hence, Z_{e} is contained in $\Psi_{\min}$. Moreover, Ψ^{e} will be the set of all portfolios in $\Psi_{\min}$ such that $\mu \geq R$. QED

Thus, whenever there exists a spanning set for Ψ^e with $m = 1$, the means, variances, and covariances of $(Z_1,...,Z_n)$ are sufficient statistics to completely determine all efficient portfolios. Such a strong set of conclusions suggests that the class of joint probability distributions for $(Z_1,...,Z_n)$ which admit a two-fund separation theorem will be highly specialized. However, as the following theorems demonstrate, the class is not empty.

Theorem 2.18

If $(Z_1,...,Z_n)$ have a joint normal probability distribution, then there exists a portfolio with return X such that (X,R) span Ψ^e.

PROOF

Using the procedure applied in the proof of Theorem 2.16, construct a risky portfolio contained in $\Psi_{\min}$, and call its return X. Define the random variables $\epsilon_k \equiv Z_k - R - a_k(X - R)$, $k = 1,...,n$. By part (c) of that theorem, $E\{\epsilon_k\} = 0$ and, by construction, $\text{cov}(\epsilon_k,X) = 0$. Because $Z_1,...,Z_n$ are normally distributed, X will be normally distributed. Hence, ϵ_k is normally distributed, and because $\text{cov}(\epsilon_k,X) = 0$, ϵ_k and X are independent. Therefore, $E\{\epsilon_k\} = E\{\epsilon_k|X\} = 0$. From Corollary 2.13 it follows that (X,R) span Ψ^e.   QED

It is straightforward to prove that if $(Z_1,...,Z_n)$ can have *arbitrary* means, variances, and covariances, and can be mutually independent, then a necessary condition for there to exist a portfolio with return X such that (X,R) span Ψ^e is that $(Z_1,...,Z_n)$ be joint normally distributed. However, it is important to emphasize both the word "arbitrary" and the prospect for independence. For example, consider a joint distribution for $(Z_1,...,Z_n)$ such that the joint probability density function $p(Z_1,...,Z_n)$ is a symmetric function. That is, for each set of admissible outcomes for $(Z_1,...,Z_n)$, $p(Z_1,...,Z_n)$ remains unchanged when any two arguments of p are interchanged. An obvious special case is when $(Z_1,...,Z_n)$ are independently and identically distributed and $p(Z_1,...,Z_n) = p(Z_1)p(Z_2)\cdots p(Z_n)$.

Theorem 2.19

If $p(Z_1,...,Z_n)$ is a symmetric function with respect to all its arguments, then there exists a portfolio with return X such that (X,R) spans Ψ^e.

PROOF

By hypothesis, $p(Z_1,...,Z_i,...,Z_n) = p(Z_i,...,Z_1,...,Z_n)$ for each set of given values $(Z_1,...,Z_n)$. Therefore, from the first-order conditions for portfolio selection, (2.4), every risk-averse investor will choose $\delta_1^* = \delta_i^*$.

But this is true for $i = 1,...,n$. Hence, all investors will hold all risky securities in the same relative proportions. Therefore, if X is the return on a portfolio with an equal dollar investment in each risky security, then (X,R) will span Ψ^e.   QED

Samuelson (1967a) was the first to examine this class of symmetric density functions in a portfolio context. Chamberlain (1983) has shown that the class of elliptical distributions characterizes the distributions that imply mean–variance utility functions for all risk-averse expected utility maximizers. However, for distributions other than Gaussian to obtain, the security returns cannot be independently distributed. Merton and Samuelson (1974) and Samuelson and Merton (1974) investigate conditions for the mean-variance criterion to provide an approximate optimum.

The Arbitrage Pricing Theory (APT) Model developed by Ross (1976a) provides an important class of linear-factor models that generate (at least approximate) spanning without assuming joint normal probability distributions. Suppose the returns on securities are generated by

$$Z_j = \bar{Z}_j + \sum_1^m a_{ij}Y_i + \epsilon_j \qquad j = 1,...,n \qquad (2.16)$$

where $E\{\epsilon_j\} = E\{\epsilon_j|Y_1,...,Y_m\} = 0$ and, without loss of generality, $E\{Y_i\} = 0$ and $\text{cov}(Y_i,Y_j) = 0$, $i \neq j$. The random variables $\{Y_i\}$ represent common factors that are likely to affect the returns on a significant number of securities. If it is possible to construct a set of m portfolios with returns $(X_1,...,X_m)$ such that X_i and Y_i are perfectly correlated, $i = 1,2,...,m$, then the conditions of Theorem 2.12 will be satisfied and $(X_1,...,X_m,R)$ will span Ψ^e.

Although in general it will not be possible to construct such a set, by imposing some mild additional restrictions on $\{\epsilon_j\}$, Ross (1976a) derives an asymptotic spanning theorem as the number of available securities, n, becomes large. While the rigorous derivation is rather tedious, a rough description goes as follows. Let Z_p be the return on a portfolio with fraction δ_j allocated to security j, $j = 1,2,...,n$. From (2.16), Z_p can be written as

$$Z_p = \bar{Z}_p + \sum_1^m a_{ip}Y_i + \epsilon_p \qquad (2.17)$$

where $\bar{Z}_p = R + \Sigma_1^n\delta_j(\bar{Z}_j - R)$, $a_{ip} \equiv \Sigma_1^n\delta_ja_{ij}$, and $\epsilon_p \equiv \Sigma_1^n\delta_j\epsilon_j$. Consider the set of portfolios (called *well-diversified portfolios*) that have the property $\delta_j \equiv \mu_j/n$, where $|\mu_j| \leq M_j < \infty$ and M_j is independent of n, $j = 1,...,n$. Virtually by the definition of a common factor, it is reasonable to assume that, for every $n \gg m$, a significantly positive fraction λ_i of all securities have $a_{ij} \neq 0$, and this will be true for each common factor i, $i = 1,...,m$. Similarly, because the $\{\epsilon_j\}$ denote the variations in securities' returns not explained by common factors, it is also reasonable to assume for large n that, for each j, ϵ_j is uncorrelated with virtually all other securities' returns. Hence, if the number of common factors, m, is fixed, then for all $n \gg m$ it should be possible to construct a set of well-diversified portfolios $\{X_k\}$ such that, for X_k, $a_{ik} = 0$, $i = 1,...,m$, $i \neq k$, and $a_{kk} \neq 0$. It follows from (2.17) that X_k can be written as

$$X_k = \overline{X}_k + a_{kk}Y_k + \frac{1}{n} \sum_1^n \mu_j^k \epsilon_j \qquad k = 1,...,m$$

But $|\mu_j^k|$ is bounded, independently of n, and virtually all the ϵ_j are uncorrelated. Therefore, by the Law of Large Numbers, as $n \to \infty$, $X_k \to \overline{X}_k + a_{kk}Y_k$. So, as n becomes very large, X_k and Y_k become perfectly correlated, and by Theorem 2.12 asymptotically $(X_1,...,X_m,R)$ will span Ψ^e. In particular, if $m = 1$, then asymptotically two-fund separation will obtain independent of any other distributional characteristics of Y_1 or the $\{\epsilon_j\}$.

As can be seen from Theorem 2.3 and its corollary, all efficient portfolios in the APT model are well-diversified portfolios. Unlike in the mean–variance model, returns on all efficient portfolios need not, however, be perfectly correlated. The model is also attractive because, at least in principle, the equilibrium structure of expected returns and risks of securities can be derived without explicit knowledge of investors' preferences or endowments. Indeed, whenever nontrivial spanning of Ψ^e obtains and the set of risky spanning portfolios can be identified, much of the structure of individual securities' returns can be empirically estimated. For example, if we know of a set of portfolios $\{X_i\}$ such that $E\{\epsilon_j | X_1,...,X_m\} = 0$, $j = 1,...,n$, then by Theorem 2.12, $(X_1,...,X_m,R)$ span Ψ^e. By Proposition 2.3, ordinary least-squares regression of the realized excess returns on security j, $Z_j - R$, on the realized excess returns of the spanning portfolios $(X_1 - R,...,X_m - R)$ will always give unbiased estimates of the a_{ij}. Of course, to apply time series estimation, it must be assumed that the spanning portfolios $(X_1,...,X_m)$ and $\{a_{ij}\}$ are intertemporally stable. For these estimators to be efficient, further restrictions on the $\{\epsilon_j\}$ are required to satisfy the Gauss–Markov theorem.

Early empirical studies of stock-market securities' returns rarely found more than two or three statistically significant common factors.[13] Given that there are tens of thousands of different corporate liabilities traded in

---

13   Cf. King (1966), Livingston (1977), Farrar (1962), Feeney and Hester (1967), and Farrell (1974). Unlike standard "factor analysis," the number of common

US securities markets, there appears to be empirical foundation for the assumptions of the APT model. More recent studies have concluded, however, that the number of common factors may be considerably larger, and some have raised serious questions about the prospect for identifying the factors by using stock-return data alone.[14]

Although the analyses derived here have been expressed in terms of restrictions on the joint distribution of security returns without explicitly mentioning security prices, it is obvious that these derived restrictions impose restrictions on prices through the identity that $Z_j \equiv V_j/V_{j0}$, where V_j is the random variable end-of-period aggregate value of security j and V_{j0} is its initial value. Hence, given the characteristics of any two of these variables, the characteristics of the third are uniquely determined. For the study of equilibrium pricing, the usual format is to derive equilibrium V_{j0} given the distribution of V_j.

Theorem 2.20

If $(X_1,\ldots,X_m)$ denote a set of linearly independent portfolios that satisfy the hypothesis of Theorem 2.12, and all securities have finite variances, then a necessary condition for equilibrium in the securities' market is that

$$V_{j0} = \frac{\overline{V}_j - \Sigma_1^m \Sigma_1^m v_{ik} \, \mathrm{cov}(X_k, V_j)(\overline{X}_i - R)}{R} \qquad j = 1,\ldots,n \quad (2.18)$$

where v_{ik} is the ikth element of Ω_X^{-1}.

PROOF

By linear independence, Ω_X is nonsingular. From the identity $V_j \equiv Z_j V_{j0}$ and Theorem 2.12, $V_j = V_{j0}[R + \Sigma_1^m a_{ij}(X_i - R) + \epsilon_j]$, where $E\{\epsilon_j | X_1,\ldots,X_m\} = E\{\epsilon_j\} = 0$. Taking expectations, we have that $\overline{V}_j = V_{j0}[R + \Sigma_1^m a_{ij}(\overline{X}_i - R)]$. Noting that $\mathrm{cov}(X_k,V_j) = V_{j0} \, \mathrm{cov}(X_k,Z_j)$, we have from Proposition 2.3 that $V_{j0} \, a_{ij} = \Sigma_1^m v_{ik} \, \mathrm{cov}(X_k,V_j)$. By substituting for a_{ij} in the $\overline{V}_j$ expression and rearranging terms, the theorem is proved.   QED

factors here does not depend upon the fraction of total variation in an individual security's return that can be "explained." Rather, what is important is the number of factors necessary to "explain" the *covariation* between pairs of individual securities.

14   There is considerable controversy on this issue. See Brown (1989), Chamberlain and Rothschild (1983), Connor and Korajczyk (1988), Constantinides (1989). Dhrymes, Friend, and Gultekin (1984, 1985), Dybvig and Ross (1985), Lehmann and Modest (1988), Roll and Ross (1980), Rothschild (1986), Shanken (1982, 1985), and Trzcinka (1986).

Hence, from Theorem 2.20, a sufficient set of information to determine the equilibrium value of security j is the first and second moments for the joint distribution of $(X_1,...,X_m,V_j)$. Moreover, the valuation formula has the following important "linearity" properties.

Corollary 2.20a

If the hypothesized conditions of Theorem 2.20 hold and if the end-of-period value of a security is given by $V = \Sigma_1^n \lambda_j V_j$, then in equilibrium

$$V_0 = \Sigma_1^n \lambda_j V_{j0}$$

The proof of the corollary follows by substitution for V in formula (2.18). This property of formula (2.18) is called "value additivity."

Corollary 2.20b

If the hypothesized conditions of Theorem 2.20 hold and if the end-of-period value of a security is given by $V = qV_j + u$, where $E\{u\} = E\{u|X_1,...,X_m\} = \bar{u}$ and $E\{q\} = E\{q|X_1,...,X_m,V_j\} = \bar{q}$, then in equilibrium

$$V_0 = \bar{q}V_{j0} + \bar{u}/R$$

The proof follows by substitution for V in formula (2.18) and by applying the hypothesized conditional expectation conditions to show that $\text{cov}(X_k,V) = \bar{q}\,\text{cov}(X_k,V_j)$. Hence, to value two securities whose end-of-period values differ only by multiplicative or additive "noise," we can simply substitute the expected values of the noise terms.

As discussed in Merton (1982a, pp. 642–51), Theorem 2.20 and its corollaries are central to the theory of optimal investment decisions by business firms. To finance new investments, the firm can use internally available funds, issue common stock, or issue other types of financial claims (e.g. debt, preferred stock, and convertible bonds). The selection from the menu of these financial instruments is called the firm's financing decision. Although the optimal investment and financing decisions by a firm generally require simultaneous determination, under certain conditions the optimal investment decision can be made independently of the method of financing.

Consider firm j with random variable end-of-period value V^j and q different financial claims. The kth such financial claim is defined by the function $f_k(V^j)$, which describes how the holders of this security will share in the end-of-period value of the firm. The production technology and choice of investment intensity, $V_j(I_j;\theta_j)$ and I_j, are taken as given (θ_j is a random variable). If it is assumed that the end-of-period value of the firm is independent of its choice of financial liabilities,[15] then $V^j = V_j(I_j;\theta_j)$, and $\Sigma_1^q f_k \equiv V_j(I_j;\theta_j)$ for every outcome θ_j.

Suppose that, if firm j were all equity financed, there exists an equilibrium such that the initial value of firm j is given by $V_{j0}(I_j)$.

Theorem 2.21

If firm j is financed by q different claims defined by the functions $f_k(V^j)$, $k = 1,\ldots, q$, and if there exists an equilibrium such that the return distribution of the efficient portfolio set remains unchanged from the equilibrium in which firm j was all equity financed, then

$$\sum_1^q f_{k0} = V_{j0}(I_j)$$

where f_{k0} is the equilibrium initial value of financial claim k.

PROOF

In the equilibrium in which firm j is all equity financed, the end-of-period random variable value of firm j is $V_j(I_j;\theta_j)$ and the initial value $V_{j0}(I_j)$ is given by formula (2.18) where $(X_1,\ldots,X_m,R)$ span the efficient set. Consider now that firm j is financed by the q different claims. The random variable end-of-period value of firm j, $\Sigma_1^q f_k$, is still given by $V_j(I_j;\theta_j)$. By hypothesis, there exists an equilibrium such that the distribution of the efficient portfolio set remains unchanged, and therefore the distribution of $(X_1,\ldots,X_m,R)$ remains unchanged. By inspection of formula (2.18), the initial value of firm j will remain unchanged, and therefore $\Sigma_1^q f_{k0} = V_{j0}(I_j)$.
                                                                                QED

Hence, for a given investment policy, the way in which the firm finances its investment will not affect the market value of the firm unless the choice of financial instruments changes the return distributions of the efficient portfolio set. Theorem 2.21 is representative of a class of theorems that describe the impact of financing policy on the market value of a firm when

15 This assumption formally rules out financial securities that alter the tax liabilities of the firm (e.g. interest deductions) or ones that can induce "outside" costs (e.g. bankruptcy costs). However, by redefining $V_j(I_j;\theta_j)$ as the pre-tax-and-bankruptcy value of the firm and letting one of the f_k represent the government's tax claim and another the lawyers' bankruptcy-cost claim, the analysis in the text will be valid for these extended securities as well. Further discussion can be found in Chapter 13.

the investment decision is held fixed, and this class is generally referred to as the *Modigliani–Miller Hypothesis*, after the pioneering work in this direction by Modigliani and Miller.[16]

Clearly, a sufficient condition for Theorem 2.21 to obtain is that each of the financial claims issued by the firm are "redundant securities" whose payoffs can be replicated by combining already existing securities. This condition is satisfied by the subclass of corporate liabilities that provide for *linear* sharing rules (i.e. $f_k(V) = a_k V + b_k$ where $\Sigma_1^q a_k = 1$ and $\Sigma_1^q b_k = 0$). Unfortunately, as will be shown in Chapters 11–14, most common types of financial instruments issued by corporations have nonlinear payoff structures. As Stiglitz (1969, 1974) has shown for the Arrow–Debreu model and the static Capital Asset Pricing Model (CAPM), linearity of the sharing rules is not a necessary condition for Theorem 2.21 to obtain. Nevertheless, the existence of nonlinear payoff structures among wide classes of securities makes the establishment of conditions under which the hypothesis of Theorem 2.21 is valid no small matter.

Beyond the issue of whether firms can optimally separate their investment and financing decisions, the fact that many securities have nonlinear sharing rules raises serious questions about the robustness of spanning models. As already discussed, the APT model, for example, has attracted much interest because it makes no explicit assumptions about preferences and places seemingly few restrictions on the joint probability distribution of security returns. In the APT model, $(X_1,\ldots,X_m,R)$ span the set of optimal portfolios and there exist m numbers $(a_{1k},\ldots,a_{mk})$ for each security k, $k = 1,\ldots, n$ such that $Z_k = \Sigma_1^m a_{ik}(X_i - R) + R + \epsilon_k$ where $E\{\epsilon_k\} = E\{\epsilon_k | X_1,\ldots,X_m\} = 0$.

Suppose that security k satisfies this condition and security q has a payoff structure that is given by $Z_q = f(Z_k)$, where f is a nonlinear function. If security q is to satisfy this condition, then there must exist numbers $(a_{1q},\ldots,a_{mq})$ so that for all possible values of $(X_1,\ldots,X_m)$

$$E\left\{ f\left[\sum_1^m a_{ik}(X_i - R) + R + \epsilon_k \right] \middle| X_1,\ldots,X_m \right\}$$

$$= \sum_1^m a_{iq}(X_i - R) + R$$

However, unless $\epsilon_k \equiv 0$ and $\epsilon_q \equiv 0$, such a set of numbers cannot be found for a general nonlinear function f.

---

16 Modigliani and Miller (1958) and Miller and Modigliani (1961). See also Stiglitz (1969, 1974), Fama (1978), and Miller (1977). The Modigliani–Miller concept has also been applied in other parts of monetary economics as in Wallace (1981).

Since the APT model only has practical relevance if, for most securities, $\text{var}(\epsilon_k) > 0$, it appears that the reconciliation of nontrivial spanning models with the widespread existence of securities with nonlinear payoff structures requires further restrictions on either the probability distributions of securities' returns or investor preferences. How restrictive these conditions are cannot be answered in the abstract. First, the introduction of general equilibrium pricing conditions on securities will impose some restrictions on the joint distribution of returns. Second, the discussed benefits to individuals from having a set of spanning mutual funds may induce the creation of financial intermediaries or additional financial securities that together with pre-existing securities will satisfy the conditions of Theorem 2.13. Using the intertemporal continuous-time model, we explore these possibilities in detail in Chapters 12, 13, 15, and 16.

An alternative approach to the development of nontrivial spanning theorems is to derive a class of utility functions for investors such that, even with arbitrary joint probability distributions for the available securities, investors within the class can generate their optimal portfolios from the spanning portfolios. Let Ψ^u denote the set of optimal portfolios selected from Ψ^f by investors with strictly concave von Neumann–Morgenstern utility functions $\{U_i\}$. Cass and Stiglitz (1970) have proved the following theorem.

Theorem 2.22

There exists a portfolio with return X such that (X,R) span Ψ^u if and only if $A_i(W) = 1/(a_i + bW) > 0$, where A_i is the absolute risk-aversion function for investor i in Ψ^u.[17]

The family of utility functions whose absolute risk-aversion functions can be written as $1/(a + bW) > 0$ is called the Hyperbolic Absolute Risk Aversion (HARA) family.[18] By appropriate choices for a and b, various members of the family will exhibit increasing, decreasing, or constant absolute and relative risk aversion. Hence, if each investor's utility function could be approximated by some member of the HARA family, then it might appear that this alternative approach would be fruitful. However, it should be emphasized that the b in the statement of Theorem 2.22 does not have a subscript i, and therefore, for separation to obtain, all investors in Ψ^u must have virtually the same utility function.[19] Moreover,

---

17 For this family of utility functions, the probability distribution for securities cannot be completely arbitrary without violating the von Neumann–Morgenstern axioms. For example, it is required that, for every realization of W, $W > -a_i/b$ for $b > 0$ and $W < -a_i/b$ for $b < 0$. The latter condition is especially restrictive.

18 The HARA family is examined in greater detail in Chapters 5 and 6.

19 As discussed in footnote 17, the range of values for a_i cannot be arbitrary for a given b. Moreover, the sign of b uniquely determines the sign of $A_i'(W)$.

they must agree on the joint probability distribution for $(Z_1,...,Z_n)$. Hence, the only significant way in which investors can differ is in their endowments of initial wealth.

Cass and Stiglitz (1970) also examine the possibilities for more general nontrivial spanning (i.e. $1 \leqslant m < n$) by restricting the class of utility functions and conclude, "...it is the requirement that there be *any* mutual funds, and not the limitation on the *number* of mutual funds, which is the restrictive feature of the property of separability" (p. 144). Hence, the Cass and Stiglitz analysis is essentially a negative report on this approach to developing spanning theorems.

In closing, two further points should be made. First, although virtually all the spanning theorems require the generally implausible assumption that all investors agree upon the joint probability distribution for securities, it is not so unreasonable when applied to the theory of financial intermediation and mutual-fund management. In a financial world where the economic concepts of "division of labor" and "comparative advantage" have content, then it is quite reasonable to expect that an efficient allocation of resources would lead to some individuals (the "fund managers") gathering data and actively estimating the joint probability distributions and the rest either buying this information directly or delegating their investment decisions by "agreeing to agree" with the fund managers' estimates. If the distribution of returns is such that nontrivial spanning of Ψ^e does not obtain, then there are no gains to financial intermediation over the direct sale of the distribution estimates. However, if nontrivial spanning does obtain and the number of risky spanning portfolios, m, is small, then a significant reduction in redundant information processing and transactions can be produced by the introduction of mutual funds. If a significant coalition of individuals can agree upon a common source for the estimates and if they know that, based on this source, a group of mutual funds spans Ψ^e, then they need only be provided with the joint distribution for these mutual funds to form their optimal portfolios. On the supply side, if the characteristics of a set of spanning portfolios can be identified, then the mutual-fund managers will know how to structure the portfolios of the funds they offer. We explore in detail these roles for financial intermediation in Chapter 14.

The second point concerns the riskless security. It has been assumed throughout that there exists a riskless security. Although some of the specifications will change slightly, virtually all the derived theorems can be shown to be valid in the absence of a riskless security.[20] However, the existence of a riskless security vastly simplifies many of the proofs.

---

20 Cf. Ross (1978) for spanning proofs in the absence of a riskless security. Black (1972) and Merton (1972a) derive the two-fund theorem for the mean–variance model with no riskless security. For analysis of the no-riskless-security case in the continuous-time dynamic model, see Merton (1970b, 1971; this volume, Sections 11.6 and 5.5).

3

On the Mathematics and Economics Assumptions of Continuous-Time Models

3.1 INTRODUCTION

The mathematical tools required for the formal manipulations used in continuous-time uncertainty analysis are somewhat specialized and therefore may not be familiar. For example, the sample paths for stochastic variables generated by diffusion processes, while continuous, are almost nowhere differentiable in the usual sense; therefore a more general type of differential equation is required to express the dynamics of such processes. While there is substantial mathematics literature on these generalized stochastic equations,[1] the derivations, although elegant, are often cryptic and difficult to follow. Moreover, these derivations provide little insight into the relations between the formal mathematical assumptions and the corresponding economics assumptions. This chapter attempts to bridge the gap by using only elementary probability theory and calculus to derive the basic theorems required for continuous-time analysis and, as part of the derivations, to make explicit the economics assumptions implicitly embedded in the mathematical assumptions. The latter is especially important because the way in which the economics assumptions are frequently stated in the substantive economics literature can make them appear to be more

Reproduced from *Financial Economics*: *Essays in Honor of Paul Cootner*, W. F. Sharpe and C. M. Cootner, eds. © 1982 Reprinted by permission of Prentice-Hall Inc., Englewood Cliffs, New Jersey. Aid from the National Science Foundation is gratefully acknowledged.

1 See Arnold (1974), Cox and Miller (1968), Chung and Williams (1983), Friedman (1975), Gihman and Skorohod (1972), Harrison (1985), Itô (1951, 1987), Itô and McKean (1964), McKean (1969), McShane (1974), and Rogers and Williams (1987) for the general mathematics associated with diffusion processes and stochastic differential equations. Bensoussan (1982, 1983), Dreyfus (1965), Fleming and Rishel (1975), Krylov (1980), and Kushner (1967) present the optimal control and stability analysis for the dynamics described by these processes. Bergstrom (1988) provides a history of continuous-time econometric models. See also Duncan and Pasik-Duncan (1989b), He (1989, Ch. 3), Lo (1986, 1988), and Marsh and Rosenfeld (1983).

restrictive than they really are. While the general approach is to keep the assumptions as weak as possible, assumptions which are more restrictive than necessary are made in those places where the "tradeoff" between the losses in generality and the reduction in mathematical complexity appears to be favorable. To motivate the study of continuous-time analysis, we begin with a brief review of the role that it has played in the development of financial economics during the last two decades.

The substantive contributions of continuous-time analysis to financial economic theory are, of course, the subject matter of this book. Therefore, only the most cryptic description of these contributions is made here.[2] The twin assumptions that trading takes place continuously in time and that the underlying stochastic variables follow diffusion-type motions with continuous sample paths lead to a set of behavioral equations for intertemporal portfolio selection that are both simpler and richer than those derived from the corresponding discrete-trading model. Moreover, these same assumptions provide the foundation for a unified theory of financial-security and capital-asset pricing that is both theoretically elegant and empirically tractable.

Of course continuous trading, like any other continuous revision process, is an abstraction from physical reality. However, if the length of time between revisions is very short (or indeterminately small), then the continuous-trading solution will be a reasonable approximation to the discrete-trading solution. Whether or not the length of time between revisions is short enough for the continuous solution to provide a good approximation must be decided on a case-by-case basis by making a relative comparison with other time scales in the problem. The analysis in this chapter is presented in the context of a securities market where, in fact, the length of time between observed transactions ranges from at most a few days to less than a minute.

However, continuous analysis can provide a good approximation even if the length of time between revisions is not this short. For example, in the analysis of long-run economic growth in a neoclassical capital model, it is the practice to neglect "short-run" business cycle fluctuations and to assume a full-employment economy. Moreover, the exogenous factors usually assumed to affect the time path of the economy in such models are either demographic or technological changes. Since major changes in either generally take place over rather long periods of time, the length of time between revisions in the capital stock, while hardly instantaneous, may well be quite short relative to the scale of the exogenous factors.[3]

2 For other overviews on the application of continuous-time analysis in the economic theory of uncertainty, see Duffie (1988), Malliaris and Brock (1982), Merton (1975b, 1982a, 1990a), and Smith (1976, 1979).
3 See Bourguignon (1974), Bismut (1975), and Merton (1975a; this volume, Ch. 17) for neoclassical growth models under uncertainty that use diffusion processes.

The application of continuous-time analysis in the empirical study of financial economic data is, by comparison, more recent and less developed. However, it shows promise of providing new approaches to resolving some of the major issues in the empirical study of speculative-price time series as outlined in Cootner (1964, pp. 79–83 and 189–97) and Fama (1970a).

It was standard practice in early studies to assume that the logarithm of the ratio of successive prices had a Gaussian distribution with time-homogeneous independent increments and stationary parameters. However, the sample characteristics of the time series were frequently inconsistent with these assumed population properties. One of the more important inconsistencies was that the empirical distributions of price changes were often too "peaked" to be consistent with the Gaussian distribution, i.e. the frequency of extreme observations was too high to be consistent with samples from a normal distribution.

Attempts to resolve these discrepancies proceeded along two separate paths. The first, pioneered by Mandelbrot (1963a, b) and Fama (1963, 1965b), maintains the independent increments and stationarity assumptions but replaces the Gaussian assumption with a more general stable (Pareto–Levy) distribution assumption. Although non-Gaussian members of the stable family frequently fit the tails of the empirical distributions better than the Gaussian, there is little empirical evidence to support adoption of the stable Paretian hypothesis over that of any leptokurtotic distribution. Moreover, as discussed by Cootner (1964, pp. 333–7), the infinite variance property of the non-Gaussian stable distributions implies that most of our statistical tools which are based upon finite-moment assumptions (e.g. least squares) are useless. It also implies that even the first-moment or expected value of the *arithmetic* price change does not exist.

The considerable theoretical and empirical difficulties with the stable Paretian hypothesis led Cootner (1964) and others to consider the alternative path of finite-moment processes whose distributions are nonstationary. It is in this approach where the continuous-time analysis shows promise. The general continuous-time framework, which requires that the underlying process be a mixture of diffusion and Poisson-directed processes, can accommodate a wide range of specific hypotheses including the "reflecting barrier" model proposed by Cootner (1964, pp. 231–52). Rosenberg (1972) shows that a Gaussian model with a changing (and forecastable) variance rate appears to "explain" the observed fat-tail characteristics of stock-market returns. Rosenfeld (1980) has developed statistical techniques for estimating the parameters of continuous-time processes and has applied them in constructing a likelihood test for choosing between a diffusion process with a changing variance rate and a mixed diffusion and Poisson-directed process. As discussed by Merton (1976a (this volume, Ch. 9), 1980), if the parameters are slowly varying functions of time, then it is possible to exploit the different "time scales" of the component parts of continuous-time processes to identify and estimate these parameters.

Of course, considerably more research is required before a judgment can be made as to the success of this approach. However, the extensive mathematics literature on the distributional characteristics of these processes together with their finite-moment properties make the development of hypothesis tests considerably easier for these processes than for the stable Pareto–Levy processes.[4]

With this as a background, we now turn to the formal development of the mathematics and economics assumptions of continuous-time models.

Let h denote the trading horizon which is the *minimum* length of time between which successive transactions by investors can be made in the securities market. In an intertemporal analysis, h is the length of time between successive market openings and is, of course, part of the specification of the structure of markets in the economy. While this structure will depend upon the tradeoff between the costs of operating the market and its benefits, this time scale is not determined by the individual investor and is the same for all investors in the economy. If $X(t)$ denotes the price of a security at time t, then the change in the price of the security between time $t = 0$ and time $T \equiv nh > 0$ can be written as

$$X(T) - X(0) = \sum_{1}^{n} [X(k) - X(k - 1)] \tag{3.1}$$

where n is the number of trading intervals between time 0 and T and $X(k) - X(k - 1)$, which is shorthand for $X(kh) - X[(k - 1)h]$, is the change in price over the kth trading interval, $k = 1, 2, \ldots, n$.

The continuous-trading assumption implies that the trading interval h is equal to the continuous-time infinitesimal dt, and, as is usual for differential calculus, all terms of higher order than dt will be neglected. To derive the economic implications of continuous trading, it is necessary to derive the mathematical properties of the time series of price changes in this environment. Specifically, the limiting distributional properties are derived for both the price change over a single trading interval and the change over a fixed finite time interval T as the length of the trading interval becomes

4   Samuelson (1967b) derived a few theorems about the portfolio-selection behavior of risk-averse investors facing stable Pareto–Levy-distributed investments. However, to my knowledge, no one has derived any such behavioral equations when the investments are log-stable distributed. This is, of course, the distributional assumption made in those empirical studies with logarithmic returns distributed stable. This lack of theory makes the development of testable model specifications under the stable Paretian hypothesis quite difficult.

very small and the number of trading intervals n in $[0, T]$ becomes very large. In interpreting this limit analysis it may be helpful to think of the process as a sequence of market structures where in each stage of the sequence the institutionally imposed length of the trading interval is reduced from the previous stage. So, for example, the limiting mathematical analysis shows how the distribution of a given security's price change over one year will change as a result of changing the trading intervals from monthly to weekly. As I have emphasized elsewhere,[5] it is unreasonable to assume that the equilibrium distribution of returns on a security over a specified time period (e.g. one year) will be invariant to the trading interval for that security because investors' optimal demand functions will depend upon how frequently they can revise their portfolios. Therefore, it should be pointed out that nowhere in the analysis presented here is it assumed that the distribution of $X(T) - X(0)$ is invariant to h.

Define the conditional expectation operator E_t to be the expectation operator conditional on knowing all relevant information revealed as of time t or before. Define the random variables $\epsilon(k)$ by

$$\epsilon(k) \equiv X(k) - X(k - 1) - E_{k-1}\{X(k) - X(k - 1)\} \qquad k = 1,...,n \tag{3.2}$$

where "time k" is used as shorthand for "time kh." By construction, $E_{k-1}\{\epsilon(k)\} = 0$, and $\epsilon(k)$ is the *unanticipated* price change in the security between $k - 1$ and k, conditional on being at time $k - 1$. Moreover, by the properties of conditional expectation, it follows that $E_{k-j}\{\epsilon(k)\} = 0$ for $j = 1,...,k$. Hence the partial sums $S_n \equiv \Sigma_1^n \epsilon(k)$ form a *martingale*.[6] As will be seen, the mathematical analysis to follow depends heavily on the properties of martingales. The theory of martingales is usually associated in the financial economics literature with the "Efficient-Market Hypothesis" of Fama and Samuelson.[7] Therefore, the reader may be tempted to connect the martingale property of the unanticipated returns derived here with an implicit assumption that "securities are priced correctly." However, the martingale property of the unanticipated returns here is

---

5 See Merton (1975b).

6 For a formal definition of the martingale and discussions of its properties, see Feller (1966, pp. 210–15 and 234–8). Important mathematical analyses of martingales in continuous-time processes are by Dellacherie and Meyer (1982) and Kunita and Watanabe (1967).

7 See Fama (1965a, 1970a, 1991), Samuelson (1965b, 1973), and also Cootner (1964). The theory of martingales provides a powerful technique for the analysis of equilibrium security prices in continuous-time models. See Harrison and Kreps (1979), Kreps (1981), Harrison and Pliska (1981, 1983), Duffie and Huang (1985, 1986), Duffie (1986, 1988), Huang (1985a, b, 1987), Pliska (1986), and Cox and Huang (1989a, b, 1991).

purely a result of construction, and therefore imposes no such economics assumption. However, two economics assumptions that will be imposed are as follows.

Assumption 1

For each finite time interval $[0,T]$ there exists a number $A_1 > 0$, independent of the number of trading intervals n, such that $\text{var}(S_n) \geq A_1$ where $\text{var}(S_n) \equiv E_0\{[\Sigma_1^n \epsilon(k)]^2\}$.

Assumption 2

For each finite time interval $[0,T]$, there exists a number $A_2 < \infty$, independent of n, such that $\text{var}(S_n) \leq A_2$.

Assumption 1 ensures that the uncertainty associated with the unanticipated price changes is not "washed out" or eliminated even in the limit of continuous trading. That is, even as $h \to dt$, the "end-of-period" price at time k will be uncertain relative to time $k - 1$. This assumption is essential for the continuous-trading model to capture this fundamental property of stock-price behavior.

Assumption 2 ensures that the uncertainty associated with the unanticipated price changes over a finite period of time is not so great that the variance becomes unbounded. It rules out the possibility that the very act of allowing more frequent trading will induce sufficient price instability to cause the limiting variance of $X(T) - X(0)$ to become unbounded, and it also rules out the Pareto–Levy stable distributions with infinite variances.

Define $V(k) \equiv E_0\{\epsilon^2(k)\}$, $k = 1,2,...,n$, to be the variance of the dollar return on the security between time $k - 1$ and k based upon information available as of time zero, and define $V \equiv \max_k V(k)$.

Assumption 3

There exists a number A_3, $1 \geq A_3 > 0$, independent of n, such that for $k = 1,...,n$, $V(k)/V \geq A_3$.

Assumption 3 is closely related to Assumption 1 and in effect rules out the possibility that all the uncertainty in the unanticipated price changes over $[0, T]$ is concentrated in a few of the many trading periods. In other words, there is significant price uncertainty in virtually all trading periods.[8]

8 Actually, the analysis will follow even if Assumption 3 is weakened to allow $V(k) = 0$ in some of the trading intervals provided that the number of such intervals has an upper bound independent of n. However, since virtually all "real-world" financial securities with uncertain returns exhibit some price uncertainty over even very small time intervals, the assumption as stated in the text should cover most empirically relevant cases.

So, for example, Assumption 3 rules out a lottery ticket where the drawing will take place at time T. In that case, the price of the lottery ticket will just appreciate at the riskless rate of interest until the final moment when the draw is made. Hence, for every n, $V(k) = 0$ for $k = 1, 2, ..., n - 1$ and $V(n) = \sigma^2$ where σ^2 is the variance of the dollar payoffs in the lottery.

At this point, I make a brief digression to define some mathematical symbols that will be used throughout the analysis. Let $\psi(h)$ and $\lambda(h)$ be functions of h. Define the *asymptotic order symbols* $O[\lambda(h)]$ and $o[\lambda(h)]$ by $\psi(h) = O[\lambda(h)]$ if $\lim[\psi(h)/\lambda(h)]$ is bounded as $h \to 0$ and by $\psi(h) = o[\lambda(h)]$ if $\lim[\psi(h)/\lambda(h)] = 0$ as $h \to 0$. So, for example, if $\psi(h) = ch^{1/2} \exp(h)$, then $\psi(h) = O(h^\gamma)$ for any value of $\gamma \leq \frac{1}{2}$. To see this, note that $\psi(h)/h^\gamma$ equals $ch^{1/2-\gamma} \exp(h)$ and the limit of this expression as $h \to 0$ is bounded for $\gamma \leq \frac{1}{2}$. Moreover, $\psi(h) = o(h^\gamma)$ for $\gamma < \frac{1}{2}$ because the limit of $\psi(h)/h^\gamma$ as $h \to 0$ is zero for $\gamma < \frac{1}{2}$. If $\psi(h) = O[\lambda(h)]$ and $\psi(h) \neq o[\lambda(h)]$, then $\psi(h) \sim \lambda(h)$ as $h \to 0$, where the symbol $\sim$ means "is asymptotically proportional to." In the above example, $\psi(h) \sim h^{1/2}$. In essence, the asymptotic order symbols, $O(\cdot)$, $o(\cdot)$, and $\sim$ are used to describe the behavior of the function $\psi(h)$ relative to the function $\lambda(h)$ for values of h close to zero.

Proposition 3.1

If Assumptions 1, 2, and 3 hold, then $V(k) \sim h$, $k = 1, ..., n$. That is, $V(k) = O(h)$ and $V(k) \neq o(h)$, and $V(k)$ is asymptotically proportional to h where the proportionality factor is positive.

PROOF

$$\mathrm{var}(S_n) = E_0 \left\{ \sum_1^n \sum_1^n \epsilon(k)\epsilon(j) \right\} = \sum_1^n \sum_1^n E_0 \left\{ \epsilon(k)\epsilon(j) \right\}$$

Consider a typical term in the double sum $E_0\{\epsilon(k)\epsilon(j)\}$. Suppose $k \neq j$. Choose $k > j$. Then, $E_0\{\epsilon(k)\epsilon(j)\} = E_0\{\epsilon(j)E_j\{\epsilon(k)\}\}$. But, by construction, $E_j\{\epsilon(k)\} = 0$, $j < k$. Hence, $E_0\{\epsilon(k)\epsilon(j)\} = 0$ for $k \neq j$. Therefore, $\mathrm{var}(S_n) = \Sigma_1^n V(k)$. From Assumptions 3 and 2, $nVA_3 \leq \Sigma_1^n V(k) \leq A_2$, and therefore $V(k) \leq A_2 h/A_3 T$ where $0 < A_2/A_3 < \infty$. Hence, $V(k) = O(h)$. From Assumptions 3 and 1, $V(k) \geq A_1 A_3 h/T$ where $A_1 A_3 > 0$. Hence, $V(k) \neq o(h)$.   QED

Armed with Proposition 3.1 we now turn to a detailed examination of the return distribution over a single trading interval. For some trading interval $[k - 1, k]$, suppose that $\epsilon(k)$ can take on any one of m distinct values denoted by $\epsilon_j(k)$, $j = 1, ..., m$ where m is finite. Whenever there is no ambiguity about the epoch of time k, we will denote $\epsilon_j(k)$ by simply ϵ_j.

Suppose further that there exists a number $M < \infty$, independent of n, such that $\epsilon_j^2 \leq M$. While the assumption of a discrete distribution of bounded range for $\epsilon(k)$ clearly restricts the class of admissible distributions, this assumption enormously simplifies the formal mathematical arguments without imposing any significant economic restrictions.[9] If $p_j(k) \equiv \text{prob}\{\epsilon(k) = \epsilon_j | \text{information available as of time zero}\}$, then from Proposition 3.1 it follows that

$$\sum_{1}^{m} p_j \epsilon_j^2 = O(h) \tag{3.3}$$

and because m is finite it follows from (3.3) that

$$p_j \epsilon_j^2 = O(h) \qquad j = 1,...,m \tag{3.4}$$

Any event j such that $p_j \epsilon_j^2 = o(h)$ will asymptotically contribute a negligible amount to the variance of (3.1) because $V(k) \neq o(h)$. Because m is finite, it follows that there exist at least two events such that $p_j \epsilon_j^2 \neq o(h)$, and from (3.4) $p_j \epsilon_j^2 \sim h$ for such events. Moreover, these events will determine the asymptotic characteristics of the distributions as one goes to the limit of continuous time. Hence, without loss of generality, it is assumed that $p_j \epsilon_j^2 \neq o(h)$, $j = 1,...,m$, and therefore $p_j \epsilon_j^2 \sim h$, $j = 1,2,...,m$.

Assumption 4

For $j = 1,2,...,m$, p_j and ϵ_j are sufficiently "well-behaved" functions of h that there exist numbers q_j and r_j such that $p_j \sim h^{q_j}$ and $\epsilon_j \sim h^{r_j}$.

While Assumption 4 is a convenient assumption for expositional purposes, it is stronger than is necessary. For example, if $p_j \sim h \log(1/h)$ in a neighborhood of $h = 0$, then Assumption 4 would not be satisfied. However, the results to be derived would still obtain if p_j behaved in this fashion.

From Assumption 4, we have that $p_j \epsilon_j^2 \sim h^{q_j + 2r_j}$. But $p_j \epsilon_j^2 \sim h$. Hence, it follows that the values taken on by q_j and r_j cannot be arbitrary, and indeed must satisfy

9 The class can be expanded to include continuous distributions with bounded ranges and most well-behaved continuous distributions with unbounded ranges (e.g. the normal distribution). However, to do so, the mathematical analysis required to prove the results derived in the text would be both longer and more complex. Because this additional mathematical complexity would provide few, if any, additional insights into the economics assumptions, to have included this larger class would have been at cross purposes with this chapter's objectives.

$$q_j + 2r_j = 1 \qquad j = 1,2,\ldots,m \qquad (3.5)$$

Because we are interested in the properties of these functions in a neighborhood of $h = 0$ and $h \ll 1$, those events with large values for r_j will have smaller-in-magnitude outcomes than those events with small values for r_j. Similarly, those events with large values for q_j are less likely to occur than those events with small values for q_j. Equation (3.5) defines the relation between these two numbers that must be satisfied for each event j. In essence, (3.5) says that "the larger the magnitude of the outcome, the smaller the likelihood that the event will occur." Because $p_j \le 1$ and ϵ_j^2 is bounded, both q_j and r_j must be nonnegative, and therefore, from (3.5), it follows that $0 \le q_j \le 1$ and $0 \le r_j \le \frac{1}{2}, j = 1,2,\ldots,m$.

As will be shown, those outcomes located at the extremes of the permissible range for r_j will determine the asymptotic distributional properties of $\epsilon(k)$. It will therefore be useful to partition its outcomes into three types: a "type I" outcome is one such that $r_j = \frac{1}{2}$; a "type II" outcome is one such that $0 < r_j < \frac{1}{2}$; and a "type III" outcome is one such that $r_j = 0$.

Let J denote the set of events j such that the outcomes ϵ_j are of type I. It follows from (3.5) that, for $j \in J$, $q_j = 0$, and therefore $p_j \ne o(1)$. Moreover, for all events $j \in J^c$ (i.e. events with types II or III outcomes), $p_j = o(1)$, and because m is finite, $\Sigma p_j = o(1)$, $j \in J^c$. Hence, because $\Sigma_1^m p_j = 1$, the set J cannot be empty and, indeed, virtually all the probability mass for $\epsilon(k)$ will be on events contained in J. In other words, for small trading intervals h, virtually all observations of $\epsilon(k)$ will be type I outcomes, and therefore an apt name for J^c might be "the set of rare events." This finding suggests a natural hierarchy for analysis: first, the asymptotic properties for $\epsilon(k)$ are derived for the case where all outcomes are of type I; second, the properties are derived for the case where outcomes can be type I and type II; and finally, they are derived for the general case where outcomes can be type I, type II, and type III.

3.2 CONTINUOUS-SAMPLE-PATH PROCESSES WITH "NO RARE EVENTS"

In this section, it is assumed that all possible outcomes for $\epsilon(k)$, $k = 1,\ldots,n$, are of type I, and therefore J^c is empty – i.e. there are no rare events, and each possible outcome $\epsilon_j, j = 1,\ldots,m$, can occur with noninfinitesimal probability.

Define the conditional expected dollar return per unit time on the security, α_k, by

$$\alpha_k \equiv E_{k-1}\{X(k) - X(k - 1)\}/h \qquad k = 1,\ldots,n \qquad (3.6)$$

Assumption 5

For every h, it is assumed that α_k exists, $k = 1,...,n$, and that there exists a number $\alpha < \infty$, independent of h, such that $|\alpha_k| \leq \alpha$.

Assumption 5 simply ensures that for all securities with a finite price the expected rate of return per unit time over the trading horizon is finite, no matter how short that horizon is. Note that it is not assumed that α_k is a constant over time, and indeed α_k may itself be a random variable relative to information available as of dates earlier than $k - 1$. From (3.2) and (3.6), we can write the dollar return on the security between $k - 1$ and k as

$$X(k) - X(k - 1) = \alpha_k h + \epsilon(k) \qquad k = 1,...,n \qquad (3.7)$$

As discussed in Section 3.1, an important assumption usually made in continuous-trading models is that the sample paths for security prices are continuous over time. The discrete-time analog to continuity of the sample path is that, in short intervals of time, prices cannot fluctuate greatly. Because type I outcomes are $O(h^{1/2})$, it may come as no surprise that this continuity assumption will be satisfied when all possible outcomes are of this type.

Proposition 3.2

If, for $k = 1,..., n$, all possible outcomes for $\epsilon(k)$ are type I outcomes, then the continuous-time sample path for the price of the security will be continuous.

PROOF

Let $Q_k(\delta)$ be the probability that $|X(k) - X(k - 1)| \geq \delta$ conditional on knowing all information available as of time $k - 1$. A necessary and sufficient condition[10] for continuity of the sample path for X is that, for every $\delta > 0$, $Q_k(\delta) = o(h)$. Define $\bar{u} = \max_{(j)} |\epsilon_j|/h^{1/2}$. By hypothesis all outcomes for $\epsilon(k)$ are type I, and therefore $\bar{u} = O(1)$. For each number $\delta > 0$, define the function $h^+(\delta)$ as the solution to the equation $\delta = \alpha h^+ + \bar{u}(h^+)^{1/2}$. Because α and $\bar{u}$ are $O(1)$, $h^+(\delta) > 0$ for every $\delta > 0$. Clearly, for all $h < h^+(\delta)$ and every possible outcome $X(k)$, $|X(k) - X(k - 1)| < \delta$. Therefore, for every h, $0 \leq h < h^+(\delta)$, $Q_k(\delta) \equiv 0$, and hence $\lim[Q_k(\delta)/h] = 0$ as $h \to 0$.   QED

10 This condition is called the "Lindeberg condition." See Feller (1966, pp. 321 and 491) for a discussion.

As illustrated in Figure 3.1, while the sample path for $X(t)$ is continuous, it is almost nowhere differentiable. Consider the change in X between $k - 1$ and k when the realization for $\epsilon(k) = \epsilon_j$. It follows that $[X(k) - X(k -1)]/h = \alpha_k + \epsilon_j/h$. But ϵ_j is asymptotically proportional to $h^{1/2}$, and hence $[X(k) - X(k - 1)]/h \sim 1/h^{1/2}$ which diverges as $h \to 0$. Thus, the usual calculus and standard theory of differential equations cannot be used to describe the dynamics of stock-price movements. However, there exists a generalized calculus and corresponding theory of stochastic differential equations which can be used instead.

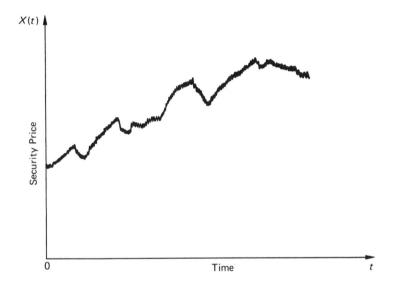

Figure 3.1 Continuous-Time Sample Path for Security Price "Type I" Outcomes.

In preparation for the derivation of this generalized calculus, it will be useful to establish certain moment properties for $X(k) - X(k - 1)$. Define the conditional variance per unit time of the dollar return on the security, σ_k^2, by

$$\sigma_k^2 \equiv E_{k-1}\{\epsilon^2(k)\}/h \qquad k = 1,...,n \qquad (3.8)$$

Because for every outcome ϵ_j, $\epsilon_j^2 = O(h)$, it follows that $\sigma_k^2 = O(1)$. Moreover, from Assumptions 1 and 3, it follows that $\sigma_k^2 > 0$ for all h. Because α_k is bounded, it follows that

$$E_{k-1}\{[X(k) - X(k - 1)]^2\} = \sigma_k^2 h + o(h) \qquad k = 1,...,n \qquad (3.9)$$

Hence, to order h, the conditional second central and noncentral moments of $X(k) - X(k - 1)$ are the same. Note that it is not assumed that σ_k^2 is constant through time, and indeed it can be a random variable when viewed from dates earlier than $k - 1$.

Consider now the Nth unconditional absolute moment of $\epsilon(k)$, $2 < N < \infty$. Using the same definition for $\bar{u}$ as given in the proof of Proposition 3.2, we have that for $k = 1,2,\ldots,n$

$$
\begin{aligned}
E_0\{|\epsilon(k)|^N\} &= \Sigma_1^m p_j |\epsilon_j|^N \\
&\leq \Sigma_1^m p_j (\bar{u})^N h^{N/2} \\
&\leq \bar{u}^N h^{N/2} = o(h) \quad \text{for } N > 2
\end{aligned}
\tag{3.10}
$$

Thus, all the absolute moments of $\epsilon(k)$ higher than the second are asymptotically insignificant by comparison with the first two moments. Similarly, we have that

$$
\begin{aligned}
E_0\{|X(k) - X(k-1)|^N\} &\leq (\alpha h + \bar{u}h^{1/2})^N \\
&= \bar{u}^N h^{N/2} + o(h^{N/2})
\end{aligned}
\tag{3.11}
$$

Hence, to order $h^{N/2}$, the unconditional Nth central and noncentral absolute moments of $X(k) - X(k-1)$ are the same.

Since the order relations among the moments derived in (3.10) and (3.11) depend only upon the $\{\epsilon_j\} = O(h^{1/2})$ and the boundedness of α_k and not upon the probabilities of specific outcomes $\{p_j\}$, it follows immediately that the order relations among the conditional moments will be the same as for the unconditional moments. Therefore,

$$
E_{k-1}\{|\epsilon(k)|^N\} = o(h) \quad \text{for } N > 2
\tag{3.12}
$$

and

$$
E_{k-1}\{|X(k) - X(k-1)|^N\} = E_{k-1}\{|\epsilon(k)|^N\} + o(h^{N/2})
\tag{3.13}
$$

Define the random variable $u(k)$, $k = 1,\ldots,n$, by

$$
u(k) \equiv \epsilon(k)/(\sigma_k^2 h)^{1/2}
\tag{3.14}
$$

where, by construction, $u_j \equiv \epsilon_j/(\sigma_k^2 h)^{1/2} = O(1), j = 1,\ldots,m; E_{k-1}\{u(k)\} = 0; E_{k-1}\{u^2(k)\} = 1;$ and $E_{k-1}\{|u(k)|^N\} = O(1), N > 2$. We can rewrite (3.7) as

$$
X(k) - X(k-1) = \alpha_k h + \sigma_k u(k) h^{1/2} \qquad k = 1,\ldots,n
\tag{3.15}
$$

Hence, whenever the unanticipated price changes of a security have only type I outcomes, the dynamics for the price change can be written as a stochastic difference equation in the form of equation (3.15) where all the explicit random variables on the right-hand side are $O(1)$ and are therefore neither degenerate nor explosive in the limit as $h \to 0$. Moreover, as of time $k - 1$, the only random variable is $u(k)$, and in this case (3.15) is called a conditional stochastic difference equation.

The form of (3.15) makes explicit an important property frequently observed in security returns: namely, because α_k, σ_k, and $u(k)$ are all $O(1)$, the realized return on a security over a very short trading interval will be completely dominated by its unanticipated component $\sigma_k u(k) h^{1/2}$. For example, it is not uncommon to find stocks with annual standard deviations of their percentage returns of between 15 and 20 percent. This would imply that price changes of the order of 1 percent in a trading day are not uncommon. However, as appears to be the case empirically, if the expected annual rate of return on a stock is of the same order as its annual standard deviation, say 15 percent, then the expected rate of return per trading day will be the order of 0.05 percent which is negligible by comparison with the standard deviation. Of course, this point was implicitly made in the earlier discussion of moments when it was shown that, to order h, the second central and noncentral moments of $X(k) - X(k - 1)$ were the same. However, it does not follow that in choosing an optimal portfolio, even with continuous trading, the investor should neglect differences in the expected returns among stocks. As is well known, it is the moments of the returns which matter, and, as was already shown, the first and second moments of the returns are of the same order of magnitude: namely h.

Having established many of the essential asymptotic properties for $X(k) - X(k - 1)$, we now derive the distributional characteristics of random variables which are themselves functions of security prices. These distributional characteristics are especially important to the theories of portfolio selection and contingent-claims pricing. One example of such a contingent claim is a common-stock call option that gives its owner the right to purchase a specified number of shares of stock at a specified price on or before a specified date. Clearly, the price of the option will be a function of the underlying stock's price.

Let $F(t)$ be a random variable given by the rule that $F(t) = f(X, t)$ if $X(t) = X$, where f is a C^2 function with bounded third partial derivatives.[11] Following the convention established for $X(t)$, we use the shorthand $F(k)$ for $F(kh)$ and $f[X(k), k]$ for $f[X(kh), kh]$. Suppose we are at time $k - 1$ and therefore know the values of $X(k - 1)$, α_k, σ_k^2, and $\{p_j'\}$ where p_j' is defined to be the conditional probability that $u(k) = u_j$, $j = 1,...,m$,

---

11   The assumption that f has bounded third derivatives is not essential to the analysis but is simply made for analytical convenience. Actually, all that is required is that the third derivatives be bounded in a small neighborhood of $X(t) = X$.

conditional on information available as of time $k - 1$. Denote by X the known value of $X(k - 1)$. Define the numbers $\{X_j\}$ by

$$X_j \equiv X + \alpha_k h + \sigma_k u_j h^{1/2} \qquad j = 1,\ldots,m \qquad (3.16)$$

For each value X_j, we can use Taylor's theorem to write $f(X_j, k)$ as

$$f(X_j, k) = f(X, k - 1) + f_1(X, k - 1)(\alpha_k h + \sigma_k u_j h^{1/2}) + f_2(X, k - 1)h$$
$$+ \tfrac{1}{2} f_{11}(X, k - 1)(\alpha_k h + \sigma_k u_j h^{1/2})^2 + R_j$$
$$j = 1,\ldots,m \qquad (3.17)$$

where subscripts on f denote partial derivatives and R_j is defined by

$$R_j \equiv \tfrac{1}{2} f_{22}(X, k - 1)h^2 + f_{12}(X, k - 1)(\alpha_k h + \sigma_k u_j h^{1/2})h$$
$$+ \tfrac{1}{6} f_{111}(\eta_j, \zeta_j)(X_j - X)^3 + \tfrac{1}{2} f_{112}(\eta_j, \zeta_j)(X_j - X)^2 h$$
$$+ \tfrac{1}{2} f_{122}(\eta_j, \zeta_j)(X_j - X)h^2 + \tfrac{1}{6} f_{222}(\eta_j, \zeta_j)h^3 \qquad (3.18)$$

where $\eta_j \equiv X + \theta_j(X_j - X)$ and $\zeta_j \equiv (k - 1) + v_j$ for some θ_j, v_j such that $0 \le \theta_j \le 1$ and $0 \le v_j \le 1$. Because all third partial derivatives of f are bounded and $u_j = O(1)$, $j = 1,\ldots,m$, we have by substitution for X_j from (3.16) into (3.18) that, for each and every j,

$$|R_j| = O(h^{3/2}) = o(h) \qquad j = 1,\ldots,m \qquad (3.19)$$

Noting that $(\alpha_k h + \sigma_k u_j h^{1/2})^2 = \sigma_k^2 u_j^2 h + o(h)$, we can rewrite (3.17) as

$$f(X_j, k) = f(X, k - 1) + f_1(X, k - 1)(\alpha_k h + \sigma_k u_j h^{1/2}) + f_2(X, k - 1)h$$
$$+ \tfrac{1}{2} f_{11}(X, k - 1)\sigma_k^2 u_j^2 h + o(h) \qquad j = 1,\ldots,m \qquad (3.20)$$

Since (3.20) holds for each and every j, we can describe the dynamics for $F(k)$ in the form of an (approximate) conditional stochastic difference equation by

$$F(k) - F(k - 1) = \{f_1[X(k - 1), k - 1]\alpha_k + f_2[X(k - 1), k - 1]$$
$$+ \tfrac{1}{2} f_{11}[X(k - 1), k - 1]\sigma_k^2 u^2(k)\}h$$
$$+ f_1[X(k - 1), k - 1]\sigma_k u(k)h^{1/2} + o(h)$$
$$k = 1,\ldots,n \qquad (3.21)$$

where (3.21) is conditional on knowing $X(k - 1)$, α_k, and σ_k.

Formally applying the conditional expectation operator E_{k-1} to both sides of (3.21) leads to the same result as the rigorous operation of multiplying both sides of (3.20) by p_j' and then summing from $j = 1,...,m$. Noting that the derivatives of f on the right-hand side of (3.21) are evaluated at $X(k - 1)$ and are therefore nonstochastic relative to time $k - 1$, we have that, for $k = 1,...,n$,

$$E_{k-1}[F(k) - F(k - 1)] = \{f_1[X(k - 1), k - 1]\alpha_k + f_2[X(k - 1), k - 1]$$

$$+ \tfrac{1}{2}f_{11}[X(k - 1), k - 1]\sigma_k^2\}h + o(h)$$

$$(3.22)$$

Define $\mu_k \equiv E_{k-1}[F(k) - F(k - 1)]/h$ to be the conditional expected change in F per unit time, and from (3.22) we have that, for $k = 1,...,n$,

$$\mu_k = \{f_1[X(k - 1), k - 1]\alpha_k + f_2[X(k - 1), k - 1]$$

$$+ \tfrac{1}{2}f_{11}[X(k - 1), k - 1]\sigma_k^2\} + o(1) \qquad (3.23)$$

Like α_k, $\mu_k = O(1)$, and to that order it is completely determined by knowing $X(k - 1)$ and only the first two moments for the change in X.
  Substituting from (3.23), we can rewrite (3.21) as

$$F(k) - F(k - 1) = \mu_k h + \tfrac{1}{2}f_{11}[X(k - 1), k - 1]\sigma_k^2[u^2(k) - 1]h$$

$$+ f_1[X(k - 1), k - 1]\sigma_k u(k)h^{1/2} + o(h) \qquad (3.24)$$

Inspection of (3.24) shows that, to order h, the conditional stochastic difference equation for $F(k) - F(k - 1)$ is essentially of the same form as equation (3.15) for $X(k) - X(k - 1)$ except for the additional $O(h)$ stochastic component. In an analogous fashion to the discussion of (3.15), it is clear that the realized change in F over a very short time interval is completely dominated by the $f_1[X(k - 1), k - 1]\sigma_k u(k)h^{1/2}$ component of the unanticipated change. Indeed, from (3.24), we can write the conditional moments for $F(k) - F(k - 1)$ as

$$E_{k-1}\{[F(k) - F(k - 1)]^2\} = \{f_1[X(k - 1), k - 1]\sigma_k\}^2 h + o(h)$$

$$(3.25)$$

and

$$E_{k-1}\{[F(k) - F(k - 1)]^N\} = O(h^{N/2}) = o(h) \qquad N > 2 \quad (3.26)$$

Hence, the order relation for the conditional moments of $F(k) - F(k - 1)$ is the same as for the conditional moments of $X(k) - X(k - 1)$, and the $O(h)$

stochastic component makes a negligible contribution to the moments of $F(k) - F(k - 1)$.

Indeed, not only is the order relation of the own moments for the changes in F and X the same, but the co-moments between them of contemporaneous changes have the same order relation. Namely, from (3.15) and (3.24), we have that

$$E_{k-1}\{[F(k) - F(k - 1)][X(k) - X(k - 1)]\}$$
$$= \{f_1[X(k - 1), k - 1]\sigma_k^2\}h + o(h) \tag{3.27}$$

and

$$E_{k-1}\{[F(k) - F(k - 1)]^j[X(k) - X(k - 1)]^{N-j}\} = O(h^{N/2}) = o(h)$$
$$j = 1,...,N, N > 2 \tag{3.28}$$

Although (3.27) and (3.28) are the noncentral co-moments, the difference between the central and noncentral co-moments will be $o(h)$, and therefore the two can be used interchangeably. For example, the covariance between the changes in F and X will differ from the right-hand side of (3.27) by $-\mu_k\alpha_k h^2 = o(h)$.

Finally, we have the rather powerful result that, to order h, the contemporaneous changes in F and X are perfectly correlated. Thus, if ρ_k is defined to be the conditional correlation coefficient per unit time between contemporaneous changes in F and X, then, from (3.25) and (3.27),

$$\rho_k = 1 + o(1) \quad \text{if } f_1[X(k - 1), k - 1] > 0$$
$$= -1 + o(1) \quad \text{if } f_1[X(k - 1), k - 1] < 0 \tag{3.29}$$

Hence, even if F is a nonlinear function of X, in the limit of continuous time their instantaneous contemporaneous changes will be perfectly correlated.

Having demonstrated that the $O(h)$ stochastic term contributes a negligible amount to the variation in F over a very short time interval, we now study its contribution to the change in F over a finite, and not necessarily small, time interval. Define the random variable $G(t)$ by

$$G(k) - G(k - 1) \equiv F(k) - F(k - 1) - \mu_k h$$
$$- f_1[X(k - 1), k - 1]\sigma_k u(k)h^{1/2}$$
$$k = 1,...,n \tag{3.30}$$

Hence, $G(k) - G(k - 1)$ is the random variable error from approximating $F(k) - F(k - 1)$ by $\mu_k h + f_1\sigma_k u(k)h^{1/2}$. If we define

$$y(k) \equiv \{f_{11}[X(k - 1), k - 1]\sigma_k^2[u^2(k) - 1]/2$$

then from (3.24) we can rewrite (3.30) as

$$G(k) - G(k - 1) = y(k)h + o(h) \qquad k = 1,\ldots,n \qquad (3.31)$$

By construction, $E_{k-1}\{y(k)\} = 0$, and therefore $E_{k-j}[y(k)] = 0, j = 1,\ldots,k$. Therefore, the partial sums $\Sigma_1^n y(k)$ form a martingale. Because $E_0\{\Sigma_1^n y^2(k)/k^2\} < \infty$ as $n \to \infty$, it follows from the Law of Large Numbers for martingales[12] that

$$\lim\left[h \sum_1^n y(k) \right] = T \lim\left[\frac{1}{n} \sum_1^n y(k) \right] \to 0 \text{ as } n \to \infty \qquad (3.32)$$

From (3.31), we have that for fixed $T (\equiv nh) > 0$

$$G(T) - G(0) = h \sum_1^n y(k) + \sum_1^n o(h)$$

$$= h \sum_1^n y(k) + o(1) \qquad (3.33)$$

Taking the limit of (3.33) as $n \to \infty$ $(h \to 0)$, we have from (3.32) that $G(T) - G(0) \to 0$. That is, the cumulative error of the approximation goes to zero with probability one.

Hence, for $T > 0$, we have from (3.30) that in the limit of continuous time (as $h \to 0$)

$$F(T) - F(0) = \sum_1^n [F(k) - F(k - 1)]$$

$$= \sum_1^n \mu_k h + \sum_1^n f_1[X(k - 1),k - 1]\sigma_k u(k)h^{1/2} \qquad (3.34)$$

with probability one. Hence, in the limit of continuous time, the $O(h)$ stochastic term in (3.24) will have a negligible effect on the change in F over a finite time interval.

It is natural to interpret the limiting sums in (3.34) as integrals. For each k, $k = 1,\ldots,n$, define $t \equiv kh$. By the usual limiting arguments for Riemann integration, we have that

---

12   For a statement and proof of the Law of Large Numbers for martingales, see Feller (1966, p. 238, Theorem 2).

$$\lim_{n \to \infty} \left(\sum_{1}^{n} \mu_k h \right) = \int_{0}^{T} \mu(t) \, dt \qquad (3.35)$$

where $\mu(t)$ is the continuous time limit of μ_k and is called the instantaneous conditional expected change in F per unit time, conditional on information available at time t. Of course, because of the $h^{1/2}$ coefficient, the second sum will not satisfy the usual Riemann integral conditions. However, we can proceed formally and define the stochastic integral as the limiting sum given by

$$\lim_{n \to \infty} \left\{ \sum_{1}^{n} f_1[X(k-1), k-1] \sigma_k u(k) h^{1/2} \right\} \equiv \int_{0}^{T} f_1[X(t), t] \sigma(t) u(t) (dt)^{1/2}$$

$$(3.36)$$

where the formalism $(dt)^{1/2}$ is used to distinguish this integral from the usual Riemann integral in (3.35). Hence, we have from (3.34) that the change in F between 0 and T can be written

$$F(T) - F(0) = \int_{0}^{T} \mu(t) \, dt + \int_{0}^{T} f_1[X(t), t] \sigma(t) u(t) (dt)^{1/2} \quad (3.37)$$

where equality in (3.37) is understood to hold with probability one.

Given this stochastic integral representation for the change in F over a finite time interval, we proceed formally to define the stochastic differential for F by

$$dF(t) = \mu(t) \, dt + f_1[X(t), t] \sigma(t) u(t) (dt)^{1/2} \qquad (3.38)$$

where the differential form dF is used rather than the usual time derivative notation, dF/dt, to underscore the previously discussed result that the sample paths are almost nowhere differentiable in the usual sense.

In an analogous fashion to the difference equations (3.15) and (3.24), (3.38) can be interpreted as a conditional stochastic differential equation, conditional on information available as of time t which includes $\mu(t)$, $X(t)$, and $\sigma(t)$, but not, of course, $u(t)$ which is the source of the random change in F from $F(t)$ to $F(t + dt)$. Taking the formal limit of (3.24) as $h \to dt$ and neglecting terms of order $o(dt)$, it appears that (3.38) has left out an $O(dt)$ term: namely, $\frac{1}{2} f_{11}[X(t), t] \sigma^2(t) [u^2(t) - 1] \, dt$. However, as has been shown, the contribution of this $O(dt)$ stochastic term to the moments of dF over the infinitesimal interval dt is $o(dt)$, and over finite intervals it disappears by the Law of Large Numbers. Hence, with probability one, the distribution implied by the process described in (3.38) is indistinguishable from the one implied by including the extra $O(dt)$ stochastic term. While $\mu(t) \, dt$ is of the same order as the neglected O(dt) stochastic term, it cannot be neglected over the infinitesimal interval because it is the first moment for the change in F which is of the same order as the second moment. It cannot be neglected over the finite interval $[0,T]$ because, unlike the O(dt) stochastic term, the partial sums of μ_k dt do not form a martingale, and the Law of Large Numbers does not apply.

The corresponding stochastic integral and differential representations for the dynamics of $X(t)$ itself can be written down immediately from (3.37) and (3.38) by simply choosing $f(X, t) = X$: namely, from (3.37),

$$X(T) - X(0) = \int_0^T \alpha(t) \, dt + \int_0^T \sigma(t)u(t)(dt)^{1/2} \qquad (3.39)$$

and

$$dX(t) = \alpha(t) \, dt + \sigma(t)u(t)(dt)^{1/2} \qquad (3.40)$$

where in this case the neglected O(dt) stochastic term is identically zero because $f_{11} \equiv 0$.

Throughout this analysis, the only restrictions on the distribution for $u(t)$ were (a) $E\{u(t)\} = 0$, (b) $E\{u^2(t)\} = 1$, (c) $u(t) = O(1)$, and (d) the distribution for $u(t)$ is discrete. Restrictions (a) and (b) are purely by construction, and (c) and (d) can be weakened to allow most well-behaved continuous distributions including ones with unbounded domain. In particular, it was not assumed that the $\{u(t)\}$ were either identically distributed or serially independent. However, to develop the analysis further requires an additional economics assumption.

Assumption 6

The stochastic process for $X(t)$ is a Markov process.[13] In other words, the conditional probability distribution for future values of X, conditional on being at time t, depends only on the current value of X and the inclusion of further information available as of that date will not alter this conditional probability.

While this assumption may appear to be quite restrictive, many processes that are formally not Markov can be transformed into the Markov format by the method of "expansion of the states,"[14] and therefore

---

13 See Feller (1966, pp. 311–43) for a formal definition and a discussion of the properties of Markov processes. The Markov assumption is almost universal among substantive models of stock-price returns.
14 See Cox and Miller (1968, pp. 16–18) for a brief discussion and further references on this method.

Assumption 6 could be weakened to say that the conditional probabilities for X depend upon only a finite amount of past information. From Assumption 6 we can write the conditional probability density for $X(T) = X$ at time T, conditional on $X(t) = x$, as

$$p(x, t) \equiv p(x, t; X, T) = \text{prob}\{X(T) = X | X(t) = x\} \qquad t < T$$
$$(3.41)$$

where suppression of the explicit arguments X and T will be understood to mean holding these two values fixed. Hence, for fixed X and T, $p[X(t), t]$ (viewed from dates earlier than t) is a random variable which is itself a function of the security price at time t. Therefore, provided that p is a well-behaved function of x and t, it will satisfy all the properties previously derived for $F(t)$. In particular, in the limit of continuous trading, dp will satisfy (3.38) where $\mu(t)$ is the conditional expected change per unit time in p. However, p is a probability density, and therefore its *expected* change is zero. Taking the limit of (3.23) as $h \to 0$ and applying the condition that $\mu(t) = 0$, we have that

$$0 = \tfrac{1}{2}\sigma^2(x, t)p_{11}(x, t) + \alpha(x, t)p_1(x, t) + p_2(x, t) \qquad (3.42)$$

where the subscripts on p denote partial derivatives. Moreover, by the Markov Assumption 6, $\alpha(t)$ and $\sigma^2(t)$ are, at most, functions of $x(t)$ and t. Hence, we make this dependence explicit by rewriting these functions as $\alpha(x, t)$ and $\sigma^2(x, t)$ respectively. Inspection of (3.42) shows that it is a linear partial differential equation of the parabolic type and is sometimes called the "Kolmogorov backward equation."[15] Therefore, subject to boundary conditions, (3.42) completely specifies the transition probability densities for the security price. Hence, in the limit of continuous trading, knowledge of the two functions $\sigma^2(x, t)$ and $\alpha(x, t)$ is sufficient to determine the probability distribution for the change in a security's price between any two dates.

It follows, therefore, that the only characteristics of the distributions for the $\{u(t)\}$ that affect the asymptotic distribution for the security price are the first and second moments, and, by construction, they are constant through time. That is, except for the scaling requirement on the first two moments, the distributional characteristics of the $\{u(t)\}$ can be chosen almost arbitrarily without having any effect upon the asymptotic distribution for the price of the security. Hence, in the limit of continuous trading, nothing of economic content is lost by assuming that the $\{u(t)\}$ are independent and identically distributed, and therefore for the rest of this section we make this assumption. *Warning*: this assumption *does not* imply that changes in $X(t)$ or $F(t)$ have these properties. Indeed, if either $\alpha(t)$ or

15   See Cox and Miller (1968, p. 215).

$\sigma^2(t)$ is a function of $X(t)$, then changes in $X(t)$ will be neither independent nor identically distributed.

Define $Z(t)$ to be a random variable whose change in value over time is described by a stochastic difference equation like (3.15) but with $\alpha_k \equiv 0$ and $\sigma_k \equiv 1$, $k = 1,\ldots,n$. In other words, the conditional expected change in $Z(t)$ per unit time is zero and the conditional variance of that change per unit time is one. Therefore,

$$Z(T) - Z(0) = \sum_{1}^{n} [Z(k) - Z(k-1)]$$

$$= h^{1/2} \sum_{1}^{n} u(k)$$

$$= T^{1/2} \frac{\sum_{1}^{n} u(k)}{n^{1/2}} \tag{3.43}$$

The $\{u(k)\}$ are independent and identically distributed with a zero mean and unit variance. Therefore, by the Central Limit Theorem,[16] in the limit of continuous trading, $\{\sum_{1}^{n} u(k)/n^{1/2}\}$ will have a standard normal distribution. It follows from (3.43) that, asymptotically, $Z(T) - Z(0)$ will be normally distributed with a zero mean and a variance equal to T for all $T > 0$. Indeed, the solution to (3.42) with $\sigma^2 = 1$ and $\alpha = 0$ is

$$p(x, t; X, T) = \frac{\exp[-(X - x)^2/2(T - t)]}{[2\pi(T - t)]^{1/2}} \tag{3.44}$$

which is a normal density function.

Since the distributional choice for $\{u(t)\}$ can be made almost arbitrarily and the limiting distribution for $Z(T) - Z(0)$ is Gaussian for all finite T, it is natural and convenient to assume that the $\{u(t)\}$ are standard normally distributed. In an analogous fashion to (3.40), we can write the stochastic differential equation representation for $Z(t)$ as

$$dZ(t) = u(t)(dt)^{1/2} \tag{3.45}$$

In the case where the $\{u(t)\}$ are independent and distributed standard normal, the dZ process described in (3.45) is called a Wiener or Brownian motion process,[17] and we shall reserve the notation dZ to denote such a process throughout this chapter.

16   See Feller (1966, p. 488, Theorem 1).
17   See McKean (1969) for an excellent rigorous discussion of Wiener processes. Cox and Miller (1968, Ch. 5) provides a less formal approach.

Since this distributional choice for $\{u(t)\}$ does not affect the limiting distribution for X, without loss of generality we can rewrite the stochastic integral and differential representations for the dynamics of $X(t)$, equations (3.39) and (3.40), as

$$X(T) - X(0) = \int_0^T \alpha[X(t), t] \, dt + \int_0^T \sigma[X(t), t] \, dZ(t) \qquad (3.46)$$

and

$$dX(t) = \alpha[X(t), t] \, dt + \sigma[X(t), t] \, dZ(t) \qquad (3.47)$$

The class of continuous-time Markov processes whose dynamics can be written in the form of (3.46) and (3.47) are called Itô processes, and are a special case of a more general class of stochastic processes called strong diffusion processes.

It follows immediately from (3.37) and (3.38) that, if the dynamics of $X(t)$ can be described by an Itô process, then the dynamics of well-behaved functions of $X(t)$ will also be described by an Itô process. This relation between the dynamics of $X(t)$ and $F(t)$ is formalized in the following lemma.

Itô's Lemma

Let $f(X, t)$ be a C^2 function defined on $R \times [0, \infty]$ and take the stochastic integral defined by (3.46), then the time-dependent random variable $F \equiv f$ is a stochastic integral and its stochastic differential is

$$dF = f_1(X, t) \, dX + f_2(X, t) \, dt + \tfrac{1}{2} f_{11}(X, t)(dX)^2$$

where the product of the differentials is defined by the multiplication rules $(dZ)^2 = dt$, $dZ \, dt = 0$, and $(dt)^2 = 0$.

The proof of Itô's lemma[18] follows from (3.23), (3.35), (3.37), and (3.38). Itô's lemma provides the differentiation rule for the generalized

18 For a rigorous proof of Itô's lemma, see McKean (1969, p. 32). Fischer (1975, appendix) and Smith (1979, appendix) provide intuitive developments of the multiplication rules. Stochastic differential equations and Itô's lemma are the key mathematical tools used in the analysis of continuous-time models of economic processes. Their first applications in economics were in Merton (1969a, 1971; this volume, Chs 4 and 5). Stratonovich (1968) develops an alternative theory of stochastic differential equations that satisfy the differentiation rules of the ordinary calculus. However, this representation is not as well suited to the analysis of economic dynamics as the Itô formulation. 1992 note: see also Sethi and Lehoczky (1981).

stochastic calculus, and as such is analogous to the fundamental theorem of the calculus for standard time derivatives.

With the derivation of Itô's lemma, the formal mathematical analysis of this section is complete and a summary is in order. Suppose that the economic structure to be analyzed is such that Assumptions 1–6 obtain and unanticipated security-price changes can have only type I outcomes (i.e. there are no "rare events"). Then, in continuous-trading models of that structure, security-price dynamics can always be described by Itô processes with no loss of generality. Indeed, possibly because the integral of a Wiener process is normally distributed, it is not uncommon in the financial economics literature to find the price dynamics assumption stated as "the change in the security price over short intervals of time, $X(t + h) - X(t)$, is approximately normally distributed" instead of stating the formal equation (3.47). If it is appropriately interpreted, there is no harm in stating the price dynamics assumption in this fashion. However, it can be misleading in at least two ways.

First, stating the assumption in this fashion carries with it the implication that the $\{u(t)\}$ are independently and identically distributed standard normal. Hence, one might be led to the belief that the normality assumption is essential to the analysis rather than merely a convenience. For example, the derived continuous-trading dynamics are equally valid if $\{u(t)\}$ has a binomial distribution provided that the parameters of that distribution are chosen so as to satisfy $E\{u(t)\} = 0$ and $E\{u^2(t)\} = 1$.[19] While in the sequence-of-market structure analysis the corresponding sequence of distribution functions for $X(t + h) - X(t)$ will depend upon the distribution of the $\{u(t)\}$, the limit distribution of that sequence does not. Moreover, independently of the distribution of $\{u(t)\}$, the continuous-trading solutions will provide a uniformly valid approximation (of $o(h)$) to the discrete-trading solutions. Therefore, the normality assumption for the $\{u(t)\}$ imposes no further restrictions on the process beyond those of Assumptions 1–6.

Second, because $X(T) - X(0) = \Sigma_1^n[X(k) - X(k - 1)]$, stating the assumption in this fashion might lead one to believe that the distribution for the security-price change over a finite interval $[0, T]$ will be (approximately) normally distributed, and this is clearly not implied by equation (3.47). For example, if $\alpha(X, t) = aX$ and $\sigma(X, t) = bX$, with a and b constant, then, by solving equation (3.42), $X(T)$ can be shown to have a log-normal distribution with

---

19 The binomial distribution which satisfies these conditions must have $u_1 = 1$ with probability 1/2 and $u_2 = -1$ with probability 1/2. Hence, in this special case, $u^2(t) = 1$ with probability one, and therefore the $O(h)$ stochastic term analyzed in equations (3.24), (3.30), (3.31), (3.32), and (3.33) will be zero even for finite h. Cf. Cox, Ross and Rubinstein (1979).

$$E_0\{X(T)\} = X(0)\,\exp[aT]$$

and

$$\mathrm{var}\{\log[X(T)]\} = b^2 T$$

for all $T > 0$, and the normal and log-normal distributions are not the same. Indeed, a normal distribution for $X(T) - X(0)$ implies a positive probability that $X(T)$ can be negative while a log-normal distribution implies that $X(T)$ can never be negative.

Along these lines, a less misleading way to state the assumed price dynamics would be: "For very short trading intervals, one may treat the change in the security price over a trading interval 'as if' it were normally distributed." However, this simply restates the conditions summarized by (3.13) and (3.26): namely, for short trading intervals, only the first two moments "matter."

The substantive benefits from using continuous-time models with Itô process price dynamics have been amply demonstrated in the financial economics literature, and therefore only a few brief remarks will be made here. For example, in solving the intertemporal portfolio-selection problem, the optimal portfolio demand functions will depend only upon the first two moments of the security return distributions. Not only does this vastly reduce the amount of information about the returns distributions required to choose an optimal portfolio, but it also guarantees that the first-order conditions are linear in the demand functions, and therefore explicit solutions for these functions can be obtained by simple matrix inversion.

The analysis of corporate liability and option pricing is also simplified by using Itô's lemma which provides a direct method for deriving the dynamics and transition probabilities for functions of security prices. Moreover, while the analysis presented here is for scalar processes, it can easily be generalized to vector processes.[20]

Of course, all the results derived in this section are based upon the assumption that changes in the security price are all type I outcomes. As discussed in Section 3.1, this class of processes is only a subset of the set of processes which satisfy economics Assumptions 1–6. Hence, to complete the study of the mathematics of continuous-trading models, we now provide a companion analysis of those processes which allow for the possibility of "rare events."

---

20   See McKean (1969, p. 44) for the proof of Itô's lemma for vector processes. Also see Cox and Miller (1968, pp. 246–8).

3.3   CONTINUOUS-SAMPLE-PATH PROCESSES WITH "RARE EVENTS"

In this section, it is assumed that the outcomes for $\epsilon(k)$, $k = 1,...,n$, can be either of type I or type II, but not type III. Thus, we allow for the possibility of rare events with type II outcomes although, as was shown in Section 3.1, virtually all observations of $\epsilon(k)$ will be type I outcomes.

The format of the analysis presented here is essentially the same as in the previous section. Indeed, the principal conclusion of this analysis will be that, in the limit of continuous trading, the distributional properties of security returns are indistinguishable from those of Section 3.2. In other words, rare events with type II outcomes "do not matter."

To show this, we begin by proving that, in the limit of continuous trading, the sample paths for security prices are continuous over time. For each time period k, define $r \equiv \min r_j$ where the lead order term for ϵ_j is h^{r_j}, $j = 1,...,m$. Because all outcomes are either type I or type II, $r > 0$, and $|\epsilon_j| = O(h^r)$, $j = 1,...,m$.

Proposition 3.3

If, for $k = 1,...,n$, all possible outcomes for $\epsilon(k)$ are either type I or type II outcomes, then the continuous-time sample path for the price of the security will be continuous.

PROOF

Let $Q_k(\delta)$ be the probability that $|X(k) - X(k - 1)| \geq \delta$ conditional on knowing all information available as of time $k - 1$. As in the proof of Proposition 3.2, a necessary and sufficient condition for continuity of the sample path for X is that, for every $\delta > 0$, $Q_k(\delta) = o(h)$. Define $\bar{u} \equiv \max_{\{j\}}|\epsilon_j|h^{-r}$. By the definition of r, $\bar{u} = O(1)$. For each number $\delta > 0$, define the function $h^+(\delta)$ as the solution to the equation $\delta = \alpha h^+ + \bar{u}(h^+)^r$ where, by Assumption 5, α is $O(1)$. Because $r > 0$ and α and $\bar{u}$ are both $O(1)$, there exists a solution $h^+(\delta) > 0$ for every $\delta > 0$. Therefore, for all $h < h^+(\delta)$ and every possible outcome $X(k)$, $|X(k) - X(k - 1)| < \delta$. Hence, for every h, $0 \leq h < h^+(\delta)$, $Q_k(\delta) \equiv 0$, and $\lim[Q_k(\delta)/h] = 0$ as $h \to 0$.   QED

Having established the continuity of the sample path, we now show that the moment properties for $X(k) - X(k - 1)$ are the same as in Section 3.2. From Assumption 5, $E_{k-1}\{X(k) - X(k - 1)\}$ is asymptotically proportional to h, and therefore so is $E_0\{X(k) - X(k - 1)\}$. Therefore, from

Proposition 3.1 and equation (3.5), the unconditional variance of $X(k) - X(k - 1)$ is asymptotically proportional to h. The Nth unconditional absolute moment of $\epsilon(k)$, $2 < N < \infty$, can be written as

$$E_0\{|\epsilon(k)|^N\} = \sum_1^m p_j|\epsilon_j|^N$$

$$= O\left(\sum_1^m h^{(N-2)r_j+1} \right) \qquad \text{from equation (3.5)}$$

$$= O(h^{(N-2)r+1})$$

$$= o(h) \quad N > 2 \tag{3.48}$$

because $r > 0$. Thus, all the absolute moments of $\epsilon(k)$ higher than the second are asymptotically insignificant by comparison with the first two moments. Moreover, by Assumption 5, these same order relations will obtain for both the central and noncentral moments of $X(k) - X(k - 1)$.

Provided that the order relations between the unconditional and conditional probabilities remain the same, the conditional moments of $X(k) - X(k - 1)$ have the same order properties as the unconditional moments: namely

$$E_{k-1}\{[X(k) - X(k - 1)]^2\} = \sigma_k^2 h + o(h) \qquad k = 1,\dots,n \tag{3.49}$$

where σ_k^2 is the conditional variance per unit time defined in (3.8) and $\sigma_k^2 > 0$ and O(1), and

$$E_{k-1}\{|X(k) - X(k - 1)|^N\} = o(h) \quad \text{for } N > 2 \tag{3.50}$$

Hence, the moment relations for $X(k) - X(k - 1)$ are identical with those derived in Section 3.2 where only type I outcomes were allowed.

To complete the analysis, we examine the distributional characteristics of random variables which are functions of security prices. Let $F(t)$ be a random variable given by the rule that $F(t) = f(X)$ if $X(t) = X$. The reader will note that, unlike the parallel analysis in Section 3.2, the explicit dependence of f on t has been eliminated. This is done solely to keep both the notation and the analysis relatively simple. However, including the explicit time dependence would not change either the method of derivation or the conclusions.

Define K to be the smallest integer such that $Kr \geq 1$. Because $r > 0$, K is finite. If f is a C^2 function with a bounded $(K + 1)$th order derivative, then from Taylor's theorem and (3.49) and (3.50) we have that

$$E_{k-1}\{F(k) - F(k-1)\} = \{f^{(1)}[X(k-1)]\alpha_k + \tfrac{1}{2}f^{(2)}[X(k-1)]\sigma_k^2\}h + o(h)$$
$$(3.51)$$

where $f^{(i)}[\cdot]$ denotes the ith derivative of f. Note that (3.51) is identical with the corresponding equation (3.22) in Section 3.2 when f is not an explicit function of time. Moreover, it is straightforward to show that the conditional moments for $F(k) - F(k - 1)$ here are the same as those derived in equations (3.25) and (3.26) of Section 3.2: namely,

$$E_{k-1}\{[F(k) - F(k - 1)]^2\} = \{f^{(1)}[X(k - 1)]\sigma_k\}^2 h + o(h) \quad (3.52)$$

and

$$E_{k-1}\{[F(k) - F(k - 1)]^N\} = o(h) \quad \text{for } N > 2 \quad (3.53)$$

Hence, the order relation for the conditional moments of $F(k) - F(k - 1)$ is the same as for the conditional moments of $X(k) - X(k - 1)$. Therefore, over short intervals of time, the unanticipated part of the change in F here will be dominated by the $f^{(1)}[X(k - 1)]\epsilon(k)$ term in the same fashion that it dominated the change in F in Section 3.2.

Having studied the change in F over a very short time interval, we now examine the stochastic properties for the change in F over a finite, and not necessarily small, time interval. For each k, $k = 1,\ldots,n$, define the random variables $\{y_j(k)\}$ by

$$y_j(k) \equiv f^{(j)}[X(k - 1)] \frac{[X(k) - X(k - 1)]^j - E_{k-1}\{[X(k) - X(k - 1)]^j\}}{j!}$$

$$j = 2,\ldots,K \quad (3.54)$$

Further define the random variable $G(t)$ by

$$G(k) - G(k - 1) \equiv F(k) - F(k - 1) - E_{k-1}\{F(k) - F(k - 1)\}$$
$$- f^{(1)}[X(k - 1)]\epsilon(k) \qquad k = 1,\ldots,n \quad (3.55)$$

which by Taylor's theorem can be rewritten as

$$G(k) - G(k - 1) = \sum_{j=2}^{K} y_j(k) + R_{K+1} \quad (3.56)$$

where R_{K+1} is defined by

$$R_{K+1} \equiv f^{(K+1)}[\theta X(k-1) + (1-\theta)X(k)]$$

$$\times \frac{[X(k) - X(k-1)]^{K+1} - E_{k-1}\{[X(k) - X(k-1)]^{K+1}\}}{(K+1)!}$$

(3.57)

for some θ, $0 \le \theta \le 1$. But $f^{(K+1)}$ is bounded and

$$[\alpha_k h + \epsilon(k)]^{K+1} = O(h^{r(K+1)})$$

for every possible outcome for $\epsilon(k)$. Hence, because $rK \ge 1$, $R_{K+1} = o(h)$. Therefore, we can rewrite (3.56) as

$$G(k) - G(k-1) = \sum_{j=2}^{K} y_j(k) + o(h) \qquad k = 1,\ldots,n \quad (3.58)$$

From (3.58), we can write the unconditional variance of $G(k) - G(k-1)$ as

$$\mathrm{var}[G(k) - G(k-1)]$$

$$= E_0\left\{ \sum_2^K \sum_2^K y_i(k)y_j(k) \right\} + o(h)$$

$$\le \sum_2^K \sum_2^K M_i M_j E_0 | \{[X(k) - X(k-1)]^i$$

$$- E_{k-1}[X(k) - X(k-1)]^i\} \{[X(k) - X(k-1)]^j$$

$$- E_{k-1}[X(k) - X(k-1)]^j\} | / i!j! + o(h)$$

(3.59)

where M_i is the least upper bound on $|f^{(i)}|$, $i = 2,\ldots,K$. From (3.48) and (3.59), we have, therefore, that

$$\mathrm{var}[G(k) - G(k-1)] = O(h^{2r+1}) + o(h)$$

$$= o(h) \qquad (3.60)$$

because $r > 0$. For the finite time interval $[0,T]$, we have that

$$G(T) - G(0) = \sum_{k=1}^{n} [G(k) - G(k - 1)]$$

$$= \sum_{1}^{n} \sum_{2}^{K} y_j(k) + o(1) \tag{3.61}$$

$\Sigma_1^n \Sigma_2^K y_j(k)$ forms a martingale, and therefore the unconditional variance of $G(T) - G(0)$ can be written as

$$\text{var}[G(T) - G(0)] = \sum_{1}^{n} \text{var}[G(k) - G(k - 1)] + o(1) \tag{3.62}$$

But, from (3.60) and (3.62), it follows that

$$\text{var}[G(T) - G(0)] = O(h^{2r}) + o(1)$$
$$= o(1) \tag{3.63}$$

and therefore, in the limit of continuous trading as $h \to 0$, the variance of $G(T) - G(0)$ goes to zero for every finite time interval $[0, T]$.

Hence, for $T > 0$, we have from (3.51), (3.52), (3.53), and (3.63) that in the limit as $h \to 0$

$$F(T) - F(0) = \sum_{1}^{n} [F(k) - F(k - 1)]$$

$$= \sum_{1}^{n} \mu_k h + \sum_{1}^{n} f^{(1)}[X(k - 1)]\epsilon(k) \tag{3.64}$$

with probability one where μ_k is the conditional expected change in F per unit time defined in (3.23). In a similar fashion to the analysis in Section 3.2, we can formally express the limiting sum in (3.64) as the sum of two integrals: namely,

$$F(T) - F(0) = \int_0^T \mu(t)\, dt + \int_0^T f^{(1)}[X(t)]\epsilon(t) \tag{3.65}$$

where (3.65) is understood to hold with probability one. As in (3.38) of Section 3.2, we can formally define the stochastic differential for F by

$$dF(t) = \mu(t) \, dt + f^{(1)}[X(t)]\epsilon(t) \qquad (3.66)$$

Moreover, if the Markov assumption (Assumption 6) obtains, then the limiting transition probabilities for X will satisfy equation (3.42). Finally, although it is not the case that $[\epsilon(t)]^2 = O(h)$ with probability one, the formal differentiation rules provided by Itô's lemma still apply. Hence, in the limit of continuous trading, processes with type I and type II outcomes are indistinguishable from processes with type I outcomes only.

3.4 DISCONTINUOUS-SAMPLE-PATH PROCESSES WITH "RARE EVENTS"

In this concluding section, the general case is analyzed where the outcomes for $\epsilon(k)$, $k = 1,...,n$ can be type I, type II, or type III. As was true for the processes in Section 3.3, virtually all observations of $\epsilon(k)$ will be type I outcomes. However, unlike the findings in Section 3.3, the possibility of rare events with type III outcomes "does matter." While the type III outcomes with their probabilities proportional to h are the "rarest" of the admissible outcomes, the magnitudes of these outcomes are also the largest. Indeed, because these outcomes are $O(1)$, it follows that X can have nonlocal changes in value, even over an infinitesimal time interval, and therefore the resulting sample path for X will be discontinuous. The analysis demonstrating this and other important properties can be simplified by neglecting the type II outcomes, and in the light of the conclusions reached in Section 3.3, this simplification can be made with no loss in generality.

Proposition 3.4

If, for $k = 1,...,n$, at least one possible outcome for $\epsilon(k)$ is a type III outcome, then the continuous-time sample path for the price of the security will not be continuous.

PROOF

Let $Q_k(\delta)$ be the probability that $|X(k) - X(k - 1)| \geq \delta$ conditional on knowing all information available as of time $k - 1$. As in the proofs of Propositions 3.2 and 3.3, a necessary and sufficient condition for continuity of the sample path for X is that, for every $\delta > 0$, $Q_k(\delta) = o(h)$. By renumbering, if necessary, for each k, suppose event j denotes a type III outcome for $\epsilon(k)$ where $\epsilon(k) = \epsilon_j$ and ϵ_j is $O(1)$. If p_j is the conditional probability as of time $k - 1$ that event j occurs, then, from (3.5), p_j can be written as $\lambda_j h$ where $\lambda_j = O(1)$. Pick a number θ such that $0 < \theta < 1$.

Define h^+ by $h^+ = \infty$ if $\alpha_k \epsilon_j \geq 0$ and $h^+ = (\theta - 1)\epsilon_j/\alpha_k$ if $\alpha_k \epsilon_j < 0$. Note that $h^+ > 0$, independent of h. Define $\delta^+ \equiv \theta|\epsilon_j|$. Note that $\delta^+ > 0$, independent of h. For all h such that $0 < h \leq h^+$, it follows that, if $\epsilon(k) = \epsilon_j$, then $|X(k) - X(k-1)| > \delta^+$. Hence, for $0 < h \leq h^+$ and any δ such that $0 < \delta \leq \delta^+$, $|X(k) - X(k-1)| > \delta$ if $\epsilon(k) = \epsilon_j$, and therefore $Q_k(\delta) \geq \lambda_j h = O(h)$ because $\lambda_j = O(1)$. Hence, the sample path is not continuous.   QED

As illustrated in Figure 3.2, a typical sample path will contain mostly local or continuous changes with infrequent nonlocal changes or "jumps" corresponding to the relatively rare type III outcomes.

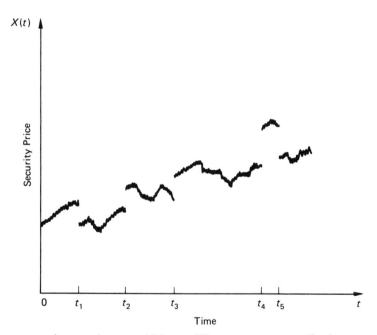

t_i denotes times at which type III outcomes were realized.

Figure 3.2 Continuous-Time Sample Path for Security Price "Type I" and "Type III" Outcomes.

These fundamental discontinuities in the sample path manifest themselves in the moment properties of $X(k) - X(k-1)$. Like the processes in Sections 3.2 and 3.3, the first and second unconditional moments of $X(k) - X(k-1)$ are asymptotically proportional to h. However, unlike the processes in those sections, the Nth unconditional absolute moments, $2 < N < \infty$, are asymptotically proportional to h as well. That is,

$$E_0\{|\epsilon(k)|^N\} = \sum_1^m p_j|\epsilon_j|^N$$

$$= O\left(\sum_1^m h^{(N-2)r_j+1} \right) \quad \text{from equation (3.5)}$$

$$= O(h) \quad N > 2 \tag{3.67}$$

because $r_j = 0$ for all type III outcomes. Hence, all the absolute moments of $X(k) - X(k-1)$ are of the same order of magnitude, and therefore none of the moments can be neglected even in the limit of continuous trading. However, the contributions of the type I outcomes for $\epsilon(k)$ to the moments higher than the second will be shown to be asymptotically insignificant. To show this along with the other results, it is useful to formally partition the outcomes for $\epsilon(k)$ into its type I and type III components.

Define the conditional random variable $u(k)$ by $u(k) \equiv \epsilon(k)/h^{1/2}$ conditional on $\epsilon(k)$ having a type I outcome. Similarly, define the conditional random variable $y(k)$ by $y(k) \equiv \epsilon(k)$ conditional on $\epsilon(k)$ having a type III outcome. If $\lambda(k)h$ denotes the conditional probability as of time $k - 1$ that $\epsilon(k)$ has a type III outcome, then, as of time $k - 1$, we can rewrite $\epsilon(k)$ as

$$\epsilon(k) = u(k)h^{1/2} \quad \text{with probability } 1 - \lambda(k)h$$
$$= y(k) \quad \text{with probability } \lambda(k)h \tag{3.68}$$

and, by construction, $u(k)$, $y(k)$, and $\lambda(k)$ are all $O(1)$.

If E^y_{k-1} denotes the conditional expectation as of time $k - 1$ over the distribution function for $y(k)$ and E^u_{k-1} denotes the corresponding conditional expectation over the distribution for $u(k)$, then

$$\bar{y}(k) \equiv E^y_{k-1}\{y(k)\} = E_{k-1}\{\epsilon(k)| \text{ type III outcome}\}$$

and

$$\bar{u}(k)h^{1/2} \equiv h^{1/2}E^u_{k-1}\{u(k)\} = E_{k-1}\{\epsilon(k)| \text{ type I outcome}\}$$

Because $E_{k-1}\{\epsilon(k)\} = 0$, it follows immediately from the properties of conditional expectation that

$$\bar{u}(k) = -\frac{\lambda(k)\bar{y}(k)h^{1/2}}{1 - \lambda(k)h}$$

$$= -\lambda\bar{y}h^{1/2} + o(h) \tag{3.69}$$

where we suppress the explicit dependence of u, y, and λ on k whenever there is no ambiguity about the time.

If σ_k^2 is the conditional variance per unit time for $\epsilon(k)$, then $E_{k-1}\{\epsilon^2(k)\} = \sigma_k^2 h$, and it follows that

$$
\begin{aligned}
\sigma_u^2 &= \frac{\sigma_k^2 - \lambda \sigma_y^2}{1 - \lambda h} \\
&= \sigma_k^2 - \lambda \sigma_y^2 + O(h)
\end{aligned}
\tag{3.70}
$$

where σ_u^2 is the conditional variance of $u(k)$ and σ_y^2 is the conditional variance of $y(k)$. Note that σ_k^2, σ_u^2, and σ_y^2 are all O(1). Further, for $N > 2$, it follows that

$$
E_{k-1}\{\epsilon^N(k)\} = \lambda(k)E_{k-1}^y\{y^N(k)\}h + o(h)
\tag{3.71}
$$

Thus, while both the type I and type III contribute significantly to the mean and variance of $\epsilon(k)$, the contributions of the type I outcomes to the higher moments of $\epsilon(k)$ are asymptotically insignificant.

As was done in the earlier sections, we complete the analysis by examining the distributional characteristics of random variables which are functions of security prices. As in Section 3.2, let $F(t)$ be a random variable given by the rule that $F(t) = f(X, t)$ if $X(t) = X$, where f is a C^2 function with bounded third partial derivatives.

For a given outcome $y(k) = y$, we have by Taylor's theorem that

$$
\begin{aligned}
f[X(k-1) + \alpha_k h + y, k] = {} & f[X(k-1) + y, k-1] \\
& + f_1[X(k-1) + y, k-1]\alpha_k h \\
& + f_2[X(k-1) + y, k-1]h + o(h)
\end{aligned}
\tag{3.72}
$$

where, as in Section 3.2, subscripts on f denote partial derivatives.

Similarly, for a given outcome $u(k) = u$, we have that

$$
\begin{aligned}
f[X(k-1) + \alpha_k h + u h^{1/2}, k] = {} & f[X(k-1), k-1] \\
& + f_1[X(k-1), k-1]\,(\alpha_k h + u h^{1/2}) \\
& + f_2[X(k-1), k-1]h \\
& + \tfrac{1}{2} f_{11}[X(k-1), k-1]u^2 h + o(h)
\end{aligned}
\tag{3.73}
$$

By the properties of conditional expectation, it follows that

$$E_{k-1}\{F(k) - F(k - 1)\} = \lambda(k)hE^y_{k-1}\{F(k) - F(k - 1)\}$$
$$+ [1 - \lambda(k)h]E^u_{k-1}\{F(k) - F(k - 1)\}$$

(3.74)

Substituting from (3.72) and (3.73) into (3.74) and eliminating explicit representation of terms that are $o(h)$, we can rewrite (3.74) as

$$E_{k-1}\{F(k) - F(k - 1)\}$$
$$= (\tfrac{1}{2}f_{11}[X(k - 1), k - 1]\sigma_u^2 + f_1[X(k - 1), k - 1](\alpha_k - \lambda\bar{y})$$
$$+ f_2[X(k - 1), k - 1] + \lambda E^y_{k-1}\{f[X(k - 1) + y(k), k - 1]$$
$$- f[X(k - 1), k - 1]\})h + o(h)$$

(3.75)

If in a corresponding fashion to equation (3.23) we define the conditional expected change in F per unit time to be $\mu_k \equiv E_{k-1}\{F(k) - F(k - 1)\}/h$, then by dividing (3.75) by h and taking the limit as $h \to 0$, we can write the instantaneous conditional expected change in F per unit time, $\mu(t)$, as

$$\mu(t) = \tfrac{1}{2}f_{11}[X(t), t]\sigma_u^2(t) + f_1[X(t), t][\alpha(t) - \lambda(t)\bar{y}(t)] + f_2[X(t), t]$$
$$+ \lambda(t)E^y_t\{f[X(t) + y(t), t] - f[X(t), t]\}$$

(3.76)

Note that in the special case when $\lambda(t) = 0$ and there are no type III outcomes, the expression for $\mu(t)$ in (3.76) reduces to the corresponding limiting form of (3.23) derived in Section 3.2.

In a similar fashion, the higher conditional moments for the change in F can be written as

$$E_{k-1}\{[F(k) - F(k - 1)]^2\}$$
$$= \left(\lambda E^y_{k-1}\{f[X(k - 1) + y(k), k - 1] - f[X(k - 1), k - 1]\}^2\right.$$
$$\left. + f_1^2[X(k - 1), k - 1]\sigma_u^2\right) h + o(h)$$

(3.77)

and, for $N > 2$,

$$E_{k-1}\{[F(k) - F(k - 1)]^N\}$$
$$= \lambda E^y_{k-1}\{f[X(k - 1) + y(k), k - 1] - f[X(k - 1), k - 1]\}^N h + o(h)$$

(3.78)

As was the case for the moments of $X(k) - X(k - 1)$, all the moments of $F(k) - F(k - 1)$ are of the same order of magnitude, and only the type III outcomes contribute significantly to the moments higher than the second. Hence, in the limit of continuous trading, the only characteristics of $u(k)$ which matter are its first two moments.

If we now reintroduce Assumption 6 that the stochastic process for $X(t)$ is Markov, then $\lambda(k) = \lambda[X(k - 1), k - 1]$; $\alpha_k = \alpha_k[X(k - 1), k - 1]$; $\sigma_u^2(k) = \sigma_u^2[X(k - 1), k - 1]$; and $g_k(y)$, the conditional density function for $y(k)$, can be written as $g[y(k); X(k - 1), k - 1]$. As defined in (3.41) of Section 3.2, let $p(x,t)$ denote the conditional probability density for $X(T) = X$ at time T, conditional on $X(t) = x$. For fixed X and T, $p[X(t), t]$ is a random variable which is a function of the security price at time t. Hence, in the limit of continuous trading, the instantaneous expected change in p per unit time will satisfy (3.76). However, because p is a probability density, its expected change is zero. Substituting the condition that $\mu(t) = 0$ into (3.76), we have that p must satisfy

$$0 = \tfrac{1}{2} \sigma_u^2 p_{11}(x, t) + (\alpha - \lambda \bar{y}) p_1(x, t) + p_2(x, t)$$

$$+ \lambda \int [p(x + y, t) - p(x, t)] g(y; x, t) \, dy \qquad (3.79)$$

which is a linear partial differential–difference equation for the transition probabilities $p(x, t)$. Hence, knowledge of the functions σ_u^2, α, λ, and g is sufficient to determine the probability distribution for the change in X between any two dates. Moreover, from (3.79), it can be shown that the asymptotic distribution for $X(t)$ is identical with that of a stochastic process driven by a linear superposition of a continuous-sample-path diffusion process and a "Poisson-directed" process.[21] That is, let $Q(t + h) - Q(t)$ be a Poisson-distributed random variable with characteristic parameter $\lambda[X(t),t]h$. Define formally the differential $dQ(t)$ to be the limit of $Q(t + h) - Q(t)$ as $h \to dt$. It follows from the Poisson density function, therefore, that

$$\begin{aligned} dQ(t) &= 0 \quad \text{with probability} \quad 1 - \lambda[X(t), t] \, dt + o(dt) \\ &= 1 \quad \text{with probability} \quad \lambda[X(t), t] \, dt + o(dt) \\ &= N \quad \text{with probability} \quad o(dt), \, N \geqslant 2 \end{aligned} \qquad (3.80)$$

---

21 See Cox and Miller (1968, pp. 237–46) for the formal analysis of "mixed" processes of this type where it is shown that such processes will have transition probabilities which satisfy (3.79). For "jump" processes alone, see Feller (1966, pp. 316–20).

Define the random variable $X_1(t)$ by the process $dX_1(t) = y(t) \, dQ(t)$ where $y(t)$ is a $O(1)$ random variable with probability density $g[y; X(t), t]$. Then, dX_1 is an example of a "Poisson-directed" process. Note that the instantaneous expected change in dX_1 is $\lambda \bar{y}(t) \, dt$. Define a second random variable $X_2(t)$ by the process $dX_2(t) = \alpha' dt + \sigma' dZ$ where dZ is a Wiener process as defined by (3.45) in Section 3.2. From (3.47) in Section 3.2, dX_2 is a diffusion process with a continuous sample path. If the function α' is chosen such that $\alpha' \equiv \alpha[X(t), t] - \lambda[X(t), t]\bar{y}(t)$ and $\sigma' \equiv \sigma_u[X(t), t]$, then from (3.79) the limiting process for the change in X, $dX(t)$, will be identical with the process described by $dX_1(t) + dX_2(t)$.

Hence, with no loss in generality, we can always describe the continuous-trading dynamics for $X(t)$ by the stochastic differential equation

$$dX(t) = \{\alpha[X(t), t] - \lambda[X(t), t]\bar{y}(t)\} \, dt + \sigma[X(t), t] \, dZ(t) + y(t) \, dQ(t)$$
$$(3.81)$$

where α is the instantaneous expected change in X per unit time; σ^2 is the instantaneous variance of the change in X, conditional on the change being a type I outcome; λ is the probability per unit time that the change in X is a type III outcome; and $y(t)$ is the random variable outcome for the change in X, conditional on the change being a type III outcome. As was discussed in Section 3.2, the stochastic differential representation in (3.81) is actually defined by a stochastic integral $X(T) - X(0) = \int_0^T dX(t)$. Of course, if $\lambda \equiv 0$ and only type I outcomes can occur, then (3.81) reduces to (3.47) in Section 3.2.

In a similar fashion, it can be shown that the stochastic differential representation for F can be written as

$$dF(t) = \{\tfrac{1}{2}\sigma^2 f_{11}[X(t), t] + (\alpha - \lambda\bar{y})f_1[X(t), t] + f_2[X(t), t]\} \, dt$$

$$+ \sigma f_1[X(t), t] \, dZ(t) + \{f[X(t) + y(t), t] - f[X(t), t]\} \, dQ(t)$$

$$(3.82)$$

Thus, if the dynamics of $X(t)$ can be described by a superposition of diffusion and Poisson-directed processes, then the dynamics of well-behaved functions of $X(t)$ can be described in the same way. Hence, (3.82) provides the transformation rule corresponding to Itô's lemma for pure diffusion processes.

In summary, if the economic structure to be analyzed is such that Assumptions 1–5 obtain, then in continuous-trading models security-price dynamics can always be described by a "mixture" of continuous-sample-path diffusion processes and Poisson-directed processes with no loss in generality. The diffusion process component describes the frequent local changes in prices and is, indeed, sufficient in structures where the magnitudes of the state variables cannot change "radically" in a short period of time. The Poisson-directed process component is used to capture those rare events when the state variables have nonlocal changes and security prices "jump."[22]

While the introduction of a "jump" component provides a significant complication to the analysis over a pure diffusion process, the analysis for the general continuous-trading model is still much simpler than for its discrete-trading counterpart. As (3.79) demonstrates, the transition probabilities are completely specified by only the four functions α, σ, λ, and g. Not only does this simplify the structural analysis, but it makes the testing of these model structures empirically feasible. Indeed, because, for a given magnitude of change, each of the components has a different "time scale," it should be possible to design tests such that these various functions can be identified. For example, by using time series data with very short time intervals between observations, one could identify any "nonlocal" price movement between observations, as a "jump," and hence, calculate an estimate of λ. Similarly, the squares of local price movements between observations could be used to estimate σ^2. Finally, armed with λ and σ^2, the price movements over relatively long time periods could be used to estimate α and $\bar{y}$.[23]

22 For examples of Poisson-directed processes in intertemporal portfolio selection, see Merton (1971; this volume, Section 5.8). For studies of the impact on corporate liabilities pricing theory when the underlying state variables have "jump" components, see Cox and Ross (1976) and Merton (1976a; this volume, Ch. 9).
23 For an early attempt along these lines, see Rosenfeld (1980). See also Jorion (1988).

Part II

Optimum Consumption and Portfolio Selection in Continuous-Time Models

4

Lifetime Portfolio Selection Under Uncertainty: The Continuous-Time Case

4.1 INTRODUCTION

Most models of portfolio selection have been one-period models. I examine the combined problem of optimal portfolio selection and consumption rules for an individual in a continuous-time model where his income is generated by returns on assets and these returns or instantaneous "growth rates" are stochastic. P. A. Samuelson (1969) has developed a similar model in discrete time for more general probability distributions in a companion paper.

I derive the optimality equations for a multiasset problem when the rates of return are generated by a Wiener Brownian-motion process. A particular case examined in detail is the two-asset model with constant relative risk aversion or isoelastic marginal utility. An explicit solution is also found for the case of constant absolute risk aversion. The general technique employed can be used to examine a wide class of intertemporal economic problems under uncertainty.

In addition to the Samuelson (1969) paper, there is the multiperiod analysis of Tobin (1965). Phelps (1962) has used a model to determine the optimal consumption rule for a multiperiod example where income is partly generated by an asset with an uncertain return. Mirrlees (1965) has developed a continuous-time optimal consumption model of the neoclassical type with random technical progress.

Reproduced from *Review of Economics and Statistics*, 51, August, 1969, 247–57 © the President and Fellows of Harvard College. This work was done during the tenure of a National Defense Education Act Fellowship. Aid from the National Science Foundation is gratefully acknowledged. I am indebted to Paul A. Samuelson for many discussions and helpful suggestions. I wish to thank Stanley Fischer, Massachusetts Institute of Technology, for his comments on Section 4.7 and John S. Flemming for his criticism of an earlier version.

4.2   DYNAMICS OF THE MODEL: THE BUDGET EQUATION

In the usual continuous-time model under certainty, the budget equation is a differential equation. However, when uncertainty is introduced by a random variable, the budget equation must be generalized to become a stochastic differential equation. To see the meaning of such an equation, it is easiest to work out the discrete-time version and then pass to the limit of continuous time.

Define $W(t)$ to be the total wealth at time t, $X_i(t)$ the price of the ith asset at time t, $i = 1,...,m$, $C(t)$ the consumption per unit time at time t, and $w_i(t)$ the proportion of total wealth invested in the ith asset at time t, $i = 1,...,m$. Note that

$$\sum_{i=1}^{m} w_i(t) \underset{t}{\equiv} 1$$

The budget equation can be written as

$$W(t) = \left[\sum_{i=1}^{m} w_i(t_0) \frac{X_i(t)}{X_i(t_0)} \right] \left[W(t_0) - C(t_0)h \right] \tag{4.1}$$

where $t \equiv t_0 + h$ and the time interval between periods is h. By subtracting $W(t_0)$ from both sides and using $\Sigma_{i=1}^{m} w_i(t_0) = 1$, we can rewrite (4.1) as

$$W(t) - W(t_0) = \left[\sum_{i=1}^{m} w_i(t_0) \frac{X_i(t) - X_i(t_0)}{X_i(t_0)} \right] \left[W(t_0) - C(t_0)h \right] - C(t_0)h$$

$$= \left[\sum_{i=1}^{m} w_i(t_0)\{\exp[g_i(t)h] - 1\} \right] \left[W(t_0) - C(t_0)h \right]$$

$$- C(t_0)h$$

$$\tag{4.2}$$

where $g_i(t)h \equiv \log[X_i(t)/X_i(t_0)]$, the logarithmic rate of return per unit time on the ith asset. The $\{g_i(t)\}$ are assumed to be generated by a stochastic process.

In discrete time, I make the further assumption that $g_i(t)$ is determined as follows:

$$g_i(t)h = (\alpha_i - \sigma_i^2/2)h + \Delta Y_i \tag{4.3}$$

where α_i, the "expected" rate of return, is constant, and $Y_i(t)$ is generated by a Gaussian random walk as expressed by the stochastic difference equation

$$Y_i(t) - Y_i(t_0) \equiv \Delta Y_i = \sigma_i Z_i(t) h^{1/2} \tag{4.4}$$

where each $Z_i(t)$ is a serially independent variate with a standard normal distribution for every t, σ_i^2 is the variance per unit time of the process Y_i, and the mean of the increment ΔY_i is zero.

Substituting for $g_i(t)$ from (4.3), we can rewrite (4.2) as

$$W(t) - W(t_0) = \sum_1^m w_i(t_0)\left\{\exp\left[\left(\alpha_i - \frac{\sigma_i^2}{2}\right)h + \Delta Y_i\right] - 1\right\}[W(t_0) - C(t_0)h]$$
$$- C(t_0)h \tag{4.5}$$

Before passing in the limit to continuous time, there are two implications of (4.5) which will be useful later in this chapter.

$$E(t_0)\{W(t) - W(t_0)\} = \left[\sum_1^m w_i(t_0)\alpha_i W(t_0) - C(t_0)\right]h + o(h) \tag{4.6}$$

and

$$E(t_0)\{[W(t) - W(t_0)]^2\} = \sum_{i=1}^m \sum_{j=1}^m w_i(t_0)w_j(t_0)E(t_0)\{\Delta Y_i \Delta Y_j\}W^2(t_0)$$
$$+ o(h) \tag{4.7}$$

where $E(t_0)$ is the conditional expectation operator (conditional on the knowledge of $W(t_0)$), and $o(\cdot)$ is the usual asymptotic order symbol meaning "smaller order than."

The limit of the process described in (4.4) as $h \to 0$ (continuous time) can be expressed by the formalism of the stochastic differential equation[1]

$$dY_i = \sigma_i Z_i(t)(dt)^{1/2} \tag{4.4a}$$

and $Y_i(t)$ is said to be generated by a Wiener process.

1 See Itô (1951) for a rigorous discussion of stochastic differential equations.

By applying the same limit process to the discrete-time budget-equation dynamics, we write (4.5) as

$$dW = \left[\sum_{1}^{m} w_i(t)\alpha_i W(t) - C(t) \right] dt$$

$$+ \sum_{1}^{m} w_i(t)\sigma_i Z_i(t) W(t)(dt)^{1/2} \qquad (4.5a)$$

The stochastic differential equation (4.5a) is the generalization of the continuous-time budget-equation dynamics under uncertainty.

A more familiar dynamical equation would be the *averaged* budget equation derived as follows: from (4.5), we have

$$E(t_0) \left\{ \frac{W(t) - W(t_0)}{h} \right\} = \sum_{1}^{m} w_i(t_0)\alpha_i[W(t_0) - C(t_0)h] - C(t_0) + o(1)$$
$$(4.8)$$

Now, take the limit as $h \to 0$, so that (4.8) becomes the following expression for the defined "mean rate of change of wealth":

$$\overset{\circ}{W}(t_0) \underset{\text{def.}}{\equiv} \lim_{h \to 0} E(t_0) \left\{ \frac{W(t) - W(t_0)}{h} \right\} = \sum_{1}^{m} w_i(t_0)\alpha_i W(t_0) - C(t_0) \qquad (4.8a)$$

4.3   THE TWO-ASSET MODEL

For simplicity, I first derive the optimal equations and properties for the two-asset model and then, in Section 4.8, display the general equations and results for the m-asset case.

Define $w_1(t) \equiv w(t)$ to be the proportion invested in the risky asset, $w_2(t) = 1 - w(t)$ to be the proportion invested in the sure asset, $g_1(t) = g(t)$ to be the return on the risky asset (var $g_1 > 0$), and $g_2(t) = r$ to be the return on the sure asset (var $g_2 = 0$). Then, for

$$g(t)h = (\alpha - \sigma^2/2)h + \Delta Y$$

equations (4.5), (4.5a), (4.6), (4.7), and (4.8a) can be written as

$$W(t) - W(t_0) = (w(t_0) \{\exp[(\alpha - \sigma^2/2)h + \Delta Y] - 1\} + [1 - w(t_0)]$$
$$\times [\exp(rh) - 1])(W(t_0) - C(t_0)h) - C(t_0)h \qquad (4.9)$$

$$E(t_0)\{W(t) - W(t_0)\} = \{[w(t_0)(\alpha - r) + r]W(t_0) - C(t_0)\}h + o(h)$$
$$(4.10)$$

$$E(t_0)\{[W(t) - W(t_0)]^2\} = w^2(t_0)W^2(t_0)E(t_0)\{(\Delta Y)^2\} + \mathrm{o}(h)$$
$$= w^2(t_0)W^2(t_0)\sigma^2 h + \mathrm{o}(h) \qquad (4.11)$$

$$\mathrm{d}W = \{[w(t)(\alpha - r) + r]W(t) - C(t)\}\mathrm{d}t + w(t)\sigma Z(t)W(t)(\mathrm{d}t)^{1/2} \qquad (4.12)$$

$$\mathring{W}(t) = [w(t)(\alpha - r) + r]W(t) - C(t) \qquad (4.13)$$

The problem of choosing optimal portfolio selection and consumption rules is formulated as follows:

$$\max E\left\{ \int_0^T \exp(-\rho t)U[C(t)]\,\mathrm{d}t + B[W(T),T] \right\} \qquad (4.14)$$

subject to the budget constraint (4.12),

$$C(t) \geq 0; \; W(t) > 0; \; W(0) = W_0 > 0$$

and where $U(C)$ is assumed to be a strictly concave utility function (i.e. $U'(C) > 0$; $U''(C) < 0$), where $g(t)$ is a random variable generated by the previously described Wiener process. T is the date of death and $B[W(T), T]$ is a specified "bequest valuation function" (also referred to in production growth models as the "scrap function," and usually assumed to be concave in $W(T)$). E in (4.14) is short for $E(0)$, the conditional expectation operator, given $W(0) = W_0$ as known.

To derive the optimality equations, I restate (4.14) in a dynamic programming form so that the Bellman principle of optimality[2] can be applied. To do this, define

$$I[W(t),t] \equiv \max_{\{C(s),w(s)\}} E(t)\left\{ \int_t^T \exp(-\rho s)U[C(s)]\,\mathrm{d}s + B[W(T),T] \right\} \qquad (4.15)$$

where (4.15) is subject to the same constraints as (4.14). Therefore,

$$I[W(T),T] = B[W(T),T] \qquad (4.15a)$$

In general, from definition (4.15),

$$I[W(t_0),t_0] = \max_{\{C(s),w(s)\}} E(t_0)\left\{ \int_{t_0}^t \exp(-\rho s)U[C(s)]\,\mathrm{d}s + I[W(t),t] \right\} \qquad (4.16)$$

2   The basic derivation of the optimality equations in this section follows that of Dreyfus (1965, Ch. 7).

and, in particular, (4.14) can be rewritten as

$$I(W_0,0) = \max_{\{C(s),w(s)\}} E\left\{ \int_0^t \exp(-\rho s)U[C(s)] \, ds + I[W(t), t]\right\} \quad (4.14a)$$

If $t \equiv t_0 + h$ and the third partial derivatives of $I[W(t_0), t_0]$ are bounded, then by Taylor's theorem and the Mean Value Theorem for integrals, (4.16) can be rewritten as

$$I[W(t_0), t_0] = \max_{\{C,w\}} E(t_0)\left\{ \exp(-\rho\bar{t})U[C(\bar{t})]h + I[W(t_0),t_0] + \frac{\partial I[W(t_0),t_0]}{\partial t}h \right.$$

$$+ \frac{\partial I[W(t_0),t_0]}{\partial W}[W(t) - W(t_0)]$$

$$\left. + \frac{1}{2}\frac{\partial^2 I[W(t_0),t_0]}{\partial W^2}[W(t) - W(t_0)]^2 + o(h)\right\} \quad (4.17)$$

where $\bar{t} \in [t_0, t]$.

In (4.17), take the $E(t_0)$ operator onto each term and, noting that $I[W(t_0),t_0] = E(t_0)\{I[W(t_0),t_0]\}$, subtract $I[W(t_0),t_0]$ from both sides. Substitute from equations (4.10) and (4.11) for $E(t_0)\{W(t) - W(t_0)\}$ and $E(t_0)\{[W(t) - W(t_0)]^2\}$, and then divide the equation by h. Take the limit of the resultant equation as $h \to 0$ and (4.17) becomes a continuous-time version of the Bellman–Dreyfus fundamental equation of optimality:

$$0 = \max_{\{C(t),w(t)\}} \left(\exp(-\rho t)U[C(t)] + \frac{\partial I_t}{\partial t} + \frac{\partial I_t}{\partial W}\{[w(t)(\alpha - r) + r]W(t) - C(t)\} \right.$$

$$\left. + \frac{1}{2}\frac{\partial^2 I_t}{\partial W^2}\sigma^2 w^2(t)W^2(t) \right) \quad (4.17a)$$

where I_t is short for $I[W(t),t]$ and the subscript on t_0 has been dropped to reflect that (4.17a) holds for any $t \in [0,T]$.

If we define[3]

$$\phi(w, C; W; t) \equiv \exp(-\rho t)U(C) + \frac{\partial I_t}{\partial t} + \frac{\partial I_t}{\partial W}\{[w(t)(\alpha - r) + r]W(t)$$

$$- C(t)\} + \frac{1}{2}\frac{\partial^2 I_t}{\partial W^2}\sigma^2 w^2(t)W^2(t)$$

---

3 $\phi(w, C; W; t)$ is short for the rigorous $\phi(w, C; \partial I_t/\partial t; \partial I_t/\partial W; \partial^2 I_t/\partial W^2; I_t; W; t)$.

then (4.17a) can be written in the more compact form

$$\max_{\{C,w\}} \phi(w,C;W;t) = 0 \qquad (4.17b)$$

The first-order conditions for a regular interior maximum to (4.17b) are

$$\phi_C(w^*,C^*;W;t) = 0 = \exp(-\rho t)\, U'(C^*) - \frac{\partial I_t}{\partial W} \qquad (4.18)$$

and

$$\phi_w(w^*,C^*;W;t) = 0 = (\alpha - r)\, W\, \frac{\partial I_t}{\partial W} + \frac{\partial^2 I_t}{\partial W^2}\, w^* W^2 \sigma^2 \qquad (4.19)$$

A set of sufficient conditions for a regular interior maximum is

$$\phi_{ww} < 0 \qquad \phi_{CC} < 0 \qquad \det\begin{bmatrix} \phi_{ww} & \phi_{wC} \\ \phi_{Cw} & \phi_{CC} \end{bmatrix} > 0$$

$\phi_{wC} = \phi_{Cw} = 0$, and if $I[W(t),t]$ were strictly concave in W, then

$$\phi_{CC} = \exp(-\rho t) U''(C) < 0 \qquad (4.20)$$

by the strict concavity of U and

$$\phi_{ww} = W^2(t)\sigma^2\, \frac{\partial^2 I_t}{\partial W^2} < 0 \qquad (4.21)$$

by the strict concavity of I_t,[4] and the sufficient conditions would be satisfied. Thus a candidate for an optimal solution which causes $I[W(t),t]$ to be strictly concave will be any solution of the conditions (4.17a)–(4.21).

The optimality conditions can be rewritten as a set of two algebraic equations and one partial differential equation to be solved for $w^*(t)$, $C^*(t)$, and $I[W(t),t]$:

---

4   By the substitution of the results of (4.18) into (4.19) at (C^*, w^*), we have the condition $w^*(t)(\alpha - r) > 0$ if and only if $\partial^2 I_t/\partial W^2 < 0$.

In this chapter, we consider only interior optimal solutions. The problem could have been formulated in the more general Kuhn–Tucker form in which case the equalities of (4.18) and (4.19) would be replaced with inequalities.

$$\begin{cases} \phi[w^*,C^*;W;t] = 0 & (4.17b) \\ \phi_C[w^*,C^*;W;t]= 0 & (4.18) \\ \phi_w[w^*,C^*;W;t]= 0 & (4.19) \\ \quad \text{subject to the boundary condition} \\ \quad I[W(T),T] = B[W(T),T] \text{ and the solution} \\ \quad \text{being a feasible solution to (4.14)} \end{cases}$$

(*)

4.4 CONSTANT RELATIVE RISK AVERSION

The system (*) of a nonlinear partial differential equation coupled with two algebraic equations is difficult to solve in general. However, if the utility function is assumed to be of the form yielding constant relative risk aversion (i.e. isoelastic marginal utility), then (*) can be solved explicitly. Therefore, let $U(C) = (C^\gamma-1)/\gamma$, $\gamma < 1$ and $\gamma \neq 0$, or $U(C) = \log C$ (the limiting form for $\gamma = 0$) where $-U''(C)C/U'(C) = 1 - \gamma \equiv \delta$ is Pratt's (1964) measure of relative risk aversion. Then, system (*) can be written in this particular case as

$$\begin{cases} 0 = \dfrac{1 - \gamma}{\gamma}\left(\dfrac{\partial I_t}{\partial W}\right)^{\gamma/(\gamma-1)} \exp\left(\dfrac{-\rho t}{1 - \gamma}\right) + \dfrac{\partial I_t}{\partial t} \\ \\ \quad + \dfrac{\partial I_t}{\partial W}rW - \dfrac{(\alpha - r)^2}{2\sigma^2}\dfrac{(\partial I_t/\partial W)^2}{\partial^2 I_t/\partial W^2} \qquad (4.17b) \\ \\ C^*(t) = \left[\exp(\rho t)\dfrac{\partial I_t}{\partial W}\right]^{1/(\gamma-1)} \qquad\qquad\qquad (4.18) \\ \\ w^*(t) = \dfrac{-(\alpha - r)}{\sigma^2 W}\dfrac{\partial I_t/\partial W}{\partial^2 I_t/\partial W^2} \qquad\qquad\qquad (4.19) \\ \\ \text{subject to } I[W(T),T] = \epsilon^{1-\gamma}\exp(-\rho T)\,[W(T)]^\gamma/\gamma \ \ \text{for } 0 < \epsilon \ll 1 \end{cases}$$

(*')

where a strategically simplifying assumption has been made as to the particular form of the bequest valuation function $B[W(T), T]$.[5]

5 The form of the bequest valuation function (the boundary condition), as is usual for partial differential equations, can cause major changes in the solution to (*). The particular form of the function chosen in (*') is used as a proxy for the "no-bequest" condition ($\epsilon = 0$). A slightly more general form which can be used without altering the resulting solution substantively is $B[W(T), T] = G(T)[W(T)]^\gamma/\gamma$ for arbitrary positive $G(T)$. If B is not of the isoelastic family, systematic effects of age will appear in the optimal decision-making.

To solve (4.17b) of (*′), take as a trial solution

$$\bar{I}_t[W(t),t] = \frac{b(t)}{\gamma} \exp(-\rho t)\, [W(t)]^\gamma \tag{4.22}$$

By substitution of the trial solution into (4.17b), a necessary condition that $\bar{I}_t[W(t),t]$ be a solution to (4.17b) is found to be that $b(t)$ must satisfy the following ordinary differential equation:

$$\dot{b}(t) = \mu b(t) - (1 - \gamma)\, [b(t)]^{-\gamma/(1-\gamma)} \tag{4.23}$$

subject to $b(T) = \epsilon^{1-\gamma}$, and where $\mu \equiv \rho - \gamma[(\alpha - r)^2/2\sigma^2(1 - \gamma) + r]$. The resulting decision rules for consumption and portfolio selection, $C^*(t)$ and $w^*(t)$, are then from equations (4.18) and (4.19) of (*′)

$$C^*(t) = [b(t)]^{1/(\gamma-1)}W(t) \tag{4.24}$$

and

$$w^*(t) = \frac{\alpha - r}{\sigma^2(1 - \gamma)} \tag{4.25}$$

The solution to (4.23) is

$$b(t) = \left\{ \frac{1 + (\nu\epsilon - 1)\, \exp[\nu(t - T)]}{\nu} \right\}^{1-\gamma} \tag{4.26}$$

where $\nu \equiv \mu/(1 - \gamma)$.

A sufficient condition for $I[W(t),t]$ to be a solution to (*′) is that $I[W(t),t]$ satisfy

1 $\bar{I}_t[W(t),\, t]$ be real (feasibility)

2 $\dfrac{\partial^2 \bar{I}_t}{\partial W^2} < 0$ (concavity for a maximum)

3 $C^*(t) \geqslant 0$ (feasibility)

The condition that (1), (2), and (3) are satisfied in the isoelastic case is that

$$\frac{1 + (\nu\epsilon - 1)\, \exp[\nu(t - T)]}{\nu} > 0 \qquad 0 \leqslant t \leqslant T \tag{4.27}$$

which is satisfied for all values of ν when $T < \infty$.

Because (4.27) holds, the optimal consumption and portfolio selection rules are[6]

$$C^*(t) = \frac{\nu}{1 + (\nu\epsilon - 1) \exp[\nu(t - T)]} W(t) \quad \text{for } \nu \neq 0$$

$$= \frac{1}{T - t + \epsilon} W(t) \qquad\qquad \text{for } \nu = 0 \qquad (4.28)$$

and

$$w^*(t) = \frac{\alpha - r}{\sigma^2(1 - \gamma)} \equiv w^* \qquad\qquad (4.29)$$

a constant independent of W or t.

4.5   DYNAMIC BEHAVIOR AND THE BEQUEST VALUATION FUNCTION

The purpose behind the choice of the particular bequest valuation function in (*') was primarily mathematical. The economic motive is that the "true" function for no bequests is $B[W(T), T] = 0$ (i.e. $\epsilon = 0$). From (4.28), $C^*(t)$ will have a pole at $t = T$ when $\epsilon = 0$. So, to examine the dynamic behavior of $C^*(t)$ and to determine whether the pole is a mathematical "error" or an implicit part of the economic requirements of the problem, the parameter ϵ was introduced.

From Figure 4.1 $(C^*/W)_{t=T} \to \infty$ as $\epsilon \to 0$. However, one must not interpret this as an infinite rate of consumption. Because there is zero utility associated with positive wealth for $t > T$, the mathematics reflects this by requiring the optimal solution to drive $W(t) \to 0$ as $t \to T$. Because C^* is a flow and $W(t)$ is a stock and, from (4.28), C^* is proportional to $W(t)$, C^*/W must become larger and larger as $t \to T$ to make $W(T) = 0$.[7]

---

6   Although not derived explicitly here, the special case $(\gamma = 0)$ of Bernoulli logarithmic utility has (4.29) with $\gamma = 0$ as a solution, and the limiting form of (4.28), namely $C^*(t) = (\rho/\{1 + (\rho\epsilon - 1) \exp[\rho(t - T)]\})W(t)$.

7   The problem described is essentially one of exponential decay. If $W(t) = W_0 \exp[-f(t)]$, $f(t) > 0$, finite for all t, and $W_0 > 0$, then it will take an infinite length of time for $W(t) = 0$. However, if $f(t) \to \infty$ as $t \to T$, then $W(t) \to 0$ as $t \to T$.

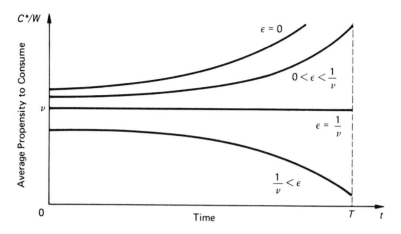

Figure 4.1 Effect of Bequest Motive on Average Propensity to Consume.

In fact, if $W(T-) > 0$, an "impulse" of consumption would be required to make $W(T) = 0$. Thus, equation (4.28) is valid for $\epsilon = 0$.

To examine some of the dynamic properties of $C^*(t)$, let $\epsilon = 0$ and define $V(t) \equiv C^*(t)/W(t)$, the instantaneous average (in this case also marginal) propensity to consume out of wealth. Then, from (4.28),

$$\dot{V}(t) = [V(t)]^2 \exp[\nu(t - T)] \qquad (4.30)$$

and, as observed in Figure 4.1 (for $\epsilon = 0$), $V(t)$ is an increasing function of time. In a generalization of the half-life calculation of radioactive decay, define τ as that $t \in [0, T]$ such that $V(\tau) = nV(0)$ (i.e. τ is the length of time required for $V(t)$ to grow to n times its initial size). Then, from (4.28),

$$\tau = \frac{\log[\exp(\nu T)(1 - 1/n) + 1/n]}{\nu} \qquad \text{for } \nu \neq 0$$

$$= \frac{n - 1}{n} T \qquad \qquad \text{for } \nu = 0 \qquad (4.31)$$

To examine the dynamic behavior of $W(t)$ under the optimal decision rules, it only makes sense to discuss the expected or "averaged" behavior because $W(t)$ is a function of a random variable. To do this, we consider equation (4.13), the averaged budget-equation dynamics, and evaluate it at the optimal (w^*, C^*) to form

$$\frac{\overset{\circ}{W}(t)}{W(t)} = \alpha_* - V(t) \qquad (4.13a)$$

where

$$\alpha* = \frac{(\alpha - r)^2}{\sigma^2(1 - \gamma)} + r$$

and, in Section 4.7, $\alpha*$ will be shown to be the expected return on the optimal portfolio.

By differentiating (4.13a) and using (4.30), we get

$$\frac{d}{dt}\left(\frac{\overset{\circ}{W}}{W}\right) = -\dot{V}(t) < 0 \qquad (4.32)$$

which implies that, for all finite-horizon optimal paths, the expected rate of growth of wealth is a diminishing function of time. Therefore, if $\alpha* < V(0)$, the individual will disinvest (i.e. he will *plan* to consume more than his expected income, $\alpha*W(t)$). If $\alpha* > V(0)$, he will plan to increase his wealth for $0 < t < \bar{t}$ and then disinvest for $\bar{t} < t < T$ where $\bar{t}$ is defined as the solution to

$$\bar{t} = T + \frac{1}{\nu}\log\left(\frac{\alpha* - \nu}{\alpha*}\right) \qquad (4.33)$$

Further, $\partial \bar{t}/\partial \alpha* > 0$ which implies that the length of time for which the individual is a net saver increases with increasing expected returns on the portfolio. Thus, in the case $\alpha* > V(0)$, we find the familiar result of "hump saving."[8]

4.6   INFINITE TIME HORIZON

Although the infinite-time-horizon case $(T = \infty)$ yields essentially the same substantive results as the finite-time-horizon case, it is worth examining separately because the optimality equations are easier to solve than for finite time. Therefore, for solving more complicated problems of this type, the infinite-time-horizon problem should be examined first.

---

8   "Hump saving" has been widely discussed in the literature. (See Graaff (1950) and the Life-Cycle Hypothesis of Modigliani and Brumberg (1954) for such a discussion.) Usually "hump saving" is discussed in the context of work and retirement periods. Clearly, such a phenomenon can occur without these assumptions as the example in this chapter shows.

The equation of optimality is, from Section 4.3,

$$0 = \max_{\{C, w\}} \left(\exp(-\rho t)U(C) + \frac{\partial I_t}{\partial t} \right.$$

$$+ \frac{\partial I_t}{\partial W} \{[w(t)\,(\alpha - r) + r]W(t) - C(t)\}$$

$$\left. + \frac{1}{2} \frac{\partial^2 I_t}{\partial W^2} \sigma^2 w^2(t)W^2(t) \right) \tag{4.17a}$$

However, (4.17a) can be greatly simplified by eliminating its explicit time dependence. Define

$$J[W(t),\, t] \equiv \exp(\rho t)\, I[W(t),\, t]$$

$$= \max_{\{C, w\}} E(t) \left\{ \int_t^\infty \exp[-\rho(s - t)]U(C)\, ds \right\}$$

$$= \max_{\{C, w\}} E \left\{ \int_0^\infty \exp(-\rho v)U(C)\, dv \right\} \tag{4.34}$$

independent of explicit time. Thus, write $J[W(t),t] = J(W)$ to reflect this independence. Substituting $J(W)$, dividing by $\exp(-\rho t)$, and dropping all t subscripts, we can rewrite (4.17a) as

$$0 = \max_{\{C,w\}} (U(C) - \rho J(W) + J'(W)\{[w(\alpha - r) + r]W - C\}$$

$$+ \tfrac{1}{2} J''(W)\sigma^2 w^2 W^2) \tag{4.35}$$

Note that, when (4.35) is evaluated at the optimum (C^*, w^*), it becomes an *ordinary* differential equation instead of the usual partial differential equation of (4.17a). For the isoelastic case, (4.35) can be written as

$$0 = \frac{1 - \gamma}{\gamma}[J'(W)]^{-\gamma/(1-\gamma)} - \rho J(W)$$

$$- \frac{(\alpha - r)^2}{2\sigma^2} \frac{[J'(W)]^2}{J''(W)} + rWJ'(W) \tag{4.36}$$

where the functional equations for C^* and w^* have been substituted in (4.36).

The first-order conditions corresponding to (4.18) and (4.19) are

$$0 = U'(C) - J'(W) \tag{4.37}$$

and

$$0 = (\alpha - r)WJ'(W) + J''(W)wW^2\sigma^2 \tag{4.38}$$

and assuming that $\lim_{T\to\infty} B[W(T),T] = 0$, the boundary condition becomes the transversality condition

$$\lim_{t\to\infty} E\{I[W(t),t]\} = 0 \tag{4.39}$$

or

$$\lim_{t\to\infty} E\{\exp(-\rho t)J[W(t)]\} = 0$$

which is a condition for convergence of the integral in (4.14). A solution to (4.14) must satisfy (4.39) plus conditions (1), (2), and (3) of Section 4.4. Conditions (1), (2), and (3) will be satisfied in the isoelastic case if

$$V^* \equiv \nu = \frac{\rho}{1-\gamma} - \gamma \left[\frac{(\alpha-r)^2}{2\sigma^2(1-\gamma)^2} + \frac{r}{1-\gamma} \right] > 0 \tag{4.40}$$

holds, where (4.40) is the limit of condition (4.27) in Section 4.4 as $T \to \infty$, and $V^* = C^*(t)/W(t)$ when $T = \infty$.

We now show that, if (4.40) obtains, then the transversality condition (4.39) is satisfied, and the limit of the finite-horizon optimal rules is the optimum for the infinite-horizon case. From (4.22) and (4.26), the limit as $T \to \infty$ of the finite horizon $I_t[W(t),t]$ is $\nu \exp(-\rho t) [W(t)]^\gamma/\gamma$. If the portfolio rule (4.25) and the consumption rule $C^*(t) = V^*W(t)$ are substituted into (4.12), then it can be shown that

$$E\left\{ \frac{\nu}{\gamma} \exp(-\rho t) [W(t)]^\gamma \right\} = \frac{\nu}{\gamma} [W(0)]^\gamma \exp(-\nu t) \tag{4.41}$$

If (4.40) obtains, then $V^* = \nu > 0$ and, from (4.41), the limit as $t \to \infty$ of $E\{I_t[W(t), t]\} = 0$.

Condition (4.40) is thus a generalization of the usual assumption required in deterministic optimal consumption growth models when the production function is linear: namely, that $\rho > \gamma\beta$ where β is the yield on capital.[9] If a "diminishing-returns" strictly concave "production" function for wealth were introduced, then a positive ρ would suffice.

If it is assumed that ρ satisfies (4.40), then the rest of the derivation is the same as for the finite-horizon case and the optimal decision rules are

$$C_\infty^*(t) = \left\{ \frac{\rho}{1-\gamma} - \gamma \left[\frac{(\alpha-r)^2}{2\sigma^2(1-\gamma)^2} + \frac{r}{1-\gamma} \right] \right\} W(t) \qquad (4.42)$$

and

$$w_\infty^*(t) = \frac{\alpha-r}{\sigma^2(1-\gamma)} \qquad (4.43)$$

The ordinary differential equation (4.35), $J'' = f(J,J')$, has "extraneous" solutions other than the one that generates (4.42) and (4.43). However, these solutions are ruled out by the transversality condition, (4.39) and conditions (1), (2), and (3) of Section 4.4. As was shown, $\lim_{T\to\infty} C^*(t) = C_\infty^*(t)$ and $\lim_{T\to\infty} w^*(t) = w_\infty^*(t)$.

The main purpose of this section was to show that the partial differential equation (4.17a) can be reduced in the case of infinite time horizon to an ordinary differential equation.

4.7 ECONOMIC INTERPRETATION OF THE OPTIMAL DECISION RULES FOR PORTFOLIO SELECTION AND CONSUMPTION

An important result is the confirmation of the theorem proved by Samuelson (1969) for the discrete-time case, stating that, for isoelastic marginal utility, the portfolio-selection decision is independent of the consumption decision. Further, for the special case of Bernoulli logarithmic utility ($\gamma = 0$), the separation goes both ways, i.e. the consumption decision is independent of the financial parameters and is only dependent upon the level of wealth. This is a result of two assumptions: (a) constant relative risk aversion (isoelastic marginal utility) which implies that one's attitude toward financial risk is independent of one's wealth level, and (b) the stochastic process which generates the price changes (i.e. α, r, and σ^2 are constants and the independent increments assumption of the Wiener

9   If one takes the limit as $\sigma_*^2 \to 0$ (where σ_*^2 is the variance of the composite portfolio) of condition (4.40), then (4.40) becomes the condition that $\rho > \gamma\alpha^*$ where α^* is the yield on the composite portfolio. Thus, the deterministic case is the limiting form of (4.40).

process). With these two assumptions, the only feedbacks of the system, the price change and the resulting level of wealth, have zero relevance for the portfolio decision, and hence it is constant.

The optimal proportion in the risky asset,[10] w^*, can be rewritten in terms of Pratt's relative risk aversion measure δ as

$$w^* = \frac{\alpha - r}{\sigma^2 \delta} \tag{4.29a}$$

The qualitative results that $\partial w^*/\partial \alpha > 0$, $\partial w^*/\partial r < 0$, $\partial w^*/\partial \sigma^2 < 0$, and $\partial w^*/\partial \delta < 0$ are intuitively clear and need no discussion. However, because the optimal portfolio-selection rule is constant, one can define the optimum composite portfolio and it will have a constant mean and variance, namely

$$\begin{aligned}
\alpha_* &= E\{w^*(\alpha + \Delta Y) + (1 - w^*)r\} \\
&= w^*\alpha + (1 - w^*)r \\
&= \frac{(\alpha - r)^2}{\sigma^2 \delta} + r
\end{aligned} \tag{4.44}$$

$$\begin{aligned}
\sigma_*^2 &= \mathrm{var}[w^*(\alpha + \Delta Y) + (1 - w^*)r] \\
&= w^{*2}\sigma^2 \\
&= \frac{(\alpha - r)^2}{\sigma^2 \delta^2}
\end{aligned} \tag{4.45}$$

After having determined the optimal w^*, one can now think of the original problem as having been reduced to a simple Phelps–Ramsey problem, in which we seek an optimal consumption rule given that income is generated by the uncertain yield of a (composite) asset.

Thus, the problem becomes a continuous-time analog of the one examined by Phelps (1962) in discrete time. Therefore, for consistency, $C_\infty^*(t)$ should be expressible in terms of α_*, σ_*^2, δ, ρ, and $W(t)$ only. To show that this is in fact the result, (4.42) can be rewritten as[11]

---

10 Note that no restriction on borrowing or going short was imposed on the problem, and therefore w^* can be greater than one or less than zero. Thus, if $\alpha < r$, the risk averter will short some of the risky asset, and if $\alpha > r + \sigma^2\delta$, he will borrow funds to invest in the risky asset. If one wished to restrict $w^* \in [0, 1]$, then such a constraint could be introduced and handled by the usual Kuhn–Tucker methods with resulting inequalities.

11 Because this section is concerned with the qualitative changes in the solution with respect to shifts in the parameters, the simpler form of the infinite-time-horizon case is examined. The essential difference between $C_\infty^*(t)$ and $C^*(t)$ is the

$$C^*(t) = \left[\frac{\rho}{\delta} + (\delta - 1) \left(\frac{\alpha*}{\delta} - \frac{\sigma*^2}{2} \right) \right] W(t) = VW(t) \qquad (4.46)$$

where V is the marginal propensity to consume out of wealth.

The tools of comparative statics are used to examine the effect of shifts in the mean and variance on consumption behavior in this model. The comparison is between two economies with different investment opportunities, but with the individuals in both economies having the same utility function.

If θ is a financial parameter, then define $(\partial C^*/\partial \theta)_{\bar{I}_0}$, the partial derivative of consumption with respect to θ, $I_0(W_0)$ being held fixed, as the intertemporal generalization of the Hicks–Slutsky "substitution" effect, $(\partial C^*/\partial \theta)_{\bar{U}}$ for static models. $\partial C^*/\partial \theta - (\partial C^*/\partial \theta)_{\bar{I}_0}$ will be defined as the intertemporal "income" or "wealth" effect. Then, from (4.22) with I_0 held fixed, one derives by total differentiation

$$0 = - \frac{1}{\delta - 1} \frac{\partial b(0)}{\partial \theta} W_0 + b(0) \left(\frac{\partial W_0}{\partial \theta} \right)_{\bar{I}_0} \qquad (4.47)$$

From (4.24) and (4.46), $b(0) = V^{-\delta}$, and so solving for $(\partial W_0/\partial \theta)_{\bar{I}_0}$ in (4.47) we can write it as

$$\left(\frac{\partial W_0}{\partial \theta} \right)_{\bar{I}_0} = \frac{-\delta W_0}{(\delta - 1)V} \frac{\partial V}{\partial \theta} \qquad (4.48)$$

Consider the case where $\theta = \alpha*$; then from (4.46)

$$\frac{\partial V}{\partial \alpha*} = \frac{\delta - 1}{\delta} \qquad (4.49)$$

and from (4.48)

$$\left(\frac{\partial W_0}{\partial \alpha*} \right)_{\bar{I}_0} = - \frac{W_0}{V} \qquad (4.50)$$

Thus, we can derive the substitution effect of an increase in the mean of the composite portfolio as follows:

$$\left(\frac{\partial C^*}{\partial \alpha*} \right)_{\bar{I}_0} = \left(\frac{\partial V}{\partial \alpha*} W_0 + V \frac{\partial W_0}{\partial \alpha*} \right)_{\bar{I}_0} = - \frac{W_0}{\delta} < 0 \qquad (4.51)$$

explicit time dependence of $C^*(t)$ which was discussed in Section 4.5. For simplicity, the subscript ∞ in $C_\infty^*(t)$ will be dropped for the rest of this section.

Because $\partial C^*/\partial \alpha_* = (\partial V/\partial \alpha_*)W_0 = [(\delta - 1)/\delta]W_0$, the income or wealth effect is

$$\frac{\partial C^*}{\partial \alpha_*} - \left(\frac{\partial C^*}{\partial \alpha_*}\right)_{\bar{I}_0} = W_0 > 0 \qquad (4.52)$$

Therefore, by combining the effects of (4.51) and (4.52), one can see that individuals with low relative risk aversion $(0 < \delta < 1)$ will choose to consume less now and save more to take advantage of the higher yield available (i.e. the substitution effect dominates the income effect). For high risk averters $(\delta > 1)$, the reverse is true and the income effect dominates the substitution effect. In the borderline case of Bernoulli logarithmic utility $(\delta = 1)$, the income and substitution effects just offset one another.[12]

In a similar fashion, consider the case of $\theta = -\sigma_*^2$,[13] then from (4.46) and (4.48) we derive

$$\left(\frac{\partial W_0}{\partial(-\sigma_*^2)}\right)_{\bar{I}_0} = \frac{-\delta W_0}{2V} \qquad (4.53)$$

and

$$\left(\frac{\partial C^*}{\partial(-\sigma_*^2)}\right)_{\bar{I}_0} = \frac{-W_0}{2} < 0 \qquad (4.54)$$

which is the substitution effect. Further, $\partial C^*/\partial(-\sigma_*^2) = (\delta - 1)W_0/2$, and so

$$\frac{\partial C^*}{\partial(-\sigma_*^2)} - \left(\frac{\partial C^*}{\partial(-\sigma_*^2)}\right)_{\bar{I}_0} = \frac{\delta}{2}W_0 > 0 \qquad (4.55)$$

which is the income effect.

To compare the relative effect on consumption behavior of an upward shift in the mean versus a downward shift in variance, we examine the elasticities. Define the elasticity of consumption with respect to the mean as

12   Many writers have independently discovered that Bernoulli utility is a borderline case in various comparative statics situations. See, for example, Phelps (1962) and Arrow (1965).
13   Because increased variance for a fixed mean usually (always for normal variates) decreases the desirability of investment for the risk averter, it provides a more symmetric discussion to consider the effect of a decrease in variance.

$$E_1 \equiv \alpha_* \frac{\partial C^*/\partial \alpha_*}{C^*} = \alpha_* \frac{\delta - 1}{\delta V} \qquad (4.56)$$

and similarly the elasticity of consumption with respect to the variance as

$$E_2 \equiv \sigma_*^2 \frac{\partial C^*/\partial \sigma_*^2}{C^*} = -\sigma_*^2 \frac{\delta - 1}{2V} \qquad (4.57)$$

For graphical simplicity, in Figure 4.2 we plot $e_1 \equiv VE_1/\alpha_*$ and $e_2 \equiv -VE_2/\alpha_*$ and define $k \equiv \sigma_*^2/2\alpha_*$. e_1 and e_2 are equal at $\delta = 1$, $1/k$. The particular case drawn is for $k < 1$.

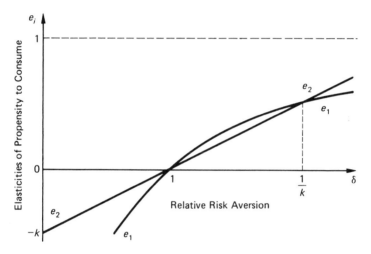

Figure 4.2 Effect on Consumption of Shifts in Expected Return and Risk.

For relatively high variance ($k > 1$), the high risk averter ($\delta > 1$) will always increase present consumption more with a decrease in variance than for the same percentage increase in mean. Because a high risk averter prefers a steadier flow of consumption at a lower expected level than a more erratic flow at a higher expected level, it makes sense that a decrease in variance would have a greater effect than an increase in mean. On the other hand, for relatively low variance ($k < 1$), a low risk averter ($0 < \delta < 1$) will always decrease his present consumption more with an increase in the mean than for the same percentage decrease in variance because such an individual (although a risk averter) will prefer to accept a more erratic flow of consumption in return for a higher expected level of consumption. Of course, these qualitative results will vary depending upon the size of k. If the riskiness of the returns is very small (i.e. $k \ll 1$), the high risk averter will increase his present consumption more with an upward shift in mean. Similarly, if the risk level is very high (i.e. $k \gg 1$), the low risk averter will change his consumption more with decreases in variance.

The results of this analysis can be summed up as follows. Because all individuals in this model are risk averters, when risk is a dominant factor (i.e. $k \gg 1$), a decrease in risk will have the larger effect on their consumption decisions. When risk is unimportant (i.e. $k \ll 1$) they all react more strongly to an increase in the mean yield. For all degrees of relative riskiness, the low risk averter will give up some present consumption to attain a higher expected future consumption while the high risk averter will always choose to increase the amount of present consumption.

4.8   EXTENSION TO MANY ASSETS

The model presented in Section 4.4 can be extended to the m-asset case with little difficulty. For simplicity, the solution is derived in the infinite-time-horizon case, but the result is similar for finite time. Assume the mth asset to be the only certain asset with an instantaneous rate of return $\alpha_m = r$.[14] Using the general equations derived in Section 4.2, and substituting for $w_m(t) = 1 - \Sigma_{i=1}^{n} w_i(t)$ where $n \equiv m - 1$, equations (4.6) and (4.7) can be written as

$$E(t_0)\{W(t) - W(t_0)\}$$
$$= [w'(t_0)\,(\alpha - \hat{r}) + r]\,W(t_0)h - C(t_0)h + \mathrm{o}(h) \qquad (4.6)$$

and

$$E(t_0)\{[W(t) - W(t_0)]^2\}$$
$$= w'(t_0)\Omega w(t_0)W^2(t_0)h + \mathrm{o}(h) \qquad (4.7)$$

where $w'(t_0) \equiv [w_1(t_0),\dots,w_n(t_0)]$, an n-vector; $\alpha' \equiv [\alpha_1,\dots,\alpha_n]$; $\hat{r}' \equiv [r,\dots,r]$, an n-vector; and $\Omega \equiv [\sigma_{ij}]$, the $n \times n$ variance–covariance matrix of the risky assets, which is symmetric and positive definite. Then, the general form of (4.35) for m assets is, in matrix notation,

$$0 = \max_{\{C,w\}}(U(C) - \rho J(W) + J'(W)\{[w'(\alpha - \hat{r}) + r]W - C\}$$

$$+ \tfrac{1}{2} J''(W)w'\Omega w W^2) \qquad (4.58)$$

14   Clearly, if there were more than one certain asset, the one with the highest rate of return would dominate the others.

and, instead of two, there will be m first-order conditions corresponding to a maximization of (4.35) with respect to $w_1,\ldots,w_n$ and C. The optimal decision rules corresponding to (4.42) and (4.43) in the two-asset case are

$$C_\infty^*(t) = \left\{\frac{\rho}{1-\gamma} - \gamma\left[\frac{(\alpha-\hat{r})'\Omega^{-1}(\alpha-\hat{r})}{2(1-\gamma)^2} + \frac{r}{1-\gamma}\right]\right\} W(t) \tag{4.59}$$

and

$$w_\infty^*(t) = \frac{1}{1-\gamma}\Omega^{-1}(\alpha-\hat{r}) \tag{4.60}$$

where $w_\infty^{*\prime}(t) = [w_1^*(t),\ldots,w_n^*(t)]$.

4.9 CONSTANT ABSOLUTE RISK AVERSION

System (*) of Section 4.3 can be solved explicitly for a second special class of utility functions of the form yielding constant absolute risk aversion. Let $U(C) = -\exp(-\eta C)/\eta$, $\eta > 0$, where $-U''(C)/U'(C) = \eta$ is Pratt's (1964) measure of absolute risk aversion. For convenience, I return to the two-asset case and infinite-time-horizon form of system (*) which can be written in this case as

$$(*'') \begin{cases} 0 = \dfrac{-J'(W)}{\eta} - \rho J(W) + J'(W)rW + \dfrac{J'(W)}{\eta}\log[J'(W)] \\[2mm] \qquad - \dfrac{(\alpha-r)^2}{2\sigma^2}\dfrac{[J'(W)]^2}{J''(W)} \hfill (4.17b) \\[4mm] C^*(t) = -\dfrac{1}{\eta}\log[J'(W)] \hfill (4.18) \\[4mm] w^*(t) = -J'(W)(\alpha-r)/\sigma^2 W J''(W) \hfill (4.19) \\[3mm] \text{subject to} \\[2mm] \lim_{t\to\infty} E\{\exp(-\rho t)J[W(t)]\} = 0 \end{cases}$$

where $J(W) \equiv \exp(\rho t)I[W(t),t]$ as defined in Section 4.6.

To solve (4.17b) of (*″), take as a trial solution

$$\bar{J}(W) = \frac{-P}{q} \exp(-qW) \qquad (4.61)$$

By substitution of the trial solution into (4.17b), a necessary condition that $\bar{J}(W)$ will be a solution to (4.17b) is found to be that p and q must satisfy the following two algebraic equations:

$$q = \eta^r \qquad (4.62)$$

and

$$p = \exp\left[\frac{r - \rho - (\alpha - r)^2/2\sigma^2}{r}\right] \qquad (4.63)$$

The resulting optimal decision rules for portfolio selection and consumption are

$$C^*(t) = rW(t) + \left[\frac{\rho - r + (\alpha - r)^2/2\sigma^2}{\eta r}\right] \qquad (4.64)$$

and

$$w^*(t) = \frac{\alpha - r}{\eta r \sigma^2 W(t)} \qquad (4.65)$$

Comparing equations (4.64) and (4.65) with their counterparts for the constant relative risk-aversion case, (4.42) and (4.43), one finds that consumption is no longer a constant proportion of wealth (i.e. marginal propensity to consume does not equal the average propensity) although it is still linear in wealth. Instead of the proportion of wealth invested in the risky asset being constant (i.e. $w^*(t)$ a constant), the total dollar value of wealth invested in the risky asset is kept constant (i.e. $w^*(t)W(t)$ a constant). As a person becomes wealthier, the proportion of his wealth invested in the risky asset falls and asymptotically, as $W \to \infty$, he invests virtually all his wealth in the certain asset and consumes all his (certain) income. Although one can do the same type of comparative statics for this utility function as was done in Section 4.7 for the case of constant relative risk aversion, it will not be done in this chapter for brevity and because I find this special form of the utility function behaviorally less plausible than constant relative risk aversion. It is interesting to note that the substitution effect in this case, $(\partial C/\partial \theta)_{\bar{I}_0}$, is zero except when $r = \theta$.

4.10 OTHER EXTENSIONS OF THE MODEL

The requirements for the general class of probability distributions which could be acceptable in this model are that

1 the stochastic process must be Markovian, and
2 the first two moments of the distribution must be proportional to Δt and the higher-order moments $o(\Delta t)$.

So, for example, the simple Wiener process postulated in this model could be generalized to include $\alpha_i = \alpha_i(X_1,\ldots, X_m, W, t)$ and $\sigma_i = \sigma_i(X_1,\ldots,X_m,W,t)$ where X_i is the price of the ith asset. In this case, there will be $m + 1$ state variables and (4.17a) will be generated from the general Taylor series expansion of $I(X_1,\ldots,X_m,W,t)$ for many variables. A particular example would be if the ith asset is a bond which fluctuates in price for $t < t_i$, but will be called at a fixed price at time $t = t_i$. Then $\alpha_i = \alpha_i(X_i,t)$ and $\sigma_i = \sigma_i(X_i,t) > 0$ when $t < t_i$ and $\sigma_i = 0$ for $t > t_i$.

A more general production function of a neoclassical type could be introduced to replace the simple linear one of this model. Mirrlees (1965) has examined this case in the context of a growth model with random Harrod-neutral technical progress. His equations (19) and (20) correspond to my equations (4.35) and (4.37) with the obvious proper substitutions for variables.

Thus, the technique employed for this model can be extended to a wide class of economic models.[15] However, because the optimality equations involve a partial differential equation, computational solution of even a slightly generalized model may be quite difficult.[16]

*15   In later work, Constantinides (1983) and Hamilton (1987) analyze the effects of taxation on saving and portfolio choice in the model. He and Pearson (1991) and He (1989, Ch. 1) derive the optimal portfolio strategies when there are constraints against short-sales. Heath and Jarrow (1987) study the effects of margin requirements on the feasible set of continuous-trading portfolio strategies. Svensson (1989) examines portfolio choice with a non-expected utility criterion.
*16   See Merton (1971; this volume, Ch. 5), Richard (1975), Aase (1984), Karatzas et al. (1986), and Cox and Huang (1989b) for examples of more general models with closed-form solutions.

Optimum Consumption and Portfolio Rules in a Continuous-Time Model

5.1 INTRODUCTION

A common hypothesis about the behavior of (limited-liability) asset prices in perfect markets is the random walk of returns or (in its continuous-time form) the "geometric Brownian motion" hypothesis which implies that asset prices are log-normally distributed with temporally constant parameters. A number of investigators of the behavior of stock and commodity prices have questioned the accuracy of the hypothesis.[1] In particular, Cootner (1964) and others have criticized the independent increments assumption and have examined the assumption of constant parameters. Mandelbrot (1963a, b) and Fama (1965b) argue that stock and commodity price changes follow a stable Paretian distribution with infinite second moments. The nonacademic literature on the stock market is also filled with theories of stock-price patterns and trading rules to "beat the market," rules often called "technical analysis" or "charting," and that presupposes a departure from random price changes.

In an earlier paper (Merton, 1969a; this volume, Ch. 4), I examined the continuous-time consumption-portfolio problem for an individual whose income is generated by capital gains on investments in assets with prices assumed to satisfy the "geometric Brownian motion" hypothesis; i.e. I studied max $E\{\int_0^T U(C,t)\, \mathrm{d}t\}$ where U is the instantaneous utility function,

Reproduced from *Journal of Economic Theory*, 3, December 1971, 373–413. Copyright © 1971 by Academic Press, Inc. I would like to thank P. A. Samuelson, R. M. Solow, P. A. Diamond, J. A. Mirrlees, J. S. Flemming, and D. T. Scheffman for their helpful discussions. Of course, all errors are mine. Aid from the National Science Foundation is gratefully acknowledged. An earlier version of the paper was presented at the Second World Congress of the Econometric Society, August 1970, Cambridge, England.

1   For a number of interesting papers on the subject, see Cootner (1964). Fama (1970a) provides an excellent survey article.

C is consumption, and E is the expectation operator. Under the additional assumption of a constant relative or constant absolute risk aversion utility function, explicit solutions for the optimal consumption and portfolio rules were derived. The changes in these optimal rules with respect to shifts in various parameters such as expected return, interest rates, and risk were examined by the technique of comparative statics.

This chapter extends these results for more general utility functions, price behavior assumptions, and for income generated also from non-capital gains sources. It is shown that if the "geometric Brownian motion" hypothesis is accepted, then a general "separation" or "mutual-fund" theorem can be proved such that, in this model, the classical Markowitz–Tobin mean–variance rules hold without the objectionable assumptions of quadratic utility or of normality of distributions for prices. Hence, when asset prices are generated by a geometric Brownian motion, one can work with the two-asset case without loss of generality. If the further assumption is made that the utility function of the individual is a member of the family of utility functions called the Hyperbolic Absolute Risk Aversion (HARA) family, explicit solutions for the optimal consumption and portfolio rules are derived and a number of theorems are proved. In the last parts of the chapter, the effects on the consumption and portfolio rules of alternative asset-price dynamics, in which changes are neither stationary nor independent, are examined along with the effects of introducing wage income, uncertainty of life expectancy, and the possibility of default on (formerly) "risk-free" assets.

5.2   A DIGRESSION ON ITÔ PROCESSES

To apply the dynamic programming technique in a continuous-time model, the state variable dynamics must be expressible as Markov stochastic processes defined over time intervals of length h, no matter how small h is. Such processes are referred to as infinitely divisible in time. The two processes of this type[2] are functions of Gauss–Wiener Brownian motions which are continuous in the "space" variables and functions of Poisson processes which are discrete in the space variables. Because neither of these processes is differentiable in the usual sense, a more general type of differential equation must be developed to express the dynamics of such processes. A particular class of continuous-time Markov processes of the

---

2   I ignore those infinitely divisible processes with infinite moments which include those members of the stable Paretian family other than the normal.

first type called Itô processes are defined as the solution to the stochastic differential equation[3]

$$dP = f(P,t) \, dt + g(P,t) \, dz \tag{5.1}$$

where P, f, and g are n-vectors and $z(t)$ is an n-vector of standard normal random variables. Then $dz(t)$ is called a multidimensional Wiener process (or Brownian motion).[4]

The fundamental tool for formal manipulation and solution of stochastic processes of the Itô type is Itô's lemma stated as follows.[5]

Lemma 5.1

Let $F(P_1,\ldots,P_n,t)$ be a C^2 function defined on $R^n \times [0, \infty)$ and take the stochastic integrals

$$P_i(t) = P_i(0) + \int_0^t f_i(P,s) \, ds + \int_0^t g_i(P,s) \, dz_i \qquad i = 1,\ldots,n$$

Then the time-dependent random variable $Y \equiv F$ is a stochastic integral and its stochastic differential is

$$dY = \sum_1^n \frac{\partial F}{\partial P_i} dP_i + \frac{\partial F}{\partial t} dt + \frac{1}{2} \sum_1^n \sum_1^n \frac{\partial^2 F}{\partial P_i \partial P_j} dP_i \, dP_j$$

3   Itô processes are a special case of a more general class of stochastic processes called strong diffusion processes (see Kushner, 1967, p. 22). Equation (5.1) is a short-hand expression for the stochastic integral $P(t) = P(0) + \int_0^t f(P, s) \, ds + \int_0^t g(P, s) \, dz$ where $P(t)$ is the solution to (5.1) with probability one.

A rigorous discussion of the meaning of a solution to equations like (5.1) is not presented here. Only those theorems needed for formal manipulation and solution of stochastic differential equations are in the text and these appear without proof. For a complete discussion of Itô processes, see the seminal paper of Itô (1951), Itô and McKean (1964), and McKean (1969). For a short description and some proofs, see Kushner (1967, pp. 12–18). For a heuristic discussion of continuous-time Markov processes in general, see Cox and Miller (1968, Ch. 5).

4   dz is often referred to in the literature as "Gaussian White Noise." There are some regularity conditions imposed on the functions f and g. It is assumed throughout the chapter that such conditions are satisfied. For the details, see Kushner (1967) or McKean (1969).

5   See McKean (1969, pp. 32–5, 44) for proofs of the lemma in 1 and n dimensions.

where the products of the differentials $dP_i\, dP_j$ are defined by the multiplication rule

$$dz_i\, dz_j = \rho_{ij}\, dt \qquad i, j = 1,\ldots,n$$

$$dz_i\, dt = 0 \qquad i = 1,\ldots,n$$

where ρ_{ij} is the instantaneous correlation coefficient between the Wiener processes dz_i and dz_j.[6]

Armed with Itô's lemma, we are now able to formally differentiate most smooth functions of Brownian motions (and hence integrate stochastic differential equations of the Itô type).[7]

Before proceeding to the discussion of the asset-price behavior, another concept useful for working with Itô processes is the differential generator (or weak infinitesimal operator) of the stochastic process $P(t)$. Define the function $\overset{\circ}{G}(P,t)$ by

$$\overset{\circ}{G}(P,t) \equiv \lim_{h \to 0} E_t \left\{ \frac{G[P(t + h), t + h] - G[P(t), t]}{h} \right\} \tag{5.2}$$

when the limit exists and where E_t is the conditional expectation operator, conditional on knowing $P(t)$. If the $P_i(t)$ are generated by Itô processes, then the differential generator of P, $\mathscr{L}_P$, is defined by

$$\mathscr{L}_p \equiv \sum_1^n f_i \frac{\partial}{\partial P_i} + \frac{\partial}{\partial t} + \frac{1}{2} \sum_1^n \sum_1^n a_{ij} \frac{\partial^2}{\partial P_i\, \partial P_j} \tag{5.3}$$

where $f = (f_1,\ldots,f_n)$, $g = (g_1,\ldots,g_n)$, and $a_{ij} \equiv g_i g_j \rho_{ij}$. Further, it can be shown that

$$\overset{\circ}{G}(P,t) = \mathscr{L}_P[G(P,t)] \tag{5.4}$$

6 This multiplication rule has given rise to the formalism of writing the Wiener process differentials as $dz_i = \mathscr{S}_i(dt)^{1/2}$ where the $\mathscr{S}_i$ are standard normal variates (cf. Cox and Miller, 1968).

7 Warning: derivatives (and integrals) of functions of Brownian motions are similar to, but different from, the rules for deterministic differentials and integrals. For example, if $P(t) = P(0)\exp(\int_0^t dz - \frac{1}{2}t) = P(0)\exp[z(t) - z(0) - \frac{1}{2}t]$, then $dP = P\, dz$. Hence $\int_0^t dP/P = \int_0^t dz \neq \log[P(t)/P(0)]$. Stratonovich (1968) has developed a symmetric definition of stochastic differential equations which formally follows the ordinary rules of differentiation and integration. However, this alternative to the Itô formalism will not be discussed here. 1992 note: see Itô (1974) and Sethi and Lehoczky (1981).

$\overset{\circ}{G}$ can be interpreted as the "average" or expected time rate of change of the function $G(P,t)$ and as such is the natural generalization of the ordinary time derivative for deterministic functions.[8]

5.3 ASSET-PRICE DYNAMICS AND THE BUDGET EQUATION

Throughout the chapter, it is assumed that all assets are of the limited-liability type, that there exist continuously trading perfect markets with no transactions costs for all assets, and that the prices per share, $\{P_i(t)\}$, are generated by Itô processes, i.e.

$$\frac{\mathrm{d}P_i}{P_i} = \alpha_i(P, t) \, \mathrm{d}t + \sigma_i(P, t) \, \mathrm{d}z_i \tag{5.5}$$

where α_i is the instantaneous conditional expected percentage change in price per unit time and σ_i^2 is the instantaneous conditional variance per unit time. In the particular case where the "geometric Brownian motion" hypothesis is assumed to hold for asset prices, α_i and σ_i will be constants. For this case, prices will be log-normally distributed and it will be shown that this assumption about asset prices simplifies the continuous-time model in the same way that the assumption of normality of prices simplifies the static one-period portfolio model.

To derive the correct budget equation, it is necessary to examine the discrete-time formulation of the model and then to take limits carefully to obtain the continuous-time form. Consider a period model with periods of length h, where all income is generated by capital gains, and wealth $W(t)$ and $P_i(t)$ are known at the *beginning* of period t. Let the decision variables be indexed such that the indices coincide with the period in which the decisions are implemented. Namely, let

$N_i(t) \equiv$ number of shares of asset i purchased and held during
period t, i.e. between t and $t + h$

and $\tag{5.6}$

$C(t) \equiv$ amount of consumption per unit time during period t

---

8 A heuristic method for finding the differential generator is to take the conditional expectation of $\mathrm{d}G$ (found by Itô's lemma) and "divide" by $\mathrm{d}t$. The result of this operation will be $\mathscr{L}_P(G)$, i.e. formally, $E_t(\mathrm{d}G)/\mathrm{d}t = \overset{\circ}{G} = \mathscr{L}_P(G)$. The $\mathscr{L}_P$ operator is often called a Dynkin operator and written as D_P.

The model assumes that the individual "comes into" period t with wealth invested in assets so that

$$W(t) = \sum_1^n N_i(t - h)P_i(t) \tag{5.7}$$

Notice that it is $N_i(t - h)$ because $N_i(t - h)$ is the number of shares purchased for the portfolio in period $t - h$ and it is $P_i(t)$ because $P_i(t)$ is the *current* value of a share of the ith asset. The amount of consumption for the period, $C(t)h$, and the new portfolio, $N_i(t)$, are simultaneously chosen, and if it is assumed that all trades are made at (known) current prices, then we have that

$$-C(t)\, h = \sum_1^n [N_i(t) - N_i(t - h)]P_i(t) \tag{5.8}$$

The "dice" are rolled and a new set of prices is determined, $P_i(t + h)$, and the value of the portfolio is now $\sum_1^n N_i(t)P_i(t + h)$. So the individual "comes into" period $t + h$ with wealth $W(t + h) = \sum_1^n N_i(t)P_i(t + h)$ and the process continues.

Incrementing (5.7) and (5.8) by h to eliminate backward differences, we have that

$$
\begin{aligned}
-C(t + h)\, h &= \sum_1^n [N_i(t + h) - N_i(t)]P_i(t + h) \\
&= \sum_1^n [N_i(t + h) - N_i(t)][P_i(t + h) - P_i(t)] \\
&\quad + \sum_1^n [N_i(t + h) - N_i(t)]P_i(t)
\end{aligned}
\tag{5.9}
$$

and

$$W(t + h) = \sum_1^n N_i(t)P_i(t + h) \tag{5.10}$$

Taking the limits as $h \to 0$,[9] we arrive at the continuous versions of (5.9)

---

9 We use here the result that Itô processes are right-continuous (Kushner, 1967, p. 15) and hence $P_i(t)$ and $W(t)$ are right-continuous. It is assumed that $C(t)$ is a right-continuous function, and, throughout the chapter, the choice of $C(t)$ is restricted to this class of functions.

and (5.10):

$$-C(t)\,dt = \sum_1^n dN_i(t)\,dP_i(t) + \sum_1^n dN_i(t)\,P_i(t) \qquad (5.9a)$$

and

$$W(t) = \sum_1^n N_i(t)P_i(t) \qquad (5.10a)$$

Using Itô's lemma, we differentiate (5.10a) to get

$$dW = \sum_1^n N_i\,dP_i + \sum_1^n dN_i\,P_i + \sum_1^n dN_i\,dP_i \qquad (5.11)$$

The last two terms, $\sum_1^n dN_i\,P_i + \sum_1^n dN_i\,dP_i$, are the net value of additions to wealth from sources other than capital gains.[10] Hence, if $dy(t) = $ (possibly stochastic) instantaneous flow of noncapital gains (wage) income, then we have that

$$dy - C(t)\,dt = \sum_1^n dN_i\,P_i + \sum_1^n dN_i\,dP_i \qquad (5.12)$$

From (5.11) and (5.12), the budget or accumulation equation is written as

$$dW = \sum_1^n N_i(t)\,dP_i + dy - C(t)\,dt \qquad (5.13)$$

It is advantageous to eliminate $N_i(t)$ from (5.13) by defining a new variable, $w_i(t) \equiv N_i(t)P_i(t)/W(t)$, the fraction of wealth invested in the ith asset at time t. Substituting for dP_i/P_i from (5.5), we can write (5.13) as

$$dW = \sum_1^n w_iW\alpha_i\,dt - C\,dt + dy + \sum_1^n w_iW\sigma_i\,dz_i \qquad (5.14)$$

where, by definition, $\sum_1^n w_i \underset{t}{\equiv} 1$.[11]

10 This result follows directly from the discrete-time argument used to derive (5.9a) where $-C(t)\,dt$ is replaced by a general $dv(t)$ where $dv(t)$ is the instantaneous flow of funds from all noncapital gains sources.

It was necessary to derive (5.12) by starting with the discrete-time formulation because it is not obvious from the continuous version directly whether $dy - C(t)\,dt$ equals $\sum_1^n dN_i\,P_i + \sum_1^n dN_i\,dP_i$ or just $\sum_1^n dN_i\,P_i$.

11 There are no other restrictions on the individual w_i because borrowing and short-selling are allowed.

Until Section 5.7, it will be assumed that $dy \equiv 0$, i.e. all income is derived from capital gains on assets. If one of the n assets is "risk-free" (by convention, the nth asset), then $\sigma_n = 0$, the instantaneous rate of return α_n will be called r, and (5.14) is rewritten as

$$dW = \sum_1^m w_i(\alpha_i - r)W \, dt + (rW - C) \, dt + dy + \sum_1^m w_i W \sigma_i \, dz_i$$

(5.14a)

where $m \equiv n - 1$ and the $w_1,\dots,w_m$ are unconstrained by virtue of the fact that the relation $w_n = 1 - \Sigma_1^m w_i$ will ensure that the identity constraint in (5.14) is satisfied.

5.4   OPTIMAL PORTFOLIO AND CONSUMPTION RULES: THE EQUATIONS OF OPTIMALITY

The problem of choosing optimal portfolio and consumption rules for an individual who lives T years is formulated as follows:

$$\max E_0 \left\{ \int_0^T U[C(t),t] \, dt + B[W(T),T] \right\}$$

(5.15)

subject to $W(0) = W_0$ and the budget-constraint dynamics, (5.14), which in the case of a "risk-free" asset becomes (5.14a), and where the utility function U (during life) is assumed to be strictly concave in C and the "bequest" function B is assumed also to be concave in W.[12]

To derive the optimal rules, the technique of stochastic dynamic programming is used. Define

$$J(W,P,t) \equiv \max_{\{C,w\}} E_t \left\{ \int_t^T U(C,s) \, ds + B[W(T),T] \right\}$$

(5.16)

where, as before, E_t is the conditional expectation operator, conditional on $W(t) = W$ and $P_i(t) = P_i$. Define

$$\phi(C, w; W, P, t) \equiv U(C, t) + \mathcal{L}(J)$$

(5.17)

---

12   When there is no "risk-free" asset, it is assumed that no asset can be expressed as a linear combination of the other assets, implying that the $n \times n$ variance–covariance matrix of returns $\Omega = [\sigma_{ij}]$, where $\sigma_{ij} \equiv \rho_{ij} \sigma_i \sigma_j$, is non-singular. In the case when there is a "risk-free" asset, the same assumption is made about the "reduced" $m \times m$ variance–covariance matrix.

given $w_i(t) = w_i$, $C(t) = C$, $W(t) = W$, and $P_i(t) = P_i$. $\mathscr{L}$ is short for the rigorous $\mathscr{L}_{P,W}^{w,C}$, the Dynkin operator over the variables P and W for a given set of controls w and C:

$$
\mathscr{L} \equiv \frac{\partial}{\partial t} + \left(\sum_1^n w_i \alpha_i W - C \right) \frac{\partial}{\partial W} + \sum_1^n \alpha_i P_i \frac{\partial}{\partial P_i}
$$

$$
+ \frac{1}{2} \sum_1^n \sum_1^n \sigma_{ij} w_i w_j W^2 \frac{\partial^2}{\partial W^2} + \frac{1}{2} \sum_1^n \sum_1^n P_i P_j \sigma_{ij} \frac{\partial^2}{\partial P_i \, \partial P_j}
$$

$$
+ \sum_1^n \sum_1^n P_i W w_j \sigma_{ij} \frac{\partial^2}{\partial P_i \, \partial W}
$$

From the theory of stochastic dynamic programming, the following theorem provides the method for deriving the optimal rules C^* and w^*.

Theorem 5.1

If the $P_i(t)$ are generated by a strong diffusion process, U is strictly concave in C, and B is concave in W, then there exists a set of optimal rules (controls), w^* and C^*, satisfying $\Sigma_1^n w_i^* = 1$ and $J(W, P, T) = B(W, T)$ and these controls satisfy

$$
0 = \phi(C^*, w^*; W, P, t) \geq \phi(C, w; W, P, t)
$$

for $t \in [0, T]$.[13]

From Theorem 5.1, we have that

$$
0 = \max_{\{C, w\}} \ \phi(C, w; W, P, t) \tag{5.18}
$$

In the usual fashion of maximization under constraint, we define the Lagrangian $L \equiv \phi + \lambda(1 - \Sigma_1^n w_i)$ where λ is the multiplier and find the extreme points from the first-order conditions

$$
0 = L_C(C^*, w^*) = U_C(C^*, t) - J_W \tag{5.19}
$$

$$
0 = L_{w_k}(C^*, w^*) = -\lambda + J_W \alpha_k W + J_{WW} \sum_1^n \sigma_{kj} w_j^* W^2
$$

13   For a heuristic proof of this theorem and the derivation of the stochastic Bellman equation, see Dreyfus (1965) and Merton (1969a; this volume, Ch. 4). For a rigorous proof and discussion of weaker conditions, see Kushner (1967, Ch. 4, especially Theorem 7).

$$+ \sum_{1}^{n} J_{jW} \sigma_{kj} P_j W \qquad\qquad k = 1,\ldots,n \qquad (5.20)$$

$$0 = L_\lambda(C^*, w^*) = 1 - \sum_{1}^{n} w_i^* \qquad\qquad (5.21)$$

where the notation for partial derivatives is $J_W \equiv \partial J/\partial W$, $J_t \equiv \partial J/\partial t$, $U_C \equiv \partial U/\partial C$, $J_i \equiv \partial J/\partial P_i$, $J_{ij} \equiv \partial^2 J/\partial P_i \partial P_j$, $J_{WW} \equiv \partial^2 J/\partial W^2$, and $J_{iW} \equiv \partial^2 J/\partial P_i \partial W$.

Because $L_{CC} = \phi_{CC} = U_{CC} < 0$, $L_{Cw_k} = \phi_{Cw_k} = 0$, $L_{w_k w_k} = \sigma_k^2 W^2 J_{WW}$, $L_{w_k w_j} = J_{WW} W^2 \sigma_{kj}$, $k \neq j$, and $[\sigma_{ij}]$ is a positive-definite matrix, a sufficient condition for a unique interior maximum is that $J_{WW} < 0$ (i.e. that J be strictly concave in W). Under that condition, as an immediate consequence of differentiating (5.19) totally with respect to W, we have

$$\frac{\partial C^*}{\partial W} > 0 \qquad\qquad (5.22)$$

To solve explicitly for C^* and w^*, we solve the $n + 2$ nondynamic implicit equations (5.19)–(5.21) for C^*, w^*, and λ as functions of J_W, J_{WW}, J_{iW}, W, P, and t. Then, C^* and w^* are substituted in (5.18) which now becomes a second-order partial differential equation for J, subject to the boundary condition $J(W, P, T) = B(W, T)$. Having (in principle at least) solved this equation for J, we then substitute back into (5.19)–(5.21) to derive the optimal rules as functions of W, P, and t. Define the inverse function $G \equiv [U_C]^{-1}$. Then, from (5.19),

$$C^* = G(J_W, t) \qquad\qquad (5.23)$$

To solve for the w_i^*, note that (5.20) is a linear system in w_i^* and hence it can be solved explicitly. Define

$$\Omega \equiv [\sigma_{ij}] \quad \text{the } n \times n \text{ variance–covariance matrix}$$

$$[\nu_{ij}] \equiv \Omega^{-1} {}^{14} \qquad\qquad (5.24)$$

$$\Gamma \equiv \sum_{1}^{n} \sum_{1}^{n} \nu_{ij}$$

Eliminating λ from (5.20), the solution for w_k^* can be written as

14 Ω^{-1} exists by the assumption on Ω in footnote 12.

$$w_k^* = h_k(P, t) + m(P, W, t)\, g_k(P, t) + f_k(P, W, t) \qquad k = 1,\dots, n \tag{5.25}$$

where $\Sigma_1^n h_k \equiv 1$, $\Sigma_1^n g_k \equiv 0$, and $\Sigma_1^n f_k \equiv 0$.

$$h_k(P, t) \equiv \sum_1^n \frac{\nu_{kj}}{\Gamma} \qquad m(P, W, t) \equiv \frac{-J_W}{W J_{WW}}$$

$$g_k(P, t) \equiv \frac{1}{\Gamma} \sum_1^n \nu_{kl}\left(\Gamma\alpha_l - \sum_1^n \sum_1^n \nu_{ij}\alpha_j\right)$$

$$f_k(P, W, t) \equiv - \left(\Gamma J_{kW}P_k - \sum_1^n J_{iW}P_i \sum_1^n \nu_{kj}\right)\bigg/ \Gamma W J_{WW}$$

Substituting for w^* and C^* in (5.18), we arrive at the fundamental partial differential equation for J as a function of W, P, and t:

$$0 = U(G, t) + J_t + J_W\left(\frac{\Sigma_1^n \Sigma_1^n \nu_{kj}\alpha_k W}{\Gamma} - G\right)$$

$$+ \sum_1^n J_i\alpha_i P_i + \frac{1}{2}\sum_1^n \sum_1^n J_{ij}\sigma_{ij}P_iP_j + \frac{W}{\Gamma}\sum_1^n J_{jW}P_j$$

$$- \frac{J_W}{\Gamma J_{WW}}\left(\sum_1^n \Gamma J_{kW}P_k\alpha_k - \sum_1^n J_{jW}P_j \sum_1^n \sum_1^n \nu_{kl}\alpha_l\right)$$

$$+ \frac{J_{WW}W^2}{2\Gamma} - \frac{1}{2\Gamma J_{WW}}\left[\sum_1^n \sum_1^n J_{jW}J_{kW}P_jP_k\sigma_{kj}\Gamma - \left(\sum_1^n J_{iW}P_i\right)^2\right]$$

$$- \frac{J_W^2}{2\Gamma J_{WW}}\left[\sum_1^n \sum_1^n \nu_{kl}\alpha_k\alpha_l\Gamma - \left(\sum_1^n \sum_1^n \nu_{kl}\alpha_k\right)^2\right] \tag{5.26}$$

subject to the boundary condition $J(W, P, T) = B(W, T)$. If (5.26) were solved, the solution J could be substituted into (5.23) and (5.25) to obtain C^* and w^* as functions of W, P, and t.

For the case where one of the assets is "risk-free," the equations are somewhat simplified because the problem can be solved directly as an unconstrained maximum by eliminating w_n as was done in (5.14a). In this case, the optimal proportions in the risky assets are

$$w_k^* = - \frac{J_W}{J_{WW}W} \sum_1^m \nu_{kj}(\alpha_j - r) - \frac{J_{kW}P_k}{J_{WW}W} \qquad k = 1,\dots, m \tag{5.27}$$

The partial differential equation for J corresponding to (5.26) becomes

$$0 = U(G, t) + J_t + J_W(rW - G) + \sum_1^m J_i\alpha_iP_i$$

$$+ \frac{1}{2}\sum_1^m\sum_1^m J_{ij}\sigma_{ij}P_iP_j - \frac{J_W}{J_{WW}}\sum_1^m J_{jW}P_j(\alpha_j - r)$$

$$- \frac{J_W^2}{2J_{WW}}\sum_1^m\sum_1^m \nu_{ij}(\alpha_i - r)(\alpha_j - r) - \frac{1}{2J_{WW}}\sum_1^m\sum_1^m J_{iW}J_{jW}\sigma_{ij}P_iP_j$$

$$(5.28)$$

subject to the boundary condition $J(W, P, T) = B(W, T)$.

Although (5.28) is a simplified version of (5.26), neither (5.26) nor (5.28) lend themselves to easy solution. The complexities of (5.26) and (5.28) are caused by the basic nonlinearity of the equations and the large number of state variables. Although there is little that can be done about the nonlinearities, in some cases it may be possible to reduce the number of state variables.

5.5 LOG-NORMALITY OF PRICES AND THE CONTINUOUS-TIME ANALOG TO TOBIN–MARKOWITZ MEAN–VARIANCE ANALYSIS

When, for $k = 1, ..., n$, α_k and σ_k are constants, the asset prices have log-normal distributions. In this case, J will be a function of W and t only and not P. Then (5.26) reduces to

$$0 = U(G, t) + J_t + J_W\left(\frac{\sum_1^n\sum_1^n\nu_{kj}\alpha_k}{\Gamma}W - G\right) + \frac{J_{WW}W^2}{2\Gamma}$$

$$- \frac{J_W^2}{2\Gamma J_{WW}}\left[\sum_1^n\sum_1^n \nu_{kl}\alpha_k\alpha_l\Gamma - \left(\sum_1^n\sum_1^n \nu_{kl}\alpha_k\right)^2\right] \quad (5.29)$$

From (5.25), the optimal portfolio rule becomes

$$w_k^* = h_k + m(W, t)g_k \quad (5.30)$$

where $\sum_1^n h_k \equiv 1$ and $\sum_1^n g_k \equiv 0$ and h_k and g_k are constants.

From (5.30), the following "separation" or "mutual-fund" theorem can be proved.[15]

Theorem 5.2

Given n assets with prices P_i that are log-normally distributed, then (a) there exists a unique (up to a nonsingular transformation) pair of "mutual funds" constructed from linear combinations of these assets such that, independent of preferences (i.e. the form of the utility function), wealth distribution, or time horizon, individuals will be indifferent between choosing from a linear combination of these two funds or a linear combination of the original n assets. (b) If P_f is the price per share of either fund, then P_f is log-normally distributed. Further, (c) if δ_k is the percentage of one mutual fund's value held in the kth asset and if λ_k is the percentage of the other mutual fund's value held in the kth asset, then one can find that

$$\delta_k = h_k + \frac{1 - \eta}{\nu} g_k \qquad k = 1,\dots,n$$

and

$$\lambda_k = h_k - \frac{\eta}{\nu} g_k \qquad k = 1,\dots,n$$

where ν and η are arbitrary constants $(\nu \neq 0)$.

PROOF

(a) Equation (5.30) is a parametric representation of a line in the hyperplane defined by $\Sigma_1^n w_k^* = 1$.[16] Hence, there exist two linearly independent vectors (namely, the vectors of asset proportions held by the two mutual funds) which form a basis for all optimal portfolios chosen by the individuals. Therefore, each individual would be indifferent between choosing a linear combination of the mutual-fund shares or a linear combination of the original n assets.

(b) Let $V \equiv N_f P_f$ be the total value of (either) fund where N_f is the number of shares of the fund outstanding. Let N_k be the number of shares

15   See Cass and Stiglitz (1970) for a general discussion of separation theorems. The only degenerate case is when all the assets are identically distributed (i.e. symmetry), in which case only one mutual fund is needed.
16   See Cass and Stiglitz (1970, p. 15).

of asset k held by the fund and $\mu_k \equiv N_k P_k / V$ be the fraction of total value invested in the kth asset. Then $V = \Sigma_1^n N_k P_k$ and

$$dV = \sum_1^n N_k \, dP_k + \sum_1^n P_k \, dN_k + \sum_1^n dP_k \, dN_k$$

$$= N_f \, dP_f + P_f \, dN_f + dP_f \, dN_f \tag{5.31}$$

But

$$\sum_1^n P_k \, dN_k + \sum_1^n dP_k \, dN_k = \text{net inflow of funds from noncapital gains}$$
$$\text{sources}$$
$$= \text{net value of new shares issued}$$
$$= P_f \, dN_f + dN_f \, dP_f \tag{5.32}$$

From (5.31) and (5.32), we have that

$$N_f \, dP_f = \sum_1^n N_k \, dP_k \tag{5.33}$$

By the definition of V and μ_k, (5.33) can be rewritten as

$$\frac{dP_f}{P_f} = \sum_1^n \mu_k \frac{dP_k}{P_k}$$

$$= \sum_1^n \mu_k \alpha_k \, dt + \sum_1^n \mu_k \sigma_k \, dz_k \tag{5.34}$$

By Itô's lemma and (5.34), we have that

$$P_f(t) = P_f(0) \exp\left[\left(\sum_1^n \mu_k \alpha_k - \frac{1}{2} \sum_1^n \sum_1^n \mu_k \mu_j \sigma_{kj} \right) t + \sum_1^n \mu_k \sigma_k \int_0^t dz_k \right] \tag{5.35}$$

So, $P_f(t)$ is log-normally distributed.

(c) Let $a(W, t; U)$ be the fraction of wealth invested in the first mutual fund by an individual with utility function U and wealth W at time t. Then, $1 - a$ must equal the fraction of wealth invested in the second mutual fund. Because the individual is indifferent between these asset holdings or an optimal portfolio chosen from the original n assets, it must be that

$$w_k^* = h_k + m(W, t)g_k = a\delta_k + (1 - a)\lambda_k \qquad k = 1,\dots,n \tag{5.36}$$

All the solutions to the linear system (5.36) for all W, t, and U are of the form

$$\delta_k = h_k + \frac{1 - \eta}{\nu} g_k \qquad k = 1,\ldots,n$$

$$\lambda_k = h_k - \frac{\eta}{\nu} g_k \qquad k = 1,\ldots,n \qquad (5.37)$$

$$a = \nu m(W, t) + \eta \qquad \nu \neq 0$$

Note that

$$\sum_1^n \delta_k = \sum_1^n \left(h_k + \frac{1 - \eta}{\nu} g_k \right) \equiv 1$$

and

$$\sum_1^n \lambda_k = \sum_1^n \left(h_k - \frac{\eta}{\nu} g_k \right) \equiv 1 \qquad \text{QED}$$

For the case when one of the assets is "risk-free," there is a corollary to Theorem 5.2.

Corollary 5.2

If one of the assets is "risk-free," then the proportions of each asset held by the mutual funds are

$$\delta_k = \frac{1 - \eta}{\nu} \sum_1^m v_{kj}(\alpha_j - r) \ \lambda_k = -\frac{\eta}{\nu} \sum_1^m v_{kj}(\alpha_j - r) \quad \text{for } k = 1,\ldots, m$$

$$\delta_n = 1 - \sum_1^m \delta_k \qquad \lambda_n = 1 - \sum_1^m \lambda_k$$

PROOF

By the assumption of log-normal prices, (5.27) reduces to

$$w_k^* = m(W, t) \sum_1^m v_{kj}(\alpha_j - r) \qquad k = 1,\ldots, m \qquad (5.38)$$

and

$$w_n^* = 1 - \sum_1^m w_k^* = 1 - m(W, t) \sum_1^m \sum_1^m v_{kj}(\alpha_j - r) \quad (5.39)$$

By the argument used in the proof of Theorem 5.2, (5.38) and (5.39) define a line in the hyperplane defined by $\Sigma_1^n w_i^* = 1$, and by the same technique used in Theorem 5.2 we derive the fund proportions stated in the corollary with $a(W, t; U) = vm(W, t) + \eta$, where v and η are arbitrary constants $(v \neq 0)$.   QED

Thus, if we have an economy where all asset prices are log-normally distributed, the investment decision can be divided into two parts by the establishment of two financial intermediaries (mutual funds) to hold all individual securities and to issue shares of their own for purchase by individual investors. The separation is complete because the "instructions" given the fund managers, namely, to hold proportions δ_k and λ_k of the kth security, $k = 1,...,n$, depend only on the price distribution parameters and are independent of individual preferences, wealth distribution, or age distribution.

The similarity of this result to that of the classical Tobin–Markowitz analysis is clearest when we choose one of the funds to be the risk-free asset (i.e. $\eta = 0$) and the other fund to hold only risky assets (which is possible by setting $v = \Sigma_1^m \Sigma_1^m v_{ij}(\alpha_j - r)$, provided that the double sum is not zero). Consider the investment rule given to the "risky" fund's manager when there exists a "risk-free" asset. It is easy to show that the δ_k proportions prescribed in Corollary 5.2 are derived by finding the locus of points in the (instantaneous) mean–standard deviation space of composite returns which minimize variance for a given mean (i.e. the efficient risky-asset frontier), and then by finding the point where a line drawn from the point $(0, r)$ is tangent to the locus. This point determines the δ_k as illustrated in Figure 5.1.

Given the α^*, the δ_k are determined. So the log-normal assumption in the continuous-time model is sufficient to allow the same analysis as in the static mean–variance model but without the objectionable assumptions of quadratic utility or normality of the distribution of absolute price changes. (Log-normality of price changes is much less objectionable, since this does invoke "limited liability" and, by the Central Limit Theorem, is the only regular solution to any continuous-space infinitely divisible process in time.)

An immediate advantage for the present analysis is that whenever log-normality of prices is assumed, we can work, without loss of generality, with just two assets, one "risk-free" and the other risky with its price

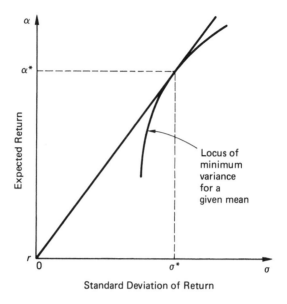

Figure 5.1 Determination of the Optimal Combination of Risky Assets.

log-normally distributed. The risky asset can always be thought of as a composite asset with price $P(t)$ defined by the process

$$\frac{\mathrm{d}P}{P} = \alpha \, \mathrm{d}t + \sigma \, \mathrm{d}z \tag{5.40}$$

where

$$\alpha \equiv \sum_{1}^{m} \delta_k \alpha_k$$

$$\sigma^2 \equiv \sum_{1}^{m} \sum_{1}^{m} \delta_k \delta_j \sigma_{kj}$$

$$\mathrm{d}z \equiv \sum_{1}^{m} \frac{\delta_k \sigma_k \, \mathrm{d}z_k}{\sigma}$$

$$\delta_k \equiv \sum_{1}^{m} v_{kj}(\alpha_j - r) \bigg/ \sum_{1}^{m} \sum_{1}^{m} v_{ij}(\alpha_j - r) \qquad k = 1,\dots,m \tag{5.41}$$

5.6   EXPLICIT SOLUTIONS FOR A PARTICULAR CLASS OF UTILITY FUNCTIONS

With the assumption of log-normality of prices, some characteristics of the asset demand functions were shown. If a further assumption about the preferences of the individual is made, then (5.28) can be solved in closed form and the optimal consumption and portfolio rules can be derived explicitly. Assume that the utility function for the individual, $U(C, t)$, can be written as $U(C, t) = \exp(-\rho t) V(C)$, where V is a member of the family of utility functions whose measure of absolute risk aversion is positive and hyperbolic in consumption, i.e.

$$A(C) \equiv -\frac{V''}{V'} = 1 \Big/ \left(\frac{C}{1 - \gamma} + \frac{\eta}{\beta} \right) > 0$$

subject to the restrictions

$$\gamma \neq 1, \quad \beta > 0, \quad \frac{\beta C}{1 - \gamma} + \eta > 0, \quad \eta = 1 \text{ if } \gamma = -\infty \qquad (5.42)$$

All members of the Hyperbolic Absolute Risk Aversion (HARA) family can be expressed as

$$V(C) = \frac{1 - \gamma}{\gamma} \left(\frac{\beta C}{1 - \gamma} + \eta \right)^{\gamma} \qquad (5.43)$$

This family is rich, in the sense that by suitable adjustment of the parameters one can have a utility function with absolute or relative risk aversion increasing, decreasing, or constant (Table 5.1).

Without loss of generality, assume that there are two assets, one "risk-free" asset with return r and the other a "risky" asset whose price is log-normally distributed satisfying (5.40). From (5.28), the optimality equation for J is

$$0 = \frac{(1 - \gamma)^2}{\gamma} \exp(-\rho t) \left(\frac{\exp(\rho t) J_W}{\beta} \right)^{\gamma/(\gamma-1)} + J_t + \left[\frac{(1 - \gamma)\eta}{\beta} + rW \right] J_W$$

$$- \frac{J_W^2}{J_{WW}} \frac{(\alpha - r)^2}{2\sigma^2} \qquad (5.44)$$

Table 5.1   Properties of Hyperbolic Absolute Risk Aversion Utility Functions

$$A(C) = \left(\frac{C}{1-\gamma} + \frac{\eta}{\beta}\right)^{-1} > 0 \qquad \text{(implies } \eta > 0 \text{ for } \gamma > 1\text{)}$$

$$A'(C) = -\left[(1-\gamma)\left(\frac{C}{1-\gamma} + \frac{\eta}{\beta}\right)^2\right]^{-1} \qquad \begin{array}{l} < 0 \text{ for } -\infty < \gamma < 1 \\ > 0 \text{ for } 1 < \gamma < \infty \\ = 0 \text{ for } \gamma = +\infty \end{array}$$

Relative risk aversion $R(C) \equiv -V''C/V' = A(C)C$

$$R'(C) = \frac{\eta}{\beta}\left[\left(\frac{C}{1-\gamma} + \frac{\eta}{\beta}\right)^2\right]^{-1} \qquad \begin{array}{l} > 0 \text{ for } \eta > 0 \ (-\infty \leqslant \gamma \leqslant \infty, \\ \hspace{5.5cm} \gamma \neq 1) \\ = 0 \text{ for } \eta = 0 \\ < 0 \text{ for } \eta < 0 \ (-\infty < \gamma < 1) \end{array}$$

Note that included as members of the HARA family are the widely used isoelastic (constant relative risk aversion), exponential (constant absolute risk aversion), and quadratic utility functions. As is well known for the quadratic case, the members of the HARA family with $\gamma > 1$ are only defined for a restricted range of consumption, namely $0 < C < (\gamma - 1)\eta/\beta$. Cass and Stiglitz (1970), Fischer (1969), Hakansson (1970), Leland (1968), Merton (1969a; this volume, Ch. 4), and Samuelson (1969) discuss the properties of various members of the HARA family in a portfolio context. Although this is not done here, the HARA definition can be generalized to include the cases when γ, β, and η are functions of time subject to the restrictions in (5.42).

subject to $J(W, T) = 0$.[17] The equations for the optimal consumption and portfolio rules are

$$C^*(t) = \frac{1-\gamma}{\beta}\left(\frac{\exp(\rho t)J_W}{\beta}\right)^{1/(\gamma-1)} - \frac{(1-\gamma)\eta}{\beta} \qquad (5.45)$$

and

$$w^*(t) = -\frac{J_W}{J_{WW}W}\frac{\alpha-r}{\sigma^2} \qquad (5.46)$$

17   It is assumed for simplicity that the individual has a zero bequest function, i.e. $B \equiv 0$. If $B(W, T) = H(T)(aW + b)^\gamma$, the basic functional form for J in (5.47) will be the same. Otherwise, systematic effects of age will be involved in the solution.

where $w^*(t)$ is the optimal proportion of wealth invested in the risky asset at time t. A solution[18] to (5.44) is

$$J(W, t) = \frac{\delta \beta^\gamma}{\gamma} \exp(-\rho t) \left(\frac{\delta\{1 - \exp[-(\rho - \gamma\nu)(T - t)/\delta]\}}{\rho - \gamma\nu} \right)^\delta$$

$$\times \left(\frac{W}{\delta} + \frac{\eta}{\beta r} \{1 - \exp[-r(T - t)]\} \right)^\gamma \tag{5.47}$$

where $\delta \equiv 1 - \gamma$ and $\nu \equiv r + (\alpha - r)^2/2\delta\sigma^2$.

From (5.45)–(5.47), the optimal consumption and portfolio rules can be written in explicit form as

$$C^*(t) = \frac{(\rho - \gamma\nu) \left(W(t) + \frac{\delta\eta}{\beta r} \{1 - \exp[r(t - T)]\} \right)}{\delta \left\{ 1 - \exp\left[\frac{(\rho - \gamma\nu)(t - T)}{\delta} \right] \right\}} - \frac{\delta\eta}{\beta} \tag{5.48}$$

and

$$w^*(t)\, W(t) = \frac{\alpha - r}{\delta\sigma^2} W(t) + \frac{\eta(\alpha - r)}{\beta r \sigma^2} \{1 - \exp[r(t - T)]\} \tag{5.49}$$

The manifest characteristic of (5.48) and (5.49) is that the demand functions are linear in wealth. It will be shown that the HARA family is the only class of concave utility functions which imply linear solutions. For notation purposes, define, $I(X,t) \subset \text{HARA}(X)$ if $-I_{XX}/I_X = 1/(\alpha X + \beta) > 0$, where α and β are, at most, functions of time and I is a strictly concave function of X.

Theorem 5.3

Given the model specified in this section, then $C^* = aW + b$ and $w^*W = gW + h$ where a, b, g, and h are, at most, functions of time if and only if $U(C, t) \subset \text{HARA}(C)$.

18 By Theorem 5.1, there is no need to be concerned with uniqueness although, in this case, the solution is unique. For $\gamma > 1$, (5.47) is valid only if $W(t) \leq (\gamma - 1)\eta\{1 - \exp[-r(T - t)]\}/\beta r$. Otherwise, the individual is satiated and the optimal rule is to hold all wealth in the riskless asset.

PROOF

The "if" part is proved directly by (5.48) and (5.49). For the "only if" part, suppose $w^*W = gW + h$ and $C^* = aW + b$. From (5.19), we have that $U_C(C^*, t) = J_W(W, t)$. Differentiating this expression totally with respect to W, we have that $U_{CC} \, dC^*/dW = J_{WW}$ or $aU_{CC} = J_{WW}$ and hence

$$- \frac{U_{CC}a}{U_C} = - \frac{J_{WW}}{J_W} \tag{5.50}$$

From (5.46), $w^*W = gW + h = -J_W(\alpha - r)/J_{WW}\sigma^2$ or

$$- \frac{J_{WW}}{J_W} = \left(\frac{\sigma^2 g}{\alpha - r} W + \frac{\sigma^2 h}{\alpha - r} \right)^{-1} \tag{5.51}$$

So, from (5.50) and (5.51), we have that U must satisfy

$$- \frac{U_{CC}}{U_C} = \frac{1}{a'C^* + b'} \tag{5.52}$$

where $a' \equiv \sigma^2 g/(\alpha - r)$ and $b' \equiv (a\sigma^2 h - b\sigma^2 g)/(\alpha - r)$. Hence $U \subset \text{HARA}(C)$.   QED

As an immediate result of Theorem 5.3, a second theorem can be proved.

Theorem 5.4

Given the model specified in this section, $J(W, t) \subset \text{HARA}(W)$ if and only if $U \subset \text{HARA}(C)$.

PROOF

The "if" part is proved directly by (5.47). For the "only if" part, suppose $J(W, t) \subset \text{HARA}(W)$. Then, from (5.46), $w^* W$ is a linear function of W. If (5.28) is differentiated totally with respect to wealth and given the specific price behavior assumptions of this section, we have that C^* must satisfy

$$C^* = rW + \frac{J_{tW}}{J_{WW}} + \frac{rJ_W}{J_{WW}} - \frac{J_W}{J_{WW}} \frac{(\alpha - r)^2}{\sigma^2} + \frac{J_{WWW}}{2J_{WW}} \left(\frac{J_W}{J_{WW}} \right)^2 \frac{(\alpha - r)^2}{\sigma^2} \tag{5.53}$$

But if $J \subset \text{HARA}(W)$, then (5.53) implies that C^* is linear in wealth. Hence, by Theorem 5.3, $U \subset \text{HARA}(C)$.   QED

Given (5.48) and (5.49), the stochastic process which generates wealth when the optimal rules are applied can be derived. From the budget-dynamics equation (5.14a), we have that

$$dW = \{[w^*(\alpha - r) + r]W - C^*\}\, dt + \sigma w^* W\, dz$$

$$= \left(\left\{\frac{(\alpha - r)^2}{\sigma^2 \delta} - \frac{\mu}{1 - \exp[\mu(t - T)]}\right\} dt + \frac{\alpha - r}{\sigma \delta} dz\right) X(t)$$

$$+ r\left(W + \frac{\delta \eta}{\beta r}\right) dt \tag{5.54}$$

where $X(t) \equiv W(t) + (\delta \eta / \beta r)\{1 - \exp[r(t - T)]\}$ for $0 \leqslant t \leqslant T$ and $\mu \equiv (\rho - \gamma \nu)/\delta$. By Itô's lemma, $X(t)$ is the solution to

$$\frac{dX}{X} = \left\{r + \frac{(\alpha - r)^2}{\sigma^2 \delta} - \frac{\mu}{1 - \exp[\mu(t - T)]}\right\} dt + \frac{\alpha - r}{\sigma \delta} dz \tag{5.55}$$

Again using Itô's lemma, integrating (5.55) we have that

$$X(t) = X(0) \exp\left\{\left[r - \mu + (1 - 2\gamma)\frac{(\alpha - r)^2}{2\sigma^2 \delta^2}\right] t + \frac{\alpha - r}{\sigma \delta} \int_0^t dz\right\}$$

$$\times \frac{1 - \exp[\mu(t - T)]}{1 - \exp(-\mu T)} \tag{5.56}$$

and hence $X(t)$ is log-normally distributed. Therefore,

$$W(t) = X(t) - \frac{\delta \eta}{\beta r}\{1 - \exp[r(t - T)]\}$$

is a "displaced" or "three-parameter" log-normally distributed random variable. By Itô's lemma, solution (5.56) to (5.55) holds with probability one and, because $W(t)$ is a continuous process, we have with probability one that

$$\lim_{t \to T} W(t) = 0 \tag{5.57}$$

From (5.48), with probability one,

$$\lim_{t \to T} C^*(t) = 0 \tag{5.58}$$

Further, from (5.48), $C^* + \delta\eta/\beta$ is proportional to $X(t)$ and, from the definition of $U(C^*,t)$, $U(C^*,t)$ is a log-normally distributed random variable.[19] The following theorem shows that this result holds only if $U(C, t) \subset \text{HARA}(C)$.

Theorem 5.5

Given the model specified in this section and the time-dependent random variable $Y(t) \equiv U(C^*, t)$, then Y is log-normally distributed if and only if $U(C, t) \subset \text{HARA}(C)$.

PROOF

For the "if" part, it was previously shown that, if $U \subset \text{HARA}(C)$, then Y is log-normally distributed. For the "only if" part, let $C^* \equiv g(W, t)$ and $w^*W \equiv f(W, t)$. By Itô's lemma

$$dY = U_C \, dC^* + U_t \, dt + \tfrac{1}{2}U_{CC}(dC^*)^2$$
$$dC^* = g_W \, dW + g_t \, dt + \tfrac{1}{2}g_{WW}(dW)^2 \qquad (5.59)$$
$$dW = [f(\alpha - r) + rW - g] \, dt + \sigma f \, dz$$

Because $(dW)^2 = \sigma^2 f^2 \, dt$, we have that

$$dC^* = [g_W f(\alpha - r) + g_W rW - gg_W + \tfrac{1}{2}g_{WW}\sigma^2 f^2 + g_t] \, dt + \sigma f g_W \, dz \qquad (5.60)$$

and

$$dY = \{U_C[g_W f(\alpha - r) + rg_W W - gg_W + \tfrac{1}{2}g_{WW}\sigma^2 f^2 + g_t] + U_t + \tfrac{1}{2}U_{CC}\sigma^2 f^2 g_W^2\} \, dt + \sigma f g_W U_C \, dz \qquad (5.61)$$

A necessary condition for Y to be log-normal is that Y satisfy

$$\frac{dY}{Y} = F(Y) \, dt + b \, dz \qquad (5.62)$$

where b is, at most, a function of time. If Y is log-normal, from (5.61) and (5.62), we have that

---

19   $U = [(1 - \gamma)/\gamma][\beta C/(1 - \gamma) + \eta]^\gamma \exp(-\rho t)$ and products and powers of log-normal variates are log-normal with one exception: the logarithmic utility function ($\gamma = 0$) is a singular case where $U(C^*, t) = \log C^*$ is normally distributed. Marginal utility, both U_C and J_W, will be log-normally distributed for all members of the family.

$$b(t) = \sigma f g_W U_C / U \tag{5.63}$$

From the first-order conditions, f and g must satisfy

$$U_{CC} g_W = J_{WW} \qquad f = -\frac{J_W(\alpha - r)}{\sigma^2 J_{WW}} \tag{5.64}$$

But (5.63) and (5.64) imply that

$$\frac{bU}{\sigma U_C} = f g_W = -(\alpha - r)\frac{U_C}{\sigma^2 U_{CC}} \tag{5.65}$$

or

$$-\frac{U_{CC}}{U_C} = \eta(t)\frac{U_C}{U} \tag{5.66}$$

where $\eta(t) \equiv (\alpha - r)/\sigma b(t)$. Integrating (5.66), we have that

$$U = [(\eta + 1)(C + \mu)\zeta(t)]^{1/(\eta+1)} \tag{5.67}$$

where $\zeta(t)$ and μ are, at most, functions of time, and hence $U \subset \text{HARA}(C)$. QED

For the case when asset prices satisfy the "geometric" Brownian motion hypothesis and the individual's utility function is a member of the HARA family, the consumption-portfolio problem is completely solved. From (5.48) and (5.49), one could examine the effects of shifts in various parameters on the consumption and portfolio rules by the methods of comparative statics as was done for the isoelastic case in Merton (1969a; this volume, Ch. 4).

5.7 NONCAPITAL GAINS INCOME: WAGES

In the previous sections, it was assumed that all income was generated by capital gains. If a (certain) wage income flow, $dy = Y(t) \, dt$, is introduced, the optimality equation (5.18) becomes

$$0 = \max_{\{C,w\}} [U(C, t) + \overline{\mathcal{L}}(J)] \tag{5.68}$$

where the operator $\overline{\mathcal{L}}$ is defined by $\overline{\mathcal{L}} \equiv \mathcal{L} + Y(t) \, \partial/\partial W$. This new complication causes no particular computational difficulties. If a new control variable $\tilde{C}(t)$ and new utility function $V(\tilde{C}, t)$ are defined by

$$\tilde{C}(t) \equiv C(t) - Y(t)$$

and

$$V(\tilde{C}, t) \equiv U[\tilde{C}(t) + Y(t), t]$$

then (5.68) can be rewritten as

$$0 = \max_{\{\tilde{C}, w\}} [V(\tilde{C}, t) + \mathcal{L}(J)] \tag{5.69}$$

which is the same equation as the optimality equation (5.18) when there is no wage income and where consumption has been redefined as consumption in excess of wage income.

In particular, if $Y(t) \equiv Y$, a constant, and $U \subset \text{HARA}(C)$, then the optimal consumption and portfolio rules corresponding to (5.48) and (5.49) are

$$C^*(t) = \frac{(\rho - \gamma\nu)\left(W + \dfrac{Y\{1 - \exp[r(t - T)]\}}{r} + \dfrac{\delta\eta}{\beta r}\{1 - \exp[r(t - T)]\}\right)}{\delta\left\{1 - \exp\left[\dfrac{(\rho - \gamma\nu)(t - T)}{\delta}\right]\right\}}$$

$$- \frac{\delta\eta}{\beta} \tag{5.70}$$

and

$$w^*W = \frac{\alpha - r}{\delta\sigma^2}\left(W + \frac{Y\{1 - \exp[r(t - T)]\}}{r}\right)$$

$$+ \frac{\eta(\alpha - r)}{\beta r\sigma^2}\{1 - \exp[r(t - T)]\} \tag{5.71}$$

Comparing (5.70) and (5.71) with (5.48) and (5.49), one finds that, in computing the optimal decision rules, the individual capitalizes the lifetime flow of wage income at the market (risk-free) rate of interest and then treats the capitalized value as an addition to the current stock of wealth.[20]

---

20 As Hakansson (1970) has pointed out, (5.70) and (5.71) are consistent with the Friedman Permanent-Income and the Modigliani Life-Cycle Hypotheses. However, in general this result will not hold if wage income is not tradeable.

The introduction of a stochastic wage income will cause increased computational difficulties although the basic analysis is the same as for the no-wage income case. For a solution to a particular example of a stochastic wage problem, see the second example in Section 5.8.

5.8 POISSON PROCESSES

The previous analyses always assumed that the underlying stochastic processes were smooth functions of Brownian motions and therefore continuous in both the time and state spaces. Although such processes are reasonable models for the price behavior of many types of liquid assets, they are rather poor models for the description of other types. The Poisson process is a continuous-time process which allows discrete (i.e. discontinuous) changes in the variables. The simplest independent Poisson process defines the probability of an event's occurring during a time interval of length h (where h is as small as you like) as follows:

prob{the event does not occur in the time interval $(t, t + h)$}

$$= 1 - \lambda h + \mathrm{o}(h)$$

prob{the event occurs once in the time interval $(t, t + h)$}   (5.72)

$$= \lambda h + \mathrm{o}(h)$$

prob{the event occurs more than once in the time interval

$$(t, t + h)\} = \mathrm{o}(h)$$

where $\mathrm{o}(h)$ is the asymptotic order symbol defined by

$$\psi(h) \text{ is } \mathrm{o}(h) \quad \text{if} \quad \lim_{h \to 0}[\psi(h)/h] = 0 \qquad (5.73)$$

and λ is the mean number of occurrences per unit time.

Given the Poisson process, the "event" can be defined in a number of interesting ways. To illustrate the degree of latitude, three examples of applications of Poisson processes in the consumption-portfolio choice problem are presented below. Before examining these examples, it is first necessary to develop some of the mathematical properties of Poisson processes. There is a theory of stochastic differential equations for Poisson processes similar to the one for Brownian motion discussed in Section 5.2. Let $q(t)$ be an independent Poisson process with probability structure as described in (5.72). Let the event be that a state variable $x(t)$ has a jump in amplitude of size $g(x, t)\mathscr{S}$ where $\mathscr{S}$ is a random variable whose probability measure has compact support. Then a Poisson differential equation for $x(t)$ can be written as

$$dx = f(x, t) \, dt + g(x, t) \, dq \qquad (5.74)$$

and the corresponding differential generator $\mathcal{L}_x$ is defined by

$$\mathcal{L}_x[h(x, t)] \equiv h_t + f(x, t)h_x + E_t\{\lambda[h(x + \mathcal{S}g, t) - h(x, t)]\} \quad (5.75)$$

where E_t is the conditional expectation over the random variable $\mathcal{S}$, conditional on knowing $x(t) = x$, and where $h(x, t)$ is a C^1 function of x and t.[21] Further, Theorem 5.1 holds for Poisson processes.[22]

Returning to the consumption-portfolio problem, consider first the two-asset case. Assume that one asset is a common stock whose price is log-normally distributed and that the other asset is a "risky" bond which pays an instantaneous rate of interest r when not in default but, in the event of default, has a price of zero.[23]

From (5.74), the process which generates the bond's price can be written as

$$dP = rP \, dt - P \, dq \qquad (5.76)$$

where dq is as previously defined, $g = -P$, and $\mathcal{S} \equiv 1$ with probability one. Substituting the explicit price dynamics into (5.14a), the budget equation becomes

$$dW = [wW(\alpha - r) + rW - C] \, dt + w\sigma W \, dz - (1 - w)W \, dq \qquad (5.77)$$

From (5.75), (5.77), and Theorem 5.1, we have that the optimality equation can be written as

$$0 = U(C^*, t) + J_t(W, t) + \lambda[J(w^*W, t) - J(W, t)]$$
$$+ J_W(W, t)\{[w^*(\alpha - r) + r]W - C^*\} + \tfrac{1}{2}J_{WW}(W, t)\sigma^2 w^{*2}W^2 \qquad (5.78)$$

where C^* and w^* are determined by the implicit equations

$$0 = U_C(C^*, t) - J_W(W, t) \qquad (5.79)$$

---

21   For a short discussion of Poisson differential equations and a proof of (5.75) as well as other references, see Kushner (1967, pp. 18–22).
22   See Dreyfus (1965, p. 225) and Kushner (1967, Ch. 4).
23   That the price of the bond is zero in the event of default is an extreme assumption made only to illustrate how a default can be treated in the analysis. One could make the more reasonable assumption that the price in the event of default is a random variable. The degree of computational difficulty caused by this more reasonable assumption will depend on the choice of distribution for the random variable as well as the utility function of the individual.

and

$$0 = \lambda J_W(w^*W, t) + J_W(W, t)(\alpha - r) + J_{WW}(W, t)\,\sigma^2 w^* W \quad (5.80)$$

To see the effect of default on the portfolio and consumption decisions, consider the particular case when $U(C, t) \equiv C^\gamma/\gamma$, for $\gamma < 1$. The solutions to (5.79) and (5.80) are[24]

$$C^*(t) = \frac{AW(t)}{(1 - \gamma)\{1 - \exp[A(t - T)/(1 - \gamma)]\}} \quad (5.79a)$$

where

$$A \equiv -\gamma \left[\frac{(\alpha - r)^2}{2\sigma^2(1 - \gamma)} + r \right] + \lambda \left[1 - \frac{2 - \gamma}{2} w^{*\gamma} - \frac{\gamma(\alpha - r)}{2\sigma^2(1 - \gamma)} w^{*\gamma-1} \right]$$

and

$$w^* = \frac{\alpha - r}{\sigma^2(1 - \gamma)} + \frac{\lambda}{\sigma^2(1 - \gamma)} (w^*)^{\gamma-1} \quad (5.80a)$$

As might be expected, the demand for the common stock is an increasing function of λ and, for $\lambda > 0$, $w^* > 0$ holds for all values of α, r, or σ^2.

For the second example, consider an individual who receives a wage $Y(t)$ which is incremented by a constant amount ϵ at random points in time. Suppose that the event of a wage increase is a Poisson process with parameter λ. Then the dynamics of the wage-rate state variable are described by

$$dY = \epsilon\,dq \quad \text{with } \mathcal{S} \equiv 1 \text{ with probability one} \quad (5.81)$$

Suppose further that the individual's utility function is of the form $U(C, t) \equiv \exp(-\rho t)V(C)$ and that his time horizon is infinite (i.e. $T = \infty$).

As shown in Section 4.6, if $U = \exp(-\rho t)V(C)$ and U is bounded or ρ is sufficiently large to ensure convergence of the integral and if the underlying stochastic processes are not explicitly time dependent, then the optimality equation (5.18) can be written, independent of explicit time, as

$$0 = \max_{\{C, w\}} [V(C) + \overline{\mathcal{L}}(I)] \quad (5.82)$$

---

24 Note that (5.79a) and (5.80a) with $\lambda = 0$ reduce to the solutions (5.48) and (5.49) when $\eta = \rho = 0$ and $\delta = 1 - \gamma$.

where $\overline{\mathscr{L}} \equiv \mathscr{L} - \rho - \dfrac{\partial}{\partial t}$ and $I(W, P) \equiv \exp(\rho t) J(W, P, t)$.

A solution to (5.82) is called the "stationary" solution to the consumption portfolio problem. Because the time state variable is eliminated, solutions to (5.82) are computationally easier to find than for the finite-horizon case. Thus, for the two-asset case of Section 5.6, the optimality equation can be written as

$$0 = V(C^*) - \rho I(W, Y) + \lambda[I(W, Y + \epsilon) - I(W, Y)]$$

$$+ I_W(W, Y)\{[w^*(\alpha - r) + r]W + Y - C^*\}$$

$$+ \tfrac{1}{2}I_{WW}(W, Y)\,\sigma^2 w^{*2} W^2 \qquad (5.83)$$

where $I(W, Y) \equiv \exp(\rho t) J(W, Y, t)$. If it is further assumed that $V(C) = -\exp(-\eta C)/\eta$, then the optimal consumption and portfolio rules, derived from (5.83), are

$$C^*(t) = r\left[W(t) + \frac{Y(t)}{r} + \frac{\lambda}{r^2}\frac{1 - \exp(-\eta\epsilon)}{\eta}\right] + \frac{1}{\eta r}\left[\rho - r + \frac{(\alpha - r)^2}{2\sigma^2}\right]$$

$$(5.84)$$

and

$$w^*(t)W(t) = \frac{\alpha - r}{\eta\sigma^2 r} \qquad (5.85)$$

In (5.84), $W(t) + Y(t)/r + \lambda[1 - \exp(-\eta\epsilon)]/\eta r^2$ is the general wealth term, equal to the sum of present wealth and capitalized future wage earnings. If $\lambda = 0$, then (5.84) reduces to (5.70) in Section 5.7, where the wage rate was fixed and known with certainty. When $\lambda > 0$,

$$\lambda[1 - \exp(-\eta\epsilon)]/\eta r^2$$

is the capitalized value of (expected) future increments to the wage rate, *capitalized at a somewhat higher rate than the risk-free market rate reflecting the risk aversion of the individual.*

(The usual expected present discounted value of the increments to the wage flow is

$$E_t\left\{\int_t^\infty \exp[-r(s - t)][Y(s) - Y(t)]\,ds\right\} = \int_t^\infty \lambda\epsilon \exp[-r(s - t)](s - t)\,ds$$

$$= \frac{\lambda\epsilon}{r^2}$$

which is greater than $\lambda[1 - \exp(-\eta\epsilon)]/\eta r^2$ for $\epsilon > 0$.) Let $X(t)$ be the "certainty-equivalent wage rate at time t" defined as the solution to

$$U[X(t)] = E_0\{U[Y(t)]\} \tag{5.86}$$

For this example, $X(t)$ is calculated as follows:

$$-\frac{\exp[-\eta X(t)]}{\eta} = -\frac{1}{\eta} E_0 \{\exp[-\eta Y(t)]\}$$

$$= -\frac{1}{\eta} \exp[-\eta Y(0)] \sum_{k=0}^{\infty} \frac{(\lambda t)^k}{k!} \exp(-\lambda t) \exp(-\eta k\epsilon)$$

$$= -\frac{1}{\eta} \exp[-\eta Y(0) - \lambda t + \lambda t \exp(-\eta\epsilon)] \tag{5.87}$$

Solving for $X(t)$ from (5.87), we have that

$$X(t) = Y(0) + \lambda t[1 - \exp(-\eta\epsilon)]/\eta \tag{5.88}$$

The capitalized value of the certainty-equivalent wage income flow is

$$\int_0^\infty \exp(-rs)X(s) \, ds = \int_0^\infty Y(0) \exp(-rs) \, ds + \int_0^\infty \frac{\lambda[1 - \exp(-\eta\epsilon)]}{\eta}$$

$$\times s \exp(-rs) \, ds$$

$$= \frac{Y(0)}{r} + \frac{\lambda[1 - \exp(-\eta\epsilon)]}{\eta r^2} \tag{5.89}$$

Thus, for this example,[25] the individual, in computing the present value of future earnings, determines the certainty-equivalent flow and then capitalizes this flow at the (certain) market rate of interest.

The third example of a Poisson process differs from the first two because the occurrence of the event does not involve an explicit change in a state variable. Consider an individual whose age of death is a random variable. Further assume that the event of death at each instant of time is an

---

25 The reader should not infer that this result holds in general. Although (5.86) is a common definition of certainty equivalent in one-period utility-of-wealth models, it is not satisfactory for dynamic consumption-portfolio models. The reason it works for this example is due to the particular relation between the J and U functions when U is exponential.

independent Poisson process with parameter λ. Then, the age of death, τ, is the first time that the event (of death) occurs and is an exponentially distributed random variable with parameter λ. The optimality criterion is to

$$\max E_0 \left\{ \int_0^\tau U(C, t) \, dt + B[W(\tau), \tau] \right\} \tag{5.90}$$

and the associated optimality equation is

$$0 = U(C^*, t) + \lambda[B(W, t) - J(W, t)] + \mathscr{L}(J) \tag{5.91}$$

To derive (5.91), an "artificial" state variable $x(t)$ is constructed with $x(t) = 0$ while the individual is alive and $x(t) = 1$ in the event of death. Therefore, the stochastic process which generates x is defined by

$$dx = dq \text{ and } \mathscr{S} \equiv 1 \text{ with probability one} \tag{5.92}$$

and τ is now defined by x as

$$\tau = \min[t \mid t > 0 \text{ and } x(t) = 1] \tag{5.93}$$

The derived utility function J can be considered a function of the state variables W, x, and t subject to the boundary condition

$$J(W, x, t) = B(W, t) \quad \text{when } x = 1 \tag{5.94}$$

In this form, the third example is shown to be of the same type as the first and second examples in that the occurrence of the Poisson event causes a state variable to be incremented, and (5.91) is of the same form as (5.78) and (5.83).

A comparison of (5.91) for the particular case when $B \equiv 0$ (no bequests) with (5.82) suggested the following theorem.[26]

Theorem 5.6

If τ is as defined in (5.93) and U is such that the integral $E_0\{\int_0^\tau U(C, t) \, dt\}$ is absolutely convergent, then the maximization of $E_0\{\int_0^\tau U(C, t) \, dt\}$ is equivalent to the maximization of $\mathscr{E}_0\{\int_0^\infty \exp(-\lambda t)U(C, t) \, dt\}$ where E_0 is the conditional expectation operator over all random variables including τ

---

26 I believe that a similar theorem has been proved by J. A. Mirrlees, but I have no reference. Cass and Yaari (1967, p. 262) also prove a similar theorem.

and $\mathscr{E}_0$ is the conditional expectation operator over all random variables excluding τ.

PROOF

τ is distributed exponentially and is independent of the other random variables in the problem. Hence, we have that

$$E_0 \left\{ \int_0^\tau U(C, t) \, dt \right\} = \int_0^\infty \lambda \exp(-\lambda\tau) \, d\tau \, \mathscr{E}_0 \left\{ \int_0^\tau U(C, t) \, dt \right\}$$

$$= \int_0^\infty \int_0^\tau \lambda g(t) \exp(-\lambda\tau) \, dt \, d\tau \tag{5.95}$$

where $g(t) \equiv \mathscr{E}_0\{U(C, t)\}$. Because the integral in (5.95) is absolutely convergent, the order of integration can be interchanged, i.e.

$$\mathscr{E}_0 \left\{ \int_0^\tau U(C, t) \, dt \right\} = \int_0^\tau \mathscr{E}_0 \left\{ U(C, t) \right\} \, dt$$

By integration by parts, (5.95) can be rewritten as

$$\int_0^\infty \int_0^\tau \lambda \exp(-\lambda\tau) g(t) \, dt \, d\tau = \int_0^\infty \exp(-\lambda s) g(s) \, ds$$

$$= \mathscr{E}_0 \left\{ \int_0^\infty \exp(-\lambda t) U(C, t) \, dt \right\}$$

(5.96)
QED

Thus, an individual who faces an exponentially distributed uncertain age of death acts as if he will live forever, but with a subjective rate of time preference equal to his "force of mortality," i.e. to the reciprocal of his life expectancy.

5.9 ALTERNATIVE PRICE EXPECTATIONS TO THE GEOMETRIC BROWNIAN MOTION

The assumption of the geometric Brownian motion hypothesis is a rich one because it is a reasonably good model of observed stock-price behavior and it allows the proof of a number of strong theorems about the optimal consumption and portfolio rules, as was illustrated in the previous sections. However, as mentioned in Section 5.1, there have been some disagreements with the underlying assumptions required to accept this hypothesis. The geometric Brownian motion hypothesis best describes a stationary equilibrium economy where expectations about future returns have settled down, and, as such, really describes a "long-run" equilibrium model for asset prices. Therefore, to explain "short-run" consumption and portfolio selection behavior one must introduce alternative models of price behavior which reflect the dynamic adjustment of expectations.

In this section, alternative price behavior mechanisms are postulated which attempt to capture in a simple fashion the effects of changing expectations, and then comparisons are made between the optimal decision rules derived under these mechanisms with those derived in the previous sections. The choices of mechanisms are not exhaustive nor are they necessarily representative of observed asset-price behavior. Rather they have been chosen as representative examples of price adjustment mechanisms commonly used in economic and financial models.

Little can be said in general about the form of a solution to (5.28) when α_k and σ_k depend in an arbitrary manner on the price levels. If it is specified that the utility function is a member of the HARA family, i.e.

$$U(C, t) = \frac{1 - \gamma}{\gamma} F(t) \left(\frac{\beta C}{1 - \gamma} + \eta \right)^{\gamma} \qquad (5.97)$$

subject to the restrictions in (5.42), then (5.28) can be simplified because $J(W, P, t)$ is separable into a product of functions, one depending on W and t and the other on P and t.[27] In particular, if we take $J(W, P, t)$ to be of the form

$$J(W, P, t) = \frac{1 - \gamma}{\gamma} H(P, t)F(t) \left(\frac{W}{1 - \gamma} + \frac{\eta}{\beta r} \left\{ 1 - \exp[r(t - T)] \right\} \right)^{\gamma} \qquad (5.98)$$

substitute for J in (5.28), and divide out the common factor

$$F(t) \left(\frac{W}{1 - \gamma} + \frac{\eta}{\beta r} \left\{ 1 - \exp[r(t - T)] \right\} \right)^{\gamma}$$

27 This separability property was noted in Cass and Stiglitz (1970), Fischer (1969), Hakansson (1970), Leland (1968), Merton (1969a; this volume, Ch. 4), and Samuelson (1969). It is assumed throughout this section that the bequest function satisfies the conditions of footnote 17.

then we derive a "reduced" equation for H,

$$
0 = \frac{(1 - \gamma)^2}{\gamma} \left(\frac{H}{\beta}\right)^{\gamma/(\gamma-1)} + \frac{1 - \gamma}{\gamma} \left(\frac{\dot{F}}{F} H + H_t\right) + (1 - \gamma)rH
$$

$$
+ \frac{1 - \gamma}{\gamma} \sum_1^m \alpha_i P_i H_i + \frac{1 - \gamma}{2\gamma} \sum_1^m \sum_1^m \sigma_{ij} P_i P_j H_{ij}
$$

$$
+ \sum_1^m (\alpha_i - r)P_i H_i + \frac{H}{2} \sum_1^m \sum_1^m v_{ij}(\alpha_i - r)(\alpha_j - r)
$$

$$
+ \frac{1}{2H} \sum_1^m \sum_1^m \sigma_{ij} P_i P_j H_i H_j \tag{5.99}
$$

and the associated optimal consumption and portfolio rules are

$$
C^*(t) = \frac{1 - \gamma}{\beta} \left[\left(\frac{H}{\beta}\right)^{1/(\gamma-1)} \left(\frac{W}{1 - \gamma} + \frac{\eta}{\beta r} \left\{1 - \exp[r(t - T)]\right\}\right) - \eta \right] \tag{5.100}
$$

and

$$
w_k^*(t)W = \left[\sum_1^m v_{kj}(\alpha_j - r) + \frac{H_k P_k}{H} \right] \left(\frac{W}{1 - \gamma} + \frac{\eta}{\beta r} \left\{1 - \exp[r(t - T)]\right\}\right)
$$

$$
k = 1,\ldots,m \tag{5.101}
$$

Although (5.99) is still a formidable equation from a computational point of view, it is less complex than the general equation (5.28), and it is possible to obtain an explicit solution for particular assumptions about the dependence of α_k and σ_k on the prices. Notice that both consumption and the asset demands are linear functions of wealth.

For a particular member of the HARA family, namely the Bernoulli logarithmic utility ($\gamma = 0 = \eta$ and $\beta = 1 - \gamma = 1$) function, (5.28) can be solved in general. In this case, J will be of the form

$$
J(W, P, t) = a(t) \log W + H(P, t) \tag{5.102}
$$

with $H(P, T) = a(T) = 0$ and with $a(t)$ independent of the α_k and σ_k (and hence the P_k). For the case when $F(t) \equiv 1$, we find $a(t) = T - t$ and the optimal rules become

$$C^* = \frac{W}{T - t} \tag{5.103}$$

and

$$w_k^* = \sum_1^m v_{kj}(\alpha_j - r) \qquad k = 1,\ldots,m \tag{5.104}$$

Thus, for the log case, the optimal rules are identical with those derived when α_k and σ_k were constants, with the understanding that the α_k and σ_k are evaluated at current prices. Hence, although we can solve this case for general price mechanisms, it is not an interesting case because different assumptions about price behavior have no effect on the decision rules.

The first of the alternative price mechanisms considered is called the "asymptotic 'normal' price-level" hypothesis which assumes that there exists a "normal" price function $\bar{P}(t)$ such that

$$\lim_{t \to \infty} E_T\{P(t)/\bar{P}(t)\} = 1 \quad \text{for } 0 \le T < t < \infty \tag{5.105}$$

i.e. independent of the current level of the asset price, the investor expects the "long-run" price to approach the normal price. A particular example which satisfies the hypothesis is that

$$\bar{P}(t) = \bar{P}(0) \exp(vt) \tag{5.106}$$

and

$$\frac{\mathrm{d}P}{P} = \beta \left\{ \phi + vt - \log\left[\frac{P(t)}{P(0)}\right] \right\} \mathrm{d}t + \sigma \, \mathrm{d}z \tag{5.107}$$

where $\phi \equiv k + v/\beta + \sigma^2/4\beta$ and $k \equiv \log[\bar{P}(0)/P(0)]$.[28] For the purpose of analysis, it is more convenient to work with the variable $Y(t) \equiv \log[P(t)/P(0)]$ rather than $P(t)$. Substituting for P in (5.107) by using Itô's lemma, we can write the dynamics for Y as

$$\mathrm{d}Y = \beta[\mu + vt - Y] \, \mathrm{d}t + \sigma \, \mathrm{d}z \tag{5.108}$$

---

28 In the notation used in previous sections, (5.107) corresponds to (5.5) with $\alpha(P, t) \equiv \beta\{\phi + vt - \log[P(t)/P(0)]\}$. Note that "normal" does not mean "Gaussian" in the above use, but rather the normal long-run price of Alfred Marshall. Thus, unlike the geometric Brownian motion case, prices under this hypothesis follow a stationary process with a trend given by the exponential growth rate v.

where $\mu \equiv \phi - \sigma^2/2\beta$. Before examining the effects of this price mechanism on the optimal portfolio decisions, it is useful to investigate the price behavior implied by (5.106) and (5.107). Equation (5.107) implies an exponentially regressive price adjustment toward a normal price, adjusted for trend. By inspection of (5.108), Y is a normally distributed random variable generated by a Markov process and does not have independent increments.[29] Therefore, from the definition of Y, $P(t)$ is log-normal and Markov. Using Itô's lemma, one can solve (5.108) for $Y(t)$, conditional on knowing $Y(T)$, as

$$
Y(t) - Y(T) = \left[k + \nu T - \frac{\sigma^2}{4\beta} - Y(T) \right] [1 - \exp(-\beta\tau)]
$$

$$
+ \nu\tau + \sigma \exp(-\beta t) \int_T^t \exp(\beta s) \, dz
$$

$$(5.109)$$

where $\tau \equiv t - T > 0$. The instantaneous conditional variance of $Y(t)$ is

$$
\mathrm{var}[Y(t)|Y(T)] = \frac{\sigma^2}{2\beta} [1 - \exp(-2\beta\tau)] \tag{5.110}
$$

Given the characteristics of $Y(t)$, it is straightforward to derive the price behavior. For example, the conditional expected price can be derived from (5.110) and written as

$$
E_T\{P(t)/P(T)\}
$$
$$
= E_T\{\exp[Y(t) - Y(T)]\}
$$
$$
= \exp\left\{ \left[k + \nu T - \frac{\sigma^2}{4\beta} - Y(T) \right] [1 - \exp(-\beta\tau)] + \nu\tau \right.
$$
$$
\left. + \frac{\sigma^2}{4\beta} [1 - \exp(-2\beta\tau)] \right\} \tag{5.111}
$$

It is easy to verify that (5.105) holds by applying the appropriate limit process to (5.111). Figure 5.2 illustrates the behavior of the conditional expectation mechanism over time.

For computational simplicity in deriving the optimal consumption and portfolio rules, the two-asset model is used with the individual having an

---

29 Processes such as (5.108) are called Ornstein–Uhlenbeck processes and are discussed, for example, in Cox and Miller (1968, p. 225).

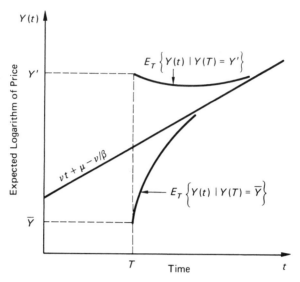

Figure 5.2 The Time Pattern of the Expected Value of the Logarithm of Price Under the "Normal" Price-Level Hypothesis.

infinite time horizon and a constant absolute risk aversion utility function, $U(C, t) = -\exp(-\eta C)/\eta$. The fundamental optimality equation then is written as

$$0 = -\exp(-\eta C^*)/\eta + J_t + J_W\{w^*[\beta(\phi + vt - Y) - r]W + rW - C^*\}$$
$$+ \tfrac{1}{2}J_{WW}w^{*2}W^2\sigma^2 + J_Y\beta(\mu + vt - Y) + \tfrac{1}{2}J_{YY}\sigma^2 + J_{YW}w^*W\sigma^2$$
$$(5.112)$$

and the associated equations for the optimal rules are

$$w^*W = -\frac{J_W[\beta(\phi + vt - Y) - r]}{J_{WW}\sigma^2} - \frac{J_{YW}}{J_{WW}} \qquad (5.113)$$

and

$$C^* = -\frac{\log(J_W)}{\eta} \qquad (5.114)$$

Solving (5.112), (5.113), and (5.114), we write the optimal rules in explicit form as

$$w^*W = \frac{1}{\eta r \sigma^2}\left\{\left(1 + \frac{\beta}{r}\right)[\alpha(P,\, t) - r] + \frac{\beta^2}{r^2}\left(\frac{\sigma^2}{2} + \nu - r\right)\right\}$$

(5.115)

and

$$C^* = rW + \frac{\beta^2}{2\sigma^2\eta r}Y^2 - \frac{\beta}{\eta r \sigma^2}\left[\beta\nu t + \beta\phi - r + \frac{\beta}{r}\left(\nu + \frac{\sigma^2}{2} - r\right)\right]Y$$

$$+\ a(t)$$

(5.116)

where

$$a(t) \equiv \frac{1}{\eta}\left\{\frac{\beta^2}{2r^2} - 1 + \frac{\beta\phi - r}{r\sigma^2}\left[\frac{1}{2}\left(1 + \frac{2\beta}{r}\right)\left(\beta\phi - r\right) + \frac{\beta^2}{r^2}\left(\frac{\sigma^2}{2} + \nu - r\right)\right.\right.$$

$$\left. - \frac{\beta}{r}\left(\beta\phi - \frac{\sigma^2}{2}\right)\right] + \frac{\beta\nu}{r^2\sigma^2}\left(\frac{\beta\nu}{r} + \beta\phi - r - \beta + \frac{\beta\sigma^2}{2r}\right)$$

$$- \frac{\beta^2}{r^3\sigma^2}\left(\beta\phi - \frac{\sigma^2}{2}\right)\left(\frac{\sigma^2}{2} + \nu - r\right) + \frac{\beta\nu t}{r\sigma^2}\left(\frac{\beta\nu}{r} + \frac{\beta\sigma^2}{2r} + \beta\phi - r - \beta\right)$$

$$+ \frac{\beta^2\nu^2 t^2}{2\sigma^2 r}\bigg\}$$

and where $\alpha(P,\, t)$ is the instantaneous expected rate of return defined explicitly in footnote 28. To provide a basis for comparison, the solutions when the geometric Brownian motion hypothesis is assumed are presented as[30]

$$w^*W = \frac{\alpha - r}{\eta r \sigma^2}$$

(5.117)

and

$$C^* = rW + \frac{1}{\eta r}\left[\frac{(\alpha - r)^2}{2\sigma^2} - r\right]$$

(5.118)

To examine the effects of the alternative "normal-price" hypothesis on the consumption-portfolio decisions, the (constant) α of (5.117) and (5.118) is

30 For a derivation of (5.117) and (5.118), see Merton (1969a; this volume, equations (4.64) and (4.65)).

chosen equal to $\alpha(P, t)$ of (5.115) and (5.116) so that, in both cases, the *instantaneous* expected return and variance are the same at the point of time of comparison. Comparing (5.115) with (5.117), we find that the proportion of wealth invested in the risky asset is always larger under the "normal-price" hypothesis than under the geometric Brownian motion hypothesis.[31] In particular, notice that even if $\alpha < r$, unlike in the geometric Brownian motion case, a positive amount of the risky asset may be held. Figure 5.3 illustrates the behavior of the optimal portfolio holdings.

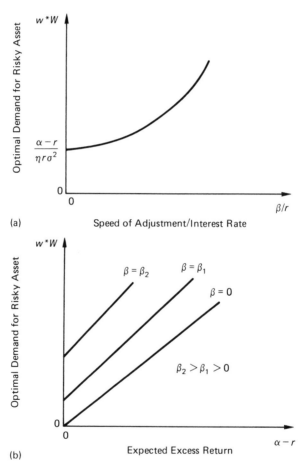

Figure 5.3 (a) The Demand for the Risky Asset as a Function of the Speed of Adjustment; (b) The Demand for the Risky Asset as a Function of the Expected Return.

31 It is assumed that $\nu > r$, i.e. the "long-run" rate of growth of the "normal" price is greater than the sure rate of interest so that something of the risky asset will be held in the short and long run.

The most striking feature of this analysis is that, despite the ability to make continuous portfolio adjustments, a person who believes that prices satisfy the "normal-price" hypothesis will hold more of the risky asset than one who believes that prices satisfy the geometric Brownian motion hypothesis, even though they both have the same utility function and the same expectations about the instantaneous mean and variance.

The primary interest in examining these alternative price mechanisms is to see the effects on portfolio behavior, and so little will be said about the effects on consumption other than to present the optimal rule.

The second alternative price mechanism assumes the same type of price dynamics equation as was assumed for the geometric Brownian motion, namely,

$$\frac{dP}{P} = \alpha \, dt + \sigma \, dz \tag{5.119}$$

However, instead of the instantaneous expected rate of return α being a constant, it is assumed that α is itself generated by the stochastic differential equation

$$d\alpha = \beta(\mu - \alpha) \, dt + \delta \left(\frac{dP}{P} - \alpha \, dt \right)$$

$$= \beta(\mu - \alpha) \, dt + \delta\sigma \, dz \tag{5.120}$$

The first term in (5.120) implies a long-run regressive adjustment of the expected rate of return toward a "normal" rate of return μ, where β is the speed of adjustment. The second term implies a short-run extrapolative adjustment of the expected rate of return of the "error-learning" type, where δ is the speed of adjustment. I will call the assumption of a price mechanism described by (5.119) and (5.120) the "De Leeuw" hypothesis for it was Frank De Leeuw who first introduced this type of mechanism to explain interest rate behavior.

To examine the price behavior implied by (5.119) and (5.120), we first derive the behavior of α, and then P. The equation for α, (5.120), is of the same type as (5.108) described previously. Hence, α is normally distributed and is generated by a Markov process. The solution of (5.120), conditional on knowing $\alpha(T)$, is

$$\alpha(t) - \alpha(T) = [\mu - \alpha(T)][1 - \exp(-\beta\tau)] + \delta\sigma \exp(-\beta t) \int_T^t \exp(\beta s) \, dz \tag{5.121}$$

where $\tau \equiv t - T > 0$. From (5.121), the conditional mean and variance of $\alpha(t) - \alpha(T)$ are

$$E_T\{\alpha(t) - \alpha(T)\} = [\mu - \alpha(T)][1 - \exp(-\beta\tau)] \qquad (5.122)$$

and

$$\text{var}[\alpha(t) - \alpha(T)|\alpha(T)] = \frac{\delta^2\sigma^2}{2\beta}[1 - \exp(-2\beta\tau)] \qquad (5.123)$$

To derive the dynamics of P, note that, unlike α, P is not Markov although the joint process $[P, \alpha]$ is. Combining the results derived for $\alpha(t)$ with (5.119), we solve directly for the price, conditional on knowing $P(T)$ and $\alpha(T)$:

$$Y(t) - Y(T) = (\mu - \tfrac{1}{2}\sigma^2)\tau - \frac{\mu - \alpha(T)}{\beta}[1 - \exp(-\beta\tau)]$$

$$+ \sigma\delta \int_T^t \int_T^s \exp[-\beta(s - s')] \, dz(s') \, ds + \sigma \int_T^t dz$$
$$(5.124)$$

where $Y(t) \equiv \log[P(t)]$. From (5.124), the conditional mean and variance of $Y(t) - Y(T)$ are

$$E_T\{Y(t) - Y(T)\} = (\mu - \tfrac{1}{2}\sigma^2)\tau - \frac{\mu - \alpha(T)}{\beta}[1 - \exp(-\beta\tau)]$$
$$(5.125)$$

and

$$\text{var}[Y(t) - Y(T)|Y(T)] = \sigma^2\tau + \frac{\sigma^2\delta^2}{\beta^3}\{\beta\tau - 2[1 - \exp(-\beta\tau)]$$

$$+ \tfrac{1}{2}[1 - \exp(-2\beta\tau)]\}$$

$$+ \frac{2\delta\sigma^2}{\beta^2}\{\beta\tau - [1 - \exp(-\beta\tau)]\} \qquad (5.126)$$

From (5.122) and (5.123), the equilibrium or "long-run" (i.e. $\tau \to \infty$) distribution for $\alpha(t)$ is stationary and normal with mean μ and variance $\delta^2\sigma^2/2\beta$. The equilibrium distribution for $P(t)/P(T)$ is log-normal with the mean of $\log[P(t)/P(T)]$ equal to $(\mu - \sigma^2/2)\tau$ and variance $\sigma^2(1 + \delta/\beta)^2\tau$. Hence, the long-run behavior of prices under the De Leeuw hypothesis approaches the geometric Brownian motion. Because $P(t)/P(T)$ is log-normal, it is straightforward to derive the moments for $P(t)$ from (5.124)–(5.126). Figure 5.4 illustrates the behavior of the expected price mechanism.

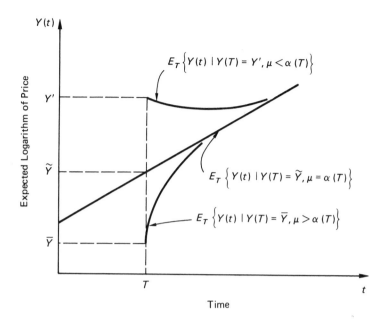

Figure 5.4 The Time Pattern of the Expected Value of the Logarithm of Price Under the De Leeuw Hypothesis.

Again, the two-asset model is used with the individual having an infinite time horizon and a constant absolute risk aversion utility function $U(C, t) = -\exp(-\eta C)/\eta$. The fundamental optimality equation is written as

$$0 = -\frac{\exp(-\eta C^*)}{\eta} + J_t + J_W[w^*(\alpha - r)W + rW - C^*]$$

$$+ \tfrac{1}{2}J_{WW}w^{*2}W^2\sigma^2 + J_\alpha\beta(\mu - \alpha) + \tfrac{1}{2}J_{\alpha\alpha}\delta^2\sigma^2 + J_{W\alpha}\delta\sigma^2 w^*W$$

(5.127)

Notice that the state variables of the problem are W and α, which are both Markov, as is required for the dynamic programming technique. The optimal portfolio rule derived from (5.127) is

$$w^*W = -\frac{J_W(\alpha - r)}{J_{WW}\sigma^2} - \frac{J_{W\alpha}\delta}{J_{WW}}$$

(5.128)

The optimal consumption rule is the same as in (5.114). Solving (5.127) and (5.128), the explicit solution for the portfolio rule is

$$w^*W = \frac{1}{\eta r \sigma^2 (r + 2\delta + 2\beta)} \left[(r + \delta + 2\beta)(\alpha - r) - \frac{\delta\beta(\mu - r)}{r + \delta + \beta} \right]$$

$$(5.129)$$

Comparing (5.129) with (5.117) and assuming that $\mu > r$, we find that under the De Leeuw hypothesis the individual will hold a smaller amount of the risky asset than under the geometric Brownian motion hypothesis. Note also that w^*W is a decreasing function of the long-run normal rate of return μ. The interpretation of this result is that, as μ increases for a given α, the probability increases that future αs will be more favorable relative to the current α, and so there is a tendency to hold more of one's current wealth in the risk-free asset as a "reserve" for investment under more favorable conditions.

The last type of price mechanism examined differs from the previous two in that it is assumed that prices satisfy the geometric Brownian motion hypothesis. However, it is also assumed that the investor does not know the true value of the parameter α, but must estimate it from past data. Suppose P is generated by equation (5.119) with α and σ constants, and the investor has price data back to time $-\tau$. Then, the best estimator for α, $\hat{\alpha}(t)$, is

$$\hat{\alpha}(t) = \frac{1}{t + \tau} \int_{-\tau}^{t} \frac{dP}{P} \qquad (5.130)$$

where we assume, arbitrarily, that $\hat{\alpha}(-\tau) = 0$. From (5.130), we have that $E\{\hat{\alpha}(t)\} = \alpha$, and so, if we define the error term $\epsilon_t \equiv \alpha - \hat{\alpha}(t)$, then (5.119) can be rewritten as

$$\frac{dP}{P} = \hat{\alpha} \, dt + \sigma \, d\hat{z} \qquad (5.131)$$

where $d\hat{z} \equiv dz + \epsilon_t \, dt/\sigma$. Further, by differentiating (5.130), we have the dynamics for $\hat{\alpha}$, namely

$$d\hat{\alpha} = \frac{\sigma}{t + \tau} \, d\hat{z} \qquad (5.132)$$

Comparing (5.131) and (5.132) with (5.119) and (5.120), we see that this "learning" model is equivalent to the special case of the De Leeuw hypothesis of pure extrapolation (i.e. $\beta = 0$), where the degree of extrapolation (δ) is decreasing over time. If the two-asset model is assumed with an investor who lives to time T with a constant absolute risk aversion utility function, and if (for computational simplicity) the risk-free asset is money (i.e. $r = 0$), then the optimal portfolio rule is

$$w^*W = \frac{t + \tau}{\eta\sigma^2} \log\left(\frac{T + \tau}{t + \tau}\right)\hat{\alpha}(t) \tag{5.133}$$

and the optimal consumption rule is

$$C^* = \frac{W}{T - t} - \frac{1}{\eta}\left(\frac{1}{2(T - t)}\left\{(T - t)[2 - \log(T + \tau)]\right.\right.$$

$$\left. + (2t + \tau + T) \log\left(\frac{t + \tau}{T + \tau}\right)\right\}$$

$$+ \frac{\hat{\alpha}^2}{2\sigma^2}\left[\frac{(t + \tau)^2}{T - t}\right]\left[\log\left(\frac{T + \tau}{t + \tau}\right) - \frac{T - t}{t + \tau}\right]\right) \tag{5.134}$$

By differentiating (5.133) with respect to t, we find that w^*W is an increasing function of time for $t < \bar{t}$, reaches a maximum at $t = \bar{t}$, and then is a decreasing function of time for $\bar{t} < t < T$, where $\bar{t}$ is defined by

$$\bar{t} = [T + (1 - e)\tau]/e \tag{5.135}$$

The reason for this behavior is that, early in life (i.e. for $t < \bar{t}$), the investor learns more about the price equation with each observation, and hence investment in the risky asset becomes more attractive. However, as he approaches the end of life (i.e. for $t > \bar{t}$), he is generally liquidating his portfolio to consume a larger fraction of his wealth, so that, although investment in the risky asset is more favorable, the absolute dollar amount invested in the risky asset declines.

Consider the effect on (5.133) of increasing the number of available previous observations (i.e. increase τ). As expected, the dollar amount invested in the risky asset increases monotonically. Taking the limit of (5.133) as $\tau \to \infty$, we have that the optimal portfolio rule is, with probability one,

$$w^*W = \frac{T - t}{\eta\sigma^2}\alpha \quad \text{as } \tau \to \infty \tag{5.136}$$

which is the optimal rule for the geometric Brownian motion case when α is known with certainty. Figure 5.5 illustrates graphically how the optimal rule changes with τ.

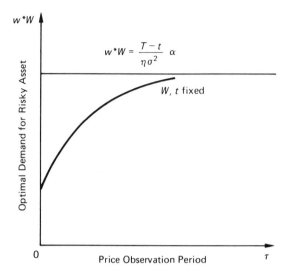

Figure 5.5 The Demand for the Risky Asset as a Function of the Duration of the Price Observation Period.

5.10 CONCLUSION

By the introduction of Itô's lemma and the fundamental theorem of stochastic dynamic programming (Theorem 5.1), we have shown how to systematically construct and analyze optimal continuous-time dynamic models under uncertainty. The basic methods employed in studying the consumption-portfolio problem are applicable to a wide class of economic models of decision-making under uncertainty.

A major advantage of the continuous-time model over its discrete time analog is that one need only consider two types of stochastic processes: functions of Brownian motions and Poisson processes. This result limits the number of parameters in the problem and allows one to take full advantage of the enormous literature written about these processes. Although I have not done so here, it is straightforward to show that the limits of the discrete-time model solutions as the period spacing goes to zero are the solutions of the continuous-time model.[32]

A basic simplification gained by using the continuous-time model to analyze the consumption-portfolio problem is the justification of the Tobin–Markowitz portfolio efficiency conditions in the important case when asset-price changes are log-normally distributed with constant parameters. With earlier writers (Hakansson, 1970; Leland, 1968; Fischer,

32 For a general discussion of this result, see Samuelson (1970). 1992 note: for later research, see He (1991) and Willinger and Taqqu (1991).

1969; Samuelson, 1969; and Cass and Stiglitz, 1970), we have shown that the assumption of the HARA utility function family simplifies the analysis and a number of strong theorems were proved about the optimal solutions. The introduction of stochastic wage income, risk of default, uncertainty about life expectancy, and alternative types of price dynamics serve to illustrate the power of the techniques as well as to provide insight into the effects of these complications on the optimal rules.

6

Further Developments in the Theory of Optimal Consumption and Portfolio Selection

6.1 INTRODUCTION

The application of continuous-time analysis to the intertemporal consumption and portfolio-selection problem in the preceding chapters produced a number of strong results about optimal asset demands and lifetime consumption allocations. Among the more important findings were the establishment of plausible conditions under which the simple mean–variance portfolio rules of Markowitz and Tobin apply; the derivation of mutual-fund theorems that allow efficient separation of the individual-asset investment decisions from the more macro allocational choices among classes of assets; and the verification of the Modigliani–Brumberg Life-Cycle Hypothesis in an uncertain environment. The models in these chapters all assume a single consumption good and investor preferences that are additive and independent, with no intertemporal complementarity of consumption. The technique of analysis is stochastic dynamic programming. In this chapter, we generalize the model in several dimensions and show that the key results of Chapters 4 and 5 are robust.

Stochastic dynamic programming is a powerful tool for the study of intertemporal optimization under uncertainty. It does have two important limitations, however:[1] first, even if an optimal solution exists, dynamic

---

1 A third limitation is that the dynamics of the variables in the problem must be described by a Markov process. However, as discussed in Chapters 3 and 15, many processes that are formally non-Markov can be transformed into Markov processes by the expansion-of-the-states technique (cf. Cox and Miller, 1968, pp. 16–18). Although dynamic programming can no longer be used, Duffie and Huang (1985), Huang and Kreps (1985), Duffie and Zame (1989), and Hindy and Huang (1989) have shown that the important substantive results of the continuous-time consumption-portfolio analysis derived here will obtain even in an environment of completely path-dependent processes that cannot be transformed into a Markov format.

programming can only be used to find it if the derived-utility (or program-valuation) function J is continuously differentiable. Second, determination of the optimal controls generally requires that the Bellman equation be solved for J and its derivatives.[2] Because it is a nonlinear partial differential equation, the Bellman equation is difficult to solve either in closed form or by numerical methods. Moreover, there are no easily applied general conditions that ensure existence of a solution.[3]

Using a martingale representation technology,[4] Cox and Huang (1989b, 1991) derive an alternative method for solving the optimal consumption-portfolio problem that does not require differentiability of the derived-utility function. Their method is presented in Section 6.2. This approach has the further rather remarkable feature that the optimal consumption and portfolio policies can be determined by solving one algebraic transcendental equation and a *linear* partial differential equation of the classic parabolic type. Unlike the Bellman equation, general existence and uniqueness conditions for a solution to this type of linear equation are well known. Further, this finding is a major computational breakthrough because there is substantial literature on numerical methods for solving this equation when no closed-form solution can be found.[5] The importance of the Cox–Huang methodology is underscored in Section 6.3, and again in Chapters 14 and 16 where it is applied to a variety of problems that cannot easily be solved using the dynamic programming approach.

Because neither negative consumption nor negative wealth is physically possible, to be feasible, a consumption–investment strategy must satisfy

2 Examples of the Bellman equation are (5.26) and (5.28). It is not always necessary, however, to solve for J to derive the essential characteristics of the optimal controls. As we saw in Chapter 5, the important properties of optimal portfolio demands (including the mutual-fund theorems) can be deduced from the first-order conditions alone. Indeed, because individual preferences are not observable, most of the testable hypotheses of the continuous-time model can be determined in this way (cf. Chapter 15).

3 General existence conditions are particularly difficult to obtain if, as is the case in our models, the set of values for admissible optimal controls is not compact. The only general approach to proving existence of an optimum is the verification theorem. That is, because satisfaction of the Bellman equation is a sufficient condition for an optimum, if a solution to that equation can be found, it is the optimum.

4 The martingale representation technology was first applied in finance by Harrison and Kreps (1979). Cox and Huang (1991) and Pliska (1986) use this technology to derive existence conditions for optimal consumption and portfolio policies without the requirement of compactness on the values of admissible optimal controls.

5 As demonstrated in later chapters, the same type of partial differential equations plays a central role in the theory of value for options and other contingent-claim securities. For this reason, there is considerable finance literature on both closed-form and numerical solutions of this equation.

these nonnegativity conditions.[6] In formulating the static portfolio problem in Chapter 2, we noted that imposition of these conditions captures the effects of personal bankruptcy on investors' choices. However, as also noted there, explicit recognition of these constraints in models of portfolio selection is relatively rare. The models in Chapters 4 and 5 are no exception. Therefore, in Section 6.2, we reformulate the optimal consumption–investment problem to include these feasibility conditions and show that the structure of portfolio demands remains essentially unchanged. Thus, the general results of Sections 5.4 and 5.5 are shown to obtain even with personal bankruptcy.

A sufficient condition for the unconstrained optimal strategies to satisfy these nonnegativity constraints is that, for each time t, there exists a nonnegative level of "subsistence" consumption at which the investor's marginal utility of consumption is infinite. Unfortunately, as Karatzas et al. (1986) and Sethi and Taksar (1988) show, this sufficiency condition is not satisfied by some members of the Hyperbolic Absolute Risk Aversion (HARA) family of utility functions analyzed in Sections 4.9 and 5.6. As is evident by inspection of (5.48), (5.54), and (5.56), some of the unconstrained solutions presented there violate these feasibility conditions.[7] Hence, in Section 6.3, we rederive the optimal consumption and portfolio rules for those members of the HARA family whose unconstrained optimal policies are not feasible.

In Section 6.4, we analyze the optimal consumption–investment problem for investors with preferences that depend on other variables in addition to current consumption and time. The analysis covers models in which investors can (at least partially) control the time path of these variables and ones in which they cannot. Specific examples explored include multiple consumption goods, money-in-the-utility function and preferences with nonzero intertemporal complementarity of consumption.

6   An arbitrage opportunity exists if there is a feasible transaction requiring no investment that produces a positive payoff with certainty. To rule out the possibility of arbitrage, zero wealth must be an absorbing state. That is, if an investor's total wealth (including capitalized future wage income, gifts, bequests, and welfare payments) reaches zero, then it remains there.

7   Although optimal rules that violate the nonnegativity constraints are not globally feasible, Cox and Huang (1989b) show that such rules are asymptotically valid as wealth becomes large. Because the unconstrained optimal rules for exponential utility are in this class, the examples in Section 5.8 and 5.9 that use this preference function should be restricted to the case $W \geqslant 0$.

6.2 THE COX–HUANG ALTERNATIVE TO STOCHASTIC DYNAMIC PROGRAMMING

In this section, we develop the Cox–Huang (1989b) approach to finding the optimal consumption and portfolio-selection rules in the continuous-time model of Chapters 4 and 5. As indicated in Section 6.1, this approach does not use dynamic programming. Unlike the analyses in Chapters 4 and 5, their formulation explicitly includes the restrictions that consumption and wealth must be nonnegative. The derivation of their technique uses a particular optimal portfolio called the "growth-optimum" portfolio. Therefore, before proceeding with the derivation, we digress to develop the properties of this portfolio.

6.2.1 THE GROWTH-OPTIMUM PORTFOLIO STRATEGY

If $W(t)$ denotes the value of a portfolio at time t that reinvests all earnings, then $W(T)/W(t)$ is the cumulative total return per dollar from investing in the portfolio between t and T. Let $\text{ACCR}(t, T)$ denote the average continuously compounded return on the portfolio over the period. Because the portfolio reinvests all earnings, $\text{ACCR}(t, T) = \log[W(T)/W(t)]/(T - t)$, the average compound growth rate of the value of the portfolio. Consider a portfolio policy chosen so as to maximize the expected value of $\text{ACCR}(t, T)$ at time t, $t < T$. The portfolio generated by this strategy is called the "growth-optimum" portfolio. By definition,

$$E_t\{\text{ACCR}(t, T)\} = E_t\{\log[W(T)] - \log[W(t)]\}/(T - t)$$

Because $W(t)$ is known at t and $T - t > 0$, the objective of maximizing the expected growth rate of the portfolio can be restated as max $E_t\{\log[W(T)]\}$. Therefore, the growth-optimum portfolio will be the same as the optimal portfolio selected by an investor in Section 5.4, equation (5.15), with preferences $U[C(t),t] = 0$ and $B[W(T),T] = \log[W(T)]$. Hence, the growth-optimum portfolio is an efficient portfolio as defined in Section 2.2.[8]

---

8   As will be shown in Theorem 6.5, the growth-optimum portfolio policy is also the optimal solution to the following problem: Given an initial wealth $W(0)$ and a "target" level of wealth $\overline{W} > W(0)$, find the portfolio strategy that minimizes $E_0(\tau)$ where τ is the first time that the value of the portfolio equals $\overline{W}$. From time to time, some have attached special normative importance to the growth-optimum strategy by claiming that it is the only rational policy for an investor with a very long time horizon. However, by examining the limiting optimal strategies for $E_0\{B[W(T), T]\}$ as $T \to \infty$, Samuelson (1971), Goldman (1974), and Merton and Samuelson (1974) have shown that such claims are not valid.

For the general asset-return dynamics posited in Chapter 5, we have from Section 5.9, equation (5.104), that the optimal portfolio fractions for an investor with logarithmic preferences at time t, $\{w_k^g(t)\}$, can be written as[9]

$$w_k^g(t) = \sum_1^m v_{kj}(t)[\alpha_j(t) - r(t)] \qquad k = 1,\ldots,m \qquad (6.1)$$

where $\alpha_j(t)$ is the instantaneous expected return on risky asset j at time t, $r(t)$ is the interest rate, and $v_{kj}(t)$ is the $k-j$ element of the inverse of the instantaneous variance–covariance matrix of returns $[\sigma_{ij}(t)]$. The fraction allocated to the riskless asset is given by $1 - \Sigma_1^m w_k^g(t)$.

By inspection of (6.1), the fractional allocations in the growth-optimum strategy at each point in time depend only on the current values of the investment opportunity set $\{\alpha_j(t), r(t), \sigma_{ij}(t)\}$, independently of whether or not these values will change in the future. The optimal fractions are also independent of both the level of the portfolio's value and the planning horizon T over which the expected average growth rate is maximized. Portfolio rules with these features are called "myopic" policies.

Let $X(t)$ denote the value of the growth-optimum portfolio at time t. From (6.1) and the posited asset-price dynamics in (5.5), we can express the dynamics for $X(t)$ in stochastic differential equation form as

$$dX = \left[\sum_1^m w_k^g\left(\frac{dP_k}{P_k} - r\,dt\right) + r\,dt \right]X$$

$$= (\mu^2 + r)X\,dt + \mu X\,dz \qquad (6.2)$$

where $\mu^2 = \mu^2(P_1,\ldots,P_m,t) \equiv \Sigma_1^m\Sigma_1^m v_{kj}(\alpha_j - r)(\alpha_k - r) > 0$ and $dz \equiv [\Sigma_1^m\Sigma_1^m v_{kj}(\alpha_j - r)\sigma_k\,dz_k]/\mu$ is a standard Wiener process. Although in general $X(t)$ is not by itself a Markov process, it is *jointly* Markov in X and P.[10]

Because $X = 0$ is an absorbing state, it follows that, if $X(t) = 0$, then $X(t + \tau) = 0$ for all $\tau > 0$. Thus, if $X(t) = 0$, then

---

9 Strictly, the optimal rules in (5.104) were derived for an investor with preferences $U(C, t) = \log(C)$ and $B[W(T), T] = 0$. However, it is straightforward to show that (5.104) is the optimal fractional rule for all investors with preferences of the form $U(C, t) = a(t) \log(C)$ and $B[W(T), T] = b(T) \log[W(T)]$ for any nonnegative $a(t)$ and $b(T)$ and at least one of them positive. For $a(t) > 0$, there will, of course, be withdrawals for consumption prior to T.

10 As in Chapter 5, we assume for simplicity that r is nonstochastic over time. For notational convenience, we use P for the vector $(P_1,\ldots,P_m)$ and drop the explicit recognition of the time dependence of variables, except where required for clarity.

$$E_t\{\partial B[X(T), T]/\partial X\} = E_t\{1/X(T)\} = \infty$$

But (6.1) is the optimal rule for maximizing $E_t\{\text{ACCR}(t, T)\}$ and there is always a feasible strategy of holding just the riskless asset such that $E_t\{\text{ACCR}(t, T)\} = r$. Therefore, it must be that

$$\text{prob}\{X(t) > 0 | X(0) > 0\} = 1 \quad \text{for all } t \geq 0 \qquad (6.3)$$

That is, the growth-optimum policy never risks ruin and will never violate the nonnegativity condition on the value of the portfolio.

In the proof of Theorem 2.16 it is shown that if a portfolio is mean–variance efficient, then its portfolio fractions can be written as

$$\delta_k = \lambda \sum_1^m v_{kj}(\alpha_j - r) \qquad k = 1,\ldots,m \qquad (6.4)$$

where λ equals the ratio of the portfolio's variance to its expected excess return. By inspection of (6.2), the (instantaneous) expected excess return on the growth-optimum portfolio is $\mu^2 + r - r = \mu^2$ and its instantaneous variance rate is μ^2. Hence, $\lambda = 1$. Setting $\lambda = 1$ in (6.4) and comparing it with (6.1), we have that $w_k^g = \delta_k$, $k = 1,\ldots,m$. Therefore, in the continuous-time model, the growth-optimum portfolio is instantaneously mean–variance efficient.

If the elements of the investment opportunity set $\{\alpha_j, r, \sigma_{ij}\}$ are constant over time, then, as shown in Section 5.5, the risky-asset returns are jointly log-normally distributed. In that special case, the $\{w_k^g\}$ are constant over time, and the growth-optimum strategy calls for a continuous rebalancing of the portfolio holdings to maintain these constant proportions. Because μ^2 and r are now constants, we have from (6.2) that $X(t)$ is, by itself, a Markov process. Moreover, (6.2) can be explicitly integrated so that, for $\tau > 0$ and for all t,

$$X(t + \tau) = X(t) \exp\left\{\left(r + \frac{\mu^2}{2}\right)\tau + \mu[z(t + \tau) - z(t)]\right\} \qquad (6.5)$$

By inspection of (6.5), $X(t + \tau)$ is log-normally distributed with $E_t\{X(t + \tau)\} = X(t) \exp[(\mu^2 + r)\tau]$ and $\text{var}_t\{\log[X(t + \tau)]\} = \mu^2\tau$.

An alternative expression for $X(t + \tau)$, obtained from integration of (6.2) with $\{w_k^g\}$ constant, is given by

$$X(t + \tau) = X(t) \exp(a\tau) \prod_1^m \left[\frac{P_k(t + \tau) \exp(-b_k\tau)}{P_k(t)}\right]^{w_k^g} \qquad (6.6)$$

where $a \equiv r - \mu^2/2$ and $b_k \equiv r - \sigma_k^2/2$, $k = 1,...,m$. Therefore, conditional on knowing the value of the growth-optimum portfolio and the risky-asset prices for some time t, we need only know the risky-asset prices $\{P_k(t + \tau)\}$ to determine the value of the growth-optimum portfolio at any future date $t + \tau$. That is, given the initial conditions, the value of the growth-optimum portfolio is solely a function of the contemporaneous risky-asset prices and time.

As we have seen, $X(t)$ is a mean–variance efficient portfolio. It follows from Corollary 5.2 that, when the investment opportunity set is constant, all investors' optimal portfolios can be generated by a simple combination of the growth-optimum portfolio and the riskless asset.[11] With this, we end our digression on the properties of the growth-optimum portfolio in the continuous-time model.

6.2.2 THE COX–HUANG SOLUTION OF THE INTERTEMPORAL CONSUMPTION–INVESTMENT PROBLEM

Consider the lifetime consumption and portfolio-selection problem as formulated in Section 5.4, where the investor chooses a set of optimal consumption and portfolio rules so as to

$$\max E_0 \left\{ \int_0^T U[C(t), t] \, dt + B[W(T), T] \right\} \qquad (6.7)$$

subject to the budget constraint dynamics (5.14a) and the appended feasibility restrictions that $C(t) \geq 0$ and $W(t) \geq 0$ for all $t \leq T$. In the dynamic programming approach to solving this problem (Theorem 5.1), $J[W(t), P(t), t]$ denotes the value of the optimized program in (6.7) at time t and the optimal consumption and portfolio rules are in the "feedback-control" form $C^*(t) = C^*[W(t), P(t), t]$ and $w_k^*(t) = w_k^*[W(t), P(t), t]$, $k = 1,...,m$. The conditional expectation operator E_0 in (6.7) is computed over the joint probability distribution for the exogenously specified asset-price dynamics and the endogenously determined dynamics for the investor's wealth.

Consider now the seemingly different optimization problem in which the investor chooses a consumption path $\{\hat{C}(t)\}$ and a bequest of wealth $\hat{W}(T)$ so as to

$$\max E_0' \left\{ \int_0^T U[\hat{C}(t), t] \, dt + B[\hat{W}(T), T] \right\} \qquad (6.8)$$

---

11   In the corollary, the growth-optimum portfolio corresponds to the risky-asset mutual fund with parameter values $\nu = 1$ and $\eta = 0$.

subject to the constraints that $\hat{C}(t) \geq 0$, $\hat{W}(T) \geq 0$, and

$$X(0)E_0'\left\{\int_0^T \frac{\hat{C}(t)}{X(t)}\,dt + \frac{\hat{W}(T)}{X(T)}\right\} \leq W(0) \qquad (6.8a)$$

where $X(t)$ is the value of the growth-optimum portfolio as defined in Section 6.2.1.

From (6.2), we have that the dynamics of $X(t)$ are jointly Markov in X and P. Hence, the conditional expectation operator E_0' in (6.8) and (6.8a) is computed over the joint probability distribution for the individual asset prices and the value of the growth-optimum portfolio. Thus, we can denote the value at time t of the optimized program in (6.8) by $\hat{J}[X(t), P(t), t]$. The optimal consumption path and terminal wealth functions will have the form $\hat{C}^*(t) \equiv G[X(t), P(t), t]$ and $\hat{W}^*(T) \equiv H[X(T), P(T), T]$, where both G and H depend parametrically on $X(0)$, $P(0)$, and $W(0)$. Unlike the optimal rules for (6.7), $\hat{C}^*(t)$ and $\hat{W}^*(T)$ are *not* feedback controls, because the choices for $\hat{C}(t)$ and $\hat{W}(T)$ do not affect the time paths of either $X(t)$ or $P(t)$.

The connection between the optimization problems (6.7) and (6.8) is established in the following theorem proved by Cox and Huang.[12]

Theorem 6.1

Under quite mild regularity conditions, there exists a solution to (6.7) if and only if (a) there exists a solution to (6.8) and (b) $C^*(t) = \hat{C}^*(t)$ for $t \leq T$ and $W(T) = \hat{W}^*(T)$.

It follows as an immediate corollary that $J[W(t), P(t), t] = \hat{J}[X(t), P(t), t]$ for all $t \leq T$. The substantive economic intuition underlying the equivalence of these two optimization problems will be considerably more apparent after the development in later chapters of the pricing theories for contingent claims and capital assets. We therefore postpone that discussion until Chapter 16 and proceed here using Theorem 6.1 in a strictly formal fashion.

Because the joint probability distribution for $X(t)$ and $P(t)$ is not affected by the investor's choices for $\hat{C}(t)$ and $\hat{W}(T)$, (6.8) has the structure of a static optimization problem that can be solved by the classical Lagrange–Kuhn–Tucker methods for constrained optimization. We can therefore rewrite (6.8) as

---

12 Theorem 6.1 is actually presented as an assumption (Assumption 2.3) in Cox and Huang (1989b). However, in their other paper (1991, Sections 2–4), they derive specific regularity conditions to assure the validity of the theorem.

$$\max E_0' \left\{ \int_0^T U[\hat{C}(t), t] \, dt + B[\hat{W}(T), T] + \lambda_1 \left[W(0) - \frac{X(0)\hat{W}(T)}{X(T)} \right. \right.$$

$$\left. - \int_0^T \frac{X(0)\hat{C}(t)}{X(t)} \, dt \right] + \int_0^T \lambda_2(t)\hat{C}(t) \, dt + \lambda_3 \hat{W}(T) \right\} \qquad (6.9)$$

where λ_1, $\lambda_2(t)$, and λ_3 are the usual Kuhn–Tucker multipliers reflecting the shadow costs of the constraints (6.8a), $\hat{C}(t) \geq 0$, and $\hat{W}(T) \geq 0$.

For all $t \leq T$ and all values of $X(t)$ and $P(t)$ that can occur with positive probability, the first-order conditions associated with (6.9) can be written as

$$U_C[\hat{C}^*(t), t] = \lambda_1 \frac{X(0)}{X(t)} - \lambda_2(t) \qquad (6.10a)$$

and

$$B_W[\hat{W}^*(T), T] = \lambda_1 \frac{X(0)}{X(T)} - \lambda_3 \qquad (6.10b)$$

where subscripts on U and B denote partial derivatives.

If the investor's preferences are such that he becomes satiated at some finite level of consumption, $\overline{C}(t)$, then $U_C[\overline{C}(t), t] = 0$. However, for $C(t) < \overline{C}(t)$, $U_C[C(t), t] > 0$ and $U_{CC}[C(t), t] < 0$. Similarly, if there exists a finite number $\overline{W}(T)$ such that $B_W[\overline{W}(T), T] = 0$, then $B_W[W(T), T] > 0$ and $B_{WW}[W(T), T] < 0$ for $W(T) < \overline{W}(T)$. If, for any t, $W(t) \geq \overline{W}(t)$ where

$$\overline{W}(t) \equiv \int_t^T \overline{C}(\tau) \exp[-r(\tau - t)] \, d\tau + \exp[-r(T - t)] \, \overline{W}(T) \qquad (6.11)$$

then the investor will be satiated in wealth because he can achieve the absolutely maximal program of consumption and bequests by simply investing in the riskless asset. Therefore, we assume for the balance of the analysis that the investor's initial wealth is such that he is not satiated (i.e. $W(0) < \overline{W}(0)$). This assumption assures us that strict equality applies in constraint (6.8a) for the optimal program and that the shadow price of wealth, λ_1, is strictly positive.

If, for any t, there exists a subsistence level of consumption $\underline{C}(t) \geq 0$ such that $U_C[\underline{C}(t), t] = \infty$, then a necessary condition for any optimal program is that $\hat{C}^*(t) > \underline{C}(t) \geq 0$ and the nonnegativity constraint on $\hat{C}(t)$

will not be binding. In that case, because $\lambda_2(t)\hat{C}^*(t) = 0$, $\lambda_2(t) = 0$ for all t. Similarly, if there exists a number $\underline{W}(T) \geq 0$ such that $B_W[\underline{W}(T), T] = \infty$, then $\hat{W}^*(T) > \underline{W}(T)$ and $\lambda_3 = 0$.[13] Therefore, as noted in Section 6.1, these marginal utility conditions applying for all $t \leq T$ are sufficient to ensure that the unconstrained solution to (6.8) and (6.8a) is a feasible solution.

In the general case, we have from the condition $\lambda_2(t)\hat{C}^*(t) = 0$ and (6.10a) that

$$\lambda_2(t) = \max\left[0, \lambda_1 \frac{X(0)}{X(t)} - U_C(0, t)\right] \tag{6.12}$$

and from $\lambda_3 \hat{W}^*(T) = 0$ and (6.10b) that

$$\lambda_3 = \max\left[0, \lambda_1 \frac{X(0)}{X(T)} - B_W(0, T)\right] \tag{6.13}$$

Because $U_{CC} < 0$ and $B_{WW} < 0$, both U_C and B_W are invertible. Hence, let $Q(y, t) \equiv U_C^{-1}(y)$ and $R(y, T) \equiv B_W^{-1}(y)$. From (6.10), (6.12), and (6.13), we have that

$$\hat{C}^*(t) = \max\left\{0, Q\left[\lambda_1 \frac{X(0)}{X(t)}, t\right]\right\} \qquad t \leq T \tag{6.14a}$$

and

$$\hat{W}^*(T) = \max\left\{0, R\left[\lambda_1 \frac{X(0)}{X(T)}, T\right]\right\} \tag{6.14b}$$

To complete the solution for the optimal program, we need only determine λ_1. Under the assumption of no satiation, (6.8a) is a strict equality for the optimal program, and therefore λ_1 can be determined as the solution to the transcendental algebraic equation given by

13   If for any $t \leq T$,

$$W(t) < \underline{W}(t) \equiv \int_t^T \underline{C}(\tau)\exp[-r(\tau - t)] \, d\tau + \underline{W}(T)\exp[-r(T - t)]$$

then the optimization problem is not well defined because there exists no feasible strategy that assures at least the subsistence level of consumption and bequests. We therefore assume that $W(0) \geq \underline{W}(0)$ which is sufficient to guarantee an optimal policy such that $W(t) \geq \underline{W}(t)$ for all $t \leq T$.

$$0 = -\frac{W(0)}{X(0)} + E_0'\left\{ \int_0^T \frac{\max\{0, Q[\lambda_1 X(0)/X(t), t]\}}{X(t)}\, dt \right.$$

$$\left. + \frac{\max\{0, R[\lambda_1 X(0)/X(T), T]\}}{X(T)} \right\} \qquad (6.15)$$

Because E_0' is conditioned on the initial value of the growth-optimum portfolio and individual risky-asset prices, the solution to (6.15) will have the form $\lambda_1 = \lambda_1[X(0), P(0), W(0)]$. Substituting for λ_1 in (6.14a) and (6.14b), we have a complete solution for the time path of optimal consumption and the bequest of wealth. For compactness in notation, we express these optimal policies as[14]

$$\hat{C}^*(t) \equiv G[X(t), P(t), t] \qquad (6.16a)$$

and

$$\hat{W}^*(T) \equiv H[X(T), P(T), T] \qquad (6.16b)$$

where the parametric dependence of G and H on the initial conditions $X(0)$, $P(0)$, and $W(0)$ is suppressed.

In sharp contrast with the dynamic programming technique of Chapters 4 and 5, the Cox–Huang method requires only the solution of a single transcendental algebraic equation to derive a complete description of the optimal intertemporal consumption–bequest allocation.[15] However, from inspection of (6.16) alone, we cannot determine the dynamic portfolio strategy that the investor must follow to achieve this optimal allocation. Nevertheless, given G and H in (6.16), we can derive the optimal portfolio strategy.

14   By inspection of (6.14a) and (6.14b), $\hat{C}^*(t)$ and $\hat{W}^*(T)$ do not depend on asset prices at times other than $t = 0$. However, we include the possibility of such dependence in (6.16) in anticipation of later analyses that include a broader class of preferences which are state dependent (cf. Section 6.4, Section 14.5, Chs 15 and 16). If, for example, $U = U[C(t), P(t), t]$ and $B = B[W(T), P(T), T]$, then $U_C^{-1}(y) = Q[y, P(t), t]$ and $B_W^{-1}(y) = R[y, P(T), T]$. It is straightforward to show that the Cox–Huang solution technique applies to this extended class of preference functions and that the optimal policies will depend on $P(t)$ in addition to $X(t)$ and t.

15   This assumes that we know the functional form for the joint probability distribution, $\text{prob}\{X(t), P(t)|X(0), P(0)\}$, for all $t \leq T$, an assumption not required for the dynamic programming approach. However, as we saw in (3.42), this probability function is itself the solution of a *linear* partial differential equation of the parabolic type. Thus, the Cox–Huang technique requires at most the solution of a transcendental equation and a linear partial differential equation. From (6.14) and (5.23), both solution techniques require that U_C be inverted.

For all $t \leq T$, define the function $F[X(t), P(t), t]$ by

$$F[X(t), P(t), t] \equiv X(t)E_t'\left\{\int_t^T \frac{G[X(\tau), P(\tau), \tau]}{X(\tau)}\, d\tau + \frac{H[X(T), P(T), T]}{X(T)}\right\}$$

(6.17)

where E_t' is conditioned on $X(t)$ and $P(t)$. From (6.8a) and (6.17), we have that $F[X(0), P(0), 0] = W(0)$. Suppose that the investor who solved (6.8) for his optimal intertemporal program at $t = 0$ reexamines his decisions at some time t, $0 < t \leq T$. At that time, his optimal problem will be to

$$\max E_t'\left\{\int_t^T U[\hat{C}(\tau), \tau]\, d\tau + B[\hat{W}(T), T]\right\}$$

(6.18)

subject to the constraint

$$X(t)E_t'\left\{\int_t^T \frac{\hat{C}(\tau)}{X(\tau)}\, d\tau + \frac{\hat{W}(T)}{X(T)}\right\} \leq W(t)$$

(6.18a)

However, (6.16a) and (6.16b) are intertemporally optimal solutions. Hence, by the "time-consistency" condition for an intertemporal optimum, (a) $W(t)$ must be such that $\hat{C}(\tau) = G[X(\tau), P(\tau), \tau]$, $t \leq \tau \leq T$, and $\hat{W}(T) = H[X(T), P(T), T]$ are feasible choices, and (b) G and H are the optimal rules that the investor would select as the solutions to (6.18). Under the maintained assumption of no initial satiation (i.e. $W(0) < \overline{W}(0)$), it follows that (6.18a) is satisfied as a strict equality for $\hat{C}(\tau) = G$ and $\hat{W}(T) = H$. By inspection of (6.17) and (6.18a), we have therefore that

$$W(t) = F[X(t), P(t), t] \qquad 0 \leq t \leq T$$

(6.19)

where $W(t)$ is the wealth of the investor at time t, *conditional* on his having followed the optimal allocation strategy in (6.16) from time 0 to time t.

Provided that F is a twice continuously differentiable function,[16] we can use Itô's lemma to derive the dynamics of the investor's optimally allocated wealth. That is, given the dynamics of risky-asset prices in (5.5) and the dynamics for X in (6.2), we have that

$$dF = \bar{\alpha}F\, dt + F_x\mu X\, dz + \sum_1^m F_k\sigma_k P_k\, dz_k$$

(6.20)

16   See Assumptions 2.1 and 2.2 and Theorem 2.1 in Cox and Huang (1989b) for the regularity conditions that ensure the required smoothness on F.

with $\bar{\alpha}$ defined by

$$\bar{\alpha}F \equiv \frac{1}{2}\,\mu^2 X^2 F_{xx} + \sum_1^m F_{xk}\sigma_{xk}XP_k + \frac{1}{2}\sum_1^m\sum_1^m F_{kj}\sigma_{kj}P_kP_j$$

$$+ (\mu^2 + r)XF_x + \sum_1^m \alpha_kP_kF_k + F_t \qquad (6.20a)$$

where subscripts on F denote partial derivatives and σ_{xk} denotes the instantaneous covariance between the returns on the growth-optimum portfolio and risky asset k, $k = 1,...,m$.[17] From (6.19), $dW = dF$ and therefore, by inspection of (6.20), $\bar{\alpha}$ is the instantaneous expected rate of growth of the investor's optimally allocated wealth.

Theorem 6.2

If there exists an optimal solution to (6.8), $[\hat{C}^*(t), \hat{W}^*(T)]$, then for $t \leqslant T$ the optimal portfolio strategy $\{w_k^*(t)\}$ that achieves this allocation is given by

$$w_k^*(t)W(t) = F_x[X(t), P(t), t]w_k^g(t)X(t) + F_k[X(t), P(t), t]P_k(t)$$

$$k = 1,...,m$$

with the balance of the investor's wealth in the riskless asset, where $w_k^g(t)$ is given in (6.1).

PROOF

From Theorem 6.1, if there exists a solution to (6.8), then there exists a solution to (6.7) such that $C^*(t) = \hat{C}^*(t)$ for $t \leqslant T$ and $W(T) = \hat{W}^*(T)$. Hence, the time path of optimally allocated wealth in (6.7) is identical with the time path for optimally allocated wealth in (6.8). Therefore the portfolio strategies required to implement this common allocation are also identical. Let $\{w_k^*(t)\}$ denote the optimal portfolio fractions in the risky assets. From (5.14a) the dynamics of the investor's optimally allocated wealth can be written as

17 $F_x \equiv \partial F/\partial X$, $F_k \equiv \partial F/\partial P_k$, $F_t \equiv \partial F/\partial t$, $F_{kj} \equiv \partial^2 F/\partial P_k\,\partial P_j$, and $F_{xk} \equiv \partial^2 F/\partial X\,\partial P_k$. From (6.1) and (6.2), $\sigma_{xk} \equiv \Sigma_1^m w_i^g\sigma_{ik} = \Sigma_1^m\Sigma_1^m v_{ij}(\alpha_j - r)\sigma_{ik} = \Sigma_1^m(\alpha_j - r) \times \Sigma_1^m v_{ij}\sigma_{ik} = \alpha_k - r$, because $\Sigma_1^m v_{ij}\sigma_{ik}$ is zero for $j \neq k$ and unity for $j = k$.

$$dW = \left\{ \left[\sum_1^m w_k^*(t)(\alpha_k - r) + r \right] W(t) - C^*(t) \right\} dt + \sum_1^m w_k^*(t)W(t)\sigma_k \, dz_k$$

From (6.19), $W(t) = F[X(t), P(t), t]$, and therefore $dW - dF \equiv 0$ for all $t \leqslant T$. But, from (6.20), this condition is satisfied if and only if

(i) $\quad \bar{\alpha} F = \left[\sum_1^m w_k^*(t)(\alpha_k - r) + r \right] W(t) - C^*(t)$

and

(ii) $\quad F_x \mu X(t) \, dz + \sum_1^m F_k \sigma_k P_k \, dz_k = \sum_1^m w_k^*(t)W(t)\sigma_k \, dz_k$

From (6.2), $\mu \, dz \equiv \Sigma_1^m w_k^g(t)\sigma_k \, dz_k$. By rearranging terms, we can rewrite (ii) as

$$\sum_1^m [F_x w_k^g(t)X(t) + F_k P_k - w_k^*(t)W(t)]\sigma_k \, dz_k \equiv 0$$

for all $t \leqslant T$. Because dz_k is not perfectly correlated with dz_j, $k \neq j$, this condition can only be satisfied if

$$F_x[X(t), P(t), t]w_k^g(t)X(t) + F_k[X(t), P(t), t]P_k(t) = w_k^*(t)W(t)$$

$$k = 1,\dots,m$$

From the portfolio balance condition, the riskless-asset holding is given by $[1 - \Sigma_1^m w_k^*(t)]W(t)$. QED

The Cox-Huang technique for solving the lifetime consumption-portfolio problem is summarized as follows: (a) determine the joint probability density function for $X(t)$ and $P(t)$, which, as noted in footnote 15, involves at most the solution of a linear partial differential equation; (b) determine the optimal intertemporal consumption–bequest allocations (6.16), which requires solution of the transcendental algebraic equation (6.15); (c) determine $F[X(t), P(t), t]$ from (6.17), which requires mere quadrature; and (d) determine the optimal portfolio strategy for each t from the formula in Theorem 6.2.

In closing this section, we present an alternative method to quadrature for determining $F[X(t), P(t), t]$ that will be used in later applications of the Cox–Huang technique in Section 6.3 and in Chapters 14 and 16.

Theorem 6.3

If F, as defined in (6.17), is twice continuously differentiable, then F is a solution to the linear partial differential equation[18]

$$0 = \frac{1}{2}\mu^2 X^2 F_{xx} + \sum_1^m F_{xk}\sigma_{xk}XP_k + \frac{1}{2}\sum_1^m \sum_1^m F_{kj}\sigma_{kj}P_k P_j + rXF_x$$

$$+ \sum_1^m rP_k F_k + F_t - rF + G$$

subject to the boundary condition that $F(X, P, T) = H(X, P, T)$, where G and H are as defined in (6.16).

PROOF

In the proof of Theorem 6.2, we showed that

$$\bar{\alpha}F = [\Sigma_1^m w_k^*(t)(\alpha_k - r) + r]W(t) - C^*(t)$$

for all $t \le T$, where $\bar{\alpha}$ is defined in (6.20a). From (6.19), $W(t) = F[X(t), P(t), t]$, and from Theorem 6.1, $C^*(t) = G[X(t), P(t), t]$ for all $t \le T$. From inspection of (6.2), $\mu^2 = \Sigma_1^m w_k^g(t)(\alpha_k - r)$. Substituting for $\{w_k^*(t)\}$ from the formula in Theorem 6.2, we have that

$$\left[\sum_1^m w_k^*(t)(\alpha_k - r) + r \right]W(t) - C^*(t)$$

$$= F_x\mu^2 X(t) + \sum_1^m F_k(\alpha_k - r)P_k + rF - G = \bar{\alpha}F$$

Substituting for $\bar{\alpha}F$ from (6.20a) and rearranging terms, we have that

$$0 = \frac{1}{2}\mu^2 X^2 F_{xx} + \sum_1^m F_{xk}\sigma_{xk}XP_k + \frac{1}{2}\sum_1^m \sum_1^m F_{kj}\sigma_{kj}P_k P_j + rXF_x$$

$$+ \sum_1^m rP_k F_k + F_t - rF + G$$

18 As shown in Cox and Huang (1989b, Assumptions 2.1 and 2.2), under mild regularity conditions on $\{\alpha_k, \sigma_{kj}, G, H\}$, the necessary additional boundary conditions are supplied to ensure that F is the unique solution to the partial differential equation.

From the definition in (6.17), we have that

$$F[X(T), P(T), T] = H[X(T), P(T), T] \qquad \text{QED}$$

6.2.3 THE RELATION BETWEEN THE COX–HUANG AND DYNAMIC PROGRAMMING SOLUTIONS

The formulation of the dynamic programming problem (6.7) is the same as in Theorem 5.1 except that we now impose the nonnegativity constraints on consumption and wealth. That is, the optimal consumption and portfolio rules, C^* and $\{w_k^*\}$, will satisfy $0 = \phi(C^*, w^*; W, P, t) \geqslant \phi(C, w; W, P, t)$ subject to the conditions $\Sigma_1^n w_k^* = 1$; $J(W, P, T) = B(W, T)$; $C^*(t) \geqslant 0$, and $W(t) \geqslant 0$.[19] To capture the requirement that $W(t) \geqslant 0$ and that $W(t) = 0$ is an absorbing state, we add the boundary condition that $J(0, P, t) = \int_t^T U(0, \tau)\mathrm{d}\tau + B(0, T)$, for $t \leqslant T$.[20] As in (5.18), the constrained maximization problem is written as

$$0 = \max_{\{C, w\}} \left[\phi(C, w; W, P, t) + \gamma_1 \left(1 - \sum_1^n w_k\right) + \gamma_2 C \right] \quad (6.21)$$

where γ_1 and γ_2 are the Kuhn–Tucker multipliers associated with the "adding-up" condition on the portfolio weights and the nonnegativity of consumption, respectively.

The first-order conditions for (6.21) corresponding to (5.19) and (5.20) are

$$0 = U_C(C^*, t) - J_W + \gamma_2 \qquad (6.22)$$

and

$$0 = -\gamma_1 + J_W \alpha_k W + J_{WW} \sum_1^n \sigma_{kj} w_j^* W^2 + \sum_1^n J_{jW} \sigma_{kj} P_j W \quad k = 1,\ldots,n$$

$$(6.23)$$

From (6.22) and the condition that $\gamma_2 C^* = 0$, we have that

$$\gamma_2 = \max[0, J_W - U_C(0, t)] \qquad (6.24)$$

---

19 $\phi(C, w; W, P, t) \equiv U(C, t) + \mathcal{L}(J)$ as defined in (5.17).
20 In the Karatzas et al. (1986) formulation, they permit the possibilities of "bankruptcy or welfare subsidies" to the investor that allow $J(0, P, t) > \int_t^T U(0, \tau)\,\mathrm{d}\tau + B(0, T)$. However, in their analysis, $W(t) = 0$ is still an absorbing state.

For $U_C(0, t) < \infty$, $B_W(0, T) < \infty$, and $\int_t^T U(0, \tau)\, d\tau + B(0, T) > -\infty$, the nonnegativity constraints on consumption and wealth will in general lead to a different solution for J than the unconstrained solution in Chapter 5. However, as in the unconstrained problem, $J_W > 0$ and $J_{WW} < 0$ for nonsatiated investors. Moreover, by inspection, (6.23) and (5.20) have identical structures. That is, as for the unconstrained solution (5.25), the optimal portfolio rules from (6.23) can be written as

$$w_k^* = h_k(P, t) + m(P, W, t)g_k(P, t) + f_k(P, W, t) \qquad k = 1,...,n \quad (6.25)$$

where h_k and g_k are independent of the investor's preferences and endowment, and therefore are the *same* functions in both the constrained and unconstrained solutions. Hence, all the optimal portfolio results derived in Chapters 4 and 5 that do not depend on explicit evaluations of J and its derivatives also obtain when the nonnegativity constraints on consumption and wealth are binding. In particular, the conditions under which the mean–variance portfolio rules and mutual-fund theorems of Chapter 5 apply are unaffected by these constraints.[21] It follows that these results from Chapters 4 and 5 are not changed by the introduction of personal bankruptcy into the model. The issues surrounding both personal and corporate bankruptcy are studied in greater detail in Chapters 13 and 14.

To derive the optimal feedback controls for the dynamic programming problem from the Cox–Huang solutions, we proceed as follows. Cox and Huang (1989b, Proposition 2.2) show that $\partial F/\partial X > 0$ if $F > 0$ and therefore, if $\partial F/\partial X = 0$, then $F = 0$. If $W(t)$ is the wealth of an investor who follows his optimal dynamic programming strategy, then, from (6.19), $W(t) = F[X(t), P(t), t]$. For $W(t) = F = 0$, the optimal strategy is, trivially, $C^*(t) = 0$ and $w_k^*(t)W(t) = 0$, $k = 1,...,n$. For $W(t) = F > 0$, $\partial F/\partial X > 0$, and therefore F is an invertible function in X. That is, for $W > 0$

$$\begin{aligned} X(t) &= F^{-1}[W(t)] \\ &\equiv L[W(t), P(t), t] \end{aligned} \qquad (6.26)$$

From Theorem 6.1, $C^*(t) = \hat{C}^*(t)$. Therefore, from (6.16a) and (6.26), we can write the dynamic programming optimal consumption policy as

$$\begin{aligned} C^*(t) &= C^*(W, P, t) \\ &= G[L(W, P, t), P, t] \end{aligned} \qquad (6.27)$$

---

21 For a general proof see Karatzas et al. (1986, pp. 268–70).

where $W = W(t)$ and $P = P(t)$. From Theorem 6.2 and equation (6.26), the feedback optimal portfolio rules are given by

$$
\begin{aligned}
w_k^*(t)W &= w_k^*(W, P, t)W \\
&= F_x[L(W, P, t), P, t]w_k^g(t)L(W, P, t) + F_k[L(W, P, t), P, t]P_k \\
&\qquad k = 1,\ldots,m \quad (6.28)
\end{aligned}
$$

where $m \equiv n - 1$ and the demand for asset n, the riskless security, is $[1 - \Sigma_1^m w_k^*(t)]W$.

To determine the critical level of wealth below which the investor will choose to consume nothing, we note from (6.10a) and (6.12) that $\hat{C}^*(t) = 0$ if and only if $U_C(0, t) \leq \lambda_1 X(0)/X(t)$. Hence, $C^*(t) = 0$ for $W(t) \leq W^+(t)$ where

$$
W^+(t) = F\left[\frac{\lambda_1 X(0)}{U_C(0, t)}, P(t), t\right] \quad (6.29)
$$

To derive the dynamic programming optimal rules from the Cox–Huang solutions, it is not necessary to compute either the indirect utility function J or its derivatives. However, to complete the analysis, note that $\hat{J}[X(t), P(t), t]$ is the value of the optimal program in (6.18). By Theorem 6.1, $J[W(t), P(t), t] = \hat{J}[X(t), P(t), t]$. Therefore, from (6.26), we have that

$$
J(W, P, t) = \hat{J}[L(W, P, t), P, t] \quad \text{for } W > 0 \quad (6.30a)
$$

and

$$
J(0, P, t) = \int_t^T U(0, \tau)\, d\tau + B(0, T) \quad \text{for } W = 0 \quad (6.30b)
$$

where $W = W(t)$ and $P = P(t)$.

Although the Cox–Huang methodology does not dominate the dynamic programming approach for all analyses of the intertemporal consumption–investment problem, it is a powerful new tool that will surely have widespread application in finance. As we will see in the section to follow, this technique is especially well suited for solving problems in which the nonnegativity constraints on consumption and wealth are binding.

6.3　OPTIMAL PORTFOLIO RULES WHEN THE NONNEGATIVITY CONSTRAINT ON CONSUMPTION IS BINDING

In Section 5.6, the unconstrained optimal consumption and portfolio rules for the HARA family of utility functions were derived in an environment in which the returns on assets are jointly log-normally distributed. As noted in Section 6.1, these unconstrained policies are not feasible for some members of the HARA family because they violate the nonnegativity conditions on consumption and wealth. Assuming the same constant investment opportunity set, Karatzas et al. (1986) use dynamic programming to make an extensive study of the effects of the nonnegativity constraints on optimal policies and, in particular, they solve for the optimal rules for HARA utility. In this section, we also use dynamic programming to analyze the portfolio behavior of long-lived investors for whom the nonnegativity constraint on consumption is binding. However, we apply the Cox–Huang technique to determine the optimal consumption and portfolio rules for those HARA preference functions for which the unconstrained solutions of Chapter 5 are invalid.

In Chapters 4 and 5, the assumption of an infinite-time-horizon investor with exponential time preference greatly simplified the solutions for the optimal consumption and portfolio rules. Because the focus here is on the effects of the nonnegativity constraints on optimal policies, we concentrate our analysis on this simplifying case. Consider therefore an investor with an infinite time horizon ($T = \infty$) with preferences given by[22]

$$U(C, t) = \exp(-\rho t)V(C) \tag{6.31}$$

for $C = C(t)$, where (a) $V'(C) > 0$ and $V''(C) < 0$ for $C \geq 0$; (b) ρ is sufficiently large to satisfy the transversality condition;[23] and (c) $V'(C) \leq M < \infty$ for all $C \geq 0$ and some fixed number M. Conditions (a) and (b) ensure the existence of an optimal policy. Condition (c) implies that, for each t, there exists a level of wealth $W^+(t) > 0$ such that $C^*(t) = 0$ for $W(t) \leq W^+(t)$. From (a), (b), and (c), we can posit with no loss in

---

22　As shown in Theorem 5.6, ρ can also be interpreted as the "force of mortality" for an investor with no time preference and no bequest motive but who faces an uncertain date of death.

23　The general transversality condition is given by (4.39). See also condition (2.6) in Karatzas et al. (1986, p. 264) for the case of log-normally distributed asset returns.

generality that $V(0) = 0$ and therefore that $V(C) > 0$ for $C > 0$.[24]

As in Sections 5.5 and 5.6, we assume throughout this section that asset returns are jointly log-normally distributed. Hence, from Theorem 5.2 and its corollary, all investors' optimal portfolios can be generated by combinations of a mean–variance-efficient portfolio and the riskless security. From (6.4) in Section 6.2, the growth-optimum portfolio strategy is mean–variance efficient. Moreover, for the posited constant investment opportunity set, we have from (6.5) that $X(t + \tau)/X(t)$ is log-normally distributed for all t and $\tau > 0$. Therefore, without loss of generality, we can assume that all investors select their optimal portfolios from just two assets: the growth-optimum portfolio and the riskless security. Thus, our model is identical with that in Section 4.6 (with $\alpha = \mu^2 + r$ and $\sigma^2 = \mu^2$) except, of course, that we now take account of the nonnegativity constraints on consumption and wealth.

From (4.34) and (4.35), we can transform the indirect utility function so that the equation of optimality can be written as

$$0 = \max_{\{C, w\}} \{V(C) - \rho J(W) + J'(W)[(w\mu^2 + r)W - C] + \tfrac{1}{2}J''(W)\mu^2 w^2 W^2\}$$

(6.32)

subject to the constraint $C \geqslant 0$ and the boundary conditions

$$J(0) = 0 \qquad\qquad (6.32a)$$

and

$$\lim_{t \to \infty} E\{\exp(-\rho t)\, J[W(t)]\} = 0 \qquad\qquad (6.32b)$$

where the indirect utility function is $\exp(-\rho t)J(W)$ and J is solely a function of W, independent of explicit time or asset prices.[25] Hence, the Bellman equation reduces to an ordinary differential equation.

Rather than solve for the optimal strategies using Kuhn–Tucker multipliers as in Section 6.2, equation (6.21), we use a different method that exploits the special structure of (6.32). By inspection of (6.32), the optimal consumption and portfolio rules will depend only on current wealth (i.e. for $W = W(t)$, $C^*(t) = C^*(W)$ and $w^*(t)W = w^*(W)W$). Hence, from condition (c) of (6.31), W^+, the critical level of wealth such that

---

24   From these continuity and boundedness conditions, $V(0)$ is finite. For $\rho > 0$, $E_t\{\int_t^\infty \exp(-\rho s)[V(C) - V(0)]\, ds\} = E_t\{\int_t^\infty \exp(-\rho s)V(C)\, ds\} - \exp(-\rho t)V(0)/\rho$, and hence the optimal rules for either criterion will be identical. For $\rho = 0$, technically, we cannot make this shift, because existence requires that $V(0) < 0$. However, as we shall see, if an optimal solution exists, it will be the set of optimal policies that obtain in the limit as $\rho \to 0$.

25   Condition (6.32a) ensures that $W(t) \geqslant 0$ and that $W(t) = 0$ is an absorbing state. From the boundary condition for (6.21), $\exp(-\rho t)J(0) = \int_t^\infty \exp(-\rho s) \times V(0)\, ds = 0$, because $V(0) = 0$. Equation (6.32b) is the transversality condition.

$C^*(W) = 0$ for $0 \le W \le W^+$, is a constant, independent of time or asset prices. With this condition on W^+, we can express (6.32) as two linked but unconstrained optimization problems. Define $J_1(W) \equiv J(W)$ for $0 \le W \le W^+$ and $J_2(W) \equiv J(W)$ for $W > W^+$. The existence of a dynamic programming solution in (6.32) requires that J be twice continuously differentiable for $0 < W < \infty$. From condition (c) of (6.31), $0 < W^+ < \infty$. Thus, we require that J_1 and J_2 satisfy

$$J_1(W^+) = J_2(W^+)$$
$$J_1'(W^+) = J_2'(W^+)$$
$$J_1''(W^+) = J_2''(W^+) \tag{6.33}$$

Because $C^*(W) = 0$ for $W \le W^+$ and $V(0) = 0$, we have from (6.32) for $0 \le W \le W^+$

$$0 = \max_{\{w\}} \left[-\rho J_1(W) + J_1'(W)(w\mu^2 + r)W + \tfrac{1}{2}J_1''(W)\mu^2 w^2 W^2 \right] \tag{6.34}$$

subject to $J_1(0) = 0$ and (6.33). Because $C^*(W) > 0$ for $W > W^+$, $J_2(W)$ will satisfy (6.32) with (6.32a) replaced by (6.33).

The first-order condition for (6.34) is given by

$$0 = J_1'(W)\mu^2 W + J_1''(W)\mu^2 W^2 w^* \tag{6.35}$$

For $\mu^2 > 0$ and $W > 0$, we have from (6.35) that, for $0 < W \le W^+$,

$$w^* = -\frac{J_1'(W)}{J_1''(W)W} \tag{6.36}$$

In the usual dynamic programming fashion, we substitute for w^* in (6.34) from (6.36) to arrive at the Bellman equation

$$0 = -\rho J_1(W) + rWJ_1'(W) - \frac{1}{2}\frac{\mu^2[J_1'(W)]^2}{J_1''(W)} \tag{6.37}$$

For $\rho > 0$, two solutions to (6.37) are given by[26]

---

26   As in footnote 24, for $\rho = 0$, V cannot be normalized so that $V(0) = 0$. Hence, in that case, replace $-\rho J_1(W)$ with $V(0)$ (< 0) in (6.34) and $J_1(0) = -\infty$. The solution is $J_1(W) = [-2V(0)/(2r + \mu^2)] \log (W/W^+) + J_2(W^+)$ and, from (6.36), $w^* = 1$.

$$J_1(W) = J_2(W^+)(W/W^+)^{\beta_i} \qquad i = 1,2 \tag{6.38}$$

where

$$\beta_1 \equiv \frac{r + \rho + \mu^2/2 - [(r + \rho + \mu^2/2)^2 - 4r\rho]^{1/2}}{2r}$$

and

$$\beta_2 \equiv \frac{r + \rho + \mu^2/2 + [(r + \rho + \mu^2/2)^2 - 4r\rho]^{1/2}}{2r}$$

For $\rho > 0$ and $\mu^2 > 0$, $0 < \beta_1 < 1$ and $\beta_2 > 1$.[27]

To determine which of the solutions in (6.38) is the optimum, we apply the boundary conditions from (6.34). Both solutions satisfy $J_1(0) = 0$ and $J_1(W^+) = J_2(W^+)$. By differentiation of (6.38),

$$J_1'(W) = J_2(W^+)(W/W^+)^{\beta_i - 1}(\beta_i/W^+)$$

and

$$J_1''(W) = J_2(W^+)(W/W^+)^{\beta_i - 2}[\beta_i(\beta_i - 1)]/(W^+)^2$$

Evaluating these derivatives at $W = W^+$ and applying the conditions in (6.33), we have that, for $i = 1,2$,

$$\frac{J_2'(W^+)}{J_2(W^+)} = \frac{\beta_i}{W^+} \tag{6.39a}$$

and

$$\frac{J_2''(W^+)}{J_2(W^+)} = \frac{\beta_i(\beta_i - 1)}{(W^+)^2} \tag{6.39b}$$

From (6.31), $V(C) \geq 0$, $V'(C) > 0$ and $V''(C) < 0$ for $C \geq 0$. Therefore, for $W \geq W^+$, $J_2(W)$ is a positive, strictly increasing and concave function. Because both β_1 and β_2 are positive, each solution in (6.38) is consistent with $J_2'(W^+)/J_2(W^+) > 0$ and (6.39a). However, only $0 < \beta_i < 1$ is consistent with $J_2''(W^+)/J_2(W^+) < 0$ and (6.39b). Hence, the optimal solution J for $0 \leq W \leq W^+$ is given by

---

27 For $r = 0$, $\beta_1 = 2\rho/(2\rho + \mu^2)$ and β_2 $(= \infty)$ does not exist.

$$J_1(W) = J_2(W^+)(W/W^+)^\beta \tag{6.40}$$

where $\beta \equiv \{r + \rho + \mu^2/2 - [(r + \rho + \mu^2/2)^2 - 4r\rho]^{1/2}\}/2r$ for $r > 0$ and $\beta \equiv 2\rho/(2\rho + \mu^2)$ for $r = 0$.

To determine J for $W > W^+$, we have from (6.39a) and (6.39b) that $J_2(W)$ satisfies (6.32) subject to (6.32b) and the conditions

$$J_2'(W^+)/J_2(W^+) = \beta/W^+ \quad \text{and} \quad J_2''(W^+)/J_2'(W^+) = (\beta - 1)/W^+$$

The seemingly "extra" boundary condition is required to uniquely determine both $J_2(W)$ *and* the optimal boundary point W^+.

We summarize our findings for optimal portfolio behavior in the region where the nonnegativity constraint on consumption is binding in the following theorem and its corollaries.

Theorem 6.4

If asset returns are jointly log-normally distributed and if an investor's preferences satisfy (6.31), then for every t such that $C^*(t) = 0$, the optimal portfolio strategy is a constant-proportion levered combination of the growth-optimum portfolio and the riskless security, with fraction $w^*(t) = 1/(1 - \beta) > 1$ allocated to the growth-optimum portfolio and fraction $1 - w^*(t) = -\beta/(1 - \beta) < 0$ in the riskless security.

PROOF

$C^*(t) = 0$ if and only if $0 \leq W(t) \leq W^+$. Hence, $J = J_1[W(t)]$ as given in (6.40). By differentiation of (6.40) twice and substitution of J_1' and J_1'' in (6.36), we have that for $0 \leq W(t) \leq W^+$, $w^*(t) = 1/(1 - \beta)$. From the definition of β in (6.40), β is a constant such that $0 < \beta < 1$. Hence, $w^*(t)$ is a constant greater than unity. Thus the fraction invested in the riskless security is $1 - w^*(t) < 0$.   QED

To determine the investor's optimal allocations among individual risky assets under the hypothesized conditions of Theorem 6.4, we have that, for $0 \leq W(t) \leq W^+$,

$$w_k^*(t) = \frac{w_k^g(t)}{1 - \beta}$$

$$= \sum_1^m \frac{v_{kj}(\alpha_j - r)}{1 - \beta} \quad k = 1,\ldots,m \tag{6.41}$$

where $w_k^g(t)$ is given in (6.1). By inspection of (6.41) and the definition of β in (6.40), when the nonnegativity constraint on consumption is binding, the optimal portfolio fractions depend only on the investment opportunity set $\{\alpha_j, r, \sigma_{ij}, i, j = 1,...,m\}$ and the investor's rate of time preference ρ. The portfolio allocations do not depend on the functional form of $V(C)$, the investor's current wealth, explicit time, or W^+. As an immediate consequence, we have the following.

Corollary 6.4a

If the hypothesized conditions of Theorem 6.4 obtain, then, at each t, all investors with the same constant rate of time preference, and for whom $C^*(t) = 0$, will (a) hold the identical optimal portfolio fractions and (b) choose their portfolios "as if" they had in common the isoelastic utility function $U(C, t) = 0$ and $B(W, T) = W^\beta/\beta$ for any $T > t$.

PROOF

As noted, β depends only on the investment opportunity set and ρ. From Theorem 6.4, if $C^*(t) = 0$, then $w^*(t) = 1/(1 - \beta)$. Thus, all investors with the same rate of time preference ρ, and for whom $C^*(t) = 0$, will choose at time t the same portfolio allocation, given by (6.41). From (4.29), an investor with preferences such that $U(C, t) = 0$ and $B(W, T) = W^\gamma/\gamma$, $\gamma < 1$, for some $T > t$, will hold optimal portfolio fraction in the risky asset, $w^*(t) = (\alpha - r)/\sigma^2(1 - \gamma)$, independently of $W(t)$, t, or T. Here, $\mu^2 = \alpha - r$ and $\sigma^2 = \mu^2$. Hence, for $\gamma = \beta$, such an investor's optimal portfolio allocation is $w^*(t) = 1/(1 - \beta)$.   QED

Corollary 6.4b

If the hypothesized conditions of Theorem 6.4 obtain and if an investor's optimal consumption satisfies $C^*(s) = 0$ for $\bar{t} \leq s \leq t^+$, then the investor's wealth at time s, $\bar{t} \leq s \leq t^+$, can be expressed as

$$W(s) = W(\bar{t}) \exp\left[-(a - 1)\left(r + \frac{a\mu^2}{2}\right)(s - \bar{t})\right]\left[\frac{X(s)}{X(\bar{t})}\right]^a$$

where $a \equiv 1/(1 - \beta) > 1$ and β is as defined in Theorem 6.4.

PROOF

By hypothesis, for $s \in [\bar{t}, t^+]$, $C^*(s) = 0$ and therefore from Theorem 6.4, $w^*(s) = 1/(1 - \beta) \equiv a$, for all $s \in [\bar{t}, t^+]$. Hence, from (6.2), the dynamics of the investor's wealth can be written as $dW/W = a \, dX/X + (1 - a)r \, dt = (a\mu^2 + r) \, dt + a\mu \, dz$ for $\bar{\imath} \leq s \leq t^+$. Using Itô's lemma, we can integrate this stochastic differential equation to obtain $W(s)/W(\bar{\imath}) = \exp[-(a - 1)(r + a\mu^2/2)(s - \bar{\imath})][X(s)/X(\bar{\imath})]^a$ for $\bar{\imath} \leq s \leq t^+$.   QED

Corollary 6.4c

If the hypothesized conditions of Theorem 6.4 obtain, if the investor's initial wealth $W(0)$ is positive, and if $X(0) > 0$, then, for all $t \geq 0$, (a) $W(t) = 0$ only if $X(t) = 0$ and (b) prob$\{W(t) > 0 | W(0) > 0\} = 1$.

PROOF

By hypothesis, $W(0) > 0$, and from (6.31), $W^+ > 0$. Trivially, for all t such that $W(t) \geq W^+$, $W(t) > 0$. Because the investor's optimally invested wealth has a continuous sample path and because $W(0) > 0$, if $W(t) = 0$ for some $t > 0$, then there exists a time $\bar{\imath}$ such that $W(\bar{\imath}) = \overline{W}$ and $W(s) \leq \overline{W}$ for all $s \in [\bar{\imath}, t]$ where $0 < \overline{W} < W^+$. Hence, the hypothesized conditions of Corollary 6.4b are satisfied for $s \in [\bar{\imath}, t]$. By inspection of the formula for $W(t)$ in Corollary 6.4b, $W(t) = 0$ only if $X(t) = 0$, which proves (a). From Section 6.2, equation (6.3), prob$\{X(t) > 0 | X(0) > 0\} = 1$. Hence, from (a), prob$\{W(t) > 0 | W(0) > 0\} = 1$, which proves (b).[28]
                                                                        QED

From Corollary 6.4c, we have that all investors with preferences that satisfy (6.31) will choose optimal portfolio strategies that do not risk ruin, and hence the probability of bankruptcy (i.e. $W(t) = 0$) is zero. Therefore, even when the nonnegativity constraint on consumption is binding, the nonnegativity constraint on wealth is not. This no-bankruptcy result was shown to obtain in the special case of infinite-lived investors and a constant investment opportunity set.[29] However, as proved in Theorem 16.2, it will also obtain for finite-lived investors facing relatively general stochastic investment opportunity sets.[30]

---

28   An alternative proof follows from (b) of Corollary 6.4a. Because the isoelastic utility function with the optimal portfolio policy $w^*(t) = 1/(1 - \beta)$ has infinite marginal utility at $W = 0$, this policy must have the feature that $W(t) > 0$, almost certainly, for all t.
29   Karatzas et al. (1986, p. 265, 3a) show this result. Cox and Huang (1989b, Proposition 3.1) derive the result for finite-lived investors.
30   The proof requires that $r(t) > -\infty$ and $0 < \mu^2(t)$ for all t. Although the purpose of the analysis is not to investigate general equilibrium pricing, the no-bankruptcy result simplifies the proofs of existence and uniqueness of equilibrium prices. Because all indirect utility functions will exhibit infinite marginal utility at $W = 0$, "corner" solutions with $W = 0$ are ruled out.

Having formally established the properties of optimal portfolios when the nonnegativity constraint on consumption is binding, we now try our hand at providing some intuition as to why Theorem 6.4 and its corollaries obtain, this to be followed by that promised analysis of the HARA utility functions.

Define the random variable time interval $\Delta \hat{t}$, conditional on $W(t) = W$, by

$$\Delta \hat{t} \equiv \inf\{s \in [0, \infty) \text{ such that } W(t + s) \geq W^+\} \qquad (6.42)$$

$\Delta \hat{t}$ is thus the first-passage time interval from time t such that $C^*(t + s) = 0$ for $0 \leq s < \Delta \hat{t}$ and $C^*(t + \Delta \hat{t}) > 0$. Obviously, for $W > W^+$, $C^*(t) > 0$ and $\Delta \hat{t} = 0$. For $W < W^+$, $\Delta \hat{t}$ is a nondegenerate random time interval whose distribution depends on W and the investor's portfolio strategy between t and $t + \Delta \hat{t}$. For each investor with $C^*(t) = 0$ and for all s, $0 \leq s < \Delta \hat{t}$, $C^*(t + s) = 0$, and hence, $V[C^*(t + s)] = 0$. Therefore, at time t, the indirect utility function for such an investor can be expressed as

$$\exp(-\rho t)J(W) = \max_{\{w\}} E_t\{\exp[-\rho(t + \Delta \hat{t})]J_2(W^+)\}$$

$$= \exp(-\rho t) J_2(W^+) \max_{\{w\}} E_t\{\exp(-\rho\Delta \hat{t})\} \qquad (6.43)$$

because $J_2(W^+) > 0$ and is nonstochastic. By inspection, the maximizing strategy in (6.43) depends at most on W and W^+.

Clearly, the strategy that maximizes $E_t\{\exp(-\rho\Delta \hat{t})\}$ also minimizes $E_t\{[1 - \exp(-\rho\Delta \hat{t})]/\rho\}$ for $\rho > 0$. However, the latter representation has the rather intuitive interpretation of minimizing the expected time until optimal consumption is positive, where time is measured by the appropriate clock. To see this, consider first the limiting case as $\rho \to 0$. In the limit, the criterion becomes min $E_t\{\Delta \hat{t}\}$. For $\rho > 0$, imagine a clock that keeps time according to the time scale $\tau(\rho)$, where

$$\tau(\rho) \equiv [1 - \exp(-\rho t)]/\rho \qquad (6.44)$$

Note that $\tau(\rho)$ has the dimension of time and that $d\tau(\rho) = \exp(-\rho t)dt$ $= [1 - \rho\tau(\rho)]\,dt > 0$. Initially, $\tau(\rho) = t = 0$ and $d\tau(\rho) = dt$. However, as time passes, the $\tau(\rho)$ clock moves ever more slowly as measured against ordinary-clock time. Indeed, for $t = \infty$, $\tau(\rho) = 1/\rho$. Moreover, the larger is ρ, the slower is the $\tau(\rho)$ clock.

From (6.42) and (6.44), we can express the first-passage time interval until optimal consumption is positive in terms of $\tau(\rho)$-clock time as

$$\Delta \bar{\tau}(\rho) \equiv \frac{1 - \exp[-\rho(t + \Delta \hat{t})]}{\rho} - \frac{1 - \exp(-\rho t)}{\rho}$$

$$= \frac{\exp(-\rho t)[1 - \exp(-\rho \Delta \hat{t})]}{\rho} \qquad (6.45)$$

Theorem 6.5

If $\{w^+(t)\}$ is the portfolio strategy at time t that minimizes $E_t\{\Delta \bar{\tau}(\rho)\}$ for $\rho \geq 0$ and $0 < W(t) < W^+$, then

(i) $w^+(t) = 1/(1 - \beta)$

and

(ii) $\partial w^+(t)/\partial \rho > 0$

where

$$\beta = \frac{r + \rho + \mu^2/2 - [(r + \rho + \mu^2/2)^2 - 4r\rho]^{1/2}}{2r}$$

PROOF

Define $I(W, t) \equiv \min E_t\{\Delta \bar{\tau}(\rho)\}$ for $W = W(t) < W^+$. It follows from (6.45) that $I(W, t) = \min E_t\{\int_t^T \exp(-\rho s) \, ds\}$ where $T \equiv t + \Delta \hat{t}$. By the principle of dynamic programming, $I(W, t)$ will satisfy (a)

$$0 = \min\left[\exp(-\rho t) + I_t(W, t) + I_W(W, t)(w^+\mu^2 + r)W \right.$$

$$\left. + \frac{I_{WW}(W, t)(w^+)^2\mu^2 W^2}{2} \right]$$

subject to the conditions $I(0, t) = \exp(-\rho t)/\rho$, because $\Delta \hat{t} = \infty$ if $W(t) = 0$, and $I(W^+, t) = 0$, because $\Delta \hat{t} = 0$ and $t = T$ if $W(t) = W^+$. Let $I_1(W) \equiv \exp(\rho t)I(W, t)$. By substitution into (a), we have that (b)

$$0 = \min\left\{ 1 - \rho I_1(W) + I_1'(W)[w^+\mu^2 + r]W + \frac{I_1''(W)(w^+)^2\mu^2 W^2}{2} \right\}$$

subject to $I_1(0) = 1/\rho$ and $I_1(W^+) = 0$. For $\rho = 0$,

$$I(W, t) = I_1(W) = \frac{\log(W^+/W)}{r + \mu^2/2}$$

and $w^+(t) = 1$.[31] For $\rho > 0$, define $I_2(W) \equiv 1 - \rho I_1(W)$. Multiplying (b) by -1, which changes "min" to "max," and substituting for $I_1(W)$, we have that (c)

$$0 = \max\left\{ -\rho I_2(W) + I_2'(W)[w^+\mu^2 + r]W + \frac{I_2''(W)(w^+)^2\mu^2 W^2}{2} \right\}$$

subject to $I_2(0) = 0$ and $I_2(W^+) = 1$. The first-order condition is $0 = \mu^2 W[I_2'(W) + I_2''(W)w^+W]$. The second-order condition for a maximum is $I_2''(W) < 0$ for $W > 0$. By inspection, (c) here is identical with (6.34) with $J_2(W^+) = 1$. Hence, $I_2(W)$ is given by (6.38) with $J_2(W^+) = 1$. Because $I_2''(W) < 0$, we have from (6.40) that $I_2(W) = (W/W^+)^\beta$ and $w^+(t) = 1/(1 - \beta)$. Note that for $\rho = 0$, $\beta = 0$, and (i) is proved.

$$\frac{\partial w^+(t)}{\partial \rho} = \frac{\partial \beta/\partial \rho}{(1 - \beta)^2}$$

From the definition of β, $\beta < 1$ for $\rho \geq 0$, and therefore,

$$\frac{\partial \beta}{\partial \rho} = \frac{1 - \beta}{[(r + \rho + \mu^2/2)^2 - 4r\rho]^{1/2}} > 0$$

Hence, $\partial w^+(t)/\partial \rho > 0$, which proves (ii). QED

As indicated by (6.43), we have from Theorems 6.4 and 6.5 that the optimal portfolio strategy when the nonnegativity constraint on consumption is binding, $\{w^*(t)\}$, is identical with the strategy that minimizes the expected time until optimal consumption becomes positive, with time measured with a $\tau(\rho)$ clock. Investors with the same rate of time preference have the same $\tau(\rho)$ clock. Because the minimizing strategy, $\{w^+(t)\}$, is independent of either current wealth or the "target" level of wealth W^+, all such investors will follow the same portfolio strategy.

Although the proof of Theorem 6.5 analyzed the optimal strategies in ordinary-clock time, one can formulate the investor's entire optimal

---

31 As indicated in footnote 8, we thus have that for log-normally-distributed asset returns, the growth-optimum portfolio policy is the optimal solution to the problem: given initial wealth $W(0)$ and any "target" level of wealth $W^+ > W(0)$, find the portfolio strategy that minimizes $E_0\{\Delta t\}$ where Δt is the first time that wealth equals W^+.

consumption–investment problem using $\tau(\rho)$-clock time. Suppose each investor uses a $\tau(\rho)$ clock with his own rate of time preference to keep track of time. So, for example, the passage of one "hour" according to one investor's clock could correspond to the passage of a "day" according to a less impatient (i.e. smaller ρ) investor's clock. From Cox and Miller (1968, pp. 228–9), a Wiener process measured in $\tau(\rho)$-clock and ordinary-clock times satisfies the relations

$$dz'[\tau(\rho)] = \exp\left(-\frac{\rho t}{2}\right) dz(t) \tag{6.46a}$$

and

$$dz(t) = \frac{dz'[\tau(\rho)]}{[1 - \rho\tau(\rho)]^{1/2}} \tag{6.46b}$$

where $z'[\tau(\rho)]$ is the Wiener process in $\tau(\rho)$-clock time. Hence, if asset-return dynamics can be described by diffusion processes in ordinary-clock time, then they are also described by diffusion processes in $\tau(\rho)$-clock time. Therefore, if a prime on a variable denotes its measurement in $\tau(\rho)$-clock time, then the dynamics of the investor's wealth can be written as

$$dW' = \{[w'(\mu')^2 + r']W' - C'\} \, d\tau + w'\mu'W' \, dz'(\tau) \tag{6.47}$$

where $\mu' \equiv \mu/(1 - \rho\tau)^{1/2}$, $r' \equiv r/(1 - \rho\tau)$ and $C'(\tau) \equiv C(t)/(1 - \rho\tau)$. The investor's program objective, $\max E_0\{\int_0^\infty \exp(-\rho t)V[C(t)] \, dt\}$, is transformed into[32]

$$\max E_0'\left\{ \int_0^T V\left[\frac{(T - \tau)C'(\tau)}{T}\right] d\tau \right\} \tag{6.48}$$

where $T \equiv 1/\rho$ and $1 - \rho\tau = (T - \tau)/T$.

Although all investors have infinite time horizons in ordinary-clock time, from (6.48) we see that in the appropriate clock time these horizons

---

32 This transformation can be applied more generally for investor preferences of the form $U(C, t) = g(t)V(C)$ provided that $g(t) > 0$ and $\int_0^\infty g(s) \, ds \equiv T < \infty$. τ-clock time is measured by $\tau \equiv \int_0^t g(s) \, ds$. Because $g > 0$, τ and t are in one-to-one correspondence, and hence we can define $f(\tau) \equiv g(t)$. The program objective can be expressed in τ-clock time as $\max E_0'\{\int_0^T V[f(\tau)C'(\tau)] \, d\tau\}$, a finite-horizon program. Provided that $T < \infty$, the validity of this transformation does not require that $g(t)$ be monotonic in t. Although the formulation in τ-clock time will not in general make the determination of explicit solutions any easier, it may be a helpful form to derive conditions for existence of an optimal solution, because T is finite.

become finite and have different durations depending on each investor's rate of time preference. In this sense, investors with different rates of impatience have different time horizons. Moreover, because $dT/d\rho < 0$, the greater the rate of time preference is, the shorter is the effective horizon.

For an investor with $0 < W(0) < W^+$ (and hence $C^*(0) = 0$), the optimal portfolio strategy formulated in $\tau(\rho)$-clock time can be expressed as the solution to

$$\min E_0'\{\min[\Delta\tilde{\tau}(\rho), T]\} \qquad (6.49)$$

By inspection of (6.49), the investor weights all $\Delta\tilde{\tau}(\rho)$ values greater than or equal to T as if they were T. This indifference follows because, once $\Delta\tilde{\tau}(\rho)$ exceeds his time horizon, the implications for his optimal consumption program are the same: he consumes nothing. The larger is ρ, the smaller is T and the shorter is the time interval at which the investor becomes indifferent. The greater degree of concavity in (6.49) induced by this truncation of the distribution for $\Delta\tilde{\tau}(\rho)$ reflects an urgency to get wealth up to the W^+ level before it does not matter. Perhaps this provides an intuitive explanation of why investors with greater temporal impatience for consumption choose more aggressive investment strategies (i.e. $\partial w^+(t)/\partial\rho > 0$).

In summary, explicit solutions have been derived for the optimal portfolio behavior of investors with preferences given by (6.31) and for whom the nonnegativity constraint on consumption is currently binding. Hence, to determine the global optimal consumption and portfolio behavior for such investors, (6.32) need only be solved in the region $W^+ \leqslant W < \infty$. To do so, the boundary condition (6.32a) is replaced with the conditions

$$\frac{J'(W^+)}{J(W^+)} = \frac{\beta}{W^+} \qquad (6.50a)$$

and

$$\frac{J''(W^+)}{J'(W^+)} = -\frac{(1 - \beta)}{W^+} \qquad (6.50b)$$

with $\beta = \{r + \rho + \mu^2/2 - [(r + \rho + \mu^2/2)^2 - 4r\rho]^{1/2}\}/2r$. These two conditions are sufficient to uniquely determine $J(W)$ and W^+. Because $W^+ \geqslant 0$ and $C^*(t) \geqslant 0$ for $W(t) \geqslant W^+$, there is no need to explicitly impose the nonnegativity constraints on consumption and wealth. Therefore, (6.32), subject to (6.50a) and (6.50b), can be solved as an unconstrained optimization problem as in Chapters 4 and 5.

The HARA family of utility functions defined in Section 5.6 can be expressed in terms of (6.31) as

$$V(C) = \frac{1 - \gamma}{\gamma} \left(\frac{\zeta C}{1 - \gamma} + \eta \right)^{\gamma} \qquad (6.51)$$

subject to the parameter constraints $\gamma \neq 1$; $\zeta > 0$; $\eta > 0$ for $\gamma > 1$; $\eta = 1$ if $\gamma = -\infty$; and the domain of C restricted so that $\zeta C/(1 - \gamma) + \eta > 0$. To ensure that $C = 0$ falls within this domain and that $V'(0)$ is finite, as required by condition (c) of (6.31), we consider only those HARA functions with $\eta > 0$.

Let $\delta \equiv 1/(1 - \gamma)$ so that $0 \leq \delta < \infty$ for $\gamma < 1$ and $-\infty < \delta < 0$ for $1 < \gamma < \infty$. Define $q(\delta) \equiv r/[r - (r - \rho - \mu^2/2)\delta - \delta^2 \mu^2/2]$. Provided that the parameter values satisfy the condition that[33]

$$0 < q(\delta) < \infty \qquad (6.52a)$$

we have from (5.48) and (5.49) that the unconstrained optimal consumption and portfolio policies for $T = \infty$ can be written as

$$C_u^*(t) = \frac{r}{q(\delta)} W(t) + \frac{\eta}{\zeta q(\delta)} \frac{1 - q(\delta)}{\delta} \qquad \text{for } W(t) < \overline{W}$$

$$= r\overline{W} \qquad \text{for } W(t) \geq \overline{W} \qquad (6.52b)$$

and

$$w_u^*(t)W(t) = \delta W(t) + \frac{\eta}{\zeta r} \qquad \text{for } W(t) < \overline{W}$$

$$= 0 \qquad \text{for } W(t) \geq \overline{W} \qquad (6.52c)$$

where $\overline{W}$ is the satiation level of wealth defined in (6.11). Hence, $\overline{W} = -\eta/\delta\zeta r$ for $\delta < 0$ and $\overline{W} = \infty$ for $\delta \geq 0$.

Using the Cox–Huang technique of Section 6.2, we now determine the optimal policies subject to the nonnegativity constraints on consumption and wealth. From (6.51), $U_C(C, t) = \zeta \exp(-\rho t)[\zeta C/(1 - \gamma) + \eta]^{\gamma - 1}$.

---

33   For $\delta > 0$ (i.e. $-\infty < \gamma < 1$), (6.52a) implies satisfaction of the transversality condition given in (4.40), which is also required for a constrained optimal solution to exist. For $\delta < 0$ (i.e. $\gamma > 1$), violation of (6.52a) implies that the optimal solution is to consume at the satiation level of consumption, $\eta(\gamma - 1)/\zeta$, until wealth is exhausted and consume nothing thereafter.

From (6.14a) and (6.16a), the investor's optimal consumption path can be written as

$$C^*(t) = G[X(t), P(t), t]$$

$$= \frac{\max\{0, [\zeta y(t)/\lambda_1 y(0)]^\delta - \eta\}}{\zeta \delta} \tag{6.53}$$

where $y(t) \equiv \exp(-\rho t)X(t)$, and by inspection, $G = G[y(t)]$ does not otherwise depend on $P(t)$ or explicit time. By inspection of (6.53), $y^+ \equiv \lambda_1 y(0)\eta^{1/\delta}/\zeta$ is the critical value such that $C^*(t) = 0$ for $y(t) \leq y^+$ and $C^*(t) > 0$ for $y(t) > y^+$.

From Section 6.2, equation (6.19), the investor's optimally invested wealth will satisfy $W(t) = F[X(t), t]$ where F is defined in (6.17). From Theorem 6.3, F satisfies[34]

$$0 = \tfrac{1}{2}\mu^2 X^2 F_{xx} + rXF_x + F_t - rF + G \tag{6.54}$$

The boundary conditions for (6.54) are determined as follows. From Corollary 6.4c, $W(t) = 0$ only if $X(t) = 0$, and from (6.26), $\partial F/\partial X > 0$ for $0 < F < \overline{W}$. Hence

$$F(0, t) = 0 \tag{6.54a}$$

From the condition $\partial F/\partial X > 0$ for $0 < F < \overline{W}$, we have that, as $X \to \infty$, $F \to \overline{W}$. But as $W \to \overline{W}$ the optimal consumption policy approaches from below the unconstrained optimal policy given by (6.52b). Therefore, from (6.52b) with $W = F$,

$$\lim_{X \to \infty} \left[\frac{F(X, t)}{\overline{W}} \right] = 1 \qquad \text{for } \delta < 0$$

$$\lim_{X \to \infty} \left[\frac{G(X, t)}{F(X, t)} \right] = \frac{r}{q(\delta)} \qquad \text{for } \delta \geq 0 \tag{6.54b}$$

Define $f \equiv F[\exp(\rho t)y, t]$. Noting that G depends only on y, we have by inspection of (6.54) and its boundary conditions that $f = f(y)$, independent of t. By substitution of $\exp(\rho t)y$ for X and f for F, (6.54) can be rewritten as an ordinary differential equation given by

$$0 = \tfrac{1}{2}\mu^2 y^2 f''(y) + (r - \rho)yf'(y) - rf(y) + G(y) \tag{6.55}$$

---

34 Unlike in the general case of Theorem 6.3, F does not depend on $P(t)$ here because the investment opportunity set is assumed to be constant over time.

subject to

$$f(0) = 0 \tag{6.55a}$$

and

$$\lim_{y \to \infty} \left[\frac{f(y)}{\overline{W}} \right] = 1 \qquad \text{for } \delta < 0$$

$$\lim_{y \to \infty} \left[\frac{G(y)}{f(y)} \right] = \frac{r}{q(\delta)} \qquad \text{for } \delta \geqslant 0 \tag{6.55b}$$

The general homogeneous (i.e. $G = 0$) solution to (6.55) can be expressed as

$$f_h(y) = Ay^a + By^b \tag{6.56}$$

where

$$a \equiv \frac{-(r - \rho - \mu^2/2) + [(r - \rho - \mu^2/2)^2 + 2r\mu^2]^{1/2}}{\mu^2} > 0$$

$$b \equiv -\frac{(r - \rho - \mu^2/2) + [(r - \rho - \mu^2/2)^2 + 2r\mu^2]^{1/2}}{\mu^2} < 0$$

and A and B are arbitrary constants. If $\psi(\lambda) \equiv \mu^2\lambda^2/2 + (r - \rho - \mu^2/2) \times \lambda - r$, then $\psi(a) = \psi(b) = 0$, and $\psi(\lambda) = (\mu^2/2)(\lambda - a)(\lambda - b)$. For $\rho > 0$, $a > 1$, and for $\rho = 0$, $a = 1$.

In the region $0 \leqslant y \leqslant y^+$, $G(y) = 0$, and $f(y) = f_h(y)$ for the appropriate selection of A and B. From (6.55a), $f(0) = 0$, which implies that $B = 0$ because $b < 0$. Replacing A by $f(y^+)(y^+)^{-a}$, where $f(y^+)$ is a number yet to be determined, we have that

$$f(y) = f(y^+)(y/y^+)^a \quad \text{for } 0 \leqslant y \leqslant y^+ \tag{6.57}$$

By the definitions of q and ψ, we have that $q(\delta) = -r/\psi(\delta)$. For existence of a nontrivial optimal policy, the parameters δ, r, μ^2, and ρ must satisfy (6.52a). It follows that, for this admissible set, $\psi(\delta) < 0$. Therefore, $b < \delta < a$.

In the region $y^+ < y$ in which $G(y) > 0$, we have from (6.53) and (6.55) that, for $b < \delta < a$, the solution for f is given by

$$f(y) = A'y^a + B'y^b + \frac{\eta[q(\delta)(y/y^+)^\delta - 1]}{\zeta r \delta} \tag{6.58}$$

where A' and B' are constants to be determined. Because $a > \delta > b$, the boundedness condition (6.55b) is satisfied if and only if $A' = 0$. From Theorem 6.3, $f(y)$ is twice continuously differentiable and therefore, from (6.57), $f'(y^+)/f(y^+) = a/y^+$ and $f''(y^+)/f'(y^+) = (a-1)/y^+$. Imposing these conditions on (6.58), we have that

$$B' = \frac{-\eta q(\delta)}{b\zeta r}\frac{a-\delta}{a-b}(y^+)^{-b}$$

$$= \frac{\eta a}{\zeta r(a-b)(\delta-b)}(y^+)^{-b} > 0 \tag{6.59}$$

Substituting for B' in (6.58) and evaluating f at $y = y^+$, we have that

$$W^+ = f(y^+)$$

$$= \frac{-\eta b}{\zeta r(a-b)(a-\delta)} > 0 \tag{6.60}$$

From (6.57)–(6.60), the investor's optimally invested wealth at time t can be written as

$$f[y(t)] = W^+\left[\frac{y(t)}{y^+}\right]^a \qquad \text{for } 0 \leqslant y(t) \leqslant y^+$$

$$= W^+ + \frac{q(\delta)}{r}\left\{C^*(t) - \frac{\eta}{\zeta}\frac{(a-\delta)}{(a-b)}\frac{[y(t)/y^+]^b - 1}{b}\right\}$$

$$\text{for } y^+ < y(t) \tag{6.61}$$

where $C^*(t) = \eta\{[y(t)/y^+]^\delta - 1\}/\zeta\delta$ and $y(t) = \exp(-\rho t)X(t)$.

From (6.52b), (6.53), and (6.61), we can write the difference between the unconstrained optimal consumption rule and the constrained rule as

$$C_u^*(t) - C^*(t) = -\frac{(a-\delta)\eta}{\zeta b(a-b)} + \frac{\eta(\delta-b)}{\zeta a(a-b)}\left\{\left[\frac{y(t)}{y^+}\right]^a - 1\right\}$$

$$\text{for } 0 \leqslant W(t) \leqslant W^+$$

$$= -\frac{(a-\delta)\eta}{\zeta b(a-b)}\left[\frac{y(t)}{y^+}\right]^b \qquad \text{for } W^+ < W(t) < \overline{W} \tag{6.62}$$

where $W(t) = f[y(t)]$. Noting that $\partial W/\partial y = f'(y) > 0$, we have from (6.62) that

$$\partial[C_u^*(t) - C^*(t)]/\partial W > 0 \qquad \text{for } W(t) < W^+$$

and

$$\partial[C_u^*(t) - C^*(t)]/\partial W < 0 \qquad \text{for } W(t) > W^+$$

$C_u^*(t) - C^*(t)$ is a continuous function for all W, but it is not differentiable at $W = W^+$ because $C^*(t)$ has a kink at that point. By inspection of (6.62), we confirm for large $W(t)$ that in the limit as $W(t) \to \overline{W}$ (and $y(t) \to \infty$), the constrained solution approaches the unconstrained solution.

From Theorem 6.2, the optimal demand for the growth-optimum portfolio is given by $f'[y(t)]y(t)$. Hence, from (6.61), the optimal risky-asset holding can be written as

$$w^*(t)W(t) = aW(t) \qquad \text{for } 0 \leq W(t) \leq W^+$$

$$= \frac{\eta q(\delta)}{\zeta r(a - b)}\left\{(a - b)\left[\frac{y(t)}{y^+}\right]^\delta - (a - \delta)\left[\frac{y(t)}{y^+}\right]^b\right\}$$

$$\text{for } W^+ \leq W(t) \leq \overline{W} \qquad (6.63)$$

From (6.63), $\partial[w^*(t)W(t)]/\partial W > 0$ for $\delta \geq 0$. For $\delta < 0$, $\partial[w^*(t)W(t)]/\partial W > 0$ for $0 \leq W(t) < f(\hat{y})$ and $\partial[w^*(t)W(t)]/\partial W < 0$ for $W(t) > f(\hat{y})$ where $\hat{y} \equiv y^+[(a - b)\delta/(a - \delta)b]^{1/(b - \delta)} > y^+$ because $a > 0 > \delta > b$.

From (6.52c) and (6.63), we can write the difference between the unconstrained and constrained optimal demand functions for the growth-optimum risky asset as

$$[w_u^*(t) - w^*(t)]W(t) = \frac{\eta a}{\zeta r(a-b)}\left(1 - \frac{b}{a}\left\{1 - \left[\frac{y(t)}{y^+}\right]^a\right\}\right)$$

$$\text{for } 0 \leq W(t) \leq W^+$$

$$= \frac{\eta a}{\zeta r(a-b)}\left[\frac{y(t)}{y^+}\right]^b$$

$$\text{for } W^+ \leq W(t) \leq \overline{W} \qquad (6.64)$$

where $W(t) = f[y(t)]$. By inspection of (6.64), $[w_u^*(t) - w^*(t)]W(t) > 0$ for all $W(t) < \overline{W}$. However, $\partial\{[w_u^*(t) - w^*(t)]W(t)\}/\partial W < 0$ for all $W(t)$ and δ, and, as with optimal consumption, the optimal constrained demand equals the optimal unconstrained demand in the limit as $W(t) \to \overline{W}$ and $y(t) \to \infty$. At the critical wealth level W^+, where optimal consumption becomes positive, $w^*(t)/w_u^*(t) = -b/(a - \delta - b)$.

As noted at the outset, the constrained optimal solutions for HARA utility functions with finite time horizons are more complicated. The interested reader can find those solutions expressed as definite integrals in Cox and Huang (1989b).

6.4 GENERALIZED PREFERENCES AND THEIR IMPACT ON OPTIMAL PORTFOLIO DEMANDS

Throughout the preceding analyses, it was assumed that preferences can be represented by max $E_0\{\psi\}$ where $\psi \equiv \int_0^T U[C(t), t]\,dt + B[W(T), T]$. This assumption implies that utility depends only on age and the time path of consumption and wealth. Moreover, by inspection, $\partial^2\psi/\partial C(t)\partial C(s) = 0$ and $\partial^2\psi/\partial C(t)\partial W(T) = 0$ for all t and s, $t \neq s$. Hence, the marginal utility of consumption at each time t is unaffected by the amount of consumption at any other time s, no matter how close s is to t. I need hardly mention that such preference orderings are rather specialized. It is therefore of some interest to explore the robustness of previously derived results with respect to more general utility functions.

In this section, we begin this exploration by examining the generic case where utility is additive in time but depends on other variables in addition to current consumption, wealth, and age. This analysis is then used to investigate some specific examples of particular interest. We close with an evaluation of optimal portfolio behavior for a class of nonadditive preferences. As shown in Chapter 15, many of the structural changes in optimal portfolio behavior caused by introducing these generalized preferences are also induced by a stochastic investment opportunity set, even in the standard model with preferences described by ψ. Therefore, to isolate the impact of generalized preferences on behavior, we assume throughout the analysis here that α_i, r, and σ_{ij} are constants over time, i, $j = 1,\ldots,m$.

Let $S(t) \equiv [S_1(t),\ldots,S_M(t)]$ denote a vector of generic state variables at time t. In analogous fashion to (6.7), we now assume that the investor selects his optimal lifetime consumption program according to

$$\max E_0\left\{ \int_0^T U[C(t), S(t), t]\,dt + B[W(T), S(T), T] \right\} \qquad (6.65a)$$

with the dynamics for $S(t)$ written as the vector Itô process

$$\mathrm{d}S = F(S)\,\mathrm{d}t + G(S)\,\mathrm{d}Q \qquad (6.65b)$$

where F is the vector $(f_1, f_2, \ldots, f_M)$; G is a diagonal matrix with diagonal elements $(g_1, g_2, \ldots, g_M)$; $\mathrm{d}Q$ is the vector Wiener process $(\mathrm{d}q_1, \mathrm{d}q_2, \ldots, \mathrm{d}q_M)$; and ν_{ij} is the instantaneous correlation coefficient between $\mathrm{d}q_i$ and $\mathrm{d}q_j$, $i, j = 1, \ldots, M$. By convention, $g_i \geq 0$, $i = 1, \ldots, M$. To complete the dynamics description, we let η_{ij} denote the instantaneous correlation coefficient between $\mathrm{d}q_i$ and $\mathrm{d}z_j$ where $\mathrm{d}P_j/P_j = \alpha_j\,\mathrm{d}t + \sigma_j\,\mathrm{d}z_j$ is the return on risky asset j, $i = 1, \ldots, M$ and $j = 1, \ldots, m$.

Define $J[W(t), S(t), t] \equiv \max E_t\{\int_t^T U[C(\tau), S(\tau), \tau]\,\mathrm{d}\tau + B[W(T), S(T), T]\}$. Along the lines of the dynamic programming development in Chapters 4 and 5, we have that the optimality conditions for an investor who acts according to (6.65a) in choosing his consumption–investment program can be written as

$$
\begin{aligned}
0 = \max_{\{C,w\}} \Bigg(& U(C, S, t) + J_t + J_W\Bigg\{\Bigg[\sum_1^m w_i(\alpha_i - r) + r\Bigg]W - C\Bigg\} \\
& + \sum_1^M J_i f_i + \frac{1}{2} J_{WW} \sum_1^m \sum_1^m w_i w_j \sigma_{ij} W^2 + \sum_1^M \sum_1^m J_{iW} w_j W g_i \sigma_j \eta_{ij} \\
& + \frac{1}{2} \sum_1^M \sum_1^M J_{ij} g_i g_j \nu_{ij} \Bigg)
\end{aligned}
\qquad (6.66)
$$

subject to $J(W, S, T) = B(W, S, T)$, where subscripts on J denote partial derivatives with respect to W, t, and S_i, $i = 1, \ldots, M$. As we have already investigated the effects of imposing the nonnegativity constraints on consumption and wealth, we neglect them here.

The first-order conditions derived from (6.66) are

$$0 = U_C(C^*, S, t) - J_W(W, S, t) \qquad (6.67)$$

and

$$0 = J_W(\alpha_i - r) + J_{WW} \sum_1^m w_j^* W \sigma_{ij} + \sum_1^M J_{jW} g_j \sigma_i \eta_{ji} \qquad i = 1, \ldots, m \qquad (6.68)$$

where $C^* = C^*(W, S, t)$ and $w_i^* = w_i^*(W, S, t)$ are the optimal consumption and portfolio rules as functions of the state variables. By inspection of (6.68), the important linearity characteristic of the optimal portfolio demands derived in our preceding analyses still obtains. Hence, these demands can be solved explicitly by matrix inversion:

$$w_i^* W = Ab_i + \sum_{1}^{M} H_k h_{ki} \qquad i = 1,...,m \qquad (6.69)$$

where $b_i \equiv \Sigma_1^m v_{ij}(\alpha_j - r)$; $h_{ki} \equiv \Sigma_1^m \sigma_j g_k \eta_{kj} v_{ij}$; $\{v_{ij}\}$ are the elements of the inverse of the instantaneous variance–covariance matrix of returns $[\sigma_{ij}]$; $A \equiv -J_W/J_{WW}$; and $H_k \equiv -J_{kW}/J_{WW}$, $k = 1,...,M$. A and H_k, $k = 1,...,M$, depend on the individual investor's preferences, age, and endowment. However, b_i and h_{ki} are determined entirely by the dynamic structure for the generic state variables and asset-price returns. Hence, these "techno-logical" parameters are the same for all investors.

To analyze the impact of state-dependent preferences on optimal portfolio demands, note first that if preferences are not state dependent (i.e. $U_k \equiv \partial U/\partial S_k \equiv 0$, $k = 1,...,M$), then $H_k \equiv 0$, $k = 1,...,M$. In that case, we have from (6.69) that $w_i^* W = Ab_i$, $i = 1,...,m$, which is identical with (5.38). Hence, the important effects on the structure of optimal portfolio demands are captured by examining the "differential-demand" functions

$$\Delta d_i^* \equiv w_i^* W - Ab_i = \sum_{1}^{M} H_k h_{ki} \qquad i = 1,...,m \qquad (6.70)$$

Define a "systematic" state variable as one whose unanticipated change is correlated with the return on at least one traded asset. That is, S_k is systematic if, for some j, $\eta_{kj} \neq 0$. If S_k is such that $\eta_{kj} = 0$, $j = 1,...,m$, then S_k is called a "nonsystematic" or "idiosyncratic" state variable. If S_k is idiosyncratic, then, by definition, $h_{ki} \equiv 0$, $i = 1,...,m$. In that case, since h_{ki} is the same for all investors, it follows that, for every investor, the H_k term does not appear in the differential-demand functions (6.70). Hence, if an investor's preferences depend only on idiosyncratic state variables, then $\Delta d_i^* = 0$, $i = 1,...,m$, and the structure of his portfolio demands is indistinguishable from that of an investor with state-independent pref-erences. Thus, although idiosyncratic state variables can affect the investor's risk aversion and consumption behavior, only systematic state variables differentially affect the structure of his portfolio demands.

To develop further intuition on the effects of state-dependent prefer-ences, it is helpful to study the special case where, for each state variable, there exists a security whose instantaneous return is perfectly correlated with the unanticipated change in the state variable.[35] By renumbering securities if necessary, we choose the convention that $\eta_{kk} = 1$,

---

35 A particular example can be found in the model of Section 5.4, where the state variables are the asset prices themselves (i.e. $S_k(t) = P_k(t)$). In that case, $g_k \equiv \sigma_k P_k$, and, as we shall see, the differential-demand function in (6.71) is the same as that derived from (5.27).

$k = 1,...,M$, and assume that $M < m$. If $\eta_{kk} = 1$, then $dq_k = dz_k$, and $\eta_{kj} = \rho_{kj} = \sigma_{kj}/\sigma_k\sigma_j$, $j = 1,...,m$. It follows that $h_{ki} = (g_k/\sigma_k) \Sigma_1^m \sigma_{kj}v_{ij}$, $i = 1,...,m$. But $[v_{ij}] = [\sigma_{ij}]^{-1}$. Hence, $\Sigma_1^m \sigma_{kj}v_{ij}$ is zero if $k \neq i$ and unity if $k = i$. Therefore, in this special case, $h_{kk} = g_k/\sigma_k$ and $h_{ki} = 0$ for $k \neq i$. Substituting for h_{ki}, we can rewrite (6.70) as

$$\Delta d_i^* = H_i g_i/\sigma_i \qquad i = 1,...,M$$

$$= 0 \qquad i = M + 1,...,m \qquad (6.71)$$

By the strict concavity of U with respect to C, $J_{WW} < 0$. Hence, $H_i = -J_{iW}/J_{WW}$ is positively proportional to J_{iW}. Thus, relative to an investor with state-independent preferences but the same current level of absolute risk aversion (i.e. $A = -J_W/J_{WW}$), the investor with state-dependent preferences will hold more of asset i if $J_{iW} > 0$ and less if $J_{iW} < 0$, $i = 1,...,M$.

If $J_{iW} > 0$, then, at least locally, the investor's marginal utility for wealth increases if S_i increases and decreases if S_i declines. By holding more of asset i, the investor assures himself of larger wealth in the event that S_i increases and wealth becomes more important. He "pays" for this by accepting smaller wealth in the event that S_i decreases and wealth is less important. The behaviorial description for $J_{iW} < 0$ is, of course, just the reverse. Thus, we see that in addition to holding securities to attain a preferred risk-return tradeoff in wealth, investors also use securities to "hedge" against unanticipated and unfavorable changes in the other state variables that enter into their preferences.

As noted, optimal portfolio demand structures like (6.68)–(6.71) are also induced by a stochastic investment-opportunity set, even when investors' direct utility functions are not state dependent. In Chapter 15, we expand on this discussion of the hedging function of securities in the context of an intertemporal equilibrium theory of asset pricing. In particular, we show that the same intuition provided by the special case leading to (6.71) applies in the general case.

Under the posited condition of a constant investment-opportunity set, Corollary 5.2 implies that all investors with state-independent preferences will hold the same relative proportions of risky assets, and therefore all such optimal portfolios have perfectly positively correlated returns. By inspection of (6.69)–(6.71), it is readily apparent that w_i^*/w_j^* will not be the same for all investors here. The richer role for securities when preferences are state dependent thus causes the two-fund separation theorem of Chapter 5 to fail. However, in Chapter 15, a generalized $(m + 2)$-fund theorem is proved, and if $M < m - 1$, then nontrivial spanning of the efficient portfolio set obtains. Having analyzed the generic case of state-dependent preferences, we turn now to specific applications.

Instead of a single consumption good, suppose that there are M different consumption goods where we let $S_k(t)$ denote the price per unit of commodity k at time t. We assume that the dynamics of these prices can be expressed by (6.65b) where F and G are suitably restricted to ensure that $S_k(t) \geq 0$. The investor's lifetime preference function is written as

$$\max E_0\left\{ \int_0^T V[C_1(t),\ldots,C_M(t), t]\, dt + B[W(T), T] \right\} \qquad (6.72)$$

where $C_k(t)$ denotes his consumption of commodity k at time t and V is a strictly concave function of $(C_1,\ldots,C_M)$.

As Breeden (1979) and Fischer (1975) show, the solution for the optimal program for (6.72) can be decomposed into two parts. First, at each t, solve for the utility-maximizing consumption of individual goods, subject to an overall consumption expenditure constraint. Second, solve for the optimal level of expenditures on consumption at time t and the optimal portfolio allocation of wealth.

The first part is simply the classical static consumer-choice problem under certainty

$$\max_{\{C_1,\ldots,C_M\}} V(C_1,\ldots,C_M, t) \qquad (6.73)$$

subject to the constraint that $C(t) = \Sigma_1^M C_k S_k(t)$, where $C(t)$ is total expenditures on consumption at time t. The first-order conditions for the optimal consumption bundle $(C_1^*,\ldots,C_M^*)$ are given by

$$\frac{V_k(C_1^*,\ldots,C_M^*, t)}{S_k(t)} = \frac{V_j(C_1^*,\ldots,C_M^*, t)}{S_j(t)} \qquad k, j = 1,\ldots,M \qquad (6.74)$$

subject to $C(t) = \Sigma_1^M C_k^* S_k(t)$, where subscripts on V denote partial derivatives. It follows from (6.74) that $C_k^* = C_k^*[C(t), S(t), t]$, $k = 1,\ldots,M$.

Define $U[C(t), S(t), t] \equiv \max V(C_1,\ldots,C_M, t) = V(C_1^*,\ldots,C_M^*, t)$. U is thus the standard indirect utility function. To solve for the optimal intertemporal expenditure path, we substitute U for V in (6.72):

$$\max E_0\left\{ \int_0^T U[C(t), S(t), t]\, dt + B[W(T), S(T), T] \right\} \qquad (6.75)$$

where we have generalized the bequest function in (6.72) to permit the sensible possibility that utility of bequests will depend on both the amount bequeathed and the prices of consumption goods. By inspection of (6.75), we have transformed (6.72) into the form of (6.65), and therefore the analysis of (6.65) applies here.

Although in this application the direct utility function is not state dependent, intertemporal uncertainty about relative consumption good prices induces optimal dynamic behavior like that of an investor with a single consumption good and state-dependent preferences. As in the generic case, the investor will select his portfolio to hedge against unanticipated and unfavorable changes in commodity prices. Hence, as long as we permit state-dependent preferences, intertemporal consumption–investment behavior, without loss of generality, can be analyzed as if there is a single consumption good.

In consumer-choice models that are used to study the demand for money, it is common practice (e.g. Fischer, 1983, Section 4) to include real money balances as one of the arguments of the utility function. Because money is not consumed in the usual sense of commodities, the rationale for this specification is that money is required in a transactions technology that provides utility or labor-saving services. In general, the benefits of money in facilitating transactions may be different for different combinations of consumption goods. However, the purpose here is only to illustrate how such models can be incorporated into the framework of our general intertemporal model. Therefore, we assume for simplicity that the utility derived from money depends only on the total consumption expenditure at each point in time.

If $S(t)$, $W(t)$, and $C(t)$ are expressed in nominal terms so that the price of a unit of money is unity and if $Q(t)$ denotes the quantity of money held by the investor at time t, then to capture the optimal individual demand for money we simply modify (6.75) as follows:

$$\max E_0\left\{ \int_0^T U[C(t), Q(t), S(t), t]\, dt + B[W(T), S(T), T] \right\} \quad (6.76)$$

We can use nominal balances of money in (6.76) since $C(t)$ and $S(t)$ are already included as arguments of U. Because the nominal rate of return on money is always zero, the nominal cost of holding $Q(t)$ between t and $t+dt$ is $rQ(t)\, dt$. Hence, the nominal accumulation equation for wealth is written as

$$dW = \left\{ \left[\sum_1^m w_j(t)(\alpha_j - r) + r \right] W(t) - C(t) - rQ(t) \right\} dt$$
$$+ \sum_1^m w_j(t) W \sigma_j\, dz_j$$

Thus, to solve (6.76), we modify (6.66) accordingly. The first-order conditions (6.67) and (6.68) still apply. However, in addition, we now have that

$$0 = U_Q(C^*, Q^*, S, t) - rJ_W \qquad (6.77)$$

where $U_Q \equiv \partial U/\partial Q$ and $Q^* = Q^*(t)$ is the optimal quantity of money. From (6.67) and (6.77), it follows that C^* and Q^* satisfy $U_Q(C^*, Q^*, S, t) = rU_C(C^*, Q^*, S, t)$. If $U_Q(C, 0, S, t)$ is finite, then one must, of course, explicitly impose a nonnegativity constraint on Q. Otherwise, if the investor could "print" money without restriction, there would be an arbitrage between money and the interest-bearing riskless asset. Because the form of (6.68) remains unaffected by including money balances in the utility function, (6.69) obtains. Therefore, the inclusion of money for commodity transactions in this way does not change the basic structure of optimal portfolio demands.

Grossman and Laroque (1990) develop a different model of the transactions technology for consumer goods. They use a single-good model like that in Section 5.5 but in addition posit that the good is durable and illiquid in the sense that a transaction cost is paid whenever the good is sold. They further assume that the level of consumption services can be changed only by selling the existing durable and purchasing a new one. Although transactions costs are proportional to the value of the durable, its effect on optimal consumption behavior in the continuous-time model is like that of a fixed cost in an optimal stopping-time problem.[36] In the model with money in the utility function, the envelope condition (6.67) obtains and therefore, by Itô's lemma, the instantaneous change in optimal consumption, dC^*, is always positively correlated with the contemporaneous change in wealth, dW. In sharp contrast, optimal behavior in the Grossman–Laroque model is to maintain a constant level of consumption until wealth either rises or falls to optimally determined thresholds. If either threshold is attained, the investor changes his level of consumption services to a new target value. Thus, in their model, $dC^* = 0$ most of the time and the *instantaneous* changes in consumption and wealth are uncorrelated almost always. Hence, unlike the preceding models of this chapter and Chapters 4 and 5, the envelope condition (6.67) does not obtain even if $C^*(t) > 0$. However, Grossman and Laroque also show that optimal portfolio behavior continues to satisfy (6.68) and (6.69). Therefore, such transactions costs in consumption do not affect the basic structure of the portfolio demand functions in the continuous-time model.

The models derived from (6.65), (6.75), or (6.76), as well as the Grossman–Laroque model, maintain the assumption that lifetime preferences are additive in time and exhibit zero intertemporal complementarity of consumption (i.e. $\partial^2\psi/\partial C(t)\partial C(s) = 0$ for $t \neq s$). However, Ryder and

---

36 The structure is similar to an optimal inventory-control problem with fixed and proportional costs of adjustment. For the mathematics of such control problems, see Eastham and Hastings (1988), Harrison and Taylor (1978), and Richard (1977).

Heal (1973), Sundaresan (1985, 1989), Bergman (1985), Huang and Kreps (1985), Briys, Crouhy, and Schlesinger (1988), Detemple and Zapatero (1992), Duffie and Epstein (1992), Hindy and Huang (1992), and Constantinides (1990) have all developed versions of the continuous-time model that allow for intertemporal complementarity of consumption.

To illustrate the effects of relaxing the assumption of intertemporal separability, we analyze a model following the lines of Ryder and Heal (1973), Sundaresan (1985, 1989), and Briys, Crouhy, and Schlesinger (1988). Let $S(t)$ denote an exponentially weighted average of past consumption defined by

$$S(t) \equiv \delta \int_0^t \exp[-\delta(t - \tau)] \, C(\tau) \, d\tau \qquad (6.78)$$

where $\delta > 0$ is a constant. From (6.78), the change in S is instantaneously nonstochastic with

$$dS(t) = \delta[C(t) - S(t)] \, dt \qquad (6.79)$$

The investor's lifetime program is written as

$$\max E_0 \left\{ \int_0^T U[C(t), S(t), t] \, dt + B[W(T), S(T), T] \right\} \qquad (6.80)$$

and therefore instantaneous utility at time t depends on both current consumption and the time path of past consumption, where the more recent past consumption is given greater weight than the more distant past.

The structure of (6.80) differs from the generic version (6.65) in two ways: the instantaneous change in the state variable is nonstochastic and the dynamics of the state variable are controllable by the investor. In similar fashion to (6.66), the optimality conditions for an investor who acts according to (6.80) in choosing his consumption–investment program can be written as

$$0 = \max_{\{C, w\}} \left(U(C, S, t) + J_t + J_W \left\{ \left[\sum_1^m w_i(\alpha_i - r) + r \right] W - C \right\} \right.$$

$$\left. + J_S \delta(C - S) + \frac{1}{2} J_{WW} \sum_1^m \sum_1^m w_i w_j \sigma_{ij} W^2 \right) \qquad (6.81)$$

subject to $J(W, S, T) = B(W, S, T)$. The first-order conditions derived from (6.81) are

$$0 = U_C(C^*, S, t) - J_W(W, S, t) + \delta J_S(W, S, t) \qquad (6.82)$$

and

$$0 = J_W(\alpha_i - r) + J_{WW} \sum_1^m w_j^* W \sigma_{ij} \qquad i = 1,...,m \qquad (6.83)$$

By inspection of (6.82) and (6.67), the introduction of nonzero intertemporal complementarity of consumption leads to failure of the envelope condition that the marginal utility of current consumption equals the marginal utility of current wealth. However, by comparing (6.83) with (6.68), we see that the structure of the optimal portfolio demand functions is, once again, unaffected by this generalization of preferences.

In an early contribution to the continuous-time model with nonzero intertemporal complementarity of consumption, Meyer (1970) posits a multiplicative (rather than additive) separable form for lifetime preferences. The Meyer-type lifetime utility function can be written as

$$\left(1 - \exp\left\{ -\beta \int_0^T U[C(t), t]\, dt \right\} \right) \Big/ \beta \qquad (6.84)$$

where β is a nonnegative constant and U is a strictly concave and increasing function of C as in the additive-separable case. Note that, for $\beta = 0$, (6.84) reduces to the standard additive preference orderings of Chapters 4 and 5.

The Bellman equation for optimal decisions with preferences given by (6.84) can be derived along the lines used in Section 4.3. Define the derived utility-of-wealth function J by

$$J[W(t), t] \equiv \max E_t\left\{ 1 - \exp\left(-\beta \int_t^T U[C(\tau), \tau]\, d\tau \right) \right\} \Big/ \beta \qquad (6.85)$$

for $0 \leqslant t \leqslant T$. The Bellman principle of optimality states that, for a program to be optimal between t and T, it must be optimal between $t + h$ and T whatever rules are followed between t and $t + h$. Hence, from this principle and the properties of conditional expectations, we can rewrite (6.85) as

$$J[W(t), t] = \max E_t\left\{ 1 - \exp\left(-\beta \int_t^{t+h} U[C(\tau), \tau]\, d\tau \right)\right.$$
$$\left. \times \max E_{t+h}\left\{ \exp\left(-\beta \int_{t+h}^T U[C(\tau), \tau]\, d\tau \right) \right\}\right\} \Big/ \beta$$

$$= \max E_t \left\{ 1 + \exp\left(-\beta \int_t^{t+h} U[C(\tau), \tau]\, d\tau \right) \right.$$

$$\left. \times \left(\beta J[W(t+h), t+h] - 1 \right) \right\} \Big/ \beta \qquad (6.86)$$

where the "outer" max in (6.86) is over decisions between t and $t + h$ and the "inner" max is over decisions between $t + h$ and T, conditional on the rules followed between t and $t + h$.

If the optimal consumption path is right-continuous, then by the Mean Value Theorem there exists a $\bar{t}$, $t \le \bar{t} \le t + h$, such that $\int_t^{t+h} U[C(\tau), \tau]\, d\tau = U[C(\bar{t}), \bar{t}]h$. By Taylor's theorem,

$$\exp\{-\beta U[C(\bar{t}), \bar{t}]h\} = 1 - \beta U[C(\bar{t}), \bar{t}]h + o(h)$$

Substituting into (6.86) and rearranging terms, we have that

$$J[W(t), t] = \max E_t\{U[C(\bar{t}), \bar{t}](1 - \beta J[W(t+h), t+h])h$$

$$+ J[W(t+h), t+h]\} + o(h) \qquad (6.87)$$

As in (4.17), expand $J[W(t+h), t+h]$ in a Taylor's series around the point $(W(t), t)$ and apply the expectation operator E_t in (6.87) term by term. We can thus rewrite (6.87) as

$$J[W(t), t] = \max\left(U[C(\bar{t}), \bar{t}]\{1 - \beta J[W(t), t]\}h + J[W(t), t] + J_t[W(t), t]h \right.$$

$$+ J_W[W(t), t]\left\{ \left[\sum_1^m w_j(t)(\alpha_j - r) + r \right] W(t) - C(t) \right\}h$$

$$\left. + \frac{1}{2} J_{WW}[W(t), t] \sum_1^m \sum_1^m w_i(t)w_j(t)\sigma_{ij}W^2(t)h + o(h) \right) \qquad (6.88)$$

where subscripts on J denote partial derivatives. Subtract $J[W(t), t]$ from both sides of (6.88) and divide by h. Take the limit of the resulting equation as $h \to 0$ and (6.88) becomes

$$0 = \max_{\{C, w\}}\left(U(C, t)(1 - \beta J) + J_t + J_W\left\{ \left[\sum_1^m w_i(\alpha_i - r) + r \right] W - C \right\} \right.$$

$$\left. + \frac{1}{2} J_{WW} \sum_1^m \sum_1^m w_i w_j \sigma_{ij} W^2 \right) \qquad (6.89)$$

subject to $J(W, T) = 0$. Note that, from (6.85), $1 - \beta J > 0$ for $U < \infty$. For the limiting additive case, $\beta = 0$, (6.89) reduces to the state-independent version of (6.66). The first-order conditions derived from (6.89) are

$$0 = U_C(C^*, t)(1 - \beta J) - J_W \qquad (6.90)$$

and

$$0 = J_W(\alpha_i - r) + J_{WW} \sum_1^m w_j^* W \sigma_{ij} \qquad i = 1,\ldots,m \qquad (6.91)$$

where $C^* = C^*(W, t)$ and $w_i^* = w_i^*(W, t)$ are the optimal consumption and portfolio rules.

By inspection of (6.90), the intertemporal complementarity of consumption for $\beta > 0$ causes the envelope condition (6.67) to fail so that the marginal utility of current consumption is not equal to the marginal utility of current wealth. By differentiating (6.90) with respect to W and rearranging terms, we can write the investor's instantaneous absolute risk aversion function $A = -J_{WW}/J_W$ as

$$A = \frac{-U_{CC}(C^*, t)}{U_C(C^*, t)} \frac{\partial C^*}{\partial W} + \beta U_C(C^*, t) \qquad (6.92)$$

Hence, for the same instantaneous absolute risk aversion of consumption and the same marginal propensity to consume, the multiplicative utility investor will have a larger absolute risk aversion for investments than his additive counterpart. For the same instantaneous absolute risk aversion of both consumption and wealth, the multiplicative utility investor will have a smaller marginal propensity to consume. However, by comparing (6.91) with (6.68), we see that the structure of optimal portfolio demands is unaffected by introducing intertemporal complementarity of consumption in this fashion. In particular, from (6.69), the relative holdings of risky assets, $w_i^*/w_j^* = b_i/b_j$, will be the same whether state-independent preferences are additive or multiplicative.

If we generalize preferences in (6.84) to be state dependent by setting $U = U[C(t), S(t), t]$, it is straightforward to show that the optimality condition corresponding to (6.89) will be the same as (6.66) with an additional term, $-\beta U(C, S, t)J$. In this more general case, (6.90) remains unchanged and (6.91) becomes identical with (6.68). Thus, the structure of optimal portfolio demands is the same for state-dependent utilities whether they be additive or multiplicative.

In Chapters 15 and 16, we prove a general mutual-fund theorem as part of a theory for risk-pooling and risk-sharing financial intermediation. In those chapters, we also aggregate optimal portfolio demand functions to derive the structure of intertemporal equilibrium asset prices. In the analyses, it is assumed that there is a single consumption good and that all investor's preferences have the form given in (6.65a) here. However, those analyses depend only on the structure of individual investors' optimal portfolio demands. Hence, from the analysis in this section, we have that the results derived in Chapters 15 and 16 are robust with respect to multiple consumption goods, transactions costs for commodities, and more general types of preferences that allow for intertemporal complementarity of consumption.

Part III
Warrant and Option Pricing Theory

A Complete Model of Warrant Pricing that Maximizes Utility

(with Paul A. Samuelson)

7.1 INTRODUCTION

In a paper written in 1965, Samuelson developed a theory of rational warrant pricing.[1] Although the model is quite complex mathematically, it is open to the charge of oversimplification on the grounds that it is only a "first-moment" theory.[2] We now propose to sketch a simple model that overcomes such deficiencies. In addition to its relevance to warrant pricing, the indicated general theory is of interest for the analysis of other securities since it constitutes a full supply-and-demand determination of the outstanding amounts of securities.

7.2 CASH-STOCK PORTFOLIO ANALYSIS

Consider a common stock whose current price X_t will give rise n periods later to a finite-variance multiplicative probability distribution of subsequent prices X_{t+n} of the form

$$\text{prob}\{X_{t+n} \leqslant X | X_t = Y\} = P(X, Y; n) \equiv P(X/Y; n) \qquad (7.1)$$

where the price ratios $X_{t+n}/X_t = Z = Z_1 Z_2 \ldots Z_n$ are assumed to be products of uniformly and independently distributed distributions, of the form $\text{prob}\{Z_1 \leqslant Z\} = P(Z; 1)$, and where, for all integral n and m, the Chapman–Kolmogorov relation $P(Z; n + m) = \int_0^\infty P(Z/z; n) \, dP(z; m)$ is satisfied. This is the "geometric Brownian motion," which at least asymp-

Reproduced from *Sloan Management Review*, Winter 1969, pp. 17–46, by permission of the publisher. Copyright © 1969 by the Sloan Management Review Association.

1   See Samuelson (1965a).
2   See Kassouf (1968).

totically approaches the familiar log-normal. Ignoring for simplicity any dividends, we know that a risk averter, one with concave utility and diminishing marginal utility, will hold such a security in preference to zero-yielding safe cash only if the stock has an expected positive gain:

$$0 < E\{Z\} - 1 = \int_0^\infty Z \, dP(Z; n) - 1 = \exp(\alpha n) - 1 \qquad (7.2)$$

i.e. $\alpha > 0$ where the integral is the usual Stieltjes integral that handles discrete probabilities and densities, and α is the mean expected rate of return on the stock per unit time. (We have ensured that α is constant, independent of n.)

A special case would be, for $n = 1$, the following discrete distribution, where $\lambda > 1$:

$$X_{t+1} = \lambda X_t \qquad \text{with probability } p \geqslant 0$$
$$X_{t+1} = \lambda^{-1} X_t \qquad \text{with probability } 1 - p \geqslant 0 \qquad (7.3)$$

This simple geometric binomial random walk leads asymptotically to the log-normal distribution. Condition (7.2) becomes, in this special case, $0 < E\{Z\} - 1 = p\lambda + (1 - p)\lambda^{-1} - 1$. If, for example, $\lambda = 1.1$ and $p = 1 - p = 0.5$, then $E\{Z\} - 1 = (\frac{1}{2})(1.1 + 10/11) - 1 = 0.004545$. If our time units are measured in months, this represents a mean gain of almost one-half a percent per month, or about $5\frac{1}{2}$ percent per year, a fair approximation to the recent performance of a typical common stock.

To deduce what proportion cash holding will bear to the holding of such a stock, we must make some definite assumption about risk aversion. A fairly realistic postulate is that everyone acts now to maximize his expected utility at the end of n periods and that his utility function is strictly concave. Then by portfolio analysis[3] in the spirit of the classical papers of Domar–Musgrave and Markowitz (but free of their approximations), the expected utility is maximized when $w = w^*$, where w is the fraction of wealth in the stock:

$$\max_w \overline{U}(w) = \max_w \int_0^\infty U[(1 - w) + wZ] \, dP(Z; n) \qquad (7.4)$$

3 See Samuelson (1967a), where theorems like this are proved without making the mean–variance approximations of the now classical Markowitz–Tobin type.

Since units are arbitrary, we can take any prescribed wealth level and by dimensional convention make it unity in all our formulas. This enables expressions like wW to be written simply as w where W is total wealth. As will be specified later, working with isoelastic marginal utility functions that are uniform for all investors will make the scale of prescribed wealth of no importance.

where $w = w^*$ is the root of the regular condition for an interior maximum

$$0 = \overline{U}'(w^*)$$

$$= \int_0^\infty \{ZU'[(1 - w^*) + w^*Z] - U'[(1 - w^*) + w^*Z]\} \, dP(Z; n) \tag{7.5}$$

or

$$1 = \frac{\int_0^\infty ZU'[(1 - w^*) + w^*Z] \, dP(Z; n)}{\int_0^\infty U'[(1 - w^*) + w^*Z] \, dP(Z; n)}$$

Since U is a concave function, U'' is everywhere negative, and the critical point does correspond to a definite maximum of expected utility. (Warning: equations like (7.4) posit that no portfolio changes can be made before the n periods are up, an assumption modified later.)

If zero-yielding cash were dominated by a safe asset yielding an instantaneous force of interest r, and hence $\exp(rn)$ in n periods, terms like $1 - w$ would be multiplied by $\exp(rn)$ and (7.5) would become

$$\exp(rn) = \frac{\int_0^\infty ZU'[(1 - w^*)\exp(rn) + w^*Z] \, dP(Z; n)}{\int_0^\infty U'[(1 - w^*)\exp(rn) + w^*Z] \, dP(Z; n)} < \exp(\alpha n)$$

$$\text{if } w^* > 0 \tag{7.5a}$$

This relationship might well be called the Fundamental Equation of Optimizing Portfolio Theory. Its content is worth commenting on. But first we can free it from any dependence on the existence of a perfectly safe asset. Rewriting (7.4) to involve any number m of alternative investment outlets, subject to any joint probability distribution, gives the multiple integral

$$\max_{\{w_j\}} \overline{U}(w_1, \ldots, w_m) = \max_{\{w_j\}} \int_0^\infty U\left(\sum_{j=1}^m w_j Z_j \right) dP(Z_1, \ldots, Z_m; n) \tag{7.4a}$$

Introducing the constraint $\Sigma_{j=1}^m w_j = 1$ into the Lagrangian expression $L = \overline{U} + \gamma(1 - \Sigma_{j=1}^m w_j)$, we derive as necessary conditions for a regular interior maximum:[4]

$$\frac{\partial L}{\partial w_k} = 0 = \int_0^\infty Z_k U'\left(\sum_{j=1}^m w_j Z_j\right) \, \mathrm{d}P(Z_1,\dots,Z_m; n) - \gamma \quad \text{for } k = 1,\dots,m$$

Dividing through by a normalizing factor, we get the fundamental equation

$$\int_0^\infty Z_1 \, \mathrm{d}Q(Z_1,\dots,Z_m; n) = \int_0^\infty Z_2 \, \mathrm{d}Q(Z_1,\dots,Z_m; n)$$

$$= \dots$$

$$= \int_0^\infty Z_m \, \mathrm{d}Q(Z_1,\dots,Z_m; n) \qquad (7.5\mathrm{b})$$

where

$$\mathrm{d}Q(Z_1,\dots,Z_m; n) = \frac{U'(\Sigma_{j=1}^m w_j^* Z_j) \, \mathrm{d}P(Z_1,\dots,Z_m; n)}{\int_0^\infty U'(\Sigma_{j=1}^m w_j^* Z_j) \, \mathrm{d}P(Z_1,\dots,Z_m; n)}$$

The probability-cum-utility function $Q(Z; n)$ has all the properties of a probability distribution, but it weights the probability of each outcome so to speak by the marginal utility of wealth in that outcome.

Figure 7.1 illustrates the probability density of good and bad outcomes; Figure 7.2 shows the diminishing marginal utility of money; and Figure 7.3 plots the "effective probability" density whose integral $\int_0^z \mathrm{d}Q(Z; n)$ defines Q.[5] Conditions (7.5), (7.5a), and (7.5b) state, in words, that the "effective-probability" mean of every asset must be equal in every use, and, of course, be equal to the yield of a safe asset if such an asset is held. Note that $\overline{U}'(0) = U'[\exp(rn)][E\{Z\} - \exp(rn)] = U'[\exp(rn)][\exp(\alpha n)$

---

4   The concavity of U is sufficient to achieve the negative semidefiniteness of the constrained quadratic forms and bordered Hessian minors of L needed to insure that any solution to the first-order conditions does provide a global as well as a local maximum. Although the maximum is unique, the portfolio proportions could take on more than one set of optimizing values in singular cases where the quadratic forms were semidefinite rather than definite, e.g. where a perpetual warrant and its common stock are perfectly linearly correlated, making the choice between them indifferent and not unique. This example will be presented later.

5   At a Washington conference in 1953, Samuelson once shocked the late J. M. Clark by saying, "Although the probability of a serious 1954 recession is only one-third, that probability should be treated as though it were two-thirds." This was a crude and nonmarginal use of a util–prob notion akin to dQ.

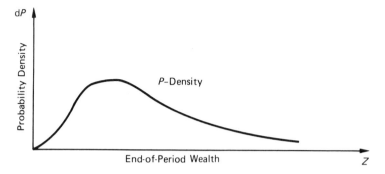

Figure 7.1 Probability Density Function for Wealth.

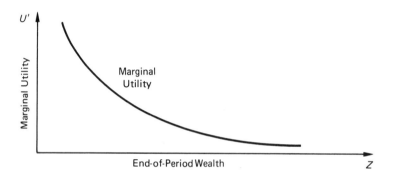

Figure 7.2 Marginal Utility of Wealth.

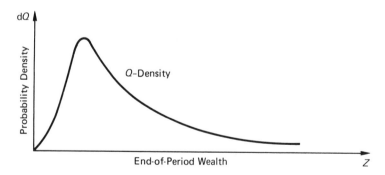

Figure 7.3 Util–Prob Density Function for Wealth.

$- \exp(rn)]$, and this must be positive if w^* is to be positive. Also $\overline{U}'(1) = E\{U'(Z)Z\} - \exp(rn) E\{U'(Z)\}$, and this cannot be positive if the safe asset is to be held in positive amount. By Kuhn–Tucker methods, interior conditions of (7.5) could be generalized to the inequalities needed if borrowing or short-selling are ruled out.

For the special probability process in (7.3) with $p = \frac{1}{2}$ and Bernoulli logarithmic utility, we can show that expected utility turns out to be maximized when wealth is always divided equally between cash and the stock, i.e. $w^* = \frac{1}{2}$ for all λ:

$$\max_{w} \overline{U}(w) = \max_{w} \left[\tfrac{1}{2} \log(1 - w + w\lambda) + \tfrac{1}{2} \log(1 - w + w\lambda^{-1})\right]$$

$$= \tfrac{1}{2} \log(\tfrac{1}{2} + \tfrac{1}{2}\lambda) + \tfrac{1}{2} \log(\tfrac{1}{2} + \tfrac{1}{2}\lambda^{-1}) \text{ for all } \lambda \qquad (7.6)$$

The maximum condition corresponding to (7.5) is

$$0 = \overline{U}'(w^*) = \frac{\tfrac{1}{2}}{\tfrac{1}{2} + \tfrac{1}{2}\lambda}(-1 + \lambda) + \frac{\tfrac{1}{2}}{\tfrac{1}{2} + \tfrac{1}{2}\lambda^{-1}}(-1 + \lambda^{-1}) \qquad (7.7)$$

and $w^* \equiv \frac{1}{2}$ for all λ.   QED

(The portfolio division is here so definitely simple because we have postulated the special case of an "unbiased" logarithmic price change coinciding with a Bernoulli logarithmic utility function; otherwise changing the probability distribution and the typical person's wealth level would generally change the portfolio proportions.)

7.3   RECAPITULATION OF THE 1965 SAMUELSON MODEL

Under what conditions will everyone be willing to hold a warrant (giving the right to buy a share of the common stock for an exercise price of one dollar per share at any time in the next n periods), and at the same time be willing to hold the stock and cash? Since the warrant's price will certainly move with the common rather than provide an opposing hedge against its price movements, if its expected rate of return were not in excess of the safe asset's yield, the warrant would not get held. In the 1965 paper, it was arbitrarily postulated that the warrant must have a specified gain per dollar which was as great or greater than the expected return per dollar invested in the common stock. Thus, if we write $Y_t(n)$ for the price at time t of a warrant with n periods still to run, the 1965 paper assumed for stock and warrant

$$E\{X_{t+T}/X_t\} = \exp(\alpha T) \geq \exp(rT) \qquad (7.8a)$$

$$E\{Y_{t+T}(n - T)/Y_t(n)\} = \exp(\beta T) \geq \exp(\alpha T) \qquad (7.8b)$$

if the warrant is to be held. In (7.8b), we recognize that after the passage of T periods of time, the warrant has $n - T$ rather than n periods left to run until its exercise privilege expires. It should be stressed that the warrant can be exercised *any* time (being of "American" rather than "European" option type) and hence in (7.8b) the warrant prices can never fall below their arbitrage exercise value, which in appropriate units (i.e. defining the units of common so that the exercise price of the warrant is unity) is given by $\max(0, X_t - 1)$. Thus, we can always convert the warrant into the common stock and sell off the stock (commissions are here neglected).

In the 1965 model, the expected percentage gain β of a warrant and the expected percentage gain α of a common were arbitrarily postulated as exogenously given data, instead of being deduced from knowledge of the risk aversion properties of U. Postulating a priori knowledge of α and β, the model was derived by beginning with the known arbitrage value of a warrant about to expire, namely

$$Y_t(0) = \max(0, X_t - 1) = F_0(X_t) \tag{7.9}$$

Then, if the warrant is to be held, we can solve (7.8b) for $Y_t(1) = F_1(X_t)$ from the equation

$$\exp(\beta) = E\{F_0(XZ)/F_1(X)|X\}$$

$$= \frac{\int_0^\infty F_0(XZ) \, dP(Z; 1)}{F_1(X)} \tag{7.10}$$

In this integral and elsewhere we can write X for X_t. If (7.10) is not achievable, the warrant will be converted, and will now be priced at its $F_0(X)$ value. Hence, in every case,

$$F_1(X) = \exp(-\beta) \int_0^\infty F_0(XZ) \, dP(Z; 1) \qquad \text{if held}$$

$$= X - 1 \geq \exp(-\beta) \int_0^\infty F_0(XZ) \, dP(Z; 1) \qquad \begin{matrix} \text{if now} \\ \text{converted} \end{matrix}$$

$$= \max\left[0, X - 1, \exp(-\beta) \int_0^\infty F_0(XZ) \, dP(Z; 1)\right] \qquad \text{in all cases} \tag{7.10a}$$

Successively putting in these expressions F_2 and F_1 for F_1 and $F_0,\ldots,F_{n+1}$ and F_n for F_1 and F_0, the 1965 model deduced rational warrant price formulas $F_n(X) = F_n(X_t) = Y_t(n)$ for any length of life; and the important perpetual warrant case $F_\infty(X) = F(X)$ can be deduced by letting $n \to \infty$:

$$F(X) = \exp(-\beta) \int_0^\infty F(XZ)\, dP(Z; 1) \qquad\qquad \text{if } X \leqslant C(\alpha, \beta)$$

$$= X - 1 \geqslant \exp(-\beta) \int_0^\infty F(XZ)\, dP(Z; 1) \quad \text{if } X \geqslant C(\alpha, \beta)$$

$$\tag{7.11}$$

where $C(\alpha, \beta)$ is the critical level at which the warrant will be worth more dead than alive. This critical level will be defined by the above relations and will be finite if $\beta > \alpha$.[6]

The special case of the 1965 theory in which $\alpha = \beta$ is particularly simple, and its mathematics turn out to be relevant to the new utility theory presented here. In this case, where conversion is never profitable (for reasons which will be spelled out even more clearly in the present chapter), the value of the warrants of any duration can be evaluated by mere quadrature, as the following linear integrals show:

$$F_n(X) = \exp(-\alpha T) \int_0^\infty F_{n-T}(XZ)\, dP(Z; T)$$

$$= \exp(-\alpha n) \int_0^\infty F_0(XZ)\, dP(Z; n)$$

$$= \exp(-\alpha n) \int_{1/X}^\infty (XZ - 1)\, dP(Z; n) \tag{7.12}$$

In concluding this recapitulation, let us note that the use of short discrete periods here gives a good approximation to the mathematically difficult limiting case of continuous time in the 1965 paper and its appendix.

---

6   In the earlier paper (1965a, pp. 30–1) it was mentioned that the possibility of hedges, in which the common stock is sold short in some proportion and the warrant is bought long, would be likely to set limits on the discrepancies that, in the absence of dividend payments, could prevail between β and α. In an unpublished paper "Restrictions on Rational Option Pricing: A Set of Arbitrage Conditions," Merton develops arbitrage formulas on warrants and puts and calls which show how severely limited are such $\beta - \alpha$ discrepancies as a result of instantaneous, almost sure-thing arbitrage transformations.

7.4 DETERMINING AVERAGE STOCK YIELD

To see how we can deduce rather than postulate in the 1965 manner the mean return that a security must provide, let us first assume away the existence of a warrant and try to deduce the mean return of a common stock. The answer must depend on supply and demand: supply as dependent upon risk averters' willingness to part with safe cash, and demand as determined by the opportunities nature affords to invest in real risky processes along a schedule of diminishing returns.

To be specific, suppose one can invest today's stock of real output (chocolates or dollars when chocolates always sell for one dollar each) either (a) in a safe (storage-type) process – *cash*, so to speak – that yields in the next period exactly one chocolate, or (b) in a *common stock*, which in the special case (7.3) gives for each chocolate "invested" today λ chocolates tomorrow with probability p, or λ^{-1} chocolates with probability $1 - p$. If we allocate today's stock of chocolates so as to maximize the expected utility, we shall shun the risk process unless its expected yield is positive. For the special case,[7] $p = 1 - p = \frac{1}{2}$, this will certainly be realized, and as seen in the earlier discussion of (7.7), for all λ, a Bernoulli utility maximizer will choose to invest half of present resources in the safe (cash) process and half in the risky (common-stock) process.

Now suppose that the risky process – say growing chocolate on the shady side of hills where the crop has a 0.5 chance of being large or small – is subject to diminishing returns. With the supply of hill land scarce, the larger is the number of chocolates planted, rather than merely stored, the lower is the mean return per chocolate (net of any competitive land rents for which the limited supply of such land will be bid to at each level of total investment in risk chocolates). Although it is admittedly a special-case assumption, suppose that λ in (7.3) drops toward unity as the absolute number of chocolates invested in the risky process rises but that $p = 1 - p = \frac{1}{2}$ throughout. Then the expected yield $a = \exp(\alpha) - 1$ drops toward zero as λ drops toward unity.

Given the initial supply of chocolates available for safe or risk allocations, the expected yield a of the common stock will be determined at the equilibrium intersection of total supply and demand – in our simple case at

---

7 If the probability of good and bad crops were not equal or if the safe investment process had a nonzero yield, the proportion of the risk asset held would be a function of the λ yield factor; and for utility functions other than the Bernoulli log form and a probability distribution different from the simple binomial, w^* would be a more complicated calculable function.

the level determined by the λ and a yields on the diminishing returns curve where exactly half of the available chocolates go into the risk process.[8]

7.5 DETERMINING WARRANT HOLDINGS AND PRICES

Using the general method outlined above, we can now deduce what warrants must yield if a prescribed amount of them is to be held alongside of cash and the common stock by a maximizer of expected utility.

Specifically, assume that cash in an insured bank account, or a safe process, has a sure yield of $\exp(r) - 1$ per unit time. Assume that each dollar invested in the common stock has a mean *ex ante* yield

$$\int_0^\infty Z \, dP(Z; 1) - 1 = \exp(\alpha) - 1$$

per period. It will be desirable now to specialize slightly our assumption of concave total utility so that the behavior of a group of investors can be treated as if it resulted from the deliberation of a single mind. In order that asset totals should behave in proportions independent of the detailed allocations of wealth among individuals, we shall assume that every person has a constant elasticity of marginal utility at every level of wealth and that the value of this constant is the same for all individuals.[9] Just as assuming uniform homothetic indifference curves frees demand curve analysis in nonstochastic situations from problems of disaggregation, a similar trick comes in handy here.

---

8   Strictly speaking, a will probably be a function of time, a_{t+1} being high in the period following a generally poor crop when the λ_t^{-1} yield factor, rather than λ_t, has just occurred and the investable surplus is small. We have here a stationary time series in which total output vibrates around an equilibrium level. Spelling all this out would be another story: here a will be taken as a constant.

9   For the family $U(X) = a + b(X^{(e-1)/e} - 1)/[(e-1)/e]$, $0 < e \neq 1$, $- U'(X)/XU''(X) = e$. The singular case where $e = 1$ can be found by L'Hospital's evaluation of an indeterminate form to correspond to the Bernoulli case, $U(X) = a + b \log X$. As Arrow (1965), Pratt (1964), and others have shown, optimal portfolio proportions are independent of the absolute size of wealth for any function that is a member of this utility family.

Actually, we can free our analysis from the assumption of isoelastic marginal utility if we are willing to apply it to any single individual and determine from it the critical warrant price patterns at which he would be neither a buyer nor seller, or would hold some specified proportion of his wealth in the form of warrants. By pitting the algebraic excess demands of one set of individuals against the other, we could determine the market clearing pattern.

Finally, we must specify how many of the warrants are to be outstanding and in need of being voluntarily held. There is a presumption that to induce people to hold a larger quantity of warrants, their relative yields will have to be sweetened. Let the amounts of total wealth W to be invested in cash, common stock, and warrants be respectively w_1, w_2, and w_3. As already seen, there is no loss of generality in setting $W = 1$. Then, subject to the constraint[10] $w_1 + w_2 + w_3 = W = 1$, we consider the following special case of (7.4a) and generalization of (7.4):

$$\max_{\{w_j\}} \overline{U}[w_1, w_2, w_3] = \max_{\{w_j\}} \int_0^\infty U\left[w_1 \exp(rT) + w_2 Z \right.$$

$$\left. + w_3 \frac{F_n(XZ)}{F_{n+T}(X)}\right] dP(Z;T)$$

$$(7.13)$$

where, as before, we assume that the decision is made for a period of length T. (Setting $T = 1$, a small period, would be typical.) To explain (7.13), note that $\exp(rT)$ is the sure return to a dollar invested in cash. Since we can with one dollar buy $1/F_{n+T}(X)$ units of a warrant with $n + T$ periods to go, and since these turn out after T periods to have the random variable price $F_n(XZ)$, clearly w_3 is to be multiplied by the per-dollar return $F_n(XZ)/F_{n+T}(X)$ as indicated.[11] As in (7.4a), we seek a critical point for the Lagrangian expression $L = \overline{U} + \gamma(1 - \Sigma_{j=1}^3 w_j)$ to get the counterpart of (7.5b), namely

$$\frac{\partial L}{\partial w_1} = 0$$

$$= -\gamma + \int_0^\infty \exp(rT)\, U'\left[w_1\exp(rT) + w_2 Z + w_3 \frac{F_n(XZ)}{F_{n+T}(X)}\right] dP(Z; T)$$

$$\frac{\partial L}{\partial w_2} = 0$$

$$= -\gamma + \int_0^\infty Z U'\left[w_1 \exp(rT) + w_2 Z + w_3 \frac{F_n(XZ)}{F_{n+T}(X)}\right] dP(Z; T)$$

10   U being concave assures a maximum. The problem could be formulated with Kuhn–Tucker inequalities to cover the no-borrowing restriction $w_1 \geq 0$, and the no-short-selling restriction $w_2 \geq 0$.

11   The F_n function in (7.13) is the "utility-warranted" price of the warrant, which is not the same as the "rational" warrant price of the 1965 theory discussed above, even though we use the same symbol for both.

$$\frac{\partial L}{\partial w_3} = 0$$

$$= -\gamma + \int_0^\infty \frac{F_n(XZ)}{F_{n+T}(X)} U'\left[w_1 \exp(rT) + w_2 Z + w_3 \frac{F_n(XZ)}{F_{n+T}(X)} \right] dP(Z; T)$$

$$\frac{\partial L}{\partial \gamma} = 0 = 1 - w_1 - w_2 - w_3 \tag{7.14}$$

Eliminating γ, we end up with special cases of (7.5b), namely

$$\exp(rT) = \frac{1}{C} \int_0^\infty ZU'\left[(1 - w_2^* - w_3^*) \exp(rT) + w_2^* Z \right.$$

$$\left. + w_3^* \frac{F_n(XZ)}{F_{n+T}(X)} \right] dP(Z; T) \tag{7.15}$$

$$\exp(rT) = \frac{1}{C} \int_0^\infty \frac{F_n(XZ)}{F_{n+T}(X)} U'\left[(1 - w_2^* - w_3^*) \exp(rT) + w_2^* Z \right.$$

$$\left. + w_3^* \frac{F_n(XZ)}{F_{n+T}(X)} \right] dP(Z; T) \tag{7.16}$$

where we have the normalizing factor

$$C = \int_0^\infty U'\left[(1 - w_2^* - w_3^*) \exp(rT) + w_2^* Z + w_3^* \frac{F_n(XZ)}{F_{n+T}(X)} \right] dP(Z; T)$$

so that, as in (7.5b)

$$dQ(Z; T) = \frac{1}{C} \left\{ U'\left[(1 - w_2^* - w_3^*) \exp(rT) + w_2^* Z \right. \right.$$

$$\left. \left. + w_3^* \frac{F_n(XZ)}{F_{n+T}(X)} \right] dP(Z; T) \right\}$$

If the w_j^* were prescribed – e.g. as the solution to a simultaneous-equation supply and demand process that auctions off the exogenously given supplies of common stock and warrants at the prices that will just get them held voluntarily[12] – then, for $T = 1$, (7.16) would become an implicit

---

12 This would be a generalization of the analysis above to three rather than only two assets. In the next section, we digress to discuss briefly in these terms the simplest case of pricing a given supply of one-period warrants. This illustrates a general theory.

equation enabling us to solve for the unknown function $F_{n+1}(X)$ recursively in terms of the assumed known function $F_n(X)$. Since $F_0(X)$ is known from arbitrage-conversion considerations, (7.16) does provide an alternative theory to the 1965 first-moment theory.

Let us now call attention to the fact that the implicit equation in (7.16) for $F_{n+T}(X)$ can be enormously simplified in the special case where the number of warrants held is "small." Thus, for $w_3^* = 0$, or nearly so, the dependence of $U'(\cdot)$ on $F_{n+T}(X)$ becomes zero, or negligible; and (7.16) becomes a simple *linear* relationship for determining $F_{n+T}(\cdot)$ recursively from $F_n(\cdot)$. If $w_3^* = 0$, (7.15) and (7.16) become

$$\exp(rT) = \frac{1}{C} \int_0^\infty ZU'[(1 - w_2^*)\exp(rT) + w_2^* Z] \, dP(Z; T) \qquad (7.15a)$$

$$\exp(rT) = \frac{1}{C} \int_0^\infty \frac{F_n(XZ)}{F_{n+T}(X)} U'[(1 - w_2^*)\exp(rT) + w_2^* Z] \, dP(Z;T) \quad (7.16a)$$

Our task will thus be simplified when we specify that the number of warrants to be held is "small"; i.e. warrant pricing is to be determined at the critical level just necessary to induce an incipient amount of them to be voluntarily held. This is an interesting case because it is also the critical level at which hedging transactions, involving buying the common and selling a bit of the warrant short, just become desirable.[13] Most of this chapter will be concerned with this interesting "incipient-warrant" case based on (7.15a) and (7.16a), but we will first digress briefly to show how one might deduce the quantitative level of all w_j^* in terms of given supplies of the various securities.

7.6   DIGRESSION: GENERAL EQUILIBRIUM PRICING

To illustrate how warrants would have to be priced if their exogenously given supply is to be absorbed voluntarily by utility maximizers, it suffices to consider the simplest case of one-period warrants that are available in a fixed amount $\overline{V}$. And let us assume for expositional simplicity that diminishing returns (e.g. in connection with the chocolate-growing hillsides above) operate so slowly that we can take the probability distribution of common-stock price changes as exogenously given, with $P(Z; 1)$ given and

---

13   Thorp and Kassouf (1967) advocate hedged short-sales of overpriced warrants about to expire. The analysis here defines the levels at which one who holds the stock long can just benefit in the maximizing expected utility sense from short-sale hedges in the warrant.

the common stock's expected return a known parameter exp(α). Assume that the present common-stock price is known to be at the level $\overline{X} = x$. Also let the amount of the safe asset ("money" or "near-money") be prescribed at the level $\overline{M}$, with a prescribed safe return exp(r) being a parameter of the problem.

We can now deduce, for utility maximizers, the equilibrium values for the unknown number S of shares of common stock held and the unknown equilibrium pattern of warrant prices $F_1(x)$. Our equations are the balance sheet identities, definitions, and supply conditions:

$$W = \overline{M} \times 1 + Sx + \overline{V}F_1(x)$$

$$= \overline{M}\left(1 + \frac{w_2}{w_1} + \frac{1 - w_1 - w_2}{w_1}\right) \tag{7.17}$$

$$S = \frac{w_2}{w_1}\frac{\overline{M}}{x} \tag{7.18}$$

$$\overline{V}F_1(x) = \frac{1 - w_1 - w_2}{w_1}\overline{M} \tag{7.19}$$

and also our earlier equations (7.15) and (7.16) with $T = 1$ and $n = 0$:

$$\exp(r) = \frac{1}{C}\int_0^\infty ZU'\left[w_1\exp(r) + w_2Z + (1 - w_1 - w_2)\frac{F_0(xZ)}{F_1(x)}\right]$$

$$dP(Z; 1) \tag{7.15b}$$

$$\exp(r) = \frac{1}{C}\int_0^\infty \frac{F_0(xZ)}{F_1(x)}$$

$$\times U'\left[w_1\exp(r) + w_2Z + (1 - w_1 - w_2)\frac{F_0(xZ)}{F_1(x)}\right]dP(Z; 1) \tag{7.16b}$$

Equations (7.19), (7.15b), and (7.16b) are independent equations for the three unknowns w_1^*, w_2^*, and $F_1(x)$. Hence we do have a determinate system.[14] When $\overline{V} \to 0$, we have the simpler theory of the rest of this chapter.

---

14 Strictly speaking, F_1 is a function of more than X alone; it can be written as $F_1(X; r; V/M)$. Likewise, the equilibrium S is of the form $G(X; r; V/M)M$, where

7.7 UTILITY-MAXIMIZING WARRANT PRICING: THE IMPORTANT "INCIPIENT" CASE

After our digression, we go back to equation (7.16a), rearranging its factors to get, for $T = 1$,

$$F_{n+1}(X) = \exp(-r) \int_0^\infty F_n(XZ) \, dQ(Z; 1) \qquad (7.20)$$

where $dQ(Z; 1)$ is short for

$$dQ(Z; 1; r, w_2^*) = \frac{U'[(1 - w_2^*) \exp(r) + w_2^* Z] \, dP(Z; 1)}{\int_0^\infty U'[(1 - w_2^*) \exp(r) + w_2^* Z] \, dP(Z; 1)}$$

Here w_2^* is a parameter already determined from solving (7.15a), and indeed is precisely the same as the w^* determined earlier from solving equation (7.5a). It will be recalled that $Q(Z; 1)$ is a kind of util–prob distribution. Precisely because of (7.15a), we know that the expected value of Z, calculated not in terms of the true objective probability distribution $dP(Z; 1)$ but rather in terms of the util–prob distribution $dQ(Z; 1)$, has a "yield" per unit time exactly equal to that of the safe asset. Rearranging (7.15a), we have

$$\int_0^\infty Z \, dQ(Z; 1) = \exp(r) < \exp(\alpha) = \int_0^\infty Z \, dP(Z; 1) \qquad (7.21)$$

Taken together with the initial condition from (7.9), $F_0(X) = \max(0, X - 1)$, equations (7.20) and (7.21) give us *linear* recursion relationships to solve our problems completely, provided we can be sure that they always yield $F_n(X)$ values that definitely exceed the conversion value of

both G and F_1 are functionals of the probability distribution function $P(Z; 1)$. There is a formal similarity here to the quantity theory of money and prices, due, of course, to the "homogeneity" assumption made about tastes. It should be fairly evident that in the same fashion by which we have here deduced the $F_1(\cdot)$ function from the known $F_0(\cdot)$ function, one could in general deduce recursively $F_{n+1}(\cdot)$ in terms of a known $F_0(\cdot)$ function. Similar homogeneity properties in terms of (V, M) and V/M would hold. Finally, instead of assuming completely inelastic V supply and completely elastic common-stock supply dependent on a hard parameter, one could formulate a completely general equilibrium model in which r, α, and the probability distribution $P(Z; 1)$ were all determined simultaneously.

$F_0(X)$. Because of (7.21), we are here in a mathematical situation similar to the 1965 special case in which $\alpha = \beta$, and indeed no premature conversion is ever possible. But of course there is this significant difference: in the 1965 case, dP rather than dQ is used to compute α and β, and to emphasize this we write $\alpha = \alpha_P = \beta_P$ for that case; in the present case, where dQ is used in the computation, we write α_Q and β_Q, recognizing from (7.21) that $\alpha_Q = r$ and from (7.20) that $\beta_Q = r = \alpha_Q < \alpha_P = \alpha$. The α_Q and β_Q "yields" are purely "hypothetical" or subjective; they should not be identified with the higher "objective" α_P and β_P yields computed with actual probability dP. These are the true *ex ante* expected percentage yields calculated from actual dollar gains and losses; they are objective in the sense that Monte Carlo experiments replicated a large number of times, within this probability model characterized by $P(Z; 1)$, will actually average out *ex post* with mean yields of α_P and β_P on the common stock and warrants, respectively.[15]

The mathematics does not care about this dP and dQ distinction. The same kind of step-by-step algorithm is yielded whatever the interpretation of the probability distribution used. But this new approach does raise an awkward question. In the 1965 paper, it could be taken as almost self-evident that conversion can never be mandatory if both warrant and stock have the same *ex ante* yield. In this case, where the yields calculated with $dQ(Z; 1)$ are of a hypothetical kind, it is desirable to provide a rigorous proof that our new theory of warrant pricing never impinges on the inequalities set by arbitrage as discussed above and in the 1965 paper.

If we are assured of nonconversion, the value of a perpetual warrant can be determined from the linear integral equation (7.20). For n so large that n and $n + 1$ are indistinguishable, we can write

$$F_n(X) = F_{n+1}(X) = F_\infty(X) = F(X)$$

and (7.20) becomes

$$F(X) = \exp(-r) \int_0^\infty F(XZ)\, dQ(Z; 1) \qquad (7.22)$$

Substituting $F(X) \equiv X$ into (7.22) does turn out to provide a solution. So too would cX, but only for $c = 1$ can we satisfy the two-sided arbitrage conditions $X \geq F(X) \geq X - 1$.

Actually, the homogeneous integral equation (7.22) has other solutions of the form cX^m, where substitution entails

15 We will show later that $\beta_P > \alpha_P$ for finite-duration warrants, falling toward equality as the duration time becomes perpetual.

$$cX^m = \exp(-r) \, cX^m \int_0^\infty Z^m \, dQ(Z; 1)$$

$$1 = \exp(-r) \int_0^\infty Z^m \, dQ(Z; 1) = \phi(m) \qquad (7.23)$$

This last equation will usually be a transcendental equation for m, with an infinite number of complex roots of which only $m = 1$ is relevant in view of our boundary conditions.[16]

That our new theory leads to the perpetual warrant's being priced equal to the common stock may seem paradoxical, just as in the 1965 special case where $\alpha_P = \beta_P$. We shall return to this later.

7.8 EXPLICIT SOLUTIONS

In a sense, our new theory is completed by the step-by-step solution of (7.20). In the 1965 theory, however, it was possible to display explicit formulas for nonconverted warrants by quadrature or direct integration over the original $F_0(X)$ function. The same procedure is possible here by introducing some further generalizations of our util–prob distribution $Q(Z; 1)$.

There are some by-no-means obvious complications in our new theory. Given the quadrature formula

$$F_1(X) = \exp(-r) \int_0^\infty F_0(XZ) \, dQ(Z; 1) \qquad (7.24)$$

one is tempted at first to write, as would be possible in the 1965 case where dP replaced dQ,

$$F_2(X) = \exp(-2r) \int_0^\infty F_0(XZ) \, dQ(Z; 2) \qquad (7.25)$$

...

...

---

16 The Hertz–Herglotz–Lotka methods of renewal theory are closely related, once we replace X and Z by their logarithms. However, the fact that our dQ involves Zs on *both* sides of unity with positive weights introduces some new complications. Later, without regard to formal expansions of this type, we prove that $F_n(X) \to F_\infty(X) \equiv X$. For references to this literature, including work by Fellner, see Lopez (1961).

or, in general,

$$F_n(X) = \exp(-nr) \int_0^\infty F_0(XZ) \, dQ(Z; n) \qquad (7.26)$$

where, as in (7.5b), we define

$$dQ(Z; n) = \frac{U'[w_1^* \exp(rn) + w_2^* Z] \, dP(Z; n)}{\int_0^\infty U'[w_1^* \exp(rn) + w_2^* Z] \, dP(Z; n)}$$

But these relations are *not* valid. They would be valid only if, say in the case $n = 2$, we locked ourselves in at the beginning to a choice of portfolio that is frozen for both periods, regardless of the fact that after one period has elapsed we have learned the outcomes of X_{t+1} and by (7.20) would want to act anew to create the proper w_j^* proportions for the final period. (For example, suppose as in (7.7) that we have $U = \log W$ and there is an equal chance of the stock's doubling or halving, with $\lambda = 2$, $p = \frac{1}{2} = 1 - p$. Suppose we put half our wealth into cash at the beginning and freeze our portfolio for two periods. Then we are violating the step-by-step solution of (7.20) if, after we have learned that the stock has doubled, we do not sell out half our gain and put it into cash for the second period.)[17] In summary, (7.25) is not consistent with (7.24) and

---

17   There is a further complication. If decisions are frozen for n periods, then (7.26) is valid, superseding (7.24) and (7.20). Or put differently, n of the old time periods are now equivalent to one new time period; and in terms of this new time period, (7.20) would be rewritten to have exactly the same content as (7.26). Now (7.24) or (7.25) would simply be irrelevant. One must not suppose that this change in time units is merely a representational shift to new dimensional units, as from seconds to minutes. If our portfolio is to be frozen for six months, that differs substantively from its being frozen for six weeks, even though we may choose to write six months as 26 weeks. But now for the complication: one would not expect the $U(W)$ function relevant for a six-week frozen-decision period to be relevant for a six-month period as well. Strictly speaking then, in using (7.26) for a long-frozen-period analysis, we should require that the $U'(W)$ function which enters into $dQ(Z; n)$ be written as dependent on n, or as $\partial U(W; n)/\partial W$. Two papers showing proper lifetime portfolio decisions are those by P. A. Samuelson, "Lifetime Portfolio Selection by Dynamic Stochastic Programming" (1969) and R. C. Merton, "Lifetime Portfolio Selection Under Uncertainty: The Continuous-Time Case" (1969a; this volume, Ch. 4).

One further remark. Consider the "incipient-cash" case, where $w_1^* = 0$ because the common stock dominates the safe asset, with $\alpha \gg r$. Combining this case with our incipient-warrant case, w_2^* remains at unity in every period, no matter what we learn about the outcomes within any larger period. In this case, the results of (7.20) and those of (7.26) are compatible and the latter does give us by mere quadrature a one-step solution to the problem. The 1965 proof that $F_n(X) \to X$ as $n \to \infty$ can then be applied directly.

$$F_2(X) = \exp(-r) \int_0^\infty F_1(XZ)\, dQ(Z; 1) \qquad (7.27)$$

If direct quadrature with $Q(Z; n)$ is not valid, what is? What we need are new iterated integrals $Q_2(Z),\ldots,Q_n(Z)$ which reflect the compound probabilities for $2,\ldots,n$ periods ahead when the proper nonfrozen portfolio changes have been made. Rather than derive these by tortuous economic intuition, let us give the mathematics its head and merely make successive substitutions. Thus, from (7.20) applied twice, we get

$$F_{n+2}(X) = \exp(-r) \int_0^\infty F_{n+1}(XZ)\, dQ(Z; 1)$$

$$= \exp(-r) \int_0^\infty \left[\exp(-r) \int_0^\infty F_n(XZV)\, dQ(V; 1) \right] dQ(Z; 1)$$

$$= \exp(-2r) \int_0^\infty F_n[X(ZV)]\, d \int_0^\infty Q\left[\frac{(ZV)}{Z}; 1 \right] dQ(Z; 1)$$

$$= \exp(-2r) \int_0^\infty F_n(XR)\, dQ_2(R) \qquad (7.28)$$

where

$$Q_2(R) = \int_0^\infty Q\left(\frac{R}{Z}; 1 \right) dQ(Z; 1)$$

and where the indicated interchange in the order of integration of the double integral can be straightforwardly justified.

This suggests defining the iterated integrals[18] by a process which becomes quite like that of convolution when we replace our variables by their logarithms, namely, relations like those of Chapman–Kolmogorov:

$$Q_1(Z) \equiv Q(Z; 1) \text{ by definition}$$

$$Q_2(Z) = \int_0^\infty Q_1\left(\frac{Z}{V} \right) dQ_1(V) \neq Q(Z; 2)$$

$$\ldots$$

18 If, as mentioned in footnote 9, we free the analysis from the assumption of isoelastic marginal utility, the definitions of (7.29) must be generalized to take account of the changing $\{w_j^*\}$ optimizing decisions, which will now be different depending on changing wealth levels that are passed through.

...

$$Q_{n+1}(Z) = \int_0^\infty Q_n\left(\frac{Z}{V}\right) dQ_1(V) \tag{7.29}$$

Then, by repeated use of (7.28)'s substitutions, the results of the step-by-step solution of (7.20) can be written in terms of mere quadratures, namely,

$$F_1(X) = \exp(-r) \int_0^\infty F_0(XZ) \, dQ_1(Z)$$

$$F_2(X) = \exp(-2r) \int_0^\infty F_0(XZ) \, dQ_2(Z)$$

...

...

$$F_n(X) = \exp(-nr) \int_0^\infty F_0(XZ) \, dQ_n(Z) \tag{7.30}$$

Fortunately, the "subjective yields" α_Q and β_Q, calculated for the new generalized util–prob functions $Q_t(Z)$, do all equal r per unit time. That is, we can prove by induction

$$\int_0^\infty Z \, dQ_1(Z) = \exp(r) < \exp(\alpha)$$

$$\int_0^\infty Z \, dQ_2(Z) = \exp(2r)$$

...

...

$$\int_0^\infty Z \, dQ_n(Z) = \exp(nr) \tag{7.31}$$

This is an important fact, needed to ensure that the solutions to our new theory never fall below the arbitrage levels at which conversion would be mandatory.

7.9 WARRANTS NEVER TO BE CONVERTED

It was shown in the 1965 paper that, for $\beta > \alpha$ and β a constant, the warrants would always be converted at a finite stock-price level. We will show that in the present model with its explicit assumption of no dividends the warrants are never converted (i.e. $F_n(X) > F_0(X)$).[19]

Theorem 7.1

If $\int_0^\infty Z \, dQ_n(Z) = \exp(rn)$ and $F_n(X) = \exp(-rn) \int_0^\infty F_0(XZ) \, dQ_n(Z)$, then

$$F_n(X) \geq F_0(X) = \max(0, X - 1)$$

and we are in the case where the warrants need never be converted prior to expiration.

PROOF

Since $F_0(X) \geq X - 1$, it is sufficient to show that

$$X - 1 \leq \exp(-rn) \int_0^\infty F_0(XZ) \, dQ_n(Z) \equiv \phi_n(X; r) \qquad (7.32)$$

holds for all $r > 0$, $n > 0$, and $X > 0$. We show this as follows:

$$\phi_n(X; r) \geq \exp(-rn) \int_0^\infty (XZ - 1) \, dQ_n(Z)$$

because $F_0(XZ) \geq XZ - 1$ and $dQ_n(Z) \geq 0$. Therefore,

$$\phi_n(X; r) \geq X \exp(-rn) \int_0^\infty Z \, dQ_n(Z) - \exp(-rn)$$

$$\geq X - \exp(-rn) \geq X - 1$$

from (7.31) for all $r \geq 0$, $n > 0$, and $X \geq 0$. Therefore (7.32) holds and the theorem is proved. QED

---

19 The results of this section hold also for calls. See Appendix 7B for the results for dividend-paying stocks.

Thus, we have validated the step-by-step relations of (7.20) or the one-step quadrature formula of (7.30). As an easy corollary of this theorem, we verify that longer life of a warrant can at most enhance its value, i.e. $F_{n+1}(X) \geq F_n(X)$. For, from the theorem itself $F_1(X) \geq F_0(X)$, and hence

$$F_2(X) = \exp(-r) \int_0^\infty F_1(XZ) \, dQ(Z; 1)$$

$$\geq \exp(-r) \int_0^\infty F_0(XZ) \, dQ(Z; 1) = F_1(X)$$

And, inductively, if $F_t(X) \geq F_{t-1}(X)$ for all $t \leq n$, it follows that

$$F_{n+1}(X) = \exp(-r) \int_0^\infty F_n(XZ) \, dQ(Z; 1)$$

$$\geq \exp(-r) \int_0^\infty F_{n-1}(XZ) \, dQ(Z; 1) = F_n(X)$$

If $Q(Z; 1) > 0$ for all $Z > 0$ and $Q(Z; 1) < 1$ for all $Z < \infty$, we can write strong inequalities $F_{n+1}(X) > F_n(X) > F_{n-1}(X) > \cdots > F_1(X) > F_0(X)$.

The log-normal case belongs to this class. If, however, as in the example generated from (7.3), $Q(Z; 1) = 0$ for $Z < \lambda^{-1} < 1$, then $F_1(X)$ will vanish for some of the same X values where $F_0(X)$ vanishes. Hence, our weak inequalities are needed in general. The crucial test is this: if for a given X, one can in T steps end up above the conversion price of 1, then for $r > 0$, $F_T(X) > F_0(X)$ and $F_{n+T}(X) > F_n(X)$.

7.10   EXACT SOLUTION TO THE PERPETUAL WARRANT CASE

We now shall show that the stationary solution to (7.30), $F(X) \equiv X$,[20] is indeed the limit of the finite-duration warrant prices as $n \to \infty$. From (7.30),

$$F_n(X) = \exp(-rn) \int_0^\infty F_0(XZ) \, dQ_n(Z)$$

$$= \exp(-rn) \int_{1/X}^\infty (XZ - 1) \, dQ_n(Z)$$

20   This is the limiting case where equations (7.30) and (7.31) become identical. The bordered Hessian becomes singular and w_2^* and w_3^* become indistinguishable, i.e. the warrant and the stock cease to be distinguishable assets.

$$= \exp(-rn) \int_0^\infty (XZ - 1) \, \mathrm{d}Q_n(Z) + \exp(-rn)$$

$$\times \frac{\int_0^{1/X} (1 - XZ) \, \mathrm{d}Q_n(Z)}{\int_0^{1/X} \mathrm{d}Q_n(Z)} \int_0^{1/X} \mathrm{d}Q_n(Z)$$

$$= X - \exp(-rn) + \exp(-rn) \, \theta_1(X; n) \, \theta_2(X; n) \qquad (7.33)$$

from (7.31). But $|\theta_i(X; n)| \leq 1$ for $i = 1,2$. So, as $n \to \infty$, $r > 0$,

$$F(X) = \lim_{n \to \infty} F_n(X) = X$$

Thus, the result is shown for $r > 0$. For $r = 0$, the proof is similar and follows closely the proof on page 23 of the 1965 paper. For $r = 0$, (7.30) becomes

$$F_n(X) = \int_{1/X}^\infty (XZ - 1) \, \mathrm{d}Q_n(Z)$$

$$= X - 1 + \theta_1(X; n)\theta_2(X; n)$$

where as before

$$\theta_1(X; n) = \frac{\int_0^{1/X}(1 - XZ) \, \mathrm{d}Q_n(Z)}{\int_0^{1/X} \mathrm{d}Q_n(Z)} = 1 - \frac{X \int_0^{1/X} Z \, \mathrm{d}Q_n(Z)}{\int_0^{1/X} \mathrm{d}Q_n(Z)}$$

and

$$\lim_{n \to \infty} \theta_1(X; n) = 1 - \frac{X \int_0^{1/X} Z \, \mathrm{d}Q_\infty(Z)}{\int_0^{1/X} \mathrm{d}Q_\infty(Z)}$$

$$= 1 - 0 \qquad (7.34)$$

because $Q_\infty(0^+, X) = 1$ for precisely the same reasons that $P(0^+, X; \infty) = 1$ as proved in Samuelson (1965a, p. 17). The paradox of almost-certain, almost-total ruin for fair-game betters who re-bet their proceeds is also involved here, but with respect to the distribution Q instead of the distribution P. Consider a hypothetical multiplicative probability process $Y_0 = X$, $Y_1 = XZ_1$, $Y_2 = XZ_1Z_2,..., Y_n = XZ_1...Z_n$ where X is a constant and each Z_i is independently distributed according to the probability distribution $\mathrm{prob}\{Z_i \leq Z\} = Q_1(Z)$. Then it directly follows that $\mathrm{prob}\{XZ_1Z_2 \leq XZ\} = Q_2(Z)$, and ... $\mathrm{prob}\{XZ_1...Z_n \leq XZ\} = Q_n(Z)$. Since $E\{Z\} = \int_0^\infty Z \, \mathrm{d}Q_1(Z) = e^0 = 1$, and $P(X; 1)$ and $Q_1(Z)$ involve some positive dispersion, the geometric mean of $\mathrm{d}Q_1(Z)$ lies below the arithmetic mean of $1 = E\{Z\}$. Hence, $E\{\log Z_i\} = \int_0^\infty \log Z \, dQ_1(Z) = \nu < 0$. By the Central Limit Theorem applied to $\log X + \Sigma_1^n \log Z_i = \log Y_n$, $E\{\log Y_n\} = \log X + n\nu$ and $E\{\log Y_n\} \to -\infty$ as $n \to \infty$, so that all the probability becomes spread out to the left of any fixed number Z. Thus, $Q_n(Z) \to 1$ as $n \to \infty$ for all $Z > 0$. (Note that a fair-game ($r = 0$) in Q-space implies a better-than-fair game ($\alpha > 0$) in P-space from equation (7.21).)

Warning: although $Q_\infty(Z)$ becomes a log-normal distribution, say, $L(Z; \nu, \delta, n)$, it is quite wrong to think that necessarily

$$X = F_\infty(X) = \lim_{n\to\infty} \exp(-rn) \int_0^\infty F_0(XZ) \, dQ_n(Z)$$

$$= \int_0^\infty F_0(XZ) \lim_{n\to\infty} \exp(-rn) \, dL(Z; \nu, \delta, n)$$

$$= \int_0^\infty F_0(XZ) \, dQ^*(Z)$$

Such interchanging of limits will generally not be permissible.

It follows that

$$\lim_{n\to\infty} \theta_2(X; n) = \int_0^{1/X} dQ_\infty(Z) = 1$$

because $Q_\infty(0^+, X) = 1$. Therefore,

$$\lim_{n\to\infty} F_n(X) = X - 1 + \lim_{n\to\infty} \theta_1(X; n) \, \theta_2(X; n)$$

$$= X - 1 + 1 = X$$

So the result is shown for $r = 0$.

Admittedly, our new theory has arrived at the same paradoxical result as the special case of the 1965 theory, namely that a perpetual warrant should sell for as much as the common stock itself. Such a result would seem empirically bizarre. In real life, perpetual warrants generally do sell for less, and since the common stock is equivalent to a perpetual right to itself at zero exercise price, one would have thought it would dominate a perpetual warrant exercisible at one dollar. Indeed, one of the purposes of the general 1965 theory was to construct a model that would keep perpetual warrants down to a price below the common.

What is there to do about the paradox? First, one can recognize that the common stock may be paying dividends now or can be expected to pay dividends at some time in the future. Therefore, the analysis presented in Appendix 7B may be deemed appropriate, and this will serve to dispel the paradox. Second, one might have thought that dropping the $w_j^* = 0$ incipient case would dispel the paradox. But such a guess would seem to be erroneous, since $w_3^* > 0$ is compatible with having a warrant price, like $F_\infty(X) = X$, because the variance of a perpetual warrant and the common stock are the same. Finally, we may dispel the paradox by accepting it as prosaic. If a stock's mean gain is almost certain to rise indefinitely above the exercise price in the distant future, and that is what $a > 0$ implies, why should not the one dollar exercise price be deemed of negligible percentage importance relative to the future value of the common? (Recall too that the one dollar is not paid now, but only after an infinite time.) Hence, why should not the perpetual warrant sell for essentially the same price as the common? And, if people believe this will be the case, it will be a self-fulfilling belief. (If most people doubt this, the person who believes in it will average a greater gain by buying warrants.)

7.11   ILLUSTRATIVE EXAMPLE

Now that the general theory is complete, it is of interest to give a complete solution in the easy case of the binomial process with Bernoulli utility as was described in (7.3), where $\lambda > 1$:

$$X_{t+1} = \lambda X_t \quad \text{with probability } p = \tfrac{1}{2}$$

$$X_{t+1} = \lambda^{-1} X_t \text{ with probability } 1 - p = \tfrac{1}{2} \tag{7.3a}$$

and the Bernoulli logarithmic total utility function $U(W) = \log W$. We further assume that the yield on cash is zero (i.e. $r = 0$), and the mean yield a of the common stock is

$$a = \tfrac{1}{2}(\lambda + \lambda^{-1}) - 1 \tag{7.35}$$

The utility maximum equation corresponding to (7.13), for $T = 1$, is

$$\max_{\{w_j\}} \overline{U} = \max_{\{w_j\}} \left\{ \tfrac{1}{2} \log\left[w_1 + w_2\lambda + w_3 \frac{F_n(X\lambda)}{F_{n+1}(X)} \right] \right.$$

$$\left. + \tfrac{1}{2} \log\left[w_1 + w_2\lambda^{-1} + w_3 \frac{F_n(X\lambda^{-1})}{F_{n+1}(X)} \right] \right\} \tag{7.36}$$

Since we already know that $w_1^* = w_2^* = \frac{1}{2}$ is optimal for w_3^* imposed at zero from the previous analysis of (7.6) and (7.7), the first-order conditions corresponding to equations (7.14) reduce to a single equation:

$$0 = \frac{\frac{1}{2} + \frac{1}{2}\lambda - F_n(X\lambda)/F_{n+1}(X)}{\frac{1}{2} + \frac{1}{2}\lambda} + \frac{\frac{1}{2} + \frac{1}{2}\lambda^{-1} - F_n(X\lambda^{-1})/F_{n+1}(X)}{\frac{1}{2} + \frac{1}{2}\lambda^{-1}} \qquad (7.37)$$

Solving for the warrant prices corresponding to (7.20), we have

$$F_{n+1}(X) = (1 + \lambda)^{-1}F_n(X\lambda) + (1 + \lambda^{-1})^{-1}F_n(X\lambda^{-1}) \qquad (7.38)$$

We have previously shown that the arbitrage conditions imposing premature conversion are not binding. Therefore, (7.38) and the initial condition

$$F_0(X) = \max(0, X - 1) \qquad (7.39)$$

are sufficient to determine the warrant prices.

The coefficients in (7.38) can easily be interpreted by our new notion of the util–prob function. They are dQ's discrete probabilities (q_1, q_{-1}) corresponding to the original dP discrete probabilities $(P_1, P_{-1}) = (\frac{1}{2}, \frac{1}{2})$ being related by

$$
\begin{aligned}
q_i &= \frac{P_i U'(\frac{1}{2} + \frac{1}{2}\lambda^i)}{P_{-1}U'(\frac{1}{2} + \frac{1}{2}\lambda^{-1}) + P_1 U'(\frac{1}{2} + \frac{1}{2}\lambda)} \\[2mm]
&= \frac{\frac{1}{2}/(\frac{1}{2} + \frac{1}{2}\lambda^i)}{\frac{1}{2}/(\frac{1}{2} + \frac{1}{2}\lambda^{-1}) + \frac{1}{2}/(\frac{1}{2} + \frac{1}{2}\lambda)} \\[2mm]
&= (1 + \lambda^i)^{-1} \quad \text{for } i = \pm 1
\end{aligned}
$$

As in the 1965 paper, we convert (7.38) into a standard random-walk stochastic process by means of a logarithmic or exponential transformation in which $X = \lambda^k$, $k = \log_\lambda X$. It will suffice for an example to consider only integer values of k. Finally, write $F_n(\lambda^k) = F_{k,n}$. Then (7.38) becomes the familiar partial difference equation[21] of the classical random walk

$$F_{k,n+1} = q_1 F_{k+1,n} + q_{-1} F_{k-1,n} \qquad q_1 + q_{-1} = 1 \qquad (7.40)$$

Table 7.1 illustrates, in the familiar form of Pascal's triangle, calculation

---

21 This partial difference equation can presumably be solved by the methods of Lagrange and Laplace, but there are complexities involved due to the boundary conditions of arbitrage which we do not wish to go into at this time.

Table 7.1 Warrant Prices for Geometric Binomial Random Walk

					k				
n	-4	-3	-2	-1	0	1	2	3	4
0	0	0	0	0	0	0.1000	0.2100	0.3310	0.4641
1		0	0	0	0.0476	0.1000	0.2100	0.3310	
2			0	0.0227	0.0476	0.1249	0.2100		
3				0.0227	0.0714	0.1249			
4					0.0714				

of the warrant prices for our special case. The arrows in the table illustrate the step-by-step calculations: thus, $F_1(1) = F_1(\lambda^0) = F_{01}$ is calculated, for $\lambda = 1.1$, as

$$F_{01} = \frac{1}{1 + 1.1} F_{10} = 0.0476$$

and $F_{13} = F_3(1.1)$ is calculated as

$$F_{13} = \frac{1}{2.1} F_{22} + \frac{1.1}{2.1} F_{02} = 0.1249$$

For $\lambda = 1.1$, we calculate

$$q_1 = \frac{1}{2.1} = 0.4762 \qquad q_{-1} = \frac{1.1}{2.1} = 0.5238$$

Note that there are several recurring patterns within the table which are not due to the particular choice of λ. For example, in the $k = 0$ column, successive odd and even entries repeat themselves: $F_{01} = F_{02}$; $F_{03} = F_{04}$; ...; $F_{0,2n+1} = F_{0,2n+2}$ for all λ.

What is the profitability of holding the warrant as against holding the common or holding cash? We can compute this from our table, using the actual dP probabilities of $(\frac{1}{2}, \frac{1}{2})$. Thus, the outcomes $F_0(\lambda^{\pm 1})$ that emerge from buying $F_1(1)$ have a mean yield of $\frac{1}{2}(2.1) + \frac{1}{2}(0) - 1 = 0.05$ percent per month.

This turns out to be a higher actual yield than the postulated $\alpha = 0.04545$ percent per month of the common stock. (We are here speaking of *actual* α_P and β_P yields and not the *hypothetical* $\alpha_Q = r$ and $\beta_Q = r$ yields referred to in earlier sections.) One can easily verify from any other entry in the table that, in every case, the warrant's β yield exceeds the fixed α yield of the common. Indeed, from the general formulas for any λ and not just for $\lambda = 1.1$, one finds $\beta > \alpha$. Thus, to find the mean yield from buying a one-period warrant at $X_t = 1$ at the rational price $F_1(1)$ for any $\lambda > 1$, we calculate from (7.38) the price $F_1(1)$:

$$F_1(1) = (1 + \lambda)^{-1}F_0(\lambda) + (1 + \lambda^{-1})^{-1}F_0(\lambda^{-1})$$

$$= \frac{\lambda - 1}{\lambda + 1} \qquad + 0$$

Our mean gain b per dollar is

$$E\left\{\frac{F_0(X_{t+1})}{F_1(1)} \,\bigg|\, X_t = 1\right\} = \frac{1}{2}\frac{\lambda - 1}{(1 + \lambda)^{-1}(\lambda - 1)} - 1$$

$$= \frac{\lambda - 1}{2} = b$$

For $\lambda > 1$,

$$\frac{\lambda - 1}{2} > \frac{\lambda - 1 + \lambda^{-1} - 1}{2} = a$$

from (7.35), or $b > a$, and $\beta > \alpha$. Is this a surprising finding? When one reflects that the warrants have higher "volatility" than does the common, it would seem intuitively reasonable that they should have to afford a higher yield than the common if they are to be held in the same portfolio. Moreover, since the degree of volatility can be expected to vary with the price of the common and the duration of the warrant, there is no *a priori* reason to expect that the actual β should be a constant; instead it is reasonable to expect that it must be written as a function of X and n, namely, $\beta(X, n)$.

Actually, this expectation that $\beta(X, n) > \alpha$, which was based on our illustrative case and on *a priori* reasoning, turns out to be true for even the most general case. In the next section, by means of an important lemma, we shall prove the above inequality. Of course, in the limit when the perpetual warrant approaches the value of the common stock, the divergence $\beta(X, n) - \alpha$ will go to zero as $n \to \infty$.

7.12 PROOF OF THE SUPERIORITY OF YIELD OF WARRANTS OVER YIELD OF COMMON STOCK

First we wish to state an important lemma upon which this proof and other results rest. Proof of this lemma and indeed of a wider lemma of which this is a special case is relegated to Appendix 7A. Broadly speaking, what we wish to show is that if two perfectly positively dependent securities are to be held in the same portfolio, with the outcome of one being a monotone-increasing function of the other but with its possessing greater "volatility" in the sense of its elasticity with respect to the other exceeding unity, the mean yield of the volatile security must exceed the mean yield of the less volatile security.

We define the elasticity of the function $\Psi(Y)$ with respect to Y, E_Ψ, in the usual fashion as

$$E_\Psi \equiv \frac{d(\log \Psi)}{d(\log Y)} = \frac{Y\Psi'(Y)}{\Psi(Y)}$$

Although we work here with functions possessing a derivative, this could be dispensed with by working with finite-difference arc elasticities.

Lemma 7.1

(i) Let $\Psi(Y)$ be a differentiable nonnegative function whose elasticity E_Ψ is strictly greater than unity for all $Y \in (0, \infty)$.

(ii) Let $v(Y)$ be a positive monotone-decreasing differentiable weighting function (i.e. $v(Y) > 0$, $v'(Y) < 0$) and let $dP(Y)$ be a probability distribution function over nonnegative Y such that its cumulative distribution function must grow at more than one positive point (so that $P(Y)$ takes on at least three positive values for positive Ys).

If

$$\int_0^\infty \Psi(Y)v(Y) \ dP(Y) = \int_0^\infty Yv(Y) \ dP(Y)$$

then

$$\int_0^\infty \Psi(Y) \ dP(Y) > \int_0^\infty Y \ dP(Y)$$

With this lemma, we can then proceed to state and prove the following theorem.

Theorem 7.2

If $F_n(X)$ is generated by the process described in equations (7.20) and (7.21), or in (7.29), (7.30), and (7.31), and if the actual yield $\beta(X, n)$ is defined by

$$\exp[\beta(X,n)] = \int_0^\infty \frac{F_n(XZ)}{F_{n+1}(X)}\, dP(Z; 1)$$

then, for all finite n, $\beta(X, n) > \alpha$.

PROOF

Now, writing $F_n(XZ)/F_{n+1}(X) = \Psi(Z)$, we must show that Ψ has the properties hypothesized by part (i) of Lemma 7.1, i.e. $\Psi \geq 0$ and $E_\Psi > 1$. Clearly, $\Psi(Z) \geq 0$ and, even more, because F_n is an increasing function of its argument, $\Psi'(Z) > 0$ for all $Z > 0$. From equation (7.30) and the definition of $F_0(X)$, for all $X > 0$ such that $F_n(X) > 0$, we have

$$0 \leq \frac{F_n'(X)}{F_n(X)} = \frac{\int_{1/X}^\infty Z\, dQ_n(Z)}{\int_{1/X}^\infty (XZ - 1)\, dQ_n(Z)}$$

$$= \frac{1}{X - \int_{1/X}^\infty dQ_n(Z)/\int_{1/X}^\infty Z\, dQ_n(Z)} > \frac{1}{X} \qquad (7.41)$$

So, for $X > 0$ such that $F_n(X) > 0$,

$$\frac{XF_n'(X)}{F_n(X)} > 1 \qquad (7.42)$$

Therefore, from (7.42),

$$E_\Psi = \frac{Z[F_n'(XZ)X/F_{n+1}(X)]}{[F_n(XZ)/F_{n+1}(X)]} = \frac{(XZ)F_n'(XZ)}{F_n(XZ)} > 1$$

If we write $v(Z) = U'[(1 - w_2^*)\exp(r) + w_2^*Z]$, we must show that U' satisfies condition (ii) of Lemma 7.1. Clearly, by the definition of U, $U' > 0$ and $U'' < 0$, condition (ii) is satisfied. From (7.29), (7.30), and (7.31), with $n = 1$, all the conditions for the hypothesis of Lemma 7.1 are satisfied:

$$\int_0^\infty \frac{F_n(XZ)}{F_{n+1}(X)} \, dQ(Z; 1) = \exp(r) = \int_0^\infty Z \, dQ(Z; 1)$$

Therefore, by Lemma 7.1,

$$\int_0^\infty \frac{F_n(XZ)}{F_{n+1}(X)} \, dP(Z; 1) > \int_0^\infty Z \, dP(Z; 1)$$

or

$$\exp[\beta(X, n)] > \exp(\alpha)$$

Therefore,

$$\beta(X, n) > \alpha \qquad\qquad \text{QED}$$

Using Lemma 7.1, as generalized in Appendix 7A, one could give a second proof that the common itself, being more "volatile" than the safe asset, must have a greater expected yield: namely $\alpha > r$ as expressed earlier in equation (7.21).

7.13   CONCLUSION

This completes the theory of utility-warranted warrant pricing. We leave to another occasion the calculation by a computer of tables of values for $F_n(X)$ based upon certain empirical assumptions about the volatility and trend of the $P(X_{t+n}/X_t; n)$ process. Using the general mathematical methods of the 1965 paper, but with different economic interpretations, we can also prepare tables of $F_n(X)$ for the Appendix 7B case of dividend-paying stocks.

Appendix 7A

The generalization and proof of Lemma 7.1 to prove the theorem that $\beta(X, n) > \alpha$ is as follows.[22]

---

22   The proofs of the general Lemma 7.2, Corollary 7.2, and Lemma 7.3 are by David T. Scheffman, Ph.D. candidate at MIT.

Lemma 7.2

Let Ψ, ϕ, and v be Riemann–Stieltjes integrable with respect to P where $dP(Y)$ is a probability distribution function and v is a monotone-decreasing function on $[0, \infty)$ and $v(Y) > 0$ for $Y > 0$. Suppose

(i) there exists $\overline{Y} \in (0, \infty)$ such that $\Psi(Y) \leqslant \phi(Y)$ for all $Y < \overline{Y}$ and $\phi(Y) \leqslant \Psi(Y)$ for all $Y > \overline{Y}$, and

(ii) $\int_0^\infty \Psi(Y)v(Y)\,dP(Y) = \int_0^\infty \phi(Y)v(Y)\,dP(Y)$.

Then $\int_0^\infty \Psi(Y)\,dP(Y) \geqslant \int_0^\infty \phi(Y)\,dP(Y)$.

PROOF

$$\int_0^{\overline{Y}} [\Psi(Y) - \phi(Y)]v(Y)\,dP(Y) \leqslant 0$$

$$\int_{\overline{Y}}^\infty [\Psi(Y) - \phi(Y)]v(Y)\,dP(Y) \geqslant 0 \tag{7A.1}$$

because $v(Y) \geqslant 0$.

$$-\int_0^{\overline{Y}} [\Psi(Y) - \phi(Y)]v(Y)\,dP(Y)$$

$$= \int_{\overline{Y}}^\infty [\Psi(Y) - \phi(Y)]v(Y)\,dP(Y) \tag{7A.2}$$

from (ii).

Let $\overline{v} = v(\overline{Y}) > 0$. Then

$$v(Y) \geqslant \overline{v} \quad \text{for } Y \leqslant \overline{Y}$$

$$v(Y) \leqslant \overline{v} \quad \text{for } Y \geqslant \overline{Y} \tag{7A.3}$$

by hypothesis. Then

$$-\int_0^{\overline{Y}} [\Psi(Y) - \phi(Y)]\overline{v}\,dP(Y) \leqslant \int_{\overline{Y}}^\infty [\Psi(Y) - \phi(Y)]\overline{v}\,dP(Y) \tag{7A.4}$$

from (7A.2) and (7A.3). Therefore,

$$\int_0^\infty \Psi(Y)\,dP(Y) \geqslant \int_0^\infty \phi(Y)\,dP(Y) \qquad \text{QED}$$

To show that Lemma 7.1 in the text is a special case of this general lemma and to get the sharper inequality result of Lemma 7.1, it is necessary to prove a corollary to Lemma 7.2 and also another lemma to the corollary.

Corollary 7.2

Let Ψ, ϕ, and dP be as in Lemma 7.2, and let dP not have the property

$$dP = \begin{cases} p & Y = 0 \\ 1-p & Y = \overline{Y} \\ 0 & \text{otherwise} \end{cases}$$

Suppose that $v(Y)$ is *strictly* monotone decreasing and nonnegative on $[0, \infty)$. Suppose that

(i') there exists $\overline{Y} \in (0, \infty)$ such that $\Psi(Y) < \phi(Y)$ for all $Y \in (0, \overline{Y})$ and $\phi(Y) < \Psi(Y)$ for all $Y \in (\overline{Y}, \infty)$, and

(ii) $\int_0^\infty \Psi(Y)v(Y)\,dP(Y) = \int_0^\infty \phi(Y)v(Y)\,dP(Y)$.

Then $\int_0^\infty \Psi(Y)\,dP(Y) > \int_0^\infty \phi(Y)\,dP(Y)$.

PROOF

$$\int_0^{\overline{Y}} [\Psi(Y) - \phi(Y)]v(Y)\,dP(Y) < 0$$

$$\int_{\overline{Y}}^\infty [\Psi(Y) - \phi(Y)]v(Y)\,dP(Y) > 0$$

by the property of dP and $v \geqslant 0$.

$$-\int_0^{\overline{Y}} [\Psi(Y) - \phi(Y)]v(Y)\,dP(Y)$$

$$= \int_{\overline{Y}}^\infty [\Psi(Y) - \phi(Y)]v(Y)\,dP(Y)$$

from (ii).
   Let $\overline{v} = v(\overline{Y}) > 0$. Then

$$v(Y) > \overline{v}, \; Y < \overline{Y}$$
$$v(Y) < \overline{v}, \; Y > \overline{Y}$$

by hypothesis. Then

$$-\int_0^{\bar{Y}} [\Psi(Y) - \phi(Y)]\bar{v} \, dP(Y) < \int_{\bar{Y}}^{\infty} [\Psi(Y) - \phi(Y)]\bar{v} \, dP(Y)$$

(Note that the posited property of dP was needed for this step.) Therefore,

$$\int_0^{\infty} \Psi(Y) \, dP(Y) > \int_0^{\infty} \phi(Y) \, dP(Y) \qquad \text{QED}$$

Thus, the strict inequality form of Lemma 7.1 used in the text is proved.

Although it is clear that the strict inequality of Corollary 7.2 would not hold for the pathological $dP(Y)$ case ruled out in the hypothesis of the corollary and of Lemma 7.1, it is instructive to give an example of this case. Let $dP(Y)$ be such that

$$\text{prob}\{Z = 0\} = \tfrac{1}{2}$$
$$\text{prob}\{Z = 3\} = \tfrac{1}{2}$$

(Note that $\Psi(3) = 3$, from below.) Suppose that we have Bernoulli logarithmic utility. Then we have $1 + a = 1.5$ or $a = 0.5$, the mean yield of the stock. From the utility maximum equation (7.38) for $n = 1$,

$$F_1(X) = \tfrac{1}{3}F_0(3X)$$

and by the usual recursive process, we get

$$F_n(X) = (\tfrac{1}{3})^n F_0(3^n X)$$

The mean warrant yield b is defined as follows:

$$b = E\left[\frac{F_n(XZ)}{F_{n+1}(X)}\right] - 1$$

$$= \frac{1}{2} \frac{(\tfrac{1}{3})^n F_0(3^n X \times 3)}{(\tfrac{1}{3})^{n+1} F_0(3^{n+1}X)} - 1$$

$$= 1.5 - 1 = 0.5$$

So, $b = a$ or $\beta(X, n) \equiv \alpha$ in this singular case.

In retrospect, the reason for $\beta(X, n) = \alpha$ for this type of distribution is that in it the stock and warrant are equally "volatile" with the chance of losing everything being the same for both stock and warrant.

We must show now the equivalence of the elasticity hypothesis of Lemma 7.1 in the text to the hypotheses of general Lemma 7.2. To do so, we prove the following lemma to the corollary.

Lemma 7.3

Let Ψ, ϕ, and dP be as in the general Lemma 7.2, and, in addition, Ψ and ϕ are continuous. Suppose either (a) there exists a $\Sigma > 0$ such that $\Psi(Y) = 0$, $Y \leqslant \Sigma$; $\phi(0) \geqslant 0$; $E_\Psi > E_\phi > 0$, for all $Y > \Sigma$; $E_\phi > 0$ for all $Y > 0$ and (ii) holds; or (b) $E_\Psi > E_\phi > 0$ for all $Y > 0$ and (ii) holds. Then condition (i) of the corollary holds.

PROOF

(I) If $\phi(\overline{Y}) = \Psi(\overline{Y})$ for some $\overline{Y} > 0$, then there does not exist $\check{Y} \neq \overline{Y}$, $\check{Y} > 0$, such that $\phi(\check{Y}) = \Psi(\check{Y})$.

For, consider any point $Y > 0$ where $\phi(Y) = \Psi(Y)$. Under condition (a), $Y > \Sigma$ because $\phi(0) \geqslant 0$, $E_\phi > 0$, for all $Y > 0$. Thus Y is such that $E_\Psi(Y) > E_\phi(Y)$, i.e. Ψ cuts ϕ from below at Y. But since $E_\Psi > E_\phi$, for all $Y > \Sigma$, Ψ can cut ϕ from below only once.

(II) There exists a $\delta > 0$ such that $\Psi(Y) < \phi(Y)$ for all $Y \in (0, \delta)$.

For (a) this holds trivially by setting $\delta = \Sigma$, in view of the restrictions on ϕ and Ψ. For (b), suppose such a δ does not exist. Then, given any $\Sigma > 0$, there exists a Y such that $Y \in (0, \Sigma)$ and $\Psi(Y) > \phi(Y)$. But since $E_\Psi > E_\phi$ for all $Y > 0$, this implies that $\Psi(Y) > \phi(Y)$ for all $Y > 0$. But this contradicts (ii).

Thus,

$$\int_0^\delta [\Psi(Y) - \phi(Y)]v(Y) \, dP(Y) < 0$$

and therefore

$$\int_\delta^\infty [\Psi(Y) - \phi(Y)]v(Y) \, dP(Y) > 0$$

Thus,

$$\Psi(Y) < \phi(Y) \text{ for some } Y \in (0, \delta)$$

$$\Psi(Y) > \phi(Y) \text{ for some } Y \in (\delta, \infty)$$

This implies, since Ψ and ϕ are assumed continuous, that there exists $\overline{Y} > 0$ such that $\phi(\overline{Y}) = \Psi(\overline{Y})$. By (I) we know that $\overline{Y}$ is unique in $(0, \infty)$. Therefore $\Psi(Y) < \phi(Y)$, $0 < Y \leqslant \Sigma$ and $E_\Psi > E_\phi$ for $Y > \Sigma$, so that $\overline{Y}$ is such that $\Psi(Y) < \phi(Y)$ for all $Y < \overline{Y}$ and $\phi(Y) < \Psi(Y)$ for all $Y > \overline{Y}$.

QED

Thus, from Corollary 7.2 and Lemma 7.3 and by taking $\phi(Y) = Y$ (and therefore, $E_\phi \equiv 1$), we have proved Lemma 7.1 used in the text. It was necessary in Lemma 7.3 to include the alternative hypothesis (a) because in the case where

$$\Psi(Z) = \frac{F_n(XZ)}{F_{n+1}(X)}$$

it is possible that $F_n(XZ) \equiv 0$ for positive XZ in the neighborhood of $XZ = 0$, in which case E_Ψ will not be properly defined. One can see that this has no effect on Lemma 7.1 because

$$\int_0^\infty \Psi(Y)v(Y) \, dP(Y) = \int_R \Psi(Y)v(Y) \, dP(Y)$$

where $R = \{Y | Y \in (0, \infty) \text{ and } \Psi(Y) > 0\}$ and similarly

$$\int_0^\infty \Psi(Y) \, dP(Y) = \int_R \Psi(Y) \, dP(Y)$$

Thus, we could go through the entire derivation considering only $Y \in R$ where E_Ψ is well defined and then at the end substitute the integrals over all nonnegative Y.

It should be emphasized that the proof of the general Lemma 7.2 did not even require continuity of Ψ, ϕ, and v and that the probability distribution dP can be discrete, entailing corners in the $F_n(X)$ functions. Thus, it holds for quite general types of assets and probability distributions. A simple extension of the corollary would prove the following general theorem of portfolio analysis.

Theorem 7.3

Let $\Psi_1, \Psi_2, \ldots, \Psi_n$ be the set of price ratios for n perfectly correlated assets and let their elasticities, E_{Ψ_i}, be such that $E_{\Psi_1} > E_{\Psi_2} > \cdots > E_{\Psi_n}$. Let Ψ_i, v, dP be as defined in Corollary 7.2.

If

$$\int_0^\infty \Psi_i(Y)v(Y) \, dP(Y) = \int_0^\infty \Psi_j(Y)v(Y) \, dP(Y)$$

for $i, j = 1, ..., n$, then $E[\Psi_1] > E[\Psi_2] > \cdots > E[\Psi_n]$.

Appendix 7B

If a common stock permanently pays no dividend, the theory of the text is applicable. If it does pay a dividend, the nice simplifications of the 1965 nonconversion special case are lost and we are back in all the 1965 complex inequalities. If we work with continuous rather than discrete time, the complicated McKean 1965 appendix methods are needed; and many unsolvable problems remain, problems that can be solved to any degree of accuracy only by taking smaller and smaller discrete time intervals. Here we shall sidestep all complexities stemming from continuous time, and can do so with a clearer conscience since the utility maximization is taken always to be over some prescribed finite interval (e.g. six months and a day to achieve capital gains tax privileges).

The simplest assumption about dividends is that the common priced at X_t, after any prescribed period, say T, will pay a dividend proportional to its price X_{t+T}. The dividend will then be $X_{t+T}[\exp(\delta T) - 1]$ where δ is the "force" or instantaneous rate of dividend yield. By convention, we may set $T = 1$; and each common that costs us X_t today brings us

$$X_{t+1} + X_{t+1}[\exp(\delta) - 1] = X_{t+1} \exp(\delta)$$

after one period. (We neglect all taxation throughout, despite the earlier remark about six-month holding periods.) Now our maximum problem becomes

$$\max_{\{w_j\}} \overline{U}(w_1, w_2, w_3)$$

$$= \max_{\{w_j\}} \int_0^\infty U\left[w_1 \exp(r) + w_2 \exp(\delta) \, Z + w_3 \frac{F_n(XZ)}{F_{n+1}(X)} \right] dP(Z; 1)$$

subject to $w_1 + w_2 + w_3 = 1$.

The conditions for the critical point of the Lagrangian

$$L = \overline{U} + \gamma(1 - \Sigma_1^3 w_j)$$

are exactly as in (7.14), (7.15a), and (7.16a) except that $w_2^* \exp(\delta)$ always appears where previously w_2^* alone appeared. Hence, the basic equations of the present theory, (7.15a) and (7.16a), become

$$F_{n+1}(X) = \exp(-r) \int_0^\infty F_n(XZ)\, dQ(Z; 1) \qquad (7B.1)$$

$$\int_0^\infty Z\, dQ(Z; 1) = \exp(r - \delta) \qquad (7B.2)$$

where, of course, dQ now involves δ along with its other suppressed parameters. Now $\beta_Q = r$ as before; but $\alpha_Q = r - \delta < \beta_Q$ and we are in the difficult $\beta > \alpha$ area of the 1965 analysis.

Now the values deduced from (7B.1) will fall below $F_0(X)$ conversion levels for large enough X, and conversion will be mandatory. Hence, the recursion relation (7B.1) above must be superseded by the inequalities

$$F_1(X) = \max\left[0, X - 1, \exp(-r) \int_0^\infty F_0(XZ)\, dQ(Z; 1)\right]$$

$$F_2(X) = \max\left[0, X - 1, \exp(-r) \int_0^\infty F_1(XZ)\, dQ(Z; 1)\right]$$

$$\cdots$$

$$\cdots$$

$$F_{n+1}(X) = \max\left[0, X - 1, \exp(-r) \int_0^\infty F_n(XZ)\, dQ(Z; 1)\right]$$

$$\cdots$$

$$\cdots$$

$$F_\infty(X) = F(X) = \max\left[0, X - 1, \exp(-r) \int_0^\infty F(XZ)\, dQ(Z; 1)\right]$$
$$(7B.3)$$

By the 1965 methods, one can show that for given $r = \beta$ and $\delta = \beta - \alpha$, we can find conversion values ($X^* = c_1, c_2, \ldots, c_\infty$) which are in ascending order and for which

$$F_n(X) > F_0(X), \qquad X < c_n$$
$$\equiv X - 1, \qquad X > c_n$$

Actually, for the perpetual warrant case, we have the following Fredholmlike integral equation of the second kind to solve for $F_\infty(X) = F(X)$, namely for $X < c = c_\infty$,

$$F(X) = \exp(-r) \int_0^\infty F(XZ) \, dQ(Z; 1)$$

$$= \exp(-r) \int_0^{c/X} F(XZ) \, dQ(Z; 1) + \exp(-r) \int_{c/X}^\infty (XZ - 1) \, dQ(Z; 1)$$

$$= \exp(-r) \int_0^{c/X} F(XZ) \, dQ(Z; 1) + \phi(X; c) \qquad (7B.4)$$

where ϕ is a known function. If dQ corresponds to a probability density $q(Z)dZ$, we can tranform this to

$$F(X) = \exp(-r) \int_0^c \frac{1}{X} q\left(\frac{v}{X}\right) F(v) dv + \phi(X; c)$$

Suppose this is solved by any of the well-known methods, for each possible c, and let $F(X; c)$ be the solution. Then we can solve for the unknown $c = c_\infty$ as the root of the joining-up equation

$$F(X; c) = X - 1 \text{ at } X = c_\infty \qquad (7B.5)$$

or

$$F(c_\infty; c_\infty) = c_\infty - 1$$

Thus the perpetual warrant case can be solved without going through the calculations of $F_n(X)$.

Actually, if the probabilities of price changes are bunched around $Z = 1$ with a finite range so that $P(Z; 1) = Q(Z; 1) = 0$ for $Z < \lambda^* < 1$ and $P(Z; 1) = Q(Z; 1) = 1$ for $Z > \lambda^{**} > 1$, this Fredholm-type equation can be solved as a Volterra-like equation, which, after a logarithmic transformation, becomes almost of the Poisson or Wiener–Hopf type. This can be seen as follows: consider an X small enough so that $c_\infty/\lambda^{**} > X$. Such an X exists because λ^{**} is finite. For Xs satisfying this inequality, we have

$$F(X) = \exp(-r) \int_{\lambda^*}^{\lambda^{**}} F(XZ) \, dQ(Z; 1) > X - 1 \qquad (7B.6)$$

and we can now use the method of analysis shown in Section 7.7. There is

an infinite number of solutions to the homogeneous integral equation
(7B.6) of the form cX^m. Substituting in (7B.6), we have

$$cX^m = \exp(-r)\, cX^m \int_{\lambda^*}^{\lambda^{**}} Z^m \, dQ(Z;\, 1)$$

$$1 = \exp(-r) \int_{\lambda^*}^{\lambda^{**}} Z^m \, dQ(Z;\, 1) = \phi(m) \qquad (7B.7)$$

This is the same as the transcendental equation (7.23). However, in this
case, because $r = \beta_Q > \alpha_Q = r - \delta$, $m = 1$ is no longer a solution. The
relevant real root, satisfying the boundary conditions, is $m > 1$, giving us
the power formula of the 1965 paper:

$$F_\infty(X) = aX^m = (c_\infty - 1) \left(\frac{X}{c_\infty}\right)^{c_x/(c_x - 1)}$$

8

Theory of Rational Option Pricing

The long history of the theory of option pricing began in 1900 when the French mathematician Louis Bachelier deduced an option pricing formula based on the assumption that stock prices follow a Brownian motion with zero drift. Since that time, numerous researchers have contributed to the theory. The present chapter begins by deducing a set of restrictions on option pricing formulas from the assumption that investors prefer more to less. These restrictions are necessary conditions for a formula to be consistent with a rational pricing theory. Attention is given to the problems created when dividends are paid on the underlying common stock and when the terms of the option contract can be changed explicitly by a change in exercise price or implicitly by a shift in the investment or capital structure policy of the firm. Since the deduced restrictions are not sufficient to uniquely determine an option pricing formula, additional assumptions are introduced to examine and extend the seminal Black–Scholes theory of option pricing. Explicit formulas for pricing both call and put options as well as for warrants and the new "down-and-out" option are derived. The effects of dividends and call provisions on the warrant price are examined. The possibilities for further extension of the theory to the pricing of corporate liabilities are discussed.

8.1 INTRODUCTION

The theory of warrant and option pricing has been studied extensively in both the academic and trade literature.[1] The approaches taken range from

Reproduced from *Bell Journal of Economics and Management Science*, 4, Spring 1973, 141–83. Reprinted with permission of the RAND Corporation. The paper is a substantial revision of sections of Merton (1970b). I am particularly grateful to Myron Scholes for reading an earlier draft and for his comments. I have benefited from discussion with P. A. Samuelson and F. Black. I thank Robert K. Merton for editorial assistance. Any errors remaining are mine. Aid from the National Science Foundation is gratefully acknowledged.

*1   The original paper has a substantial bibliography. Those papers not cited in the text have been excluded from the composite bibliography here.

sophisticated general equilibrium models to *ad hoc* statistical fits. Because options are specialized and relatively unimportant financial securities, the amount of time and space devoted to the development of a pricing theory might be questioned. One justification is that, since the option is a particularly simple type of contingent-claim asset, a theory of option pricing may lead to a general theory of contingent-claims pricing. Some have argued that all such securities can be expressed as combinations of basic option contracts, and, as such, a theory of option pricing constitutes a theory of contingent-claims pricing.[2] Hence, the development of an option pricing theory is, at least, an intermediate step toward a unified theory to answer questions about the pricing of a firm's liabilities, the term and risk structure of interest rates, and the theory of speculative markets. Further, there exist large quantities of data for testing the option pricing theory.

The first part of the chapter concentrates on laying the foundations for a rational theory of option pricing. It is an attempt to derive theorems about the properties of option prices based on assumptions sufficiently weak to gain universal support. To the extent that it is successful, the resulting theorems become necessary conditions to be satisfied by any rational option pricing theory.

As one might expect, assumptions weak enough to be accepted by all are not sufficient to determine uniquely a rational theory of option pricing. To do so, more structure must be added to the problem through additional assumptions at the expense of losing some agreement. The Black and Scholes formulation[3] is a significant "breakthrough" in attacking the option problem. The second part of the chapter examines their model in detail. An alternative derivation of their formula shows that it is valid under weaker assumptions than they postulate. Several extensions to their theory are derived.

8.2 RESTRICTIONS ON RATIONAL OPTION PRICING

An "American"-type warrant is a security, issued by a company, giving its owner the right to purchase a share of stock at a given ("exercise") price on or before a given date. An "American"-type call option has the same terms as the warrant except that it is issued by an individual instead of a company. An "American"-type put option gives its owner the right to sell a share of stock at a given exercise price on or before a given date. A "European"-type option has the same terms as its "American" counterpart except that it cannot be surrendered ("exercised") before the last date of

2 See Black and Scholes (1973) and Merton (1970b; this volume, Ch. 11).
3 In Black and Scholes (1973).

the contract. Samuelson (1965a) has demonstrated that the two types of contracts may not have the same value. All the contracts may differ with respect to other provisions such as antidilution clauses, exercise price changes, etc. Other option contracts such as strips, straps, and straddles are combinations of put and call options.

The principal difference between valuing the call option and the warrant is that the aggregate supply of call options is zero while the aggregate supply of warrants is generally positive. The "bucket shop" or "incipient" assumption of zero aggregate supply[4] is useful because the probability distribution of the stock-price return is unaffected by the creation of these options, which is not in general the case when they are issued by firms in positive amounts.[5] The "bucket shop" assumption is made throughout the chapter although many of the results derived hold independently of this assumption.

The notation used throughout is as follows: $F(S, \tau; E)$ is the value of an American warrant with exercise price E and τ years before expiration, when the price per share of the common stock is S; $f(S, \tau; E)$ is the value of its European counterpart; $G(S, \tau; E)$ is the value of an American put option; and $g(S, \tau; E)$ is the value of its European counterpart.

From the definition of a warrant and limited liability, we have that

$$F(S, \tau; E) \geq 0; \quad f(S, \tau; E) \geq 0 \tag{8.1}$$

and when $\tau = 0$, at expiration, both contracts must satisfy

$$F(S, 0; E) = f(S, 0; E) = \max(0, S - E) \tag{8.2}$$

Further, it follows from conditions of arbitrage that

$$F(S, \tau; E) \geq \max(0, S - E) \tag{8.3}$$

In general, a relation like (8.3) need not hold for a European warrant.

---

4 See Samuelson and Merton (1969; this volume, Section 7.7) for a discussion of "incipient" analysis. Essentially, the incipient price is such that a slightly higher price would induce a positive supply. In this context, the term "bucket shop" was coined in oral conversation by Paul Samuelson and is based on the (now illegal) 1920s practice of side-bets on the stock market.

Myron Scholes has pointed out that if a company sells a warrant against stock already *outstanding* (not just authorized), then the incipient analysis is valid as well (e.g. Amerada Hess selling warrants against shares of Louisiana Land and Exploration stock that it owns and City Investing selling warrants against shares of General Development Corporation stock that it owns).

5 See Merton (1970b; this volume, Section 11.2).

Definition

Security (portfolio) A is *dominant* over security (portfolio) B if, on some known date in the future, the return on A will exceed the return on B for some possible states of the world, and will be at least as large as on B in all possible states of the world.

Note that in perfect markets with no transactions costs and the ability to borrow and short-sell without restriction, the existence of a dominated security would be equivalent to the existence of an arbitrage situation. However, it is possible for dominated securities to exist without arbitrage in imperfect markets. If one assumes something like "symmetric market rationality" and assumes further that investors prefer more wealth to less,[6] then any investor willing to purchase security B would prefer to purchase A.

Assumption 1

A necessary condition for a rational option pricing theory is that the option be priced such that it is neither a dominant nor a dominated security.

Given two American warrants on the same stock and with the same exercise price, it follows from Assumption 1 that

$$F(S, \tau_2; E) \geq F(S, \tau_1; E) \text{ if } \tau_2 > \tau_1 \qquad (8.4)$$

and that

$$F(S, \tau; E) \geq f(S, \tau; E) \qquad (8.5)$$

Further, two warrants, identical in every way except that one has a larger exercise price than the other, must satisfy

$$\begin{aligned} F(S, \tau; E_2) &\leq F(S, \tau; E_1) \\ f(S, \tau; E_2) &\leq f(S, \tau; E_1) \text{ if } E_2 > E_1 \end{aligned} \qquad (8.6)$$

Because the common stock is equivalent to a perpetual ($\tau = \infty$) American warrant with a zero exercise price ($E = 0$), it follows from (8.4) and (8.6) that

$$S \geq F(S, \tau; E) \qquad (8.7)$$

6 See Miller and Modigliani (1961, p. 427) for a definition of "symmetric market rationality."

and, from (8.1) and (8.7), the warrant must be worthless if the stock is, i.e.

$$F(0, \tau; E) = f(0, \tau; E) = 0 \tag{8.8}$$

Let $P(\tau)$ be the price of a riskless (in terms of default) discounted loan (or "bond") which pays one dollar, τ years from now. If it is assumed that current and future interest rates are positive, then

$$1 = P(0) > P(\tau_1) > P(\tau_2) > \cdots > P(\tau_n) \text{ for } 0 < \tau_1 < \tau_2 < \cdots < \tau_n \tag{8.9}$$

at a given point in calendar time.

Theorem 8.1

If the exercise price of a European warrant is E and if no payouts (e.g. dividends) are made to the common stock over the life of the warrant (or, alternatively, if the warrant is protected against such payments), then $f(S, \tau; E) \geq \max[0, S - EP(\tau)]$.

PROOF

Consider the following two investments.

A   Purchase the warrant for $f(S, \tau; E)$;
     Purchase E bonds at price $P(\tau)$ per bond.
         Total investment: $f(S, \tau; E) + EP(\tau)$.
B   Purchase the common stock for S.
         Total investment: S.

Suppose at the end of τ years the common stock has value S^*. Then the value of B will be S^*. If $S^* \leq E$, then the warrant is worthless and the value of A will be $0 + E = E$. If $S^* > E$, then the value of A will be $(S^* - E) + E = S^*$. Therefore, unless the current value of A is at least as large as B, A will dominate B. Hence, by Assumption 1, $f(S, \tau; E) + EP(\tau) \geq S$, which together with (8.1) implies that $f(S, \tau; E) \geq \max [0, S - EP(\tau)]$.   QED

From (8.5), it follows directly that Theorem 8.1 holds for American warrants with a fixed exercise price over the life of the contract. The right to exercise an option prior to the expiration date always has nonnegative value. It is important to know when this right has zero value, since in that case the values of a European and American option are the same. In practice, almost all options are of the American type while it is always easier to solve analytically for the value of a European option. Theorem

8.1 significantly tightens the bounds for rational warrant prices over (8.3). In addition, it leads to the following two theorems.

Theorem 8.2

If the hypothesized conditions for Theorem 8.1 hold, an American warrant will never be exercised prior to expiration, and hence it has the same value as a European warrant.

PROOF

If the warrant is exercised, its value will be $\max(0, S - E)$. But from Theorem 8.1, $F(S, \tau; E) \geq \max[0, S - EP(\tau)]$, which is larger than $\max(0, S - E)$ for $\tau > 0$ because, from (8.9), $P(\tau) < 1$. Hence, the warrant is always worth more "alive" than "dead."   QED

Theorem 8.2 suggests that if there is a difference between the American and European warrant prices which implies a positive probability of a premature exercise, it must be due to unfavorable changes in the exercise price or to lack of protection against payouts to the common stocks. This result is consistent with the findings of Samuelson and Merton (1969; this volume, Section 7.9 and Appendix 7B).

It is a common practice to refer to $\max(0, S - E)$ as the *intrinsic value* of the warrant and to state that the warrant must always sell for at least its intrinsic value (condition (8.3)). In light of Theorems 8.1 and 8.2, it makes more sense to define $\max[0, S - EP(\tau)]$ as the intrinsic value. The latter definition reflects the fact that the amount of the exercise price need not be paid until the expiration date, and $EP(\tau)$ is just the present value of that payment. The difference between the two values can be large, particularly for long-lived warrants, as the following theorem demonstrates.

Theorem 8.3

If the hypothesized conditions for Theorem 8.1 hold, the value of a perpetual ($\tau = \infty$) warrant must equal the value of the common stock.

PROOF

From Theorem 8.1, $F(S, \infty; E) \geq \max[0, S - EP(\infty)]$. But $P(\infty) = 0$ since, for positive interest rates, the value of a discounted loan payable at infinity is zero. Therefore, $F(S, \infty; E) \geq S$. But from (8.7), $S \geq F(S, \infty; E)$. Hence, $F(S, \infty; E) = S$.   QED

Samuelson (1965a), Samuelson and Merton (1969; this volume, Ch. 7), and Black and Scholes (1973) have shown that the price of a perpetual warrant equals the price of the common stock for their particular models. Theorem 8.3 demonstrates that it holds independently of any stock price distribution or risk-averse behavioral assumptions.[7]

The inequality of Theorem 8.1 demonstrates that a finite-lived rationally determined warrant price must be a function of $P(\tau)$. For if it were not, then, for some sufficiently small $P(\tau)$ (i.e. large interest rate), the inequality of Theorem 8.1 would be violated. From the form of the inequality and previous discussion, this direct dependence on the interest rate seems to be "induced" by using the exercise price instead of the present value of the exercise price as a variable (i.e. I conjecture that the pricing function $F[S, \tau; E, P(\tau)]$ can be written as $W(S, \tau; e)$, where $e = EP(\tau)$).[8] If this is so, then the qualitative effect of a change in P on the warrant price would be similar to a change in the exercise price, which, from (8.6), is negative. Therefore the warrant price should be an increasing function of the interest rate. This finding is consistent with the theoretical models of Samuelson and Merton (1969; this volume, Ch. 7) and Black and Scholes (1973) and with the empirical study by Van Horne (1969).

Another argument for the reasonableness of this result comes from recognizing that a European warrant is equivalent to a long position in the common stock levered by a limited-liability discount loan, where the borrower promises to pay E dollars at the end of τ periods, but in the event of default is only liable to the extent of the value of the common stock at that time.[9] If the present value of such a loan is a decreasing function of the interest rate, then, for a given stock price, the warrant price will be an increasing function of the interest rate.

We now establish two theorems about the effect of a change in exercise price on the price of the warrant.

---

7 It is a bit of a paradox that a perpetual warrant with a positive exercise price should sell for the same price as the common stock (a "perpetual warrant" with a zero exercise price), and, in fact, the few such outstanding warrants do not sell for this price. However, it must be remembered that one assumption for the theorem to obtain is that no payouts to the common stock will be made over the life of the contract which is almost never true in practice. See Samuelson and Merton (1969; this volume, Section 7.10) for further discussion of the paradox.

8 The only case where the warrant price does not depend on the exercise price is the perpetuity, and the only case where the warrant price does not depend on $P(\tau)$ is when the exercise price is zero. Note that, in both cases, $e = 0$ (the former because $P(\infty) = 0$, and the latter because $E = 0$), which is consistent with our conjecture.

9 Stiglitz (1969, p. 788) introduces this same type of loan as a sufficient condition for the Modigliani–Miller theorem to obtain when there is a positive probability of bankruptcy.

Theorem 8.4

If $F(S, \tau; E)$ is a rationally determined warrant price, then F is a convex function of its exercise price E.

To prove convexity, we must show that if

$$E_3 \equiv \lambda E_1 + (1 - \lambda)E_2$$

then, for every λ, $0 \leq \lambda \leq 1$,

$$F(S, \tau; E_3) \leq \lambda F(S, \tau; E_1) + (1 - \lambda)F(S, \tau; E_2)$$

We do so by a dominance argument similar to the proof of Theorem 8.1. Let portfolio A contain λ warrants with exercise price E_1 and $1 - \lambda$ warrants with exercise price E_2 where, by convention, $E_2 > E_1$. Let portfolio B contain one warrant with exercise price E_3. If S^* is the stock price on the date of expiration, then by the convexity of $\max(0, S^* - E)$ the value of portfolio A,

$$\lambda \max(0, S^* - E_1) + (1 - \lambda) \max(0, S^* - E_2)$$

will be greater than or equal to the value of portfolio B,

$$\max[0, S^* - \lambda E_1 - (1 - \lambda)E_2]$$

Hence, to avoid dominance, the current value of portfolio B must be less than or equal to the current value of portfolio A. Thus, the theorem is proved for a European warrant. Since nowhere in the argument is any factor involving τ used, the same results would obtain if the warrants in the two portfolios were exercised prematurely. Hence, the theorem holds for American warrants.   QED

Theorem 8.5

If $f(S, \tau; E)$ is a rationally determined European warrant price, then for $E_1 < E_2$, $-P(\tau)(E_2 - E_1) \leq f(S, \tau; E_2) - f(S, \tau; E_1) \leq 0$. Further, if f is a differentiable function of its exercise price, $-P(\tau) \leq \partial f(S, \tau; E)/\partial E \leq 0$.

PROOF

The right-hand inequality follows directly from (8.6). The left-hand inequality follows from a dominance argument. Let portfolio A contain a warrant to purchase the stock at E_2 and $E_2 - E_1$ bonds at price $P(\tau)$ per bond. Let portfolio B contain a warrant to purchase the stock at E_1. If S^* is the stock price on the date of expiration, then the terminal value of portfolio A,

$$\max(0, S^* - E_2) + (E_2 - E_1)$$

will be greater than the terminal value of portfolio B, $\max(0, S^* - E_1)$, when $S^* < E_2$, and equal to it when $S^* \geq E_2$. So, to avoid dominance, $f(S, \tau; E_1) \leq f(S, \tau; E_2) + P(\tau)(E_2 - E_1)$. The inequality on the derivative follows by dividing the discrete-change inequalities by $E_2 - E_1$ and taking the limit as E_2 tends to E_1. QED

If the hypothesized conditions for Theorem 8.1 hold, then the inequalities of Theorem 8.5 hold for American warrants. Otherwise, we only have the weaker inequalities $-(E_2 - E_1) \leq F(S, \tau; E_2) - F(S, \tau; E_1) \leq 0$ and $-1 \leq \partial F(S, \tau; E)/\partial E \leq 0$.

Let $Q(t)$ be the price per share of a common stock at time t and $F_Q(Q, \tau; E_Q)$ be the price of a warrant to purchase one share of stock at price E_Q on or before a given date τ years in the future, when the current price of the common stock is Q.

Theorem 8.6

If k is a positive constant, $Q(t) = kS(t)$, $E_Q = kE$, then $F_Q(Q, \tau; E_Q) \equiv kF(S, \tau; E)$ for all S, τ, E and each k.

PROOF

Let S^* be the value of the common stock with initial value S when both warrants either are exercised or expire. Then, by the hypothesized conditions of the theorem, $Q = Q^* \equiv kS^*$ and $E_Q = kE$. The value of the warrant on Q will be $\max(0, Q^* - E_Q) = k \max(0, S^* - E)$ which is k times the value of the warrant on S. Hence, to avoid dominance of one over the other, the value of the warrant on Q must sell for exactly k times the value of the warrant on S. QED

The implications of Theorem 8.6 for restrictions on rational warrant pricing depend on what assumptions are required to produce the hypothesized conditions of the theorem. In its weakest form, it is a dimensional theorem where k is the proportionality factor between two units of account (e.g. $k = 100$ cents per dollar). If the stock and warrant markets are purely competitive, then it can be interpreted as a scale theorem. Namely, if there are no economies of scale with respect to transactions costs and no problems with indivisibilities, then k shares of stock will always sell for exactly k times the value of one share of stock. Under these conditions, the theorem states that a warrant to buy k shares of stock for a total of kE dollars when the stock price per share is S dollars is equal in value to k times the price of a warrant to buy one share of the stock for E dollars, all other terms being the same. Thus, the rational warrant pricing function is homogeneous of degree one in S and E with respect to scale, which reflects the usual constant returns to scale results of competition.

Hence, one can always work in standardized units of $E = 1$ where the stock price and warrant price are quoted in units of exercise price by choosing $k = 1/E$. Not only does this change of units eliminate a variable from the problem, but it is also a useful operation to perform prior to making empirical comparisons across different warrants where the dollar amounts may be of considerably different magnitudes.

Let $F_i(S_i, \tau_i; E_i)$ be the value of a warrant on the common stock of firm i with current price per share S_i when τ_i is the time to expiration and E_i is the exercise price.

Assumption 2

If $S_i = S_j = S$, $\tau_i = \tau_j = \tau$, $E_i = E_j = E$, and the returns per dollar on the stocks i and j are identically distributed, then $F_i(S, \tau; E) = F_j(S, \tau; E)$.

Assumption 2 implies that, from the point of view of the warrant holder, the only identifying feature of the common stock is its (*ex ante*) distribution of returns.

Define $z_i(t)$ to be the one-period random variable return per dollar invested in the common stock of firm i in period t. Let $Z_i(\tau) \equiv \Pi_{t=1}^{\tau} z_i(t)$ be the τ-period return per dollar.

Theorem 8.7

If $S_i = S_j = S$, $i, j = 1,2,\ldots,n$,

$$Z_{n+1}(\tau) \equiv \sum_1^n \lambda_i Z_i(\tau)$$

for $\lambda_i \in [0, 1]$ and $\Sigma_1^n \lambda_i = 1$, then

$$F_{n+1}(S, \tau; E) \leq \sum_{1}^{n} \lambda_i F_i(S, \tau; E)$$

PROOF

By construction, one share of the $(n + 1)$th security contains λ_i shares of the common stock of firm i, and by hypothesis the price per share $S_{n+1} = \Sigma_1^n \lambda_i S_i = S\Sigma_1^n \lambda_i = S$. The proof follows from a dominance argument. Let portfolio A contain λ_i warrants on the common stock of firm i, $i = 1,2,...,n$. Let portfolio B contain one warrant on the $(n + 1)$th security. Let S_i^* denote the price per share on the common stock of the ith firm on the date of expiration, $i = 1,2,...,n$. By definition, $S_{n+1}^* = \Sigma_1^n \lambda_i S_i^*$. On the expiration date, the value of portfolio A, $\Sigma_1^n \lambda_i \max(0, S_i^* - E)$, is greater than or equal to the value of portfolio B, $\max(0, \Sigma_1^n \lambda_i S_i^* - E)$, by the convexity of $\max(0, S - E)$. Hence, to avoid dominance,

$$F_{n+1}(S, \tau; E) \leq \sum_{1}^{n} \lambda_i F_i(S, \tau; E) \qquad \text{QED}$$

Loosely, Theorem 8.7 states that a warrant on a portfolio is less valuable than a portfolio of warrants. Thus, from the point of view of warrant value, diversification "hurts," as the following special case of Theorem 8.7 demonstrates.

Corollary 8.7

If the hypothesized conditions of Theorem 8.7 hold and if, in addition, the $\{z_i(t)\}$ are identically distributed, then

$$F_{n+1}(S, \tau; E) \leq F_i(S, \tau; E)$$

for $i = 1,2,...,n$.

PROOF

From Theorem 8.7, $F_{n+1}(S, \tau; E) \leq \Sigma_1^n \lambda_i F_i(S, \tau; E)$. By hypothesis, the $z_i(t)$ are identically distributed, and hence so are the $\{Z_i(\tau)\}$. Therefore, by Assumption 2, $F_i(S, \tau; E) = F_j(S, \tau; E)$ for $i, j = 1,2,...,n$. Since $\Sigma_1^n \lambda_i = 1$, it then follows that $F_{n+1}(S, \tau; E) \leq F_i(S, \tau; E)$, $i = 1,2,...,n$. QED

Theorem 8.7 and its corollary suggest the more general proposition that, the more risky the common stock, the more valuable the warrant. Just as with the broadly accepted dictum that "diversification reduces risk," so the validity of this proposition depends critically on the definition of "riskiness" or "volatility."[10]

Definition

Security one is *more risky* than security two if $Z_1(\tau) = qZ_2(\tau) + \epsilon$ where the random variables q, $Z_2(\tau)$, and ϵ are mutually independent; $E(q) = 1$; and $E(\epsilon) = 0$.

Theorem 8.8

The rationally determined warrant price is a nondecreasing function of the riskiness of its associated common stock.

PROOF

Let $Z(\tau)$ be the τ-period return on a common stock with warrant price $F_Z(S, \tau; E)$. Let $Z_i(\tau) = q_iZ(\tau) + \epsilon_i$, $i = 1,...,n$, where the ϵ_i are independently and identically distributed with $E(\epsilon_i) = 0$, $i = 1,...,n$, the q_i are independently and identically distributed with $E(q_i) = 1$, $i = 1,...,n$, and ϵ_i, q_j, $Z(\tau)$ are mutually independent, $i, j = 1,...,n$. By definition, security i is more risky than security Z, for $i = 1,...,n$. Define the random variable return

$$Z_{n+1}(\tau) \equiv \frac{1}{n} \sum_1^n Z_i(\tau) = Z(\tau) + \left[\frac{1}{n} \sum_1^n (q_i - 1)\right]Z(\tau) + \frac{1}{n} \sum_1^n \epsilon_i$$

Note that, by construction, the $Z_i(\tau)$ are identically distributed. Hence, by Corollary 8.7 with $\lambda_i = 1/n$, $F_{n+1}(S, \tau; E) \leq F_i(S, \tau; E)$ for $i = 1,...,n$. By the Law of Large Numbers, $Z_{n+1}(\tau)$ converges in probability to $Z(\tau)$ as $n \to \infty$, and hence, by Assumption 2,

$$\lim_{n\to\infty} F_{n+1}(S, \tau; E) = F_Z(S, \tau; E)$$

Therefore, $F_Z(S, \tau; E) \leq F_i(S, \tau; E)$ for $i = 1,...,n$.   QED

---

*10   For a discussion of the conditions under which diversification reduces risk, see Merton (1983a, pp. 113–16). In the original paper (Merton, 1973a, p. 148), I defined "riskiness" for the purpose of the proposition about warrant price as: "Security one is *more risky* than security two if $Z_1(\tau) = Z_2(\tau) + \epsilon$ where ϵ is a random variable with the property $E[\epsilon|Z_2(\tau)] = 0$." This definition corresponds to the Rothschild and Stiglitz (1970, p. 225) definition of more risky and includes the definition of the text here as a special case. However, Jagannathan (1984) has shown that this original broader definition is not sufficient for the proposition to obtain.

Thus, the more uncertain one is about the outcomes on the common stock, the more valuable is the warrant.[11] This finding is consistent with the empirical study by Van Horne (1969).

To this point in the chapter, no assumptions have been made about the properties of the distribution of returns on the common stock. If it is assumed that the $\{z(t)\}$ are independently distributed,[12] then the distribution of the returns per dollar invested in the stock is independent of the initial level of the stock price, and we have the following theorem.

Theorem 8.9

If the distribution of the returns per dollar invested in the common stock is independent of the level of the stock price, then $F(S, \tau; E)$ is homogeneous of degree one in the stock price per share and exercise price.

PROOF

Let $z_i(t)$ be the return per dollar if the initial stock price is S_i, $i = 1,2$. Define $k = S_2/S_1$ and $E_2 = kE_1$. Then, by Theorem 8.6, $F_2(S_2, \tau; E_2) \equiv kF_2(S_1, \tau; E_1)$. By hypothesis, $z_1(t)$ and $z_2(t)$ are identically distributed. Hence, by Assumption 2, $F_2(S_1, \tau; E_1) = F_1(S_1, \tau; E_1)$. Therefore, $F_2(kS_1, \tau; kE_1) \equiv kF_1(S_1, \tau; E_1)$ and the theorem is proved.   QED

Although similar in a formal sense, Theorem 8.9 is considerably stronger than Theorem 8.6, in terms of restrictions on the warrant pricing function. Namely, given the hypothesized conditions of Theorem 8.9, one would expect to find, in a table of rational warrant values for a given maturity, that the value of a warrant with exercise price E when the common stock is at S will be exactly k times as valuable as a warrant on the same stock with exercise price E/k when the common stock is selling for S/k. In general, this result will not obtain if the distribution of returns depends on the level of the stock price as is shown by a counter-example in Appendix 8A.

Theorem 8.10

If the distribution of the returns per dollar invested in the common stock is independent of the level of the stock price, then $F(S, \tau; E)$ is a convex function of the stock price.

11 It should also be noted that it is the *total* risk, and not just the *systematic* or portfolio risk, of the common stock that is important to warrant pricing.
12 Cf. Samuelson (1965a).

PROOF

To prove convexity, we must show that if

$$S_3 \equiv \lambda S_1 + (1 - \lambda)S_2$$

then, for every λ, $0 \le \lambda \le 1$,

$$F(S_3, \tau; E) \le \lambda F(S_1, \tau; E) + (1 - \lambda)F(S_2, \tau; E)$$

From Theorem 8.4,

$$F(1, \tau; E_3) \le \gamma F(1, \tau; E_1) + (1 - \gamma)F(1, \tau; E_2)$$

for $0 \le \gamma \le 1$ and $E_3 = \gamma E_1 + (1 - \gamma)E_2$. Take $\gamma \equiv \lambda S_1/S_3$, $E_1 \equiv E/S_1$, and $E_2 \equiv E/S_2$. Multiplying both sides of the inequality by S_3, we have that

$$S_3 F(1, \tau; E_3) \le \lambda S_1 F(1, \tau; E_1) + (1 - \lambda)S_2 F(1, \tau; E_2)$$

From Theorem 8.9, F is homogeneous of degree one in S and E. Hence,

$$F(S_3, \tau; S_3 E_3) \le \lambda F(S_1, \tau; S_1 E_1) + (1 - \lambda)F(S_2, \tau; S_2 E_2)$$

By the definition of E_1, E_2, and E_3, this inequality can be rewritten as $F(S_3, \tau; E) \le \lambda F(S_1, \tau; E) + (1 - \lambda)F(S_2, \tau; E)$.   QED

Although convexity is usually assumed to be a property which always holds for warrants, and while the hypothesized conditions of Theorem 8.10 are by no means necessary, Appendix 8A provides an example where the distribution of future returns on the common stock is sufficiently dependent on the level of the stock price to cause perverse local concavity.

Based on the analysis so far, Figure 8.1 illustrates the general shape that the rational warrant price should satisfy as a function of the stock price and time.[13]

8.3   EFFECTS OF DIVIDENDS AND CHANGING EXERCISE PRICE

A number of the theorems of the previous section depend upon the assumption that either no payouts are made to the common stock over the

---

*13   By adding the assumption that all investors are strictly risk averse, these bounds on option prices can be tightened (cf. Perrakis and Ryan, 1984; Levy, 1985; Ritchken, 1985; Perrakis, 1986; Sachdeva, 1986; Lo, 1987).

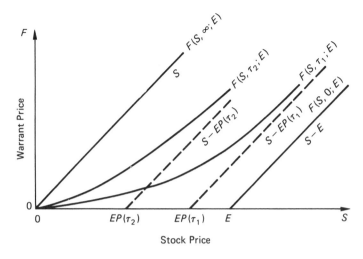

Figure 8.1 Arbitrage Boundaries of Warrant Prices.

life of the contract or the contract is protected against such payments. In this section, the adjustments required in the contracts to protect them against payouts are derived, and the effects of payouts on the valuation of unprotected contracts are investigated. The two most common types of payouts are stock dividends (splits) and cash dividends.

In general, the value of an option will be affected by unanticipated changes in the firm's investment policy, capital structure (e.g. debt–equity ratio), and payout policy. For example, if the firm should change its investment policy so as to lower the riskiness of its cash flow (and hence the riskiness of outcomes on the common stock), then, by Theorem 8.8, the value of the warrant would decline for a given level of the stock price. Similarly, if the firm changed its capital structure by raising the debt–equity ratio, then the riskiness of the common stock would increase and the warrant would become more valuable. If that part of the total return received by shareholders in the form of dividends is increased by a change in payout policy, then the value of an unprotected warrant would decline since the warrant holder has no claim on the dividends.[14]

While it is difficult to provide a set of adjustments to the warrant contract to protect it against changes in investment or capital structure policies without severely restricting the management of the firm, there do exist a set of adjustments to protect the warrant holders against payouts.

14   This is an important point to remember when valuing unprotected warrants of companies such as AT&T where a substantial fraction of the total return to shareholders comes in the form of dividends.

Definition

An option is said to be *payout protected* if, for a fixed investment policy and fixed capital structure, the value of the option is invariant to the choice of payout policy.

Theorem 8.11

If the total return per dollar invested in the common stock is invariant to the fraction of the return represented by payouts and if, on each expayout date during the life of a warrant, the contract is adjusted so that the number of shares which can be purchased for a total of E dollars is increased by the fraction d/S^x where d is the dollar amount of the payout and S^x is the expayout price per share of the stock, then the warrant will be payout protected.

PROOF

Consider two firms with identically distributed total returns per dollar invested in the common stock, $z_i(t)$, $i = 1,2$, and whose initial prices per share are the same ($S_1 = S_2 = S$). For firm i, let $\lambda_i(t)$ ($t \geq 1$) be the return per dollar in period t from payouts and $x_i(t)$ be the return per dollar in period t from capital gains, such that $z_i(t) \equiv \lambda_i(t)x_i(t)$. Let $N_i(t)$ be the number of shares of firm i which the warrant of firm i has claim on for a total price of E at time t, where $N_1(0) = N_2(0) = 1$. By definition, $\lambda_i(t) \equiv 1 + d_i(t)/S_i^x(t)$, where $S_i^x(t) = \Pi_{k=1}^{t} x_i(k)S$ is the expayout price per share at time t. Therefore, by the hypothesized conditions of the theorem, $N_i(t) = \lambda_i(t)N_i(t - 1)$. On the date when the warrants are either exercised or expire, the value of the warrant on firm i will be

$$\max[0, N_i(t)S_i^x(t) - E]$$

But

$$N_i(t)S_i^x(t) = \left[\prod_{k=1}^{t} \lambda_i(k) \right]\left[\prod_{k=1}^{t} x_i(k)S \right] = \prod_{k=1}^{t} z_i(k)S$$

Since, by hypothesis, the $z_i(t)$ are identically distributed, the distribution of outcomes on the warrants of the two firms will be identical. Therefore, by Assumption 2, $F_1(S, \tau; E) = F_2(S, \tau; E)$, independent of the particular pattern chosen for the $\{\lambda_i(t)\}$.   QED

Note that if the hypothesized conditions of Theorem 8.11 hold, then the value of a protected warrant will be equal to the value of a warrant which restricts management from making any payouts to the common stock over the life of the warrant (i.e. $\lambda_i(t) \equiv 1$). Hence, a protected warrant will satisfy all the theorems of Section 8.2 which depend on the assumption of no payouts over the life of the warrant.

Corollary 8.11a

If the total return per dollar invested in the common stock is invariant to the fraction of the return represented by payouts, if there are no economies of scale, and if, on each expayout date during the life of a warrant, each warrant to purchase one share of stock for exercise price E is exchanged for λ ($\equiv 1 + d/S^x$) warrants to purchase one share of stock for exercise price E/λ, then the warrant will be payout protected.

PROOF

By Theorem 8.11, on the first expayout date, a protected warrant will have claim on λ shares of stock at a total exercise price of E. By hypothesis, there are no economies of scale. Hence the scale interpretation of Theorem 8.6 is valid which implies that the value of a warrant on λ shares at a total price of E must be identically (in λ) equal to the value of λ warrants to purchase one share at an exercise price of E/λ. Proceeding inductively, we can show that this equality holds on each payout date. Hence, a warrant with the adjustment provision of Corollary 8.11a will be payout protected. QED

If there are no economies of scale, it is generally agreed that a stock split or dividend will not affect the distribution of future per dollar returns on the common stock. Hence, the hypothesized adjustments will protect the warrant holder against stock splits where λ is the number of postsplit shares per presplit share.[15]

The case for cash dividend protection is more subtle. In the absence of taxes and transactions costs, Miller and Modigliani (1961) have shown that, for a fixed investment policy and capital structure, dividend policy does not affect the value of the firm. Under their hypothesized conditions, it is a necessary result of their analysis that the total return per dollar invested in the common stock will be invariant to payout policy. Therefore, warrants adjusted according to either Theorem 8.11 or Corollary 8.11a will be

---

15 For any particular function $F(S, \tau; E)$, there are many other adjustments which could leave value the same. However, the adjustment suggestions of Theorem 8.11 and Corollary 8.11a are the only ones which do so for every such function. In practice, both adjustments are used to protect warrants against stock splits. See Braniff Airways 1986 warrants for an example of the former and Leasco 1987 warrants for the latter. λ could be less than unity in the case of a reverse split.

payout protected in the same sense that Miller and Modigliani mean when they say that dividend policy "doesn't matter."

The principal cause for confusion is different definitions of payout protected. Black and Scholes (1973) give an example to illustrate "that there may not be any adjustment in the terms of the option that will give adequate protection against a large dividend." Suppose that the firm liquidates all its assets and pays them out in the form of a cash dividend. Clearly, $S^x = 0$, and hence the value of the warrant must be zero no matter what adjustment is made to the number of shares it has claim on or to its exercise price.

While their argument is correct, it also suggests a much stronger definition of payout protection. Namely, their example involves changes in investment policy and, if there is a positive supply of warrants (the nonincipient case), a change in the capital structure, in addition to a payout. Hence, their definition would seem to require protection against all three.

To illustrate, consider the firm in their example, but where management is prohibited against making any payouts to the shareholders prior to expiration of the warrant. It seems that such a warrant would be called payout protected by any reasonable definition. It is further assumed that the firm has only equity outstanding (i.e. the incipient case for the warrant) to rule out any capital structure effects.[16]

Suppose the firm sells all its assets for a fair price (so that the share price remains unchanged) and uses the proceeds to buy riskless τ-period bonds. As a result of this investment policy change, the stock becomes a riskless asset and the warrant price will fall to $\max(0, S - EP)$. Note that, if $S < EP$, the warrant will be worthless even though it is payout protected. Now lift the restriction against payouts and replace it with the adjustments of Corollary 8.11a. Given that the shift in investment policy has taken place, suppose the firm makes a payment of fraction γ of the value of the firm to the shareholders. Then, $S^x = (1 - \gamma)S$ and

$$\lambda = 1 + \frac{\gamma}{1 - \gamma} = \frac{1}{1 - \gamma}$$

The value of the warrant after the payout will be

$$\lambda \max\left(0, S^x - \frac{EP}{\lambda}\right) = \max(0, S - EP)$$

---

16   The incipient case is a particularly important example since, in practice, the only contracts that are adjusted for cash payouts are options. The incipient assumption also rules out "capital structure induced" changes in investment policy by malevolent management. For an example, see Stiglitz (1972).

which is the same as the value of the warrant when the company was restricted from making payouts. In the Black and Scholes example, $\gamma = 1$ and so $\lambda = \infty$ and $E/\lambda = 0$. Hence, there is the indeterminacy of multiplying zero by infinity. However, for every $\gamma < 1$, the analysis is correct, and therefore it is reasonable to suspect that it holds in the limit.

A similar analysis in the nonincipient case would show that both investment policy and the capital structure were changed, for in this case the firm would have to purchase fraction γ of the warrants outstanding to keep the capital structure unchanged without issuing new stock. In the Black and Scholes example where $\gamma = 1$, this would require purchasing the entire issue, after which the analysis reduces to the incipient case. The Black and Scholes emphasis on protection against a "large" dividend is further evidence that they really have in mind protection against investment policy and capital structure shifts as well, since large payouts are more likely to be associated with nontrivial changes in either or both.

It should be noted that calls and puts that satisfy the incipient assumption have in practice been the only options issued with cash dividend protection clauses, and the typical adjustment has been to reduce the exercise price by the amount of the cash dividend, an adjustment that has been demonstrated to be incorrect.[17]

To this point it has been assumed that the exercise price remains constant over the life of the contract (except for the adjustments for payouts mentioned earlier). A variable exercise price is meaningless for a European warrant since the contract is not exercisable prior to expiration. However, a number of American warrants do have variable exercise prices as a function of the length of time until expiration. Typically, the exercise price increases as time approaches the expiration date.

Consider the case where there are n changes of the exercise price during the life of an American warrant, represented by the following schedule:

Exercise Price	*Time until Expiration* (τ)
E_0	$0 \leqslant \tau \leqslant \tau_1$
E_1	$\tau_1 \leqslant \tau \leqslant \tau_2$
$\vdots$	$\vdots$
E_n	$\tau_n \leqslant \tau$

---

17 By Taylor series approximation, we can compute the loss to the warrant holder of the standard adjustment for dividends: namely, $F(S - d, \tau; E - d) - F(S, \tau; E) = -dF_S(S, \tau; E) - dF_E(S, \tau; E) + o(d) = -[F(S, \tau; E) - (S - E)F_S(S, \tau; E)]$ $(d/E) + o(d)$, by the first-degree homogeneity of F in (S, E). Hence, to a first approximation, for $S = E$, the warrant will lose d/S fraction of its value by this adjustment. Clearly, for $S > E$, the percentage loss will be smaller, and for $S < E$, it will be larger.

where it is assumed that $E_{j+1} < E_j$ for $j = 0, 1,...,n - 1$. If, otherwise, the conditions for Theorems 8.1–8.11 hold, it is easy to show that, if premature exercising takes place, it will occur only at points in time just prior to an exercise price change, i.e. at $\tau = \tau_j^+$, $j = 1,2,...,n$. Hence, the American warrant is equivalent to a *modified European warrant* which allows its owner to exercise the warrant at discrete times, just prior to an exercise price change. Given a technique for finding the price of a European warrant, there is a systematic method for valuing a modified European warrant. Namely, solve the standard problem for $F_0(S, \tau; E_0)$ subject to the boundary conditions $F_0(S, 0; E_0) = \max(0, S - E_0)$ and $\tau \leqslant \tau_1$. Then, by the same technique, solve for $F_1(S, \tau; E_1)$ subject to the boundary conditions $F_1(S, \tau_1; E_1) = \max[0, S - E_1, F_0(S, \tau_1; E_0)]$ and $\tau_1 \leqslant \tau \leqslant \tau_2$. Proceed inductively by this dynamic-programming-like technique until the current value of the modified European warrant is determined. Typically, the number of exercise price changes is small, so the technique is computationally feasible.

Often the contract conditions are such that the warrant will never be prematurely exercised, in which case the correct valuation will be the standard European warrant treatment using the exercise price at expiration, E_0. If it can be demonstrated that

$$F_j(S, \tau_{j+1}; E_j) \geqslant S - E_{j+1} \quad \text{for all } S \geqslant 0 \text{ and } j = 0,1,...,n - 1 \tag{8.10}$$

then the warrant will always be worth more "alive" than "dead," and the no-premature-exercising result will obtain. From Theorem 8.1, $F_j(S, \tau_{j+1}; E_j) \geqslant \max[0, S - P(\tau_{j+1} - \tau_j)E_j]$. Hence from (8.10), a sufficient condition for no early exercising is that

$$\frac{E_{j+1}}{E_j} > P(\tau_{j+1} - \tau_j) \tag{8.11}$$

The economic reasoning behind (8.11) is identical to that used to derive Theorem 8.1. If, by continuing to hold the warrant and investing the dollars which would have been paid for the stock if the warrant were exercised, the investor can with certainty earn enough to overcome the increased cost of exercising the warrant later, then the warrant should not be exercised.

Condition (8.11) is not as simple as it may first appear, because in valuing the warrant today, one must know for certain that (8.11) will be satisfied at some future date, which in general will not be possible if interest rates are stochastic. Often, as a practical matter, the size of the exercise price change versus the length of time between changes is such that, for almost any reasonable rate of interest, (8.11) will be satisfied. For example, if the increase in exercise price is 10 percent and the length of time before the next exercise price change is five years, the yield to maturity on riskless securities would have to be less than 2 percent before (8.11) would not hold.

As a footnote to the analysis, we have the following corollary.

Corollary 8.11b

If there is a finite number of changes in the exercise price of a payout-protected perpetual warrant, then it will not be exercised and its price will equal the common stock price.

PROOF

Applying the previous analysis, consider the value of the warrant if it survives past the last exercise price change, $F_0(S, \infty; E_0)$. By Theorem 8.3, $F_0(S, \infty; E_0) = S$. Now consider the value just prior to the last change in exercise price, $F_1(S, \infty; E_1)$. It must satisfy the boundary condition

$$F_1(S, \infty; E_1) = \max[0, S - E_1, F_0(S, \infty; E_0)] = \max(0, S - E_1, S) = S$$

Proceeding inductively, the warrant will never be exercised, and, by Theorem 8.3, its value is equal to the common stock price.   QED

The analysis of the effect on unprotected warrants when future dividends or dividend policy is known[18] follows exactly the analysis of a changing exercise price. The arguments that no one will prematurely exercise his warrant except possibly at the discrete points in time just prior to a dividend payment go through, and hence the modified European warrant approach works where now the boundary conditions are $F_j(S, \tau_j; E)$ = $\max[0, S - E, F_{j-1}(S - d_j, \tau_j; E)]$ where d_j equals the dividend per share paid at τ_j years prior to expiration, for $j = 1,2,...,n$.

In the special case where future dividends and rates of interest are known with certainty, a sufficient condition for no premature exercising is that[19]

---

18 The distinction is made between knowing future dividends and knowing dividend policy. With the former one knows, currently, the actual amounts of future payments, while with the latter one knows the conditional future payments, conditional on (currently unknown) future values, such as the stock price.
19 The interpretation of (8.12) is similar to the explanation given for (8.11). Namely, if the losses from dividends are smaller than the gains which can be earned risklessly from investing the extra funds required to exercise the warrant and hold the stock, then the warrant is worth more "alive" than "dead."

$$E > \sum_{t=0}^{\tau} \frac{d(t)P(\tau - t)}{1 - P(\tau)} \tag{8.12}$$

i.e. the net present value of future dividends is less than the present value of earnings from investing E dollars for τ periods. If dividends are paid continuously at the constant rate of d dollars per unit time and if the interest rate r is the same over time, then (8.12) can be rewritten in its continuous form as

$$E > \frac{d}{r} \tag{8.13}$$

Samuelson suggests the use of discrete recursive relations, similar to our modified European warrant analysis, as an approximation to the mathematically difficult continuous-time model when there is some chance for premature exercising.[20] We have shown that the only reasons for premature exercising are lack of protection against dividends or sufficiently unfavorable exercise price changes. Further, such exercising will never take place except at boundary points. Since dividends are paid quarterly and exercise price changes are less frequent, the Samuelson recursive formulation with the discrete-time spacing matching the intervals between dividends or exercise price changes is actually the correct one, and the continuous solution is the approximation, even if warrant and stock prices change continuously!

Based on the relatively weak Assumption 1, we have shown that dividends and unfavorable exercise price changes are the only rational reasons for premature exercising, and hence the only reasons for an American warrant to sell for a premium over its European counterpart. In those cases where early exercising is possible, a computationally feasible general algorithm for modifying a European warrant valuation scheme has been derived. A number of theorems were proved putting restrictions on the structure of rational European warrant pricing theory.

8.4 RESTRICTIONS ON RATIONAL PUT OPTION PRICING

The put option, defined at the beginning of Section 8.2, has received relatively little analysis in the literature because it is a less popular option

---

20 See Samuelson (1965a, pp. 25–6, especially equation (42)). Samuelson had in mind small discrete-time intervals, while in the context of the current application, the intervals would be large. Chen (1970) also used this recursive relation in his empirical testing of the Samuelson model.

than the call and because it is commonly believed[21] that, given the price of a call option and the common stock, the value of a put is uniquely determined. This belief is false for American put options, and the mathematics of put option pricing is more difficult than that of the corresponding call option.

Using the notation defined in Section 8.2, we have that, at expiration,

$$G(S, 0; E) = g(S, 0; E) = \max(0, E - S) \qquad (8.14)$$

To determine the rational European put option price, two portfolio positions are examined. Consider taking a long position in the common stock at S dollars, a long position in a τ-year European put at $g(S, \tau; E)$ dollars, and borrowing $EP'(\tau)$ dollars where $P'(\tau)$ is the current value of a dollar payable τ years from now at the borrowing rate[22] (i.e. $P'(\tau)$ may not equal $P(\tau)$ if the borrowing and lending rates differ). The value of the portfolio τ years from now with the stock price at S^* will be $S^* + (E - S^*) - E = 0$ if $S^* \leq E$, and $S^* + 0 - E = S^* - E$ if $S^* > E$. The payoff structure is identical in every state to a European call option with the same exercise price and duration. Hence, to avoid the call option being a dominated security,[23] the put and call must be priced so that

$$g(S, \tau; E) + S - EP'(\tau) \geq f(S, \tau; E) \qquad (8.15)$$

As was the case in the similar analysis leading to Theorem 8.1, the values of the portfolio prior to expiration were not computed because the call option is European and cannot be prematurely exercised.

Consider taking a long position in a τ-year European call, a short position in the common stock at price S, and lending $EP(\tau)$ dollars. The value of the portfolio τ years from now with the stock price at S^* will be $0 - S^* + E = E - S^*$ if $S^* \leq E$, and $(S^* - E) - S^* + E = 0$ if $S^* > E$. The payoff structure is identical in every state to a European put option with the same exercise price and duration. If the put is not to be a dominated security,[24] then

---

21   See, for example, Black and Scholes (1973) and Stoll (1969).

22   The borrowing rate is the rate on a τ-year noncallable discounted loan. To avoid arbitrage, $P'(\tau) \leq P(\tau)$.

23   Because of the existent market structure, (8.15) must hold for the stronger reason of arbitrage. The portfolio did not require short-sales and it is institutionally possible for an investor to issue (sell) call options and reinvest the proceeds from the sale. If (8.15) did not hold, an investor, acting unilaterally, could make immediate positive profits with no investment and no risk.

24   In this case, we do not have the stronger condition of arbitrage discussed in footnote 23 because the portfolio requires a short-sale of shares and, under current regulations, the full proceeds cannot be reinvested. Again, intermediate values of the portfolio are not examined because the put option is European.

$$f(S, \tau; E) - S + EP(\tau) \geq g(S, \tau; E) \qquad (8.16)$$

must hold.

Theorem 8.12

If Assumption 1 holds and if the borrowing and lending rates are equal so that $P(\tau) = P'(\tau)$, then

$$g(S, \tau; E) = f(S, \tau; E) - S + EP(\tau)$$

PROOF

The proof follows directly from the simultaneous application of (8.15) and (8.16) when $P'(\tau) = P(\tau)$.   QED

Thus, the value of a rationally priced European put option is determined once one has a rational theory of the call option value. The formula derived in Theorem 8.12 is identical with the Black–Scholes equation (26) when the riskless rate r is constant (i.e. $P(\tau) = \exp(-r\tau)$). Note that no distributional assumptions about the stock price or future interest rates were required to prove Theorem 8.12.

Two corollaries to Theorem 8.12 follow directly from the above analysis.

Corollary 8.12a

$EP(\tau) \geq g(S, \tau; E)$.

PROOF

From (8.5) and (8.7), $f(S, \tau; E) - S \leq 0$, and from (8.16), $EP(\tau) \geq g(S, \tau; E)$.   QED

The intuition of this result is immediate. Because of limited liability of the common stock, the maximum value of the put option is E, and because the option is European, the proceeds cannot be collected for τ years. The option cannot be worth more than the present value of a sure payment of its maximum value.

Corollary 8.12b

The value of a perpetual ($\tau = \infty$) European put option is zero.

PROOF

The put is a limited-liability security and hence, $g(S, \tau; E) \geq 0$. From Corollary 8.12a and the condition that $P(\infty) = 0$, $0 \geq g(S, \infty; E)$. QED

Using the relation $g(S, \tau; E) = f(S, \tau; E) - S + EP(\tau)$, it is straightforward to derive theorems for rational European put pricing which are analogous to the theorems for warrants in Section 8.2. In particular, whenever f is homogeneous of degree one or convex in S and E, so g will be also. The correct adjustment for stock and cash dividends is the same as prescribed for warrants in Theorem 8.11 and Corollary 8.11a.[25]

Since the American put option can be exercised at any time, its price must satisfy the arbitrage condition

$$G(S, \tau; E) \geq \max(0, E - S) \tag{8.17}$$

By the same argument used to derive (8.5), it can be shown that

$$G(S, \tau; E) \geq g(S, \tau; E) \tag{8.18}$$

where the strict inequality holds only if there is a positive probability of premature exercising.

As shown in Section 8.2, the European and American warrant have the same value if the exercise price is constant and they are protected against payouts to the common stock. Even under these assumptions, there is almost always a positive probability of premature exercising of an American put, and hence, the American put will sell for more than its European counterpart. A hint that this must be so comes from Corollary 8.12b and arbitrage condition (8.17). Unlike European options, the value of an American option is always a nondecreasing function of its expiration date. If there is no possibility of premature exercising, the value of an American option will equal the value of its European counterpart. By Corollary 8.12b, the value of a perpetual American put would be zero, and by the proposed monotonicity argument on length of time to maturity, all American puts would have zero value. This absurd result clearly violates the arbitrage condition (8.17) for $S < E$.

To clarify this point, reconsider the two portfolios examined in the European put analysis, but with American puts instead. The first portfolio

---

25 While such adjustments for stock or cash payouts add to the value of a warrant or call option, the put option owner would prefer not to have them since lowering the exercise price of a put decreases its value. For simplicity, the effects of payouts are not considered, and it is assumed that no dividends are paid on the stock and that there are no exercise-price changes.

contains a long position in the common stock at price S, a long position in an American put at price $G(S, \tau; E)$, and borrowings of $EP'(\tau)$. As was previously shown, if held until maturity, the outcome of the portfolio will be identical with that of an American (European) warrant held until maturity. Because we are now using American options with the right to exercise prior to expiration, the interim values of the portfolio must be examined as well. If, for all times prior to expiration, the portfolio has value greater than the exercise value of the American warrant, $S - E$, then to avoid dominance of the warrant, the current value of the portfolio must exceed or equal the current value of the warrant.

The interim value of the portfolio at T years until expiration when the stock price is S^* is

$$S^* + G(S^*, T; E) - EP'(T)$$
$$= G(S^*, T; E) + (S^* - E) + E[1 - P'(T)] > S^* - E$$

Hence, condition (8.15) holds for its American counterparts to avoid dominance of the warrant, i.e.

$$G(S, \tau; E) + S - EP'(\tau) \geq F(S, \tau; E) \tag{8.19}$$

The second portfolio has a long position in an American call at price $F(S, \tau; E)$, a short position in the common stock at price S, and a loan of $EP(\tau)$ dollars. If held until maturity, this portfolio replicates the outcome of a European put, and hence must be at least as valuable at any interim point in time. The interim value of the portfolio, at T years to go and with the stock price at S^*, is

$$F(S^*, T; E) - S^* + EP(T)$$
$$= (E - S^*) + F(S^*, T; E) - E[1 - P(T)] < E - S^*$$

if $F(S^*, T; E) < E[1 - P(T)]$, which is possible for small enough S^*. From (8.17), $G(S^*, T; E) \geq E - S^*$. So, the interim value of the portfolio will be less than the value of an American put for sufficiently small S^*. Hence, if an American put was sold against this portfolio, and if the put owner decided to exercise his put prematurely, the value of the portfolio could be less than the value of the exercised put. This result would certainly obtain if $S^* < E[1 - P(T)]$. So, the portfolio will not dominate the put if inequality (8.16) does not hold, and an analog theorem to Theorem 8.12, which uniquely determines the value of an American put in terms of a call, does not exist. Analysis of the second portfolio does lead to the weaker inequality that

$$G(S, \tau; E) \leq E - S + F(S, \tau; E) \tag{8.20}$$

Theorem 8.13

If, for some $T < \tau$, there is a positive probability that $f(S, T; E) < E[1 - P(T)]$, then there is a positive probability that a τ-year American put option will be exercised prematurely and the value of the American put will strictly exceed the value of its European counterpart.

PROOF

The only reason that an American put will sell for a premium over its European counterpart is that there is a positive probability of exercising prior to expiration. Hence, it is sufficient to prove that $g(S, \tau; E) < G(S, \tau; E)$. From Assumption 1, if, for some $T \leq \tau$, $g(S^*, T; E) < G(S^*, T; E)$ for some possible value(s) of S^*, then $g(S, \tau; E) < G(S, \tau; E)$. From Theorem 8.12, $g(S^*, T; E) = f(S^*, T; E) - S^* + EP(T)$. From (8.17), $G(S^*, T; E) \geq \max(0, E - S^*)$. But $g(S^*, T; E) < G(S^*, T; E)$ is implied if $E - S^* > f(S^*, T; E) - S^* + EP(T)$, which holds if $f(S^*, T; E) < E[1 - P(T)]$. By hypothesis of the theorem, such an S^* is a possible value. QED

Since almost always there will be a chance of premature exercising, the formula of Theorem 8.12 or the Black–Scholes equation (26) will not lead to a correct valuation of an American put and, as mentioned in Section 8.3, the valuation of such options is a more difficult analytical task than valuing their European counterparts.

8.5 RATIONAL OPTION PRICING ALONG BLACK–SCHOLES LINES

A number of option pricing theories satisfy the general restrictions on a rational theory as derived in the previous sections. One such theory developed by Black and Scholes (1973) is particularly attractive because it is a complete equilibrium formulation of the problem and because the final formula is a function of "observable" variables, making the model subject to direct empirical tests.

Black and Scholes assume that (a) the standard form of the Sharpe–Lintner–Mossin Capital Asset Pricing Model (CAPM) holds for intertemporal trading, and that trading takes place continuously in time; (b) the market rate of interest r is known and fixed over time; and (c) there are no dividends or exercise price changes over the life of the contract.

To derive the formula, they assume that the option price is a function of the stock price and time to expiration. Over "short" time intervals, a hedged portfolio containing the common stock, the option, and a short-term riskless security is constructed where the portfolio weights are chosen to eliminate all "market risk." By the assumption of the CAPM, any portfolio with a zero ("beta") market risk must have an expected return equal to the risk-free rate. Hence, an equilibrium condition is established between the expected return on the option, the expected return on the stock, and the riskless rate.

Because of the distributional assumptions and because the option price is a function of the common stock price, Black and Scholes in effect make use of the Samuelson (1965a) application to warrant pricing of the Bachelier–Einstein–Dynkin derivation of the Fokker–Planck equation to express the expected return on the option in terms of the option price function and its partial derivatives. From the equilibrium condition on the option yield, such a partial differential equation for the option price is derived. The solution to this equation for a European call option is

$$f(S, \tau; E) = S\Phi(d_1) - E \exp(-r\tau)\Phi(d_2) \qquad (8.21)$$

where Φ is the cumulative standard normal distribution function, σ^2 is the instantaneous variance of the return on the common stock,

$$d_1 \equiv \frac{\log(S/E) + (r + \tfrac{1}{2}\sigma^2)\tau}{\sigma\tau^{1/2}}$$

and $d_2 \equiv d_1 - \sigma\tau^{1/2}$.

An exact formula for an asset price, based on observable variables only, is a rare finding from a general equilibrium model, and care should be taken to analyze the assumptions with Occam's razor to determine which ones are necessary to derive the formula. Some hints are to be found by inspection of their final formula (8.21) and a comparison with an alternative general equilibrium development.

The manifest characteristic of (8.21) is the number of variables that it does *not* depend on. The option price does not depend on the expected return on the common stock,[26] risk preferences of investors, or the aggregate supplies of assets. It does depend on the rate of interest (an "observable") and the *total* variance of the return on the common stock

---

26 This is an important result because the expected return is not directly observable and estimates from past data are poor because of nonstationarity. It also implies that attempts to use the option price to estimate either expected returns on the stock or risk preferences of investors are doomed to failure (e.g. see Sprenkle, 1961). However, since the formula does depend on σ^2, it is, in principle, possible to use the option price to estimate the variance rate. 1992 note: some bounds on the expected return can be deduced from option prices. See Grundy (1991) and Lo (1987).

which is often a stable number and hence accurate estimates are possible from time series data.[27]

The Samuelson and Merton (1969; this volume, Ch. 7) model is a complete, although very simple (three assets and one investor), general equilibrium formulation. Their formula[28] is

$$f(S, \tau; E) = \exp(-r\tau) \int_{E/S}^{\infty} (ZS - E) \, dQ(Z; \tau) \qquad (8.22)$$

where dQ is a probability density function with the expected value of Z over the dQ distribution equal to $\exp(r\tau)$. Equations (8.22) and (8.21) will be the same only in the special case when dQ is a log-normal density with the variance of $\log(Z)$ equal to $\sigma^2\tau$.[29] However, dQ is a risk-adjusted ("util–prob") distribution, dependent on both risk preferences and aggregate supplies, while the distribution in (8.21) is not. Black and Scholes claim that one reason that Samuelson and Merton did not arrive at formula (8.21) was because they did not consider other assets. If a result does not obtain for a simple three-asset case, it is unlikely that it would in a more general example. More to the point, it is only necessary to consider three assets to derive the Black–Scholes formula. In connection with this point, although Black and Scholes claim that their central assumption is the CAPM (emphasizing this over their hedging argument), their final formula, (8.21), depends only on the interest rate (which is exogenous to the CAPM) and on the *total* variance of the return on the common stock. It does not depend on the betas (covariances with the market) or other assets' characteristics. Hence, this assumption may be a "red herring."

Although their derivation of (8.21) is intuitively appealing, such an important result deserves a rigorous derivation. In this case, the rigorous derivation is not only for the satisfaction of the "purist," but also to give insight into the necessary conditions for the formula to obtain. The reader should be alerted that, because Black and Scholes consider only terminal boundary conditions, their analysis is strictly applicable to European options, although as shown in Sections 8.2–8.4, the European valuation is often equal to the American one.

---

*27 Subsequently, several researchers have reversed the process and have used option prices and the model to deduce implied variance rates as estimates for future volatility of the stock. Cf. Beckers (1981), Jarrow and Wiggins (1989), Latané and Rendleman (1976), Manaster and Koehler (1982), and Schmalensee and Trippi (1978). See Nelson (1991) for recent techniques for estimating variances from time series data.

28 Samuelson and Merton (1969; this volume, equation (7.30)).

29 This will occur only if (a) the objective returns on the stock are log-normally distributed; (b) the investor's utility function is isoelastic (i.e. homothetic indifference curves); and (c) the supplies of *both* options and bonds are at the incipient level.

Finally, although their model is based on a different economic structure, the formal analytical content is identical with Samuelson's (1965a) "linear, $\alpha = \beta$" model when the returns on the common stock are log-normal.[30] Hence, with different interpretation of the parameters, theorems proved in Samuelson (1965a) and in the difficult McKean (1965) appendix are directly applicable to the Black–Scholes model, and vice versa.

8.6 AN ALTERNATIVE DERIVATION OF THE BLACK–SCHOLES MODEL

Initially, we consider the case of a European option where no payouts are made to the common stock over the life of the contract. We make the following further assumptions.[31]

1 *"Frictionless" markets:* there are no transactions costs or differential taxes. Trading takes place continuously and borrowing and short-selling are allowed without restriction.[32] The borrowing rate equals the lending rate.

2 *Stock-price dynamics:* the instantaneous return on the common stock is described by the stochastic differential equation[33]

$$\frac{\mathrm{d}S}{S} = \alpha \, \mathrm{d}t + \sigma \, \mathrm{d}z \tag{8.23}$$

30 See Merton (1972b, 1983a) for a brief description of the relation between the Samuelson and Black–Scholes models.

31 Although the derivation presented here is based on assumptions and techniques different from those of the original Black–Scholes model, it is in the spirit of their formulation, and yields the same formula when their assumptions are applied.

32 The assumptions of unrestricted borrowing and short-selling can be weakened without changing the results obtained by splitting the created portfolio of the text into two portfolios: one containing the common stock and the other containing the warrant plus a long position in bonds. Then, as was done in Section 8.2, if we accept Assumption 1, the formulas of the current section follow immediately.

33 For a general description of the theory of stochastic differential equations of the Itô type, see McKean (1969) and Kushner (1967). For a description of their application to the consumption-portfolio problem, see Merton (1969a, 1971, 1973b; this volume, Chs 4, 5, and 15). Briefly, Itô processes follow immediately from the assumption of a continuous-time stochastic process which results in continuous price changes (with finite moments) and some level of independent increments. If the process for price changes were a function of stable Paretian distributions with infinite moments, it is conjectured that the only equilibrium value for a warrant would be the stock price itself, independent of the length of time to maturity. This implication is grossly inconsistent with all empirical observations.

where α is the instantaneous expected return on the common stock, σ^2 is the instantaneous variance of the return, and dz is a standard Gauss–Wiener process. α may be a stochastic variable of quite general type including being dependent on the level of the stock price or other assets' returns. Therefore no presumption is made that dS/S is an independent increments process with constant parameters, although dz clearly is. However, σ is restricted to be nonstochastic and, at most, a known function of time.

3   *Bond-price dynamics:* $P(\tau)$ is as defined in previous sections and the dynamics of its returns are described by

$$\frac{\mathrm{d}P}{P} = \mu(\tau) \, \mathrm{d}t + \delta(\tau) \, \mathrm{d}q(t; \tau) \qquad (8.24)$$

where μ is the instantaneous expected return, δ^2 is the instantaneous variance, and $\mathrm{d}q(t; \tau)$ is a standard Gauss–Wiener process for the zero-coupon bond with maturity τ. Allowing for the possibility of habitat and other term structure effects, it is not assumed that $\mathrm{d}q$ for one maturity is perfectly correlated with $\mathrm{d}q$ for another, i.e.

$$\mathrm{d}q(t; \tau) \, \mathrm{d}q(t; T) = \rho_{\tau T} \, \mathrm{d}t \qquad (8.24a)$$

where $\rho_{\tau T}$ may be less than unity for $\tau \neq T$. However, it is assumed that there is no serial correlation[34] among the (unanticipated) returns on any of the assets, i.e.

$$\mathrm{d}q(s; \tau) \, \mathrm{d}q(t; T) = 0 \text{ for } s \neq t$$
$$\mathrm{d}q(s; \tau) \, \mathrm{d}z(t) = 0 \text{ for } s \neq t \qquad (8.24b)$$

34   The reader should be careful to note that it is assumed only that the *unanticipated* returns on the bonds are not serially correlated. Cootner (1966) and others have pointed out that, since the bond price will equal its redemption price at maturity, the total returns over time cannot be uncorrelated. In no way does this negate the specification of (8.24), although it does imply that the variance of the unanticipated returns must be a function of time to maturity. The following example found in Merton (1970b; this volume, Ch. 11) illustrates that the two are not inconsistent. Suppose that bond prices for all maturities are only a function of the current (and future) short-term interest rates. Further, assume that the short-rate r follows a Gauss–Wiener process with (possibly) some drift, i.e. $\mathrm{d}r = a \, \mathrm{d}t + g \, \mathrm{d}z$, where a and g are constants. Although this process is not realistic because it implies a positive probability of negative interest rates, it will still illustrate the point. Suppose that all bonds are priced so as to yield an expected rate of return over the next period equal to r (i.e. a form of the Expectations Hypothesis): then, $P(\tau; r) = \exp(-r\tau - a\tau^2/2 + g^2\tau^3/6)$ and $\mathrm{d}P/P = r \, \mathrm{d}t - g\tau \, \mathrm{d}z$. By construction, dz is not serially correlated and in the notation of (8.24) $\delta(\tau) = -g\tau$.

which is consistent with the general Efficient Market Hypothesis of Fama (1965a) and Samuelson (1965b). $\mu(\tau)$ may be stochastic through dependence on the level of bond prices, etc. and different for different maturities. Because $P(\tau)$ is the price of a discounted loan with no risk of default, $P(0) = 1$ with certainty and $\delta(\tau)$ will definitely depend on τ with $\delta(0) = 0$. However, δ is otherwise assumed to be nonstochastic and independent of the level of P. In the special case when the interest rate is nonstochastic and constant over time, $\delta \equiv 0$, $\mu = r$, and $P(\tau) = \exp(-r\tau)$.

4 *Investor preferences and expectations:* no assumptions are necessary about investor preferences other than that they satisfy Assumption 1 of Section 8.2. All investors agree on the values of σ and δ, and on the distributional characteristics of dz and dq. It is *not* assumed that they agree on either α or μ.[35]

From the analysis in Section 8.2, it is reasonable to assume that the option price is a function of the stock price, the riskless bond price, and the length of time to expiration. If $H(S, P, \tau; E)$ is the option price function, then, given the distributional assumptions on S and P, we have, by Itô's lemma,[36] that the change in the option price over time satisfies the stochastic differential equation

$$dH = H_1 \, dS + H_2 \, dP + H_3 \, d\tau + \tfrac{1}{2}[H_{11}(dS)^2 + 2H_{12}(dS \, dP) + H_{22}(dP)^2] \tag{8.25}$$

where subscripts denote partial derivatives, and $(dS)^2 \equiv \sigma^2 S^2 \, dt$, $(dP)^2 \equiv \delta^2 P^2 dt$, $d\tau = -dt$, and $(dSdP) \equiv \rho\sigma\delta SP \, dt$ with ρ the instantaneous correlation coefficient between the (unanticipated) returns on the stock and on the bond. Substituting from (8.23) and (8.24) and rearranging terms, we can rewrite (8.25) as

$$dH = \beta H dt + \gamma H dz + \eta H dq \tag{8.26}$$

---

35 This assumption is much more acceptable than the usual homogeneous expectations. It is quite reasonable to expect that investors may have quite different estimates for current (and future) expected returns due to different levels of information, techniques of analysis, etc. However, most analysts calculate estimates of variances and covariances in the same way: namely, by using previous price data. Since all have access to the same price history, it is also reasonable to assume that their variance–covariance estimates may be the same.

36 Itô's lemma is the stochastic analog to the fundamental theorem of the calculus because it states how to differentiate functions of Wiener processes. For a complete description and proof, see McKean (1969). A brief discussion can be found in Merton (1971; this volume, Ch. 5).

where the instantaneous expected return on the warrant, β, is

$$\beta = \frac{\frac{1}{2}\sigma^2 S^2 H_{11} + \rho\sigma\delta SP H_{12} + \frac{1}{2}\delta^2 P^2 H_{22} + \alpha S H_1 + \mu P H_2 - H_3}{H}$$

$$\gamma \equiv \frac{\sigma S H_1}{H}$$

and

$$\eta \equiv \frac{\delta P H_2}{H}$$

In the spirit of the Black–Scholes formulation and the analysis in Sections 8.2–8.4, consider forming a portfolio containing the common stock, the option, and riskless bonds with time to maturity τ equal to the expiration date of the option, such that the aggregate investment in the portfolio is zero. This is achieved by using the proceeds of short-sales and borrowing to finance long positions. Let W_1 be the (instantaneous) number of dollars of the portfolio invested in the common stock, W_2 be the number of dollars invested in the option, and W_3 be the number of dollars invested in bonds. Then the condition of zero aggregate investment can be written as $W_1 + W_2 + W_3 = 0$. If dY is the instantaneous dollar return to the portfolio, it can be shown[37] that

$$dY = W_1 \frac{dS}{S} + W_2 \frac{dH}{H} + W_3 \frac{dP}{P}$$

$$= [W_1(\alpha - \mu) + W_2(\beta - \mu)]\, dt + (W_1\sigma + W_2\gamma)\, dz$$

$$+ [W_2\eta - (W_1 + W_2)\delta]\, dq \tag{8.27}$$

where $W_3 \equiv -(W_1 + W_2)$ has been substituted out.

Suppose that a strategy $W_j = W_j^*$ can be chosen such that the coefficients of dz and dq in (8.27) are always zero. Then the dollar return on that portfolio, dY^*, would be nonstochastic. Since the portfolio requires zero investment, it must be that to avoid "arbitrage"[38] profits, the expected (and realized) return on the portfolio with this strategy is zero. The two

37 See Merton (1969a, 1971; this volume, Chs 4 and 5).
38 "Arbitrage" is used in the qualified sense that the distributional and other assumptions are known to hold with certainty. A weaker form would say that, if the return on the portfolio is nonzero, either the option or the common stock would be a dominated security. See Samuelson (1968, 1972b) for a discussion of this distinction.

portfolio and one equilibrium conditions can be written as a 3×2 linear system,

$$(\alpha - \mu)W_1^* + (\beta - \mu)W_2^* = 0$$
$$\sigma W_1^* + \gamma W_2^* = 0 \qquad (8.28)$$
$$-\delta W_1^* + (\eta - \delta)W_2^* = 0$$

A nontrivial solution ($W_1^* \neq 0$; $W_2^* \neq 0$) to (8.28) exists if and only if

$$\frac{\beta - \mu}{\alpha - \mu} = \frac{\gamma}{\sigma} = \frac{\delta - \eta}{\delta} \qquad (8.29)$$

Because we make the "bucket shop" assumption, μ, α, δ, and σ are legitimate exogenous variables (relative to the option price), and β, γ, and η are to be determined so as to avoid dominance of any of the three securities. If (8.29) holds, then $\gamma/\sigma = 1 - \eta/\delta$, which implies from the definition of γ and η in (8.26) that

$$\frac{SH_1}{H} = 1 - \frac{PH_2}{H} \qquad (8.30)$$

or

$$H = SH_1 + PH_2 \qquad (8.31)$$

Although it is not a sufficient condition, by Euler's theorem, (8.31) is a necessary condition for H to be first degree homogeneous in (S, P) as was conjectured in Section 8.2.

The second condition from (8.29) is that $\beta - \mu = \gamma(\alpha - \mu)/\sigma$, which implies from the definition of β and γ in (8.26) that

$$\tfrac{1}{2}\sigma^2 S^2 H_{11} + \rho\sigma\delta SP H_{12} + \tfrac{1}{2}\delta^2 P^2 H_{22} + \alpha SH_1 + \mu PH_2 - H_3 - \mu H$$
$$= SH_1(\alpha - \mu) \qquad (8.32)$$

or, by combining terms, that

$$\tfrac{1}{2}\sigma^2 S^2 H_{11} + \rho\sigma\delta SP H_{12} + \tfrac{1}{2}\delta^2 P^2 H_{22} + \mu SH_1 + \mu PH_2 - H_3 - \mu H = 0 \qquad (8.33)$$

Substituting for H from (8.31) and combining terms, (8.33) can be rewritten as

$$\tfrac{1}{2}[\sigma^2 S^2 H_{11} + 2\rho\sigma\delta SP H_{12} + \delta^2 P^2 H_{22}] - H_3 = 0 \qquad (8.34)$$

which is a second-order linear partial differential equation of the parabolic type.

If H is the price of a European warrant, then H must satisfy (8.34) subject to the boundary conditions

$$H(0, P, \tau; E) = 0 \tag{8.34a}$$

$$H(S, 1, 0; E) = \max(0, S - E) \tag{8.34b}$$

since, by construction, $P(0) = 1$.

Define the variable $x \equiv S/EP(\tau)$, which is the price per share of stock in units of exercise-price dollars payable at a *fixed date* in the future (the expiration date of the warrant). The variable x is a well-defined price for $\tau \geq 0$, and from (8.23), (8.24), and Itô's lemma, the dynamics of x are described by the stochastic differential equation

$$\frac{dx}{x} = (\alpha - \mu + \delta^2 - \rho\sigma\delta)\, dt + \sigma\, dz - \delta\, dq \tag{8.35}$$

From (8.35), the expected return on x will be a function of S, P, etc., through α and μ, but the instantaneous variance of the return on x, $V^2(\tau)$, is equal to $\sigma^2 + \delta^2 - 2\rho\sigma\delta$, and will depend only on τ.

Motivated by the possible homogeneity properties of H, we try the change in variables $h(x, \tau; E) \equiv H(S, P, \tau; E)/EP$ where h is assumed to be independent of P and is the warrant price evaluated in the same units as x. Substituting (h, x) for (H, S) in (8.34), (8.34a), and (8.34b) leads to the partial differential equation for h

$$\tfrac{1}{2}V^2x^2h_{11} - h_2 = 0 \tag{8.36}$$

subject to the boundary conditions $y(0,T) = 0$ and $y(x,0) = \max(0, x - 1)$. From inspection of (8.36) and its boundary conditions, h is only a function of x and τ, since V^2 is only a function of τ. Hence, the assumed homogeneity property of H is verified. Further, h does not depend on E, and so H is actually homogeneous of degree one in $[S, EP(\tau)]$.

Consider a new time variable, $T \equiv \int_0^\tau V^2(s)\, ds$. Then, if we define $y(x, T) \equiv h(x, \tau)$ and substitute into (8.36), y must satisfy

$$\tfrac{1}{2}x^2y_{11} - y_2 = 0 \tag{8.37}$$

subject to the boundary conditions $y(0, T) = 0$ and $y(x, 0) = \max(0, x - 1)$. Suppose we wrote the warrant price in its "full functional form," $H(S, P, \tau; E, \sigma^2, \delta^2, \rho)$. Then,

$$y = H(x, 1, T; 1, 1, 0, 0)$$

and is the price of a warrant with T years to expiration and exercise price of one dollar, on a stock with unit instantaneous variance of return, when the market rate of interest is zero over the life of the contract.

Once we solve (8.37) for the price of this "standard" warrant, we have, by a change of variables, the price for any European warrant, namely,

$$H(S, P, \tau; E) = EP(\tau)y\left[\frac{S}{EP(\tau)}, \int_0^\tau V^2(s)\, ds\right] \qquad (8.38)$$

Hence, for empirical testing or applications, one need only compute tables for the "standard" warrant price as a function of two variables, stock price and time to expiration, to be able to compute warrant prices in general.

To solve (8.37), we first put it in standard form by the change in variables $Z \equiv \log x + T/2$ and $\phi(Z, T) \equiv y(x, T)/x$, and then substitute in (8.37) to arrive at

$$0 = \tfrac{1}{2}\phi_{11} - \phi_2 \qquad (8.39)$$

subject to the boundary conditions $|\phi(Z, T)| \leq 1$ and $\phi(Z, 0) = \max[0, 1 - \exp(-Z)]$. Equation (8.39) is a standard free-boundary problem to be solved by separation of variables or Fourier transforms.[39] Its solution is

$$y(x, T) = x\phi(Z, T) = \frac{x\,\mathrm{erfc}(h_1) - \mathrm{erfc}(h_2)}{2} \qquad (8.40)$$

where erfc is the error complement function which is tabulated,[40] $h_1 \equiv -(\log x + \tfrac{1}{2}T)/(2T)^{1/2}$, and $h_2 \equiv -(\log x - \tfrac{1}{2}T)/(2T)^{1/2}$. Equation (8.40) is identical to (8.21) with $r = 0$, $\sigma^2 = 1$, and $E = 1$. Hence, (8.38) will be identical to (8.21), the Black–Scholes formula, in the special case of a nonstochastic and constant interest rate (i.e. $\delta = 0$, $\mu = r$, $P = \exp(-r\tau)$, and $T \equiv \sigma^2\tau$).

Equation (8.37) corresponds exactly to Samuelson's equation[41] for the warrant price in his "linear" model when the stock price is log-normally distributed, with his parameters $\alpha = \beta = 0$, and $\sigma^2 = 1$. Hence, tables generated from (8.40) could be used with (8.38) for valuations of the

39 For a separation of variables solution, see Churchill (1963, pp. 154–6) and for the transform technique, see Dettman (1969, p. 390). Also see McKean (1965).
*40 The relation between the erfc function and $\Phi(x)$ in (8.21) is given by $\Phi(x) = 1 - \tfrac{1}{2}\mathrm{erfc}(x/2^{1/2})$.
41 Samuelson (1965a, p. 27).

Samuelson formula where $\exp(-\alpha\tau)$ is substituted for $P(\tau)$ in (8.38).[42] Since α in his theory is the expected rate of return on a risky security, one would expect that $\exp(-\alpha\tau) < P(\tau)$. As a consequence of the following theorem, $\exp(-\alpha\tau) < P(\tau)$ would imply that Samuelson's forecasted values for the warrants would be higher than those forecasted by Black and Scholes or the model presented here.

Theorem 8.14

For a given stock price, the warrant price is a nonincreasing function of $P(\tau)$, and hence a nondecreasing function of the τ-year interest rate.

PROOF

It follows immediately, since an increase in P is equivalent to an increase in E which never increases the value of the warrant. Formally, H is a convex function of S and passes through the origin. Hence, $H - SH_1 \leq 0$. But from (8.31), $H - SH_1 = PH_2$, and since $P \geq 0$, $H_2 \leq 0$. By definition, $P(\tau)$ is a decreasing function of the τ-year interest rate.   QED

Because we applied only the terminal boundary condition to (8.34), the price function derived is for a European warrant. The correct boundary conditions for an American warrant would also include the arbitrage boundary inequality

$$H(S, P, \tau; E) \geq \max(0, S - E) \tag{8.34c}$$

Since it was assumed that no dividend payments or exercise-price changes occur over the life of the contract, we know from Theorem 8.1 that, if the formulation of this section is a "rational" theory, then it will satisfy the stronger inequality $H \geq \max[0, S - EP(\tau)]$ (which is homogeneous in S and $EP(\tau)$), and the American warrant will have the same value as its European counterpart. Samuelson (1965a) argues that solutions to equations like (8.21) and (8.38) will always have values at least as large as $\max(0, S - E)$, and Samuelson and Merton (1969; this volume, Ch. 7) prove it under more general conditions. Hence, there is no need for formal verification here. Further, it can be shown that (8.38) satisfies all the theorems of Section 8.2.

---

42   The tables could also be used to evaluate warrants priced by the Sprenkle (1961) formula. Warning: while the Samuelson interpretation of the "$\beta = \alpha$" case implies that expected returns are equated on the warrant and the stock, the Black and Scholes interpretation does not. Namely, from (8.29), the expected return on the warrant satisfies $\beta = r + H_1 S(\alpha - r)/H$, where H_1 can be computed from (8.21) by differentiation.

As a direct result of the equal values of the European and American warrants, we have the following theorem.

Theorem 8.15

The warrant price is a nondecreasing function of the variance of the stock price return.

PROOF

From (8.38), the change in H with respect to a change in variance will be proportional to y_2. But, y is the price of a legitimate American warrant, and hence must be a nondecreasing function of time to expiration, i.e. $y_2 \geq 0$.   QED

Actually, Theorem 8.15 is a special case of the general proposition (Theorem 8.8), proved in Section 8.2, that the more risky is the stock, the more valuable is the warrant. Although, in general, increasing variance may not imply increasing risk, variance is a valid measure of risk for this model with log-normally distributed stock-price returns.

We have derived the Black–Scholes warrant pricing formula rigorously under assumptions weaker than they postulate, and have extended the analysis to include the possibility of stochastic interest rates.

Because Black and Scholes assumed constant interest rates in forming their hedge positions in the original derivation, it did not matter whether they borrowed or lent long or short maturities. The derivation here clearly demonstrates that the correct maturity to use in the hedge is the one which matches the maturity date of the option. "Correct" is used in the sense that, if the price $P(\tau)$ remains fixed while the price of other maturities changes, the price of a τ-year option will remain unchanged.

The CAPM is a sufficient assumption to derive the formula. While the assumptions of this section are necessary for the intertemporal use of the CAPM,[43] they are not sufficient, e.g. we do not assume that interest rates are nonstochastic, that the price dynamics have constant variances, or that investors have homogeneous expectations. All are required for the CAPM. Further, since we consider only the properties of three securities, we do not assume that the capital market is in full general equilibrium. Since the final formula is independent of α or μ, it may hold even if the observed stock or bond prices are transient nonequilibrium prices.

---

43 See Merton (1973b; this volume, Ch. 15) for a discussion of necessary and sufficient conditions for a Sharpe–Lintner–Mossin type model to obtain in an intertemporal context. The sufficient conditions are rather restrictive.

The key to the derivation is that any one of the securities' returns over time can be perfectly replicated by continuous portfolio combinations of the other two. A complete analysis would require that all three securities' prices be solved for simultaneously which, in general, would require the examination of all other assets, knowledge of preferences, etc. However, because of "perfect substitutability" of the securities and the "bucket shop" assumption, supply effects can be neglected, and we can apply "partial equilibrium" analysis resulting in a "causal-type" formula for the option price as a function of the stock and bond prices.

This "perfect substitutability" of the common stock and borrowing for the warrant or the warrant and lending for the common stock explains why the formula is independent of the expected return on the common stock or preferences. The expected return on the stock and the investor's preferences will determine how much capital to invest (long or short) in a given company. The decision as to whether to take the position by buying warrants or by leveraging the stock depends only on their relative prices and the cost of borrowing. As Black and Scholes point out, the argument is similar to an intertemporal Modigliani–Miller theorem. The reason that the Black–Scholes assumption of the CAPM leads to the correct formula is that, because it is an equilibrium model, it must necessarily rule out "sure-thing" profits among perfectly correlated securities, which is exactly condition (8.29). Careful study of both their derivations shows that (8.29) is the only part of the CAPM ever used.

The assumptions of this section are necessary for (8.38) and (8.40) to hold.[44] The continuous-trading assumption is necessary to establish perfect correlation among nonlinear functions which is required to form the "perfect-hedge" portfolio mix. The Samuelson and Merton (1969; this volume, Ch. 7) model is an immediate counter-example to the validity of the formula for discrete-trading intervals.

The assumption of Itô processes for the assets' returns dynamics was necessary to apply Itô's lemma. The further restriction that σ and δ be nonstochastic and independent of the price levels is required so that the option price change is due only to changes in the stock or bond prices, which was necessary to establish a perfect hedge and to establish the homogeneity property (8.31).[45] Clearly if investors did not agree on the value of $V^2(\tau)$, they would arrive at different values for the same warrant.

44 If most of the "frictionless" market assumptions are dropped, it may be possible to show that, by substituting current institutional conditions, (8.38) and (8.40) will give lower bounds for the warrant's value.

45 In the special case when interest rates are nonstochastic, the variance of the stock price return can be a function of the price level and the derivation still goes through. However, the resulting partial differential equation will not have a simple closed-form solution.

The Black–Scholes claim that (8.21) or (8.38) is the only formula consistent with capital market equilibrium is a bit too strong. It is not true that if the market prices options differently, then arbitrage profits are ensured. It is a "rational" option pricing theory relative to the assumptions of this section. If these assumptions held with certainty, then the Black–Scholes formula is the only one which all investors could agree on, and no deviant member could prove them wrong.[46]

8.7 EXTENSION OF THE MODEL TO INCLUDE DIVIDEND PAYMENTS AND EXERCISE PRICE CHANGES

To analyze the effect of dividends on unprotected warrants, it is helpful to assume a constant and known interest rate r. Under this assumption, $\delta = 0$, $\mu = r$, and $P(\tau) = \exp(-r\tau)$. Condition (8.29) simplifies to

$$\beta - r = \gamma(\alpha - r)/\sigma \qquad (8.41)$$

Let $D(S, \tau)$ be the dividend rate per share per unit time when the stock price is S and the warrant has τ years to expiration. If α is the instantaneous *total* expected return as defined in (8.23), then the instantaneous expected return from price appreciation is $\alpha - D(S, \tau)/S$. Because $P(\tau)$ is no longer stochastic, we suppress it and write the warrant price function as $W(S, \tau; E)$. As was done in (8.25) and (8.26), we apply Itô's lemma to derive the stochastic differential equation for the warrant price to be

$$dW = W_1(dS - D(S, \tau)\,dt) + W_2\,d\tau + \tfrac{1}{2}W_{11}(dS)^2$$
$$= [\tfrac{1}{2}\sigma^2 S^2 W_{11} + (\alpha S - D)W_1 - W_2]\,dt + \sigma S W_1\,dz \qquad (8.42)$$

Note that since the warrant owner is not entitled to any part of the dividend return, he only considers that part of the expected dollar return to the common stock due to price appreciation. From (8.42) and the definition of β and γ, we have that

$$\beta W = \tfrac{1}{2}\sigma^2 S^2 W_{11} + (\alpha S - D)W_1 - W_2$$
$$\gamma W = \sigma S W_1 \qquad (8.43)$$

Applying (8.41) to (8.43), we arrive at the partial differential equation for the warrant price,

---

46 This point is emphasized in a critique of Thorp and Kassouf's (1967) "sure-thing" arbitrage techniques by Samuelson (1968) and again in Samuelson (1972b, footnote 6).

$$\tfrac{1}{2}\sigma^2 S^2 W_{11} + (rS - D)W_1 - W_2 - rW = 0 \qquad (8.44)$$

subject to the boundary conditions, $W(0, \tau; E) = 0$, $W(S, 0; E) =$ max$(0, S - E)$ for a European warrant, and to the additional arbitrage boundary condition $W(S, \tau; E) \geq$ max$(0, S - E)$ for an American warrant.

Equation (8.44) will not have a simple solution, even for the European warrant and relatively simple functional forms for D. In evaluating the American warrant in the "no-dividend" case $(D = 0)$, the arbitrage boundary inequalities were not considered explicitly in arriving at a solution because it was shown that the European warrant price never violated the inequality, and the American and European warrant prices were equal. For many dividend policies, the solution for the European warrant price will violate the inequality, and for those policies, there will be a positive probability of premature exercising of the American warrant. Hence, to obtain a correct value for the American warrant from (8.44), we must explicitly consider the boundary inequality, and transform it into a suitable form for solution.

If there exists a positive probability of premature exercising, then, for every τ, there exists a level of stock price, $C[\tau]$ such that for all $S > C[\tau]$ the warrant would be worth more exercised than if held. Since the value of an exercised warrant is always $S - E$, we have the appended boundary condition for (8.44)

$$W(C[\tau], \tau; E) = C[\tau] - E \qquad (8.44a)$$

where W satisfies (8.44) for $0 \leq S \leq C[\tau]$.

If $C[\tau]$ were a known function, then, after the appropriate change of variables, (8.44) with the European boundary conditions and (8.44a) appended would be a semi-infinite boundary value problem with a time-dependent boundary. However, $C[\tau]$ is not known and must be determined as part of the solution. Therefore, an additional boundary condition is required for the problem to be well posed.

Fortunately, the economics of the problem are sufficiently rich to provide this extra condition. Because the warrant holder is not contractually obliged to exercise his warrant prematurely, he chooses to do so only in his own best interest (i.e. when the warrant is worth more "dead" than "alive"). Hence, the only rational choice for $C[\tau]$ is that time pattern which maximizes the value of the warrant. Let $f(S, \tau; E, C[\tau])$ be a solution to (8.44)–(8.44a) for a given $C[\tau]$ function. Then, the value of a τ-year American warrant will be

$$W(S, \tau; E) = \max_{\{C\}} f(S, \tau; E, C) \qquad (8.45)$$

Further, the structure of the problem makes it clear that the optimal $C[\tau]$ will be independent of the current level of the stock price. In attacking this difficult problem, Samuelson (1965a) postulated that the extra condition was "high contact" at the boundary, i.e.

$$W_1(C[\tau], \tau; E) = 1 \qquad (8.44b)$$

It can be shown[47] that (8.44b) is implied by the maximizing behavior described by (8.45). So the correct specification for the American warrant price is (8.44) with the European boundary conditions plus (8.44a) and (8.44b).

Samuelson (1965a) and Samuelson and Merton (1969; this volume, Ch. 7) have shown that for a proportional dividend policy where $D(S, \tau) = \rho S, \rho > 0$, there is always a positive probability of premature exercising, and hence the arbitrage boundary condition will be binding for sufficiently large stock prices.[48] With $D = \rho S$, (8.44) is mathematically identical to Samuelson's "nonlinear" ($\beta > \alpha$) case where his $\beta = r$ and his $\alpha = r - \rho$. Samuelson (1965a) and McKean (1965) analyze this problem in great detail. Although there are no simple closed-form solutions for finite-lived warrants, they do derive solutions for perpetual warrants which are power functions, tangent to the "$S - E$" line at finite values of S.

A second example of a simple dividend policy is the constant one where $D = d$, a constant.[49] Unlike the previous proportional policy, premature exercising may or may not occur, depending upon the values for d, r, E, and τ. In particular, a sufficient condition for no premature exercising was derived in Section 8.3, namely,

$$E > \frac{d}{r} \qquad (8.13)$$

If (8.13) obtains, then the solution for the European warrant price will be the solution for the American warrant. Although a closed-form solution

47   Let $f(x, c)$ be a differentiable function, concave in its second argument, for $0 \le x \le c$. Require that $f(c, c) = h(c)$, a differentiable function of c. Let $c = c^*$ be the c which maximizes f, i.e. $f_2(x, c^*) = 0$, where subscripts denote partial derivatives. Consider the total derivative of f with respect to c along the boundary $x = c$. Then, $df/dc = dh/dc = f_1(c, c) + f_2(c, c)$. For $c = c^*, f_2 = 0$. Hence, $f_1(c^*, c^*) = dh/dc$. In the case of the text, $h = c - E$, and the "high-contact" solution, $f_1(c^*, c^*) = 1$, is proved.

48   For $D = \rho S$, the solution for the European warrant is given by (8.21) with $S \exp(-\rho\tau)$ substituted for S everywhere in the formula. For large S, $W \sim \exp(-\rho\tau) S - E \exp(-r\tau)$ which will be less than $S - E$ for large S and $\rho > 0$. Hence, the American warrant can be worth more "dead" than "alive."

*49   Further development of option pricing theory for dividend-paying stocks can be found in Roll (1977), Geske (1978), Whaley (1979, 1981), Bensoussan (1984), Geske and Roll (1984), Blomeyer (1986), Karatzas (1988), and Kim (1990).

has not yet been found for finite τ, a solution for the perpetual warrant when $E > d/r$ is[50]

$$W(S, \infty; E) = S - \frac{d}{r}\left[1 - \frac{(2d/\sigma^2 S)^{2r/\sigma^2}}{\Gamma(2 + 2r/\sigma^2)} M\left(\frac{2r}{\sigma^2}, 2 + \frac{2r}{\sigma^2}, \frac{-2d}{\sigma^2 S}\right)\right]$$

(8.46)

where M is the confluent hypergeometric function and W is plotted in Figure 8.2.

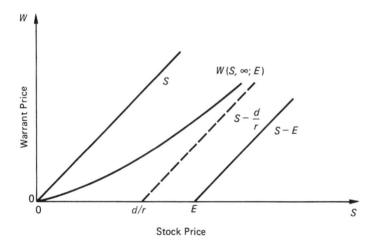

Figure 8.2 Perpetual Warrant Price with Constant Dividend Policy.

Consider the case of a continuously changing exercise price $E(\tau)$, where E is assumed to be differentiable and a decreasing function of the length of time to maturity, i.e. $dE/d\tau = -dE/dt = -\dot{E} < 0$. The warrant price will satisfy (8.44) with $D = 0$, but subject to the boundary conditions

$$W[S, 0; E(0)] = \max[0, S - E(0)]$$

50   Make the change in variables $Z \equiv \delta/S$ and $h(Z) \equiv Z^{-\gamma}W$ where $\delta \equiv -2d/\sigma^2$ and $\gamma \equiv 2r/\sigma^2$. Then, substituting in (8.44), we have the differential equation for h: $Zh'' + (\gamma + 2 - Z)h' - \gamma h = 0$, whose general solution (cf. Slater, 1966) is $h = c_1 M(\gamma, 2 + \gamma, Z) + c_2 Z^{-(\gamma+1)} M(-1, -\gamma, Z)$ which becomes (8.46) when the boundary conditions are applied. Analysis of (8.46) shows that W passes through the origin, is convex, and is asymptotic to the line $S - d/r$ for large S, i.e. it approaches the common stock value less the present discounted value of all future dividends forgone by holding the warrant.

and

$$W[S, \tau; E(\tau)] \geq \max[0, S - E(\tau)]$$

Make the change in variables $X \equiv S/E(\tau)$ and

$$F(X, \tau) \equiv W[S, \tau; E(\tau)]/E(\tau)$$

Then, F satisfies

$$\tfrac{1}{2}\sigma^2 X^2 F_{11} + \eta(\tau)XF_1 - \eta(\tau)F - F_2 = 0 \qquad (8.47)$$

subject to $F(X, 0) = \max(0, X - 1)$ and $F(X, \tau) \geq \max(0, X - 1)$ where $\eta(\tau) \equiv r - \dot{E}/E$. Notice that the structure of (8.47) is identical to the pricing of a warrant with a fixed exercise price and a variable, but nonstochastic, "interest rate" $\eta(\tau)$. (That is, substitute in the analysis of the previous section for $P(\tau)$, $\exp[-\int_0^\tau \eta(s)\, ds]$, but note that $\eta(\tau)$ can be negative for sufficiently large changes in exercise price.) We have already shown that, for $\int_0^\tau \eta(s)\, ds \geq 0$, there will be no premature exercising of the warrant, and only the terminal exercise price should matter. Noting that

$$\int_0^\tau \eta(s)\, ds = \int_0^\tau \left(r + \frac{dE/d\tau}{E} \right) ds = r\tau + \log\left[\frac{E(\tau)}{E(0)}\right]$$

formal substitution for $P(\tau)$ in (8.38) verifies that the value of the warrant is the same as for a warrant with a fixed exercise price $E(0)$ and interest rate r. We also have agreement of the current model with (8.11) of Section 8.3, because $\int_0^\tau \eta(s)\, ds \geq 0$ implies $E(\tau) \geq E(0) \exp(-r\tau)$, which is a general sufficient condition for no premature exercising.

8.8   VALUING AN AMERICAN PUT OPTION

As the first example of an application of the model to other types of options, we now consider the rational pricing of the put option, relative to the assumptions in Section 8.7. In Section 8.4, it was demonstrated that the value of a European put option is completely determined once the value of the call option is known (Theorem 8.12). Black and Scholes (1973, eq. 26) give the solution for their model. It was also demonstrated in Section 8.4 that the European valuation is not valid for the American put option because of the positive probability of premature exercising. If $G(S, \tau; E)$ is the rational put price, then, by the same technique as that used to derive (8.44) with $D = 0$, G satisfies

$$\tfrac{1}{2}\sigma^2 S^2 G_{11} + rSG_1 - rG - G_2 = 0 \qquad (8.48)$$

subject to $G(\infty, \tau; E) = 0$, $G(S, 0; E) = \max(0, E - S)$, and $G(S, \tau; E) \geq \max(0, E - S)$.

From the analysis by Samuelson (1965a) and McKean (1965) on warrants, there is no closed-form solution to (8.48) for finite τ. However, using their techniques, it is possible to obtain a solution for the perpetual put option (i.e. $\tau = \infty$). For a sufficiently low stock price, it will be advantageous to exercise the put. Define C to be the largest value of the stock such that the put holder is better off exercising than continuing to hold it. For the perpetual put, (8.48) reduces to the ordinary differential equation

$$\tfrac{1}{2}\sigma^2 S^2 G_{11} + rSG_1 - rG = 0 \qquad (8.49)$$

which is valid for the range of stock prices $C \leq S \leq \infty$. The boundary conditions for (8.49) are

$$G(\infty, \infty; E) = 0 \qquad (8.49a)$$

$$G(C, \infty; E) = E - C \qquad (8.49b)$$

and

> choose C so as to maximize the value of the option, which follows from the maximizing behavior arguments of the previous section
> $$\qquad (8.49c)$$

From the theory of linear ordinary differential equations, solutions to (8.49) involve two constants, a_1 and a_2. Boundary conditions (8.49a), (8.49b), and (8.49c) will determine these constants along with the unknown lower-bound stock price C. The general solution to (8.49) is

$$G(S, \infty; E) = a_1 S + a_2 S^{-\gamma} \qquad (8.50)$$

where $\gamma \equiv 2r/\sigma^2 > 0$. Equation (8.49a) requires that $a_1 = 0$, and (8.49b) requires that $a_2 = (E - C)C^\gamma$. Hence, as a function of C,

$$G(S, \infty; E) = (E - C)(S/C)^{-\gamma} \qquad (8.51)$$

To determine C, we apply (8.49c) and choose that value of C which maximizes (8.51), i.e. choose $C = C^*$ such that $\partial G/\partial C = 0$. Solving this condition, we have that $C^* = \gamma E/(1 + \gamma)$, and the put option price is

$$G(S, \infty; E) = \frac{E}{1 + \gamma} \left[\frac{(1 + \gamma)S}{\gamma E} \right]^{-\gamma} \qquad (8.52)$$

The Samuelson "high-contact" boundary condition

$$G_1(C^*, \infty; E) = -1$$

as an alternative specification of boundary condition (8.49c) can be verified by differentiating (8.52) with respect to S and evaluating at $S = C^*$. Figure 8.3 illustrates the American put price as a function of the stock price and time to expiration.[51]

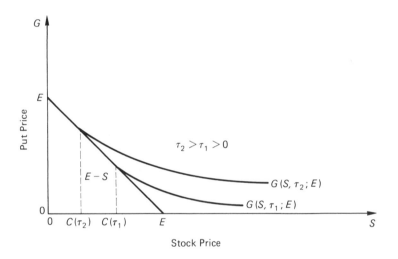

Figure 8.3 American Put Option Price.

8.9   VALUING THE "DOWN-AND-OUT" CALL OPTION

As a second example of the application of the model to other types of options, we consider the rational pricing of a new type of call option called the "down-and-out."[52] This option has the same terms with respect to

*51   Later development of put option pricing theory along these lines can be found in Brennan and Schwartz (1977a), Parkinson (1977), Johnson (1983), Bensoussan (1984), Geske and Johnson (1984), Blomeyer (1986), Barone-Adesi and Whaley (1987), Karatzas (1988), and Kim (1990).
52   See Snyder (1969) for a complete description. A number of Wall Street houses are beginning to deal in this option. See *Fortune*, November, 1971, p. 213.

exercise price, antidilution clauses, etc. as the standard call option, but with the additional feature that if the stock price falls below a stated level the option contract is nullified, i.e. the option becomes worthless.[53] Typically, the "knock-out" price is a function of the time to expiration, increasing as the expiration date nears.

Let $f(S, \tau; E)$ be the value of a European "down-and-out" call option, and $B(\tau) = bE \exp(-\eta\tau)$ be the "knock-out" price as a function of time to expiration where it is assumed that $\eta \geq 0$ and $0 \leq b \leq 1$. Then f will satisfy the fundamental partial differential equation

$$\tfrac{1}{2}\sigma^2 S^2 f_{11} + rSf_1 - rf - f_2 = 0 \tag{8.53}$$

subject to the boundary conditions

$$f[B(\tau), \tau; E] = 0$$

$$f(S, 0; E) = \max(0, S - E)$$

Note that, if $B(\tau) = 0$, then (8.53) would be the equation for a standard European call option.

Make the change in variables $x \equiv \log[S/B(\tau)]$; $T \equiv \sigma^2\tau$;

$$H(x, T) \equiv \exp(ax + \gamma\tau)f(S, \tau; E)/E$$

with $a \equiv (r - \eta - \sigma^2/2)/\sigma^2$ and $\gamma \equiv r + a^2\sigma^2/2$. Then, by substituting into (8.53), we arrive at the equation for H:

$$\tfrac{1}{2}H_{11} - H_2 = 0 \tag{8.54}$$

subject to

$$H(0, T) = 0$$

$$H(x, 0) = \exp(ax) \max[0, b \exp(x) - 1]$$

---

53   In some versions of the "down-and-out," the option owner receives a positive rebate, $R(\tau)$, if the stock price hits the "knock-out" price. Typically, $R(\tau)$ is an increasing function of the time until expiration (i.e. $R'(\tau) > 0$) with $R(0) = 0$. Let $g(S, \tau)$ satisfy (8.53) for $B(\tau) \leq S < \infty$, subject to the boundary conditions (a) $g[B(\tau), \tau] = R(\tau)$ and (b) $g(S, 0) = 0$. Then, $F(S, \tau; E) \equiv g(S, \tau) + f(S, \tau; E)$ will satisfy (8.53) subject to the boundary conditions (a) $F[B(\tau), \tau; E] = R(\tau)$ and (b) $F(S, 0; E) = \max(0, S - E)$. Hence, F is the value of a "down-and-out" call option with rebate payments $R(\tau)$, and $g(S, \tau)$ is the additional value for the rebate feature. See Dettman (1969, p. 391) for a transform solution for $g(S, \tau)$.

which is a standard semi-infinite boundary value problem to be solved by separation of variables or Fourier transforms.[54]

Solving (8.54) and substituting back, we arrive at the solution for the "down-and-out" option:

$$f(S, \tau; E) = \tfrac{1}{2} \left[S \operatorname{erfc}(h_1) - E \exp(-r\tau) \operatorname{erfc}(h_2) \right]$$

$$- \frac{1}{2} \left[\frac{S}{B(\tau)} \right]^{-\delta} \left\{ B(\tau) \operatorname{erfc}(h_3) - \frac{S}{B(\tau)} E \exp(-r\tau) \operatorname{erfc}(h_4) \right\} \tag{8.55}$$

where

$$h_1 \equiv - \frac{\log(S/E) + (r + \sigma^2/2)\tau}{(2\sigma^2\tau)^{1/2}}$$

$$h_2 \equiv - \frac{\log(S/E) + (r - \sigma^2/2)\tau}{(2\sigma^2\tau)^{1/2}}$$

$$h_3 \equiv - \frac{2 \log[B(\tau)/E] - \log(S/E) + (r + \sigma^2/2)\tau}{(2\sigma^2\tau)^{1/2}}$$

$$h_4 \equiv - \frac{2 \log[B(\tau)/E] - \log(S/E) + (r - \sigma^2/2)\tau}{(2\sigma^2\tau)^{1/2}}$$

and $\delta \equiv 2(r - \eta)/\sigma^2$. Inspection of (8.55) and (8.21) reveals that the first term with square brackets in (8.55) is the value of a standard call option, and hence the term with braces is the "discount" due to the "down-and-out" feature.

To gain a better perspective on the qualitative differences between the standard call option and the "down-and-out," it is useful to go to the limit of a perpetual option where the "knock-out" price is constant (i.e. $\eta = 0$). In this case, (8.53) reduces to the ordinary differential equation

$$\tfrac{1}{2}\sigma^2 S^2 f'' + rSf' - rf = 0 \tag{8.56}$$

subject to

$$f(bE) = 0 \tag{8.56a}$$

$$f(S) \leqslant S \tag{8.56b}$$

54   See Churchill (1963, p. 152) for a separation of variables solution and Dettman (1969, p. 391) for a transform solution.

where primes denote derivatives and $f(S)$ is short for $f(S, \infty; E)$. By standard methods, we solve (8.56) to obtain

$$f(S) = S - bE(S/bE)^{-\gamma} \tag{8.57}$$

where $\gamma \equiv 2r/\sigma^2$. Remembering that the value of a standard perpetual call option equals the value of the stock, we may interpret $bE(S/bE)^{-\gamma}$ as the "discount" for the "down-and-out" feature. Both (8.55) and (8.57) are homogeneous of degree one in (S, E) as are the standard options. Further, it is easy to show that $f(S) \geq \max(0, S - E)$, and, although a tedious exercise, it also can be shown that $f(S, \tau; E) \geq \max(0, S - E)$. Hence, the option is worth more "alive" than "dead," and therefore (8.55) and (8.57) are the correct valuation functions for the American "down-and-out."

From (8.57), the elasticity of the option price with respect to the stock price $Sf'(S)/f(S)$ is greater than unity, and so it is a "levered" security. However, unlike the standard call option, it is a concave function of the stock price, as illustrated in Figure 8.4.

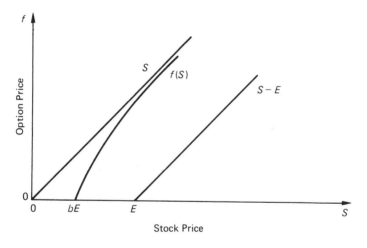

Figure 8.4 Perpetual Down-and-Out Call Option Price.

8.10   VALUING A CALLABLE WARRANT

As our third and last example of an application of the model to other types of options, we consider the rational pricing of a callable American warrant. Although warrants are rarely issued as callable, this is an important example because the analysis is readily carried over to the valuation of other types of securities such as convertible bonds which are almost always issued as callable.

We assume the standard conditions for an American warrant except that the issuing company has the right to ("call") buy back the warrant at any time for a fixed price. Because the warrant is of the American type, in the event of a call, the warrant holder has the option of exercising his warrant rather than selling it back to the company at the call price. If this occurs, it is called "forced conversion," because the warrant holder is "forced" to exercise, if the value of the warrant exercised exceeds the call price.

The value of a callable warrant will be equal to the value of an equivalent noncallable warrant less some "discount." This discount will be the value of the call provision to the company. One can think of the callable warrant as the resultant of two transactions: the company sells a noncallable warrant to an investor and, simultaneously, purchases from the investor an option to either "force" earlier conversion or to retire the issue at a fixed price.

Let $F(S, \tau; E)$ be the value of a callable American warrant, $H(S, \tau; E)$ be the value of an equivalent noncallable warrant as obtained from equation (8.21), and $C(S, \tau; E)$ be the value of the call provision. Then $H = F + C$. F will satisfy the fundamental partial differential equation

$$\tfrac{1}{2}\sigma^2 S^2 F_{11} + rSF_1 - rF - F_2 = 0 \tag{8.58}$$

for $0 \leqslant S \leqslant \bar{S}$ and subject to

$$F(0, \tau; E) = 0$$
$$F(S, 0; E) = \max(0, S - E)$$
$$F(\bar{S}, \tau; E) = \max(K, \bar{S} - E)$$

where K is the call price and $\bar{S}$ is the (yet to be determined) level of the stock price where the company will call the warrant. Unlike the case of "voluntary" conversion of the warrant (because of unfavorable dividend protection) analyzed in Section 8.7, $\bar{S}$ is not the choice of the warrant owner but of the company, and hence will not be selected to maximize the value of the warrant.

Because $C = H - F$ and H and F satisfy (8.58), C will satisfy (8.58) subject to the boundary conditions

$$C(0, \tau; E) = 0$$
$$C(S, 0; E) = 0$$
$$C(\bar{S}, \tau; E) = H(\bar{S}, \tau; E) - \max(K, \bar{S} - E)$$

Because $\bar{S}$ is the company's choice, we append the maximizing condition that $\bar{S}$ be chosen so as to maximize $C(S, \tau; E)$ making (8.58) a well-posed problem. Since $C = H - F$ and H is not a function of $\bar{S}$, the maximizing condition on C can be rewritten as a minimizing condition on F.

In general, it will not be possible to obtain a closed-form solution to (8.58). However, a solution can be found for the perpetual warrant. In this case, we know that $H(S, \infty; E) = S$, and (8.58) reduces to the ordinary differential equation

$$\tfrac{1}{2}\sigma^2 S^2 C'' + rSC' - rC = 0 \tag{8.59}$$

for $0 \leq S \leq \bar{S}$ and subject to

$$C(0) = 0$$

$$C(\bar{S}) = \bar{S} - \max(K, \bar{S} - E)$$

$$\text{choose } \bar{S} \text{ so as to maximize } C$$

where $C(S)$ is short for $C(S, \infty; E)$ and primes denote derivatives. Solving (8.59) and applying the first two conditions, we have

$$C(S) = \left[1 - \max\left(\frac{K}{\bar{S}}, 1 - \frac{E}{\bar{S}}\right)\right] S \tag{8.60}$$

Although we cannot apply the simple calculus technique for finding the maximizing $\bar{S}$, it is obviously $\bar{S} = K + E$ since, for $\bar{S} < K + E$, C is an increasing function of $\bar{S}$ and, for $\bar{S} > K + E$, it is a decreasing function. Hence, the value of the call provision is

$$C(S) = \frac{E}{K + E} S \tag{8.61}$$

and because $F = H - C$ the value of the callable perpetual warrant is

$$F(S) = \frac{K}{K + E} S \tag{8.62}$$

8.11 CONCLUSION

It has been shown that a Black–Scholes type model can be derived from weaker assumptions than in their original formulation. The main attractions of the model are that (a) the derivation is based on the relatively weak condition of avoiding dominance, (b) the final formula is a function of "observable" variables, and (c) the model can be extended in a straightforward fashion to determine the rational price of any type option.

The model has been applied with some success to empirical investigations of the option market by Black and Scholes (1972) and to warrants by Leonard (1971).

As suggested by Black and Scholes (1973) and Merton (1970b; this volume, Ch. 11), the model can be used to price the various elements of the firm's capital structure. Essentially, under conditions when the Modigliani–Miller theorem obtains, we can use the total value of the firm as a "basic" security (replacing the common stock in the formulation of this chapter) and the individual securities within the capital structure (e.g. debt, convertible bonds, common stock, etc.) can be viewed as "options" or "contingent claims" on the firm and priced accordingly. So, for example, one can derive in a systematic fashion a risk structure of interest rates as a function of the debt–equity ratio, the risk class of the firm, and the riskless (in terms of default) debt rates.

Using the techniques developed here, it should be possible to develop a theory of the term structure of interest rates along the lines of Cootner (1966) and Merton (1970b; this volume, Ch. 11). The approach would also have application in the theory of speculative markets.

Appendix 8A

Theorems 8.9 and 8.10 state that warrants whose common stock per dollar returns possess *distributions* that are independent of *stock price* levels (henceforth, referred to as DISP) are (a) homogeneous of degree one in stock price S and exercise price E (Theorem 8.9) and (b) convex in S (Theorem 8.10). This appendix[55] exhibits via counter-example the insufficiency of the posited assumptions *sans* DISP for the proof of Theorems 8.9 and 8.10.

First, we posit a very simple noncontroversial one-period European warrant pricing function W:

$$W(S, \lambda) = K \int_{E/S}^{\infty} (S\hat{Z} - E) dP(\hat{Z}; S, \lambda) \qquad (8A.1)$$

wherein $1 > K > 0$ is a discounting factor which is deemed (somewhat erroneously) to be constant at this point in time (i.e. independent of S), $\lambda \in [0, 1]$ is a parameter of the distribution dP,

$$\hat{Z} \equiv Z + \lambda g(S)\epsilon \equiv Z + U(S, \lambda) \equiv \text{common stock per dollar return}$$

$$(8A.2)$$

---

55 I thank M. B. Goldman of MIT for constructing this example and writing the appendix.

and Z and ϵ are independent random variables such that $E(\epsilon|Z) = 0$. The function $g(S)$ has the following properties for our example: $g(S) \in (0, 1)$, $dg(S)/dS < 0$, and $dP(\hat{Z}; S, \lambda)$ is the Stieltjes integral representation of the probability density which is equivalent to the convolution of the probability densities of Z and U.

In constructing the counter-example, we choose the following uniform distributions for Z and U:

$$f(\epsilon) = \tfrac{1}{2} \quad \text{for } -1 \leqslant \epsilon \leqslant 1$$

$$= 0 \quad \text{elsewhere}$$

(8A.3)

$$\rightarrow f(U) = \frac{1}{2\lambda g(S)} \quad \text{for} \quad -\lambda g(S) \leqslant U \leqslant \lambda g(S)$$

$$= 0 \qquad \text{elsewhere}$$

$$h(Z) = \tfrac{1}{2} \quad \text{for} \quad 1 \leqslant Z \leqslant 3$$

$$= 0 \quad \text{elsewhere}$$

(8A.4)

The convolved density would then be

$$\frac{dP}{d\hat{Z}}(\hat{Z}; S, \lambda) = \frac{\hat{Z} - 1 + \lambda g(S)}{4\lambda g(S)} \quad \text{for} \quad 1 - \lambda g(S) \leqslant \hat{Z} \leqslant 1 + \lambda g(S)$$

(8A.5)

$$= \tfrac{1}{2} \qquad \text{for} \quad 1 + \lambda g(S) \leqslant \hat{Z} \leqslant 3 - \lambda g(S)$$

$$= \frac{3 + \lambda g(S) - \hat{Z}}{4\lambda g(S)} \quad \text{for} \quad 3 - \lambda g(S) \leqslant \hat{Z} \leqslant 3 + \lambda g(S)$$

$$= 0 \qquad \text{elsewhere}$$

As a further convenience, we choose the exercise price E to be in the neighborhood of twice the stock price S and evaluate (8A.1):

$$W(S, \lambda) = K\left[\frac{E^2}{4S} - \frac{3E}{2} + \frac{9S}{4} + \frac{\lambda^2 g^2(S)S}{12}\right]$$

(8A.6)

By inspection of (8A.6), we notice that W is not homogeneous of degree one in S and E. Moreover, the convexity of W can be violated (locally) (i.e. d^2W/dS^2 can become negative) by choosing a sufficiently negative $d^2g(S)/dS^2$:

$$\frac{\mathrm{d}^2W}{\mathrm{d}S^2} = K\left\{\frac{E^2}{2S^3} + \frac{\lambda^2}{6}\left[2g(S)\frac{\mathrm{d}g}{\mathrm{d}S} + S\left(\frac{\mathrm{d}g}{\mathrm{d}S}\right)^2 + Sg(S)\frac{\mathrm{d}^2g}{\mathrm{d}S^2}\right]\right\} \gtreqless 0$$

(8A.7)

Thus, our example has shown Theorems 8.9 and 8.10 to be not generally consistent with a non-DISP environment; however, we can verify Theorems 8.9 and 8.10 for the DISP subcase of our example, since by construction setting $\lambda = 0$ reinstates the DISP character of the probability distribution. By inspection, we observe that when $\lambda = 0$, the right-hand side of (8A.6) is homogeneous of degree one in S and E, while the right-hand side of (8A.7) is $KE^2/2S^3 > 0$, verifying the convexity theorem.

Option Pricing When Underlying Stock Returns are Discontinuous

The validity of the classic Black–Scholes option pricing formula depends on the capability of investors to follow a dynamic portfolio strategy in the stock that replicates the payoff structure to the option. The critical assumption required for such strategy to be feasible is that the underlying stock-return dynamics can be described by a stochastic process with a continuous sample path. In this chapter, an option pricing formula is derived for the more general case when the underlying stock returns are generated by a mixture of both continuous and jump processes. The derived formula has most of the attractive features of the original Black–Scholes formula in that it does not depend on investor preferences or knowledge of the expected return on the underlying stock. Moreover, the same analysis applied to the options can be extended to the pricing of corporate liabilities.

9.1 INTRODUCTION

In their classic paper on the theory of option pricing, Black and Scholes (1973) present a mode of analysis that has revolutionized the theory of corporate liability pricing. In part, their approach was a breakthrough because it leads to pricing formulas using, for the most part, only observable variables. In particular, their formulas do not require knowledge of either investors' tastes or their beliefs about expected returns on the underlying common stock. Moreover, under specific posited

Reproduced from *Journal of Financial Economics*, 3, January–March 1976, 125–44. An earlier version of this paper with the same title appeared as a Sloan School of Management Working Paper #787–75 (April 1975). Aid from the National Science Foundation is gratefully acknowledged.

conditions, their formula must hold to avoid the creation of arbitrage possibilities.[1]

To derive the option pricing formula, Black and Scholes[2] assume "ideal conditions" in the market for the stock and option. These conditions are as follows.

1   "Frictionless" markets: there are no transactions costs or differential taxes. Trading takes place continuously in time. Borrowing and short-selling are allowed without restriction and with full proceeds available. The borrowing and lending rates are equal.
2   The short-term interest rate is known and constant through time.
3   The stock pays no dividends or other distributions during the life of the option.
4   The option is "European" in that it can only be exercised at the expiration date.
5   The stock price follows a "geometric" Brownian motion through time which produces a log-normal distribution for the stock price between any two points in time.

In a subsequent, alternative derivation of the Black–Scholes formula, Merton (1973a; this volume, Ch. 8) demonstrated that their basic mode of analysis obtains even when the interest rate is stochastic; the stock pays dividends; and the option is exercisable prior to expiration. Moreover, it was shown that as long as the stock-price dynamics can be described by a continuous-time diffusion process whose sample path is continuous with probability one,[3] then their arbitrage technique is still valid. Thorp (1973) has shown that dividends and restrictions against the use of proceeds of short-sales do not invalidate the Black–Scholes analysis. Moreover, the introduction of differential taxes for capital gains versus dividends or interest payments does not change the analysis either (see Ingersoll, 1976).

As was pointed out in Merton (1973a; this volume, Section 8.6), the critical assumptions in the Black–Scholes derivation is that trading takes place continuously in time and that the price dynamics of the stock have a continuous sample path with probability one. It would be pedantic to claim

---

1   For an alternative derivation of the Black–Scholes model and a discussion of option pricing models in general, see Merton (1973a; this volume, Ch. 8). For applications of the Black–Scholes technique to other financial instruments, see Merton (1974; this volume, Ch. 12) and Ingersoll (1976). As Samuelson (1972b, p. 16) has pointed out, violation of the Black–Scholes formula implies arbitrage opportunities only if their assumptions hold with certainty.

2   In this chapter, the term "option" refers to a call option although a corresponding analysis would apply to put options. For a list of the assumptions used to derive their formula, see Black and Scholes (1973, p. 640).

3   See Merton (1973a; this volume, Section 8.6).

that the Black–Scholes analysis is invalid because continuous trading is not possible and because no empirical time series has a continuous sample path. In Merton and Samuelson (1974, pp. 85–92), it was shown that the continuous-trading solution will be a valid asymptotic approximation to the discrete-trading solution provided that the dynamics have continuous sample paths. Under these same discrete-trading conditions, the returns on the Black–Scholes "no-risk" arbitrage portfolio will have some risk. However, the magnitude of this risk will be a bounded continuous function of the trading interval length, and the risk will go to zero as the trading interval goes to its continuous limit. Thus, provided that the interval length is not "too large," the difference between the Black–Scholes continuous-trading option price and the "correct" discrete-trading price cannot differ by much without creating a "virtual" arbitrage possibility.

However, the Black–Scholes solution is not valid, even in the continuous limit, when the stock-price dynamics cannot be represented by a stochastic process with a continuous sample path. In essence, the validity of the Black–Scholes formula depends on whether or not stock-price changes satisfy a kind of "local" Markov property. That is, in a short interval of time, the stock price can only change by a small amount.

The antipathetical process to this continuous stock price motion would be a "jump" stochastic process defined in continuous time. In essence, such a process allows for a positive probability of a stock-price change of extraordinary magnitude, no matter how small the time interval between successive observations. Indeed, since empirical studies of stock-price series[4] tend to show far too many outliers for a simple constant-variance log-normal distribution, there is a *prima facie* case for the existence of such jumps. On a less scientific basis, we have all observed price changes in stocks (usually in response to some announcement) which, at least on the surface, appear to be "jumps." The balance of this chapter examines option pricing when the stock-price dynamics include the possibility of nonlocal changes. To highlight the impact of noncontinuous stock-price dynamics on option pricing, all the other assumptions made by Black and Scholes are maintained throughout the analysis.

4 There have been a variety of alternative explanations for these observations, among them, nonstationarity in Cootner (1964); finite-variance subordinated processes in Clark (1973); nonlocal jump processes in Press (1967); nonstationary variance in Rosenberg (1972); and stable Paretian infinite-variance processes in Mandelbrot (1963b) and Fama (1965b). The latter stable Paretian hypothesis is not, in my opinion, a reasonable description of security returns because it allows for negative prices as does the corresponding finite-variance Gaussian hypothesis. Of course, limited liability can be imposed by specifying that the logarithmic returns are stable Paretian, and therefore the distribution of stock prices would be log-stable Paretian (the analog to log-normal for the Gaussian case). However, under this specification, the expected (arithmetic) return on such securities would be infinite, and it is not clear in this case that the equilibrium interest rate would be finite.

9.2 THE STOCK-PRICE AND OPTION-PRICE DYNAMICS

The total change in the stock price is posited to be the composition of two types of changes. (a) The first is the "normal" vibrations in price due, for example, to a temporary imbalance between supply and demand, changes in capitalization rates, changes in the economic outlook, or other new information that causes marginal changes in the stock's value. In essence, the impact of such information per unit time on the stock price is to produce a marginal change in the price (almost certainly). This component is modeled by a standard geometric Brownian motion with a constant variance per unit time and it has a continuous sample path.[5] (b) The second is the "abnormal" vibrations in price due to the arrival of important new information about the stock that has more than a marginal effect on price. Usually, such information will be specific to the firm or possibly its industry. It is reasonable to expect that there will be "active" times in the stock when such information arrives and "quiet" times when it does not although the "active" and "quiet" times are random. By its very nature, important information arrives only at discrete points in time. This component is modeled by a "jump" process reflecting the nonmarginal impact of the information.

To be consistent with the general Efficient Market Hypothesis of Fama (1970a) and Samuelson (1965b), the dynamics of the unanticipated part of the stock-price motions should be a martingale. Just as once the dynamics are posited to be a continuous-time process, the natural prototype process for the continuous component of the stock-price change is a Wiener process, so the prototype for the jump component is a "Poisson-driven" process.[6]

The Poisson-driven process is described as follows. The Poisson-distributed "event" is the arrival of an important piece of information about the stock. It is assumed that the arrivals are independently and identically distributed. Therefore, the probability of an event occurring during a time interval of length h (where h is as small as you like) can be written as

$$\text{prob\{the event does not occur in the time interval } (t, t + h)\}$$
$$= 1 - \lambda h + o(h)$$

---

5   The properties of this process in an economic context are discussed in Cootner (1964), Samuelson (1965a, 1972b), Merton (1971, 1973a (this volume, Chs 5 and 8); 1972b), and Merton and Samuelson (1974). For a more formal analysis, see McKean (1969), Kushner (1967), and Cox and Miller (1968).

6   Both types of processes are infinitely divisible in time and, appropriately scaled, have independent increments. See Kushner (1967) and Cox and Miller (1968).

prob{the event occurs once in the time interval $(t, t + h)$}
$$= \lambda h + o(h)$$
prob{the event occurs more than once in the time interval
$$(t, t + h)\} = o(h) \tag{9.1}$$

where $o(h)$ is the asymptotic order symbol defined by $\psi(h) = o(h)$ if $\lim_{h \to 0} [\psi(h)/h] = 0$, and λ is the mean number of arrivals per unit time.

Given that the Poisson event occurs (i.e. some important information on the stock arrives), then there is a "drawing" from a distribution to determine the impact of this information on the stock price. That is, if $S(t)$ is the stock price at time t and Y is the random variable description of this drawing, then, neglecting the continuous part, the stock price at time $t + h$, $S(t + h)$, will be the random variable $S(t + h) = S(t)Y$, given that one such arrival occurs between t and $t + h$. It is assumed throughout that Y has a probability measure with compact support and $Y \geq 0$. Moreover, the $\{Y\}$ from successive drawings are independently and identically distributed.

As discussed in Merton (1971; this volume, Ch. 5), there is a theory of stochastic differential equations to describe the motions· of continuous-sample-path stochastic processes. There is also a similar theory of stochastic differential equations for Poisson-driven processes.[7] The posited stock-price returns are a mixture of both types and can be formally written as a stochastic differential equation (conditional on $S(t) = S$), namely, as

$$\frac{dS}{S} = (\alpha - \lambda k)\, dt + \sigma\, dZ + dq \tag{9.2}$$

where α is the instantaneous expected return on the stock; σ^2 is the instantaneous variance of the return, conditional on no arrivals of important new information (i.e. the Poisson event does not occur); dZ is a standard Gauss–Wiener process; $q(t)$ is the independent Poisson process described in (9.1); dq and dZ are assumed to be independent; λ is the mean number of arrivals per unit time; $k \equiv \epsilon\{Y - 1\}$ where $Y - 1$ is the random variable percentage change in the stock price if the Poisson event occurs; and ϵ is the expectation operator over the random variable Y.

The $\sigma\, dZ$ part describes the instantaneous part of the unanticipated return due to the "normal" price vibrations, and the dq part describes the part due to the "abnormal" price vibrations. If $\lambda = 0$ (and therefore, $dq \equiv 0$), then the return dynamics would be identical with those posited in the Black and Scholes (1973) and Merton (1973a; this volume, Ch. 8) papers. Equation (9.2) can be rewritten in a somewhat more cumbersome form as

---

7 See Merton (1971; this volume, Section 5.8) and Kushner (1967, pp. 18–22).

$$\frac{dS}{S} = (\alpha - \lambda k)\,dt + \sigma\,dZ \qquad \text{if the Poisson event does not occur}$$

$$= (\alpha - \lambda k)\,dt + \sigma\,dZ + (Y - 1) \quad \text{if the Poisson event occurs}$$
$$(9.2a)$$

where, with probability one, no more than one Poisson event occurs in an instant, and if the event does occur, then $Y - 1$ is an impulse function producing a finite jump in S to SY. The resulting sample path for $S(t)$ will be continuous most of the time with finite jumps of differing signs and amplitudes occurring at discrete points in time. If α, λ, k, and σ are constants, then the random variable ratio of the stock price at time t to the stock at time zero (conditional on $S(0) = S$) can be written as

$$\frac{S(t)}{S} = \exp\left[\left(\alpha - \frac{\sigma^2}{2} - \lambda k\right)t + \sigma Z(t)\right]Y(n) \qquad (9.3)$$

where $Z(t)$ is a Gaussian random variable with a zero mean and variance equal to t; $Y(n) = 1$ if $n = 0$; $Y(n) = \Pi_{j=1}^{n} Y_j$ for $n \geqslant 1$ where the $\{Y_j\}$ are independently and identically distributed, and n is Poisson distributed with parameter λt.

In the special case when the $\{Y_j\}$ are themselves log-normally distributed, then the distribution of $S(t)/S$ will be log-normal with the variance parameter a Poisson-distributed random variable. In this form, the posited dynamics are similar to those used by Press (1967).

Having established the stock-price dynamics, I now turn to the dynamics of the option price. Suppose that the option price W can be written as a twice-continuously differentiable function of the stock price and time: namely, $W(t) = F(S, t)$. If the stock price follows the dynamics described in (9.2), then the option-return dynamics can be written in a similar form as

$$\frac{dW}{W} = (\alpha_W - \lambda k_W)\,dt + \sigma_W\,dZ + dq_W \qquad (9.4)$$

where α_W is the instantaneous expected return on the option, and σ_W^2 is the instantaneous variance of the return, conditional on the Poisson event not occurring. $q_W(t)$ is an independent Poisson process with parameter λ. $k_W \equiv \epsilon\{Y_W - 1\}$ where $Y_W - 1$ is the random variable percentage change in the option price if the Poisson event occurs and ϵ is the expectation operator over the random variable Y_W.

Using Itô's lemma for the continuous part and an analogous lemma for the jump part,[8] we have the following important relations:

$$\alpha_W \equiv \frac{\frac{1}{2}\sigma^2 S^2 F_{SS}(S, t) + (\alpha - \lambda k)SF_S(S, t) + F_t + \lambda\epsilon\{F(SY, t) - F(S, t)\}}{F(S, t)} \tag{9.5a}$$

$$\sigma_W \equiv \frac{F_S(S, t)\sigma S}{F(S, t)} \tag{9.5b}$$

where subscripts on $F(S, t)$ denote partial derivatives.

Further, the Poisson process for the option price, $q_W(t)$, is perfectly functionally dependent on the Poisson process for the stock price, $q(t)$. Namely, the Poisson event for the option price occurs if and only if the Poisson event for the stock price occurs. Moreover, if the Poisson event for the stock occurs and the random variable Y takes on the value $Y = y$, then the Poisson event for the option occurs and the random variable Y_W takes on the value $F(Sy, t)/F(S, t)$, i.e. $Y_W \equiv F(SY, t)/F(S, t)$. Warning: even though the two processes are perfectly dependent, they are *not* linearly dependent because F is a nonlinear function of S.

Consider a portfolio strategy which holds the stock, the option, and the riskless asset (with return r per unit time) in proportions w_1, w_2, and w_3 where $\Sigma_{j=1}^3 w_j = 1$. If P is the value of the portfolio, then the return dynamics on the portfolio can be written as

$$\frac{dP}{P} = (\alpha_p - \lambda k_p)\,dt + \sigma_p\,dZ + dq_p \tag{9.6}$$

where α_p is the instantaneous expected return on the portfolio, and σ_p^2 is the instantaneous variance of the return, conditional on the Poisson event not occurring. $q_p(t)$ is an independent Poisson process with parameter λ. $k_p \equiv \epsilon\{Y_p - 1\}$ where $Y_p - 1$ is the random variable percentage change in the portfolio's value if the Poisson event occurs and ϵ is the expectation operator over the random variable Y_p.

From (9.2) and (9.4), we have that

$$\alpha_p \equiv w_1(\alpha - r) + w_2(\alpha_W - r) + r \tag{9.7a}$$

$$\sigma_p \equiv w_1\sigma + w_2\sigma_W \tag{9.7b}$$

8   See Merton (1971; this volume, Lemma 5.1) for a statement of Itô's lemma. Its proof can be found in McKean (1969, pp. 32–5). For a description of the corresponding lemma for Poisson processes, see Kushner (1967, p. 20) and Merton (1971; this volume, equations (5.74) and (5.75)).

$$Y_p - 1 \equiv w_1(Y - 1) + \frac{w_2[F(SY, t) - F(S, t)]}{F(S, t)} \tag{9.7c}$$

where $w_3 = 1 - w_1 - w_2$ has been substituted out.

In the Black–Scholes analysis where $\lambda = 0$ (and therefore, $dq = dq_W = dq_p \equiv 0$), the portfolio return could be made riskless by choosing $w_1 = w_1^*$ and $w_2 = w_2^*$ so that $w_1^*\sigma + w_2^*\sigma_W = 0$. This done, it must be that to avoid arbitrage the expected (and realized) return on the portfolio with weights w_1^* and w_2^* is equal to the riskless rate r. From (9.7a) and (9.7b), this condition implies that

$$\frac{\alpha - r}{\sigma} = \frac{\alpha_W - r}{\sigma_W} \tag{9.8}$$

From (9.5a) (with $\lambda = 0$), (9.5b) and (9.8), they arrive at their famous partial differential equation for the option price, namely,

$$\tfrac{1}{2}\sigma^2 S^2 F_{SS} + rSF_S - rF + F_t = 0 \tag{9.9}$$

Unfortunately, in the presence of the jump process dq, the return on the portfolio with weights w_1^* and w_2^* will not be riskless. Moreover, inspection of (9.7c) shows that there does not exist a set of portfolio weights (w_1, w_2) that will eliminate the "jump" risk (i.e. make $Y_p \equiv 1$). The reason is that portfolio mixing is a *linear* operation and the option price is a nonlinear function of the stock price. Therefore, if Y has positive dispersion,[9] then for any w_1 and w_2, $Y_p - 1$ will take on nonzero values for some possible values of Y. Since the analysis is already in continuous time, the Black–Scholes "hedge" will not be riskless even in the continuous limit.

However, one can still work out the return characteristics on the portfolio where the Black–Scholes hedge is followed. Let P^* denote the value of the portfolio. Then, from (9.6) we have that

$$\frac{dP^*}{P^*} = (\alpha_p^* - \lambda k_p^*)\, dt + dq_p^* \tag{9.10}$$

Note that the return on the portfolio is a "pure" jump process because the continuous parts of the stock and option price movements have been

---

9   In the case where σ^2 equals zero and Y is not a random variable (i.e. a pure Poisson process), then a riskless hedge is possible. These twin assumptions are used by Cox and Ross (1976) to deduce by a different route this special case of the formula derived here.

"hedged" out. Equation (9.10) can be rewritten in an analogous form to (9.2a) as

$$\frac{dP^*}{P^*} = (\alpha_p^* - \lambda k_p^*)\, dt \qquad\qquad \text{if the Poisson event does not occur}$$

$$= (\alpha_p^* - \lambda k_p^*)\, dt + (Y_p^* - 1) \quad \text{if the Poisson event occurs} \quad (9.10a)$$

From (9.10a) it is easy to see that, "most of the time," the return on the portfolio will be predictable and will yield $\alpha_p^* - \lambda k_p^*$. However, on average, once every $1/\lambda$ units of time the portfolio's value will take an unexpected jump. Further, we can work out additional qualitative characteristics of the return. Namely, from (9.7c) and (9.5b),

$$Y_p^* - 1 = \frac{w_2^*[F(SY, t) - F(S, t) - F_S(S, t)(SY - S)]}{F(S, t)} \qquad (9.11)$$

By the strict convexity of the option price in the stock price, $F(SY, t) - F(S, t) - F_S(S, t)(SY - S)$ is positive for every value of Y. Hence, if w_2^* is positive, then $Y_p^* - 1$ will be positive, and the unanticipated return on the hedge portfolio will always be positive. If $w_2^* < 0$, then the unanticipated return will be negative. Moreover, the sign of k_p^* will be the same as the sign of w_2^*.

Thus, if an investor follows a Black–Scholes hedge where he is long the stock and short the option (i.e. $w_2^* < 0$), then most of the time he will earn more than the expected return α_p^* on the hedge because $k_p^* < 0$. However, in those "rare" occasions when the stock price jumps he will suffer a comparatively large loss. Of course, these large losses occur just frequently enough so as to, on average, offset the almost steady "excess" return $-\lambda k_p^*$. Conversely, if an investor follows a (reverse) Black–Scholes hedge where he is short the stock and long the option (i.e. $w_2^* > 0$), then most of the time he will earn less than the expected return. But if the stock price jumps, then he will make large positive returns.

Thus, in "quiet" periods when little company-specific information is arriving, writers of options will tend to make what appear to be positive excess returns, and buyers will "lose." However, in the relatively infrequent "active" periods, the writers will suffer large losses and the buyers will "win." Of course, if arrival of an "active" period is random, then there is no systematic way to exploit these findings. It should be emphasized that the large losses suffered by writers during "active" periods are not the result of an "underestimated" variance rate. In general, there is no finite variance rate that could have been used in the formula to "protect" the writer against the losses from a jump.

9.3   AN OPTION PRICING FORMULA

As was demonstrated in the previous section, there is no way to construct a
riskless portfolio of stock and options, and hence the Black–Scholes "no
arbitrage" technique cannot be employed. Of course, along the lines of
Samuelson (1965a), if one knew the required expected return on the option
(as a function of the stock price and time to expiration), then an option
pricing formula could be derived. Let $g(S,\tau)$ be the equilibrium instantaneous expected rate of return on the option when the current stock price is
S and the option expires at time τ in the future. Then, from (9.5a), we have
that F (written as a function of time until expiration instead of time) must
satisfy

$$0 = \tfrac{1}{2}\sigma^2 S^2 F_{SS} + (\alpha - \lambda k)SF_S - F_t - g(S, \tau)F + \lambda\epsilon[F(SY, \tau) - F(S, \tau)]$$
(9.12)

subject to the boundary conditions

$$F(0, \tau) = 0 \qquad\qquad\qquad (9.12a)$$

$$F(S, 0) = \max(0, S - E) \qquad\qquad (9.12b)$$

where E is the exercise price of the option.

Equation (9.12) is a "mixed" partial differential–difference equation,
and although it is linear such equations are difficult to solve. Moreover, the
power and beauty of the original Black–Scholes derivation stems from not
having to know either α or $g(S, \tau)$ to compute the option's value, and both
are required to solve (9.12).

A second approach to the pricing problem follows along the lines of the
original Black–Scholes derivation which assumed that the Capital Asset
Pricing Model[10] (CAPM) was a valid description of equilibrium security
returns. In Section 9.2, the stock-price dynamics were described as the
resultant of two components: the continuous part which is a reflection of
new information which has a marginal impact on the stock's price and the
jump part which is a reflection of important new information that has an
instantaneous nonmarginal impact on the stock. If the latter type of
information is usually firm (or even industry) specific, then it may have
little impact on stocks in general (i.e. the "market"). Examples would be
the discovery of an important new oil well or the loss of a court suit.

If the source of the jumps is such information, then the jump component
of the stock's return will represent "nonsystematic" risk, i.e. the jump

10   See Black and Scholes (1973, pp. 645–6). The CAPM is derived in Sharpe
(1964), Lintner (1965a), and Mossin (1966). An intertemporal version is derived in
Merton (1973b; this volume, Ch. 15). Jensen (1972b) provides an excellent survey
article on the model.

component will be uncorrelated with the market. Suppose that this is generally true for stocks. Return now to the P^* hedge portfolio of the previous section. Inspection of the return dynamics in equation (9.10) shows that the only source of uncertainty in the return is the jump component of the stock. But by hypothesis, such components represent only nonsystematic risk, and therefore the "beta" of this portfolio is zero. If the CAPM holds, then the expected return on all zero-beta securities must equal the riskless rate. Therefore, $\alpha_p^* = r$. But, from (9.7a), this condition implies that $w_1^*(\alpha - r) + w_2^*(\alpha_W - r) = 0$, or substituting for w_1^* and w_2^* we have that

$$\frac{\alpha - r}{\sigma} = \frac{\alpha_W - r}{\sigma_W} \qquad (9.13)$$

But (9.13) together with (9.5a) and (9.5b) imply that F must satisfy

$$0 = \tfrac{1}{2}\sigma^2 S^2 F_{SS} + (r - \lambda k)SF_S - F_\tau - rF + \lambda\epsilon\{F(SY, \tau) - F(S, \tau)\} \qquad (9.14)$$

subject to the boundary conditions (9.12a) and (9.12b). While (9.14) is formally the same type of equation as (9.12), note that (9.14) does not depend on either α or $g(S, \tau)$. Instead, as in the standard Black–Scholes case, only the interest rate r appears. Moreover, (9.14) reduces to the Black–Scholes equation (9.9) if $\lambda = 0$ (i.e. if there are no jumps). It is important to note that even though the jumps represent "pure" nonsystematic risk, the jump component does affect the equilibrium option price. That is, one cannot "act as if" the jump component was not there and compute the correct option price.

While a complete closed-form solution to (9.14) cannot be written down without a further specification of the distribution for Y, a partial solution which is in a reasonable form for computation can be.

Define $W(S, \tau; E, \sigma^2, r)$ to be the Black–Scholes option pricing formula for the no-jump case. Then W will satisfy equation (9.9) subject to the boundary conditions (9.12a) and (9.12b). From the Black and Scholes paper (1973, p. 644, equation 13), W can be written as

$$W(S, \tau; E, \sigma^2, r) = S\Phi(d_1) - E\exp(-r\tau)\,\Phi(d_2) \qquad (9.15)$$

where

$$\Phi(y) \equiv \frac{1}{(2\pi)^{1/2}} \int_{-\infty}^{y} \exp\left(-\frac{s^2}{2}\right)\mathrm{d}s$$

is the cumulative standard normal distribution function,

$$d_1 \equiv \frac{\log(S/E) + (r + \sigma^2/2)\tau}{\sigma\tau^{1/2}}$$

and

$$d_2 \equiv d_1 - \sigma\tau^{1/2}$$

Define the random variable X_n to have the same distribution as the product of n independently and identically distributed random variables, each identically distributed to the random variable Y defined in (9.2), where it is understood that $X_0 \equiv 1$. Define ϵ_n to be the expectation operator over the distribution of X_n.

The solution to equation (9.14) for the option price when the current stock price is S can be written as[11]

$$F(S, \tau) = \sum_{n=0}^{\infty} \frac{\exp(-\lambda\tau)\,(\lambda\tau)^n}{n!}\,\epsilon_n\{W[SX_n \exp(-\lambda k\tau), \tau; E, \sigma^2, r]\}$$

(9.16)

While (9.16) is not a closed-form solution, it does admit to reasonable computational approximation provided that the density functions for the $\{X_n\}$ are not too complicated.

There are two special cases where (9.16) can be vastly simplified. The first is the one described by Samuelson (1972b, p. 16, n. 6) where there is a positive probability of immediate ruin, i.e. if the Poisson event occurs, then the stock price goes to zero. In our notation, this case corresponds to $Y \equiv 0$ with probability one. Clearly, $X_n = 0$ for $n \neq 0$, and $k = -1$. So, in this case, equation (9.16) can be written as

---

11   A verification that (9.16) is indeed a solution to (9.14) is provided in the appendix. The method of obtaining this solution is as follows. In Merton (1972b, p. 38) it was pointed out that the mathematical form of the Black–Scholes equation was formally equivalent to that of Samuelson's (1965a) "first-moment" analysis where the expected return on the stock and the option in his analysis are set equal to the interest rate. That is, to obtain a solution to Black–Scholes, one can "pretend" that the required expected return on both the stock and option must equal the riskless rate. While at first a bit counter-intuitive, this result follows because the Black–Scholes solution does not depend on risk preferences. So, in particular, it must be consistent with risk-neutral preferences which require that expected returns on all securities must equal the interest rate. Cox and Ross (1976) provide an explicit demonstration of this point. Warning: while this method is valid for obtaining solutions, it does not imply that the *actual* expected return on the option is equal to the interest rate. Indeed, from (9.5b) and (9.13), we have that $\alpha_W = r + F_S S(\alpha - r)/F$, and therefore $\alpha_W \neq r$ unless $\alpha = r$.

$$F(S, \tau) = \exp(-\lambda\tau) \, W[S \exp(\lambda\tau), \tau; E, \sigma^2, r]$$
$$= W(S, \tau; E, \sigma^2, r + \lambda) \tag{9.17}$$

Formula (9.17) is identical with the standard Black–Scholes solution but with a larger "interest rate," $r' \equiv r + \lambda$, substituted in the formula. As was shown in Merton (1973a; this volume, Ch. 8), the option price is an increasing function of the interest rate, and therefore an option on a stock that has a positive probability of complete ruin is more valuable than an option on a stock that does not. This result verifies a conjecture of Samuelson.

The second special case of no little interest occurs when the random variable Y has a log-normal distribution. Let δ^2 denote the variance of the logarithm of Y and let $\gamma \equiv \log(1 + k)$. In this case, X_n will have a log-normal distribution with the variance of the logarithm of X_n equal to $\delta^2 n$ and $\epsilon_n(X_n) = \exp(n\gamma)$. Moreover, define $f_n(S, \tau)$ by

$$f_n(S, \tau) \equiv W(S, \tau; E, v_n^2, r_n) \tag{9.18}$$

where $v_n^2 \equiv \sigma^2 + n\delta^2/\tau$ and $r_n \equiv r - \lambda k + n\gamma/\tau$. $f_n(S, \tau)$ is the value of a standard Black–Scholes option where the "formal" variance per unit time on the stock is v_n^2 and the "formal" instantaneous rate of interest is r_n.[12] If Y has a log-normal distribution, then (9.16) can be written as

$$F(S, \tau) = \sum_{n=0}^{\infty} \frac{\exp(-\lambda'\tau) \, (\lambda'\tau)^n}{n!} f_n(S, \tau) \tag{9.19}$$

where $\lambda' \equiv \lambda(1 + k)$. Clearly, $f_n(S, \tau)$ is the value of the option, conditional on knowing that exactly n Poisson jumps will occur during the life of the option. The actual value of the option, $F(S, \tau)$, is just the weighted sum of each of these prices where each weight equals the probability that a Poisson random variable with characteristic parameter $\lambda'\tau$ will take on the value n.[13] From (9.19), it is clear that k does not net out of the option-price formula although the total expected return on the stock, α, does.

12   The term "formal" is used because, if the variance per unit time were really v_n^2, then the variance over the life of the option would be the limit as $m \to 0$ of $\sigma^2\tau + n\delta^2[\log(\tau) - \log(m)]$, and not $\sigma^2\tau + n\delta^2$. So actually v_n^2 is the average variance per unit time, and a similar interpretation holds true for r_n.

13   In the particular case when the expected change in the stock price is zero, given that the Poisson event occurs (i.e. $k = 0$), then $r_n = r$ and $\lambda' = \lambda$. And, with the exception of $\tau = 0$, $f_n(S, \tau)$ in (9.18) is equivalent in value to an option on a stock with no jumps, but a nonproportional-in-time variance that approaches a nonzero limit as the option approaches expiration. In this case from (9.19) each weight is the probability that exactly n jumps occur, and therefore $F(S, \tau)$ is equal to the expected value of $f_n(S, \tau)$ over the random variable n.

Formula (9.16) was deduced from the twin assumptions that securities are priced so as to satisfy the Sharpe–Lintner–Mossin CAPM and that the jump component of a security's return is uncorrelated with the market. While the CAPM has been extensively tested, its validity as a descriptor of equilibrium returns is still an open question.[14] To my knowledge, there have been no empirical studies of the correlation between the jump component of stocks' returns and the market return. So one can hardly claim strong empirical evidence to support these assumptions.

An alternative derivation of formula (9.16) follows along the lines of the Ross (1976a) model for security pricing. Namely, suppose that the jump components of stocks' returns are contemporaneously independent.[15] Suppose that there are m stocks outstanding and one forms a stock-option hedge portfolio of the type described in the previous section for each of the m stocks. If P_j^* denotes the value of the hedge portfolio using stock j, then from equation (9.10) we can write the return dynamics for this portfolio as

$$\frac{\mathrm{d}P_j^*}{P_j^*} = (\alpha_j^* - \lambda_j k_j^*)\,\mathrm{d}t + \mathrm{d}q_j^* \qquad j = 1,2,\ldots,m \qquad (9.20)$$

Consider forming a portfolio of these hedge portfolios and the riskless asset where x_j is the fraction of the portfolio invested in the jth hedge portfolio, $j = 1,2,\ldots,m$, and $1 - \Sigma_{j=1}^{m}\, x_j$ equals the fraction allocated to the riskless asset. If the value of this portfolio of hedge portfolios is H, then the return dynamics of the portfolio can be written as

$$\frac{\mathrm{d}H}{H} = (\alpha_H - \lambda_H k_H)\,\mathrm{d}t + \mathrm{d}q_H \qquad (9.21)$$

where

$$\alpha_H \equiv \sum_{j=1}^{m} x_j(\alpha_j^* - r) + r \qquad (9.21a)$$

$$\lambda_H k_H \equiv \sum_{j=1}^{m} x_j \lambda_j k_j^* \qquad (9.21b)$$

$$\mathrm{d}q_H \equiv \sum_{j=1}^{m} x_j\,\mathrm{d}q_j^* \qquad (9.21c)$$

14   See Black, Jensen, and Scholes (1972) for an empirical test of the model and a discussion of the discrepancies. Also, see Jensen (1972b) and Merton (1973b; this volume, Ch. 15) for a theoretical discussion of why such discrepancies may occur.
15   Actually, the assumption of strict independence can be weakened to allow for some dependence among stocks within groups (e.g. an industry), without affecting the results. See Ross (1976a) for a discussion of this point.

Suppose the unconstrained portfolio weights in the hedge portfolios, $\{x_j\}$, are restricted so that they can be written as $x_j \equiv \mu_j/m$ where the μ_j are finite constants, independent of the number of stocks, m. As m becomes large, Ross calls such portfolios "well diversified." If $ds_j \equiv \mu_j \, dq_j^*$, then ds_j has an instantaneous expected value per unit time of $\mu_j \lambda_j k_j^*$ and an instantaneous variance per unit time of $\lambda_j \mu_j^2 \, \text{var}(Y_j - 1)$, where $Y_j - 1$ is the random variable percentage change in the jth hedge portfolio if a jump occurs in the jth stock price. By the assumption on μ_j, the instantaneous mean and variance per unit time of ds_j are bounded and independent of m.

From (9.21c), we have that $dq_H = (\Sigma_{j=1}^m \, ds_j)/m$ where the ds_j are independent because the dq_j^* are independent. Therefore, by the Law of Large Numbers, $dq_H \to \lambda_H k_H \, dt$ with probability one as $m \to \infty$; i.e. as the number of hedge portfolios contained in a well-diversified portfolio becomes large, the variance of that portfolio tends to zero, and it becomes virtually riskless. Thus, the realized return dH/H will be its expected return $\alpha_H \, dt$ with probability one, and to rule out "virtual" arbitrage $\alpha_H = r$. Substituting this condition into (9.21a), we have that, for large m,

$$\frac{1}{m} \sum_{j=1}^m \mu_j(\alpha_j^* - r) = 0 \qquad (9.22)$$

Since the $\{\mu_j\}$ are arbitrary and (9.22) must hold for almost all choices for the $\{\mu_j\}$, we have that, almost certainly, $\alpha_j^* = r$, for $j = 1,2,\ldots,m$. But, in the first derivation, it was shown that $\alpha_j^* = r$ implies that $(\alpha - r)/\sigma = (\alpha_W - r)/\sigma_W$ (equation (9.13)). But equation (9.13) was the condition required to obtain formula (9.16) as a valid equilibrium price for the option.

While the two derivations leading to formula (9.16) use different assumptions, they have in common the same basic message, namely that, if the jump component of a stock's risk can be diversified away, then the equilibrium option price must satisfy formula (9.16). While I am not aware of any empirical tests of this proposition, the essential test would be whether the returns on well-diversified portfolios can reasonably be described as stochastic processes with continuous sample paths or whether these returns contain identifiable jump components as well.

In the "no-jump" case, Black and Scholes (1973, p. 645, equation 14) derive the number of shares of stock to be bought for each option sold that will create a riskless hedge, namely,

$$N = \partial W/\partial S$$

$$= \Phi(d_1) \qquad (9.23)$$

where W and d_1 are defined in (9.15). In the jump case, there is no such riskless mix. However, there is a mix which eliminates all systematic risk, and, in that sense, is a hedge. The number of shares required for this hedge, N^*, is equal to $\partial F/\partial S$ which can be obtained by differentiating formula (9.16). Note that while, in both cases, the appropriate number of shares is equal to the derivative of the option pricing function with respect to the stock price, the formulas for the number of shares are different. So, for example, in the special case leading to formula (9.19) the number of shares is given by

$$N^* = \sum_{n=0}^{\infty} \frac{\exp(-\lambda'\tau)\,(\lambda'\tau)^n}{n!}\,\Phi[d(n)] \qquad (9.24)$$

where

$$d(n) \equiv \frac{\log(S/E) + (r_n + \sigma^2/2)\tau + n\delta^2/2}{(\sigma^2\tau + n\delta^2)^{1/2}}$$

Of course, when $\lambda = 0$, (9.24) reduces to (9.23).

9.4 A POSSIBLE ANSWER TO AN EMPIRICAL PUZZLE

Using formula (9.16) and the strict convexity in the stock price of the Black–Scholes option-price formula (9.15), it is a straightforward exercise to show that, *ceteris paribus*, an option on a stock with a jump component in its return is more valuable than an option on a stock without a jump component (i.e. $\partial F/\partial \lambda > 0$ at $\lambda = 0$). However, a much more interesting question can be posed as follows. Suppose an investor believes that the stock-price dynamics follow a continuous-sample-path process with a constant variance per unit time, and therefore he uses the standard Black–Scholes formula (9.15) to appraise the option when the true process for the stock price is described by equation (9.2). How will the investor's appraised value, call it $F_e(S, \tau)$, based on a misspecified process for the stock, compare with the $F(S, \tau)$ value based on the correct process?

To make the analysis tractable, I assume the special case in the previous section where Y is log-normally distributed with the variance of the logarithm of Y equal to δ^2 and the expected value of Y equal to unity. Given the investor's incorrect belief about the stock process, it would be natural for him to estimate the variance by using the past time series of the logarithmic returns on the stock.

The distribution of the logarithmic returns on the stock around the mean over any observation period, conditional on exactly n Poisson jumps occurring during the period, is a normal distribution with variance per unit time equal to $\sigma^2 + n\delta^2/h$ where h is the length of time between observations. Thus, if one observation period was an (*ex post*) "active" period for the stock and a second observation period was an (*ex post*) "quiet" period, then the investor might conclude that the variance rate on the "perceived" process is not stationary. Moreover, there would appear to be a "regression" effect in the variance, which has been given by Black and Scholes (1972, pp. 405–9) as a possible explanation for certain empirical discrepancies in a test of their model.

However, I will assume that the investor has a sufficiently long time series of data so that his estimate is the true unconditional variance per unit time of the process, namely,

$$v^2(h) = \sigma^2 + \lambda\delta^2$$
$$= v^2 \qquad\qquad (9.25)$$

the same for all h. So the issue becomes, if the investor uses v^2 as his estimate of the variance rate in the standard Black–Scholes formula, then how will his appraisal of the option's value compare with the "true" solution in formula (9.19)? Define the variable, for $n = 0, 1, 2,...,$

$$T_n \equiv \sigma^2\tau + n\delta^2$$

Let N be a Poisson-distributed random variable with parameter $\lambda\tau$ and define T to be a random variable that takes on the value T_n when the random variable N takes on the value n. Let ϵ denote the expectation operator over the distribution of T. Then, the expected value of T can be written as

$$\bar{T} \equiv \epsilon\{T\}$$
$$= (\sigma^2 + \lambda\delta^2)\tau$$
$$= v^2\tau \qquad\qquad (9.26)$$

I have shown elsewhere (1973a; this volume, equation (8.38)) that

$$W(S, \tau; E, u^2, r) = E \exp(-r\tau) W(X, \tau'; 1, 1, 0) \qquad (9.27)$$

where $W(\cdot)$ is defined in (9.15); $X \equiv S \exp(r\tau)/E$; $\tau' \equiv u^2\tau$. I adopt the short-hand notation $W(X, \tau') \equiv W(X, \tau'; 1, 1, 0)$.

Inspection of (9.18) shows that, from (9.27), f_n can be rewritten as

$$F_e(S, \tau) = E \exp(-r\tau) W(X, \bar{T}) \qquad (9.28)$$

and, from (9.19), that

$$F(S, \tau) = E \exp(-r\tau)\epsilon\{W(X, T)\} \qquad (9.29)$$

Moreover, from (9.26) and (9.27), the investor's incorrect appraisal can be written as

$$F_e(S, \tau) = E \exp(-r\tau)W(X, \overline{T}) \qquad (9.30)$$

From (9.29) and (9.30), the answer to the question as to which formula gives the larger option-price estimate will depend on whether

$$\epsilon\{W(X, T)\} - W(X, \overline{T}) \gtreqless 0$$

If $W(X, \tau')$ were either a strictly convex or strictly concave function of τ', then the answer would be unambiguous by Jensen's inequality. Unfortunately, while $\partial W/\partial\tau' > 0$, the second derivative satisfies

$$\frac{\partial^2 W/\partial\tau'^2}{\partial W/\partial\tau'} = \frac{a^2 - [\tau' + (\tau')^2/4]}{2(\tau')^2}$$

$$\gtreqless 0 \qquad (9.31)$$

where $a \equiv \ln(X)$. At $a = 0$ which corresponds to $S \equiv E \exp(-r\tau)$, $W(X, \tau')$ is a concave function of τ', and therefore $F_e(S, \tau) > F(S, \tau)$ at that stock price. That is, the Black–Scholes estimate will be larger than the true value. For small values of $r\tau$ which would be the case for options, one would expect by continuity that, for stock prices sufficiently near the exercise price, this same inequality would hold. Of course, as a *percentage difference*, the difference may be small.

Similarly, for $a^2 \gg 1$, one would expect that $W(X, T)$ would be convex for most of the probable range of T, and in that case $F(S, \tau) > F_e(S, \tau)$, i.e. the Black–Scholes estimate will be smaller than the true value. But, $a^2 \gg 1$ implies either $S \gg E$ or $S \ll E$, which makes this conjecture intuitively correct. Namely, for deep-out-of-the-money options, there is relatively little probability that the stock price will exceed the exercise price prior to expiration if the underlying process is continuous. However, the possibility of a large finite jump in price significantly increases this probability, and hence makes the option more valuable. Similarly, for deep-in-the-money options, there is relatively little probability that the stock would decline below the exercise price prior to expiration if the underlying process is continuous, and hence the "insurance" value of the option would be virtually nil. However, this need not be the case with jump possibilities. Moreover, these differences will be magnified as one goes to short-maturity options.

Of course, since both $F(S, \tau)$ and $F_e(S, \tau)$ are bounded below by $S - E$ and bounded above by S, the percentage difference between $F(S, \tau)$ and $F_e(S, \tau)$ cannot be large for $S \gg E$. However, in the out-of-the-money case, the percentage difference could be substantial.[16]

It is interesting to note that the qualitative discrepancies between the two formulas correspond to what practitioners often claim to observe in market prices for options. Namely, deep-in-the-money, deep-out-of-the-money, and shorter-maturity options tend to sell for more than their Black–Scholes value, and marginally-in-the-money and longer-maturity options sell for less. It would be presumptuous to claim that the model in this paper "explains" these discrepancies from such casual empiricisms because other deviations from the original Black–Scholes assumptions might also explain them. For example, the special tax treatment of options for writers or a "no-jump" process with a stochastic variance rate for the stock's return could cause such an effect. However, the model in this chapter does suggest a direction for further careful empirical research. Indeed, since the same analysis applied here to options can be extended to pricing corporate liabilities in general,[17] the results of such further research would be of interest to all students of finance.[18]

Appendix

To verify that formula (9.16) in the text is a solution to (9.14) and boundary conditions (9.12a) and (9.12b), we proceed as follows. From (9.16), the option price formula can be rewritten as

$$F(S, \tau) = \sum_{n=0}^{\infty} P_n(\tau) \epsilon_n \{ W(V_n, \tau; E, \sigma^2, r) \} \qquad (9A.1)$$

where we define $P_n(\tau) \equiv \exp(-\lambda\tau)(\lambda\tau)^n/n!$ and $V_n \equiv SX_n \exp(-\lambda k\tau)$.

By differentiating (9A.1), we have that

$$SF_S(S, \tau) = \sum_{n=0}^{\infty} P_n(\tau) \epsilon_n \{ V_n W_1 \} \qquad (9A.2)$$

16 The parameter ranges for which the Black–Scholes solution is less than or greater than the solutions derived here are analyzed in Merton (1976b).

17 Examples of such extensions can be found in Black and Scholes (1973), Merton (1974; this volume, Ch. 12) and Ingersoll (1976).

*18 For later research on asset and option pricing with discontinuous returns, see Jones (1984), Jarrow and Rosenfeld (1984), Ball and Torous (1985), Jorion (1988), Naik and Lee (1990), and Jarrow and Madan (1991).

and

$$S^2 F_{SS}(S, \tau) = \sum_{n=0}^{\infty} P_n(\tau)\epsilon_n\{V_n^2 \, W_{11}\} \tag{9A.3}$$

where subscripts on F and W denote partial derivatives. Further, we have that

$$F_\tau(S, \tau) = -\lambda F - \lambda k \sum_{n=0}^{\infty} P_n(\tau)\epsilon_n\{V_n W_1\} + \sum_{n=0}^{\infty} P_n(\tau)\epsilon_n\{W_2\}$$

$$+ \lambda \sum_{n=1}^{\infty} \frac{(\lambda\tau)^{n-1} \exp(-\lambda\tau)}{(n-1)!} \epsilon_n\{W\}$$

$$= -\lambda F - \lambda k S F_S + \sum_{n=0}^{\infty} P_n(\tau)\epsilon_n\{W_2\}$$

$$+ \lambda \sum_{m=0}^{\infty} P_m(\tau)\epsilon_{m+1}\{W(V_{m+1}, \tau; E, \sigma^2, r)\} \tag{9A.4}$$

where the second line follows by substituting from (9A.2) and changing the summation variable in the last term by $m \equiv n - 1$. Finally, we have that

$$\epsilon_Y\{F(SY, \tau)\} = \epsilon_Y\left\{ \sum_{n=0}^{\infty} P_n(\tau)\epsilon_n\{W(V_n Y, \tau; E, \sigma^2, r)\} \right\}$$

$$= \sum_{n=0}^{\infty} P_n(\tau)\epsilon_{n+1}\{W(V_{n+1}, \tau; E, \sigma^2, r)\} \tag{9A.5}$$

where the second line follows because by the definition of X_n, X_{n+1} and YX_n are identically distributed, and the operator $\epsilon_Y \cdot \epsilon_n$ applied to a function of YX_n is identical to the operator ϵ_{n+1} applied to the same function with X_{n+1} substituted for YX_n.

From (9A.1)–(9A.5), we have that

$$\tfrac{1}{2}\sigma^2 S^2 F_{SS} + (r - \lambda k)S F_S - F_\tau - rF$$

$$= \sum_{n=0}^{\infty} P_n(\tau)\epsilon_n\{\tfrac{1}{2}\sigma^2 V_n^2 W_{11} + rV_n W_1 - W_2 - rW\}$$

$$-\lambda k S F_S + \lambda F + \lambda k S F_S - \lambda \sum_{m=0}^{\infty} P_m(\tau)\epsilon_{m+1}\{W(V_{m+1}, \tau; E, \sigma^2, r)\}$$

$$= -\lambda[\epsilon_Y\{F(SY, \tau) - F(S, \tau)\}] \tag{9A.6}$$

because W satisfies equation (9.9) in the text, and therefore

$$\tfrac{1}{2}\sigma^2 V_n^2 W_{11} + r V_n W_1 - W_2 - rW = 0$$

for each n. It follows immediately from (9A.6) that $F(S, \tau)$ satisfies equation (9.14). $S = 0$ implies that $V_n = 0$ for each n. Further, from (9.15), $W(0, \tau; E, \sigma^2, r) = 0$. Therefore, from (9A.1), $F(0, \tau) = 0$ which satisfies boundary condition (9.12a).

From (9.15) we have

$$\epsilon_n\{W(V_n, 0; E, \sigma^2, r)\} = \epsilon_n\{\max(0, V_n - E)\}$$
$$\leq \epsilon_n\{V_n\}$$
$$= S(1 + k)^n \tag{9A.7}$$

Therefore, using (9A.7),

$$\lim_{\tau \to 0} \sum_{n=1}^{\infty} P_n(\tau)\epsilon_n\{W\} \leq \lim_{\tau \to 0} \sum_{n=1}^{\infty} \frac{S \exp(-\lambda\tau)\,[(1 + k)\lambda\tau]^n}{n!}$$
$$= \lim_{\tau \to 0} S \exp(-\lambda\tau)\,\{\exp[(1 + k)\lambda\tau] - 1\}$$
$$= 0 \tag{9A.8}$$

and, from (9A.8), it follows that

$$\lim_{\tau \to 0} F(S, \tau) = \lim_{\tau \to 0}[P_0(\tau)\epsilon_0\{W(V_0, \tau; E, \sigma^2, r)\}]$$

$$= \max(0, S - E) \tag{9A.9}$$

Hence, formula (9.16) satisfies boundary condition (9.12b).

10

Further Developments in Option Pricing Theory

10.1 INTRODUCTION

The lineage of modern option pricing theory began with the 1900 Sorbonne thesis, *Theory of Speculation*, by the French mathematician, Louis Bachelier. The work is rather remarkable because, in studying the problem of option pricing, Bachelier derives much of the mathematics of probability diffusions, and this, five years before Einstein's famous development of the mathematical theory of Brownian motion.[1] Although, from today's perspective, the economics and mathematics of Bachelier's analysis are flawed, the connection of his research with the subsequent path of attempts to develop a rigorous theory of option pricing is unmistakable.[2] It was not until the publication of the Black–Scholes model, however, nearly three-quarters of a century later, that the field reached a sense of closure on the subject. This closure on methodology opened the gates to what has become a flood of research on option pricing applications, generated by both the academic and practising financial communities.

Along with the publication of the seminal Black–Scholes paper, the spring of 1973 also marked the creation of the first organized markets for options on common stocks.[3] In April of that year, the Chicago Board Options Exchange (CBOE) began trading call options on 12 companies'

1 On comparing the Bachelier and Einstein derivations, Samuelson (1972b, n. 2) writes, "But years ago when I compared the two texts, I formed the judgment (which I have not checked back on) that Bachelier's methods dominated Einstein's in every element of the vector. Thus, the Einstein–Fokker–Planck Fourier equation for diffusion of probabilities is already in Bachelier, along with subtle uses of the now-standard method of reflected images." What financial economist doesn't relish this revelation of the great debt owed to this early option pricing theorist by the mathematical physicists and probabilists, to be added to the well-known debt owed to Malthus by the Darwinian biologists?

2 For many years, Bachelier's work was unknown in the literature of option pricing. The rediscovery of his work in the early 1950s is generally credited to Samuelson via L. J. Savage. And, of course, Samuelson's own work on warrants had an important impact on the development of modern option pricing theory (cf. Merton, 1983a, pp. 106–7, 128–34).

3 At least, in modern times. From Joseph de la Vega's (1688) treatise detailing the workings of the Amsterdam stock exchange, it appears that options and

shares. Within a few years, the CBOE, together with competing exchanges, had expanded to include both calls and puts on hundreds of stocks. The success of these markets was followed by a series of new markets for trading options on fixed-income securities, currencies, stock-market and bond-market indices, and a variety of commodities. Today, trading volume in options and the related financial futures markets account for a substantial portion of total financial-market trading.

The creation and successful development of these markets was surely the primary stimulus for much of the applied options research contributed by practising financial analysts. Just as surely, a significant part of the academic empirical research on options would not have been possible without the transactions data generated by these markets.[4] However, the commercial success of these specialized financial markets is not the reason that option pricing analysis has become one of the cornerstones of general finance theory. Instead, the central role for options analysis evolves from the fact that option-like structures permeate virtually every part of the field. The continuous-time theory of option pricing forms the methodological foundation for the general theory of contingent-claims pricing.[5] As Chapters 11–14 demonstrate, contingent-claims analysis can be applied to a wide range of problems in corporate finance, financial intermediation, and capital markets, including the pricing of corporate liabilities, the determination of the term structure of interest rates, and the evaluation of complex capital budgeting decisions.

This chapter is focused exclusively on developments in the theory of option pricing, leaving to the succeeding four chapters coverage of the contributions to the derivative theory of contingent-claims pricing. We begin with a brief overview of important extensions to the theory, this to be followed by a more lengthy analysis of a selected few.

---

securities similar to modern financial futures contracts dominated trading activities in this leading financial center of the seventeenth-century world. As Miller (1986, n. 1) notes, options on commodity futures were traded on the Chicago Board of Trade in the 1920s, although they were later banned by Congress in the 1930s. From the coincidence of timing, some may perhaps be tempted to infer a causal relation between the creation of the CBOE and the research by Black and Scholes. But, of course, their basic research was completed years before. There is little doubt, however, that the existence and success of the CBOE contributed much to the unusually rapid diffusion of knowledge of their research, especially among practicing financial analysts.

4   Black and Scholes (1972) examine several thousand transactions of over-the-counter options gathered from a dealer's book to provide the first important test of their model. See Galai (1983) and Cox and Rubinstein (1985, pp. 482–4) for extensive bibliographies of subsequent empirical studies of option pricing models.

5   The observation that options are fundamental securities is not limited to the continuous-time framework. As Ross (1976b), Arditti and John (1980), Green and Jarrow (1987), and Nachman (1988) show in a discrete-time setting, the availability of a rich set of option contracts can significantly improve the allocational efficiency of capital markets.

Scholes (1976) modifies the basic Black–Scholes model to take account of the effects of taxes on both option prices and the prescribed mix of stocks and bonds in the replicating-portfolio strategy. Constantinides and Scholes (1980) and Constantinides and Ingersoll (1984) also analyze the effects of taxes on security prices by deriving the value of an investor's options to choose when to realize gains and losses on investments in an environment with personal taxes. Leland (1985), Figlewski (1989), Hodges and Neuberger (1989), Boyle and Vorst (1992), and Bensaid, Lesne, Pagès, and Scheinkman (1991) examine option pricing and the risks of imperfect hedging when there are transactions costs. Gilster and Lee (1984), Barron and Jensen (1990), and Bergman (1991) derive option prices when there is a spread between the riskless borrowing and lending rates.

As shown in Chapter 9, the option pricing methodology can be applied to options on securities with price dynamics described by combined diffusion and Poisson-directed stochastic processes. See also Cox and Ross (1976), Jones (1984), Ball and Torous (1985), and Aase (1988). Hull and White (1987), Johnson and Shanno (1987), Scott (1987), Wiggins (1987), and Goldenberg (1991) investigate option pricing with price dynamics following a diffusion process with a stochastic variance rate. Cox and Ross (1976) and Cox, Ross, and Rubinstein (1979) derive the equations of option pricing for other types of processes. The binomial model of Cox, Ross, and Rubinstein, along with the Cox–Ross "risk-neutral" method for pricing options, are analyzed in Section 10.2.

Geske (1977, 1979) uses the Black–Scholes approach to derive prices for "compound" options (e.g. an option to buy an option). His technique can produce closed-form solutions for prices of options on dividend-paying stocks. See also Selby and Hodges (1987). Geske and Johnson (1984) provide an infinite series solution for the American put. Ball and Torous (1983), Brennan and Schwartz (1983), Schaefer and Schwartz (1987), and Black, Derman, and Toy (1990) evaluate options on government bonds and other default-free debt. Johnson and Stulz (1987) examine the price effects of default on the option contract itself. Margrabe (1979) analyzes the pricing of the option to exchange one risky asset for another. Fischer (1978) develops a formula for pricing options with stochastic exercise prices and uses it to evaluate index bonds. Stulz (1982) solves the pricing problem for options that pay either the maximum or the minimum of the value of two risky assets. Johnson (1987) extends the Stulz analysis to n assets. The closely related structures of the Margrabe–Fischer–Stulz models frequently arise in other types of finance problems. Merton, Scholes, and Gladstein (1978, 1982) use historical stock returns to simulate the patterns of returns for option strategies involving a portfolio of options.

The largest-volume real-world options markets trade options on futures contracts. Assuming a constant interest rate, Black (1976a) derives pricing formulas for European options on futures. Ramaswamy and Sundaresan (1985) and Jarrow (1987) extend the analysis to an environment with stochastic interest rates. Brenner, Courtadon, and Subrahmanyam (1985), Whaley (1986), and Overdahl (1988) study the effects of early exercise on the prices of American options on futures. Garman and Kohlhagen (1983), Grabbe (1983), Shastri and Tandon (1987), Jorion (1988), and Melino and Turnbull (1990) develop models to evaluate prices of options on foreign currency. Eytan and Harpaz (1986) analyze the pricing of futures and options on the geometric Value Line Index. A brief development of the pricing theory for options on futures is presented in Section 10.3.

Chapters 8 and 9 contain a number of examples of closed-form formulas for option prices. Nevertheless, such solutions to the fundamental partial differential equation of option pricing are rare. Extensive research efforts have thus been undertaken to develop numerical methods for approximate solutions to this partial differential equation.[6] The books by Ames (1977) and Smith (1978) are general mathematical references on the finite-difference method of solution. Brennan and Schwartz (1977a) use this technique to simultaneously solve for the price of an American put and the optimal exercise boundary (see also Courtadon, 1982, and Hull and White, 1988, 1990a). Parkinson (1977) also solves the American put pricing problem but he uses a binomial-trinomial method of numerical integration. Boyle (1977) investigates the prospects for Monte Carlo simulations as a solution technique and finds mixed results. See also Hull and White (1987) and Johnson and Shanno (1987). Geske and Shastri (1985) compare and contrast the various numerical methods used in option price valuations. Boyle (1988), Boyle, Evnine, and Gibbs (1989), He (1989, Ch. 2), and Madan, Milne, and Shefrin (1989) develop computational methods for pricing options that depend on multiple stochastic variables.

For broad coverage of the developments in option pricing theory, see the survey articles by Smith (1976, 1979), Cox and Rubinstein (1983), Mason and Merton (1985), and Cox and Huang (1989a). See also the survey article on empirical work by Galai in the collection of papers on option pricing edited by Brenner (1983). There are many reference books on option pricing and option investment strategies. The books by Gastineau (1979), Bookstaber (1981), Jarrow and Rudd (1983), Cox and Rubinstein (1985), Ritchken (1987), and Hull (1989) use methodological approaches that are most closely aligned with the development here. Although not exclusively devoted to option pricing, the books by Ingersoll (1987) and Duffie (1988) also provide useful analysis in this area.

6   The numerical solution of parabolic partial differential equations has long been studied for physics and engineering applications (e.g. heat transfer). Unfortunately, many of the techniques developed cannot be used to solve the options version of this equation because of the type of boundary conditions. The problem is especially complicated if the optimal early-exercise boundary must be simultaneously determined. An alternative approach is to find an analytical solution for a security with payoffs that approximate those of the security to be priced. See Johnson (1983), Geske and Roll (1984), Blomeyer (1986), MacMillan (1986), Barone-Adesi and Whaley (1987), and Kim (1990).

10.2 COX–ROSS "RISK-NEUTRAL" PRICING AND THE BINOMIAL OPTION PRICING MODEL

The Samuelson (1965a) theory of warrant pricing, summarized in Section 7.3, posits that warrants are priced to yield a constant expected rate of return β. Samuelson proves that it is never optimal to exercise a warrant on a nondividend-paying stock before expiration if the expected returns on the warrant and the stock are the same (i.e. $\beta = \alpha$). In that special case, the value of an American warrant can be determined by simple quadrature. That is, from (7.12) with $S(t) = S$, the warrant price $F(S, t)$ can be written as

$$F(S, t) = \exp[-\alpha(T-t)] \int_0^\infty \max(0, SZ-E) \, dP(Z; T, t) \qquad (10.1)$$

where E denotes the exercise price of a warrant that expires at time T and Z is the random variable return per dollar on the stock between t and T. Equation (10.1) is the standard present-value formula in which the expected value of the warrant at expiration is discounted back at the assumed-constant required expected return on the warrant.

In the Samuelson–Merton discrete-trading model, the expected return on a finite-lived warrant will equal the expected return on the stock only if the expected return on the stock equals the interest rate. In the three-asset equilibrium version of that model, this equality of expected returns will obtain if and only if the investor's utility function is linear (i.e. preferences are "risk neutral").[7] From Chapter 8, footnote 42, the expected return on a finite-lived option in the Black–Scholes model will also equal the expected return on the stock only if the latter is equal to the interest rate. Thus, the posited conditions leading to (10.1) will rarely be satisfied in equilibrium models of warrant and option pricing. Nevertheless, formula (10.1) is important for the computation of warrant and option prices.

As shown in Section 7.7, equation (10.1) can generally be used to compute warrant values in the Samuelson–Merton theory by replacing the objective distribution dP by the subjective util–prob distribution dQ and by setting α equal to r, the riskless interest rate. Because the formal mathematics makes no distinction between the util–prob and objective distributions, warrant prices in that theory can be determined "as if" securities are priced to produce expected returns equal to the interest rate.

Under the additional assumption that the underlying stock-price dynamics follow a geometric Brownian motion with drift rate α and variance

---

7 See Sections 7.6 and 7.12.

rate σ^2, Samuelson (1965a, p. 27) shows that warrant prices given by (10.1) must satisfy the partial differential equation

$$\frac{1}{2}\sigma^2 S^2 \frac{\partial^2 F}{\partial S^2} + \alpha S \frac{\partial F}{\partial S} + \frac{\partial F}{\partial t} - \alpha F = 0 \qquad (10.2)$$

subject to the boundary conditions $S \geq F(S, t) \geq \max(0, S - E)$ and $F(S, T) = \max(0, S - E)$. As noted in Chapter 8, equation (10.2) is, by inspection, identical with the partial differential equation for the Black–Scholes call option price if α is set equal to the interest rate. Equation (10.1), however, is the unique solution to (10.2). Thus, Black–Scholes call option prices can also be computed by "pretending" that the expected returns on call options and their underlying stocks are the same and equal to the interest rate. Moreover, as shown for the put option in Section 8.8, Black–Scholes prices for all types of options must satisfy (10.2) with $\alpha = r$. Hence, the present-value formula can be used to price any European option by substituting the appropriate terminal-value function $F(SZ, T)$ for $\max(0, SZ - E)$ in (10.1).[8]

That (10.1) is the solution to (10.2) is important in the application of numerical methods to derive approximate solutions for option prices when no closed-form solution can be found. If, for example, a closed-form solution for the density function dP is known, then approximate solutions for F can be obtained by numerical integration of (10.1). For the same level of precision, numerical quadrature techniques are generally faster to compute than recursive solutions of finite-difference approximations to equation (10.2). Further, the stability conditions required to ensure uniformly valid approximations to the solution are considerably weaker for numerical integration than for finite-difference methods.

Cox and Ross (1976) were the first to generally apply the present-value formula with discounting at the riskless interest rate as a convenient computational "trick" for pricing options. More importantly, they were the first to recognize that this relation is a fundamental characteristic of "arbitrage-free" price systems in continuous-trading environments. The economic reasoning given by Cox and Ross for this relation is as follows.

---

8   As discussed in Samuelson and Merton (1969; this volume, equation (7.12)), equation (10.1) applies only to the case of no early exercise. However, the computational device of equating expected returns on the option and the stock to the interest rate works with early exercise as well. As underscored in Merton (1972b) and again in Chapter 9, footnote 11, the mathematical equivalence between the Black–Scholes and Samuelson pricing formulas is purely formal and surely does not imply that actual expected returns are equated. Indeed, as the derivation of the Black–Scholes model in Chapter 8 demonstrates, the option price can be determined without specifying the expected returns on either the underlying stock or the option.

Continuous-Time Finance

Given a posited environment of continuous trading and diffusion processes for underlying stock prices, option prices must equal Black–Scholes model prices as a necessary condition to rule out arbitrage opportunities. The absence of arbitrage opportunities, however, is a necessary condition for an equilibrium system of prices. It therefore follows that option prices must equal Black–Scholes model prices in any equilibrium model with continuous trading and diffusion processes for stock prices. In particular, the Black–Scholes model price must equal the equilibrium option price in an economy where all investors have linear utility functions. It is well known that, with risk-neutral preferences, equilibrium will obtain only if the expected returns on all securities are the same and equal to the interest rate. Hence, the Black–Scholes model price is equal to the option price derived from the assumption that the expected returns on both the option and its underlying stock are equal to the interest rate. The Cox–Ross technique is thus called the "risk-neutral" pricing method.

As we have seen, the risk-neutral pricing method can, at least formally, be applied to discrete-trading models by substitution of the util–prob distribution dQ for the objective distribution dP. However, the transformation to the util–prob distribution will in general alter the entire stochastic structure of the actual return distribution.[9] The option prices so obtained are, of course, dependent on the choice of utility function. In contrast, with continuous trading, Black–Scholes option prices are the same for all preferences, and the transformation to the Cox–Ross risk-neutral pricing distribution preserves the stochastic component of the actual return distribution. That is, if $dS/S = \alpha \, dt + \sigma \, dz$ denotes the dynamics for actual stock returns, then $dS^*/S^* = r \, dt + \sigma \, dz$ where S^* denotes the price of the stock in the associated risk-neutral equilibrium model with $S^*(0) = S(0)$. If we set $S^+(t) \equiv S^*(t)/\exp(rt)$ and $S^{++}(t) \equiv S(t)/\exp[\int_0^t \alpha(s)ds]$, then $dS^+/S^+ = \sigma \, dz = dS^{++}/S^{++}$. Hence, with $S^+(0) = S^{++}(0)$, the detrended actual stock price and the detrended risk-neutral equilibrium price have identical probability distributions for $t > 0$.

If F and F^*, respectively, denote the actual and risk-neutral equilibrium prices of the options, then $dF = \alpha_F F \, dt + (\partial F/\partial S)\sigma S \, dz$ and $dF^* = rF^* \, dt + (\partial F^*/\partial S^*)\sigma S^* \, dz$. From (10.2) and (10.1), we have that $F^*(S^*, t) = F(S, t)$ for $S^* = S$, and therefore $\partial F/\partial S = \partial F^*/\partial S^*$ for $S^* = S$. If $F^+ \equiv F^*/\exp(rt)$, then $dF^+ = (\partial F^+/\partial S^+)\sigma S^+ dz$. By the chain rule, $\partial F^+/\partial S^+ = \partial F^*/\partial S^*$ for $S^+ = S^* \exp(-rt)$, and hence, $\partial F^+/\partial S^+ = \partial F/\partial S$ for $S^+ = S \exp(-rt)$.

---

9   The only restrictions are that, with risk-averse preferences, probability mass is shifted from higher-return events to lower-return events and that for each event $dQ = 0$ if and only if $dP = 0$. The latter implies that dQ and dP are *equivalent* probability measures as defined, for example, in Harrison (1985, pp. 9–11).

The detrending of the risk-neutral equilibrium prices S^* and F^* is equivalent to choosing as numeraire one unit of a portfolio that initially invests one dollar in the riskless asset and retains all earnings. By inspection, for each t, $E_t\{dS^+\} = E_t\{dF^+\} = 0$. Therefore, risk-neutral equilibrium prices with the riskless asset as numeraire satisfy the conditions of a martingale. That is, $E_t[S^+(\tau)] = S^+(t)$ and $E_t\{F^+[S^+(\tau), \ \tau]\} = F^+[S^+(t), \ t]$ for all t and $\tau > t$. Moreover, the probability distribution governing the evolution of the martingale prices S^+ and F^+ is identical with the distribution of the martingale process for the actual detrended stock price S^{++}.

Although derived by Cox and Ross in the context of option pricing, the martingale property of risk-neutral equilibrium prices and their connection to actual prices applies in general to security prices in arbitrage-free price systems with continuous trading.[10] As is evident from the substantial body of literature on the subject, the risk-neutral pricing technique has proved to be a powerful tool for the analysis of general equilibrium pricing in continuous-trading environments.[11] Application of Cox–Ross risk-neutral pricing generally requires that trading takes place continuously and that security prices have continuous sample paths. One important exception is the Cox–Ross–Rubinstein (1979) binomial option pricing model. See also Sharpe (1978) and Rendleman and Bartter (1979) for similar models.

To derive the Cox–Ross–Rubinstein model, consider a two-period discrete-trading model in which the one-period changes in stock price have binomial conditional-probability distributions. As illustrated by the tree diagram in Figure 10.1, the catalog of possible stock prices at time t, $S(t)$, given an initial stock price $S(0) = S_0$, is as follows: at time 1, $S(1)$ will equal either S_{11} or S_{12} with $S_{11} < S_{12}$. Conditional on $S(1) = S_{11}$, $S(2)$ will equal either S_{21} or S_{22} with $S_{21} < S_{22}$. Conditional on $S(1) = S_{12}$, $S(2)$ will equal either S_{23} or S_{24} with $S_{23} < S_{24}$. Other than assuming that the conditional probabilities are nondegenerate (i.e. $\text{prob}\{S(t) = S_{tj}|S_0\} > 0$, $t = 1,2; j = 1,2,3,4$), we posit no other conditions on the probabilities. We do assume that the stock pays no dividends.

It is assumed that there is a riskless security that yields the same return per dollar each period, $R (\equiv 1 + r)$. To rule out the possibility of arbitrage between the stock and the riskless security, the possible future stock prices must satisfy

---

10 Harrison and Kreps (1979) were the first to formally derive the martingale property for general arbitrage-free price systems. Their analysis also shows the importance of carefully specifying the class of admissible trading strategies in models that use continuous-trading strategies to determine security prices.
11 See Kreps (1981), Harrison and Pliska (1981, 1983), Huang (1985a, b, 1987), Duffie and Huang (1985), Pliska (1986), Duffie (1986, 1987, 1988), Denny and Suchanek (1986), Cox and Huang (1989a, b, 1991), and Karatzas (1989). A brief discussion can also be found in Chapter 16. Girsanov (1960) provides the key mathematical theorem for applying this technique.

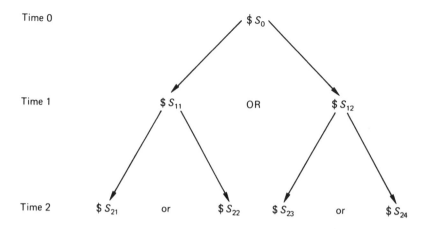

Figure 10.1 Tree Diagram of Possible Stock-Price Paths.

$$S_{11} < S_0 R < S_{12} \tag{10.3a}$$

$$S_{21} < S_{11} R < S_{22} \tag{10.3b}$$

$$S_{23} < S_{12} R < S_{24} \tag{10.3c}$$

In words, the restrictions in (10.3) ensure that in each period there is a positive probability that the stock will earn more than the riskless security and a positive probability that it will earn less.

Suppose there is a limited-liability security, call it an "option," that receives no payments at time 1 and whose value at time 2 is specified by the nonnegative function $H(S)$ for $S(2) = S$. As in the derivation of the Black–Scholes model in Chapter 8, we now show that there exists a dynamic portfolio strategy, mixing the stock with the riskless security, that exactly replicates the payoff to the option. To derive the strategy, we proceed in a backwards induction process like that of dynamic programming.

Let $N(S, t)$ denote the number of shares of the stock held in the portfolio at time t when $S(t) = S$. Let $B(S, t)$ denote the dollar amount invested in the riskless security at time t when $S(t) = S$. If $F(S, t)$ is the value of the portfolio at time t, then $F(S, t) = N(S, t)S + B(S, t)$.

Suppose that, at $t = 1$, $S(1) = S_{11}$. To exactly match the payoff to the option at time 2, the portfolio mix must satisfy $N(S_{11},1)S_{21} + B(S_{11},1)R = H(S_{21})$ in the event $S(2) = S_{21}$, and $N(S_{11},1)S_{22} + B(S_{11}, 1)R = H(S_{22})$ in the event $S(2) = S_{22}$. Solving these two linear equations, we have that

$$N(S_{11}, 1) = \frac{H(S_{22}) - H(S_{21})}{S_{22} - S_{21}} \tag{10.4a}$$

$$B(S_{11}, 1) = \frac{H(S_{21})S_{22} - H(S_{22})S_{21}}{R(S_{22} - S_{21})} \tag{10.4b}$$

It follows from (10.4a) and (10.4b) that the amount of resources required in the portfolio at time 1 to support this strategy is given by

$$F(S_{11}, 1) = \frac{p(S_{11}, 1)H(S_{22}) + [1 - p(S_{11}, 1)]H(S_{21})}{R} \tag{10.4c}$$

where $p(S_{11}, 1)$ is defined as

$$p(S_{11}, 1) \equiv \frac{RS_{11} - S_{21}}{S_{22} - S_{21}} \tag{10.4d}$$

Suppose that, at $t = 1$, $S(1) = S_{12}$. Then, at time 2, $S(2)$ will equal either S_{23} or S_{24}. Hence, by the same analysis as that leading to (10.4a) and (10.4b), we have that the portfolio strategy required to match the option value at time 2 is given by

$$N(S_{12}, 1) = \frac{H(S_{24}) - H(S_{23})}{S_{24} - S_{23}} \tag{10.5a}$$

$$B(S_{12}, 1) = \frac{H(S_{23})S_{24} - H(S_{24})S_{23}}{R(S_{24} - S_{23})} \tag{10.5b}$$

From (10.5a) and (10.5b), the value of the portfolio required to implement this strategy is

$$F(S_{12}, 1) = \frac{p(S_{12}, 1)H(S_{24}) + [1 - p(S_{12}, 1)]H(S_{23})}{R} \tag{10.5c}$$

where $p(S_{12}, 1)$ is defined as

$$p(S_{12}, 1) \equiv \frac{RS_{12} - S_{23}}{S_{24} - S_{23}} \tag{10.5d}$$

If the portfolio is to exactly replicate the return received by holding the option from $t = 0$ until expiration, then the strategy at $t = 0$ must produce a portfolio value of $F(S_{11}, 1)$ at time 1 if $S(1) = S_{11}$ and a value of $F(S_{12}, 1)$ at time 1 if $S(1) = S_{12}$. This objective can be met provided that $N(S_0, 0)S_{11} + B(S_0, 0)R = F(S_{11}, 1)$ and $N(S_0, 0)S_{12} + B(S_0, 0)R = F(S_{12}, 1)$. Solving these equations, we have that

$$N(S_0, 0) = \frac{F(S_{12}, 1) - F(S_{11}, 1)}{S_{12} - S_{11}} \tag{10.6a}$$

$$B(S_0, 0) = \frac{F(S_{11}, 1)S_{12} - F(S_{12}, 1)S_{11}}{R(S_{12} - S_{11})} \tag{10.6b}$$

The initial value of the portfolio required to undertake these positions is given by

$$F(S_0, 0) = \frac{p(S_0, 0)F(S_{12}, 1) + [1 - p(S_0, 0)]F(S_{11}, 1)}{R} \tag{10.6c}$$

where $p(S_0, 0)$ is defined as

$$p(S_0, 0) \equiv \frac{RS_0 - S_{11}}{S_{12} - S_{11}} \tag{10.6d}$$

We have thus shown that, with an initial investment of $F(S_0, 0)$, there exists a dynamic portfolio strategy involving the stock and the riskless security that exactly replicates the payoff to an option for all possible sample paths of the stock. The "recipe" for actually replicating the option is given by equations (10.4a), (10.5a), and (10.6a), that prescribe the number of shares to be held at each point in time and for each possible stock price. To rule out the possibility of arbitrage between the stock and the option at $t = 0$, the option price must equal $F(S_0, 0)$ for $S(0) = S_0$. Similarly, to rule out arbitrage at $t = 1$, the option price at that time must equal $F[S(1), 1]$. As defined by (10.4c), (10.5c), and (10.6c), $F(S, t)$ is the Cox–Ross–Rubinstein binomial option price, and it is the only binomial option pricing formula that is consistent with arbitrage-free price systems.

To replicate option payoffs in the Black–Scholes world of Chapters 8 and 9 requires a continuous-trading dynamic portfolio strategy. As shown in equation (9.23), the number of shares of stock prescribed for that strategy, $N(S, t)$, is given by the partial derivative $\partial F/\partial S$ of the Black–Scholes option pricing function with respect to the stock price. $N(S, t)$ is the number of shares of stock that an investor should short-sell to hedge against the price risk of a long position in an option on one share of the stock. $N(S, t)$ is often called the *hedge ratio* or *stock-equivalent ratio* associated with the option at time t when the stock price is S. For a call option or warrant, the hedge ratio is always nonnegative and less than or equal to one.[12] Noting that $F(S, 2) = H(S)$, the hedge ratio in the binomial option pricing model can be written as

$$N(S, t) = \frac{\Delta F}{\Delta S} \qquad (10.7)$$

where ΔF is the difference between the option prices for each of the two possible stock prices at $t + 1$ and ΔS is the difference in those stock prices. Hence, the hedge ratio $\Delta F/\Delta S$ for the discrete-sample-path binomial process is the natural analog to the hedge ratio $\partial F/\partial S$ for the continuous-sample-path process posited in the Black–Scholes model.

As indicated at the outset, the binomial option pricing formula can be derived by using the Cox–Ross risk-neutral pricing method. To see this, consider the following. From (10.3b), $RS_{11} > S_{21}$ and $S_{22} - S_{21} > RS_{11} - S_{21}$. Hence, from (10.4d), $0 < p(S_{11}, 1) < 1$. Similarly, from (10.3c) and (10.5d), $0 < p(S_{12}, 1) < 1$ and, from (10.3a) and (10.6d), $0 < p(S_0, 0) < 1$. The set $\{p(S, t)\}$ thus defines a conditional probability distribution for a binomial process. Our derivation of the binomial option pricing formula in (10.4)–(10.6) requires knowledge of the event tree of possible future stock prices. It does not, however, require specification of the probabilities for those prices. The pricing formula must therefore apply for any set of nondegenerate probabilities. In particular, it must apply for the probability set $\{p(S, t)\}$.

From (10.4d), we have that

$$E\{S(2)|S_{11}\} = p(S_{11}, 1)S_{22} + [1 - p(S_{11}, 1)]S_{21} = RS_{11}$$

and from (10.4c)

$$E\{F[S(2), 2]|S_{11}\} = p(S_{11}, 1)H(S_{22}) + [1 - p(S_{11}, 1)]H(S_{21})$$
$$= RF(S_{11}, 1)$$

From (10.5d),

$$E\{S(2)|S_{12}\} = p(S_{12}, 1)S_{24} + [1 - p(S_{12}, 1)]S_{23} = RS_{12}$$

---

12   As shown in equation (9.23), the number of shares of stock required in the replicating portfolio for a call option is given by $N(S, t) = \partial F/\partial S = \Phi(d_1)$, where Φ is the standard normal cumulative probability function and $d_1 \equiv [\log(S/E) + (r + \sigma^2/2)(T - t)]/\sigma(T - t)^{1/2}$. Hence, $0 \leqslant N(S, t) \leqslant 1$, with the strict inequalities holding for $0 < S < \infty$ and $t < T$.

and from (10.5c)

$$E\{F[S(2),\, 2]|S_{12}\} = RF(S_{12},\, 1)$$

Hence,

$$E\{S(2)|S(1)\} = RS(1)$$

and

$$E\{F[S(2),\, 2]|S(1)\} = RF[S(1),\, 1]$$

Similarly, from (10.6d),

$$E\{S(1)|S_0\} = RS_0$$

and from (10.6c)

$$E\{F[S(1),\, 1]|S_0\} = RF(S_0,\, 0)$$

If, therefore, $\{p(S, t)\}$ were the actual probabilities, then both the stock and option would be priced to yield expected returns equal to the return on the riskless security. Thus, the $\{p(S, t)\}$ applied to the actual set of possible future stock prices is the Cox–Ross risk-neutral probability distribution.

To write the binomial option pricing formula in the form of (10.1), note that the two-period probability distribution for the stock price can be expressed as

$$p_1 \equiv \text{prob}\{S(2) = S_{21}|S_0\} = [1 - p(S_0,\, 0)][1 - p(S_{11},\, 1)]$$
$$p_2 \equiv \text{prob}\{S(2) = S_{22}|S_0\} = [1 - p(S_0,\, 0)]p(S_{11},\, 1)$$
$$p_3 \equiv \text{prob}\{S(2) = S_{23}|S_0\} = p(S_0,\, 0)\,[1 - p(S_{12},\, 1)]$$
$$p_4 \equiv \text{prob}\{S(2) = S_{24}|S_0\} = p(S_0,\, 0)p(S_{12},\, 1)$$

By substitution for $F(S, 1)$ from (10.4c) and (10.5c) into (10.6c) and rearrangement of terms, we have that

$$F(S_0,\, 0) = \frac{\Sigma_1^4\, p_j H(S_{2j})}{R^2} \tag{10.8}$$

Hence, option prices for binomially distributed stock prices can be computed by the standard present-value formula with a discount rate equal to the riskless interest rate. For the call option, $H(S) = \max(0, S - E)$ and for the put option, $H(S) = \max(0, E - S)$.

As in the continuous-trading models, the transformation of the binomial distribution for actual stock prices to the Cox–Ross risk-neutral distribution does not depend upon investor preferences.[13] However, unlike in the continuous-trading case, the transformation does not preserve the "detrended" or central moments of the actual stock-price distribution. For example, if p denotes the actual probability that $S(1) = S_{12}$, then the variance of the return on the stock between $t = 0$ and $t = 1$ is $p(1 - p)(S_{12} - S_{11})^2/S_0^2$. The corresponding variance for the associated Cox–Ross risk-neutral distribution is $(RS_0 - S_{11})(S_{12} - RS_0)/S_0^2$. By inspection, the variances of the two distributions are not the same for every p, $0 < p < 1$.

The binomial option pricing formula, derived here for the two-period case, can easily be extended to n periods by the same backwards-induction process. The dynamic programming technique can also be used to solve for prices of American options and their associated early-exercise boundaries. Cox and Rubinstein (1985, Ch. 5) provide a complete development of the binomial option pricing model in the general case, including the possibility of early exercise.

The binomial option pricing model is elegantly simple. Its derivation does not require continuous trading and, hence, avoids the mathematical complexities of Itô stochastic integrals. It thus provides a powerful pedagogical tool for developing the economic intuitions underlying the pricing of options in arbitrage-free price systems. Of course, the practical applications of the model in a strictly discrete-time setting are severely limited by the assumption that the underlying stock price can only take on two possible values. However, as we now show, the model does provide a rather practical technique for computing approximate solutions to continuous-time option pricing models.

In Chapter 3, we developed the properties of diffusion processes, including Itô's lemma, by taking the limit of discrete-time type I stochastic processes with m possible outcomes in each period. That is, if T is a fixed finite time interval, we subdivided that interval into n periods of length $h = T/n$ and examined the properties of the stochastic process in the limit as $h \to 0$ (and $n \to \infty$). One such sequence is the $m = 2$ case where the outcomes in each period are binomially distributed. Indeed, in a classic application of the Central Limit Theorem, Bachelier (1900) derives

---

13 Hence, although the Samuelson–Merton util–prob distribution of Chapter 7 will in general depend on the choice of utility function, the util–prob distribution derived in Section 7.11 for the binomial process will be the same for any choice of preferences.

Brownian motion as the continuous-time limit of a properly scaled binomially distributed random walk. Extending this application to geometric Brownian motion, Samuelson (1965a, pp. 25–7) derives his partial differential equation for warrant prices – equation (10.2) here – as the limit of the discrete-time warrant pricing equation associated with binomially distributed stock returns. Cox, Ross, and Rubinstein (1979, p. 254) use a similar approach to deduce the Black–Scholes option pricing equation.

The Cox–Ross–Rubinstein binomial option pricing formula is a necessary condition to rule out arbitrage opportunities for all sample paths of the stock price. Hence, by the proper selection of a binomial process that converges to the diffusion process posited by Black and Scholes, the binomial option pricing formula will converge to the Black–Scholes option price.

Let the return per dollar on the stock between t and $t + h$, $Z(t + h) \equiv S(t + h)/S(t)$, be given by the binomial process $Z(t + h) = 1 + \sigma h^{1/2}$ with probability q and $Z(t + h) = 1 - \sigma h^{1/2}$ with probability $1 - q$, where it is understood that h is chosen small enough that $h < 1/\sigma^2$. σ is an order-one function of $S(t)$ and t, satisfying $\sup(\sigma) < \infty$. Let α denote the expected rate of return on the stock per unit time so that $\exp(\alpha h) \equiv E_t\{Z(t + h)\} = 1 + (2q - 1)\sigma h^{1/2}$. If α is an order-one bounded function for all h (Chapter 3, Assumption 5), then it follows that q must satisfy

$$q = \frac{1}{2}\left(1 + \frac{\alpha}{\sigma} h^{1/2}\right) + o(h) \tag{10.9}$$

The conditional variance of the stock return is given by $q(1 - q)4\sigma^2 h$, and hence, from (10.9), we have that

$$\text{var}_t[Z(t + h)] = \sigma^2 h + o(h) \tag{10.10}$$

From (10.4d), (10.5d), and (10.6d), the Cox–Ross risk-neutral probability assigned to the event that $Z(t + h) = 1 + \sigma h^{1/2}$ can be written as

$$p(S, t) = \frac{\exp(rh) - 1 + \sigma h^{1/2}}{2\sigma h^{1/2}}$$

$$= \frac{1}{2}\left(1 + \frac{r}{\sigma} h^{1/2}\right) + o(h) \tag{10.11}$$

where r is the continuously compounded interest rate ($R = \exp(rh)$) and σ is evaluated at $S(t) = S$. By inspection of (10.9) and (10.11), $p(S, t)$ has the same form as q with r substituted for α. Moreover, unlike in the general binomial case, the conditional variance of the return computed from the risk-neutral probability distribution is, to order $o(h)$, equal to the conditional variance of the actual return given by (10.10).

From (10.4c), (10.5c), and (10.6c), the binomial option pricing formula satisfies

$$\exp(rh)F(S, t) = p(S, t)F[S(1 + \sigma h^{1/2}), t + h]$$
$$+ [1 - p(S, t)]F[S(1 - \sigma h^{1/2}), t + h] \tag{10.12}$$

As in Chapter 3, Taylor's theorem with a remainder can be used to express the option price at time $t + h$ as a function of the option pricing formula and its derivatives evaluated at time t. That is, for each possible outcome on the stock

$$F[S(1 + \sigma h^{1/2}), t + h] = F(S, t) + F_t(S, t)h + F_S(S, t)S\sigma h^{1/2}$$
$$+ \tfrac{1}{2}F_{SS}(S, t)S^2\sigma^2 h + o(h) \tag{10.13a}$$

and

$$F[S(1 - \sigma h^{1/2}), t + h] = F(S, t) + F_t(S, t)h - F_S(S, t)S\sigma h^{1/2}$$
$$+ \tfrac{1}{2}F_{SS}(S, t)S^2\sigma^2 h + o(h) \tag{10.13b}$$

where subscripts on F denote partial derivatives. Noting that

$$\exp(rh)F(S, t) = (1 + rh)F(S, t) + o(h),$$

we have by substitution for $p(S, t)$ from (10.11) and by substitution for $F(\cdot, t + h)$ from (10.13), that (10.12) can be rewritten as

$$(1 + rh)F(S, t) = F(S, t) + F_t(S, t)h + F_S(S, t)rSh$$
$$+ \tfrac{1}{2}F_{SS}(S, t)S^2\sigma^2 h + o(h) \tag{10.14}$$

By subtracting $F(S, t)$ from both sides of (10.14), dividing by h and taking the limit as $h \to 0$, we have that in the limit of continuous time the binomial option pricing formula satisfies

$$0 = \tfrac{1}{2}\sigma^2 S^2 F_{SS}(S, t) + rSF_S(S, t) + F_t(S, t) - rF(S, t) \tag{10.15}$$

By inspection, (10.15) is the same as the Samuelson warrant pricing equation (10.2) with $\alpha = r$, and is therefore identical with the Black–Scholes option pricing equation. Thus, for the posited binomial process, the limit of the binomial option price is the Black–Scholes option price.

The derived relation between (10.12) and (10.15) suggests a numerical method for approximating the solution to (10.15). Choose σ^2 to match the variance rate of the diffusion process for the actual stock returns. If $H(S)$ denotes the value of an American option at expiration, then beginning with the terminal condition $F(S, T) = H(S)$, we have the backwards recursive condition that

$$F(S, t) = \max(H(S), \exp(-rh)\{p(S, t)F[S(1 + \sigma h^{1/2}), t + h]$$
$$+ [1 - p(S, t)]F[S(1 - \sigma h^{1/2}), t + h]\}) \qquad (10.16)$$

where (10.12) has been adjusted to reflect the possibility of early exercise. For each t, (10.16) is evaluated for a discrete number of values for S, and there are n steps backward in time to arrive at $F(S, 0)$. The accuracy of the calculated approximations to the solution of (10.15) will depend on the number of steps. That is, for fixed T, the larger is n and hence the smaller is h, the more accurate is the approximation. In the special case of the original Black–Scholes model with a constant σ, we have from (10.11) that $p(S, t)$ is a constant. However, as is evident from the derivation, this approximation procedure can handle the general diffusion case where σ depends on the level of the stock price and time.

Parkinson (1977) was among the first to apply the binomial technique as a numerical method for solving (10.15) for the American put option. As is evident from the mathematical development in Chapter 3, the binomial process is only one of many discrete-time stochastic processes that converge to diffusion processes in the limit of continuous time. Numerical approximations to the solution of (10.15) can be developed for these distributions, along the lines of (10.16).[14]

Although the binomial option pricing model provides important insights into the hedging process derived in the continuous-trading environment, we close with a note of caution on extending the intuitions of that model to the case where the option's value depends on more than one underlying security price.[15] If, for example, an option depends on the prices of two securities and if each security has two possible outcomes in each period,

14 In the cited Parkinson (1977) study, he actually uses a trinomial distribution instead of the binomial because it provides a computationally efficient means to standardize the grid sizes.
15 Examples can be found in Margrabe (1978), Fischer (1978), Stulz (1982), Boyle and Kirzner (1985), Johnson (1987), and Marcus (1987).

then, in general, for each step in time, there are four possible "states" for the vector (S_1, S_2). By the method of derivation used here, three securities plus the riskless security are necessary to hedge an option position for each possible outcome. However, in the continuous-trading model with diffusion processes, only the two underlying securities and the riskless security are needed to create a riskless hedge of the option. In the general case of an option that depends on n risky securities, the number of securities (including the riskless one) required to hedge the option for the binomial process is 2^n, whereas the number required in the corresponding continuous-trading model is $n + 1$.[16]

10.3 PRICING OPTIONS ON FUTURES CONTRACTS

As noted in Section 10.1, some of the largest-volume options markets trade options on futures contracts. Although the pricing of such options is closely related to the pricing of options on cash-market securities, they are sufficiently different to warrant separate analysis. We begin with definitions and brief analyses of forward and futures contracts, this to be followed by the derivation of the option pricing equations.

A *forward contract* on one unit of a financial security is a two-party agreement. A denotes the party who is said to be *long* the forward contract and B denotes the party who is said to be *short* the forward contract. The terms of the forward contract are that on a specified date (the "delivery date") B will deliver one unit of the security to A and A will pay B a specified price (the "delivery price"). Unlike the purchaser of a call option, party A is contractually obliged to buy the security at the delivery price. Unlike the purchaser of a put option, party B must sell the security at the delivery price.

Although collateral may be required of either party to ensure performance of the contract, the standard terms of forward contracts are that neither party makes any side-payment to the other in return for entering into the contract. Hence, at the time that they enter into the agreement, the value of the forward contract (to both parties) is zero. The *forward*

---

16 Sharpe's discussion of Marcus (1987) alludes to this difference between the discrete-time binomial and continuous-time diffusion option pricing models. For numerical approximation purposes it is, of course, always possible to construct a *particular* multidimensional binomial process that converges to a particular multidimensional diffusion process. Cf. He (1989, Ch. 2, 1990), Madan, Milne and Shefrin (1989), and Nelson and Ramaswamy (1990). The issue raised here is that the economic intuitions about the requirements for hedging in the general binomial model need not correspond to the ones for the diffusion model.

price is defined to be the delivery price that makes the value of the forward contract equal to zero.

A two-party agreement closely related to the forward contract is the *futures contract*. Let $X(t; T)$ denote the futures price at time t associated with a futures contract with delivery date T. Let h denote the settlement time interval and let $n \equiv T/h$. Define $t_k \equiv kh$ to be the kth settlement date, $k = 1,...,n$. The conditions of the futures contract are that (a) on the delivery date T, B will deliver one unit of the security to A and A will pay to B an amount equal to the then-prevailing futures price $X(T; T)$; (b) on each settlement date t_k, $k = 1,...,n$, B will pay to A an amount equal to the difference between the futures price at that date and the futures price at the previous settlement date (i.e. $X(t_k; T) - X(t_{k-1}; T)$). If this difference is negative, then A will pay $|X(t_k; T) - X(t_{k-1}; T)|$ to B.

The delivery price for a forward contract is set at the outset of the agreement and remains fixed for the life of the contract. In contrast, from conditions (a) and (b), the effective delivery prices for outstanding futures contracts are changed on each settlement date and set equal to the then-prevailing futures price. Thus, independently of the initiation dates of the contracts, the delivery price at a given point in time is the same on all futures contracts with the same delivery date. This feature permits futures contracts to be standardized, a critical requirement if an instrument is to be successfully traded in a market.

As with the forward contract, neither party makes any payment to induce the other to enter into the futures contract. Thus, at the time of entry into the contract, the futures price $X(t; T)$ must be such that the value of the contract is zero. But, at each settlement date, the futures price for both old and new contracts is the same. Therefore, on each settlement date and after the payment required by (b), the value of all futures contracts is zero. It follows immediately that the futures price on the delivery date will equal the cash-market price of the underlying security to be delivered, i.e. $X(T; T) = S(T)$. Hence, the gains and losses between the parties are settled throughout the life of the futures contract. Because the settlement time interval is in practice quite short (typically, one day), this provision for frequent settling of gains and losses substantially reduces the need for collateral.

With the terms of the forward and futures contracts established, we turn now to the determination of the forward and futures prices. Let $Y(t; T)$ be the forward price for a contract established at time t with delivery date T. Let $P(t; T)$ denote the price at time t of a default-free zero-coupon bond that pays one dollar at time T. Consider the portfolio strategy of establishing a long position in a forward contract at time t plus the purchase of $Y(t; T)$ units of the zero-coupon bond that matures on the delivery date. The value of the portfolio at time T will equal the price of the security delivered, $S(T)$, less the payment of the delivery price, $Y(t; T)$, plus the $Y(t; T)$

dollars received for the matured bonds. Thus, the value of this portfolio at time T will equal the cash-market price of the security, $S(T)$. If there were no dividends or other distributions paid on the security between t and T, then the payoff to the portfolio is identical to the payoff from purchasing the underlying security at time t and holding it to time T. To avoid arbitrage, the investment required in the portfolio at time t must equal the cash-market price of the security, $S(t)$. Because no investment is required to enter into a forward contract, the total investment in the portfolio is the cost of the bonds, $P(t; T)Y(t; T)$. It follows that, to avoid arbitrage, the forward price on a nondividend-paying security must satisfy

$$Y(t; T) = \frac{S(t)}{P(t; T)} \tag{10.17}$$

To determine the forward price on a security that does pay dividends between t and T, note that a European call option with expiration date T and exercise price equal to zero is economically equivalent to owning the underlying security but with no rights to the dividends paid on the security prior to T. Because the value of the call at time T is $S(T)$, a forward contract on the underlying security is economically identical to a forward contract on this option. But the call option pays no dividends. Therefore, from (10.17), we have that

$$Y(t; T) = \frac{W(t; T)}{P(t; T)} \tag{10.18}$$

where W is the price of the European call option.

In Section 8.7 we analyzed the pricing of call options on dividend-paying stocks with a continuous-payout rate given by $D(S, t)$. As shown in footnote 48 of that section, a closed-form formula for the European call-option price was derived in the particular case where the dividend yield $D(S(t), t)/S(t)$ is a constant ρ, for all t. Substituting $E = 0$ into that formula, we have that $W(t; T) = S(t) \exp[-\rho(T - t)]$. From (10.18), it follows that

$$Y(t; T) = S(t) \exp[-(\rho - \bar{r})(T - t)] \tag{10.19}$$

where $\bar{r} \equiv -\log[P(t; T)]/(T - t)$ is the yield-to-maturity on the zero-coupon bond. The term $1 - \exp[-(\rho - \bar{r})(T - t)]$ is called the *cost of carry* associated with the forward contract. If the cost of carry is positive, the forward price will be less than the current cash-market price of the security. If the cost of carry is negative, then the forward price will exceed the current cash-market price.

To analyze the properties of futures prices in a continuous-trading environment, it is convenient to assume that futures are continuously settled (i.e. the settlement time interval $h = dt$). As in Section 10.2, let $b(t) \equiv \exp[\int_0^t r(s) \, ds]$. Consider the following continuous-trading portfolio strategy. Initially ($t = 0$), take a long position in a futures contract with delivery date T and invest $X(0; T)$ dollars in the riskless security. Over the period from $t = 0$ to $t = T$, change the number of futures contracts in the portfolio so that $N(t)$ long positions are held between t and $t + dt$. Reinvest all interest earned on the riskless-security component of the portfolio. If dX denotes the instantaneous change in the futures price, then by condition (b) the portfolio receives a cash flow of $N(t) \, dX$ between t and $t + dt$. If $dX > 0$, the cash inflow is invested in the riskless security until T. If $dX < 0$, the cash outflow is financed by borrowing at the riskless rate until T. In either case, the investor neither adds nor withdraws any cash from the portfolio until $t = T$.[17]

The contribution to the total value of the portfolio at T from the futures positions held between t and $t + dt$ is $[b(T)/b(t)]N(t) \, dX$. If $V(t)$ denotes the value of the portfolio at t, then it follows that

$$V(T) = \int_0^T \frac{b(T)}{b(t)} N(t) \, dX + b(T)X(0; T)$$

$$= b(T) \left[\int_0^T \frac{N(t)}{b(t)} \, dX + X(0; T) \right] \qquad (10.20)$$

where the initial investment $V(0) = X(0; T)$ and $N(0) = b(0) = 1$.

Since $b(t)$ is known at time t, one such feasible strategy is $N(t) = b(t)$. From (10.20), the value of the portfolio with this strategy is

$$V(T) = b(T)X(T; T)$$

$$= b(T)S(T) \qquad (10.21)$$

because $\int_0^T dX = X(T; T) - X(0; T)$ and $X(T; T) = S(T)$. From the analysis of the portfolio strategy used to derive the forward price in (10.17), we have that an initial position of $Y(0; T)/P(0; T)$ units of a zero-coupon bond together with $1/P(0; T)$ long positions in forward contracts will produce a portfolio value of $S(T)/P(0; T)$ at the delivery date. Therefore, the difference in portfolio values between this strategy and the futures strategy leading to (10.21) is $[1/P(0; T) - b(T)]S(T)$. $1/P(0; T) - b(T)$ is the difference between the cumulative returns from investing one dollar in a long-term bond and one dollar in "rolling over"

---

17 Portfolios with this property are called "self-financing" portfolios.

the riskless security. In the special case where the dynamic path of the riskless interest rate is nonstochastic, $P(0; T) = 1/b(T)$ or there would be an arbitrage opportunity between short-term and long-term borrowing and lending. Hence, in this case, the payoffs to the forward-contract and the futures-contract strategies are identical. To avoid arbitrage opportunities between forward and futures contracts, the initial investment in the two portfolios must be the same. It follows that, in an environment of nonstochastic interest rates,

$$X(t; T) = Y(t; T) \tag{10.22}$$

The futures price will not in general equal the forward price when the dynamics of interest rates are stochastic. The development of the relation between the futures and forward prices in this general case is rather involved.[18] We therefore derive the pricing equation for options on futures under the assumption that the interest rate is constant and (10.22) obtains.

Suppose that the security underlying the futures contract is a stock that pays a constant proportional dividend at rate ρ and that the dynamics for the stock price are described by $dS/S = (\alpha - \rho) \, dt + \sigma \, dz$ where α is the expected rate of return. If the interest rate r is a constant, then from (10.19) and (10.22) the futures price can be written as

$$X(t; T) = S(t) \exp[-(\rho - r)(T - t)] \tag{10.23}$$

By applying Itô's lemma to (10.23), we have that the futures-price dynamics can be expressed as

$$dX = (\alpha - r)X \, dt + \sigma X \, dz \tag{10.24}$$

Note that although the relation between the futures price and the cash-market price of the security depends on the dividend payout rate, from (10.24), the dynamics of the futures price do not.

Let $F(X, t; E, T^*)$ denote the price of a call option on the futures contract where E is the exercise price and T^* is the expiration date ($T^* \leq T$, the delivery date of the futures contract). If the option is exercised, the holder enters into a futures contract and receives a cash payment of $X(t; T) - E$. Because the value of the futures contract is zero,

---

18 See Cox, Ingersoll, and Ross (1981), Richard and Sundaresan (1981), and Jarrow (1987) for the development of continuous-time models for futures prices in a stochastic interest rate environment. In Section 10.2, we used a price system that has as its numeraire one unit in a portfolio which holds the riskless security. Since $b(t)/b(t) \equiv 1$, the interest rate is constant and equal to zero. Thus, the futures price will equal the cash-market price in such a system.

the value of the option, if exercised, is $X(t; T) - E$. Similarly, at $t = T^*$, $F(X, T^*; E, T^*) = \max(0, X - E)$.

As in Section 8.7, equation (8.42), we apply Itô's lemma to derive the dynamics of the option price:

$$dF = [\tfrac{1}{2}\sigma^2 X^2 F_{11} + (\alpha - r)XF_1 + F_2]\, dt + \sigma XF_1\, dz \qquad (10.25)$$

where subscripts denote partial derivatives. Along the lines of the derivation in Section 8.6, consider the following portfolio strategy. At $t = 0$, buy a call option and finance the purchase by borrowing. At time t ($\geqslant 0$), hold a *short* position in $N(t)$ futures contracts. Use all cash inflows from changes in the futures price to reduce borrowings and finance all cash outflows from such changes by increasing borrowings. If $B(t)$ is the amount borrowed in the portfolio at time t, then $dB = rB(t)\, dt + N(t)\, dX$. If $V(t)$ is the value of the portfolio at time t, then $V(t) = F[X(t; T), t; E, T^*] - B(t)$, because positions in futures contracts require no investment. In particular, $V(0) = 0$.

The dynamics of the portfolio value can be written as

$$dV = dF - dB$$

$$= dF - rB\, dt - N\, dX \qquad (10.26)$$

By substitution from (10.24) and (10.25) into (10.26) and rearranging terms, we have that

$$dV = [\tfrac{1}{2}\sigma^2 X^2 F_{11} + (\alpha - r)X(F_1 - N) + F_2 - rB]\, dt + (F_1 - N)\sigma X\, dz \qquad (10.27)$$

Suppose we select the particular strategy

$$N(t) = F_1 \equiv \partial F[X(t; T), t; E, T^*]/\partial X$$

By inspection of (10.27), the change in the value of the portfolio is nonstochastic. Therefore, to rule out arbitrage, $dV = rV\, dt = r(F - B)\, dt$. From this condition and (10.27), the option price must satisfy

$$0 = \tfrac{1}{2}\sigma^2 X^2 \frac{\partial^2 F}{\partial X^2} + \frac{\partial F}{\partial t} - rF \qquad (10.28)$$

The boundary conditions to be applied to (10.28) for a European call option are as follows: for $t < T^*$, $0 \leqslant F(X, t; E, T^*) \leqslant X$ and $F(X, T^*; E, T^*) = \max(0, X - E)$. For an American option, we require further that $\max(0, X - E) \leqslant F(X, t; E, T^*)$ for all t.

By comparing (10.28) with (8.44) in Section 8.7, we see that the pricing formula for an option on a futures contract is formally identical with the one for an option on a cash-market security that pays a constant-proportional dividend equal to rX. There are, of course, no explicit dividends paid on futures contracts. However, because positions in futures contracts require no investment, there is an "implicit" dividend equal to the financing savings of carrying an otherwise equivalent cash-market security.

From Section 8.7, footnote 48, with $\rho = r$, the solution to (10.28) for a European call option can be written as

$$F(X, t; E, T^*) = \exp[-r(T^* - t)][X\Phi(d_1) - E\Phi(d_2)] \quad (10.29)$$

where $d_1 = [\log(X/E) + \sigma^2(T - t)/2]/\sigma(T - t)^{1/2}$, $d_2 = d_1 - \sigma(T - t)^{1/2}$, and Φ is the cumulative standard normal distribution function.

As also shown in footnote 48, for a sufficiently large futures price, an American call will be worth more if exercised than if held. Hence, the result that it never pays to exercise an American call option on a nondividend-paying cash-market security before expiration does not apply to options on futures. Therefore, to solve (10.28) for an American call option requires a simultaneous solution for the optimal-exercise boundary as described by equations (8.44a) and (8.44b), Section 8.7.

By an analysis similar to the one used to derive (10.28) for the call option, it can be shown that put-option prices will also satisfy (10.28) with the boundary conditions $0 \leqslant F(X, t; E, T^*) \leqslant E$ and $F(X, T^*; E, T^*) = \max(0, E - X)$ for the European put, and the further condition $\max(0, E - X) \leqslant F(X, t; E, T^*)$ for the American put.

The *swap contract* is a relatively recent, but already important derivative security that serves a similar function to forward and futures contracts. A swap is a two-party agreement to exchange contingent cash flows on specified future dates. For example, Party A agrees to pay Party B (.10 × $100 million =) $10 million on each December 31 over the next five years. In return, on each such payment date, B will pay A whatever the one-year United States Treasury (UST) bill yield was on the preceding January 2, applied to $100 million. That is, this *interest-rate* swap has A pay a "fixed" rate (10%) and receive a "floating" rate (1-year UST yield). The principal amount ($100 million) to which these rates are applied to determine the cash payments is called the *notional amount* of the swap. The contingent payments in this swap are the floating-side payments that depend on the future levels of the 1-year UST bill yield.

The types of contingent payments available in swap contracts are wide ranging. Beside interest rates, common examples are a swap of the total return on the Standard & Poor's 500 stock portfolio for the total return on a 10-year UST note and a swap of currencies such as Yen for dollars.

Commodities prices are also frequently used, such as exchanging payments based on the price of oil for payments based on the price of wheat. See Merton (1990b, pp. 266–8) for terms of a stock-market swap contract designed to reduce the efficiency losses from capital controls.

As with forward contracts, standard terms are set to make the initial value of the swap equal to zero. Of course, the subsequent value of the contract will fluctuate with changes in market conditions. Call and put options on swap contracts are called "swaptions." Hull (1989) provides an introduction to swap contracts. See Solnik (1989) and Sundaresan (1990) for application of the continuous-time model to valuation of both swaps and swaptions. Cooper and Mello (1991) analyze the valuation of swaps when there is risk of default on the payments by one of the parties.

Part IV

Contingent-Claims Analysis in the Theory of Corporate Finance and Financial Intermediation

11

A Dynamic General Equilibrium Model of the Asset Market and Its Application to the Pricing of the Capital Structure of the Firm

11.1 INTRODUCTION

In earlier papers (Merton, 1969a, 1971; this volume, Chs 4 and 5), the problem of lifetime consumption-portfolio decisions for an individual investor was examined in the context of a continuous-time model. The current chapter uses a similar approach to derive general equilibrium relations among securities in the asset market. Under the assumption that the value of the firm is independent of its capital structure, an explicit equation for pricing the individual securities within the capital structure is presented.

In Sections 11.2 and 11.3, a partial-equilibrium model for pricing the capital structure is developed to aid in the understanding of the approach and for comparison with the complete equilibrium solution in later sections. In Sections 11.4, 11.5, 11.6, and 11.7, the general model is derived and its implications for security pricing, the term structure of interest rates, and the capital structure of the firm under various assumptions are discussed.

Although the chapter concentrates on the asset markets, the model can be generalized to examine equilibrium behavior in other sectors of the economy as well.

Reproduced from Working Paper No. 497–70, A. P. Sloan School of Management, Massachusetts Institute of Technology, Cambridge, MA, 1970. An earlier version of the paper was presented at the Conference on Capital Market Theory, Massachusetts Institute of Technology, July 1970. My thanks to Myron Scholes for helpful discussion. Aid from the National Science Foundation is gratefully acknowledged.

11.2   A PARTIAL-EQUILIBRIUM ONE-PERIOD MODEL

In an earlier paper coauthored with Paul Samuelson (Samuelson and Merton, 1969; this volume, Ch. 7), we derived a theory of warrant pricing based on expected utility maximization when the individual has a portfolio choice among three assets: the warrant, the stock of the firm, and a riskless asset. The model presented in this section follows the approach used in that paper.

Consider an economy made up of one firm with current value $V(t)$. Further, assume that there exists a "representative man" for the economy who acts so as to maximize the expected utility of wealth at the end of a period of length τ.[1] That is, since the firm is the only asset in the economy, he acts so as to

$$\max E_t\{U[V(t + \tau)]\} \qquad (11.1)$$

where E_t is the conditional expectation, conditional on knowing that $V(t) = V$, and U is assumed to be strictly concave and monotonically increasing, i.e. $U' > 0$ and $U'' < 0$.

We further postulate a known probability distribution $P(Z, \tau)$ for the value of the firm at the end of the period, where the random variable Z is defined by

$$Z \equiv \frac{V(t + \tau)}{V(t)} \qquad (11.2)$$

The random variable Z reflects both the uncertainty about the cash flow (or earnings) of the firm and the changes in value of the firm's capital stock or earning assets over the period. A crucial assumption is that $P(Z, \tau)$ is independent of the particular capital structure of the firm, i.e. P is determined solely by the characteristics of the asset side of the balance sheet and is not affected by the particular instruments used by the firm to finance these assets. This assumption is consistent with the Modigliani–Miller (1958) theorem and, as such, we implicitly assume perfect capital markets and tax effects are not considered.

Consider that the firm chooses a particular set of financial instruments (debt, equity, etc.) defined by their terminal conditions. We now find the current equilibrium value of each of these future claims on the terminal

---

1   Since, in this section, we are using a period model, τ could be set equal to one. However, it will be useful for later development to carry the general symbol τ.

(random) value of the firm. For $i = 1,...,n$, define $F_i(V, \tau)$ as the current value of the ith type of security with terminal date τ from now issued by the firm.[2] The different types of securities are distinguishable by their terminal value $F_i(VZ, 0)$, contingent on the terminal value of the firm $V(t + \tau) = VZ$. For example, if one of the securities is a debt issue ($i = 1$), senior to all other claims on the firm, with a terminal claim of B dollars on the firm, then

$$F_1(VZ, 0) = \min(B, VZ) \qquad (11.3)$$

i.e. the debtholders will receive B dollars at the end of the period if the firm can pay, or, in the event that the firm cannot pay (default), they are entitled to all the assets of the firm which will have value VZ.

To determine the equilibrium values of each of the securities, note that because each of the securities appears separately in the market place, they must be priced so that when examined by the representative man he will choose his portfolio so as to hold the amount supplied, i.e.

$$V = \sum_1^n F_i(V, \tau) \qquad (11.4)$$

and, of course, $VZ = \Sigma_1^n F_i(VZ, 0)$. Define $w_i \equiv F_i(V, \tau)/V$ as the fraction of the firm's assets financed by the ith security. Then, because the firm is the only asset in the economy, w_i will also be equal to the fraction of the representative man's initial wealth invested in the ith security. We rewrite (11.1) as a maximization under constraint problem:

$$\max_{\{w_i\}} \left\{ E_t U \left[V \sum_1^n w_i \frac{F_i(VZ, 0)}{F_i(V, \tau)} \right] + \lambda \left[1 - \sum_1^n w_i \right] \right\} \qquad (11.5)$$

The first-order conditions[3] derived from (11.5) are

$$E_t \left\{ \frac{F_i(VZ, 0)}{F_i(V, \tau)} U' \left[V \sum_1^n w_i \frac{F_i(VZ, 0)}{F_i(V, \tau)} \right] \right\} = \lambda \qquad i = 1,...,n$$

$$(11.6)$$

Equation (11.6) can be rewritten in terms of util–prob distributions[4] Q as

2   Strictly, F_i will be a function of the current values of all securities senior to it, the capitalization rate, etc. in addition to V. However, in equilibrium, the F_i are perfectly positively related to changes in the value of the firm, and so these other arguments of the function will enter only as parameters.
3   The assumption of strict concavity of U is sufficient to ensure a unique interior maximum which rules out any need for inequalities in the first-order conditions.
4   See Samuelson and Merton (1969; this volume, Section 7.2) for further discussion of the util–prob concept.

$$\int_0^\infty \frac{F_i(VZ, 0)}{F_i(V, \tau)} \, dQ = \int_0^\infty \frac{F_j(VZ, 0)}{F_j(V, \tau)} \, dQ \equiv \exp(\eta\tau) \text{ for all } i, j = 1,\dots,n$$

(11.7)

where

$$dQ \equiv \frac{U'(ZV) \, dP(Z, \tau)}{\int_0^\infty U'(ZV) \, dP(Z, \tau)}$$

and $\exp(\eta\tau)$ is a new multiplier related to the original λ multiplier. Note the important substitution of VZ for $V\Sigma_1^n w_i F_i(VZ, 0)/F_i(V, \tau)$ in the definition of dQ. By the assumption that the value of the firm is independent of its capital structure, we have that dQ is independent of the functions F_i, $i = 1,\dots,n$. Therefore, (11.7) is a set of integral equations, *linear* in the F_i.[5] Hence, we can meaningfully rewrite (11.7) as

$$F_i(V, \tau) = \exp(-\eta\tau) \int_0^\infty F_i(VZ, 0) \, dQ(Z, \tau) \quad i = 1,\dots,n$$

(11.8)

Because the $F_i(VZ, 0)$ are known functions determined by the type of security, and U and $P(Z, \tau)$ are assumed known, (11.8) would be sufficient to determine the current equilibrium value of the ith security if we knew η.

From examination of (11.7) and noting again that dQ is independent of the particular capital structure chosen, we find that $\exp(\eta\tau)$ (and hence η) is independent of the particular capital structure. Since (11.7) holds for all capital structures, it must hold for the trivial capital structure, namely, when the firm issues just one type of security, equity, and $n = 1$. In this case, it is obvious that $F_1(V, \tau) = V$ and $F_1(VZ, 0) = VZ$. Substituting in (11.7), we have that

$$\exp(\eta\tau) = \int_0^\infty Z \, dQ(Z, \tau)$$

(11.9)

i.e. $\exp(\eta\tau)$ is the expected return on the firm in *util–prob* space. Equation (11.7) states that the expected return on all securities in *util–prob* space must be equated. If U was linear (i.e. the representative man was "risk neutral"), then $dQ = dP$ and (11.7) would imply the well-known result for

5   Thus, the assumption that the firm's value is independent of its capital structure provides the same mathematical simplification that the assumption of the "incipient" case for warrant pricing did in Samuelson and Merton (1969; this volume, Section 7.7).

risk neutrality that expected returns (in the ordinary sense) be equated. Hence, the util–prob distribution is the distribution of returns adjusted for risk.

11.3   SOME EXAMPLES

Using equation (11.8), we can derive the equilibrium pricing for various capital structures of the firm. In the first example it is assumed that there are two types of securities: debt and equity. Suppose that the amount of debt issued by the firm represents a terminal claim of B dollars on the firm. Let $F_1(V, \tau)$ be the current value of the debt outstanding and $F_2(V, \tau)$ be the current value of the (residual) equity. Then, from previous discussion and equation (11.3), the terminal value of the debt will be $F_1(VZ, 0)$ $= \min(B, VZ)$. From equations (11.8) and (11.3), the current value of the debt will be

$$F_1(V, \tau) = \exp(-\eta\tau)\left[\int_0^{B/V} ZV \, dQ(Z, \tau) + \int_{B/V}^{\infty} B \, dQ(Z, \tau)\right]$$
$$(11.10)$$

We can rewrite (11.10) as

$$F_1(V, \tau) = \exp(-\eta\tau)B - \exp(-\eta\tau)\int_0^{B/V} (B - ZV) \, dQ(Z, \tau)$$
$$(11.10a)$$

Suppose that the terminal claim of the debtholders is very small relative to the (current) total value of the firm (i.e. $0 < B \ll V$) or, alternatively, $dQ(Z, \tau) = 0$ for $0 \leq Z \leq B/V$. Then

$$F_1(V, \tau) \rightarrow \exp(-\eta\tau)B \text{ as } B/V \rightarrow 0 \qquad (11.11)$$

In the limit, the debt becomes riskless and so, from (11.11), we have that η must be the riskless rate of return per unit time (in both util–prob and ordinary returns space) for the period of length τ. Hence, from this point on, η will be replaced by r, the usual notation for the riskless rate. Examining (11.10a), the second term is the discounted expected loss in util–prob space due to default on the debt,[6] and as such is a risk premium charged over the riskless rate. A second useful form of (11.10) is

---

6   Throughout the chapter, all debt is assumed to be of the "discounted-loan" type with no payments prior to maturity. Similarly, it is assumed that no dividends are paid on the equity.

$$F_1(V, \tau) = \exp(-r\tau)\left[\int_0^\infty ZV \, dQ(Z, \tau) - \int_{B/V}^\infty (ZV - B) \, dQ(Z, \tau)\right]$$

$$= V - \exp(-r\tau)\int_{B/V}^\infty (ZV - B) \, dQ(Z, \tau) \tag{11.10b}$$

Since, in equilibrium, $V = F_1(V, \tau) + F_2(V, \tau)$, the current value of equity, $F_2(V, \tau)$, must satisfy

$$F_2(V, \tau) = \exp(-r\tau)\int_{B/V}^\infty (ZV - B) \, dQ(Z, \tau) \tag{11.12}$$

Equation (11.12) is identical to the warrant pricing equation derived in Samuelson and Merton (1969; this volume, Section 7.8) for a warrant with exercise price B. Because we are pricing the securities as functions of the total value of the firm, the nature of equity as a "residual" security makes it a "warrant" on the firm. Equation (11.12) could have been derived directly in a similar manner to the derivation of the debt equation (11.10) by starting with the terminal value of equity which is[7]

$$F_2(VZ, 0) = \max(0, VZ - B) \tag{11.13}$$

In the second example, consider a firm with a capital structure made up from three types of securities: debt with a terminal claim of B dollars on the firm; equity of which there are N shares outstanding with current price per share of S (i.e. $F_2(V, \tau) \equiv NS$); warrants which terminate at the end of the period and each warrant gives the holder the right to purchase one share of stock at $\bar{S}$ dollars per share. Assume that there are n warrants outstanding with current market value per warrant of W (i.e. $F_3(V, \tau) = nW$). Because the warrant is a junior security to the debt, the current value of the debt for this firm will be the same as in the first example, namely, equation (11.10). The current value of the equity will be

$$F_2(V, \tau) = \exp(-r\tau)\left[\int_{B/V}^{\gamma/V} (ZV - B) \, dQ(Z, \tau)\right.$$

$$\left. + \frac{N}{n + N}\int_{\gamma/V}^\infty (ZV + n\bar{S} - B) \, dQ(Z, \tau)\right] \tag{11.14}$$

---

7 Equation (11.13) immediately suggests a warrant "interpretation" of equity since it is the standard terminal condition for a warrant.

where γ is the maximum value of VZ such that the price per share of equity is less than or equal to $\bar{S}$ (i.e. the maximum value of the firm at the end of the period such that the warrants are not exercised). Thus, for $ZV \leqslant \gamma$, as in the first example, the equity owners receive the residual value of the firm, $ZV - B$. However, for $ZV > \gamma$, the warrantholders will exercise their warrants by turning in the warrants plus a total of $n\bar{S}$ dollars to the firm in return for n shares of equity. In this event, the original ownership of the equityholders will be diluted and they will be entitled to the fraction $N/(n + N)$ of the residual value of the firm which will be $ZV + n\bar{S} - B$.

To determine γ, let S' be the terminal price per share of equity and suppose that the warrants are not exercised, i.e. $S' \leqslant \bar{S}$, but that Z is such that $ZV > B$. Then, $VZ - B = NS'$ or $VZ = NS' + B$. But γ is defined as the maximum value of VZ such that $S' \leqslant \bar{S}$. Hence,[8]

$$\gamma = N\bar{S} + B \tag{11.15}$$

To determine the current value of the warrants, rewrite (11.14) as

$$F_2(V, \tau) = \exp(-r\tau) \left\{ \int_{B/V}^{\infty} (ZV - B) \, dQ(Z, \tau) \right.$$

$$\left. + \frac{N}{n + N} \int_{\gamma/V}^{\infty} \left[n\bar{S} + \left(1 - \frac{n + N}{N} \right)(ZV - B) \right] dQ(Z, \tau) \right\}$$

$$= V - F_1(V, \tau)$$

$$+ \frac{N \exp(-r\tau)}{n + N} \left\{ \int_{\gamma/V}^{\infty} \left[n\bar{S} - \frac{n}{N} (ZV - B) \right] dQ(Z, \tau) \right\} \tag{11.16}$$

But, in equilibrium, $F_3(V, \tau) = V - F_1(V, \tau) - F_2(V, \tau)$, and so from (11.16) we have, after rearranging terms, that

$$F_3(V, \tau) = \frac{n}{n + N} \exp(-r\tau) \int_{\gamma/V}^{\infty} (ZV - \gamma) \, dQ(Z, \tau) \tag{11.17}$$

To compare (11.17) with the warrant pricing formula derived in Samuelson and Merton (1969; this volume, Ch. 7), (11.17) is rewritten in a

---

*8   This analysis assumes that the entire warrant issue is either exercised or not. Later work by Emanuel (1983a) examines the case of a "monopolist" warrantholder who might optimally choose to exercise only a portion of the issue. See also Constantinides (1984), Constantinides and Rosenthal (1984), Galai and Schneller (1978), Spatt and Sterbenz (1988), and Crouhy and Galai (1991).

"normalized"[9] price per warrant form. Let the normalized price of the firm be defined as

$$y \equiv \frac{V}{\gamma} = \frac{V/(n+N)}{(N\overline{S}+B)/(n+N)} \tag{11.18}$$

and the normalized price of a warrant be defined as

$$w \equiv \frac{F_3(V,\tau)}{n\gamma/(n+N)} \tag{11.19}$$

Then (11.17) can be rewritten as

$$w(y,\tau) = \exp(-r\tau) \int_{1/y}^{\infty} (Zy-1)\, dQ(Z,\tau) \tag{11.20}$$

which is of the same form as equation (7.24). However, there is a difference between the two equations: namely, in Samuelson and Merton (1969; this volume, Ch. 7), we used the exercise price of the warrant, $\overline{S}$, as the normalizing price, while to derive (11.20) the "exercise" price of the firm, $\gamma/(n+N)$, was used. From the definition of γ in (11.15), the "exercise" price of the firm is $(N\overline{S}+B)/(n+N)$. If the firm holds no debt (which is implicitly assumed in Samuelson and Merton (1969), since we work directly with the stock price distribution as exogenous instead of with the distribution of the firm's value) and if one concentrates on the "incipient" case (i.e. $n = 0$), then $\gamma/(n+N) = \overline{S}$, and (11.17) is identical with equation (7.24). The advantage of the present analysis is that it explicitly takes into account in current valuation the possibility of future dilution from a large number of warrants outstanding.

For the third example, consider a firm whose capital structure contains a convertible bond issue with a total terminal claim on the firm of either B dollars or alternatively the bonds can be exchanged for a total of n shares of equity, and N shares of equity with current price per share of S dollars.[10] The terminal value of the original N shares of equity, i.e. $F_2(VZ,0)$, will be zero if $VZ < B$, equal to $VZ - B$ if $VZ > B$ and the bonds are not converted, or equal to $NVZ/(n+N)$ if the bonds are converted. The bondholders have the choice of conversion, and they will convert or not

---

9   By "normalized" price, we mean that the exercise price, instead of dollars, is used as the unit of price, so that when the "normalized" price of the stock is one, the dollar price of the stock is $\overline{S}$. See Samuelson (1965a) for a complete description of this useful standardization process.

*10   For more-recent studies of the valuation of convertible bonds, see Brennan and Schwartz (1977c, 1980), Ingersoll (1977), and McConnell and Schwartz (1986).

depending on which choice gives the larger value. Because $VZ = F_1(VZ, 0) + F_2(VZ, 0)$, this implies that

$$F_2(VZ, 0) = \max\{0, \min[VZ - B, NVZ/(n + N)]\} \quad (11.21)$$

Hence from (11.8) and (11.21), we have that the current value of equity is

$$F_2(V, \tau) = \exp(-r\tau)\left[\int_{B/V}^{\gamma/V} (VZ - B)\,dQ(Z, \tau)\right.$$

$$\left. + \frac{N}{n + N}\int_{\gamma/V}^{\infty} VZ\,dQ(Z, \tau)\right] \quad (11.22)$$

where, by a similar procedure to the previous example, γ is determined to be $(n + N)B/n$. By using the equilibrium condition that $F_1(V, \tau) = V - F_2(V, \tau)$, the current value of the convertible bond issue is derived as

$$F_1(V, \tau) = \exp(-r\tau)\left[\int_0^{B/V} VZ\,dQ(Z, \tau) + \int_{B/V}^{\infty} B\,dQ(Z, \tau)\right.$$

$$\left. + \frac{n}{n + N}\int_{\gamma/V}^{\infty} (VZ - \gamma)\,dQ(Z, \tau)\right] \quad (11.23)$$

By comparing (11.23) with (11.10) and (11.17), we have the well-known result that the value of a convertible is equal to its value as a straight bond plus a warrant with exercise price $\bar{S} = B/n$.[11]

The fourth and final example is to price the capital structure of a "dual" fund.[12] A dual fund is the same as an ordinary closed-end mutual fund on the asset side (i.e. both type funds hold marketable securities as their only assets). However, unlike the usual closed-end fund, the dual fund issues two types of securities to finance these assets: namely, *capital shares* (equity) and *income shares* (a type of bond). The difference between the income shares and the bond of the first example is that, in addition to a fixed terminal payment, the income shares are entitled to all the ordinary income (dividends, interest, etc.) of the fund while the capital shares are entitled to all the accumulated capital gains (in excess of the fixed terminal

11   This result holds provided that the bond is noncallable. Because the model is of the one-period type, we have implicitly assumed all securities to be noncallable. Few convertible bonds actually sell at their bond plus warrant value because the call feature on the bond means that *both* the bond and the warrant are callable which reduces the value of the package.

*12   For a more-recent theoretical and empirical analysis of dual funds, see Ingersoll (1976). A similar type of security is the Americus Trust with its Prime and Score securities. See Jarrow and O'Hara (1989) for an analysis.

payment). To protect the income shareholders, the fund managers may be required to invest the fund's portfolio in securities which will earn some fixed proportion of the total asset value in the form of dividends or interest. Let ρ be the instantaneous fixed proportion of total asset value earned as ordinary income. Further, if the fund managers act to maximize the capital shares return subject to the above constraints, then they will choose a portfolio which just meets the ρ requirement. Let V be the current asset value of the fund and Z the (random variable) total return on the fund including dividends, interest, and capital gains. Clearly, the distribution of asset returns is independent of the capital structure since all assets are marketable securities. Let $F_1(V, \tau)$ be the current value of the income shares with terminal claim on the fund of B dollars plus all interest and dividends earned. Let $F_2(V, \tau)$ be the current value of the capital shares. From the definition of Z and ρ, the capital gains part of the total return on the assets is $\exp(-\rho\tau)Z$. Hence, the terminal value of the capital shares will be

$$F_2(VZ, 0) = \max[0, \exp(-\rho\tau)VZ - B] \qquad (11.24)$$

From equation (11.8), we have that the current value of the capital shares is

$$F_2(V, \tau) = \exp[-(r + \rho)\tau] \int_{\gamma/V}^{\infty} (VZ - \gamma) \, dQ(Z, \tau) \qquad (11.25)$$

where $\gamma \equiv B \exp(\rho\tau)$. The current value of the income shares is

$$F_1(V, \tau) = \exp(-r\tau)\left\{ \int_{0}^{\gamma/V} VZ \, dQ(Z, \tau) + \int_{\gamma/V}^{\infty} B \, dQ(Z, \tau) \right.$$

$$\left. + \int_{\gamma/V}^{\infty} VZ[1 - \exp(-\rho\tau)] \, dQ(Z, \tau) \right\} \qquad (11.26)$$

From (11.25), one can show that the current value of the capital shares can be less than the current net asset value of the capital shares, defined to be $V - B$.[13] From (11.25), we have that

$$F_2(V, \tau) < \exp[-(\rho + r)\tau] \int_{\gamma/V}^{\infty} VZ \, dQ(Z, \tau)$$

---

13   This is the definition generally used by the *Wall Street Journal*, for example, to determine whether the capital shares are selling at a premium or a discount.

$$< \exp[-(\rho + r)\tau] \int_0^\infty VZ \, dQ(Z, \tau)$$

$$= \exp(-\rho\tau)V \tag{11.27}$$

Hence, if $\exp(-\rho\tau)V < V - B$, then $F_2(V, \tau)$ will be less than $V - B$. So for $V > B/[1 - \exp(-\rho\tau)]$, $F_2(V, \tau) < V - B$.

This concludes the examples of capital structure pricing based on the model of Section 11.2. One could extend the theory to include multiperiod analysis by the use of the iterated-integral technique employed in Samuelson and Merton (1969; this volume, Section 7.8). However, rather than extend the present partial-equilibrium one-period model further, an intertemporal equilibrium model, which includes the model of Section 11.2 as a special case, is developed in the following sections.

11.4 A GENERAL INTERTEMPORAL EQUILIBRIUM MODEL OF THE ASSET MARKET

Consider an economy with K consumers–investors and n firms with current value V_i, $i = 1,...,n$. Each consumer acts so as to

$$\max E_0\left\{ \int_0^{T^k} U^k[C^k(s), s] \, ds + B^k[W^k(T^k), T^k] \right\} \tag{11.28}$$

where E_0 is the conditional expectation operator, conditional on the value of current wealth $W^k(0) = W^k$ of the kth consumer and on the current value of the firms, $V_i(0) = V_i$, $i = 1,...,n$. $C^k(s)$ is his instantaneous consumption at time s. U^k is a strictly concave von Neumann–Morgenstern utility function; B^k is a strictly concave "bequest" or utility-of-terminal-wealth function; and T^k is the date of death of the kth consumer. Define $N_i(t)P_i(t) \equiv V_i(t)$ where $N_i(t)$ is the number of shares[14] of firm i outstanding at time t and $P_i(t)$ is the price per share at time t. It is assumed that expectations about the dynamics of the prices per share in the future are the same for all investors and these dynamics can be described by the stochastic differential equation[15]

14   In this section, the particular capital structure of the firm is not discussed, and hence one can think of each firm as having the trivial capital structure, namely, all equity. However, the assumption that the value of the firm is independent of its capital structure is retained throughout the chapter.

15   For a discussion of and further references to stochastic differential equations of the type in (11.29), see Merton (1971; this volume, Ch. 5).

$$\frac{\mathrm{d}P_i}{P_i} = \alpha_i \, \mathrm{d}t + \sigma_i \, \mathrm{d}Z_i \quad i = 1,\ldots,n \tag{11.29}$$

where the instantaneous expected rate of return, α_i, and the instantaneous standard deviation of return, σ_i, may change stochastically over time, but only in a way which is instantaneously uncorrelated with price changes (i.e. $\mathrm{d}\alpha_i \, \mathrm{d}Z_i = \mathrm{d}\sigma_i \, \mathrm{d}Z_j = 0$ for i, $j = 1,\ldots,n$). The $\mathrm{d}Z_i$ represent a simple Gauss–Wiener process with zero mean and unit variance rate (often referred to as Gaussian "white noise"). Equation (11.29) includes returns from both capital gains and dividends, and reflects both the uncertainties about future cash flows and changes in the "capitalized" value of the firm's earning assets. Notice that, if α_i and σ_i were constant, then the $P_i(t)$ would be log-normally distributed. Further assume that one of the n assets (by convention the nth one) is an "instantaneously" riskless asset[16] with instantaneous return $r(t)$ and that the dynamics of this rate are described by

$$\mathrm{d}r = f(r, t) \, \mathrm{d}t + g(r, t) \, \mathrm{d}q \tag{11.30}$$

where (11.30) is the same type of equation as (11.29) and $\mathrm{d}q$ is a simple Gauss–Wiener process. For computational simplicity, it is further assumed that α_i and σ_i, in (11.29), are functions only of $r(t)$,[17] i.e. investors only anticipate revising their expectations about returns if the interest rate changes.

From the definition of N_i and P_i, we have that the change in the value of the ith firm over time is $\mathrm{d}V = N_i \, \mathrm{d}P_i + \mathrm{d}N_i(P_i + \mathrm{d}P_i)$. The first term is that part of the changed value of the firm due to cash flow and changes in the value of its assets. The second term is that part of the changed value of the firm due to the issue (or purchase) of new shares at the new price per share $P_i + \mathrm{d}P_i$.[18] Substituting from (11.29) for $\mathrm{d}P_i/P_i$ and writing everything in percentage terms, we have that

$$\frac{\mathrm{d}V_i}{V_i} = \alpha_i \, \mathrm{d}t + \sigma_i \, \mathrm{d}Z_i + \frac{\mathrm{d}N_i}{N_i}(1 + \alpha_i \, \mathrm{d}t + \sigma_i \, \mathrm{d}Z_i) \quad i = 1,\ldots,n \tag{11.31}$$

16   What is meant by an "instantaneously" riskless asset is that, at each instant of time, each investor knows with certainty that he can earn return $r(t)$ over the next instant by holding the asset (i.e. $\sigma_n = 0$ and $\alpha_n = r$). However, the future values of $r(t)$ are not known with certainty. It is assumed here that one of the firms is characterized by this asset. Alternatively, one could postulate a government which issues (very) short bonds, or that $r(t)$ is the instantaneous private sector borrowing (and lending) rate.
17   Since $\mathrm{d}q \, \mathrm{d}Z_i$ will not be zero in general, the changes in α_i and σ_i are correlated with price changes. Hence, we modify the earlier assumption of no correlation to include this particular "indirect" correlation caused by interest rate changes.
18   For symmetry, it is assumed that firms do not pay dividends but adjust their total size by issuing or purchasing their shares in the market.

The accumulation equation for the kth investor can be written as[19]

$$dW^k = \sum_1^n w_i^k W^k \frac{dP_i}{P_i} + (y^k - C^k) \, dt \qquad (11.32)$$

where y^k is his wage income and w_i^k is the fraction of his wealth invested in the ith security (hence, $\Sigma_1^n w_i^k \equiv 1$). Therefore, his demand for the ith security, d_i^k, can be written as

$$d_i^k = w_i^k W^k = N_i^k P_i \qquad (11.33)$$

where N_i^k is the number of shares of the ith security demanded by investor k. Substituting for dP_i/P_i from (11.29) (and noting that the nth asset is riskless), we can rewrite (11.32) as

$$dW^k = \left[\sum_1^m w_i^k(\alpha_i - r) + r \right] W^k \, dt + \sum_1^m w_i^k W^k \sigma_i \, dZ_i + (y^k - C^k) \, dt \qquad (11.34)$$

where $m \equiv n - 1$ and the $w_1^k, \ldots, w_m^k$ are unconstrained[20] because w_n can always be chosen to satisfy the constraint $\Sigma_1^n w_i^k = 1$.

From the budget constraint, $W^k = \Sigma_1^n N_i^k P_i$, and from the accumulation equation (11.32) we have that

$$(y^k - C^k) \, dt = \sum_1^n dN_i^k(P_i + dP_i) \qquad (11.35)$$

i.e. the net value of shares purchased must equal the value of savings from wage income.

I have shown elsewhere[21] that the necessary optimality conditions for an individual who acts according to (11.28) in choosing his consumption–investment program are[22]

---

19   See Merton (1971; this volume, Ch. 5) for a derivation of (11.32). Although taken here to be deterministic, there are no particular problems with letting wage income be stochastic.

20   Hence, we allow borrowing and short-selling by all investors.

21   See Merton (1969a, 1971; this volume, Chs 4 and 5).

22   $J^k(W^k, r, t) \equiv \max E_t\{\int_t^{T^k} U^k(C^k, s) \, ds + B^k(W^k, T^k)\}$ and is called the "derived" utility-of-wealth function. Substituting from (11.37) and (11.38) to eliminate w^k and C^k in (11.36) makes (11.36) a partial differential equation for J^k, subject to the boundary condition $J^k(W^k, r, T^k) = B^k(W^k, T^k)$. Having solved for J^k, we then substitute for J^k and its derivatives in (11.37) and (11.38) to find the optimal rules (w^k, C^k).

$$0 = \max_{\{C^k,\, w^k\}} \left(U^k(C^k,\, t) + J_3^k(W^k,\, r,\, t) + J_{2f}^k + J_1^k\left\{ \left[\sum_1^m w_i^k(\alpha_i - r) + r \right] W^k \right.\right.$$

$$\left. + (y^k - C^k) \right\} + \tfrac{1}{2}J_{22}^k g^2 + \tfrac{1}{2}J_{11}^k \sum_1^m \sum_1^m w_i^k w_j^k \sigma_{ij}(W^k)^2$$

$$+ J_{12}^k \sum_1^m \sigma_{ir} w_i^k W^k \Bigg) \tag{11.36}$$

subject to $J^k(W^k,\, r,\, T^k) = B^k(W^k,\, T^k)$ and where subscripts on the $J^k(W^k,\, r,\, t)$ function denote partial derivatives. The σ_{ij} are the instantaneous covariances between the returns on the ith and jth assets (i.e. $(dP_i/P_i)(dP_j/P_j) \equiv \sigma_{ij}\, dt$), and σ_{ir} is the instantaneous covariance between the return on the ith asset and the change in the rate of interest (i.e. $dr\, dP_i/P_i \equiv \sigma_{ir}\, dt$). The $m + 1$ first-order conditions derived from (11.36) are[23]

$$0 = U_1^k(C^k,\, t) - J_1^k(W^k,\, r,\, t) \tag{11.37}$$

and

$$0 = J_1^k(\alpha_i - r) + J_{11}^k \sum_1^m w_j^k W^k \sigma_{ij} + J_{12}^k \sigma_{ir} \quad i = 1,\ldots,m \tag{11.38}$$

Equation (11.38) can be solved explicitly for the demand functions for each risky security as

$$d_i^k = A^k \sum_1^m v_{ij}(\alpha_j - r) + H^k \sum_1^m v_{ij}\sigma_{jr} \quad i = 1,\ldots,m \tag{11.39}$$

where the v_{ij} are the elements of the inverse of the instantaneous variance–covariance matrix of returns $\Omega = [\sigma_{ij}]$, $A^k \equiv -J_1^k/J_{11}^k$, and

23 Because in this chapter we are primarily interested in finding equilibrium conditions for the asset markets, the model assumes a single consumption good. However, C^k could have easily been taken as a vector of h different consumption goods in which case C^k in (11.34) would be replaced by $\Sigma_1^h X_i C_i^k$ where X_i is the price of the ith good. There would then be an additional $h - 1$ equations in (11.37) of the type derived in ordinary consumer demand theory. One can see how the model could be extended to examine the dynamics of consumption good demand by incorporating expectations about future commodity (relative) prices.

$H^k \equiv -J^k_{12}/J^k_{11}$. Applying the Implicit Function Theorem to (11.37), we have that

$$A^k = -U_1\Big/U_{11}\frac{\partial C^k}{\partial W^k} > 0$$

$$H^k = -\frac{\partial C^k}{\partial r}\Big/\frac{\partial C^k}{\partial W^k} \gtreqless 0$$

(11.40)

The aggregate demands for the risky securities can be derived from (11.39) by summing over all investors as follows:

$$D_i \equiv \sum_1^K d_i^k$$

$$= A\sum_1^m v_{ij}(\alpha_j - r) + H\sum_1^m v_{ij}\sigma_{jr} \quad i = 1,\ldots,m \quad .(11.41)$$

where $A \equiv \Sigma_1^K A^k$ and $H \equiv \Sigma_1^K H^k$. Equation (11.41) can be rewritten in matrix–vector form as

$$D = A\Omega^{-1}(\alpha - r) + H\Omega^{-1}\sigma_r \qquad (11.41a)$$

If it is assumed that the asset market is always in equilibrium, then $N_i = \Sigma_1^K N_i^k$ and $dN_i = \Sigma_1^K dN_i^k$ for $i = 1,\ldots,n$. Furthermore, $\Sigma_1^n N_i P_i = \Sigma_1^n D_i \equiv M$ where M is the total value of all assets, i.e. the value of the "market," in equilibrium. From the definition of M, we have that

$$dM = \sum_1^n N_i\,dP_i + \sum_1^n dN_i(P_i + dP_i)$$

$$= \sum_1^K dW^k \quad \text{in equilibrium}$$

$$= \sum_1^n D_i\frac{dP_i}{P_i} + \sum_1^K (y^k - C^k)\,dt \qquad (11.42)$$

from (11.32). Changes in the value of the market come about by capital gains on current shares outstanding (the first term in (11.42)) and by expansion of the total number of shares outstanding (the second term in (11.42)). To separate these two effects, let P_M be the price per "share" of the market (portfolio) and N be the number of "shares," i.e. $M \equiv NP_M$.

Then, $dM = N\,dP_M + dN(P_M + dP_M)$, and P_M and N are defined by

$$N\,dP_M \equiv \sum_1^n N_i\,dP_i$$

$$\text{(11.43)}$$

$$dN(P_M + dP_M) \equiv \sum_1^n dN_i(P_i + dP_i)$$

If we combine the equilibrium condition $dN_i = \Sigma_1^K dN_i^k$ with equation (11.35), then

$$dN(P_M + dP_M) = \sum_1^K (y^k - C^k)\,dt \qquad \text{(11.44)}$$

and hence, from (11.42),

$$N\,dP_M = \sum_1^n D_i \frac{dP_i}{P_i} \qquad \text{(11.45)}$$

Define $w_i \equiv N_i P_i/M = D_i/M$, the fractional contribution of the ith firm to total market value. By dividing equation (11.45) by M and substituting for dP_i/P_i from (11.29), we can rewrite (11.45) in terms of instantaneous rates of return as

$$\frac{dP_M}{P_M} = \left[\sum_1^m w_j(\alpha_j - r) + r\right]dt + \sum_1^m w_j\sigma_j dZ_j \qquad \text{(11.46)}$$

The instantaneous expected rate of return, α_M, the variance of the return, σ_M^2, the covariance with the return on the ith asset, σ_{iM}, and the covariance of the return with a change in the interest rate, σ_{Mr}, of the market portfolio can be determined from (11.46) as follows:

$$\alpha_M \equiv \sum_1^m w_j(\alpha_j - r) + r$$

$$\sigma_{iM}\,dt \equiv \frac{dP_M}{P_M}\frac{dP_i}{P_i} = \sum_1^m w_j\,\sigma_{ij}\,dt \qquad i = 1,\dots,m$$

$$\text{(11.47)}$$

$$\sigma_M^2\,dt \equiv \frac{dP_M}{P_M}\frac{dP_M}{P_M} = \sum_1^m w_j\,\sigma_{jM}\,dt$$

$$\sigma_{Mr}\,dt \equiv \frac{dP_M}{P_M}dr = \sum_1^m w_j\,\sigma_{jr}\,dt$$

By manipulating (11.41a), one can solve for the yields on individual risky assets: namely, in matrix–vector form

$$\alpha - r = \frac{1}{A} \Omega D - \frac{H}{A} \sigma_r \tag{11.48}$$

In equilibrium, $D_i = w_i M$, and hence (11.48) can be rewritten in scalar form as

$$\alpha_i - r = \frac{M}{A} \sum_{1}^{m} w_j \sigma_{ij} - \frac{H}{A} \sigma_{ir}$$

$$= \frac{M}{A} \sigma_{iM} - \frac{H}{A} \sigma_{ir} \qquad i = 1,\dots,m \tag{11.49}$$

By multiplying (11.49) by w_i and summing from 1 to m, we have that

$$\alpha_M - r = \frac{M}{A} \sigma_M^2 - \frac{H}{A} \sigma_{Mr} \tag{11.50}$$

In summary, given the distribution of returns, individual preferences, and endowments, equation (11.41a) can be used to determine the equilibrium (relative to the riskless asset) prices of the m risky assets. Given the consumption level and (11.37), the price of the riskless asset relative to the price of the consumption good can be determined, closing out the system.

Alternatively, one can assume that security prices are "correct" (i.e. equilibrium prices) and then use (11.49) to determine the equilibrium (relative to the riskless asset) expected yields of the risky assets. Then, given the consumption level, the equilibrium interest rate can be determined from (11.37).

Since prices are observable and expected yields are not, the second formulation is used. Because the emphasis is on finding equilibrium (relative) relations among assets, the consumption equation (11.37) will be ignored, and the interest rate will be treated as exogenous to the asset market.

11.5 MODEL I: A CONSTANT INTEREST RATE ASSUMPTION

Consider the particular case of the general model of the previous section when the interest rate is assumed to be constant (i.e. $f = g = 0$ in (11.30)). By examining (11.39), one can see that the ratios of an investor's demands for risky assets are the same for all investors (i.e. independent of preferences, wealth, etc.). Hence, the "mutual-fund" or separation theorem holds,[24] and all optimal portfolios can be represented as a linear combination of any two distinct efficient portfolios (mutual funds).[25] In equilibrium, the market portfolio must be efficient, and so one can choose the two efficient funds to be the market portfolio and the riskless asset. From (11.49) with $\sigma_{ir} = 0$, we see that the ratios of equilibrium relative expected yields are independent of preferences. Further, by combining (11.49) and (11.50), the term depending on preferences can be eliminated, and the equilibrium expected return on an individual security can be written as a function of the expected market return and the interest rate as

$$\alpha_i - r = \frac{\sigma_{iM}}{\sigma_M^2}(\alpha_M - r) \quad i = 1,\dots,m \tag{11.51}$$

With a slightly different interpretation of the variables, (11.51) is the equation for the Security Market Line (Sharpe, 1970, p. 89) of the Sharpe–Lintner–Mossin Capital Asset Pricing Model (CAPM) and all the implications of their model will be implied by Model I as well. The Sharpe–Lintner–Mossin model is a one-period model and implicitly must assume quadratic utility functions or Gaussian-distributed prices to be consistent with the Expected Utility Maxim. Model I is an intertemporal model which assumes that trading takes place continuously and that price changes are continuous (although not differentiable in the usual sense). If α_i and σ_i are constant, then prices are log-normally distributed (which is reasonable because "limited liability" is ensured and, by the Central Limit Theorem, it is the only regular solution to any independent multiplicative finite-moment continuous-space infinitely divisible process in time). The model as presented is consistent over time in the sense that the implications of the assumed price behavior are not *a priori* refutable. The assumption of normally distributed prices is bothersome because, no matter how compact the distribution, given enough time, one would expect to observe some negative prices. Similarly, the assumption of quadratic utility, given enough time, leads to the problem of wealth satiation or negative marginal utility.

The models are empirically distinguishable since, over time, samples drawn from log-normal distributions will differ from those drawn from normal distributions. If it is assumed that the w_i are constant over time, then from (11.46) it can be shown that P_M is log-normally distributed.[26] We can integrate (11.29) to get, conditional on $P_i(t) = P_i$,

---

24 See Merton (1971; this volume, Ch. 5) for a discussion, further references, and a proof of the separation theorem for this model.
25 See Merton (1972a) for a proof and further discussion.
26 See Merton (1971; this volume, Theorem 5.2).

$$P_i(t + \tau) = P_i \exp[(\alpha_i - \tfrac{1}{2}\sigma_i^2)\tau + \sigma_i Z_i(t; \tau)] \qquad (11.52)$$

where $Z_i(t; \tau) \equiv \int_t^{t+\tau} dZ_i$ is a normal variate with zero mean and variance τ. Similarly, we can integrate (11.46) to get

$$P_M(t + \tau) = P_M \exp[(\alpha_M - \tfrac{1}{2}\sigma_M^2)\tau + \sigma_M X(t; \tau)] \qquad (11.53)$$

where $X(t; \tau) \equiv \int_t^{t+\tau} \Sigma_1^m w_j \sigma_j \, dZ_j/\sigma_M$ is a normal variate with zero mean and variance τ. Define the variables

$$\mathcal{P}_i(t + \tau) \equiv \log\left[\frac{P_i(t + \tau)}{P_i(t)}\right] = (\alpha_i - \tfrac{1}{2}\sigma_i^2)\tau + \sigma_i Z_i(t; \tau)$$

$$\mathcal{P}_M(t + \tau) \equiv \log\left[\frac{P_M(t + \tau)}{P_M(t)}\right] = (\alpha_M - \tfrac{1}{2}\sigma_M^2)\tau + \sigma_M X(t; \tau)$$

$$(11.54)$$

Consider the ordinary least-squares regression

$$\mathcal{P}_i(t) - r = \beta_i[\mathcal{P}_M(t) - r] + \gamma_i + \epsilon_t^i \qquad (11.55)$$

After making the usual assumptions about the differences between *ex ante* expectations and *ex post* outcomes, if Model I is the "true" specification, then from (11.51) and (11.55) the following must hold:

$$\beta_i = \frac{\sigma_{iM}}{\sigma_M^2}$$

$$\gamma_i = \tfrac{1}{2}(\beta_i \sigma_M^2 - \sigma_i^2)\tau \qquad (11.56)$$

$$\epsilon_t^i = (1 - \rho_{iM}^2)^{1/2}\sigma_i Y_i(t; \tau)$$

where τ is the time period between observations, ρ_{iM} is the instantaneous correlation coefficient between the return on the ith security and the market, and $Y_i(t; \tau)$ is a normal variate with zero mean, variance τ, and a covariance with the market return of zero. In the context of Model I, the correct specification for regression is logarithmic changes in prices, and notice that the constant γ_i will *not* in general be zero.[27] Notice that for

27 This result has implications for various tests of portfolio performance (e.g. see Jensen, 1969) which have used a regression model similar to (11.55) and have assumed that the correct "benchmark" is $\gamma_i = 0$. Unfortunately, γ_i as derived in (11.56) is ambiguous in sign.

(11.55) to be a correct specification, r must be constant over time,[28] and since r does vary, our general model shows that the specification will be incorrect. This more general case is discussed in Section 11.7.

Equation (11.51) describes the equilibrium expected yield relation among firms. Using the model of this section, we return to the problem posed in Sections 11.1 and 11.2, namely, pricing the capital structure of the firm.

When the firm issued one type of security, we could define a relation $V_i(t) \equiv N_i(t)P_i(t)$. Now, $V_i(t) = \Sigma_1^k N_{ij}(t)P_{ij}(t)$ where N_{ij} is the number of units of the jth type security issued by the ith firm and P_{ij} is the price per unit. Since only one firm will be considered at a time, the i subscript will be dropped and the unsubscripted variables will be for any firm, e.g. $V(t) = \Sigma_1^k N_j(t)P_j(t)$. For simplicity, consider the first example in Section 11.2, where the firm's capital structure consists of two securities: equity and debt. It is also assumed that the firm is enjoined from the issue or purchase of securities prior to the redemption date of the debt (τ "years" from now).[29] Hence, from (11.31), we have that

$$\frac{dV}{V} = \frac{dP}{P} = \alpha \, dt + \sigma \, dZ \tag{11.57}$$

where α and σ are constants.

Let $D(t; \tau)$ be the current value of the debt with τ years until maturity and with redemption value at that time of B. Then $D(t + \tau; 0) = \min [V(t + \tau), B]$, and therefore it is reasonable to assume that $D(t; \tau)$ will depend on the interest rate and the probability of default which will be a function of the current value of the firm. Because the current value of equity is $V(t) - D(t; \tau)$, equity will only depend on the current value of the firm and the interest rate. Let $F(V, \tau)$ be the current value of equity where

---

28 It is sufficient to assume that $\sigma_{ir} = 0$ for $i = 1,...,m$ for Model I to be the correct specification. However, this assumption seems to be no more reasonable than r equal to a constant (particularly when an asset which is correlated with changes in r could (and would) easily be created if r did vary).

29 This assumption is stronger than necessary. It is sufficient that any new issues have the same terms as the current capital structure and that they be issued in the same proportions of units (*not* values) as the current structure. A more general model using the same approach as in the text could be formulated to include the expectations of future issues.

The assumption that the debt is of the discounted-loan type is not completely innocent because of the possibility of default on interim interest payments. Although the resulting mathematics is more complicated, the basic approach used here could be modified to include the case of interim payments as well. (1990 note: see Merton (1974; this volume, Section 12.6) for a solution of the risky coupon-bond case.)

the variable r has been suppressed because, in this model, it is constant. The dynamics of the return on equity can be written as

$$\frac{dF}{F} = \alpha_e\, dt + \sigma_e\, dZ \tag{11.58}$$

where α_e is the instantaneous expected rate of return, σ_e is the instantaneous standard deviation of return, and dZ is the *same* standard Wiener process as in (11.57). α_e and σ_e are not constants but functions of V and τ. Like every security in the economy, the equity of the firm must satisfy (11.51) in equilibrium, and hence

$$\alpha_e - r = \frac{\rho\sigma_e\sigma_M}{\sigma_M^2}(\alpha_M - r) \tag{11.59}$$

where ρ is the instantaneous correlation coefficient between dZ and the market return. Further, by Itô's lemma (see Merton, 1971; this volume, Lemma 5.1), we have that

$$dF = F_V\, dV + F_\tau\, d\tau + \tfrac{1}{2}F_{VV}(dV)^2 \tag{11.60}$$

where subscripts denote partial derivatives. Since τ is the length of time until maturity, $d\tau = -dt$. Substituting for dV from (11.57), we rewrite (11.60) as

$$dF = (\tfrac{1}{2}\sigma^2 V^2\, F_{VV} + \alpha V F_V - F_\tau)\, dt + \sigma V F_V\, dZ \tag{11.61}$$

where $(dV)^2 \equiv \sigma^2 V^2\, dt$. Comparing (11.58) and (11.61), it must be that

$$\alpha_e F \equiv \tfrac{1}{2}\sigma^2 V^2\, F_{VV} + \alpha V F_V - F_\tau \tag{11.62}$$

and

$$\sigma_e F \equiv \sigma V F_V \tag{11.63}$$

As previously shown, the return on holding the firm itself must satisfy equation (11.51) in equilibrium. Hence,

$$\alpha - r = \frac{\rho\sigma\sigma_M}{\sigma_M^2}(\alpha_M - r) \tag{11.64}$$

Substituting for α and α_e from (11.59) and (11.64) into (11.62), we have the Fundamental Partial Differential Equation of Security Pricing

$$0 = \tfrac{1}{2}\sigma^2 V^2 F_{VV} + rVF_V - F_\tau - rF \tag{11.65}$$

subject to the boundary condition $F(V, 0) = \max(0, V - B)$. The solution[30] to (11.65) is

$$F(V, \tau) = \exp(-r\tau) \int_{B/V}^{\infty} (VZ - B)\, d\Lambda(Z, \tau) \tag{11.66}$$

where Z is a log-normally distributed random variable with mean $\exp(r\tau)$ and variance of $\log(Z)$ $\sigma^2\tau$, and $d\Lambda$ is the log-normal density function. I call (11.65) the Fundamental Partial Differential Equation of Asset Pricing because all the securities in the firm's capital structure must satisfy it. As was true of the model in Section 11.1, securities are distinguished by their terminal claims (boundary conditions). For example, the value of the debt of the firm satisfies (11.65) subject to the boundary condition $F(V, 0) = \min(V, B)$. A comparison of (11.66) with (11.12) shows that they are the same for $dQ = d\Lambda$. Equation (11.66) can be rewritten in general form as

$$F(V, \tau) = \exp(-r\tau) \int_{0}^{\infty} F(VZ, 0)\, d\Lambda(Z, \tau) \tag{11.67}$$

where $F(VZ, 0)$ is the terminal claim of the security on the firm. Note that (11.67) depends only on the rate of interest r, which is an observable, and σ^2 which can be estimated from past data reasonably accurately; and *not* on α, which would be difficult to estimate. The actual value of F can be computed by using standard error-complement function tables. Hence, (11.67) is subject to rigorous empirical investigation.

Although (11.67) is a kind of discounted expected value formula, one should not infer that the expected return on F is r. From (11.59), (11.63), and (11.64), the expected return on F can be written as

$$\alpha_e = r + \frac{F_V V}{F}\,(\alpha - r) \tag{11.68}$$

which will vary with changes in V and τ, although it too can be computed from the error-complement function tables, given an estimate of α.

30   See Samuelson (1965a, p. 22) for solution of the $\alpha = \beta$ case.

Equation (11.65) was previously derived by Black and Scholes (1973) as a method for pricing option contracts.[31] Moreover, (11.65) actually holds without the assumption of market equilibrium used here. Because of its elegance, I derive the Black–Scholes model in an alternative fashion which makes use of Itô's lemma and the associated theory of stochastic differential equations. Consider a two-asset portfolio constructed so as to contain the firm as one security and any one of the securities in the firm's capital structure as the other. Let P be the price per unit of this portfolio, δ the fraction of the total portfolio's value invested in the firm and $1 - \delta$ the fraction in the particular security chosen from the firm's capital structure. Then, from (11.57) and (11.58),

$$\frac{dP}{P} = \delta \frac{dV}{V} + (1 - \delta) \frac{dF}{F}$$

$$= [\delta(\alpha - \alpha_e) + \alpha_e]\, dt + [\delta(\sigma - \sigma_e) + \sigma_e]\, dZ \qquad (11.69)$$

Suppose δ is chosen such that $\delta(\sigma - \sigma_e) + \sigma_e = 0$. Then, the portfolio will be "perfectly hedged" and the instantaneous return on the portfolio will be $\delta(\alpha - \alpha_e) + \alpha_e$ with certainty. By arbitrage[32] conditions, $\delta(\alpha - \alpha_e) + \alpha_e = r$, the instantaneous riskless rate of return. Combining these two conditions, we have that

$$\alpha_e - r = \frac{\sigma_e}{\sigma}(\alpha - r) \qquad (11.70)$$

Then, as was done previously, we use Itô's lemma to derive (11.62) and (11.63). By combining (11.62), (11.63), and (11.70), we arrive at (11.65). Nowhere was the market-equilibrium assumption needed.

Two further remarks must be made before we examine asset pricing in the more complex models in Section 11.6 and Section 11.7. Although the value of the firm follows a simple dynamic process with constant parameters as described in (11.57), the individual component securities follow more complex processes with changing expected returns and variances.

*31 For a brief history of the development of the Black–Scholes option pricing model, see Black (1987, 1989) and Bernstein (1992, Ch. 11).

32 The meaning of "arbitrage" here is not as strong as the usual definition since differences of opinion among investors about the value of σ^2 or the belief that F is a function of other variables besides the value of the firm, time, and interest rates would lead to different values for F without infinite profits. However, given homogeneous expectations and agreement that F is only a function of the stated variables, then (11.66) is the valuation function which all investors would agree upon and not be proved wrong at some time in the future.

Thus, in empirical examinations using a regression such as (11.55), if one were to use equity instead of firm values, systematic biases would be introduced. One can find cases where the risky debt of one firm is more comparable with the equity of another firm than the equity of one firm is to that of the other.

One possibly practical application of the equations of this section is to provide a systematic method of measuring the riskiness of debt of various firms. Hence, by using equation (11.67), one could derive a *risk structure of interest rates* as a function of the percentage of the total capital structure subordinated to the issue and the overall riskiness of the firm. It would be interesting to see how such a method of rating debt would compare with the classical methods of Moody's and Standard & Poor's.

11.6 MODEL II: THE "NO RISKLESS ASSET" CASE

In the previous two sections, one of the assets available to investors was riskless. In this section, it is assumed that no such asset exists. The rationale for this assumption is uncertain inflation. Because consumers are interested in investing only as a means to a higher (real) consumption level, a security which is "riskless" in money terms is not riskless in real terms.[33] Thus, if there are no futures markets in consumption goods or other guaranteed "purchasing power" securities available, there will be no perfect hedge against future (consumption) price changes.

In an earlier paper,[34] I derived the analogous equations to (11.36), (11.37), and (11.38) and, further, showed that a separation or mutual-fund theorem obtains in this case as well.[35]

Following the same procedure as in Section 11.4, we can derive analogous equilibrium conditions to (11.49) and (11.50), namely,

$$\alpha_i = \frac{M}{A}\sigma_{iM} + G \quad i = 1,\dots,n \tag{11.71}$$

---

33 It is possible for a "riskless" nominal asset to be riskless in real terms. If the change in the rate of inflation is sufficiently (stochastically) smooth, then by re-contracting loans sufficiently often and adjusting the interest rate, one can eliminate any risk of the loss of real purchasing power. If the changes in the price level are very fast (i.e. at Brownian motion $(dt)^{1/2}$ speed similar to the postulated asset-price behavior), then the re-contracting approach is not a solution.

34 Merton (1971; this volume, equations (5.18)–(5.20)). Although derived for a single consumer, one need only add the superscript k for each consumer to make the equations identical.

35 See Merton (1971 (this volume, Theorem 5.2); 1972a) for further discussion of the separation theorem when none of the assets is riskless.

and

$$\alpha_M = \frac{M}{A}\sigma_M^2 + G \tag{11.72}$$

where the interest rate r is no longer a variable, and hence H, σ_{ir}, σ_{Mr}, etc. are not relevant. However, a new term G (dependent on preferences) comes in, reflecting the constraint that the sum of the proportions of the risky assets in each investor's portfolio must be unity.

The nth security[36] must satisfy (11.71) in equilibrium, i.e.

$$\alpha_n = \frac{M}{A}\sigma_{Mn} + G \tag{11.73}$$

Equations (11.72) and (11.73) can be solved for M/A and G and the results substituted into (11.71) to determine the equilibrium relations among all securities in terms of the parameters of the market portfolio and the nth security:

$$\alpha_i = \frac{\sigma_{Mi} - \sigma_{Mn}}{\sigma_M^2 - \sigma_{Mn}}\alpha_M + \frac{\sigma_M^2 - \sigma_{Mi}}{\sigma_M^2 - \sigma_{Mn}}\alpha_n \quad i = 1,...,m \tag{11.74}$$

Equation (11.74) reduces to (11.51) when $\sigma_n = 0$ and $\alpha_n = r$, and so Model II contains Model I as a particular case.

In a similar fashion to the analysis in the previous section, the Fundamental Partial Differential Equation for Security Pricing for Model II can be shown to be

$$\tfrac{1}{2}\sigma^2 V^2 F_{VV} + \mu V F_V - F_\tau - \mu F = 0 \tag{11.75}$$

where $\mu \equiv (\sigma_M^2\alpha_n - \sigma_{Mn}\alpha_M)/(\sigma_M^2 - \sigma_{Mn})$, *provided* that μ is nonstochastic. If security n is such that $\sigma_{Mn} = 0$, a zero-beta security (see Black, 1972), then $\mu = \alpha_n$ and (11.74) can be rewritten as

$$\alpha_i = \beta_i\alpha_M + (1 - \beta_i)\alpha_n \quad i = 1,...,m \tag{11.74a}$$

where $\beta_i \equiv \sigma_{Mi}/\sigma_M^2$. If μ varies stochastically over time, then the fundamental equation of security pricing will be more complicated than (11.75), and this case is discussed in the following section.

36 Alternatively, one could use any other security or portfolio of securities whose rate of return is not perfectly correlated with the market portfolio.

11.7 MODEL III: THE GENERAL MODEL

We now return to the general model of Section 11.4 where the interest rate varies stochastically over time. The equilibrium conditions are (11.49) and (11.50), and we note that the standard separation theorem does not obtain. However, by an approach similar to the previous section, preferences can still be removed from (11.49). The mth security must satisfy (11.49) in equilibrium, i.e.

$$\alpha_m - r = \frac{M}{A}\sigma_{mM} - \frac{H}{A}\sigma_{mr} \qquad (11.76)$$

Hence, (11.50) and (11.76) can be solved for M/A and H/A and the results substituted into (11.49) to determine the equilibrium relations among all securities in terms of the parameters of the market portfolio, the mth security,[37] and the interest rate:

$$\alpha_k - r = \frac{\sigma_{mr}\sigma_{Mk} - \sigma_{Mn}\sigma_{kr}}{Q}(\alpha_M - r) + \frac{\sigma_M^2\sigma_{kr} - \sigma_{Mr}\sigma_{Mk}}{Q}(\alpha_m - r)$$

$$(11.77)$$

where $Q \equiv \sigma_M^2\sigma_{mr} - \sigma_{Mr}\sigma_{Mm}$ and $k = 1,...,m - 1$. The same method as was used to prove the separation theorem in Merton (1971 (this volume, Ch. 5); 1972a) can be applied to prove the following more general separation theorem.[38]

Theorem 11.1 (Three-"Fund" Theorem)

Given n assets satisfying the conditions of the model in Section 11.4, there exist three portfolios ("mutual funds") constructed from these n assets such that all risk-averse individuals, who behave according to (11.28), will be indifferent between choosing portfolios from among the original n assets or choosing portfolios from these three funds. Further, a possible choice for the three funds is the market portfolio, the riskless asset, and a portfolio which is (instantaneously) perfectly correlated with changes in the interest rate.

---

37 It is assumed that the mth security is not perfectly correlated with the market. However, it must be correlated with either the market and/or changes in the interest rate, i.e. σ_{Mm} and σ_{mr} are not both zero.

38 The theorem can be generalized to the k-fund case when other variables such as inflation, wage income, etc. are stochastic, and investors want to hedge against unfavorable outcomes by purchasing securities correlated with these variables. This would certainly be the case with many consumption goods whose relative prices are changing over time.

Equation (11.77) can be derived directly from Theorem 11.1 in the same way as (11.51) can be derived from the usual separation theorem. Notice that if the kth security has no "market risk" in the usual sense (i.e. $\sigma_{Mk} = 0$), its expected return will *not* be equal to the riskless rate r. Further, even if the market is not correlated with changes in the interest rate (i.e. $\sigma_{Mr} = 0$), this statement still holds. Hence, we have a result which differs fundamentally from the results of the static CAPM. This strictly intertemporal effect is caused by investors' attempts to hedge against possible unfavorable future investment opportunities (i.e. yields) caused by the change in the rate of interest.

Suppose there exists a security (or portfolio) whose return is perfectly correlated (instantaneously) with changes in the interest rate. Then, if this security is taken as the mth security, its dynamics are described by

$$\frac{dP_m}{P_m} = \alpha_m \, dt + \sigma_m \, dq \tag{11.78}$$

and, from (11.30), $\sigma_{Mn} \equiv \sigma_M \sigma_{Mr}/g$ and $\sigma_{mr} \equiv \sigma_m g$. Both from a theoretical and an empirical standpoint, it makes sense to choose, as the third ("interest rate hedging") mutual fund, a portfolio that is strongly correlated with interest rate changes. Throughout the rest of the section, it is assumed that the mth asset satisfies (11.78).

In the previous models, the term structure of interest rates was either trivial ("flat" as in Model I) or nonexistent (as in Model II). Model III is rich in this respect because (a) it provides an explanation for the existence of "long" default-free bonds as an efficient means of hedging against interest rate changes[39] (i.e. the existence of a term structure), (b) it gives insight into how to price these bonds (determination of the shape of the term structure), and (c) it is sufficiently flexible to be consistent with many existing theories. Nowhere in the model is it necessary to introduce concepts such as liquidity, transactions costs, time horizon, or habitat to explain the existence of a term structure where bonds of different maturities have different expected returns.

Consider, as a possible set of securities, bonds guaranteed against default, which pay one dollar at various maturity dates.[40] It is assumed that the price of these bonds is a function of the (short) interest rate and the

---

39   Although any security whose return is correlated with interest rate changes would be sufficient in theory, securities which are perfectly correlated with interest rate changes are more effective as was mentioned in the text. Because of the risk of default, to use ordinary corporate bonds instead of guaranteed ("government") bonds would require significant diversification to eliminate that risk.

40   These bonds are discounted loans. Because the payments are riskless, once these bonds are priced it is straightforward to derive the price of coupon bonds by weighting each maturity by the coupon payment and adding.

length of time until maturity.[41] Therefore, let $P(r, \tau)$ be the price of a discounted loan which pays a dollar at time τ in the future when the current interest rate is r. Then, the dynamics of P can be written as

$$\frac{dP}{P} = \alpha_\tau \, dt + \sigma_\tau \, dq \qquad (11.79)$$

where α_τ is the instantaneous expected rate of return on a τ-year bond and σ_τ is the instantaneous standard deviation. From the equilibrium condition (11.77) and the assumptions leading to (11.78), α_τ must satisfy

$$\alpha_\tau - r = \frac{\sigma_\tau}{\sigma_m}(\alpha_m - r) \qquad (11.80)$$

By Itô's lemma, α_τ and σ_τ must satisfy

$$0 = \tfrac{1}{2} g^2 P_{rr} + f P_r - P_\tau - \alpha_\tau P \qquad (11.81)$$

and

$$\sigma_\tau = \frac{P_r g}{P} \qquad (11.82)$$

where subscripts on the P denote partial derivatives with respect to r and τ. Equation (11.81) is similar to the Fundamental Equation of Security Pricing previously discussed. Given α_τ, (11.81) could be solved, subject to the boundary condition $P(r, 0) = 1$, to determine $P(r, \tau)$ and hence the term structure of interest rates. However, without some independent knowledge of α_m (and hence α_τ), we cannot determine an explicit solution for the term structure.

Suppose that one knew that the Expectations Hypothesis held. Then $\alpha_\tau \equiv r$ for all τ and the term structure is completely determined by

$$0 = \tfrac{1}{2} g^2 P_{rr} + f P_r - P_\tau - rP \qquad (11.83)$$

subject to $P(r, 0) = 1$. Further, from (11.80), it must be that in equilibrium, $\alpha_m = r$. In this case, the equilibrium condition (11.77) simplifies to

$$\alpha_k - r = \frac{\sigma_k(\rho_{kM} - \rho_{Mr}\rho_{kr})}{\sigma_M(1 - \rho_{Mr}^2)}(\alpha_M - r) \qquad k = 1,\dots,m-1 \qquad (11.84)$$

---

41 If each investor's expectations include other variables such as the relative supplies of each maturity etc., then the valuation formula presented in the text is incorrect. However, the assumption that investors believe that the only (anticipated) risk in holding government bonds is due to changing interest rates seems reasonable. Further, if each investor does have such a belief, then the "correct" price will be agreed upon by all and will not be refutable at any time in the future.

where the ρs are the instantaneous correlation coefficients defined by $\rho_{kM} \equiv \sigma_{kM}/\sigma_k\sigma_M$, $\rho_{kr} \equiv \sigma_{kr}/g\sigma_k$, and $\rho_{Mr} \equiv \sigma_{Mr}/g\sigma_M$. Hence, the individual expected returns are proportional to the market expected return as was the case in Model I. However, the proportionality factor is not σ_{Mk}/σ_M^2. If the mth security is chosen to be a portfolio of government bonds, then, given specific knowledge of the term structure, the rest of the equilibrium relations work out in a determined fashion.

Equation (11.83) cannot be solved in closed form for arbitrary f and g. However, if it is assumed that f and g are constants (i.e. r follows a Gaussian random walk with a drift), then, under the Expectations Hypothesis, we do have the explicit solution

$$P(r, \tau) = \exp\left(-r\tau - \frac{f}{2}\tau^2 + \frac{g^2}{6}\tau^3\right) \qquad (11.85)$$

Note that in (11.85), as $\tau \to \infty$, $P \to \infty$, which is not at all reasonable. Certainly, the current value of a discounted loan which will never be paid should be zero for any realistic assumption about interest rates. The reason that (11.85) gives such nonsensical results is that, by the assumption that r is Gaussian, there is a positive probability of r becoming negative. In fact, as $\tau \to \infty$, r will be negative for an arbitrary period of time with positive probability. This result illustrates how the assumption of the normal distribution for variables which are constrained to be nonnegative can lead to absurd implications. However, equation (11.83) with reasonable assumptions about f and g can be solved numerically and further research is planned in this area.[42]

By arguments similar to those used in Section 11.5, the Fundamental Equation of Security Pricing for the capital structure of the firm in Model III can be derived as

$$0 = \tfrac{1}{2}\sigma^2 V^2 F_{VV} + \tfrac{1}{2}g^2 F_{rr} + \rho g\sigma V F_{rV} + rV F_V + fF_r - F_\tau - rF \qquad (11.86)$$

subject to an appropriate boundary condition $F(V, r, 0)$, where subscripts denote partial derivatives and ρ is the instantaneous correlation coefficient

---

*42 Further development of the theory of the term structure of interest rates leading to equations like (11.81), (11.82), and (11.83) can be found in Vasicek (1977), Dothan (1978), Richard (1978), Brennan and Schwartz (1979), Cox, Ingersoll, and Ross (1979, 1985b), and Longstaff and Schwartz (1991). Torous (1985) expands the model to include taxes and Ahn and Thompson (1988) add a jump component to the process. Feldman (1989) allows for information asymmetries. Marsh and Rosenfeld (1983) develop empirical estimation techniques. Jarrow and Madan (1991) use the term structure to hedge systematic jump risks in asset returns. Models that match the empirical term structure and price other interest-rate-sensitive securities are developed in Ho and Lee (1986), Black, Derman, and Toy (1990), Hull and White (1990b), Jamshidian (1991), and Heath, Jarrow, and Morton (forthcoming).

of the return on the firm with interest rate changes. The basic difference between equations (11.86) and (11.65) of Model I is the explicit dependence of F on r which must be taken into account. Under most conditions, (11.86) will not be solvable in closed form. However, numerical solution seems quite reasonable which implies many possibilities for empirical testing both by direct statistical methods and by simulation.

11.8   CONCLUSION

A general intertemporal equilibrium model of the asset market has been derived for arbitrary preferences, time horizon, and wealth distribution. The equilibrium relations among securities were shown to depend only on certain "observable" market aggregates, and hence are subject to empirical investigation. Under the additional assumption of a constant rate of interest, these equilibrium relations are essentially the same as those of the static CAPM of Sharpe, Lintner, and Mossin. However, these results were derived without the assumption of Gaussian distributions for security prices or quadratic utility functions. When interest rates vary, some of the intuition about "market risk" and equilibrium expected returns provided by the CAPM was shown to be incorrect.[43] In addition, the model clearly differentiates between the trading-period horizon (dt, an infinitesimal) and the planning or time horizon (T^k, which is arbitrary).

Under the assumption that the value of the firm is independent of the composition of its capital structure, we have shown how to price any security in the capital structure by means of the Fundamental Equation of Security Pricing. This relation depends only on observables, and therefore is subject to empirical study. As a particular use of the model, one can derive a "risk structure" of interest rates for ranking debt and explaining differential yields on bonds. Further applications would include the examination of the effects of interest rate changes, dilution, etc. on the prices of different types of securities.

The existence of a term structure of interest rates is a direct result of the model. Further, from the Fundamental Equation of Security Pricing, a method for determining the term structure was presented.

The model does not allow for nonhomogeneous expectations, non-serially independent preferences, or transactions costs (all are areas for further research). Although not done here, the analysis of demands for consumption goods when future prices are uncertain could be made along the lines suggested in footnote 23.[44] Similarly, given a theory of the firm,

---

*43   For expansion of this point to multiple dimensions of risk along the lines of footnote 38, see Breeden (1979) and Merton (1973b (this volume, Ch. 15); 1977c, 1982a, 1990a).
*44   For this development, see Breeden (1979), Merton (1977c), and Section 6.4.

the supply dynamics of new shares can be brought explicitly into the model instead of such changes being treated as exogenous.[45] Further research along the lines of the model presented here is aimed at including these additions as well as other sectors of the economy. It is believed that this research will lead to a better understanding of the mechanism by which government actions in the securities markets affect security prices and firms' investment decisions.

The fundamental assumption which allows the model to be so general and yet yield strong results is the continuous-time assumption. If the model were formulated in discrete time with time spacing of length h between trading periods, then the results derived in this chapter no longer hold.[46] Since the option to trade continuously includes the option to trade at discrete intervals, all investors would prefer this option (at no cost). Hence, the assumption seems legitimate under the usual perfect-market assumptions of no transactions costs, no indivisibilities, costless information, etc.

The usual reason given for the discrete-time formulation is that such transactions costs exist. The approach typically taken is to assume equal time spacings of nonspecified length. If one wants to include transactions costs, however, it seems logical to incorporate them in the continuous-time model and derive the h (which almost certainly will not be equally spaced in calendar time, but will depend on the size of price changes of securities in the portfolio among other things).[47] In many empirical studies, the trading-period spacing h is implicitly assumed to coincide with the observation spacing (e.g. one year) which seems quite unreasonable. Further, even if each investor had the same trading-period spacing, different investors would most likely begin on different days, and hence the resulting "smear" of the aggregate may be more closely approximated by the continuous-trading assumption. The continuous-time assumption buys a lot of results. So, until the existence of a fundamental minimum quantum of time in economics is proved, it will be a helpful assumption to make.

*45 For development of the supply side, see Merton (1973b; this volume, Ch. 15), Breeden (1979, 1986), Brock (1982), Grinols (1984), Sundaresan (1984), Detemple (1986), and especially Cox, Ingersoll, and Ross (1985a).

46 However, the continuous-time solution is not singular in the sense that the limit, as $h \rightarrow 0$, of the discrete-time solution is the continuous-time solution. 1992 note: for subsequent research, see Willinger and Taqqu (1991) and He (forthcoming).

*47 For recent developments on transactions costs along these lines, see Magill and Constantinides (1976), Kandel and Ross (1983), Constantinides (1986), Sun (1987), Taksar, Klass, and Assaf (1988), Eastham and Hastings (1988), Davis and Norman (1990), and Dumas and Luciano (1991).

On the Pricing of Corporate Debt: The Risk Structure of Interest Rates

12.1 INTRODUCTION

The value of a particular issue of corporate debt depends essentially on three items: (a) the required rate of return on riskless (in terms of default) debt (e.g. government bonds or very high grade corporate bonds); (b) the various provisions and restrictions contained in the indenture (e.g. maturity date, coupon rate, call terms, seniority in the event of default, sinking fund, etc.); and (c) the probability that the firm will be unable to satisfy some or all of the indenture requirements (i.e. the probability of default).

While numerous theories and empirical studies have been published on the term structure of interest rates (item a), there has been no systematic development of a theory for pricing bonds when there is a significant probability of default. The purpose of this chapter is to present such a theory which might be called a theory of the risk structure of interest rates. The use of the term "risk" is restricted to the possible gains or losses to bondholders as a result of (unanticipated) changes in the probability of default and does not include the gains or losses inherent to all bonds caused by (unanticipated) changes in interest rates in general. Throughout most of the analysis, a given term structure is assumed and hence the price differentials among bonds will be solely caused by differences in the probability of default.

In a seminal paper, Black and Scholes (1973) present a complete equilibrium theory of option pricing which is particularly attractive because the final formula is a function of "observable" variables. Therefore, the model is subject to direct empirical tests which Black and Scholes (1972) performed with some success. Merton (1973a; this volume, Ch. 8) clarified and extended the Black–Scholes model. While options are highly special-

Reproduced from *Journal of Finance*, 29, May 1974, 449–70. I thank J. Ingersoll for doing the computer simulations and for general scientific assistance. Aid from the National Science Foundation is gratefully acknowledged.

ized and relatively unimportant financial instruments, both Black and Scholes (1973) and Merton (1970b, 1973a; this volume, Chs 11 and 8) recognized that the same basic approach could be applied in developing a pricing theory for corporate liabilities in general.

In Section 12.2, the basic equation for the pricing of financial instruments is developed along Black–Scholes lines. In Section 12.3, the model is applied to the simplest form of corporate debt, the discount bond where no coupon payments are made, and a formula for computing the risk structure of interest rates is presented. In Section 12.4, comparative statics are used to develop graphs of the risk structure, and the question of whether the term premium is an adequate measure of the risk of a bond is answered. In Section 12.5, the validity in the presence of bankruptcy of the famous Modigliani–Miller theorem (Modigliani and Miller, 1958) is proven, and the required return on debt as a function of the debt-to-equity ratio is deduced. In Section 12.6, the analysis is extended to include coupon and callable bonds.

12.2   ON THE PRICING OF CORPORATE LIABILITIES

To develop the Black–Scholes type of pricing model, we make the following assumptions.

1   There are no transactions costs, taxes, or problems with indivisibilities of assets.
2   There are sufficiently many investors with comparable wealth levels so that each investor believes that he can buy and sell as much of an asset as he wants at the market price.
3   There exists an exchange market for borrowing and lending at the same rate of interest.
4   Short-sales of all assets, with full use of the proceeds, is allowed.
5   Trading in assets takes place continuously in time.
6   The Modigliani–Miller theorem that the value of the firm is invariant to its capital structure obtains.
7   The term structure is "flat" and known with certainty. That is, the price of a riskless discount bond which promises a payment of one dollar at time τ in the future is $P(\tau) = \exp(-r\tau)$ where r is the (instantaneous) riskless rate of interest, the same for all time.
8   The dynamics for the value of the firm, V, through time can be described by a diffusion-type stochastic process with stochastic differential equation

$$dV = (\alpha V - C)\, dt + \sigma V\, dz$$

where α is the instantaneous expected rate of return on the firm per unit time; C is the total dollar payouts by the firm per unit time to either its shareholders or liabilities-holders (e.g. dividends or interest payments) if positive, and it is the net dollars received by the firm from new financing if negative; σ^2 is the instantaneous variance of the return on the firm per unit time; and dz is a standard Gauss–Wiener process.

Many of these assumptions are not necessary for the model to obtain but are chosen for expositional convenience. In particular, the "perfect-market" assumptions, Assumptions 1–4, can be substantially weakened. Assumption 6 is actually proved as part of the analysis and Assumption 7 is chosen so as to clearly distinguish risk structure from term structure effects on pricing. Assumptions 5 and 8 are the critical assumptions. Basically, Assumption 5 requires that the market for these securities is open for trading most of the time. Assumption 8 requires that price movements are continuous and that the (unanticipated) returns on the securities are serially independent which is consistent with the Efficient Markets Hypothesis of Fama (1965a) and Samuelson (1965b).[1]

Suppose there exists a security whose market value Y at any point in time can be written as a function of the value of the firm and time, i.e. $Y = F(V, t)$. We can formally write the dynamics of this security's value in stochastic differential equation form as

$$dY = (\alpha_y Y - C_y)\, dt + \sigma_y Y\, dz_y \qquad (12.1)$$

where α_y is the instantaneous expected rate of return per unit time on this security; C_y is the dollar payout per unit time to this security; σ_y^2 is the instantaneous variance of the return per unit time; and dz_y is a standard Gauss–Wiener process. However, given that $Y = F(V, t)$, there is an explicit functional relation between the α_y, σ_y, and dz_y in (12.1) and the corresponding variables α, σ, and dz defined in Assumption 8. In particular, by Itô's lemma,[2] we can write the dynamics for Y as

$$dY = F_V dV + \tfrac{1}{2} F_{VV}\, (dV)^2 + F_t\, dt$$

$$= [\tfrac{1}{2}\sigma^2 V^2 F_{VV} + (\alpha V - C)F_V + F_t]\, dt + \sigma V F_V\, dz \qquad (12.2)$$

---

1   Of course, this assumption does not rule out serial dependence in the earnings of the firm. See Samuelson (1973) for a discussion.

2   For a rigorous discussion of Itô's lemma, see McKean (1969). For references to its application in portfolio theory, see Merton (1971, 1973b; this volume, Chs 5 and 15).

from Assumption 8, where subscripts denote partial derivatives. Comparing terms in (12.2) and (12.1), we have that

$$\alpha_y Y = \alpha_y F \equiv \tfrac{1}{2}\sigma^2 V^2 F_{VV} + (\alpha V - C)F_V + F_t + C_y \quad (12.3a)$$

$$\sigma_y Y = \sigma_y F \equiv \sigma V F_V \quad (12.3b)$$

$$dz_y \equiv dz \quad (12.3c)$$

Note that from (12.3c) the instantaneous returns on Y and V are perfectly correlated.

Following the derivation of the Black–Scholes model presented in Merton (1973a; this volume, Section 8.6), consider forming a three-security "portfolio" containing the firm, the particular security, and riskless debt such that the aggregate investment in the portfolio is zero. This is achieved by using the proceeds of short-sales and borrowings to finance the long positions. Let W_1 be the (instantaneous) number of dollars of the portfolio invested in the firm, W_2 the number of dollars invested in the security, and W_3 ($\equiv -(W_1 + W_2)$) the number of dollars invested in riskless debt. If dx is the instantaneous dollar return to the portfolio, then

$$dx = W_1 \frac{dV + C\,dt}{V} + W_2 \frac{dY + C_y\,dt}{Y} + W_3 r\,dt$$

$$= [W_1(\alpha - r) + W_2(\alpha_y - r)]\,dt + W_1\sigma\,dz + W_2\sigma_y\,dz_y$$

$$= [W_1(\alpha - r) + W_2(\alpha_y - r)]\,dt + (W_1\sigma + W_2\sigma_y)\,dz \quad (12.4)$$

from (12.3c). Suppose the portfolio strategy $W_j = W_j^*$ is chosen such that the coefficient of dz is always zero. Then the dollar return on the portfolio, dx^*, would be nonstochastic. Since the portfolio requires zero net investment, it must be that, to avoid arbitrage profits, the expected (and realized) return on the portfolio with this strategy is zero, i.e.

$$W_1^*\sigma + W_2^*\sigma_y = 0 \qquad \text{(no risk)} \qquad (12.5a)$$

$$W_1^*(\alpha - r) + W_2^*(\alpha_y - r) = 0 \quad \text{(no arbitrage)} \qquad (12.5b)$$

A nontrivial solution ($W_j^* \neq 0$) to (12.5) exists if and only if

$$\frac{\alpha - r}{\sigma} = \frac{\alpha_y - r}{\sigma_y} \qquad (12.6)$$

But, from (12.3a) and (12.3b), we substitute for α_y and σ_y and rewrite (12.6) as

$$\frac{\alpha - r}{\sigma} = \frac{\frac{1}{2}\sigma^2 V^2 F_{VV} + (\alpha V - C)F_V + F_t + C_y - rF}{\sigma V F_V} \tag{12.6a}$$

and by rearranging terms and simplifying we can rewrite (12.6a) as

$$0 = \tfrac{1}{2}\sigma^2 V^2 F_{VV} + (rV - C)F_V - rF + F_t + C_y \tag{12.7}$$

Equation (12.7) is a parabolic partial differential equation for F, which must be satisfied by *any* security whose value can be written as a function of the value of the firm and time. Of course, a complete description of the partial differential equation requires, in addition to (12.7), a specification of two boundary conditions and an initial condition. It is precisely these boundary condition specifications which distinguish one security from another (e.g. the debt of a firm from its equity).

In closing this section, it is important to note which variables and parameters appear in (12.7) (and hence affect the value of the security) and which do not. In addition to the value of the firm and time, F depends on the interest rate, the volatility of the firm's value (or its business risk) as measured by the variance, the payout policy of the firm, and the promised payout policy to the holders of the security. However, F *does not* depend on the expected rate of return on the firm nor on the risk preferences of investors nor on the characteristics of other assets available to investors beyond the three mentioned. Thus, two investors with quite different utility functions and different expectations for the company's future but who agree on the volatility of the firm's value will, for a given interest rate and current firm value, agree on the value F of the particular security. Also all the parameters and variables except the variance are directly observable and the variance can be reasonably estimated from time series data.

12.3   ON THE PRICING OF "RISKY" DISCOUNT BONDS

As a specific application of the formulation of the previous section, we examine the simplest case of corporate debt pricing. Suppose the corporation has two classes of claims: (a) a single homogeneous class of debt and (b) the residual claim, equity. Suppose further that the indenture of the bond issue contains the following provisions and restrictions: (a) the firm promises to pay a total of B dollars to the bondholders on the specified calendar date T; (b) in the event that this payment is not met, the bondholders immediately take over the company (and the shareholders receive nothing); (c) the firm cannot issue any new senior (or of equivalent rank) claims on the firm nor can it pay cash dividends or do share repurchase prior to the maturity of the debt.

If F is the value of the debt issue, we can write (12.7) as

$$\tfrac{1}{2}\sigma^2 V^2 F_{VV} + rVF_V - rF - F_\tau = 0 \qquad (12.8)$$

where $C_y = 0$ because there are no coupon payments; $C = 0$ from restriction (c); and $\tau \equiv T - t$ is the length of time until maturity so that $F_t = -F_\tau$. To solve (12.8) for the value of the debt, two boundary conditions and an initial condition must be specified. These boundary conditions are derived from the provisions of the indenture and the limited liability of claims. By definition, $V \equiv F(V, \tau) + f(V, \tau)$ where f is the value of the equity. Because both F and f can only take on nonnegative values, we have that

$$F(0, \tau) = f(0, \tau) = 0 \qquad (12.9a)$$

Further, $F(V, \tau) \leqslant V$ implies the regularity condition

$$\frac{F(V, \tau)}{V} \leqslant 1 \qquad (12.9b)$$

which substitutes for the other boundary condition in a semi-infinite boundary problem where $0 \leqslant V < \infty$. The initial condition follows from indenture conditions (a) and (b) and the fact that management is elected by the equity owners and hence must act in their best interests. On the maturity date T (i.e. $\tau = 0$), the firm must either pay the promised payment of B to the debtholders or else the current equity will be valueless. Clearly, if at time T, $V(T) > B$, the firm should pay the bondholders because the value of equity will be $V(T) - B > 0$, whereas if they do not the value of equity would be zero. If $V(T) < B$, then the firm will not make the payment and default the firm to the bondholders because otherwise the equityholders would have to pay in additional money and the (formal) value of equity prior to such payments would be $V(T) - B < 0$. Thus, the initial condition for the debt at $\tau = 0$ is

$$F(V, 0) = \min(V, B) \qquad (12.9c)$$

Armed with boundary conditions (12.9), one could solve (12.8) directly for the value of the debt by the standard methods of Fourier transforms or separation of variables. However, we avoid these calculations by looking at a related problem and showing its correspondence to a problem already solved in the literature.

To determine the value of equity, $f(V, \tau)$, we note that $f(V, \tau) = V - F(V, \tau)$, and substitute for F in (12.8) and (12.9) to deduce the partial differential equation for f. Thus,

$$\tfrac{1}{2}\sigma^2 V^2 f_{VV} + rVf_V - rf - f_\tau = 0 \tag{12.10}$$

subject to

$$f(V, 0) = \max(0, V - B) \tag{12.11}$$

and boundary conditions (12.9a) and (12.9b). Inspection of the Black–Scholes equation (Black and Scholes, 1973, p. 643, (7)) or Merton (1973a; this volume, equation (8.34)) shows that (12.10) and (12.11) are identical with the equations for a European call option on a non-dividend-paying common stock where firm value in (12.10)–(12.11) corresponds to stock price and B corresponds to the exercise price. This isomorphic price relation between levered equity of the firm and a call option not only allows us to write down the solution to (12.10)–(12.11) directly, but in addition allows us to immediately apply the comparative statics results in these papers to the equity case and, hence, to the debt. From Black and Scholes' equation (13) when σ^2 is a constant, we have that

$$f(V, \tau) = V\Phi(x_1) - B\exp(-r\tau)\Phi(x_2) \tag{12.12}$$

where

$$\Phi(x) \equiv \frac{1}{(2\pi)^{1/2}} \int_{-\infty}^{x} \exp(-\tfrac{1}{2}z^2)\, dz$$

$$x_1 \equiv \frac{[\log(V/B) + (r + \tfrac{1}{2}\sigma^2)\tau]}{\sigma\tau^{1/2}}$$

and

$$x_2 \equiv x_1 - \sigma\tau^{1/2}$$

From (12.12) and $F = V - f$, we can write the value of the debt issue as

$$F(V, \tau) = B\exp(-r\tau)\left\{\Phi[h_2(d, \sigma^2\tau)] + \frac{1}{d}\Phi[h_1(d, \sigma^2\tau)]\right\} \tag{12.13}$$

where

$$d \equiv \frac{B \exp(-r\tau)}{V}$$

$$h_1(d, \sigma^2\tau) \equiv -\frac{\frac{1}{2}\sigma^2\tau - \log(d)}{\sigma\tau^{1/2}}$$

$$h_2(d, \sigma^2\tau) \equiv -\frac{\frac{1}{2}\sigma^2\tau + \log(d)}{\sigma\tau^{1/2}}$$

Because it is common in discussions of bond pricing to talk in terms of yields rather than prices, we can rewrite (12.13) as

$$R(\tau) - r = -\frac{1}{\tau}\log\left\{\Phi[h_2(d, \sigma^2\tau)] + \frac{1}{d}\Phi[h_1(d, \sigma^2\tau)]\right\} \quad (12.14)$$

where

$$\exp[-R(\tau)\tau] \equiv \frac{F(V, \tau)}{B}$$

and $R(\tau)$ is the yield to maturity on the risky debt provided that the firm does not default. It seems reasonable to call $R(\tau) - r$ a *risk premium* in which case (12.14) defines a risk structure of interest rates.

For a given maturity, the risk premium is a function of only two variables: (a) the variance (or volatility) of the firm's operations, σ^2, and (b) the ratio of the present value (at the riskless rate) of the promised payment to the current value of the firm, d. Because d is a debt-to-firm value ratio computed with debt valued at the riskless rate, it is a biased upward estimate of the actual (market-value) debt-to-firm value ratio.

Since Merton (1973a; this volume, Ch. 8) has solved the option pricing problem when the term structure is not "flat" and is stochastic (by again using the isomorphic correspondence between options and levered equity), we could deduce the risk structure with a stochastic term structure. The formulae (12.13) and (12.14) would be the same in this case except that we would replace $\exp(-r\tau)$ by the price of a riskless discount bond which pays one dollar at time τ in the future and $\sigma^2\tau$ by a generalized variance term defined in Merton (1973a; this volume, Section 8.6).

12.4   A COMPARATIVE STATICS ANALYSIS OF
THE RISK STRUCTURE

Examination of (12.13) shows that the value of the debt can be written, showing its full functional dependence, as $F(V, \tau, B, \sigma^2, r)$. Because of the isomorphic relation between levered equity and a European call option, we can use analytical results presented in Merton (1973a; this volume, Ch. 8) to show that F is a first-degree homogeneous concave function of V and B.[3] Further, we have that[4]

$$F_V = 1 - f_V > 0 \quad F_B = -f_B > 0$$
$$F_\tau = -f_\tau < 0 \quad F_{\sigma^2} = -f_{\sigma^2} < 0$$
$$F_r = -f_r < 0 \tag{12.15}$$

where again subscripts denote partial derivatives. The results presented in (12.15) are as one would have expected for a discount bond: namely, the value of debt is an increasing function of the current market value of the firm and the promised payment at maturity, and a decreasing function of the time to maturity, the business risk of the firm, and the riskless rate of interest.

Since we are interested in the risk structure of interest rates which is a cross-section of bond prices at a point in time, it will shed more light on the characteristics of this structure to work with the price ratio $P \equiv F(V, \tau)/B \exp(-r\tau)$ rather than the absolute price level F. P is the price today of a risky dollar promised at time τ in the future in terms of a dollar delivered at that date with certainty, and it is always less than or equal to one. From (12.13), we have that

$$P(d, T) = \Phi[h_2(d, T)] + \frac{1}{d}\Phi[h_1(d, T)] \tag{12.16}$$

where $T \equiv \sigma^2\tau$. Note that, unlike F, P is completely determined by d, the "quasi" debt-to-firm value ratio, and T, which is a measure of the volatility of the firm's value over the life of the bond, and it is a decreasing function of both. That is,

$$P_d = -\frac{\Phi(h_1)}{d^2} < 0 \tag{12.17}$$

---

3   See Merton (1973a; this volume, Theorems 8.4, 8.9, and 8.10) where it is shown that f is a first-degree homogeneous, convex function of V and B.
4   See Merton (1973a; this volume, Theorems 8.5, 8.14, and 8.15).

and

$$P_T = -\frac{\Phi'(h_1)}{2dT^{1/2}} < 0 \tag{12.18}$$

where $\Phi'(x) \equiv \exp(-x^2/2)/(2\pi)^{1/2}$ is the standard normal density function.

We now define another ratio which is of critical importance in analyzing the risk structure: namely, $g \equiv \sigma_y/\sigma$ where σ_y is the instantaneous standard deviation of the return on the bond and σ is the instantaneous standard deviation of the return on the firm. Because these two returns are instantaneously perfectly correlated, g is a measure of the relative riskiness of the bond in terms of the riskiness of the firm at a given point in time.[5] From (12.3b) and (12.13), we can deduce the formula for g to be

$$\frac{\sigma_y}{\sigma} = \frac{VF_V}{F}$$

$$= \frac{\Phi[h_1(d, T)]}{P(d, T)d}$$

$$= g(d, T) \tag{12.19}$$

In Section 12.5, the characteristics of g are examined in detail. For the purposes of this section, we simply note that g is a function of d and T only, and that from the "no-arbitrage" condition, (12.6), we have that

$$\frac{\alpha_y - r}{\alpha - r} = g(d, T) \tag{12.20}$$

where $\alpha_y - r$ is the expected excess return on the debt and $\alpha - r$ is the expected excess return on the firm as a whole. We can rewrite (12.17) and (12.18) in elasticity form in terms of g as

$$\frac{dP_d}{P} = -g(d, T) \tag{12.21}$$

---

5 Note, for example, that in the context of the Sharpe–Lintner–Mossin Capital Asset Pricing Model, g is equal to the ratio of the beta of the bond to the beta of the firm.

and

$$\frac{TP_T}{P} = -\frac{g(d,\ T)\Phi'(h_1)T^{1/2}}{2\Phi(h_1)} \tag{12.22}$$

As mentioned in Section 12.3, it is common to use yield to maturity in excess of the riskless rate as a measure of the risk premium on debt. If we define $R(\tau) - r \equiv H(d,\ \tau,\ \sigma^2)$, then from (12.14) we have that

$$H_d = \frac{1}{\tau d}g(d,\ T) > 0 \tag{12.23}$$

$$H_{\sigma^2} = \frac{1}{2T^{1/2}}g(d,\ T)\,\frac{\Phi'(h_1)}{\Phi(h_1)} > 0 \tag{12.24}$$

$$H_\tau = \left[\log(P) + \frac{T^{1/2}}{2}g(d,\ T)\,\frac{\Phi'(h_1)}{\Phi(h_1)}\right]\bigg/\tau^2 \gtrless 0 \tag{12.25}$$

As can be seen in Table 12.1 and Figures 12.1 and 12.2, the term premium is an increasing function of both d and σ^2. While from (12.25) the change in the premium with respect to a change in maturity can be either sign, Figure 12.3 shows that for $d \geq 1$, it will be negative. To complete the analysis of the risk structure as measured by the term premium, we show that the premium is a decreasing function of the riskless rate of interest, i.e.

$$\frac{\mathrm{d}H}{\mathrm{d}r} = H_d\,\frac{\partial d}{\partial r}$$

$$= -g(d,\ T) < 0 \tag{12.26}$$

It still remains to be determined whether $R - r$ is a valid measure of the riskiness of the bond. That is, can one assert that if $R - r$ is larger for one bond than for another, then the former is riskier than the latter? To answer this question, one must first establish an appropriate definition of "riskier." Since the risk structure like the corresponding term structure is a "snapshot" at one point in time, it seems natural to define the riskiness in terms of the uncertainty of the rate of return over the next trading interval. In this sense of riskier, the natural choice as a measure of risk is the (instantaneous) standard deviation of the return on the bond, $\sigma_y = \sigma g(d,\ T) \equiv G(d,\ \sigma,\ \tau)$. In addition, for the type of dynamics postulated, I have shown elsewhere[6] that the standard deviation is a sufficient statistic

6   See Merton (1973a; this volume, Theorem 8.15).

Table 12.1 Representative Values of the Term Premium, $R - r$

σ^2	d	$R - r$ (%)	σ^2	d	$R - r$ (%)
Time until Maturity = 2			Time until Maturity = 5		
0.03	0.2	0.00	0.03	0.2	0.01
0.03	0.5	0.02	0.03	0.5	0.16
0.03	1.0	5.13	0.03	1.0	3.34
0.03	1.5	20.58	0.03	1.5	8.84
0.03	3.0	54.94	0.03	3.0	21.99
0.10	0.2	0.01	0.10	0.2	0.12
0.10	0.5	0.82	0.10	0.5	1.74
0.10	1.0	9.74	0.10	1.0	6.47
0.10	1.5	23.03	0.10	1.5	11.31
0.10	3.0	55.02	0.10	3.0	22.59
0.20	0.2	0.12	0.20	0.2	0.95
0.20	0.5	3.09	0.20	0.5	4.23
0.20	1.0	14.27	0.20	1.0	9.66
0.20	1.5	26.60	0.20	1.5	14.24
0.20	3.0	55.82	0.20	3.0	24.30
Time until Maturity = 10			Time until Maturity = 25		
0.03	0.2	0.01	0.03	0.2	0.09
0.03	0.5	0.38	0.03	0.5	0.60
0.03	1.0	2.44	0.03	1.0	1.64
0.03	1.5	4.98	0.03	1.5	2.57
0.03	3.0	11.07	0.03	3.0	4.68
0.10	0.2	0.48	0.10	0.2	1.07
0.10	0.5	2.12	0.10	0.5	2.17
0.10	1.0	4.83	0.10	1.0	3.39
0.10	1.5	7.12	0.10	1.5	4.26
0.10	3.0	12.15	0.10	3.0	6.01
0.20	0.2	1.88	0.20	0.2	2.69
0.20	0.5	4.38	0.20	0.5	4.06
0.20	1.0	7.36	0.20	1.0	5.34
0.20	1.5	9.55	0.20	1.5	6.19
0.20	3.0	14.08	0.20	3.0	7.81

for comparing the relative riskiness of securities in the Rothschild–Stiglitz (1970) sense. However, it should be pointed out that the standard deviation is not sufficient for comparing the riskiness of the debt of different companies in a portfolio sense[7] because the correlations of the

7   For example, in the context of the Capital Asset Pricing Model, the correlations of the two firms with the market portfolio could be sufficiently different to make the beta of the bond with the larger standard deviation smaller than the beta of the bond with the smaller standard deviation.

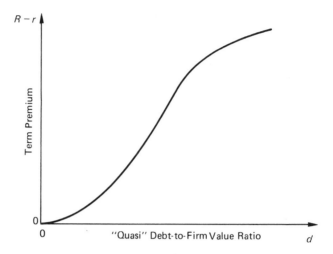

Figure 12.1 Term Premium vs "Quasi" Debt-to-Firm Value Ratio.

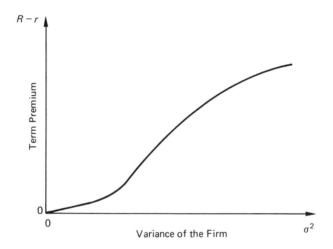

Figure 12.2 Term Premium vs Variance of the Firm.

returns of the two firms with other assets in the economy may be different. However, since $R - r$ can be computed for each bond without the knowledge of such correlations, it cannot reflect such differences except indirectly through the market value of the firm. Thus, as at least a necessary condition for $R - r$ to be a valid measure of risk, it should move in the same direction as G does in response to changes in the underlying variables. From the definition of G and (12.19), we have that

$$G_d = \frac{\sigma g^2}{T^{1/2}} \frac{\Phi(h_2)}{\Phi(h_1)} \left[\frac{\Phi'(h_2)}{\Phi(h_2)} + \frac{\Phi'(h_1)}{\Phi(h_1)} + h_1 + h_2 \right] > 0 \;^8 \tag{12.27}$$

$$G_\sigma = g \left\{ \Phi(h_1) - \Phi'(h_1) \left[\frac{T^{1/2}}{2} (1 - 2g) + \frac{\log(d)}{T^{1/2}} \right] \right\} \Bigg/ \Phi(h_1) > 0 \tag{12.28}$$

$$G_\tau = \frac{-\sigma^2 G}{2T^{1/2}} \frac{\Phi'(h_1)}{\Phi(h_1)} \left[\frac{1}{2}(1 - 2g) + \frac{\log(d)}{T} \right] \gtreqless 0 \text{ as } d \lesseqgtr 1 \tag{12.29}$$

Table 12.2 and Figures 12.4–12.6 show the standard deviation for typical values of d, σ, and τ. Comparing (12.27)–(12.29) with (12.23)–(12.25), we see that the term premium and the standard deviation change in the same direction in response to a change in the "quasi" debt-to-firm value ratio or the business risk of the firm. However, they need not change in the same direction with a change in maturity as a comparison of Figures 12.3 and 12.6 readily demonstrates. Hence, while comparing the term premiums on bonds of the same maturity does provide a valid comparison of the riskiness of such bonds, one cannot conclude that a higher term premium on bonds of different maturities implies a higher standard deviation.[9]

To complete the comparison between $R - r$ and G, the standard deviation is a decreasing function of the riskless rate of interest as was the case for the term premium in (12.26). Namely, we have that

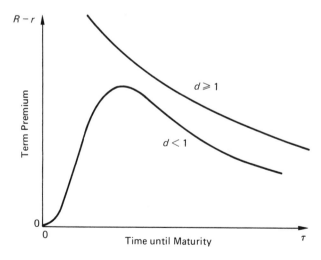

Figure 12.3 Term Premium vs Time until Maturity.

8   It is well known that $\Phi'(x) + x\Phi(x) > 0$ for $-\infty < x \leq \infty$.

9   While inspection of (12.25) shows that $H_\tau < 0$ for $d \geq 1$ which agrees with the sign of G_τ for $d > 1$, H_τ can be either-signed for $d < 1$ which does not agree with the positive sign of G_τ.

Table 12.2 Representative Values of the Standard Deviation of the Debt, G, and the Ratio of the Standard Deviation of the Debt to the Firm, g

σ^2	d	g	G	σ^2	d	g	G
Time until Maturity = 2				Time until Maturity = 5			
0.03	0.2	0.000	0.000	0.03	0.2	0.000	0.000
0.03	0.5	0.003	0.001	0.03	0.5	0.048	0.008
0.03	1.0	0.500	0.087	0.03	1.0	0.500	0.087
0.03	1.5	0.943	0.163	0.03	1.5	0.833	0.144
0.03	3.0	1.000	0.173	0.03	3.0	0.996	0.173
0.10	0.2	0.000	0.000	0.10	0.2	0.021	0.007
0.10	0.5	0.077	0.024	0.10	0.5	0.199	0.063
0.10	1.0	0.500	0.158	0.10	1.0	0.500	0.158
0.10	1.5	0.795	0.251	0.10	1.5	0.689	0.218
0.10	3.0	0.989	0.313	0.10	3.0	0.913	0.289
0.20	0.2	0.011	0.005	0.20	0.2	0.092	0.041
0.20	0.5	0.168	0.075	0.20	0.5	0.288	0.129
0.20	1.0	0.500	0.224	0.20	1.0	0.500	0.224
0.20	1.5	0.712	0.318	0.20	1.5	0.628	0.281
0.20	3.0	0.939	0.420	0.20	3.0	0.815	0.364
Time until Maturity = 10				Time until Maturity = 25			
0.03	0.2	0.003	0.001	0.03	0.2	0.056	0.010
0.03	0.5	0.128	0.022	0.03	0.5	0.253	0.044
0.03	1.0	0.500	0.087	0.03	1.0	0.500	0.087
0.03	1.5	0.745	0.129	0.03	1.5	0.651	0.113
0.03	3.0	0.966	0.167	0.03	3.0	0.857	0.148
0.10	0.2	0.092	0.029	0.10	0.2	0.230	0.073
0.10	0.5	0.288	0.091	0.10	0.5	0.377	0.119
0.10	1.0	0.500	0.158	0.10	1.0	0.500	0.158
0.10	1.5	0.628	0.199	0.10	1.5	0.573	0.181
0.10	3.0	0.815	0.258	0.10	3.0	0.691	0.219
0.20	0.2	0.196	0.088	0.20	0.2	0.324	0.145
0.20	0.5	0.358	0.160	0.20	0.5	0.422	0.189
0.20	1.0	0.500	0.224	0.20	1.0	0.500	0.224
0.20	1.5	0.584	0.261	0.20	1.5	0.545	0.244
0.20	3.0	0.719	0.321	0.20	3.0	0.622	0.278

$$\frac{dG}{dr} = G_d \frac{\partial d}{\partial r}$$

$$= -\tau d G_d < 0 \tag{12.30}$$

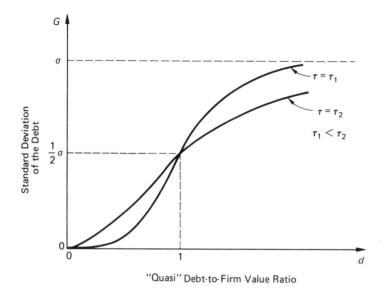

Figure 12.4 Debt Volatility vs "Quasi" Debt-to-Firm Value Ratio.

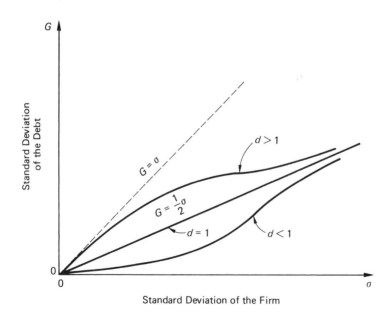

Figure 12.5 Debt Volatility vs Firm Volatility.

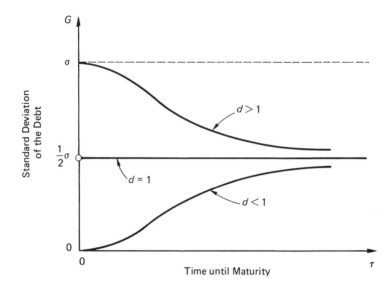

Figure 12.6 Debt Volatility vs Time until Maturity.

12.5 ON THE MODIGLIANI–MILLER THEOREM WITH BANKRUPTCY

In the derivation of the fundamental equation for pricing of corporate liabilities, (12.7), it was assumed that the Modigliani–Miller theorem held so that the value of the firm could be treated as exogenous to the analysis. If, for example, because of bankruptcy costs or corporate taxes, the Modigliani–Miller theorem does not obtain and the value of the firm does depend on the debt–equity ratio, then the formal analysis of the chapter is still valid. However, the linear property of (12.7) would be lost, and instead a nonlinear simultaneous solution, $F = F[V(F), \tau]$, would be required.

Fortunately, in the absence of these imperfections, the formal hedging analysis used in Section 12.2 to deduce (12.7), simultaneously, stands as a proof of the Modigliani–Miller theorem even in the presence of bankruptcy. To see this, imagine that there are two firms identical with respect to their investment decisions, but one firm issues debt and the other does not. The investor can "create" a security with a payoff structure identical to the risky bond by following a portfolio strategy of mixing the equity of the unlevered firm with holdings of riskless debt. The correct portfolio strategy is to hold $F_V V$ dollars of the equity and $F - F_V V$ dollars of riskless bonds where V is the value of the unlevered firm and F and F_V are determined by the solution of (12.7). Since the value of the "manufactured" risky debt is always F, the debt issued by the other firm can never sell for more than F. In a similar fashion, one could create levered equity by a portfolio strategy of holding $f_V V$ dollars of the unlevered equity and $f - f_V V$ dollars of borrowing on margin which would have a payoff structure identical to the equity issued by the levering firm. Hence, the value of the levered firm's equity can never sell for more than f. But, by construction, $f + F = V$, the value of the unlevered firm. Therefore, the value of the levered firm can be no larger than that of the unlevered firm, and it cannot be less. Note that, unlike in the analysis by Stiglitz (1969), we did not require a specialized theory of capital market equilibrium (e.g. the Arrow–Debreu model or the Capital Asset Pricing Model) to prove the theorem when bankruptcy is possible.

In the previous section, a cross-section of bonds across firms at a point in time was analyzed to describe a risk structure of interest rates. We now examine a debt issue for a single firm. In this context, we are interested in measuring the risk of the debt relative to the risk of the firm. As discussed in Section 12.4, the correct measure of this relative riskiness is $\sigma_y/\sigma = g(d, T)$ defined in (12.19). From (12.16) and (12.19), we have that

$$\frac{1}{g} = 1 + \frac{d\Phi(h_2)}{\Phi(h_1)} \tag{12.31}$$

From (12.31), we have $0 \le g \le 1$. That is, the debt of the firm can never be more risky than the firm as a whole, and, as a corollary, the equity of a levered firm must always be at least as risky as the firm. In particular, from (12.13) and (12.31), the limit as $d \to \infty$ of $F(V, \tau) = V$ and of $g(d, T) = 1$. Thus, as the ratio of the present value of the promised payment to the current value of the firm becomes large and therefore the probability of eventual default becomes large, the market value of the debt approaches that of the firm and the risk characteristic of the debt approaches that of (unlevered) equity. As $d \to 0$, the probability of default approaches zero, and $F(V, \tau) \to B \exp(-r\tau)$, the value of a riskless bond, and $g \to 0$. So, in this case, the risk characteristics of the debt become the same as riskless debt. Between these two extremes, the debt will behave like a combination of riskless debt and unlevered equity, and will change in a continuous fashion. To see this, note that in the portfolio used to replicate the risky debt by combining the equity of an unlevered firm with riskless bonds, g is the fraction of that portfolio invested in the equity and $1 - g$ is the fraction invested in riskless bonds. Thus, as g increases, the portfolio will contain a larger fraction of equity until in the limit as $g \to 1$ it is all equity.

Noting that $g = G/\sigma$, we have from (12.19) and (12.27) that

$$g_d = \frac{g}{d}\left[-(1 - g) + \frac{1}{T^{1/2}}\frac{\Phi'(h_1)}{\Phi(h_1)}\right] > 0 \qquad (12.32)$$

i.e. the relative riskiness of the debt is an increasing function of d, and

$$g_T = \frac{-g\Phi'(h_1)}{2T^{1/2}\Phi(h_1)}\left[\frac{1}{2}(1 - 2g) + \frac{\log(d)}{T}\right] \gtreqless 0 \text{ as } d \lesseqgtr 1 \qquad (12.33)$$

Further, we have that

$$g(1, T) = \tfrac{1}{2} \qquad T > 0 \qquad (12.34)$$

and

$$\lim_{T\to\infty} g(d, T) = \tfrac{1}{2} \qquad 0 < d < \infty \qquad (12.35)$$

Thus, for $d = 1$, independent of the business risk of the firm or the length of time until maturity, the standard deviation of the return on the debt equals half the standard deviation of the return on the whole firm. From (12.35), as the business risk of the firm or the time to maturity gets large, $\sigma_y \to \sigma/2$, for all d. Figures 12.7 and 12.8 show g as a function of d and T.

Contrary to what many might believe, the relative riskiness of the debt can decline as either the business risk of the firm or the time until maturity increases. Inspection of (12.33) shows that this is the case if $d > 1$ (i.e. the present value of the promised payment is less than the current value of the firm). To see why this result is not unreasonable, consider the following. For small T (i.e. σ^2 or τ small), the chances that the debt will become equity through default are large, and this will be reflected in the risk characteristics of the debt through a large g. By increasing T (through an increase in σ^2 or τ), the chances are better that the firm value will increase enough to meet the promised payment. It is also true that the chances that the firm value will be lower are increased. However, remember that g is a measure of how much the risky debt behaves like equity versus debt, since, for g large, the debt is already more aptly described by equity than riskless debt (e.g. for $d > 1$, $g > \tfrac{1}{2}$ and the "replicating" portfolio will contain more than half equity). Thus, the increased probability of meeting the promised payment dominates, and g declines. For $d < 1$, g will be less than a half, and the argument goes the opposite way. In the "watershed" case

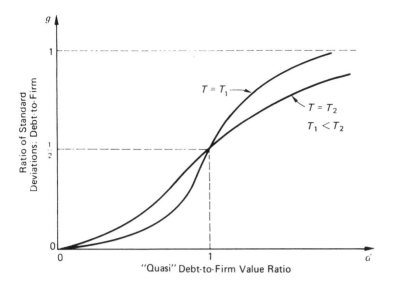

Figure 12.7 Relative Debt Volatility vs "Quasi" Debt-to-Firm Value Ratio.

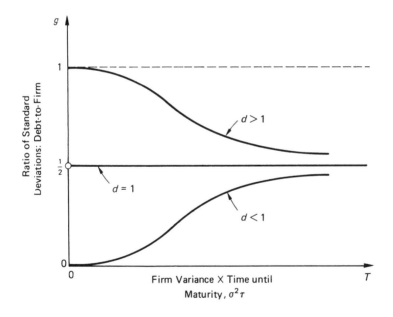

Figure 12.8 Relative Debt Volatility vs Firm Volatility-to-Maturity.

when $d = 1$, g equals a half; the "replicating" portfolio is exactly half equity and half riskless debt, and the two effects cancel leaving g unchanged.

In closing this section, we examine a classical problem in corporate finance: given a fixed investment decision, how does the required return on debt and equity change, as alternative debt–equity mixes are chosen? Because the investment decision is assumed fixed, and the Modigliani–Miller theorem obtains, V, σ^2, and α (the required expected return on the firm) are fixed. For simplicity, suppose that the maturity of the debt, τ, is fixed, and the promised payment at maturity per bond is one dollar. Then, the debt–equity mix is determined by choosing the number of bonds to be issued. Since, in our previous analysis, F is the value of the whole debt issue and B is the total promised payment for the whole issue, B will be the number of bonds (promising one dollar at maturity) in the current analysis, and F/B will be the price of one bond.

Define the market debt-to-equity ratio to be X which is equal to $F/f = F/(V - F)$. From (12.20), the required expected rate of return on the debt, α_y, will equal $r + (\alpha - r)g$. Thus, for a fixed investment policy,

$$\frac{d\alpha_y}{dX} = (\alpha - r)\frac{dg/dB}{dX/dB} \tag{12.36}$$

provided that $dX/dB \neq 0$. From the definition of X and (12.13), we have that

$$\frac{dX}{dB} = \frac{X(1 + X)(1 - g)}{B} > 0 \tag{12.37}$$

Since $dg/dB = g_d d/B$, we have from (12.32), (12.36), and (12.37) that

$$\frac{d\alpha_y}{dX} = \frac{d(\alpha - r)g_d}{X(1 + X)(1 - g)} > 0$$

$$= \frac{\alpha - r}{X(1 + X)}\left[-g + \frac{1}{T^{1/2}}\frac{\Phi'(h_2)}{\Phi(h_2)}\right] \tag{12.38}$$

Further analysis of (12.38) shows that α_y starts out as a convex function of X, passes through an inflection point where it becomes concave and approaches α asymptotically as X tends to infinity.

To determine the path of the required return on equity, α_e, as X moves between zero and infinity, we use the well-known identity that the equity return is a weighted average of the return on debt and the return on the firm. That is,

$$\alpha_e = \alpha + X(\alpha - \alpha_y)$$

$$= \alpha + (1 - g)X(\alpha - r) \tag{12.39}$$

α_e has a slope of $\alpha - r$ at $X = 0$ and is a concave function bounded from above by the line $\alpha + (\alpha - r)X$. Figure 12.9 displays both α_y and α_e. Although Figure 12.9 was not produced from computer simulation, it should be emphasized that, because both $(\alpha_y - r)/(\alpha - r)$ and $(\alpha_e - r)/(\alpha - r)$ do not depend on α, such curves can be computed up to the scale factor $\alpha - r$ without knowledge of α.

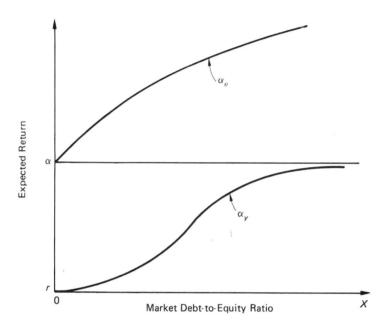

Figure 12.9 Expected Return on Debt and Equity vs Market Debt-to-Equity Ratio.

12.6   ON THE PRICING OF RISKY COUPON BONDS

In the usual analysis of (default-free) bonds in term structure studies, the derivation of a pricing relation for pure discount bonds for every maturity would be sufficient because the value of a default-free coupon bond can be written as the sum of discount bonds' values weighted by the size of the coupon payment at each maturity. Unfortunately, no such simple formula exists for risky coupon bonds. The reason for this is that, if the firm defaults on a coupon payment, then all subsequent coupon payments (and payments of principal) are also defaulted on. Thus, the default on one of the "mini" bonds associated with a given maturity is not independent of the event of default on the "mini" bond associated with a later maturity.

However, the apparatus developed in the previous sections is sufficient to solve the coupon bond problem.

Assume the same simple capital structure and indenture conditions as in Section 12.3 except modify the indenture condition to require (continuous) payments at a coupon rate per unit time, $\bar{C}$. From indenture restriction (c), we have that, in equation (12.7), $C = C_y = \bar{C}$ and hence the coupon bond value will satisfy the partial differential equation

$$0 = \tfrac{1}{2}\sigma^2 V^2 F_{VV} + (rV - \bar{C})F_V - rF - F_\tau + \bar{C} \qquad (12.40)$$

subject to the same boundary conditions (12.9). The corresponding equation for equity f will be

$$0 = \tfrac{1}{2}\sigma^2 V^2 f_{VV} + (rV - \bar{C})f_V - rf - f_\tau \qquad (12.41)$$

subject to boundary conditions (12.9a), (12.9b), and (12.11). Again, equation (12.41) has an isomorphic correspondence with an option pricing problem previously studied. Equation (12.41) is identical with equation (44) in Merton (1973a; this volume, equation (8.44)) which is the equation for the European option value on a stock which pays dividends at a constant rate per unit time of $\bar{C}$. While a closed-form solution to (12.41) for finite τ has not yet been found, one has been found for the limiting case of a perpetuity ($\tau = \infty$), and is presented in Merton (1973a; this volume, equation (8.46)). Using the identity $F \equiv V - f$, we can write the solution for the perpetual risky coupon bond as

$$F(V, \infty) = \frac{\bar{C}}{r}\left[1 - \frac{(2\bar{C}/\sigma^2 V)^{2r/\sigma^2}}{\Gamma(2 + 2r/\sigma^2)} M\left(\frac{2r}{\sigma^2}, 2 + \frac{2r}{\sigma^2}, \frac{-2\bar{C}}{\sigma^2 V}\right)\right]. \qquad (12.42)$$

where $\Gamma(\cdot)$ is the gamma function and $M(\cdot)$ is the confluent hypergeometric function. While perpetual noncallable bonds are nonexistent in the United States, there are preferred stocks with no maturity date and (12.42) would be the correct pricing function for them.

Moreover, even for those cases where closed-form solutions cannot be found, powerful numerical integration techniques have been developed for solving equations like (12.7) or (12.41). Hence, computation and empirical testing of these pricing theories is entirely feasible.

Note that, in deducing (12.40), it was assumed that coupon payments were made uniformly and continuously. In fact, coupon payments are usually only made semiannually or annually in discrete lumps. However, it is a simple matter to take this into account by replacing $\bar{C}$ in (12.40) by $\Sigma_i \bar{C}_i \delta(\tau - \tau_i)$ where $\delta(\cdot)$ is the Dirac delta function and τ_i is the length of time until maturity when the ith coupon payment of $\bar{C}_i$ dollars is made.

As a final illustration, we consider the case of callable bonds. Again, assume the same capital structure but modify the indenture to state that "the firm can redeem the bonds at its option for a stated price of $K(\tau)$ dollars" where K may depend on the length of time until maturity. Formally, equation (12.40) and boundary conditions (12.9a) and (12.9c) are still valid. However, instead of the boundary condition (12.9b) we have that, for each τ, there will be some value for the firm, call it $\overline{V}(\tau)$, such that for all $V(\tau) \geqslant \overline{V}(\tau)$ it would be advantageous for the firm to redeem the bonds. Hence, the new boundary condition will be

$$F[\overline{V}(\tau), \tau] = K(\tau) \tag{12.43}$$

Equations (12.40), (12.9a), (12.9c), and (12.43) provide a well-posed problem to solve for F provided that the $\overline{V}(\tau)$ function is known. But, of course, it is not. Fortunately, economic theory is rich enough to provide us with an answer. First, imagine that we solved the problem as if we knew $\overline{V}(\tau)$ to get $F[V, \tau; \overline{V}(\tau)]$ as a function of $\overline{V}(\tau)$. Second, recognize that it is management's option to redeem the bonds and that management operates in the best interests of the equityholders. Hence, as a bondholder, one must presume that management will select the $\overline{V}(\tau)$ function so as to maximize the value of equity, f. But, from the identity $F \equiv V - f$, this implies that the $\overline{V}(\tau)$ function chosen will be the one which minimizes $F[V, \tau; \overline{V}(\tau)]$. Therefore, the additional condition is that

$$F(V, \tau) = \min_{\{V(\tau)\}} F[V, \tau; V(\tau)] \tag{12.44}$$

To put this in appropriate boundary-condition form for solution, we again rely on the isomorphic correspondence with options and refer the reader to the discussion in Merton (1973a; this volume, Ch. 8) where it is shown that condition (12.44) is equivalent to the condition

$$F_V[\overline{V}(\tau), \tau] = 0 \tag{12.45}$$

Hence, appending (12.45) to (12.40), (12.9a), (12.9c), and (12.43), we solve the problem for the $F[V, \tau]$ and $\overline{V}(\tau)$ functions simultaneously.

12.7   CONCLUSION

We have developed a method for pricing corporate liabilities which is grounded in solid economic analysis, requires inputs which are on the whole observable, and can be used to price almost any type of financial instrument. The method was applied to risky discount bonds to deduce a risk structure of interest rates. The Modigliani–Miller theorem was shown to obtain in the presence of bankruptcy provided that there are no differential tax benefits to corporations or transactions costs. The analysis was extended to include callable coupon bonds.

On the Pricing of Contingent Claims and the Modigliani–Miller Theorem

A general formula is derived for the price of a security whose value under specified conditions is a known function of the value of another security. Although the formula can be derived using the arbitrage technique of Black and Scholes, the alternative approach of continuous-time portfolio strategies is used instead. This alternative derivation allows the resolution of some controversies surrounding the Black and Scholes methodology. Specifically, it is demonstrated that the derived pricing formula must be continuous with continuous first derivatives, and that there is not a "pre-selection bias" in the choice of independent variables used in the formula. Finally, the alternative derivation provides a direct proof of the Modigliani–Miller theorem even when there is a positive probability of bankruptcy.

13.1 INTRODUCTION

The theory of portfolio selection in continuous time has as its foundation two assumptions: (a) the capital markets are assumed to be open at all times, and therefore economic agents have the opportunity to trade continuously; and (b) the stochastic processes generating the state variables can be described by diffusion processes with continuous sample paths.[1] If these assumptions are accepted, then the continuous-time model

Reproduced from *Journal of Financial Economics*, 5, November 1977, 241–9. The paper is a substantial revision of parts of Merton (1976c) presented in seminars at Yale and Brown Universities in April 1976 and at the EIASM Workshop in Management Science, Bergamo, Italy, in October 1976. I thank the participants for their helpful comments. Aid from the National Science Foundation is gratefully acknowledged. My thanks to the referee for editorial suggestions.

1 For references to the mathematics of diffusion processes and their applications in economics, see the bibliographies of Merton (1971, 1973a; this volume, Chs 5 and 8).

can be used to derive equilibrium security prices.[2] The pricing formulas derived by this method will in general require as minimum inputs estimates of the price of risk, the covariance of the security's cash flows with the market, and the expected cash flows. These numbers are difficult to estimate. However, it is not always necessary to have these numbers to price a security.

In a seminal paper, Black and Scholes (1973) used the continuous-time analysis to derive a formula for pricing common-stock options.[3] Although their derivation uses the same assumptions and analytical tools used in the continuous-time portfolio analysis, the resulting formula expressed in terms of the price of the underlying stock does not require as inputs expected returns, expected cash flows, the price of risk, or the covariance of the returns with the market. In effect, all these variables are implicit in the stock's price. Because expected returns and market covariances are not part of the inputs, the Black–Scholes evaluation formula is robust with respect to a reasonable amount of heterogeneity of expectations among investors, and because the required inputs are for the most part observable, the formula is testable. All of this has created substantial interest in extending their analysis to the evaluation of other types of securities.

The essential reason that the Black–Scholes pricing formula requires so little information as inputs is that the call option is a security whose value on a specified future date is uniquely determined by the price of another security (the stock). As such, a call option is an example of a *contingent claim*. While call options are very specialized financial instruments, Black and Scholes and others[4] recognized that the same analysis could be applied to the pricing of corporate liabilities generally where such liabilities were viewed as claims whose values were contingent on the value of the firm. Moreover, whenever a security's return structure is such that it can be described as a contingent claim, the same technique is applicable.

In Section 13.2, I derive a general formula for the price of a security whose value under specified conditions is a known function of the value of another security. Although the formula can be derived using the arbitrage technique employed by Merton (1974; this volume, Ch. 12) to derive the price of risky debt, an alternative approach is used to demonstrate that the resulting formula will obtain even if institutional restrictions prohibit arbitrage.

---

2 See Merton (1973b; (this volume, Ch. 15) and 1975b).
3 A call option gives its owner the right to buy a specified number of shares of a given stock at a specified price (the "exercise price") on or before a specified date (the "expiration date").
4 The literature based on contingent-claims analysis is extensive. Section 13.4 provides a sampling of applications including references to general survey articles and books.

Because the formula is often used to evaluate corporate liabilities as a function of the value of the firm, it is important to know conditions under which the value of the firm will not be affected by the form of its capital structure. In Section 13.3, the Modigliani–Miller theorem (Modigliani and Miller, 1958) that the value of the firm is invariant to its capital structure is extended to the case where there is a positive probability of bankruptcy.

13.2 A GENERAL DERIVATION OF A CONTINGENT-CLAIM PRICE

To develop the contingent-claim pricing model, I make the following assumptions.

1 "*Frictionless markets*" There are no transactions costs or taxes. Trading takes place continuously in time. Borrowing and short-selling are allowed without restriction. The borrowing rate equals the lending rate.
2 *Riskless asset* There is a riskless asset whose rate of return per unit time is known and constant over time. Denote this return rate by r.
3 *Asset 1* There is a risky asset whose value at any point in time is denoted by $V(t)$. The dynamics of the stochastic process generating $V(\cdot)$ over time are assumed to be describable by a diffusion process with a formal stochastic differential equation representation of

$$dV = [\alpha V - D_1(V, t)] \, dt + \sigma V \, dZ$$

where α is the instantaneous expected rate of return on the asset per unit time, σ^2 is the instantaneous variance per unit time of the rate of return, $D_1(V, t)$ is the instantaneous payout to the owners of the asset per unit time, and dZ is a standard Wiener process. α can be generated by a stochastic process of a quite general type, and σ^2 is restricted to be at most a function of V and t.
4 *Asset 2* There is a second risky asset whose value at any date t is denoted by $W(t)$ with the following properties: for $0 \leqslant t < T$, its owners will receive an instantaneous payout per unit time, $D_2(V, t)$. For any $t \, (0 \leqslant t < T)$, if $V(t) = \overline{V}(t)$, then the value of the second asset is given by $W(t) = f[\overline{V}(t), t]$, where f is a known function. For any t $(0 \leqslant t < T)$, if $V(t) = \underline{V}(t)$, then the value of the second asset is given by $[\underline{V}(t) < \overline{V}(t)]$: $W(t) = g[\underline{V}(t), t]$, where g is a known function. For $t = T$, the value of the second asset is given by $W(T) = h[V(T)]$. Asset 2 is called a contingent claim, contingent on the value of Asset 1.
5 *Investor preferences and expectations* It is assumed that investors prefer more to less. It is assumed that investors agree upon σ^2, but it is *not* assumed that they necessarily agree on α.

6 *Other* There can be as many or as few other assets or securities as one likes.

The constant interest rate and most of the "frictionless" market assumptions are not essential to the development of the model but are chosen for expositional convenience. The critical assumptions are continuous-trading opportunities and the dynamics description for Asset 1.

If it is assumed that the value of Asset 2 can be written as a twice continuously differentiable function of the price of Asset 1 and time, then the pricing formula for Asset 2 can be derived by the same procedure as that used in Merton (1974; this volume, Sections 12.2 and 12.3) to derive the value of risky debt. If $W(t) = F[V(t), t]$ for $0 \leqslant t \leqslant T$ and for $\underline{V}(t) \leqslant V(t) \leqslant \overline{V}(t)$, then, to avoid arbitrage, F must satisfy the linear partial differential equation

$$0 = \tfrac{1}{2}\sigma^2 V^2 F_{11} + (rV - D_1)F_1 - rF + F_2 + D_2 \qquad (13.1)$$

where subscripts on F denote partial derivatives with respect to its two explicit arguments V and t. Inspection of (13.1) shows that, in addition to V and t, F will depend on σ^2 and r. However, F does *not* depend on the expected return on Asset 1, α, and it does *not* depend on the characteristics of other assets available in the economy. Moreover, investors' preferences do not enter the equation either.

To solve (13.1), boundary conditions must be specified. From Assumption 4, we have that

$$F[\overline{V}(t), t] = f[\overline{V}(t), t] \qquad (13.2a)$$

$$F[\underline{V}(t), t] = g[\underline{V}(t), t] \qquad (13.2b)$$

$$F(V, T) = h(V) \qquad (13.2c)$$

While the functions f, g, and h are required to solve for F, they are generally deducible from the terms of the specific contingent claim being priced. For example, the original case examined by Black and Scholes is a common-stock call option with an exercise price of E dollars and an expiration date of T. If V is the value of the underlying stock, then the boundary conditions can be written as

$$F/V \leqslant 1 \text{ as } V \to \infty \qquad (13.3a)$$

$$F(0, t) = 0 \qquad (13.3b)$$

$$F(V, T) = \max(0, V - E) \qquad (13.3c)$$

where (13.3a) is a regularity condition which replaces the usual boundary condition when $\overline{V}(t) = \infty$. Both (13.3a) and (13.3b) follow from limited liability and from the easy-to-prove condition that the underlying stock is always more valuable than the option. Equation (13.3c) follows from the terms of the call option which establish the exact price relation between the stock and option on the expiration date.[5]

Hence, (13.1) together with (13.2a)–(13.2c) provide the general equation for pricing contingent claims. Moreover, if the contingent claim is priced according to (13.1) and (13.2), then it follows that there is no opportunity for intertemporal arbitrage. That is, the relative prices (W, V, r) are intertemporally consistent.

Suppose there exists a twice continuously differentiable solution to (13.1) and (13.2). Because the derivation of (13.1) used the *assumption* that the pricing function satisfies this condition, it is possible that some other solution exists which does not satisfy this differentiability condition. Indeed, in discussing the Black–Scholes solution to the call option case, Smith[6] points out that there are an infinite number of continuous solutions to (13.1) and (13.3) which have discontinuous derivatives at only one interior point although the Black–Scholes solution is the only solution with continuous derivatives. He goes on to state that "the economics of the option pricing problem would suggest that the solution be continuous, but there is no obvious argument that it be differentiable everywhere."

The following alternative derivation is a direct proof that if a twice continuously differentiable solution to (13.1) and (13.2) exists, then to rule out arbitrage, it must be the pricing function.

Let F be the formal twice continuously differentiable solution to (13.1) with boundary conditions (13.2). Consider the continuous-time portfolio strategy where the investor allocates the fraction $w(t)$ of his portfolio to Asset 1 and $1 - w(t)$ to the riskless asset. Moreover, let the investor make net "withdrawals" per unit time (e.g. for consumption) of $C(t)$. If $C(t)$ and $w(t)$ are right-continuous functions and $P(t)$ denotes the value of the investor's portfolio, then I have shown elsewhere[7] that the dynamics for the value of the portfolio, P, will satisfy the stochastic differential equation

---

5   In some cases, either $\overline{V}(t)$ or $\underline{V}(t)$ must be determined simultaneously with the solution of (13.1) for F. Two examples are the American call and put options on a dividend-paying stock with the potential for early exercise. In such cases, there is usually an additional boundary condition imposed on the derivative of F which allows just enough "over-specification" to determine $\overline{V}$. See Merton (1973a; this volume, Section 8.8) for a discussion. The structural definition of Asset 2 can easily be adjusted to include these cases.

6   See Smith (1976, p. 23, fn. 21).

7   See Merton (1971; this volume, equation (5.14)).

$$dP = \{[w(\alpha - r) + r]P - C\} \, dt + w\sigma P \, dZ \qquad (13.4)$$

Suppose we pick the particular portfolio strategy with

$$w(t) = F_1(V, t)V(t)/P(t) \qquad (13.5)$$

where F_1 is the partial derivative of F with respect to V, and the "consumption" strategy

$$C(t) = D_2(V, t) \qquad (13.6)$$

By construction, F_1 is continuously differentiable, and hence is a right-continuous function. Substituting from (13.5) and (13.6) into (13.4), we have that

$$dP = F_1 \, dV + [F_1(D_1 - rV) + rP - D_2] \, dt \qquad (13.7)$$

where dV is given in Assumption 3.

Since F is twice continuously differentiable, we can use Itô's lemma[8] to express the stochastic process for F as

$$dF = [\tfrac{1}{2}\sigma^2 V^2 F_{11} + (\alpha V - D_1)F_1 + F_2] \, dt + F_1 \sigma V \, dZ \qquad (13.8)$$

But F satisfies (13.1). Hence, we can rewrite (13.8) as

$$dF = F_1 \, dV + [F_1(D_1 - rV) + rF - D_2] \, dt \qquad (13.9)$$

Let $Q(t) \equiv P(t) - F[V(t), t]$. Then, from (13.7) and (13.9), we have that

$$
\begin{aligned}
dQ &= dP - dF \\
&= r(P - F) \, dt \\
&= rQ \, dt \qquad (13.10)
\end{aligned}
$$

But (13.10) is a nonstochastic differential equation with solution

$$Q(t) = Q(0) \exp(rt) \qquad (13.11)$$

for any time t and where $Q(0) \equiv P(0) - F[V(0), 0]$. Suppose that the initial amount invested in the portfolio, $P(0)$, is chosen equal to $F[V(0), 0]$. Then from (13.11) we have that

---

8 See Merton (1971; this volume, Ch. 5) for a discussion of Itô's lemma and stochastic differential equations.

$$P(t) = F[V(t), t] \tag{13.12}$$

By construction, the value of Asset 2, $W(t)$, will equal F at the boundaries $\underline{V}(t)$ and $\overline{V}(t)$ and at the termination date T. Hence, from (13.12), the constructed portfolio's value $P(t)$ will equal $W(t)$ at the boundaries. Moreover, the interim "payments" or withdrawals available to the portfolio strategy, $D_2[V(t), t]$, are identical to the interim payments made to Asset 2.

Therefore, if $W(t) > P(t)$, then the investor could short-sell Asset 2; proceed with the prescribed portfolio strategy including all interim payments; and be guaranteed a positive return on zero investment, i.e. there would be an arbitrage opportunity. If $W(t) < P(t)$, then the investor could essentially "short-sell" the prescribed portfolio strategy; use the proceeds to buy Asset 2; and again be guaranteed a positive return on zero investment. If institutional restrictions prohibit arbitrage,[9] then a similar argument can be applied using the principle that no security should be priced so as to "dominate" another security.[10] Hence, $W(t)$ must equal $F[V(t), t]$.

While this method of proof may appear to be very close to the original derivation, unlike the original derivation it does not *assume* that the dynamics of Asset 2 can be described by an Itô process, and therefore it does not assume that Asset 2 has a smooth pricing function. Indeed, the portfolio strategy described by (13.5) and (13.6) involves only combinations of Asset 1 and the riskless asset, and therefore does not even require that Asset 2 exists! The connection between the portfolio strategy and Asset 2 is that, if Asset 2 exists, then the price of Asset 2 must equal $F[V(t), t]$ or there will be an opportunity for intertemporal arbitrage.

Not only does this alternative derivation provide the "obvious argument" why such pricing functions must be differentiable everywhere, but it also can be used to resolve other issues that have been raised about results derived using this type of analysis. In the next section, two of the more important issues are resolved.

13.3 ON THE MODIGLIANI–MILLER THEOREM WITH BANKRUPTCY

In an earlier paper (1974, p. 460; this volume, Section 12.5) I proved that, in the absence of bankruptcy costs and corporate taxes, the Modigliani–Miller theorem (Modigliani and Miller, 1958) obtains even in the presence

---

9 One example would be restrictions on short-sales.
10 See Merton (1973a; this volume, Section 8.2) and Smith (1976, p. 7) for a discussion of "dominance" in this context.

of bankruptcy. In a comment on this earlier paper, Long (1974a) has asserted that my method of proof was "logically incoherent." Rather than debate over the original proof's validity, the method of derivation used in the previous section provides an immediate alternative proof.

Let there be a firm with two corporate liabilities: (a) a single homogeneous debt issue and (b) equity. The debt issue is promised a continuous coupon payment per unit time, C, which continues until either the maturity date of the bond, T, or the total assets of the firm reach zero. The firm is prohibited by the debt indenture from issuing additional debt or paying dividends. At the maturity date, there is a promised principal payment of B to the debtholders. In the event that the payment is not made, the firm is defaulted to the debtholders, and the equityholders receive nothing. If $S(t)$ denotes the value of the firm's equity and $D(t)$ the value of the firm's debt, then the value of the (levered) firm, $V_L(t)$ is identically equal to $S(t) + D(t)$. Moreover, in the event that the total assets of the firm reach zero, $V_L(t) = S(t) = D(t) = 0$ by limited liability. Also, by limited liability, $D(t)/V_L(t) \leq 1$.

Consider a second firm with initial assets and an investment policy identical with those of the levered firm. However, the second firm is all-equity financed with total value equal to $V(t)$. To ensure the identical investment policy including scale, it follows from the well-known accounting identity that the net payout policy of the second firm must be the same as for the first firm. Hence, let the second firm have a dividend policy that pays dividends of C per unit time either until date T or until the value of its total assets reaches zero (i.e. $V = 0$). Let the dynamics of the firm's value be as posited in Assumption 3 where $D_1(V, t) = C$ for $V > 0$ and $D_1 = 0$ for $V = 0$.

Let $F(V, t)$ be the formal twice-continuously differentiable solution to (13.1) subject to the boundary conditions $F(0, t) = 0$; $F(V, t)/V \leq 1$; and $F[V(T), T] = \min[V(T), B]$. Consider the dynamic portfolio strategy of investing in the all-equity firm and the riskless asset according to the "rules" (13.5) and (13.6) of Section 13.2 where $C(t)$ is taken equal to C. If the total initial amount invested in the portfolio, $P(0)$, is equal to $F[V(0), 0]$, then from (13.12), $P(t) = F[V(t), t]$.

Because both the levered firm and the all-equity firm have identical investment policies including scale, it follows that $V(t) = 0$ if and only if $V_L(t) = 0$. And it also follows that, on the maturity date T, $V_L(T) = V(T)$.

By the indenture conditions on the levered firm's debt, $D(T) = \min[V_L(T), B]$. But since $V(T) = V_L(T)$ and $P(T) = F[V(T), T]$, it follows that $P(T) = D(T)$. Moreover, since $V_L(t) = 0$ if and only if $V(t) = 0$, it follows that $P(t) = F(0, t) = D(t) = 0$ in that event.

Thus, by following the prescribed portfolio strategy, one would receive interim payments exactly equal to those on the debt of the levered firm. Moreover, on a specified future date T, the value of the portfolio will equal the value of the debt. Hence, to avoid arbitrage or dominance, $P(t) = D(t)$.

The proof for equity follows along similar lines. Let $f(V, t)$ be the formal solution to (13.1) subject to the boundary conditions $f(0, t) = 0$, $f(V, t)/V \leq 1$; and $f[V(T), T] = \max[0, V(T) - B]$. Consider the dynamic portfolio strategy of investing in the all-equity firm and the riskless asset according to the "rules" (13.5) and (13.6) of Section 13.2 where $C(t)$ is now taken equal to zero. If the total initial amount invested in this portfolio, $p(0)$, is equal to $f[V(0), 0]$, then from (13.12), $p(t) = f[V(t), t]$.

As with debt, if $V(t) = 0$, then $p(t) = S(t) = 0$, and at the maturity date, $p(T) = \max[0, V(T) - B] = S(T)$.

Thus, by following this prescribed portfolio strategy, one would receive the same interim payments as those on the equity of the levered firm. On the maturity date, the value of the portfolio will equal the value of the levered firm's equity. Therefore, to avoid arbitrage or dominance, $p(t) = S(t)$.

If one were to combine both portfolio strategies, then the resulting interim payments would be C per unit time with a value at the maturity date of $V(T)$. That is, both strategies together are the same as holding the equity of the unlevered firm. Hence, $f[V(t), t] + F[V(t), t] = V(t)$. But it was shown that $f[V(t), t] + F[V(t), t] = S(t) + D(t) \equiv V_L(t)$. Therefore, $V_L(t) = V(t)$, and the proof is completed.

While the proof was presented in the traditional context of a firm with a single debt issue, the proof goes through in essentially the same fashion for multiple debt issues or for "hybrid securities" such as convertible bonds, preferred stock, or warrants.[11]

In his comment on my earlier paper, Long (1974a, p. 485) claims that the original derivation builds into the model that risky debt can only depend on the "prespecified explanatory variables." His point is that, in fact, bond prices could depend on "the price of beer," "the value of the market portfolio," or "the rate of inflation," but by assuming that the bond price depends only on the value of the firm, the market rate of interest, the volatility of the market value of the firm, and time until maturity, the derived model price rules out such additional dependencies. The derivation in Section 13.2 did not assume that the value of Asset 2 depends only on these prespecified variables. The assumptions used are only the stated ones, Assumptions 1–6. Hence, given the current values of Asset 1, the only way that the price of beer, the market portfolio, or the rate of inflation can affect the price of Asset 2 is if they affect σ^2, r, or the boundary conditions. While it could be argued that *in fact* σ^2 and r may

---

11 In more complicated bond indentures, the restrictions may be in terms of accounting variables rather than market values. In such cases, the analysis requires that these accounting variables can be written as functions of the market values.

depend on these other variables, such an argument would simply be a criticism of Assumptions 2 and 3, and not of the derivation itself.[12]

The Modigliani–Miller theorem holds that for a *given* investment policy, the value of the firm is invariant to the choice of financing policy. It does *not* imply that the choice of financing policy will not influence investment policy and thereby affect the value of the firm. As discussed in Stiglitz (1972) and Merton (1973a; this volume, Ch. 8, footnote 16), managers of firms with large quantities of debt outstanding may choose to undertake negative net-present-value projects that reduce the market value of the firm but increase the market value of its common stock. Myers (1977) has shown that firms with noncallable debt may not undertake positive net-present-value projects that would otherwise increase the market value of the firm but reduce the market value of equity. Thus, managers of firms should, in general, take account of the financing decision when making the capital-budgeting decision. See Merton (1990b) for further discussion of the conflict between debtholders and equityholders over the investment and financing policies of the firm.

If the choice of securities issued by the firm can alter the tax liabilities of the firm, or if there are bankruptcy costs, then the Modigliani–Miller theorem no longer obtains. As noted in Merton (1982a, 1990a) and in footnote 15 of Chapter 2, the contingent-claims pricing technique can, nevertheless, be used to value corporate liabilities. To do so, redefine $V(t)$ as the pre-tax and pre-bankruptcy-cost value of the firm at time t and include as explicit liabilities of the firm both the government's tax claim and the "deadweight" bankruptcy-cost claim. Because these additional "noninvestor" liabilities, like those held by investors, are entitled to specified payments that depend on the fortunes of the firm, the previous analyses of this section and Section 13.2 apply. Hence, for a fixed investment policy, the redefined "investor-plus-noninvestor" value of the firm will be invariant to the firm's choice of financing policy. Majd and Myers (1985, 1987) use this approach to derive the value of the government's tax claim on the firm and the value of the various liabilities held by its investors.

Although the total investor-plus-noninvestor value of the firm does not depend on the financing choice, the allocation of that value between investor and noninvestor components does. Thus, for a given investment policy, the firm's financing policy does "matter" to its management, debt-holders, and stockholders. Brennan and Schwartz (1978) and Galai (1988) apply the contingent-claims pricing methodology to the problem of optimal-capital-structure choice in the presence of corporate taxes.

*12   This paragraph marks the end of the original Merton (1977b). The balance of this chapter is new material.

13.4 APPLICATIONS OF CONTINGENT-CLAIMS ANALYSIS IN CORPORATE FINANCE

The contingent-claims pricing methodology has had and continues to have an important influence on both academic financial research and finance practice. The extraordinary impact of contingent-claims analysis (CCA) can in large part be explained by four critical elements: (a) the relatively weak assumptions required for its valid application make CCA robust; (b) the variables and parameters required as inputs in the valuation equation are either directly observable or reasonable to estimate; (c) there are several computationally feasible numerical methods for solving the partial differential equations for prices;[13] (d) the generality of the methodology permits adaptation to a wide range of finance applications and it can handle many of the complexities encountered with real-world securities and corporate capital structures. This section provides a brief overview of these applications. The reader will find more comprehensive surveys in Smith (1976, 1979), Mason and Merton (1985), Cox and Rubinstein (1985), and Ingersoll (1987).

The applications of CCA to the pricing of corporate liabilities has progressed far beyond the original Black and Scholes (1973) and Merton (1970b, 1974; this volume, Chs 11 and 12) studies of simple risky debt and levered equity. Galai and Masulis (1976) analyze the effects on debt prices of changes in the firm's investment policy. Black and Cox (1976) and Mason and Bhattacharya (1981) evaluate typical debt-indenture restrictions such as safety covenants, seniority and subordination agreements, and limits on the financing of payouts to other liability holders. Ho and Singer (1982, 1984) examine the pricing and risk characteristics of corporate debt with sinking-fund requirements. Brennan and Schwartz (1977b) and Merton (1974; this volume, Ch. 12) analyze the valuation of debt with call provisions. Stulz and Johnson (1985) evaluate secured or collateralized debt. Hawkins (1982) studies revolving credit agreements. The pricing of convertible bonds is covered in Brennan and Schwartz (1977c, 1980), Ingersoll (1977), McConnell and Schwartz (1986), and Merton (1970b; this volume, Ch. 11). Their analyses can be extended to include the pricing of bonds that are convertible into equity of other companies, commodities, or different currencies. Baldwin (1972) and Emanuel (1983b) evaluate preferred stock. Fischer (1975, 1978) uses both continuous-time portfolio analysis and the CCA methodology to price "real" bonds with payments

13 Ames (1977) and Smith (1978) are general references on the numerical solution of partial differential equations. Brennan and Schwartz (1977a, b, c, 1985b), Boyle (1977, 1988), Boyle, Evnine, and Gibbs (1989), Geske (1977), Geske and Shastri (1985), Parkinson (1977), and Schwartz (1977) develop numerical methods for solving the valuation equations of option and contingent-claims pricing. See also the bibliography in Cox and Rubinstein (1985, pp. 481–2).

linked to a commodity-price or wage index. See also Schwartz (1982). The same CCA methodology can be applied to the evaluation of stock and debt warrants, rights, and underwriters' stand-by arrangements. Buser, Hendershott, and Sanders (1985), Cox, Ingersoll, and Ross (1980), and Ramaswamy and Sundaresan (1986) analyze "floor–ceiling" agreements that limit the range of interest payments on floating-rate debt issues and adjustable-rate mortgages.

Business firms often guarantee the payments on debt issued by their subsidiaries. Government agencies also provide guarantees of private-sector debt, the most notable example being deposit insurance. As we shall see in Chapters 19 and 20, the CCA approach can be used to evaluate loan guarantees and deposit insurance.[14] Brennan and Schwartz (1976) and Boyle and Schwartz (1977) analyze the related problem of an insurance company's guarantee of a minimum cash value for equity-linked life insurance policies. Gatto, Geske, Litzenberger, and Sosin (1980) study the pricing of mutual-fund insurance. Kraus and Ross (1982) apply the continuous-time model to the problem of determining the fair rate of profit for a property-liability insurance company. Briys (1988) and Richard (1975) use the model to analyze the intertemporal life-cycle demands for life insurance. Bodie (1990) applies CCA to evaluate inflation insurance.

Financial institutions and finance-company subsidiaries of business firms can sell a portion of their financial assets by placing the assets in a trust and issuing one or more classes of securities with specified claims to the trust assets. A prime example is the mortgage-backed securities market, where thrift institutions can issue securities collateralized by packages of mortgages held in escrow. The mortgage payments of interest and principal amounts received by the issuing thrift are "passed through" to the holders of the issued securities. Brennan and Schwartz (1985b), Dunn and McConnell (1981), and Schwartz and Torous (1989) use CCA to price mortgage-backed securities in the case where the mortgages are guaranteed against default by a government agency.

In addition to providing a unified approach to the pricing of corporate securities, CCA has also been applied to the financial analysis of corporate employee-compensation plans. An obvious example is the valuation of executive stock options.[15] A more subtle one is the evaluation of both explicit and implicit labor contracts that provide wage "floors" and employment guarantees, including tenure.[16] Merton, Bodie, and Marcus

---

14   See also Jones and Mason (1980), Sosin (1980), Ronn and Verma (1986), Pennacchi (1987a, b), Selby, Franks, and Karki (1988), and Fries and Perraudin (1991).
15   The difference between the cost of the option to the granting firm and its value to the employee is significantly affected by the corporate and personal tax codes. Thus, evaluators of executive stock options should use the Scholes (1976) model that takes account of taxes.
16   Cf. McDonald (1974) on tenure and Merton (1985) on wage floors. Merton (1976c) uses a similar approach to develop a model for valuing human capital that takes account of the employee's option to withhold his labor. Dothan and Williams (1981) use option theory to analyze the decision of when to terminate one's education and enter the labor force in an uncertain environment.

(1987) analyze the insurance aspects of the integration of corporate pension plans with Social Security. Cummins (1988) evaluates the liabilities of state insurance guarantee funds that protect policy-holders against losses from insurance company insolvencies. Sharpe (1976) and Marcus (1987) use CCA to study the impact that guarantees of corporate pension liabilities by the Pension Benefit Guaranty Corporation can have on the optimal investment policy for corporate pension funds.

Among the more recent applications of CCA in corporate finance, perhaps the most significant are in the areas of capital-investment decisions and corporate strategy. Embedded in many types of production projects are operating options that are difficult to evaluate by traditional capital-budgeting techniques. For example, a production facility that can use various inputs and produces various outputs provides the firm with operating options that it would not have with a specialized facility that uses a fixed set of inputs and produces a single type of output. Examples are flexible oil refineries and chemical plants that can use different mixes of inputs to produce the same output, or the same inputs to produce various arrays of outputs. In operations management, *modularization* is the breaking apart of integrated manufacturing systems into components linked by standard interfaces. Baldwin and Clark (1992) use CCA to value the options to reconfigure the production process that modularization makes possible. CCA provides a powerful technique to weigh the benefits of these production options against the larger initial cost or lower operating efficiency of the more flexible production technology.[17]

The choice among techniques with various mixes of fixed and variable costs can be analyzed as options to change production levels. Myers and Majd (1983) analyze the value of the option to abandon a project. McDonald and Siegel (1985) extend that analysis to include the temporary shutdown of production. Brennan and Schwartz (1985a) take account of this option in the evaluation of a mine. Dixit (1989b) uses the CCA technique to analyze optimal entry and exit behaviour by firms in an industry.

Just as the option to abandon can be a significant source of value in a project, so the option to choose when to initiate a project can be valuable. Myers (1977) points out that recognition of this option is important to the proper evaluation of a firm's "growth opportunities." As has long been recognized in financial analysis, the value of a firm can exceed the market value of its projects currently in place, because the firm may have opportunities to earn returns in excess of the cost of capital on some of its future projects. Standard capital-budgeting procedures implicitly assume that the firm is committed to develop these future projects, although, in fact, it need not make such a commitment before the implementation date. CCA can capture the value of this option not to go forward.

17 See Triantis and Hodder (1990). CCA can also be used to evaluate the benefits of a more broadly trained (and hence more flexible) work force against the cost of the higher wages that must be paid whether this extra training is used or not.

Other examples, where having the option to initiate is important, are exploration projects for natural resources and the purchase or long-term lease of land for possible future development. If all natural resources discovered were required to be produced, then firms would not explore in areas where the estimated development and extraction costs exceed the expected future price for the resource. If, as is actually the case, firms can choose when to initiate such development, then it may pay to explore in high-production-cost areas, because such exploration creates an option to produce if the price of the resource, at some later date, is higher than was expected. Paddock, Siegel, and Smith (1988) evaluate offshore oil leases from this perspective. Geltner (1989) applies it to the development of urban real estate. See Chiang, Lai, and Ling (1986), Capozza and Helsley (1990), and Capozza and Schwann (1990) for other applications to real estate. McDonald and Siegel (1986) use CCA to make a general quantitative analysis of the value of waiting to invest.

The building of large-scale investment projects often requires several sequential stages of development that, in total, involve a considerable period of time. For example, the production of a new type of airplane involves engineering, prototype production, testing, and final tooling stages, which can take a decade to complete. Other examples are the construction of oil pipelines and petrochemical and electric-power generating plants. Because such projects generate no returns unless completed, the principal economic benefit of finishing one interim stage is to give the firm the option to proceed with the next stage toward completion of the project. Using CCA, Majd and Pindyck (1987) derive the optimal sequential investment rules and the project values for projects that have "construction-time flexibility." That is, for such projects, the firm can not only choose at each stage whether to continue with the project, but can also select the optimal rate of development and expenditure for each stage of the project. Pindyck (1988) generalizes this analysis to study marginal investment decisions in the context of optimal capacity choice and expansion when investment is irreversible.

In the context of a theory of value for market-timing skills, Merton (1981) shows that the equilibrium value of superior information about an asset's future price is directly related to the current market price of a put option on that asset. See also Henriksson and Merton (1981). This analysis would suggest that CCA can be applied to evaluate the decision of whether to acquire more information about a project before either rejecting it or proceeding with its implementation. For example, consider a firm that must select one from among n mutually exclusive projects. Suppose that, at a cost, the firm can acquire now all project-value information that would otherwise only become known at some later ("information-release") date. The value of acquiring this information now is equal to the current price of an option to exchange any one of these projects for any other one. The expiration date of this option is the information-release date. A natural generalization of the Margrabe–Fischer–Stulz technique for valuing such options could be used to determine whether the value of the information exceeds its acquisition cost[18].

Mason and Merton (1985, Appendix) integrate many of these operating and financing options into their contingent-claims analysis of a project financing for a hypothetical, large-scale energy project. The project is financed by equity, senior debt, and subordinated debt with outside loan guarantees. The analysis includes the possibility of posting performance bonds to discourage abandonment during construction and "throughput" or minimum-price guarantees for output produced during a specified period after construction.

Kester (1984) examines the strategic problem of the sequencing of investments among projects, and concludes that such problems can be fruitfully analyzed using CCA. For example, in the marketing of basic consumer products such as soap or paper towels, a successful brand name plays an important role, not only because of consumer recognition, but also because brand-name products are more likely to receive "shelf space" from distributors such as supermarkets. In evaluating projects to produce a number of consumer products, a firm may find it advantageous to develop these projects sequentially, instead of simultaneously. By doing so, the firm would resolve some of the uncertainty about the available shelf space needed for subsequent products before spending the resources for their development. The option to not spend resources for product development is lost if products are developed simultaneously.

Kester's sequencing-of-products analysis exemplifies a broader class of strategic and capital-budgeting decision problems, where as a direct result of investment in one project the firm acquires valuable options on one or more other projects. The value of such interproject options may be missed if a project is evaluated on a "stand-alone" basis. Neglecting such linkages can cause substantial undervaluations of certain types of projects. A good example is the research and development project whose only value is to provide the firm with options to enter new markets, expand market share, or reduce production costs.

As these few examples suggest, CCA is an especially powerful tool for the valuation of the "flexibility" components of projects. In his article on the reconciliation of finance theory and corporate strategy, Myers (1984) points out that these option-like components are precisely the ones whose values, corporate strategists often claim, are not properly measured by the traditional capital-budgeting techniques of finance. CCA thus holds forth the promise of systematic quantitative assessments for investment projects and corporate strategy decisions that heretofore were largely evaluated on an *ad hoc*, qualitative basis.

---

18   See Johnson (1987) for an extension of the Margrabe–Fischer–Stulz analysis to several assets.

14

Financial Intermediation in the Continuous-Time Model

14.1 INTRODUCTION

As discussed in Chapter 1, the core of financial economic theory is the study of the microbehavior of agents in the intertemporal deployment of their resources in an environment of uncertainty. Economic organizations are regarded as existing primarily to facilitate these allocations and are therefore endogenous to the theory. In this chapter, the continuous-time model is used to analyze the risk-pooling and risk-sharing roles of financial intermediaries and to derive some of the operating technologies that can be used to fulfill those roles. The formal analysis explores three aspects of operations: product identification, product implementation and pricing, and risk management and control for an intermediary's entire portfolio. The focus is on the economic function of financial intermediaries rather than on their specific institutional structure. Nevertheless, the institutional homes of the financial products and management techniques studied can be readily associated with current structures of banks, investment management firms, and insurance companies. A brief afterword touches upon application of the continuous-time model to policy and strategy issues in intermediation.

In Section 2.4, theorems are derived that specify the conditions under which nontrivial spanning of the efficient portfolio set will obtain. Under these conditions, all possible optimal portfolios can be generated by combinations of a relatively small and select set of portfolios. These generating portfolios have an institutional interpretation as mutual funds or investment companies. Thus, as noted in the closing remarks of Chapter 2, spanning theorems provide a basis for a beginning theory of financial intermediation.

Such theorems are a commonplace result in the continuous-time model. With joint log-normally distributed security prices, the analysis in Section 5.5 shows that, with or without a riskless security, only two mutual funds are required to span the set of optimal portfolios. In the model of Section 11.7, three funds are sufficient for spanning. As will be proved in Theorems 15.5 and 15.6, this result expands to an m-fund spanning theorem in the general case of the continuous-time model. The discussion surrounding the derivation of the theorems in Chapter 15 describes the economic function for each of the mutual funds as well as the explicit portfolio rules required for their construction. The analysis also establishes the minimum information set required to implement each fund's portfolio strategy. These mutual-fund theorems are generally used to help identify the various sources of systematic risk in multi-dimensional versions of the Capital Asset Pricing Model (CAPM). However, in the context of financial intermediation, they also serve to identify a class of investment products for which there would seem to be a natural demand. Hence, as with the theorems derived in the static environment of Chapter 2, these spanning theorems create a theoretical foundation for the role of financial intermediaries in a dynamic economic system with continuous-trading opportunities.[1]

As exemplified by the analyses in Chapters 11–13, contingent-claims analysis (CCA) has a broad range of application to the pricing of financial instruments. It should therefore come as little surprise that CCA is an important tool for developing the theory of financial intermediation. The contribution of CCA to the enrichment of that theory, however, is deeper than just the pricing of financial instruments issued or purchased by intermediaries. Contingent-claim securities with payoffs that can be expressed as functions of other traded-securities' prices are called *derivative securities*. CCA provides the "blueprints" or production technologies for financial intermediaries to manufacture derivative securities. As underscored in the general development of CCA in Chapter 13, the portfolio-replication process used to derive contingent-claim prices applies whether or not the derivative security actually exists. Thus, the specified dynamic portfolio strategy used to create an arbitrage position against a traded contingent claim is also a prescription for synthesizing an otherwise nonexistent derivative security. The initial investment required to fund the replicating portfolio becomes, in this context, the production cost to the intermediary that creates the security. In Section 14.3, we expand on this theory of production for financial intermediaries and derive the technolo-

---

1   As in the case of mutual funds, financial intermediation activities often involve the combining of diverse financial assets into a package and the issuing of a single class of securities as claims against the portfolio. However, it is also common to "reverse" the process and issue a diverse set of claims against a relatively homogeneous package of financial assets. One real-world example is the collateralized mortgage obligation in which the portfolio contains mortgages of the same expected duration. Several classes of securities (called "tranches") are issued that have claims to different components of the total cash flow generated by the portfolio. A theoretical foundation for such "stripping" of various parts of a financial asset is laid in Section 14.3 with the development of Arrow–Debreu pure securities. See also Hakansson (1976) for a theory of "stripping" in his development of the "superfund."

gies for creating and pricing Arrow–Debreu-like securities. As will be shown, these securities provide the "building blocks" for intermediaries to construct and price their financial products.

The focus of CCA is on the hedging and pricing of an individual security or financial product. However, as shown in Section 14.4, CCA, together with general dynamic portfolio theory, can be used to measure and control the total risk of an intermediary's entire portfolio. Although few in the practice of intermediation would doubt the central importance of risk management, such doubts do arise in the theory. It is, after all, standard fare that the Modigliani–Miller theorems hold (at least approximately) in economic models with well-functioning capital markets. It follows as a corollary that, at most, only the systematic-risk component of the firm's total risk warrants first-order attention by the firm's managers. In Sections 14.4 and 14.5, we examine the issue of whether, as a theoretical matter, financial intermediaries are different in this respect from other types of business firms. We conclude that the management of total risk by intermediaries can be of significant importance even in an environment where the Modigliani–Miller theorems obtain with respect to ordinary business firms. Although mainly of theoretical interest, the analysis does provide some foundation for real-world policies that selectively discriminate between intermediaries and other firms when deciding on government bailouts and loan guarantees and when setting regulations.

With all the continuous-time model seems to offer, its application to the theory of intermediation nevertheless carries with it an apparent paradox. In the standard model, investors are entirely indifferent as to whether or not derivative securities are created, because investors can themselves use the dynamic portfolio strategies of CCA to replicate the payoff patterns to these securities. Thus, each derivative security is redundant, and because it adds nothing new to the market, creation of such a security provides no social benefit. Of course, in the real world, the prescribed dynamic replications may not be feasible. But, the CCA methodology is valid only if the payoffs to the derivative security can be reproduced by trading in existing securities. Hence, we have a version of the Hakansson (1979, pp. 722–3) paradox: CCA only provides the production technology and production cost for creating securities that are of no consequence.

Much the same paradox applies to the mutual-fund theorems of the continuous-time model: investors are simply indifferent between selecting their portfolios from a group of funds that span the optimal portfolio set and selecting from all available securities. It would thus seem that the rich menu of financial intermediaries and derivative securities observed in the real world has no important economic function in an idealized environment where investors have the same information, can trade continuously, and face no transactions costs or taxes.

Such indifference is indeed the case if *all* investors can gather information and transact without cost. Hence, some types of transactions-cost structure in which financial intermediaries and market makers have a comparative advantage with respect to other investors and corporate issuers is required to provide a *raison d'être* for financial intermediation and markets for derivative securities.[2]

In Section 14.2, the binomial model of Chapter 10 is used to derive the production technology and cost for creating a derivative security in the presence of transactions costs. The derived costs of hedging both long and short positions in the same derivative security provides an endogenous specification of the relation among bid–ask price spreads for derivatives and their underlying securities. For an empirically relevant range of investor transactions costs, we show by example that the induced spreads in derivative prices can be substantial, and thereby suggest the prospect of significant benefits from efficient intermediation.

Although analytically tractable, even the simple binomial model is greatly complicated by the explicit recognition of transactions costs. As we know from the work of Constantinides (1986), Davis and Norman (1990), Dumas and Luciano (1991), Eastham and Hastings (1988), Figlewski (1989), Garman and Ohlson (1981), Hodges and Neuberger (1989), Kandel and Ross (1983), Leland (1985), Magill and Constantinides (1976), Sun (1987), and Taksar, Klass, and Assaf (1988), the impact of transactions costs on optimal portfolio behaviour and security pricing in the continuous-time model is considerably more difficult.[3] Moreover, development of a satisfactory equilibrium theory of allocations and prices in the presence of transactions costs promises still more complexity, because it requires a simultaneous endogenous determination of prices, allocations, *and* the least-cost form of market structure and financial intermediation.

To circumvent all this complexity and also preserve a role for intermediation, I introduce a continuous-time model in which many investors cannot trade costlessly, but the lowest-cost transactors (by definition, financial intermediaries) can. In this model, standard CCA can be used to determine the production costs for financial products issued by intermediaries. However, unlike in the standard zero-cost model, these products can significantly improve economic efficiency. If, moreover, the traded-

---

2 For example, in Chapter 20, the cost of surveillance by the deposit insurer is, in equilibrium, borne by the depositors in the form of a lower yield on their deposits. If all investors can transact costlessly, then none would hold deposits and instead they would invest directly in higher-yielding US Treasury bills. Thus, to justify this form of intermediation, it is necessary to assume that at least some investors face positive transactions costs for such direct investments in the market.

3 With diffusion processes and proportional transactions costs, investors cannot trade continuously, and therefore cannot perfectly hedge derivative-security positions. The reason is that, with continuous trading, transactions costs at each trade will be proportional to $|dz|$, where dz is a Brownian motion. However, for any noninfinitesimal time interval T, $\int_0^T |dz| = \infty$ almost certainly, and hence with continuous trading the total transactions cost is unbounded with probability one.

security markets and financial-services industry are competitive, then equilibrium prices of financial products will equal the production costs of the lowest-cost transactors. In Section 14.5, we analyze this model and show that, through intermediation, all investors can achieve optimal consumption–bequest allocations as if they could trade continuously without cost. Hence, in this model with transactions costs, both the contingent-claims analyses of Chapters 11–13 and the equilibrium analyses of Chapter 15 can be used to determine equilibrium allocations and prices.[4] Thus, this model provides a resolution of the Hakansson paradox by showing that mutual funds and derivative-security markets can provide important economic benefits to investors and corporate issuers, even though these securities are priced in equilibrium as if they were redundant.

· 14.2 DERIVATIVE-SECURITY PRICING WITH TRANSACTIONS COSTS

In this section, we examine the effects of transactions costs on derivative-security pricing by using the two-period version of the Cox–Ross–Rubinstein binomial option pricing model as analyzed in Section 10.2. In that model, the initial stock price $S(0)$ is given by S_0. At time 1, the stock price will equal either S_{11} or S_{12}. If $S(1) = S_{11}$, then at time 2, $S(2)$ will equal either S_{21} or S_{22}. If $S(1) = S_{12}$, then at time 2, $S(2)$ will equal either S_{23} or S_{24}. R denotes the return per dollar invested in the riskless security and is constant over both periods. To capture the effect of transactions costs, we assume that a commission must be paid on each purchase or sale of the stock and that the commission rate is a fixed proportion τ of the dollar amount of the transaction. Equivalently, we could assume a bid–ask spread in which investors pay the *ask price* for the stock, $S^a(t) \equiv (1 + \tau)S(t)$, when they buy and receive the *bid price*, $S^b(t) \equiv (1 - \tau)S(t)$, when they sell. There are no costs for transacting in the riskless security.

As shown in (10.3), the array of possible stock prices must satisfy certain conditions to rule out the possibility of arbitrage or dominance opportunities between the stock and the riskless security. The corresponding set of restrictions in the presence of transactions costs can be written as

---

4 More generally, standard CCA will provide a close approximation if the "mark-up" per unit required to cover the intermediary's transactions costs and profit is sufficiently small that, from the perspective of its customers' behavior, the additional cost is negligible. Of course, a tiny margin applied to large volume can produce substantial total profits for the financial intermediation industry.

$$S_{11} < S_0 R < \frac{(1 - \tau)S_{12}}{1 + \tau} \tag{14.1a}$$

$$S_{21} < S_{11} R < \frac{(1 - \tau)S_{22}}{1 + \tau} \tag{14.1b}$$

$$S_{23} < S_{12} R < \frac{(1 - \tau)S_{24}}{1 + \tau} \tag{14.1c}$$

Consider an intermediary that sells to a customer a call option with exercise price E and expiration date two periods from now. The terms of the option require cash settlement in which the customer is paid the in-the-money value of the call, $S(t) - E$, if the call is exercised. In the case where prices are quoted as a spread, the stock price is determined by the average of the bid and ask prices, $\bar{S}(t) \equiv [S^a(t) + S^b(t)]/2 = S(t)$.

As in the no-transactions-cost case, we determine the production cost for manufacturing the call option by deriving a dynamic portfolio strategy in the stock and riskless security that exactly replicates the payoff to the option. By following this strategy, the intermediary can completely hedge all the risk of this liability. In determining the cost, we assume that the intermediary has no initial position in the underlying stock and that all stock held at the expiration date of the option is sold in the market.[5]

If $S(t) = S$ and the commission rate is τ, then let $N(S, t; \tau)$ denote the number of shares of stock held in the portfolio at time t after adjusting the portfolio to the desired position. If $N(S, t; \tau) < 0$, then the portfolio is short $|N(S, t; \tau)|$ shares. Let $B(S, t; \tau)$ denote the amount of the riskless security held in the portfolio after the payment of the transactions costs associated with adjustments to the portfolio at time t. If $B(S, t; \tau) < 0$, then the portfolio has borrowed $|B(S, t; \tau)|$ dollars. Let $F(S, t; \tau)$ denote the value of the portfolio *before* payment of transactions costs incurred at time t.

As in the analysis of Chapter 10, we derive the replicating portfolio strategy by beginning at the expiration date and working backwards in time in a dynamic-programming-like fashion. If $S(1) = S_{11}$, then to exactly match the payoff to the option at $t = 2$, the portfolio composition must satisfy $N(S_{11}, 1; \tau)(1 - \tau)S_{21} + B(S_{11}, 1; \tau)R = H(S_{21})$ in the event $S(2) = S_{21}$, and $N(S_{11}, 1; \tau)(1 - \tau)S_{22} + B(S_{11}, 1; \tau)R = H(S_{22})$ in the

---

5 Because commissions are paid for both purchases and sales of the stock, this assumption produces the most "conservative" (i.e. highest) estimate of the cost. In practice, an intermediary with an ongoing business of writing options on this stock would avoid the double costs of liquidating stock at the expiration of one option and repurchasing stock to hedge the new issue of another. Hence, the inventory of stock held by the intermediary will affect its marginal cost of producing options and therefore the prices derived here provide an upper bound on the bid–ask spread.

event $S(2) = S_{22}$. $H(S) \equiv \max(0, S - E)$ is the schedule of payments to the customer at expiration and we have taken account of commissions paid on the sale of the stock in the portfolio. From the matching conditions, we have that

$$N(S_{11}, 1; \tau) = \frac{H(S_{22}) - H(S_{21})}{(1 - \tau)(S_{22} - S_{21})}$$

$$= \frac{N(S_{11}, 1; 0)}{1 - \tau} \qquad (14.2a)$$

and

$$B(S_{11}, 1; \tau) = \frac{H(S_{21})S_{22} - H(S_{22})S_{21}}{R(S_{22} - S_{21})}$$

$$= B(S_{11}, 1; 0) \qquad (14.2b)$$

Because $S_0 > S_{11}$, we tentatively assume (and verify later) that, in the event $S(1) = S_{11}$, the portfolio holdings of the stock should be reduced from the initial position $N(S_0, 0; \tau)$, established at $t = 0$. Hence, for $S(1) = S_{11}$, the intermediary will incur a transaction cost of $\tau[N(S_0, 0; \tau) - N(S_{11}, 1; \tau)]S_{11}$ to adjust the portfolio. Therefore, from (14.2a) and (14.2b), the total resources required in the portfolio at time 1 to support this strategy can be written as[6]

$$F(S_{11}, 1; \tau) = N(S_{11}, 1; \tau)S_{11} + B(S_{11}, 1; \tau) + \tau[N(S_0, 0; \tau)$$
$$- N(S_{11}, 1; \tau)]S_{11}$$
$$= F(S_{11}, 1; 0) + \tau N(S_0, 0; \tau)S_{11} \qquad (14.2c)$$

If instead, at $t = 1$, $S(1) = S_{12}$, then at $t = 2$, $S(2)$ will equal either S_{23} or S_{24}. By the same analysis leading to (14.2a) and (14.2b), we have that

$$N(S_{12}, 1; \tau) = \frac{H(S_{24}) - H(S_{23})}{(1 - \tau)(S_{24} - S_{23})}$$

$$= \frac{N(S_{12}, 1; 0)}{1 - \tau} \qquad (14.3a)$$

---

6 As discussed in footnote 5, the resources required to fund the portfolio depend on the inventory of stock held by the intermediary. Thus, if the same option were just being created at $t = 1$, (14.2a) and (14.2b) would still apply, but the transaction cost paid would be $\tau N(S_{11}, 1; \tau)S_{11}$. Hence, the required funding for the portfolio would be $F(S_{11}, 1; 0) + 2\tau N(S_{11}, 1; \tau)S_{11}$.

and

$$B(S_{12}, 1; \tau) = \frac{H(S_{23})S_{24} - H(S_{24})S_{23}}{R(S_{24} - S_{23})}$$

$$= B(S_{12}, 1; 0) \qquad (14.3b)$$

Because $S_{12} > S_0$, we assume that, in the event $S(1) = S_{12}$, the stock holdings in the portfolio should be increased from the level at $t = 0$. Hence, the intermediary will incur a transaction cost of $\tau[N(S_{12}, 1; \tau) - N(S_0, 0; \tau)]S_{12}$ to adjust the portfolio. From (14.3a) and (14.3b), the total portfolio value required at $t = 1$ is[7]

$$F(S_{12}, 1; \tau) = N(S_{12}, 1; \tau)S_{12} + B(S_{12}, 1; \tau) + \tau[N(S_{12}, 1; \tau)$$

$$- N(S_0, 0; \tau)]S_{12}$$

$$= F(S_{12}, 1; 0) + \tau[2N(S_{12}, 1; \tau) - N(S_0, 0; \tau)]S_{12}$$
$$(14.3c)$$

By inspection of (14.2a) and (14.3a),

$$N[S(1), 1; \tau] = N[S(1), 1; 0]/(1 - \tau)$$

and therefore the number of shares of stock held is larger with transactions costs than in the no-cost case. From (14.2b) and (14.3b), $B[S(1), 1; \tau] < 0$, and the amount borrowed is independent of the level of transactions costs. From (14.2c) and (14.3c), $F[S(1), 1; \tau]$ exceeds $F[S(1), 1; 0]$, the amount required to fund the portfolio with no transactions costs.

To exactly replicate the return on the option from $t = 0$ until expiration, the portfolio strategy at $t = 0$ must produce a portfolio value of $F(S_{11}, 1; \tau)$ at $t = 1$ if $S(1) = S_{11}$ and a value of $F(S_{12}, 1; \tau)$ if $S(1) = S_{12}$. Because $F[S(1), 1; \tau]$ includes the transactions costs for portfolio changes at $t = 1$, this funding requirement can be met if $N(S_0, 0; \tau)S(1) + B(S_0, 0; \tau) \times R = F[S(1), 1; \tau]$. It follows that

$$N(S_0, 0; \tau) = \frac{F(S_{12}, 1; \tau) - F(S_{11}, 1; \tau)}{S_{12} - S_{11}}$$

7   As in footnote 6, if the portfolio were just now being created, (14.3a) and (14.3b) would still apply, but the transaction cost paid would be $\tau N(S_{12}, 1; \tau)S_{12}$. The corresponding funding for the portfolio would be $F(S_{12}, 1; 0) + 2\tau N(S_{12}, 1; \tau)S_{12}$.

and that

$$B(S_0, 0; \tau) = \frac{F(S_{11}, 1; 0)S_{12} - F(S_{12}, 1; 0)S_{11}}{R(S_{12} - S_{11})}$$

$$- \frac{[N(S_0, 0; \tau)(1 - \tau) - N(S_0, 0; 0)]S_{11}}{R}$$

By substitution from (14.2c) and (14.3c) and the rearrangement of terms, we have that[8]

$$N(S_0, 0; \tau) = N(S_0, 0; 0)$$

$$+ \frac{2\tau[N(S_{12}, 1; \tau)S_{12} - N(S_0, 0; 0)(S_{11} + S_{12})/2]}{(1 + \tau)S_{12} - (1 - \tau)S_{11}} \qquad (14.4a)$$

and

$$B(S_0, 0; \tau) = B(S_0, 0; 0) - \frac{[N(S_0, 0; \tau)(1 - \tau) - N(S_0, 0; 0)]S_{11}}{R}$$

$$(14.4b)$$

Because $N(S_{12}, 1; 0) > N(S_0, 0; 0)$ and $S_{12} > S_{11}$, we have from (14.4a) and (14.4b) that $N(S_0, 0; \tau) > N(S_0, 0; 0) > 0$ and that $B(S_0, 0; \tau) < B(S_0, 0; 0) < 0$. Hence, the presence of transactions costs causes a larger long position in the stock and additional borrowing in the replicating portfolio.

The initial investment in the portfolio required to undertake these positions (including the transaction cost of $\tau N(S_0, 0; \tau)S_0$) can be written as

$$F(S_0, 0; \tau) = F(S_0, 0; 0) + [N(S_0, 0; \tau) - N(S_0, 0; 0)]\left(S_0 - \frac{S_{11}}{R}\right)$$

$$+ \tau N(S_0, 0; \tau)\left(S_0 + \frac{S_{11}}{R}\right) \qquad (14.4c)$$

Because $N(S_0, 0; \tau) > N(S_0, 0; 0) > 0$ and $S_0 > S_{11}/R$, we have by inspection of (14.4c) that $F(S_0, 0; \tau) > F(S_0, 0; 0)$. We thus verify that an

---

8 Using (14.2a) and (14.3a) with $H(S) = \max(0, S - E)$, we have from (14.4a) that $N(S_{11}, 1; \tau) < N(S_0, 0; \tau) < N(S_{12}, 1; \tau)$. Hence, the direction of changes in the portfolio, tentatively assumed in the derivation of (14.2c) and (14.3c), is verified.

increase in the cost of producing a call option caused by commissions charged in the stock market increases the option price charged by the intermediary. In a competitive financial-services industry, the ask price for the call option is its production cost, $F(S_0, 0; \tau)$.

To explore further the spread in call-option prices induced by transactions costs in the stock market, consider a customer who would like to sell a call option to the intermediary. To determine the (maximum) price to bid for the call option, the intermediary solves for the portfolio strategy with a return that exactly hedges the payoffs it would receive from holding the call option. If there were no transactions costs, the replicating strategy would be the mirror-image of the one used to hedge a short position in the call option. That is, the intermediary would hold short positions in the stock given by $-N[S(t), t; 0] < 0$, and hold positive amounts of the riskless security given by $-B[S(t), t; 0] > 0$. The portfolio would require a negative initial investment of $-F(S_0, 0; 0)$ and this net cash flow to the intermediary at $t = 0$ would be the maximum amount that it would pay to the customer for the call option.

Although the qualitative features of the replicating portfolio will be the same with transactions costs, the magnitudes of the positions held will not be the same because the intermediary must pay the commissions no matter which side of the transaction it undertakes. Applying the same analysis used to derive (14.2)–(14.4), we have that

$$N'(S_0, 0; \tau) = -N(S_0, 0; -\tau) \qquad (14.5a)$$

$$B'(S_0, 0; \tau) = -B(S_0, 0; -\tau) \qquad (14.5b)$$

$$F'(S_0, 0; \tau) = -F(S_0, 0; -\tau) \qquad (14.5c)$$

where the prime on each variable denotes the positions and amounts required to hedge a long position in a call option. By inspection of (14.4a)–(14.4c), it is readily apparent that $N(S_0, 0; \tau)$, $B(S_0, 0; \tau)$, and $F(S_0, 0; \tau)$ are not even functions of τ. Therefore, it follows from (14.5a)–(14.5c) that, for $\tau > 0$, the replicating strategy to hedge a long position in a call option is not simply the reverse of the replicating strategy to hedge a short position in a call option.

We can say more, however. From (14.1a), $(1 - \tau)S_{12} > (1 + \tau)S_{11}$ and from (14.3a) and (14.4a), $N(S_{12}, 1; 0) > N(S_0, 0; 0)$. Using this condition in (14.4a), we have that

$$0 < N(S_0, 0; -\tau) < N(S_0, 0; 0) < N(S_0, 0; \tau) \qquad (14.6)$$

Hence, the number of shares held short to hedge a long call position is fewer than the number held long to hedge a short call position. From manipulation of (14.4c), it can also be shown that

$$0 < F(S_0, 0; -\tau) < F(S_0, 0; 0) < F(S_0, 0; \tau) \qquad (14.7)$$

That is, the minimum price at which the intermediary would sell a call option exceeds the maximum price at which the intermediary would buy a call option. The zero-transactions-cost price of the option is between the two.

At the outset of our analysis, we saw that, with symmetric proportional transactions costs, the average of the bid and ask prices of the stock, $\bar{S}(t)$, is equal to the stock price with no transactions costs, $S(t)$. In a competitive financial-services industry, the bid price for the call option is given by $F(S_0, 0; -\tau)$. In this environment, the average of the bid and ask prices of the call option, $\bar{F}(S_0, 0; \tau)$, is equal to $[F(S_0, 0; \tau) + F(S_0, 0; -\tau)]/2$. From the conditions leading to (14.6) and (14.4c), it can be shown that

$$0 < F(S_0, 0; 0) - F(S_0, 0; -\tau) < F(S_0, 0; \tau) - F(S_0, 0; 0)$$

It follows that

$$\bar{F}(S_0, 0; \tau) > F(S_0, 0; 0) \qquad (14.8)$$

That is, the average of the bid and ask prices of the option is a biased-high estimate of its zero-transactions-cost price.[9] Thus, symmetry of the bid and ask prices of the stock around its zero-transactions-cost price does not imply a corresponding symmetry for the bid and ask prices of the call option.

To provide some indication of the size of the effect on option prices induced by transactions costs in the underlying stock, consider the following numerical example of an at-the-money two-period call option: the exercise price is \$100; the interest rate is 5 percent; and the array of stock prices is $S_0 = \$100$; $S_{11} = \$90$; $S_{12} = \$115$; $S_{21} = \$70$; $S_{22} = \$110$; $S_{23} = \$90$; $S_{24} = \$140$. The bid and ask prices for the option, $F(100, 0; -\tau)$ and $F(100, 0; \tau)$, along with the initial number of shares required to hedge the position, are presented in Table 14.1 for transactions costs of 0.1 percent, 0.5 percent, and 1 percent. With transactions costs in that range, the effect on the initial hedge ratio of shares of stock per option is small. For $\tau = 0.01$ versus the zero-cost case, the difference in the number of shares is less than 3 percent. The asymmetry between the bid and ask prices is also small. For $\tau = 0.01$, the average of the bid and ask prices is \$15.63 versus \$15.61 for the $\tau = 0$ case. However, the effect of transactions

---

9 The magnitude of the bias is O(τ^2), and therefore typically quite small.

Table 14.1 Bid and Ask Call-Option Prices with Transactions Costs

Assumed Interest Rate and Stock Price Environment

$R = 1.05$	$S_{11} = \$90$	$S_{21} = \$70$	$S_{23} = \$90$
$S_0 = \$100$	$S_{12} = \$115$	$S_{22} = \$110$	$S_{24} = \$140$

	Intermediary Sells Call Option ($E = \$100$)			Intermediary Buys Call Option ($E = \$100$)		
Commission Rate, τ	Initial Hedge Ratio $N(100, 0; \tau)$	Ask Price $F(100, 0; \tau)(\$)$	Percentage Above $F(100, 0; 0)(\%)$	Initial Hedge Ratio $-N(100, 0; -\tau)$	Bid Price $F(100, 0; -\tau)(\$)$	Percentage Below $F(100, 0; 0)(\%)$
0.000	0.7038	15.61	0.00	−0.7038	15.61	0.00
0.001	0.7054	15.76	0.98	−0.7022	15.46	0.98
0.005	0.7116	16.38	4.95	−0.6957	14.85	4.88
0.010	0.7192	17.17	9.96	−0.6873	14.10	9.69

costs on the levels of the bid and ask prices is substantial. The percentage premium of the ask price above the zero-cost price is approximately linear in τ and equal to 10τ. Thus, the percentage premium is about 1 percent for $\tau = 0.001$ and 10 percent for $\tau = 0.01$. Similar results hold for the percentage discount of the bid price below the zero-cost price. Hence, the percentage spread between the bid and ask price is approximately 20τ. Although the price of the stock is much larger than the option price, the *dollar* spread between the bid and ask prices of the option is larger than the corresponding spread for the stock. Dollar spreads of $0.20, $1.00, and $2.00 for the stock induce respective spreads in the option prices of $0.30, $1.53, and $3.07.

Care should always be exercised in drawing strong inferences from a single example of a simple model. Nevertheless, these findings seem to indicate that for investors facing high, but empirically relevant, levels of transactions costs for trading stocks, the cost of synthetically creating their own option contracts and other derivative securities can be prohibitively high.

One would, of course, expect that the costs for financial intermediaries to transact in stocks are considerably lower than for most investors. Further, even the lower transaction-cost numbers in Table 14.1 may significantly overstate the actual costs to intermediaries that create options as an ongoing business. As discussed in footnotes 5–7, the calculations leading to Table 14.1 assume that the intermediary carries no inventory of either stocks or options and that each position is perfectly hedged. As we discuss in Section 14.4, a more complete analysis would take account of the opportunities for intermediaries to create and optimally manage such inventories to net out many of the transactions otherwise required to hedge individual option exposures. Moreover, for controlling the risks of intermediaries with derivative-security liabilities contingent on many different stocks, diversification may provide a cost-reducing alternative to a complete hedge of each position.

In summary, the two-period binomial model illustrates how bid and ask prices for derivative securities can be endogenously determined from the transaction-cost structure of their underlying securities. The analysis shows that the percentage spreads in the production costs of derivative securities can be many times larger than the spreads in their underlying securities. Hence, even with modest transactions costs for investors in traded securities, there is an economic function for financial intermediaries that specialize in the creation of derivative securities and take advantage of economies of scale to produce them at a greatly reduced cost.

14.3 PRODUCTION THEORY FOR ZERO-TRANSACTION-COST FINANCIAL INTERMEDIARIES

As we have seen, transactions costs among investors and corporate issuers are virtually a requirement to justify an important economic role for financial intermediation.[10] However, as we have also seen, explicit recognition of such costs can cause even the most simple of models to become extraordinarily complex. As suggested in the introduction, a happy compromise is to assume that some agents face significant transactions costs, but that financial intermediaries, as the lowest-cost transactors in the financial markets, do not. Hence, for the balance of the chapter, we proceed under that assumption and develop the general theory for production and pricing of derivative securities by intermediaries.

An *Arrow–Debreu pure state-contingent security* is a security that pays its holder $1 if a particular state of the world obtains at a particular point in time, and otherwise pays nothing. More than a generation ago, Arrow demonstrated that the payoff structure for any state-contingent security can be exactly replicated by a portfolio combination of pure securities. Hence, to avoid arbitrage, the equilibrium price of the state-contingent security can be expressed as a weighted sum of the prices of these pure securities.[11] As discussed in preceding chapters, it was recognized from the outset that the Black–Scholes approach to option pricing could also be applied to the pricing of derivative securities in general. However, it was not until later that these two theories of valuation were explicitly connected. Ross (1976b), Hakansson (1976), Banz and Miller (1978), and Breeden and Litzenberger (1978) were among the first to show that combinations of options could be used to create pure securities and that these pure securities could be used to price derivative securities.

In this section, we derive the natural analog to Arrow–Debreu pure securities in the continuous-time model and demonstrate their application to the pricing of contingent-claim securities. This done, we go on to show

10 Information costs together with agency problems that prohibit the direct sale of information to investors can, of course, justify certain types of financial intermediation such as mutual funds. Regulation and special features of the tax laws may also induce the creation of specialized financial instruments and institutions. However, in the absence of transactions costs, it is difficult to explain the complex structure of financial intermediaries and their wide scope of activities that we observe in the real world.

11 See the classical works of Arrow (1953, 1964) and Debreu (1959) for the original development of pure state-contingent securities. There is an enormous literature based on the Arrow–Debreu model (cf. Radner, 1972, and Merton, 1982a, 1990a, Section 5).

the explicit connections between option pricing theory and the pricing of these pure securities.

In Section 13.2, we derived the price of a general derivative security with payoffs that are a function of a traded asset's price and time. Under Assumptions 1–6 of that chapter, it was shown that the price of the derivative security, $F(V, t)$, will satisfy

$$0 = \tfrac{1}{2}\sigma^2 V^2 F_{11} + (rV - D_1)F_1 - rF + F_2 + D_2 \qquad (14.9)$$

for $0 \leqslant \underline{V}(t) < V < \overline{V}(t) \leqslant \infty$ and $t < T$, subject to the boundary conditions

$$F[\overline{V}(t), t] = f[\overline{V}(t), t] \qquad (14.10a)$$

$$F[\underline{V}(t), t] = g[\underline{V}(t), t] \qquad (14.10b)$$

$$F(V, T) = h(V) \qquad (14.10c)$$

Subscripts on F in (14.9) denote partial derivatives with respect to V and t. $D_1(V, t)$ and $D_2(V, t)$ denote the cash-flow rates paid to the holders of the traded asset and its derivative security, respectively. The limited liability of the traded asset implies that $V(t) = 0$ only if $V(t + \tau) = 0$ and $D_1(0, t + \tau) = 0$ for all $\tau > 0$. Without loss of generality, we can assume that $D_2(0, t) = 0.$[12] As discussed in Chapter 13, D_2, f, g, and h specify the payoff function for the derivative security.

In the analysis to follow, we assume that the stochastic process governing the dynamics of the traded asset is such that prob$\{V(\tau) = 0 | V(t) > 0\} = 0$ for $t \leqslant \tau < \infty.$[13] Let $\pi[V(t), t; E, T]$ denote the price at time t of the particular derivative security with a payoff structure given by $D_2 = 0$, and for $V(T) = V$ and $E > 0$

$$\pi(V, T; E, T) = \delta(E - V) \qquad (14.11)$$

where $\delta(x)$ denotes the Dirac delta function with the properties that $\delta(x) = 0$ for $x \neq 0$ and $\delta(0)$ is infinite in such a way that $\int_a^b \delta(x)\,dx = 1$ for any $a < 0 < b.$[14] We now show that the derivative securities defined by

12   Because $V(t) = 0$ implies that $V(t + \tau) = 0$ for $\tau > 0$, the capitalized value of any promised payments, $D_2(0, t + \tau)$, can be incorporated into the termination function $g(0, t)$. Thereby, we can formally set $D_2(0, t + \tau) = 0$ without loss of generality.

13   That is, we assume that $V(t) = 0$ is an *inaccessible boundary* for finite t. For example, this assumption is satisfied if the underlying asset has a proportional payout policy, $D_1(V, t) = \rho(t)V, 0 \leqslant \rho(t) < \infty$ for all t and σ is a constant. General conditions are given in Karlin and Taylor (1981, pp. 226–50). See also Mandl (1968, pp. 24–5) and Merton (1975a; this volume, Appendix 17B).

14   $\delta(x)$ is not a function in the usual sense, and instead, belongs to an extended class called "generalized functions." Cf. Dettman (1969, pp. 228–9).

(14.11) for various values of E and T are essentially Arrow–Debreu pure securities, extended to an environment with a continuum of states defined by the price of the traded asset and time.[15]

Let $dE > 0$ denote the infinitesimal differential of the parameter E. Consider a portfolio strategy that at time t purchases dE units of each of the continuum of derivative securities with parameter values $E \in [E_1, E_2]$ and $0 < E_1 < E_2$. If the portfolio is held until time T and $V(T) = V$, then from (14.11), the value of the portfolio is given by

$$\int_{E_1}^{E_2} \delta(E - V) \, dE = 1 \quad \text{if} \quad E_1 < V < E_2$$

$$= 0 \quad \text{otherwise} \quad\quad (14.12)$$

The cost of acquiring this portfolio at time t is $\int_{E_1}^{E_2} \pi[V(t), t; E, T] \, dE$. If we undertake the particular limiting strategy where $E_2 = \bar{E} + dE/2$ and $E_1 = \bar{E} - dE/2$, then from (14.12), the value of the portfolio is, in the limit, \$1 if $V(T) = \bar{E}$ and \$0 otherwise. By the Mean Value Theorem, the cost of the portfolio at time t is $\pi[V(t), t; \bar{E}, T] \, dE$. Thus, for $E > 0$, $\pi[V(t), t; E, T] \, dE$ is the price at time t of an Arrow–Debreu state-contingent security that pays \$1 at time T if $V(T) = E$ and nothing otherwise.[16]

Consider the limiting portfolio strategy in which $E_2 \to \infty$ and $E_1 \to 0$. From (14.12) and the assumption that $V(T) > 0$ with probability one, the value of the portfolio at time T will be \$1 for all possible values of $V(T)$. Therefore, to rule out arbitrage between the riskless security and the derivative securities, their prices for all $V(t)$ and $t < T$ must satisfy[17]

---

15 In the usual applications of the Arrow–Debreu model, the number of states is countable, and the payoffs to the pure securities are contingent on "states of nature." That is, which state is realized is assumed to be unaffected by the actions of economic agents, either individually or collectively. We do assume here that the actions of any one agent have no effect on the time path of $V(t)$. However, $V(t)$ is a price, and hence is endogenously determined within the economic system. Thus, unlike the usual case, the state-contingent securities here depend on a state-space description that is controlled by the collective actions of economic agents. In Chapter 16, we analyze the creation and pricing of Arrow–Debreu securities in the continuous-time model with the state space defined by truly exogenous variables.
16 As is well known for state-contingent prices in the standard Arrow–Debreu model, the $\{\pi(V, t; E, T)\}$ have a functional structure like that of a conditional probability density function. As with the probability density for a diffusion process, π is an order-one function, but the probability that $V(T) = E$ is infinitesimal if $V(t) = E$ is not an absorbing-barrier point for $t \leq T$. Hence, the value of a security that pays a finite amount only in that state is also infinitesimal.
17 This result is a well-known property of pure securities in the Arrow–Debreu model. Cf. Merton (1982a, 1990a, Section 5).

$$\exp[-r(T - t)] = \int_0^\infty \pi[V(t), t; E, T] \, dE \qquad (14.13)$$

Because all possible payoffs to each of the derivative securities are nonnegative, the no-arbitrage condition requires that $\pi(V, t; E, T) \geq 0$. Hence, from (14.13), we have that $\pi(V, t; E, T)$ is a bounded function in the limit as $V \to \infty$.

If, at time t, we construct a portfolio that holds $E \, dE$ units of each of the continuum of derivative securities with parameter values $E \in (0, \infty)$, then from (14.11), the value of the portfolio at T is given by

$$\int_0^\infty E\delta(E - V) \, dE = V$$

for $V(T) = V$. An investment in one unit of the traded asset at time t will also be worth $V(T)$ at T. However, in addition, that investment will also receive all payouts to the asset, $\{D_1\}$, between t and T. Hence, to avoid arbitrage opportunities between the traded asset and the derivative securities, their prices must satisfy

$$V(t) \geq \int_0^\infty \pi[V(t), t; E, T]E \, dE \qquad (14.14)$$

From (14.14) and the nonnegativity of π, we have that $\pi(V, t; E, T)E/V$ is a bounded function in the limit as $V \to 0$. Therefore, for $E > 0$ and fixed, $\pi(V, t; E, T)/V$ is bounded in the limit as $V \to 0$.

From the derivation in Chapter 13, to avoid arbitrage opportunities, $\pi(V, t; E, T)$ must satisfy (14.9) with $D_2 = 0$, $\underline{V}(t) = 0$, and $\overline{V}(t) = \infty$ for all $E > 0$ and $t < T$. The boundary conditions required for a unique solution are that $|\pi(V, t; E, T)/V|$ is bounded and that (14.11) is satisfied. Thus, under the hypothesized conditions 1–6 of Chapter 13, we have determined the prices of a complete set of pure state-contingent securities, where the state space is defined by the price of the traded asset and time.

In the context of this chapter, $\pi(V, t; E, T)$ is the production cost to a zero-transaction-cost financial intermediary for creating this security at time t when $V(t) = V$. From Chapter 13, the production technology for replicating the payoffs to the security calls for a total portfolio investment at time t of $\pi(V, t; E, T)$ dollars with $[\partial\pi(V, t; E, T)/\partial V]V$ dollars in the traded asset and the balance in the riskless security.

The connection between these pure state-contingent securities and the theory of financial intermediation can be made apparent by examining the general class of derivative securities with payoff structures given by

(14.10a)–(14.10c), with $\underline{V}(t) = 0$ and $\overline{V}(t) = \infty$ for all t. It is well known, from the Green's functions method of solving linear differential equations, that the solution to (14.9), subject to these boundary conditions, can be written as[18]

$$F(V, t) = \int_t^T \int_0^\infty D_2(E, \tau)\pi(V, t; E, \tau) \, dE \, d\tau + \int_0^\infty h(E)\pi(V, t; E, T) \, dE \tag{14.15}$$

Just as in the standard Arrow–Debreu model, the payoff structure to this derivative security can be expressed as a linear combination of the payoff structures of the pure state-contingent securities. Thus, these securities provide the fundamental "building blocks" for constructing more complex securities. The term "building blocks" is apt because none of these pure securities, taken individually, is likely to be demanded by any customer of the intermediary. Nevertheless, once an intermediary has determined the production costs for the complete set of state-contingent securities, it can use simple quadrature in (14.15) to calculate the production cost for any derivative security with $\underline{V}(t) = 0$ and $\overline{V}(t) = \infty$ for all t.

Equation (14.15) is a powerful tool for the evaluation of derivative-security prices. It cannot, however, be applied to securities for which there is a positive probability that either $V(t) \leq \underline{V}(t)$ or $V(t) \geq \overline{V}(t)$ for some $t < T$. To see why, consider the example of an American put option. As we know from Theorem 8.13, there always exists, at each point in time, a sufficiently small but positive stock price such that it pays to exercise the put immediately. Let $\{\underline{V}(t) > 0\}$ denote the early-exercise schedule of stock prices such that the put option is exercised at t if $V(t) \leq \underline{V}(t)$. From (14.10b), $g[\underline{V}(t), t] = X - \underline{V}(t)$, and from (14.10c), $h(V) = \max(0, X - V)$, where X is the exercise price of the put. If $\underline{V}(t)$ is a continuous function of t, then a naive application of (14.15) might suggest that the put price can be written as

$$F(V, t) = \int_t^T [X - \underline{V}(\tau)]\pi[V, t; \underline{V}(\tau), \tau] \, d\tau + \int_0^X (X - E)\pi(V, t; E, T) \, dE \tag{14.16}$$

However, (14.16) gives an incorrect evaluation. For times t_1 and t_2 such that $t \leq t_1 < t_2 \leq T$, the events that $V(t_1) = \underline{V}(t_1)$ and $V(t_2) = \underline{V}(t_2)$ are not mutually exclusive. Equation (14.16) implies that, if both events occur, the put holder will receive payments of $X - \underline{V}(t_1)$ at $t = t_1$ *and* $X - \underline{V}(t_2)$ at $t = t_2$. But, of course, if the put is exercised at $t = t_1$, it cannot also be

18   See Dettman (1969, Ch. 5).

exercised at $t = t_2$. Thus, when early exercise is possible, (14.16) overstates the value of the put.[19]

The American put option is an example of a contingent-claim security with a *path-dependent* payoff structure. That is, looking forward from the perspective of date t, the payoff at time $\tau > t$ depends not only on the price of the underlying asset at τ, $V(\tau)$, but also on the time path followed by the asset's price between t and τ. In contrast, the payoff to the pure state-contingent security given by (14.11) depends only on the price of the traded asset at date T and therefore is not path dependent.[20] Thus, to have the right to a payment of $X - \underline{V}(\tau)$ dollars at time τ, contingent on both $V(\tau) = \underline{V}(\tau)$ and $V(s) > \underline{V}(s)$ for all $s \in [t, \tau)$, is not the same as owning $[X - \underline{V}(\tau)]\,d\tau$ units of a pure security that, collectively, pay $X - \underline{V}(\tau)$ dollars at time τ, contingent only on $V(\tau) = \underline{V}(\tau)$. It is that lack of equivalence that causes (14.16) to fail as a valuation formula.

The pure-securities approach to valuation can be modified to accommodate derivative securities with path-dependent payoffs. To do this, one constructs a set of state-contingent securities that are also path dependent by replacing the payoff function (14.11) with the condition that $\pi(V, T; E, T) = \delta(E - V)$ if $\underline{V}(t) < V(t) < \overline{V}(t)$ for *all* $t < T$ and $\pi(V, T; E, T) = 0$ otherwise.[21] With this modified set of pure securities, one can use quadrature in a equation like (14.15) or (14.16) to determine the prices of all derivative securities with the *same* specified schedules, $\{\underline{V}(t)\}$ and $\{\overline{V}(t)\}$. Note, however, that a different set of pure securities is required for each specification of $\{\underline{V}(t)\}$ and $\{\overline{V}(t)\}$. Unfortunately, these schedules tend to be specific to each particular derivative security.[22] Hence, with path-dependent payoff structures, there will generally be no computational advantage for this technique over the direct solution of (14.9), subject to boundary conditions (14.10), for each individual derivative security.

19　Equation (14.16), with $\underline{V}(t) \equiv 0$, does provide the correct price for a *European* put option, because $\pi(V, t; 0, \tau) = 0$ for $t \leqslant \tau \leqslant T$ and $V > 0$.

20　Path-independent and path-dependent processes are directly related to Markov processes. The returns on a security with path-dependent payoffs will not be a Markov process in $V(t)$. Because their payoffs are path independent, pure state-contingent securities' returns are Markov processes in $V(t)$.

21　Formally, we define an indicator variable $X(t)$ such that $X(t) = 1$ if $\underline{V}(s) < V(s) < \overline{V}(s)$ for all $s < t$ and $X(t) = 0$, otherwise. The path-dependent pure-security payoff function becomes $\pi(V, X, T; E, T) = X\delta(E - V)$. Although not Markov in $V(t)$ alone, $\pi[V(t), X(t), t; E, T]$ does follow a Markov process in $V(t)$ and $X(t)$. The general method of expanding the number of variables to convert a non-Markov process to a Markov process is discussed in Cox and Miller (1968, p. 262).

22　Consider, for example, a collection of American put options on the same traded asset. From Section 8.8, the optimal early-exercise boundary will depend on both the exercise price and the expiration date. Thus, $\{\underline{V}(t)\}$ will be different for each of these derivative securities.

To demonstrate the direct connection between the pricing theories of options and pure securities in the continuous-time model, we present an alternative derivation of the pure-security prices along the lines of Breeden and Litzenberger (1978). Let $F(V, t; E, T)$ denote the solution to (14.9) for a European call option with exercise price E and expiration date T. Consider an option investment strategy that at time t contains long and short positions in call options with the same expiration date T, such that one "unit" of the strategy holds a long position in an option with exercise price $E - \epsilon$; a short position in two options with exercise price E; and a long position in an option with exercise price $E + \epsilon$. This particular strategy is commonly called a "butterfly spread."[23] The payoff function at time T to one unit of this spread is given by $\max[0, V(T) + \epsilon - E] - 2\max[0, V(T) - E] + \max[0, V(T) - E - \epsilon]$. For $X \equiv E - V(T)$, let $Q(X; \epsilon)$ denote the payoff function at time T to a portfolio containing $1/\epsilon^2$ units of the butterfly spread. It follows that Q can be written as

$$
\begin{aligned}
Q(X; \epsilon) &= 0 & X &\le -\epsilon \\
&= (X + \epsilon)/\epsilon^2 & -\epsilon &< X \le 0 \\
&= (\epsilon - X)/\epsilon^2 & 0 &< X \le \epsilon \\
&= 0 & \epsilon &< X \le E \qquad (14.17)
\end{aligned}
$$

The cost of acquiring this portfolio at time t is $[F(V, t; E - \epsilon, T) - 2F(V, t; E, T) + F(V, t; E + \epsilon, T)]/\epsilon^2$ for $V(t) = V$. From (14.17), we have that the limit as $\epsilon \to 0$ of $Q(X; \epsilon)$ is $\delta(X)$, which is exactly the payoff function of a pure state-contingent security, as given in (14.11).[24] Therefore, to avoid arbitrage, the cost of acquiring the portfolio must, as $\epsilon \to 0$, approach $\pi(V, t; E, T)$. It follows that

$$
\begin{aligned}
\pi(V, t; E, T) \\
= \lim_{\epsilon \to 0} \frac{F(V, t; E - \epsilon, T) - 2F(V, t; E, T) + F(V, t; E + \epsilon, T)}{\epsilon^2} \\
= \frac{\partial^2 F(V, t; E, T)}{\partial E^2} \qquad (14.18)
\end{aligned}
$$

---

23 Cf. Cox and Rubinstein (1985, pp. 15 and 17).
24 For any $\lambda > 0$ and for all X such that $|X| \ge \lambda$, there clearly exists an $\epsilon > 0$, such that $Q(X; \epsilon) = 0$. $Q(0; \epsilon) = 1/\epsilon$, which diverges as $\epsilon \to 0$. However, $\int_{-\epsilon}^{\epsilon} Q(x; \epsilon) \, dx = [\int_{-\epsilon}^{0}(x + \epsilon) \, dx + \int_{0}^{\epsilon}(\epsilon - x) \, dx]/\epsilon^2 = 1$. Hence, in the limit as $\epsilon \to 0$, $Q(X; \epsilon)$ becomes the Dirac delta function, $\delta(E - V)$.

Thus, if one has the solutions to (14.9) for European call options of all exercise prices and expiration dates, then the prices for a complete set of pure state-contingent securities can be determined from (14.18). As an illustration, suppose that the dynamics of the traded asset are such that $D_1(V, t) = 0$ for all $t \leq T$ and σ^2 is a constant. These are the dynamics assumed by Black and Scholes (1973) and hence European call-option prices will satisfy their original formula.[25] Taking the second derivative of their formula with respect to the exercise price, we have from (14.18) that

$$\pi(V, t; E, T) = \frac{\exp[-r(T - t)]\Phi'(d_2)}{E\sigma(T - t)^{1/2}} \qquad (14.19)$$

where

$$d_2 \equiv \frac{\log(V/E) + (r - \sigma^2/2)(T - t)}{\sigma(T - t)^{1/2}}$$

and $\Phi'(y) \equiv \exp(-y^2/2)/(2\pi)^{1/2}$, the standard normal probability density function.

In Section 10.2, we developed the Cox–Ross "risk-neutral" technique for pricing options. To complete our demonstration of the connection between option pricing theory and the pure-securities approach to valuation, we now show the equivalence between the Cox–Ross pricing formula and (14.15). We begin with the special case leading to (14.19) in which the dynamics of the traded-asset price are given by $dV = \alpha V \, dt + \sigma V \, dz$.

As described in Chapter 10, the Cox–Ross procedure formally replaces the dynamics for the actual traded-asset returns with $dV^* = rV^* \, dt + \sigma V^* \, dz$, where $V^*(t)$ denotes the price of the traded asset in the associated risk-neutral equilibrium with $V^*(0) = V(0)$. The option price is then determined as the present value of an option on V^*, discounted at the riskless interest rate. Let $p(x, t; X, T) \equiv \text{prob}\{V^*(T) = X | V^*(t) = x\}$ denote the conditional probability density function for V^*. In the case in which r and σ^2 are constants, the distribution of $V^*(T)$, conditional on $V^*(t) = x$, is log-normal, and therefore

$$p(x, t; X, T) = X\Phi'(d)/[x\sigma(T - t)^{1/2}] \qquad (14.20)$$

where $d \equiv [\log(X/x) - (r - \sigma^2/2)(T - t)]/\sigma(T - t)^{1/2}$. Noting that $\Phi'(y) = \Phi'(-y)$, we have from (14.20) that (14.19) can be rewritten as

$$\pi(V, t; E, T) = \exp[-r(T - t)]p(V, t; E, T) \qquad (14.21)$$

---

25 Cf. equation (9.15). Bick (1982) modifies the Breeden–Litzenberger valuation formula for the case where there are mass points in the probability distribution for the underlying traded security.

Hence, the price of a pure state-contingent security is equal to the product of the price of a discount bond that pays \$1 at time T and the Cox–Ross risk-neutral probability density function.

With $\underline{V}(t) = 0$, $\overline{V}(t) = \infty$, and $D_1(V, t) = 0$ for all $t < T$, we have from (14.15) and (14.21) that the price of a general derivative security can be written as

$$F(V, t) = \int_0^\infty h(E)\pi(V, t; E, T)\, dE$$

$$= \exp[-r(T - t)] \int_0^\infty h(E)p(V, t; E, T)\, dE \quad (14.22)$$

But the second line of (14.22) is exactly the Cox–Ross option pricing formula applied to a general derivative security.

Consider now the general case in which $dV^* = [rV^* - D_1(V^*, t)]\, dt + \sigma V^*\, dz$, with $D_1(V^*, t) \neq 0$ and $\sigma = \sigma(V^*, t)$. In Chapter 3, it was shown in (3.42) that the conditional probability density function for this diffusion process satisfies

$$0 = \tfrac{1}{2}\sigma^2(x, t)x^2 p_{11}(x, t; X, T) + [rx - D_1(x, t)]p_1(x, t; X, T)$$

$$+ p_2(x, t; X, T) \quad (14.23)$$

subject to the boundary conditions $p(x, t; X, T)/x$ bounded for all x and $p(x, T; X, T) = \delta(X - x)$. Define

$$\hat{\pi}(V, t; E, T) \equiv \pi(V, t; E, T)/\exp[-r(T - t)]$$

By substitution of $\hat{\pi}$ for π in (14.9) with $D_2 \equiv 0$, and the rearrangement of terms, we have that

$$0 = \tfrac{1}{2}\sigma^2 V^2 \hat{\pi}_{11} + (rV - D_1)\hat{\pi}_1 + \hat{\pi}_2 \quad (14.24)$$

Moreover, $|\hat{\pi}(V, t; E, T)/V|$ is bounded for all V and $E > 0$ because $|\pi(V, t; E, T)/V|$ is so bounded. Further, from (14.11), $\hat{\pi}(V, T; E, T) = \pi(V, T; E, T) = \delta(E - V)$. By inspection of (14.23) and (14.24), together with their respective boundary conditions, we have that $\hat{\pi}(V, t; E, T) = p(V, t, E; T)$. Therefore, (14.21) and (14.22) obtain in the general case.

In Sections 10.2 and 10.3, it was convenient to choose as numeraire, $b(t) \equiv \exp[\int_0^t r(s)\, ds]$, the price at time t of one unit of a portfolio that initially invests \$1 in the riskless security and retains all earnings. Selection of that particular numeraire here leads to an interpretation of pure-security prices as probability density functions.

In this price system, the price of the traded asset is given by $V^+(t) \equiv V(t)/b(t)$, and its dynamics can be expressed as $dV^+ = \{(\alpha - r)V^+ - D_1[b(t)V^+, t]/b(t)\}\, dt + \sigma V^+\, dz$. Because the interest rate in this system is always zero, the probability density function for the associated Cox–Ross risk-neutral equilibrium price of the asset, $p^+(x, t; X, T)$, satisfies (14.23) with $r = 0$.[26] If $\pi^+[V^+(t), t; E^+, T]$ denotes the price of a pure state-contingent security with payoff function at time T given by $\delta(E^+ - V^+)$ for $V^+(T) = V^+$, then π^+ will satisfy (14.9) with $r = 0$ and $D_2 \equiv 0$. But, by inspection, (14.23) and (14.9) are identical equations if $D_2 \equiv 0$ and $r = 0$. Hence, we have that

$$\pi^+(V^+, t; E^+, T) = p^+(V^+, t; E^+, T) \qquad (14.25)$$

which is (14.21) with $r = 0$. Thus, in a price system normalized by the cumulative return on the riskless security, the prices of pure state-contingent securities are equal to the corresponding Cox–Ross risk-neutral conditional probability density functions.[27]

14.4   RISK MANAGEMENT FOR FINANCIAL INTERMEDIARIES

Financial intermediaries, like other firms, issue stock and other liability instruments to investors in order to raise capital for operations. However, intermediaries are different from other business firms because they create explicit liabilities whenever they sell their products. Although intermediaries do act as agents in some transactions, their primary function is to act as principals and provide financial instruments and products that cannot be efficiently supported by trading in organized secondary markets.[28] The

---

26   Although it has been assumed throughout this chapter that r is a constant, the results derived here with $b(t)$ as numeraire apply even if, in the original price system, the interest rate changes stochastically.

27   Equation (14.25) verifies the claim in footnote 16 that pure-security prices have a functional structure like that of a conditional probability density. In analyses using the Arrow–Debreu model, it is common practice to select a normalizing price system such that, for each point in time, the sum of pure-security prices across all possible states of the world is equal to unity. With the additional condition of nonnegative prices, it follows that all pure-security prices lie within the unit simplex. In the continuous-time model, the corresponding normalization leads to $\int_0^\infty \pi^+(V^+, t; E^+, T)\, dE^+ = 1$ for all $V^+, E^+ > 0$, and $t \leqslant T < \infty$. This condition follows immediately from (14.13) with $r = 0$.

28   In effect, the test is whether the bid–ask spread charged by the intermediary is smaller than the one that market makers would charge the customer if the instrument were traded in an organized market. A stereotypical financial intermedi-

purchasers of these products are therefore *de facto* liabilityholders of the intermediary. Indeed, as we all know, the vast bulk of a typical intermediary's liabilities are held by its customers.

In general, customers, unlike investors in the firm, prefer to have the payoffs on their contracts as insensitive as possible to the fortunes of the firm itself. For example, a customer who buys a warranty on his new car from an automobile manufacturer wants the repairs paid for in the event that the car is defective. In fact, he has a contract that pays for repairs in the joint contingency that the car is defective *and* the automobile manufacturer is financially solvent. Even if an actuarially fair reduction in the price of the warranty were made to reflect the risk of insolvency, it is likely that the customer would still prefer the warranty with the least default risk.[29] As with customers of automobile manufacturers, so with customers of financial intermediaries. Thus, the success of an intermediary depends not only on charging adequate prices to cover its production costs, but also on providing adequate assurances to its customers that promised payments will be made. Hence, an important part of the management of financial intermediaries is the measurement and control of the risk exposures created by issuing their financial products.

As we have seen, contingent-claims analysis (CCA) can be used to determine the production process and cost for an intermediary to create virtually any financial product that has the properties of a derivative security. To match a prescribed payoff function, the intermediary need only set down the appropriate boundary conditions in (14.10) and solve (14.9). Therefore, it is in principle no more difficult to create derivative securities with specialized payoff patterns than it is to create ones with standard patterns (e.g. call options). CCA thus provides the means for intermediaries to create custom financial products in an "assembly-line" fashion. In such an environment, intermediaries are likely to have a diverse array of complex financial assets and liabilities. This diversity and complexity makes measurement of the risk exposure for such intermediaries a

---

ary purchases and issues illiquid or nontraded financial instruments to its customers, and uses the financial markets to raise capital and to hedge its positions. As in the case of mutual funds, the intermediary may also create "pools" of traded assets for its customers if their individual demands for these assets are not an economic lot size for direct market purchases and sales.

29 For example, even at actuarially fair prices, customers are likely to prefer a guaranteed put option on the general stock market to one with a payoff function that is also contingent (in a significant way) on the solvency of the issuer of the option. Much the same point is made with respect to the viability of organized futures and forward markets in Section 10.3. Regulations on capital requirements, collateral, guarantees and insurance purchased from external sources, and escrows of the intermediary's assets, are among the devices used to insulate customers from the business risk of the intermediary.

difficult task, even in a theoretical model. CCA can be used to significantly reduce the difficulty of that task.

Consider an intermediary that issues derivative securities on n different traded assets. Let V_k denote the price of asset k with dynamics specified as

$$dV_k = (\alpha_k V_k - D_1^k)\,dt + \sigma_k V_k\,dz_k \qquad (14.26)$$

where α_k and σ_k are the expected rate of return and standard deviation of return respectively, and D_1^k is the payout rate on asset k, $k = 1,\dots, n$. For $i = 1,\dots, m_k$ and $k = 1,\dots, n$, let $F^{ki}(V, t)$ denote the solution to (14.9) subject to boundary conditions (14.10) that are appropriate for the ith type of derivative security, which is contingent on the price of traded asset k. If $V_k(t) = V_k$ at time t, then $F^{ki}(V_k, t)$ is the unit production cost to the intermediary and it is also the value to the intermediary of owning one unit of derivative security i. From Itô's lemma and (14.9), we have that the dollar return to the intermediary from owning one unit of the derivative security between t and $t + dt$ can be written as[30]

$$
\begin{aligned}
dF^{ki} + D_2^{ki}\,dt &= [F_1^{ki}(V_k, t)(\alpha_k - r)V_k + rF^{ki}(V_k, t)]\,dt \\
&\quad + F_1^{ki}(V_k, t)\sigma_k V_k\,dz_k \\
&= F_1^{ki}(V_k, t)(dV_k + D_1^k\,dt) + [F^{ki}(V_k, t) - F_1^{ki}(V_k, t)V_k]r\,dt
\end{aligned}
$$
$$(14.27)$$

where D_2^{ki} is the payout rate on derivative security i and subscripts on F denote partial derivatives as in (14.9). By inspection of (14.27), owning one unit of derivative security i between t and $t + dt$ produces the same dollar return as holding $F_1^{ki}(V_k, t)$ units of traded asset k and $F^{ki}(V_k, t) - F_1^{ki}(V_k, t)V_k$ dollars of the riskless security, over the same period.

If at time t the intermediary owns M_{ki} units of this derivative security,[31] then its exposure from this position between t and $t + dt$ is equivalent to owning N_{ki}^e units of traded asset k and B_{ki}^e dollars of the riskless security where $N_{ki}^e \equiv M_{ki}F_1^{ki}(V_k, t)$ and $B_{ki}^e \equiv M_{ki}[F^{ki}(V_k, t) - F_1^{ki}(V_k, t)V_k]$. Adding up the exposures from all types of derivative securities (contingent on the price of asset k), we have that the total exposure from these positions between t and $t + dt$ is equivalent to owning $N_k^e(\equiv \Sigma_1^{m_k} N_{ki}^e)$ units of asset k and $B_k^e(\equiv \Sigma_1^{m_k} B_{ki}^e)$ dollars in the riskless security. Thus, the intermediary can express its entire risk exposure on the m_k different types of derivative

---

30 By Itô's lemma, $dF^{ki} = (F_2^{ki} + \sigma_k^2 V_k^2 F_{11}^{ki}/2)\,dt + F_1^{ki}\,dV_k$. By substituting for $F_2^{ki} + \sigma_k^2 V_k^2 F_{11}^{ki}/2$ from (14.9) and rearranging terms, we arrive at (14.27).
31 If $M_{ki} < 0$, then the intermediary has a short position (i.e. a liability) of $|M_{ki}|$ units of the derivative security.

securities in terms of the risk exposure to just two traded securities: asset k and the riskless security.[32]

The intermediary can, of course, make this conversion for all derivative securities in its portfolio. If $W(t)$ denotes the net value of the financial-security holdings of the intermediary at time t, then we have that

$$W(t) = \sum_1^n \sum_1^{m_k} M_{ki}(t)F^{ki}(V_k, t) + \sum_1^n N_k(t)V_k + B(t) \quad (14.28)$$

where $B(t)$ is the dollar amount of the riskless security held at t and $N_k(t)$ is the number of units of traded asset k held at t, $k = 1,\ldots, n$. Thus, from (14.28), CCA provides the means for continuous valuation of the intermediary's portfolio, even if the bulk of its financial products and liabilities are not traded in organized secondary markets.

From (14.26), (14.27), and (14.28), the dollar return to the intermediary's portfolio between t and $t + dt$ can be written as

$$
\begin{aligned}
dW &= \sum_1^n \sum_1^{m_k} M_{ki}(dF^{ki} + D_2^{ki}\, dt) + \sum_1^n N_k(dV_k + D_1^k\, dt) + rB\, dt \\
&= \sum_1^n (N_k^e + N_k)(dV_k + D_1^k\, dt) + r\left(B + \sum_1^n B_k^e\right) dt \\
&= \left[\sum_1^n (N_k^e + N_k)V_k\alpha_k + \left(B + \sum_1^n B_k^e\right)r\right]dt + \sum_1^n (N_k^e + N_k)\sigma_k V_k\, dz_k
\end{aligned}
$$

$$(14.29)$$

By inspection of (14.29), we have that the intermediary's risk exposures to the $\Sigma_1^n m_k$ different derivative securities and the n traded assets can be expressed in terms of risk exposures to the n traded assets alone. Hence, by the application of CCA, risk management of the intermediary's complex portfolio can be reduced to the management of a relatively simple portfolio containing only traded assets.

The analysis leading to (14.29) assumes no transactions costs. It can nevertheless be used to identify management policies that reduce the

---

32   In practice, restating the risk exposures in these terms may be beneficial, even if $m_k = 1$. For example, many managers may have difficulty in assessing the exposure of a short position of a six-month call option on 1,000 shares of stock, with an exercise price of $110 per share, when the stock is currently selling for $100. Assuming that $F = \$8$ and $F_1 = 0.40$, they would perhaps understand better the equivalent risk-exposure statement, that they are short 400 shares of stock and have $32,000 in the riskless security.

volume of hedging transactions and thereby reduce the impact of such costs on financial intermediation. The derivation of bid–ask price spreads in Section 14.2 overstates the effect of transactions costs on an active financial intermediary, because it assumes no inventories of either traded assets or other derivative securities. To perfectly hedge its entire portfolio, the intermediary need only hold inventories of traded assets that are sufficient to hedge the *net* exposures created by its financial products. In the context of (14.29), a perfect hedge requires only that $N_k = -N_k^e$, $k = 1,...,n$.

To further illustrate the point, consider an intermediary with current exposures that are completely hedged. Now, suppose it issues call options on asset k with an equivalent exposure of N_{ki} and issues put options on asset k with an equivalent exposure of N_{kj}. Because for these instruments, $N_{ki} < 0$ and $N_{kj} > 0$, the dollar transaction in asset k required to jointly hedge these new exposures, $|(N_{ki} + N_{kj})|V_k$, is less than $(|N_{ki}| + |N_{kj}|)V_k$, the dollar amount required if each new exposure is treated as an isolated transaction. Thus, by offering a mix of "bullish" and "bearish" products, the intermediary can reduce the volume of hedging transactions in traded assets. If necessary, the intermediary can adjust its bid and ask prices for selected financial products so as to induce its customers to buy products that reduce the overall need for hedging transactions.

Even in the absence of new business, transactions in traded assets are required if the intermediary is to maintain a hedged position against its current inventory of financial products. If the policy is to maintain $N_k = -N_k^e$, then by Itô's lemma we have that

$$\mathrm{d}N_k = -\left(\tfrac{1}{2}\sigma_k^2 V_k^2 \frac{\partial^2 N_k^e}{\partial V_k^2} + \frac{\partial N_k^e}{\partial t}\right)\mathrm{d}t - \frac{\partial N_k^e}{\partial V_k}\mathrm{d}V_k \tag{14.30}$$

By inspection of (14.30), the volume of transactions induced by unexpected changes in traded-asset prices is proportional to the absolute magnitude of $\partial N_k^e/\partial V_k$. Hence, the size of transactions caused by changes in traded-asset prices can be minimized if the intermediary can maintain a hedged portfolio with $\partial N_k^e/\partial V_k$ close to zero. If we neglect the effect of new business (i.e. $\mathrm{d}M_{ki} = 0$, $i = 1,...,m_k$, $k = 1,...,n$), then from the definition of N_k^e, we have that

$$\frac{\partial N_k^e}{\partial V_k} = \sum_1^{m_k} M_{ki}F_{11}^{ki}(V_k, t) \tag{14.31}$$

If the production cost for a derivative security of type i is a strictly convex function of V_k, then $F_{11}^{ki}(V_k, t) > 0$. If it is a strictly concave function, then $F_{11}^{ki}(V_k, t) < 0$. Thus, by offering a mix of "convex" and "concave" products, the intermediary can reduce the volume of transactions in traded assets that is required to maintain a hedged portfolio.

In the parlance of option pricing analysis,[33] the hedge ratio, $N_{ki} = F_1^{ki}(V_k, t)$, is called the "delta" of derivative security i and the change in the hedge ratio, $\partial N_{ki}/\partial V_k = F_{11}^{ki}(V_k, t)$ is called the "gamma" of derivative security i. The gamma of the intermediary's aggregate position, $\partial N_k^e/\partial V_k$, characterizes the degree of local convexity or concavity of the position with respect to V_k. If $N_k = -N_k^e$, then the intermediary is perfectly hedged against any small ("local") changes in V_k. If, however, this locally hedged position is such that $\partial N_k^e/\partial V_k > 0$, then the intermediary will gain from any large ("nonlocal") changes in V_k, whether up or down.[34] Similarly, if $\partial N_k^e/\partial V_k < 0$, the intermediary will lose from any large change in V_k. Thus, for $N_k = -N_k^e$, the gamma of the aggregate position measures the intermediary's exposure to large moves in V_k. Our assumptions about the dynamics of traded-asset prices are such that nonlocal movements cannot occur. Such assurances cannot, of course, be given for the behavior of real-world asset prices. Hence, the assessment of one's exposure to convexity is an important element of risk management for practitioners.[35] Our analysis also neglects taxes. However, CCA and the resulting prescriptions for risk management by intermediaries can be modified to include taxes along the lines of Scholes (1976) and Constantinides and Scholes (1980).

As noted at the outset, risk management is important in large part, because customers are better served by products from intermediaries that have negligible default risk. However, especially (but not exclusively) because of transactions costs, perfect hedging of an intermediary's entire portfolio can be a suboptimal policy. In such cases, diversification can be used as a risk-management alternative to transacting in the traded assets. From (14.29), the instantaneous variance of the dollar return on an intermediary's portfolio can be expressed as

---

33   Cf. Cox and Rubinstein (1985, pp. 222–35).

34   If $H(V_k, t)$ denotes the value of the intermediary's position, then by Taylor's theorem, $H(V_k + X, t) - H(V_k, t) = H_1(V_k, t)X + H_{11}(V, t)X^2/2$, where V is some number satisfying $|V - V_k| \leq |X|$. If $N_k = -N_k^e$, then $H_1(V_k, t) = 0$. Hence, the change in the value is positive (negative), if $H_{11}(V, t) > 0 \, (< 0)$.

35   As we have stressed on several occasions in the preceding chapters, the risklessness of the derived hedges is contingent on a correct specification of the asset dynamics. The techniques presented in Chapter 9 can be adopted to formally recognize the possibility of nonlocal changes in asset prices. As is often the case, real-world applications of CCA are a compromise: practitioners typically assume the model presented here and then, using (14.31), adjust their holdings to create the desired gamma exposure to nonlocal movements in prices.

$$\sum_{1}^{n} \sum_{1}^{n} (N_k^e + N_k)(N_j^e + N_j)\sigma_k\sigma_j\rho_{kj}V_kV_j$$

where ρ_{kj} is the instantaneous correlation coefficient between returns on asset k and asset j. Diversity among the products offered and diversity among the underlying traded assets are essentially the two ways by which diversification can reduce the variance of the portfolio. As we have seen, a diverse product mix can decrease the absolute magnitude of the net exposure to each traded asset. Among traded assets with positively correlated returns ($\rho_{kj} > 0$), a product mix that leads to $N_k^e N_j^e < 0$ will also reduce the volatility of the intermediary's portfolio. For product mixes that lead to $N_k^e N_j^e > 0$, the intermediary can reduce portfolio variance by offering these products on traded assets with relatively small correlations among their returns (i.e. $\rho_{kj} \ll 1$, and preferably, $\rho_{kj} < 0$).

Regulation can be beneficial to both financial intermediaries and their customers if it reduces expenditures by customers on information gathering and monitoring. Regulation, whether beneficial or not, can significantly influence risk-management policy, even for an intermediary that can transact without cost. One common form of regulation is to require the intermediary to maintain a minimum level of net worth or capital if it is to continue in business. If the intermediation franchise has a positive net present value, then regulations of this type can cause value-maximizing financial intermediaries to exhibit risk-averse-like behavior in the management of their financial assets and liabilities. In choosing among financial assets (or liabilities) with the same net present values, the intermediary will prefer the mix that minimizes the probability of violating the regulatory constraint, because that choice maximizes the value of its franchise.[36]

Given the "cliff-edge" nature of the regulatory constraint, a risk-management strategy that meets this objective is to systematically maintain a put-option position on the entire portfolio of financial assets. By selecting an exercise price larger than the minimum capital requirement and a time until expiration of sufficient duration, the intermediary can protect itself against violation of the regulation and provide adequate time to raise any necessary additional capital. Although occasionally referred to as an *insured-equity* or *protective-put* strategy, this risk-management strategy is most commonly called *portfolio insurance*.[37]

36 See, for example, Chapter 20 on the investment behavior of banks covered by deposit insurance.
37 Cf. Leland (1980), Brennan and Solanki (1981), Rubinstein (1985), Luskin, ed. (1988), and Brennan and Schwartz (1989). There are a number of variations of the basic portfolio-insurance idea. For instance, having the exercise price of the put option grow at a specified rate over time can guarantee a minimum positive rate of return on the portfolio. For other variations, see, for example, Goldman, Sosin, Shepp (1979), Gatto, Geske, Litzenberger, and Sosin (1980). Brennan and Schwartz (1988), and Black and Perold (1992).

To implement this strategy, the intermediary could purchase insurance from another firm. However, as a minimum-cost transactor, it may find it more cost-effective to synthetically create its own portfolio insurance by using the CCA techniques of this and the preceding chapters. By pursuing this route, the intermediary, in effect, creates a captive portfolio-insurance subsidiary that sells the put to the parent and undertakes dynamic strategies to hedge its liability. One advantage of this approach is that the intermediary retains the mark-up or spread that would otherwise be paid to an external issuer of the insurance. This saving includes any noncompetitive profit to the issuer and the "deadweight" costs of redundant information gathering and surveillance that often arise in arms-length transactions. An external insurer of the intermediary's portfolio would surely place restrictions on the types of assets and liabilities held in the portfolio. Thus, self-insuring also allows greater flexibility in the intermediary's investment policy. The main disadvantage is, of course, that the self-insurer retains the risk that the dynamic hedging strategies fail to replicate the payoffs to a put option on the portfolio.[38] But, given their presumed financial expertise and continuous involvement in the financial markets, intermediaries are, almost surely, the best suited among individuals and institutions to bear this risk.

14.5   ON THE ROLE OF EFFICIENT FINANCIAL INTERMEDIATION IN THE CONTINUOUS-TIME MODEL

As is evident from the preceding analyses, the continuous-time model provides a rich analytical framework for developing a theory of financial intermediation that encompasses both the general infrastructure and the specific operational procedures of financial intermediaries. Perhaps less apparent is that the existence of a well-functioning financial intermediation sector in the economy can do much to justify the continuous-time model

---

38   Cf. the discussion in footnote 35. In recent years, several real-world institutional investors have adopted portfolio insurance as a risk-management strategy for both their equity and fixed-income portfolios. Although some purchased the insurance from intermediaries, the great majority chose to create their own by trading in stock- and bond-index futures and traded-options on these futures. The skills of both the insurers and the self-insurers in implementing these strategies were given an extreme test on Black Monday, October 19, 1987, when the Dow Jones Industrial Average fell 508 points (22.6 percent). By any standard, this unprecedented decline represented a "nonlocal" movement in traded-asset prices. The facts on how they did are not as yet known. It is a safe prediction, however, that those with a positive gamma on their otherwise hedged portfolios did well, and those with a negative gamma did poorly.

with its frictionless-market assumptions as a relevant mode of analysis for the study of general financial economic behavior. We thus close our formal analysis with an investigation of this more subtle side of the symbiotic relationship between the continuous-time model and financial intermediation.

The optimal consumption and investment rules for individual investors derived in Chapters 4–6 are valid only if the investors can trade continuously with no transactions costs. As noted in those chapters, real-world financial markets in well-developed economies are open virtually all the time, and therefore the assumption of continuous trading is a reasonable approximation to real-world trading opportunities. However, it is also readily apparent that, in the real world, individual investors generally face significant transactions costs for trading in the asset markets. This observation surely raises a question about the robustness of the model's prescriptions as an approximation to feasible behavior in the real world. In this section, we show that with efficient financial intermediation all investors can achieve the identical consumption–bequest allocations that they would have chosen if they could have traded continuously without cost. We also show that the aggregate demands for traded assets are the same as the ones that obtain in the frictionless-market models of Chapters 4–6. Thus, the consumption and asset demands derived in these earlier chapters are shown to apply in a more realistic model with transactions costs.

In Chapter 13, the pricing function for a derivative security was derived by using the techniques of dynamic portfolio theory developed in Chapter 5. Let $C(t)$ denote the consumption rate of the investor and let $w(t)$ be the fraction of the investor's portfolio allocated to the risky traded asset. If $W(t)$ denotes the value of the investor's portfolio at time t, then from (13.4) we have that

$$dW = \{[w(\alpha - r) + r]W - C\}\,dt + wW\sigma\,dz \qquad (14.32)$$

where α and σ are assumed to be functions of V and t only. To derive the replicating portfolio for a particular derivative security, we required that (a) $w(t) = F_1[V(t), t]V(t)/W(t)$; (b) $C(t) = D_2[V(t), t]$; and (c) $W(0) = F[V(0), 0]$. We then showed that, to rule out arbitrage, $W(t) = F[V(t), t]$ for all t, where $F(V, t)$ is the solution to the partial differential equation (13.1).

In this section, we "reverse" this process. Instead of searching for a feasible portfolio that exactly replicates the payoffs to a particular derivative security, we search for a feasible derivative security with payoffs that exactly match the payoffs to a particular investor's optimal portfolio. Suppose that a blueprint for constructing such a security can be found and that the price charged by a financial intermediary for the security does not exceed the investor's budget constraint. Then, as an alternative to continuously trading assets to achieve his optimal consumption–bequest allocation, the investor can buy the appropriate derivative security from the intermediary and achieve his optimal allocation without ever trading again.[39] If the information-acquisition and transactions costs are smaller for the intermediary than for the investor, then the availability of such derivative securities makes it possible for the investor to achieve welfare-improving allocations that would not otherwise be feasible if the investor had to trade directly in the asset markets.

To derive the terms of the derivative security that provides the optimal consumption–bequest allocation for a particular investor, we use the Cox–Huang approach to the optimal consumption–investment problem as analyzed in Chapter 6. Although the explicit development here assumes a single risky asset and a riskless asset, the results can be generalized to the case of n assets.[40]

Let $X(t)$ denote the price per share of a mutual fund with an investment policy to follow the growth-optimum portfolio strategy and pay no dividends to its shareholders.[41] As shown in Chapter 6, the dynamics of $X(t)$ for a single risky asset can be written as

$$dX = (\mu^2 + r)X \, dt + \mu X \, dz \qquad (14.33)$$

where $\mu = \mu(V, t) \equiv (\alpha - r)/\sigma$. If $C^*(t)$ denotes the investor's optimal consumption rate at time t and $W^*(T)$ denotes his optimal bequest of wealth, then, as shown in Chapter 6, there exist functions G and H such that

$$C^*(t) = G[X(t), V(t), t] \qquad (14.34a)$$

---

39 That investors need only transact once to achieve their lifetime optimal allocation is a well-known feature of the intertemporal version of the Arrow–Debreu model with complete markets. That this result obtains here is no coincidence, because the proposed set of derivative securities is equivalent to a complete market. See Chapter 16 for an analysis and discussion of the connection between the two models.

40 The general case is developed in a somewhat different fashion in Chapter 16.

41 From the mutual-fund theorems of Chapters 5, 11, and 15, the theory predicts that investment companies with growth-optimum portfolio strategies are natural financial products to be offered by intermediaries. In the single risky-asset case, an unambiguous statement of the investment policy for such funds is to undertake continuous trading so as to hold the portfolio fraction $w[V(t), t]$ in the risky asset, where $w[V(t), t] \equiv \{\alpha[V(t), t] - r\}/\sigma^2[V(t), t]$. If the funds are "open ended," and thereby required to either redeem or issue shares at net asset value, then the no-dividend policy of the funds does not matter to their shareholders.

and

$$W^*(T) = H[X(T), V(T)] \qquad (14.34b)$$

where G and H depend parametrically on $X(0)$, $V(0)$, and the investor's initial wealth, $W(0)$. Moreover, for any feasible consumption plan, G and H are nonnegative, and $G(0, V, t) = G(X, 0, t) = H(0, V) = H(X, 0) = 0$ for all $t \leq T$.

It follows from (14.34a) and (14.34b) that to match the optimal consumption–bequest allocation of the investor, the terms of the derivative security must be that it pays a continuous dividend rate of $G[X(t), V(t), t]$ for $t < T$ and a lump-sum payment of $H[X(T), V(T)]$ at time T. The derivation of the production technology and production cost to create this security follows along the general lines of that presented in Chapter 13. However, the development here is somewhat more complicated because the value of the derivative security depends on the prices of two traded assets in addition to the riskless one.

Define $F(X, V, t)$ to be the solution to the linear partial differential equation

$$\tfrac{1}{2}(\mu^2 X^2 F_{11} + 2\mu\sigma XV F_{12} + \sigma^2 V^2 F_{22}) + rXF_1 + rVF_2 + F_3 - rF$$
$$+ G(X, V, t) = 0 \qquad (14.35)$$

subject to the boundary conditions

$$F(0, V, t) = 0 \qquad (14.36a)$$

$$F(X, 0, t) = 0 \qquad (14.36b)$$

$$F(X, V, T) = H(X, V) \qquad (14.36c)$$

where the subscripts on F in (14.35) denote partial derivatives with respect to X, V, and t.

Let $P(t)$ denote the value of a portfolio that makes continuous payouts at the rate $G[X(t), V(t), t]$ and follows an investment strategy of allocating $w_1(t)P(t)$ dollars to the growth-optimum portfolio, $w_2(t)P(t)$ dollars to the risky asset, and the balance of the portfolio to the riskless asset, where[42]

---

42 In the single risky-asset case here, the growth-optimum fund is just a prescribed mix of the traded risky asset and the riskless asset. Therefore, as is evident from (14.33), the instantaneous return on the fund is perfectly correlated with the return on the risky asset. Thus, in this case, we can rewrite (14.37a) and (14.37b) in terms of a single combined position in the risky asset: namely, hold $w[V(t), t]w_1(t)P(t) + w_2(t)P(t)$ dollars in the risky asset (and the balance of the portfolio in the riskless asset) where $w[V(t), t]$ is defined in footnote 41.

$$w_1(t)P(t) = F_1[X(t), V(t), t]X(t) \qquad (14.37a)$$

and

$$w_2(t)P(t) = F_2[X(t), V(t), t]V(t) \qquad (14.37b)$$

It follows that the dynamics of $P(t)$ can be written as

$$dP = F_1 \, dX + F_2 \, dV + [r(P - F_1X - F_2V) - G(X, V, t)] \, dt \qquad (14.38)$$

Because F is twice-continuously differentiable, we can use Itô's lemma to express the stochastic process for $F[X(t), V(t), t]$ as

$$dF = F_1 \, dX + F_2 \, dV + [\tfrac{1}{2}(\mu^2 X^2 F_{11} + 2\mu\sigma XV F_{12} + \sigma^2 V^2 F_{22}) + F_3] \, dt \qquad (14.39)$$

But F satisfies (14.35). Hence we can rewrite (14.39) as

$$dF = F_1 \, dX + F_2 \, dV + [r(F - F_1X - F_2V) - G(X, V, t)] \, dt \qquad (14.40)$$

Let $Q(t) \equiv P(t) - F[X(t), V(t), t]$. From (14.38) and (14.40), we have that

$$dQ = dP - dF$$

$$= r(P - F) \, dt$$

$$= rQ \, dt \qquad (14.41)$$

The solution to (14.41) for any $t \leqslant T$ is $Q(t) = Q(0) \exp(rt)$. Therefore, if we choose the initial investment in the portfolio so that $P(0) = F[X(0), V(0), 0]$, then $Q(0) = 0$ and $Q(t) \equiv 0$ for all $t \leqslant T$. It follows that for all $t \leqslant T$

$$P(t) = F[X(t), V(t), t] \qquad (14.42)$$

Thus, we have derived a dynamic portfolio strategy that exactly replicates the payoffs of a derivative security that makes continuous payments at the rate $G[X(t), V(t), t]$ for $t < T$ and has a final payout of $H[X(T), V(T)]$ at time T. The production technology for creating this security is given by (14.37a) and (14.37b). The cost of producing the security at time t is $F[X(t), V(t), t]$.

The payoffs of the derivative security exactly match the consumption–bequest allocation of the investor's optimal continuous-trading strategy. Hence, the investor can achieve this allocation by simply buying the security, provided that the price of the security does not exceed his budget constraint. As discussed in Chapter 6, Cox and Huang have shown that the investor's optimally invested wealth $W(t)$ can be expressed as a function of

$X(t)$, $V(t)$, and t and that this function satisfies our partial differential equation (14.35), with boundary conditions (14.36).[43] Therefore, $W(t) = F[X(t), V(t), t]$ and, in particular, $W(0) = F[X(0), V(0), 0]$. Purchase of the derivative security by the investor is thus always feasible.

Having both derived the procedure for creating this type of security and established the feasibility of its purchase by the investor, we now examine the role of financial intermediation in making the continuous-time model more robust. Assume an institutional environment with a competitive financial-services industry in which financial intermediaries pay no transactions costs and consider an investor who must pay significant transactions costs to trade in the asset markets. Using the methods of Chapter 5, the investor can solve for the optimal lifetime consumption–investment program that he would choose if he could trade continuously with no transactions costs. Using the Cox–Huang technique of Chapter 6, this optimal program can be expressed as a stream of contingent payments, $G[X(t), V(t), t]$ for $t < T$ and a final payment of $H[X(T), V(T)]$ at time T.[44] By assumption, the investor cannot implement this strategy by trading directly in the asset markets. The investor can, however, negotiate with an intermediary for the purchase of a custom-designed derivative security with payoffs specified by G and H. By assumption, financial intermediation is a competitive industry, and therefore price equals marginal cost. Hence, $F[X(0), V(0), 0] = W(0)$.[45] Thus, if such derivative securities are generally available from intermediaries, all investors can achieve optimal consumption–bequest allocations that are identical with those that they would have selected if they could trade continuously with no transactions costs.[46]

---

43   In Chapter 6, it was shown that the investor's optimal portfolio demand for the risky asset at time t is given by $F_1[X(t), V(t), t]\mu X(t)/\sigma + F_2[X(t), V(t), t]V(t)$, with the balance of his wealth held in the riskless asset. If an intermediary follows hedging rules (14.37a) and (14.37b), it follows from footnote 42 that the intermediary's demands for traded assets to hedge the derivative security are identical with those of the investor if he could trade continuously without cost.

44   The functions G and H can, of course, be determined in a single step by solving the optimal consumption–investment problem, using the techniques of Chapter 6 directly.

45   In the spirit of footnote 4, the purely competitive assumption for financial intermediaries can be somewhat relaxed without significantly affecting the results. That is, provided that the unit mark-up for noncompetitive intermediary profits is a small fraction of each investor's wealth, the optimal allocation achieved through intermediation will be close to the competitive one, because $C^*(t)$ is a continuously differentiable function of the investor's wealth.

46   The duration of the derivative security is the lifetime T of the investor. The magnitude of the liability as assessed by the intermediary at any time $t(\leq T)$ is $F[X(t), V(t), t] = W(t)$. Hence, at any time t, a competitive intermediary would be willing to repurchase the security from the investor for $W(t)$. By such a sale, the investor can therefore recover the same wealth that he would have had if he had been able to trade continuously during the time interval $[0, t]$.

If the creation of these securities is to provide a meaningful extension to the robustness of the frictionless-market version of the continuous-time model, the assumptions about institutional structure and the partitioning of information sets among agents that are necessary for widespread distribution of these securities must be plausible. It is unlikely, for example, that trading in derivative securities of this type could be supported in organized secondary markets. The wealth of any one investor is small and the particular security demanded by each investor will in general be unique in terms of its specified payout structure G and H. The structure of these securities is ideally suited, however, for broad distribution by financial intermediaries. After the sale of such a security, an intermediary can use the proceeds to finance the hedging of its liability by trading continuously in the asset markets according to the rules (14.37a) and (14.37b). As in the preceding section, the nature of these trading rules is such that hedging of custom-designed derivative securities is no more difficult than hedging of standard ones. The intermediary simply aggregates its individual exposures, as calculated from (14.37), across all its outstanding securities and then establishes positions in a relatively small number of traded assets to hedge its net exposure.

Widespread availability of these derivative securities requires arms-length transactions, and these can only be implemented if the contracts create no important moral hazard problem for either party. The contingent payments on each derivative security depend only on time and the prices of the growth-optimum mutual fund and the risky asset. All three are observable, and hence verifiable, by the investor and the intermediary. Provided that both the investor and the intermediary are price-takers in the traded-asset markets, neither can affect the time path of either $X(t)$ or $V(t)$. Hence, there is no inherent moral hazard to either party in these contracts.

To establish and evaluate the terms of the derivative security, each party needs a specific body of information. Successful implementation of these contracts thus requires that the task of acquiring the needed information by the respective parties be a reasonable one. To create and price the derivative security, the intermediary need only know the schedules $G[X(t), V(t), t]$ and $H[X(T), V(T)]$, which are specified by the investor at the time that the security is created. The intermediary does not need to know either the investor's preferences or even that the purpose of the security is to provide an optimal lifetime allocation. Because $G \geqslant 0$ and $H \geqslant 0$, the only contractual payment by the investor to the intermediary is the initial one, $F[X(0), V(0), 0]$. Thus, we have, as a *derived* result and not as an assumption, that this type of derivative security provides limited liability for the investor. It follows that to price and hedge these securities, the intermediary does not require monitoring of the investor's endowment or creditworthiness. We thus conclude that the informational requirements for intermediaries to produce these securities are reasonable.

The information set required by the investor to determine the functions $G(X, V, t)$ and $H(X, V)$ is surely reasonable because it is no larger than the one he would use to solve for his optimal consumption and investment program in the absence of such intermediation opportunities. Moreover, this is the only information the investor needs, provided that there is no uncertainty about the ability of the issuing intermediary to make the promised contingent payments. The prospect of default on the customer-held liabilities of intermediaries raises two important issues. First, if there is significant default risk, then derivative securities with identical promised payments that are issued by different intermediaries are no longer perfect substitutes. Hence, to evaluate these securities, the investor requires information about the creditworthiness of the issuing intermediaries. Therefore, default risk imposes on the investor a burden of additional information acquisition, albeit perhaps not an unreasonable one.

A second and more serious issue is that default risk reduces the functional efficiency of the derivative securities sold to individual investors. These investors want securities with payments (contingent on X, V, and t) that match their optimal consumption–bequest allocations. Unless the risk of default on these contracts is negligible, their payments are, *de facto*, also contingent on the value of the issuing intermediary and its entire structure of outstanding liabilities. The suboptimality of the contracts induced by this unwanted dependence underscores the distinction drawn in Section 14.4 between the liabilities of the intermediary held by its customers and the liabilities held by its investors. In the model here, only zero-cost transactors would trade in the asset markets. Hence, these are the only investors to have direct holdings of the stock and other general liabilities of individual financial intermediaries. As we saw in the proof of the Modigliani–Miller theorem in Chapter 13, default risk on liabilities held by zero-cost transactors causes no loss in efficiency because such investors can, if they choose, use continuous-trading strategies in the asset markets to hedge this risk. In contrast, the customers of intermediaries are individual investors who buy the custom-designed financial products of the intermediaries precisely because they cannot transact costlessly in the asset markets. Unlike investors in intermediaries, customers cannot use trading strategies in the asset markets to shed their unwanted exposure to the fortunes of the intermediaries whose products they buy.

Customers can reduce the effects of bankruptcy risk by buying a security with promised payments of $G[X(t), V(t), t]/N$ and $H[X(T), V(T)]/N$ at a price of $F[X(t), V(t), t]/N$ from each of N financial intermediaries. Such diversification efforts alone may not, however, be sufficient to eliminate the adverse effects of default.[47] Because default risk reduces the usefulness

---

47 The degree of success of this strategy in statistically eliminating the risk of default depends on the extent to which the Law of Large Numbers applies. Valid application of this theorem requires not only that the number of intermediaries, N,

of their financial products, intermediaries have an incentive to apply risk-management techniques, make institutional arrangements, and support regulations, all designed to minimize the probability of default on customer-held liabilities. This incentive would, of course, exist in any model of financial intermediation. What distinguishes the continuous-time model is that the theory provides a feasible set of trading rules for each intermediary to unilaterally reduce the risk of default on its own products to a negligible level.[48] Hence, there exists a feasible institutional structure and partitioning of agents' information sets to support the creation of optimal default-free contracts such that each investor can buy his entire lifetime consumption–bequest allocation in a single transaction.

In Chapter 15, an intertemporal equilibrium model of allocations and asset prices is developed for an economy with frictionless markets where all investors can trade continuously without cost. This model has a simple financial sector with no explicit derivative-security markets or financial intermediaries, and further, all business firms are assumed to be financed entirely by equity. However, as noted here at the outset, derivative securities, mutual funds, and corporate liabilities with payoffs that can be replicated by continuous trading in existing assets serve no important function in an environment in which all agents can trade without cost. Because every investor can trade continuously, each investor can synthesize the payoff patterns of these financial instruments, using the existing set of traded assets alone. Hence, any allocation chosen by the investor after such instruments are added to the menu of investments could have been achieved before their introduction. Thus, the addition of these financial instruments into the model of Chapter 15 would leave unchanged the equilibrium time paths of consumption, production, and asset prices.

It follows that equilibrium in a frictionless-market model that explicitly includes all financial markets, intermediaries, and corporate-liability structures can be analyzed in two separate parts: in the first, the model of Chapter 15 with its simplified financial sector is used to determine real-sector allocations and asset prices; in the second, the equilibrium dynamics of asset prices as determined in the first part are used together with the CCA pricing methods of Chapter 13 to find the equilibrium prices of derivative securities, financial products, and corporate liabilities. Such a separation among sectors of the economy is generally called a *dichotomy*. Dichotomy occurs here because many of the financial securities, markets,

---

is large, but also that the events of default among the selected intermediaries are sufficiently statistically independent. Because many economic events that affect the fortunes of one intermediary also affect the fortunes of others, the required independence assumption may not be satisfied.

48 For the model of this section, these rules are given by (14.37a) and (14.37b). For the analogous rules in a general version of the continuous-time model, see Chapter 16.

and institutions are redundant, and hence much of the financial sector "doesn't matter."[49]

In the model of this section, the financial sector does matter because not all agents can trade continuously without cost.[50] As we have seen, there exists an institutional structure of well-functioning and competitive financial intermediaries such that every investor can achieve the same consumption–bequest allocation that he or she would have selected in a frictionless-market environment. Although these investors need only transact once to buy their optimal allocation, the issuing intermediaries must transact continuously in the asset markets to hedge their customer-held liabilities. As discussed in footnote 43, the increments to a financial intermediary's hedging demands for traded assets that are induced by the sale of an optimal allocation contract to an investor will be identical, at every point in time after the sale, to the optimal portfolio demands that this investor would have chosen in a frictionless-market model. Hence, the individual consumption functions and aggregate demand functions for traded assets in this model can be computed *as if* all investors could trade continuously without cost. It follows that the equilibrium real-sector allocations and asset prices will be the same as those derived in the model of Chapter 15.

It would seem therefore that the same dichotomy derived in the frictionless-market case applies also to our model with transactions costs. In a formal computational sense it does. We can still solve for the equilibrium asset-price dynamics in the model of Chapter 15 and then compute the prices of derivative securities, mutual funds, and corporate liabilities using CCA. There is one significant difference, however: the first-part calculation of equilibrium real-sector allocations is valid if and only if there exists a sufficiently rich set of securities and intermediaries in the financial sector to make these allocations feasible for agents who cannot trade without cost. Because of this conditioning, perhaps a more appropriate term for this separation is "quasi-dichotomy."

With the assumption that not all agents can trade continuously without cost, a significant economic role is established for derivative-security markets and financial intermediaries in the model. Somewhat paradox-

---

49 The conditions under which the creation of a new financial instrument or market can change equilibrium allocations are briefly addressed in Chapter 15 and analyzed more fully in Chapter 16. If a set of existing securities and markets leads to an equilibrium that is an unconstrained Pareto optimum, then any additional securities or markets will be redundant.

50 The term "transactions costs" can, of course, mean more than just the bid–ask spread or commissions paid for buying and selling assets. For example, if an investor literally traded his portfolio continuously, he would have no time to do anything else! Because investment management and financial intermediation involve primarily information processing and security trading, there are significant economies of scale. One would thus expect substantially lower costs for the individual investor to use intermediaries instead of transacting directly in the asset markets.

ically, we find that, if intermediation is efficient, then derivative securities and the financial products of the intermediaries will be priced *as if* they are redundant.[51] Under these conditions, quasi-dichotomy obtains, and we can derive equilibrium real-sector allocations and asset prices from the frictionless-market version of the model.

14.6 AFTERWORD: POLICY AND STRATEGY IN FINANCIAL INTERMEDIATION

In this chapter, as throughout the book, the focus has been on theory. Allusions to practice were concentrated on the micro quantitative applications of the continuous-time model to product technologies and risk management. Still, I cannot wholly resist the temptation to call attention to the model's potential for addressing broader issues in the practice of intermediation. And so this afterword shall ever so briefly touch upon implications of the model for intermediation policy and strategy in the hope that it will lead others, better qualified, to explore this matter elsewhere.

Derivative securities have long been an integral part of the financial markets,[52] but most would mark the creation of the Chicago Board Options Exchange in April 1973 as the start of the current wave of financial innovations involving derivative securities. The succeeding years have witnessed an unprecedented proliferation of organized trading markets in both equity and fixed-income derivative instruments. In turn, these markets made possible the creation of a wide range of financial products, many custom-designed to meet selected needs of investors and issuers. Concurrently, mainstream financial institutions increasingly adopted quantitative techniques including computerized trading strategies to help manage their portfolios, often on a global scale. These changes have been

---

51 Thus, our model provides a resolution to Hakansson's (1979, p. 722) "The Catch 22 of Option Pricing." Although the *equilibrium* prices of options and other derivative securities satisfy the redundancy condition of CCA, they are nevertheless needed to support the equilibrium allocations, and hence their elimination would reduce social welfare.

52 Bernstein (1992) reports that Aristotle's anecdote about Thales in Book I of *Politics* is the first recorded mention of a financial option. Schaede (1988) makes the case that the Dōjima rice market in Ōsaka was a forward market in the seventeenth century and a fully organized futures market by the eighteenth century. As discussed in Chapter 10, footnote 3, the Amsterdam stock exchange also traded options and contracts similar to financial futures in the seventeenth century. Organized futures exchanges were created in Frankfurt in 1867 and in London in 1877. The Chicago Board of Trade was founded in 1848 and the New York Cotton Exchange was incorporated in 1872. For functional discussion and historical listings of various financial instruments and innovations, see Dewing (1934), Carlton (1984), Finnerty (1988), and Tufano (1989).

accompanied by an explosion of trading volume in just about every sector of the financial markets. On these facts, all agree.

There are, however, some in the financial and regulatory communities who see all this alleged innovation as nothing more than a giant fad, driven by institutional investors and issuers with wholly unrealistic expectations of greater returns with less risk, and fueled by financial-services firms and organized exchanges that see huge profits from this vast activity. Perhaps. There have surely been instances of financial products and trading strategies that have not delivered in practice the performance promised in theory. But, notwithstanding such examples, there is another, quite different, interpretation of these events.

From the perspective of our theory, these same facts about change are seen as consistent with a real-world dynamic path evolving toward an idealized target of an efficient financial-market and intermediation system. On this premise, these changes can be interpreted as part of a "financial innovation spiral." That is, the proliferation of new trading markets makes feasible the creation of new financial products; to hedge these products, producers trade in these new markets and volume expands; increased volume reduces marginal transactions costs and thereby makes possible further implementation of new products and trading strategies, which in turn leads to still more volume. Success of these trading markets encourages investment in creating additional markets, and so on it goes . . ., spiraling toward the theoretically limiting case of zero marginal transactions costs and dynamically-complete markets.

Consider now a small sampling of the implications for strategy and policy from this view of the process. In this scenario, aggregate volume expands secularly and trading is increasingly dominated by institutions. As more institutions employ dynamic strategies to hedge their product liabilities, incentives rise for expansion to round-the-clock trading that permits more-effective implementation of these strategies. Whether the financial intermediation industry becomes more concentrated or more diffuse is not clear. The central functions of information and transactions processing would favor economies of scale. Similarly, from the analysis in Section 14.4, the greater opportunities for netting and diversifying risk exposures by an intermediary with a diverse set of products would suggest a decline in hedging transactions per dollar of product liability as size increases. On the other hand, expansion in the types of organized trading markets, reductions in transactions costs, and continued improvements in information-processing and telecommunications technologies will all make it easier for a greater variety of firms to serve the functions of a financial intermediary. Continuing the scenario, existing intermediaries will be capable of offering a broader range of financial products and servicing a wider geographic area. Traditional institutional identifications with specific types of products are likely to become increasingly blurred. Geopolitical advantages currently enjoyed by some financial institutions will be reduced.

Along that hypothesized path of development, the need to distribute a larger volume and more diverse set of products promises continued relative growth of the sales activity within financial intermediaries. The trading activity is also likely to expand to meet the execution requirements for implementing more-complex product technologies. As in other innovating industries, competition to create new products and to find new ways to produce established products at lower cost could make the research and development activity the lifeblood of the financial intermediary. Although presented prospectively, many but not all of these changes are already under way. Further, this represents one possible scenario growing out of our theoretical model of the intermediation process.

However, the dramatic increases over the past decade in the size and complexity of transactions together with the global linking of financial markets have raised concern about macro credit risk and the possibility of broad financial-market "breakdown." The crash in world stock markets in October 1987 surely heightened those concerns. The changes in practice projected by the theory imply, *ipso facto*, further increases in the interdependence among institutions and markets in the financial system. Moreover, as discussed in Sections 14.4 and 14.5, minimizing the default risk for the customer-held liabilities of financial intermediaries is a key element in our theory of efficient intermediation. As also noted, much the same point can be made about markets for standardized instruments, such as options and futures. Thus, the theory selectively concurs with the belief that credit risk is a major issue for financial markets.

Space, not source material, is the scarce resource for discussion of the credit-risk issue in this chapter. I shall therefore not even try to summarize the various detailed lines of inquiry that show promise for finding policy solutions that are congruent with evolution to an efficient financial system.[53] Instead, I use my limited space to comment on a single guideline for policy that is central from the perspective of the theory.

The overriding theme of the theory has financial innovation as the engine driving the financial system on its prospective journey to efficiency and complete markets. With its focus on product innovation, this theory largely abstracts from the concurrent changes in financial infrastructure (including institutional and regulatory practices, organization of trading facilities, and the communication and information processing systems for transactions) required to support realization of this journey. But perhaps the single most important implication for policy is the need for explicit recognition of the interdependence between product and infrastructure innovations and of the inevitable conflicts that arise between the two.

---

53 These range from finding feasible mechanisms to centralize (or at least coordinate) the clearing system and global standards of collateral for all major markets, a line more rooted in the disciplines of political science and systems analysis than finance, to the risk management of macro "jumps" in asset prices, a subject very much in the mainstream of current finance research.

As an analogy of supreme simplicity, consider the creation of a high-speed passenger train, surely a beneficial product innovation. Suppose, however, that the tracks of the current rail system are inadequate to handle such high speeds. In the absence of policy rules, the innovator, either through ignorance or a willingness to take risk, could choose to fully implement his product and run the train at high speed. If the train subsequently crashes, it is, of course, true that the innovator and his passengers will pay a dear price. But if in the process the track is also destroyed, then those, such as freight operators, who use the system for a different purpose will also be greatly damaged – hence the need for policy to safeguard the system. A simple one that fulfills that objective is to permanently fix a safe but low speed limit. But, of course, this narrowly focused policy has as a rather unfortunate consequence that the benefits of innovation will never be realized. An obviously better, if more complex, policy solution is to facilitate the needed upgrading of the track and at the same time to set transient limits on speed, while there is a technological imbalance between the product and its infrastructure.

As in this hypothetical rail system,[54] the financial system is used by many for a variety of purposes. When treated atomistically, financial innovations in products and services can be implemented unilaterally and rather quickly. Hence, these innovations take place in an entrepreneurial and opportunistic manner. In contrast, innovations in financial infrastructure must be more coordinated, and therefore take longer to implement. It is thus wholly unrealistic to expect financial innovation to proceed along a balanced path of development for all elements in the system. It is indeed possible that, at times, the imbalance between product innovation and infrastructure could become large enough to jeopardize the functioning of the system – hence the need for policy to protect against such breakdown. But, as we have seen, a single-minded policy focused exclusively on this concern could derail the engine of innovation and bring to a halt the financial system's trip to greater efficiency.

The analysis and discussion of this chapter exemplify our manifest hypothesis that the continuous-time model is a useful tool for both finance theory and finance practice. However, it goes further and suggests a second – perhaps more latent – one: as real-world financial intermediation and markets become increasingly more efficient, the continuous-time model's predictions about actual financial prices, products and institutions will become increasingly more accurate. In short, that reality will eventually imitate theory.

---

54 Underscore "hypothetical," since for purposes of the analogy I implicitly posit that the track system is a public good, an assumption which in the real world perhaps more accurately fits a public highway than a rail system.

From abstract mathematical derivations to concrete policy evaluations, this has surely been a song of unbridled praise for the continuous-time model as a synthesizing design for the theory and practice of financial intermediation. But, having opened discussion of that model's relevance to the real world, due diligence requires that I not close it without reiterating some qualifying caveats.

It is a dictum that financial markets will not long let stand prices that violate arbitrage. However, unlike with true arbitrage, the derived price relations in the continuous-time model are delicately conditional on the assumed stochastic process for the underlying securities and on the opportunity to trade continuously. Hence, with only conditional arbitrage, there are no assurances in the real world of an inexorable and swift convergence of actual prices to their theoretical model values. Thus, the simple but powerful argument of no violation of true arbitrage cannot be invoked to, *a priori*, validate the model.

Validation must therefore rely on traditional *a posteriori* assessments. Empirical study of the model is still very much in an evolving stage. Hence, I simply note that at the moment the cumulative statistical evidence appears encouraging but also contains anomalies. The clinical evaluations from more than a decade of widespread and ongoing applications of the continuous-time model by practitioners seem to provide inferentially favorable evidence of a different sort. But those who see the last decade of innovations as a fad are also likely to interpret this evidence as an instance of a self-fulfilling prophecy, serving only to confirm their hypothesis.[55] Even without accepting this polar view, we must surely concede that practitioners, like academics, are not immune from following the paths of error. Thus, although the prognosis may be good, the continuous-time model as an empirical hypothesis, strictly speaking, remains unproved.

55 That is, the proclamation that the model is widely used induces each practitioner to use it only because he believes that all others are and therefore that prices will conform to the model, independently of its economic validity. As originally formulated in R. K. Merton (1948), the concept of the self-fulfilling prophecy applies only if the prophesized event would not have occurred in the absence of its public proclamation. Hence, even if widespread public knowledge of the model's adoption leads others to use it, there is no self-fulfilling prophecy if, as our theory predicts, the model is economically valid without the proclamation.

Part V

An Intertemporal Equilibrium Theory of Finance

An Intertemporal Capital Asset Pricing Model

An intertemporal model for the capital market is deduced from the portfolio selection behavior by an arbitrary number of investors who act so as to maximize the expected utility of lifetime consumption and who can trade continuously in time. Explicit demand functions for assets are derived, and it is shown that; unlike the one-period model, current demands are affected by the possibility of uncertain changes in future investment opportunities. After aggregating demands and requiring market clearing, the equilibrium relations among expected returns are derived, and contrary to the classical Capital Asset Pricing Model, expected returns on risky assets may differ from the riskless rate even when they have no systematic or market risk.

15.1   INTRODUCTION

One of the more important developments in modern capital market theory is the Sharpe–Lintner–Mossin mean–variance equilibrium model of exchange, commonly called the Capital Asset Pricing Model (CAPM).[1]

Reproduced from *Econometrica*, 41, September 1973, 867–87. The original paper was a substantial revision of parts of Merton (1970b; this volume, Ch. 11) and was presented in various forms at the NBER Conference on Decision Rules and Uncertainty, Massachusetts Institute of Technology, February 1971, and at the Wells Fargo Conference on Capital Market Theory, San Francisco, July 1971. I am grateful to the participants for helpful comments. I thank Myron Scholes and Fischer Black for many useful discussions, and Robert K. Merton for editorial assistance. Aid from the National Science Foundation is gratefully acknowledged.

1   See Sharpe (1964, 1970), Lintner (1965a, b), and Mossin (1966). While more general and elegant than the CAPM in many ways, the general equilibrium model of Arrow (1953, 1964) and Debreu (1959, Ch. 7) has not had the same impact, principally because of its empirical intractability and the rather restrictive assumption that there exist as many securities as states of nature (see Stiglitz, 1972). The "growth-optimum" model of Hakansson (1971) can be formulated as an equilibrium model although it is consistent with expected utility maximization only if all investors have logarithmic utility functions (see Samuelson, 1971; Merton and Samuelson, 1974). However, Roll (1973) has shown that the model fits the data about as well as the CAPM.

Although the model has been the basis for more than a hundred academic papers and has had significant impact on the nonacademic financial community,[2] it is still subject to theoretical and empirical criticism. Because the model assumes that investors choose their portfolios according to the Markowitz mean–variance criterion, it is subject to all the theoretical objections to this criterion, of which there are many.[3] It has also been criticized for the additional assumptions required,[4] especially homogeneous expectations and the single-period nature of the model. The proponents of the model who agree with the theoretical objections, but who argue that the capital market operates as if these assumptions were satisfied, are themselves not beyond criticism. While the model predicts that the expected excess return from holding an asset is proportional to the covariance of its return with the market portfolio (its "beta"), the careful empirical work of Black, Jensen and Scholes (1972) has demonstrated that this is not the case. In particular, they found that "low beta" assets earn a higher return on average and "high beta" assets earn a lower return on average than is forecast by the model.[5] Nonetheless, the model is still used because it is an equilibrium model which provides a strong specification of the relation among asset yields that is easily interpreted, and the empirical evidence suggests that it does explain a significant fraction of the variation in asset returns.

This chapter develops an equilibrium model of the capital market which (a) has the simplicity and empirical tractability of the CAPM; (b) is consistent with expected utility maximization and the limited liability of assets; and (c) provides a specification of the relation among yields that is more consistent with empirical evidence. Such a model cannot be constructed without costs. The assumptions, principally homogeneous expectations,[6] that it holds in common with the classical model, make the new model subject to some of the same criticisms.

2 For academic references, see Sharpe (1970) and Jensen's (1972b) survey article. For a summary of the model's impact on the financial community, see Welles (1971).

3 See Borch (1969), Feldstein (1969), and Hakansson (1971). For a list of the conditions necessary for the validity of mean–variance analysis, see Samuelson (1967a, 1970).

4 See Sharpe (1970, pp. 77–8) for a list of the assumptions required.

5 Friend and Blume (1970) also found that the empirical capital-market line was "too flat." Their explanation was that the borrowing–lending assumption of the model is violated. Black (1972) provides an alternative explanation based on the assumption of no riskless asset. Other less important, stylized facts in conflict with the model are that investors do not hold the same relative proportions of risky assets, and short-sales occur in spite of unfavorable institutional requirements.

*6 In subsequent development, Williams (1977) has extended the model to allow for heterogeneous beliefs among investors.

The CAPM is a static (single-period) model although it is generally treated as if it holds intertemporally. Fama (1970b) has provided some justification for this assumption by showing that, if preferences and future investment opportunity sets are not state dependent, then intertemporal portfolio maximization can be treated as if the investor had a single-period utility function. However, these assumptions are rather restrictive as will be seen in later analysis.[7] Merton (1971; this volume, Ch. 5) has shown in a number of examples that portfolio behavior for an intertemporal maximizer will be significantly different when he faces a changing investment opportunity set instead of a constant one.

The model presented here is based on consumer–investor behavior as described in Merton (1971; this volume, Ch. 5), and for the assumptions to be reasonable ones, it must be intertemporal. Far from being a liability, the intertemporal nature of the model allows it to capture effects which would never appear in a static model, and it is precisely these effects which cause the significant differences in specification of the equilibrium relation among asset yields that obtain in the new model and the classical model.

15.2 CAPITAL MARKET STRUCTURE

It is assumed that the capital market is structured as follows:

1 All assets have limited liability.
2 There are no transactions costs, taxes, or problems with indivisibilities of assets.
3 There is a sufficient number of investors with comparable wealth levels so that each investor believes that he can buy and sell as much of an asset as he wants at the market price.
4 The capital market is always in equilibrium (i.e. there is no trading at nonequilibrium prices).
5 There exists an exchange market for borrowing and lending at the same rate of interest.
6 Short-sales of all assets, with full use of proceeds, is allowed.
7 Trading in assets takes place continually in time.

Assumptions 1–6 are the standard assumptions of a perfect market, and their merits have been discussed extensively in the literature. Although Assumption 7 is not standard, it follows almost directly from Assumption 2. If there are no costs to transacting and assets can be exchanged on any

---

7 Fama recognizes the restrictive nature of the assumptions as evidenced by discussion in Fama and Miller (1972).

scale, then investors would prefer to be able to revise their portfolios at any time (whether they actually do so or not). In reality, transactions costs and indivisibilities do exist, and one reason given for finite trading-interval (discrete-time) models is to give implicit, if not explicit, recognition to these costs. However, this method of avoiding the problem of transactions costs is not satisfactory since a proper solution would almost certainly show that the trading intervals are stochastic and of nonconstant length.[8] Further, the portfolio demands and the resulting equilibrium relations will be a function of the specific trading interval that is chosen.[9] An investor making a portfolio decision which is irrevocable ("frozen") for ten years will choose quite differently than the one who has the option (even at a cost) to revise his portfolio daily. The essential issue is the market structure and not investors' tastes, and for well-developed capital markets, the time interval between successive market openings is sufficiently small to make the continuous-time assumption a good approximation.[10]

15.3 ASSET VALUE AND RATE OF RETURN DYNAMICS

Having described the structure of the capital market, we now develop the dynamics of the returns on assets traded in the market. It is sufficient for

*8 For recent developments on this point, see Constantinides (1986), Davis and Norman (1990), Dumas and Luciano (1991), Eastham and Hastings (1988), Kandel and Ross (1983), Magill and Constantinides (1976), Sun (1987), and Taksar, Klass, and Assaf (1988). As discussed in Chapter 14, to properly incorporate transactions costs into an equilibrium analysis generally requires explicit recognition and endogenous determination of the structure of markets and financial intermediation. However, for the equilibrium results derived here, it is not necessary that Assumptions 2, 5, and 6 apply to all investors and business firms. As shown in Section 14.5, if we assume instead that marginal transactions costs for financial intermediaries are negligible, then we have that (a) explicit recognition of the financial-services industry is not necessary in the analysis ("quasi-dichotomy") and (b) equilibrium allocations and prices will be as if Assumptions 1–7 were valid for all investors and business firms.

9 A simple example from the Expectations Theory of the term structure will illustrate the point. It is well known (see, for example, Stiglitz, 1970) that bonds cannot be priced to equate expected returns over *all* holding periods. Hence, one must select a "fundamental" period (usually one "trading" period, our h) to equate expected returns. Clearly, the prices which satisfy this relation will be a function of h. Similarly, the demand functions of investors will depend on h. We have chosen for our interval the smallest h possible. For processes which are well defined for every h, it can be shown that the limit of every discrete-time solution as h tends to zero will be the continuous solution derived here [see Samuelson (1970), He (forthcoming), and Willinger and Taqqu (1991)].

10 What is "small" depends on the particular process being modeled. For the orders of magnitude typically found for the moments (mean, variance, skewness, etc.) of annual returns on common stocks, daily intervals ($h = 1/270$) are small.

his decision-making that the consumer–investor know at each point in time (a) the transition probabilities for returns on each asset over the next trading interval (the *investment opportunity set*) and (b) the transition probabilities for returns on assets in future periods (i.e. knowledge of the stochastic processes of the changes in the investment opportunity set). Unlike a single-period maximizer who, by definition, does not consider events beyond the present period, the intertemporal maximizer in selecting his portfolio takes into account the relation between current period returns and returns that will be available in the future. For example, suppose that the current return on a particular asset is negatively correlated with changes in yields ("capitalization" rates). Then, by holding this asset, the investor expects a higher return on the asset if, *ex post*, yield opportunities next period are lower than were expected.

A brief description of the supply side of the asset market will be helpful in understanding the relation between current returns on assets and changes in the investment opportunity set.

An asset is defined as a production technology which is a probability distribution for cash flow (valued in consumption units) and physical depreciation as a function of the amount of capital, $K(t)$ (measured in physical units, e.g. number of machines), employed at time t. The price per unit capital in terms of the consumption good is $P_k(t)$, and the value of an asset at time t, $V(t)$, equals $P_k(t)K(t)$. The return on the asset over a period of length h will be the cash flow, X, plus the value of undepreciated capital, $(1 - \lambda)P_k(t + h)K(t)$ (where λ is the rate of physical depreciation of capital), minus the initial value of the asset, $V(t)$. The total change in the value of the asset outstanding, $V(t + h) - V(t)$, is equal to the sum of the return on the asset plus the value of gross new investment in excess of cash flow, $P_k(t + h)[K(t + h) - (1 - \lambda)K(t)] - X$.

Each firm in the model is assumed to invest in a single asset and to issue one class of securities, called equity.[11] Hence, the terms "firm" and "asset" can be used interchangeably. Let $N(t)$ be the number of shares of the firm outstanding and let $P(t)$ be the price per share, where $N(t)$ and $P(t)$ are defined by the difference equations

$$P(t + h) \equiv \frac{X + (1 - \lambda)P_k(t + h)K(t)}{N(t)} \tag{15.1}$$

The essential test is: for what h does the distribution of returns become sufficiently "compact" in the Samuelson (1970) sense?

11 It is assumed that there are no economies or diseconomies to the "packaging" of assets (i.e. no "synergism"). Hence, any "real" firm holding more than one type of asset will be priced as if it held a portfolio of the "firms" in the text. Similarly, it is assumed that all financial leveraging and other capital structure differences are carried out by investors (possibly through financial intermediaries).

and

$$N(t + h) \equiv N(t) + \frac{P_k(t + h)[K(t + h) - (1 - \lambda)K(t)] - X}{P(t + h)} \quad (15.2)$$

subject to the initial conditions $P(0) = P$, $N(0) = N$, and $V(0) = N(0)P(0)$. If we assume that all dividend payments to shareholders are accomplished by share repurchase, then from (15.1) and (15.2), $[P(t + h) - P(t)]/P(t)$ is the rate of return on the asset over the period, in units of the consumption good.[12]

Since movements from equilibrium to equilibrium through time involve both price and quantity adjustment, a complete analysis would require a description of both the rate of return and the change in asset-value dynamics. To do this would require a specification of firm behavior in determining the supply of shares, which in turn would require knowledge of the real asset structure (i.e. technology, whether capital is "putty" or "clay", etc.). In particular, the current returns on firms with large amounts (relative to current cash flow) of nonshiftable capital with low rates of depreciation will tend to be strongly affected by shifts in capitalization rates because, in the short run, most of the adjustment to the new equilibrium will be done by prices.

Since this chapter examines only investor behavior to derive the demands for assets and the relative yield requirements in equilibrium,[13] only the rate of return dynamics will be examined explicitly. Hence, certain variables, taken as exogenous in the model, would be endogenous to a full-equilibrium system.[14]

From the assumption of continuous trading (Assumption 7), it is assumed that the returns and the changes in the opportunity set can be

---

12 In an intertemporal model, it is necessary to define two quantities, such as number of shares and price per share, to distinguish between the two ways in which a firm's value can change. The return part, (15.1), reflects new additions to wealth, while (15.2) reflects a reallocation of capital among alternative assets. The former is important to the investor in selecting his portfolio while the latter is important in (determining) maintaining equilibrium through time. The definition of price per share used here (except for cash dividends) corresponds to the way open-ended mutual funds determine asset value per share, and seems to reflect accurately the way the term is normally used in a portfolio context.

13 While the analysis is not an equilibrium one in the strict sense because we do not develop the supply side, the derived model is as much an equilibrium model as the "exchange" model of Mossin (1966). Because his is a one-period model, he could take supplies as fixed. To assume this over time is nonsense.

*14 See Brock (1982), Grinols (1984), Sundaresan (1984), Cox, Ingersoll, and Ross (1985a), Breeden (1986), Detemple (1986), Huang (1987), Duffie (1988), Dumas (1989), and Chapter 16 for subsequent developments of general equilibrium versions of the model.

described by continuous-time stochastic processes. However, it will clarify the analysis to describe the processes for discrete trading intervals of length h, and then to consider the limit as h tends to zero.

We assume the following:

8 The vector set of stochastic processes describing the opportunity set and its changes is a time-homogeneous[15] Markov process.
9 Only local changes in the state variables of the process are allowed.
10 For each asset in the opportunity set at each point in time t, the expected rate of return per unit time defined by

$$\alpha \equiv E_t \left\{ \frac{P(t + h) - P(t)}{P(t)} \right\} \Big/ h$$

and the variance of the return per unit time defined by

$$\sigma^2 \equiv E_t \left\{ \left[\frac{P(t + h) - P(t)}{P(t)} - \alpha h \right]^2 \right\} \Big/ h.$$

exist, are finite with $\sigma^2 > 0$, and are (right) continuous functions of h, where E_t is the conditional expectation operator, conditional on the levels of the state variables at time t. In the limit as h tends to zero, α is called the instantaneous expected return and σ^2 the instantaneous variance of the return.

Assumption 8 is not too restrictive since it is not required that the stochastic processes describing returns be Markov by themselves but only that, by the "expansion of the state" (supplementary variables) technique (Cox and Miller, 1968, p. 262) to include (a finite number of) other variables describing the changes in the transition probabilities, the entire (expanded) set be Markov. This generalized use of the Markov assumption for the returns is important because one would expect that the required returns will depend on other variables besides the price per share (e.g. the relative supplies of assets).

Assumption 9 is the discrete-time analog to the continuous-time assumption of continuity in the state variables (i.e. if $X(t + h)$ is the random state variable, then, with probability one, $\lim_{h \to 0}[X(t + h) - X(t)] = 0$). In words, it says that, over small time intervals, price changes (returns) and changes in the opportunity set are small. This restriction is nontrivial since

---

15 While it is not necessary to assume that the processes are independent of calendar time, nothing of content is lost by it. However, when a state variable is declared as constant in the text, we really mean nonstochastic. Thus, the term "constant" is used to describe variables which are deterministic functions of time.

the implied "smoothness" rules out Pareto–Levy or Poisson-type jump processes.[16]

Assumption 10 ensures that, for small time intervals, the uncertainty neither "washes out" (i.e. $\sigma^2 = 0$) nor dominates the analysis (i.e. $\sigma^2 = \infty$). Actually, Assumption 10 follows from Assumptions 8 and 9 (see Feller, 1966, p. 321).

If we let $\{X(t)\}$ stand for the vector stochastic process, then Assumptions 8–10 imply that, in the limit as h tends to zero, $X(t)$ is a diffusion process with continuous state-space changes and that the transition probabilities will satisfy a (multidimensional) Fokker–Planck or Kolmogorov partial differential equation.

Although these partial differential equations are sufficient for study of the transition probabilities, it is useful to write down the explicit return dynamics in stochastic difference equation form and then, by taking limits, in stochastic differential equation form. From the previous analysis, we can write the returns dynamics as

$$\frac{P(t + h) - P(t)}{P(t)} = \alpha h + \sigma y(t) h^{1/2} \qquad (15.3)$$

where, by construction, $E_t(y) = 0$ and $E_t(y^2) = 1$, and $y(t)$ is a purely random process; i.e. $y(t)$ and $y(t + s)$, for $s > 0$, are identically distributed and mutually independent.[17] If we define the stochastic process $z(t)$ by

$$z(t + h) = z(t) + y(t) h^{1/2} \qquad (15.4)$$

then $z(t)$ is a stochastic process with independent increments. If it is further assumed that $y(t)$ is Gaussian distributed,[18] then the limit as h tends to zero of $z(t + h) - z(t)$ describes a Wiener process or Brownian motion. In the formalism of stochastic differential equations,

$$dz \equiv y(t)(dt)^{1/2} \qquad (15.5)$$

16   While a similar analysis can be performed for Poisson-type processes (see Kushner, 1967; Merton, 1971 (this volume, Ch. 5)) and for the subordinated processes of Press (1967) and Clark (1973), most of the results derived under the continuity assumption will not obtain in these cases. 1992 note: for some results, see Jarrow and Rosenfeld (1984), Jorion (1988), and Naik and Lee (1991).

17   It is sufficient to assume that the $y(t)$ are uncorrelated and that the higher-order moments are $o(1/h^{1/2})$. This assumption is consistent with a weak form of the Efficient Market Hypothesis of Samuelson (1965b) and Fama (1965a). See Merton and Samuelson (1974) for further discussion.

18   While the Gaussian assumption is not necessary for the analysis, the generality gained by not making that assumption is more apparent than real, since it can be shown that all continuous diffusion processes can be described as functions of Brownian motion (see Feller, 1966, p. 326; Itô and McKean, 1964).

In a similar fashion, we can take the limit of (15.3) to derive the stochastic differential equation for the instantaneous return on the ith asset as

$$\frac{dP_i}{P_i} = \alpha_i \, dt + \sigma_i \, dz_i \tag{15.6}$$

Processes such as (15.6) are called Itô processes and, while they are continuous, they are not differentiable.[19]

From (15.6), a sufficient set of statistics for the opportunity set at a given point in time is $\{\alpha_i, \sigma_i, \rho_{ij}\}$ where ρ_{ij} is the instantaneous correlation coefficient between the Wiener processes dz_i and dz_j. The vector of return dynamics as described in (15.6) will be Markov only if α_i, σ_i, and ρ_{ij} are, at most, functions of the Ps. In general, one would not expect this to be the case since, at each point in time, equilibrium clearing conditions will define a set of implicit functions between equilibrium market values, $V_i(t) = N_i(t)P_i(t)$, and the α_i, σ_i, and ρ_{ij}. Hence, one would expect the changes in required expected returns to be stochastically related to changes in market values, and dependence on P solely would obtain only if changes in N (changes in supplies) were nonstochastic. Therefore, to close the system, we append the dynamics for the changes in the opportunity set over time: namely

$$d\alpha_i = a_i \, dt + b_i \, dq_i$$
$$d\sigma_i = u_i \, dt + v_i \, dx_i \tag{15.7}$$

where we do assume that (15.6) and (15.7), together, form a Markov system,[20] with dq_i and dx_i standard Wiener processes.

Under the assumptions of continuous trading and the continuous Markov structure of the stochastic processes, it has been shown that the instantaneous first two moments of the distributions are sufficient statistics.[21] Further, by the existence and boundedness of α and σ, P equal to

19 See Merton (1971; this volume, Ch. 5) for a discussion of Itô processes in a portfolio context. For a general discussion of stochastic differential equations of the Itô type, see Itô and McKean (1964), McKean (1969), and Kushner (1967).

20 It is assumed that the dynamics of α and σ reflect the changes in the supply of shares as well as other factors such as new technical developments. The particular derivation of the dz_i in the text implies that the ρ_{ij} are constants. However, the analysis could be generalized by appending an additional set of dynamics to include changes in the ρ_{ij}.

21 Because these are sufficient statistics, if there are $n + 1$ assets and n is finite, then our assumption of a finite number of dimensions for the vector X can be satisfied. From (15.6) and (15.7), there are three dynamics equations for P, α, and σ for each of the n risky assets and one equation for $d\alpha_{n+1} \equiv dr$, the dynamics of the riskless asset. Thus, X will, in general, have dimension $3n + 1$.

zero is a natural absorbing barrier ensuring limited liability of all assets.

For the rest of the chapter, it is assumed that there are n distinct[22] risky assets and one "instantaneously riskless" asset. "Instantaneously riskless" means that, at each instant of time, each investor knows with certainty that he can earn rate of return $r(t)$ over the next instant by holding the asset (i.e. $\sigma_{n+1} = 0$ and $\alpha_{n+1} \equiv r(t)$). However, the future values of $r(t)$ are not known with certainty (i.e. $b_{n+1} \neq 0$ in (15.7)). We interpret this asset as the exchange asset and $r(t)$ as the instantaneous private-sector borrowing (and lending) rate. Alternatively, the asset could represent (very) short government bonds.

15.4 PREFERENCE STRUCTURE AND BUDGET-EQUATION DYNAMICS

We assume that there are K consumer–investors with preference structures as described in Merton (1971; this volume, Ch. 5): namely, the kth consumer acts so as to

$$\max E_0 \left\{ \int_0^{T^k} U^k[c^k(s), s] \, ds + B^k[W^k(T^k), T^k] \right\} \tag{15.8}$$

where E_0 is the conditional expectation operator, conditional on the current value of his wealth, $W^k(0) = W^k$; the state variables of the investment opportunity set; and the distribution for his age of death, T^k (which is assumed to be independent of investment outcomes). His instantaneous consumption flow at age t is $c^k(t)$.[23] U^k is a strictly concave von Neumann–Morgenstern utility function for consumption and B^k is a strictly concave "bequest" or utility of terminal wealth function.

Dropping the superscripts (except where required for clarity), we can write the accumulation equation for the kth investor as[24]

22 "Distinct" means that none of the assets' returns can be written as an (instantaneous) linear combination of the other assets' returns. Hence, the instantaneous variance–covariance matrix of returns, $\Omega = [\sigma_{ij}]$, is nonsingular.

23 Because we are primarily interested in finding equilibrium conditions for the asset markets, the model assumes a single consumption good. The model could be generalized by making c^k a vector and introducing as state variables the relative prices. While the analysis would be similar to the one-good case, there would be systematic effects on the portfolio demands reflecting hedging behavior against unfavorable shifts in relative consumption goods prices (i.e. in the consumption opportunity set).

24 See Merton (1971; this volume, Ch. 5) for a derivation of (15.9).

$$dW = \sum_{1}^{n+1} w_i W \frac{dP_i}{P_i} + (y - c)\, dt \qquad (15.9)$$

where $w_i \equiv N_i P_i / W$ is the fraction of his wealth invested in the ith asset, N_i is the number of shares of the ith asset he owns, and y is his wage income. Substituting for dP_i / P_i from (15.6), we can rewrite (15.9) as

$$dW = \left[\sum_{1}^{n} w_i(\alpha_i - r) + r \right] W\, dt + \sum_{1}^{n} w_i W \sigma_i\, dz_i + (y - c)\, dt$$
$$(15.10)$$

where his choice for $w_1, w_2, \ldots, w_n$ is unconstrained because w_{n+1} can always be chosen to satisfy the budget constraint $\sum_{1}^{n+1} w_i = 1$.

From the budget constraint, $W = \sum_{1}^{n+1} N_i P_i$, and the accumulation equation (15.9), we have that

$$(y - c)\, dt = \sum_{1}^{n+1} dN_i(P_i + dP_i) \qquad (15.11)$$

i.e. the net value of new shares purchased must equal the value of savings from wage income.

15.5 THE EQUATIONS OF OPTIMALITY: THE DEMAND FUNCTIONS FOR ASSETS

For computational simplicity, we will assume that investors derive all their income from capital gains sources (i.e. $y \equiv 0$),[25] and for notational simplicity, we introduce the state-variable vector X whose m elements x_i denote the current levels of P, α, and σ. The dynamics for X are written as the vector Itô process

$$dX = F(X)\, dt + G(X)\, dQ \qquad (15.12)$$

where F is the vector $[f_1, f_2, \ldots, f_m]$, G is a diagonal matrix with diagonal elements $[g_1, g_2, \ldots, g_m]$, dQ is the vector Wiener process $[dq_1, dq_2, \ldots, dq_m]$, η_{ij} is the instantaneous correlation coefficient between dq_i and dz_j, and ν_{ij} is the instantaneous correlation coefficient between dq_i and dq_j.

---

25 The analysis would be the same with wage income, provided that investors can issue shares against future income, since we can always redefine wealth as including capitalized future wage income. However, since institutionally this cannot be done, the introduction of wage income will cause systematic effects on the portfolio and consumption decisions.

I have shown elsewhere[26] that the necessary optimality conditions for an investor who acts according to (15.8) in choosing his consumption–investment program are that, at each point in time

$$0 = \max_{\{c,\, w\}} \left(U(c, t) + J_t + J_W \left\{ \left[\sum_1^n w_i(\alpha_i - r) + r \right] W - c \right\} \right.$$

$$+ \sum_1^m J_i f_i + \frac{1}{2} J_{WW} \sum_1^n \sum_1^n w_i w_j \sigma_{ij} W^2$$

$$\left. + \sum_1^m \sum_1^n J_{iW} w_j W g_i \sigma_j \eta_{ij} + \frac{1}{2} \sum_1^m \sum_1^m J_{ij} g_i g_j \nu_{ij} \right) \qquad (15.13)$$

subject to $J(W, T, X) = B(W, T)$, where subscripts on the "derived" utility of wealth function J denote partial derivatives. The σ_{ij} are the instantaneous covariances between the returns on the ith and jth assets ($\equiv \sigma_i \sigma_j \rho_{ij}$).

The $n + 1$ first-order conditions derived from (15.13) are

$$0 = U_c(c, t) - J_W(W, t, X) \qquad (15.14)$$

and

$$0 = J_W(\alpha_i - r) + J_{WW} \sum_1^n w_j W \sigma_{ij} + \sum_1^m J_{jW} g_j \sigma_i \eta_{ji} \qquad i = 1, 2, \ldots, n$$

$$(15.15)$$

where $c = c(W, t, X)$ and $w_i = w_i(W, t, X)$ are the optimal consumption and portfolio rules as functions of the state variables. Equation (15.14) is the usual intertemporal envelope condition to equate the marginal utility of current consumption to the marginal utility of wealth (future consumption). The manifest characteristic of (15.15) is its linearity in the portfolio demands; hence, we can solve explicitly for these functions by matrix inversion,

$$w_i W = A \sum_1^n v_{ij}(\alpha_j - r) + \sum_1^m \sum_1^n H_k \sigma_j g_k \eta_{kj} v_{ij} \qquad i = 1, 2, \ldots, n$$

$$(15.16)$$

26 See Merton (1969a, 1971; this volume, Chs 4 and 5). $J(W, t, X) \equiv \max E_t\{\int_t^T U(c, s)ds + B[W(T), T]\}$ and is called the "derived" utility of wealth function. Substituting from (15.14) and (15.15) to eliminate w_i and c in (15.13) makes (15.13) a partial differential equation for J, subject to the boundary condition $J(W, T, X) = B(W, T)$. Having solved for J, we then substitute for J and its derivatives into (15.14) and (15.15) to find the optimal rules (w_i, c).

where the v_{ij} are the elements of the inverse of the instantaneous variance–covariance matrix of returns, $\Omega = [\sigma_{ij}]$, $A \equiv -J_W/J_{WW}$, and $H_k \equiv -J_{kW}/J_{WW}$.

Some insight into interpreting (15.16) can be gained by expressing A and H_k in terms of the utility and consumption functions: namely, by the Implicit Function Theorem applied to (15.14),

$$A = - \frac{U_c}{U_{cc}(\partial c/\partial W)} > 0 \qquad (15.17)$$

and

$$H_k = - \frac{\partial c/\partial x_k}{\partial c/\partial W} \lesseqgtr 0 \qquad (15.18)$$

From (15.17) and (15.18), we can interpret the demand function (15.16) as having two components. The first term, $A\Sigma_1^n v_{ij}(\alpha_j - r)$, is the usual demand function for a risky asset by a single-period mean–variance maximizer, where A is proportional to the reciprocal of the investor's absolute risk aversion.[27] The second term, $\Sigma_1^m \Sigma_1^n H_k \sigma_j g_k \eta_{kj} v_{ij}$, reflects his demand for the asset as a vehicle to hedge against "unfavorable" shifts in the investment opportunity set. An "unfavorable" shift in the opportunity set variable x_k is defined as a change in x_k such that (future) consumption will fall for a given level of (future) wealth. An example of an unfavorable shift would be if $\partial c/\partial x_k < 0$ and x_k increased.

It can be shown, by differentiating (15.16) with respect to η_{ij}, that all risk-averse utility maximizers will attempt to hedge against such shifts in the sense that, if $\partial c/\partial x_k < (>) 0$, then, *ceteris paribus*, they will demand more of the ith asset, the more positively (negatively) correlated its return is with changes in x_k. Thus, if the *ex post* opportunity set is less favorable than was anticipated, the investor will expect to be compensated by a higher level of wealth through the positive correlation of the returns. Similarly, if *ex post* returns are lower, he will expect a more favorable investment environment.

Although this behavior implies a type of intertemporal consumption "smoothing," it is not the traditional type of maintenance of a constant level of consumption, but rather it reflects an attempt to minimize the (unanticipated) variability in consumption over time. A simple example will illustrate the point. Assume a single risky asset, a riskless asset with return r, and X a scalar (e.g. $X = r$). Further, require that $\alpha = r$. Standard portfolio analysis would show that a risk-averse investor would invest all

---

27   See Merton (1972a, equation (36)).

his wealth in the riskless asset (i.e. $w = 0$). Consider the (instantaneous) variance of the change in consumption which, by Itô's lemma,[28] can be written as $c_x^2 g^2 + c_W^2 w^2 W^2 \sigma^2 + 2 c_x c_W w W g \sigma \eta$, where subscripts denote partial derivatives of the (optimal) consumption function. Simple differentiation will show that this variance is minimized at $wW = -c_x \eta g / \sigma c_W$, which is exactly the demand given by (15.16), and for $c_x < 0$ and $\eta > 0$, $w > 0$. Thus, an intertemporal investor who currently faces a 5 percent interest rate and a possible interest rate of either 2 or 10 percent next period will have portfolio demands different from a single-period maximizer in the same environment or an intertemporal maximizer facing a constant interest rate of 5 percent over time.

We have derived explicit expressions for the portfolio demands and have given some interpretations of their meaning. However, further analysis at this level of generality is complex and hence the resulting economic interpretations may be less intuitive than in a more specialized setting. While some simplification could be gained by restricting the class of utility functions (see Merton, 1971; this volume, equations (5.99)–(5.101)), a more fruitful approach is to add some additional (simplifying) assumptions to restrict the structure of the investment opportunity set. Therefore, to provide the basic economic intuition, equilibrium asset prices are derived in two special, but important, cases. We then return to the model of this section and develop the intertemporal CAPM for the general case.

15.6 CONSTANT INVESTMENT OPPORTUNITY SET

The simplest form of the model occurs when the investment opportunity set is constant through time (i.e. α, r, and Ω are constants), and from (15.6) the distributions for price per share will be log-normal for all assets. This form of the model is examined in detail in Merton (1971; this volume, Section 5.5), and hence the main results are presented without proof.

In this case, the demand for the ith asset by the kth investor, (15.16), reduces to

$$w_i^k W^k = A^k \sum_1^n v_{ij}(\alpha_j - r) \qquad i = 1, 2, \dots, n \qquad (15.19)$$

which is the same demand that a one-period[29] risk-averse mean–variance

---

28   Itô's lemma is the analog to the Fundamental Theorem of the Calculus for Itô processes. See Merton (1971; this volume, Section 5.2) for a brief description and McKean (1969, p. 32) for a formal proof.
29   Of course, since "one period" is an instant, a meaningful interpretation is that investors behave myopically.

investor would have. If all investors agree on the investment opportunity set (homogeneous expectations), then the ratio of the demands for risky assets will be independent of preferences and the same for all investors. Further, we have the following theorem.[30]

Theorem 15.1

Given n risky assets whose returns are log-normally distributed and a riskless asset, then (a) there exists a unique pair of efficient portfolios ("mutual funds"), one containing only the riskless asset and the other only risky assets, such that, independent of preferences, wealth distribution, or time horizon, all investors will be indifferent between choosing portfolios from among the original $n + 1$ assets or from these two funds; (b) the distribution of the return on the risky fund is log-normal; (c) the proportion of the risky fund's assets invested in the kth asset is

$$\sum_1^n v_{kj}(\alpha_j - r) \bigg/ \sum_1^n \sum_1^n v_{ij}(\alpha_j - r) \quad k = 1,2,...,n$$

Theorem 15.1 is the continuous-time version of the Markowitz–Tobin separation theorem and the holdings of the risky fund correspond to the Optimal Combination of Risky Assets (see Sharpe, 1970, p. 69).

Using the condition that the market portfolio is efficient in equilibrium, it can be shown (see Merton, 1972a) that, for this version of the model, the equilibrium returns will satisfy

$$\alpha_i - r = \beta_i(\alpha_M - r) \quad i = 1,2,..., n \quad (15.20)$$

where $\beta_i \equiv \sigma_{iM}/\sigma_M^2$, σ_{iM} is the covariance of the return on the ith asset with the return on the market portfolio, and α_M is the expected return on the market portfolio. Equation (15.20) is the continuous-time analog to the Security Market Line of the classical CAPM.

Hence, the additional assumption of a constant investment opportunity set is a sufficient condition for investors to behave as if they were single-period maximizers and for the equilibrium return relation specified

---

30 Theorem 15.1 is stated and proved in a more general form, including the possibility of no riskless asset, in Merton (1971; this volume, Theorem 5.2). The uniqueness of the two funds is ensured by the requirement that one fund hold only the riskless asset and the other only risky assets, and that both funds be efficient. Otherwise, the funds are unique only up to a nonsingular linear transformation. A further requirement is that $r < \sum_1^n \sum_1^n v_{ij}\alpha_j/\sum_1^n \sum_1^n v_{ij}$. However, since this is a necessary condition for equilibrium, it is assumed to be satisfied. See Merton (1972a) for a complete discussion of this point.

by the CAPM to obtain. Except for some singular cases, this assumption is also necessary. Thus, this version of our model represents a watershed between the static and dynamic models of equilibrium asset prices.

15.7 GENERALIZED SEPARATION: A THREE-FUND THEOREM

Unfortunately, the assumption of a constant investment opportunity set is not consistent with the facts, since there exists at least one element of the opportunity set which is directly observable, namely the interest rate, and it is definitely changing stochastically over time. The simplest form of the model consistent with this observation occurs if it is assumed that a single state variable is sufficient to describe changes in the opportunity set. We further assume that this variable is the interest rate (i.e. $\alpha_i = \alpha_i(r)$ and $\sigma_i = \sigma_i(r)$).

The interest rate has always been an important variable in portfolio theory, general capital theory, and to practitioners. It is observable, satisfies the condition of being stochastic over time, and, while it is surely not the sole determinant of yields on other assets,[31] it is an important factor. Hence, one should interpret the effects of a changing interest rate in the forthcoming analysis in the way economists have generally done in the past: namely, as a single (instrumental) variable representation of shifts in the investment opportunity set. For example, $\partial c/\partial r$ is the change in consumption due to a change in the opportunity set for a fixed level of wealth.

This assumed, we can write the kth investor's demand function for the ith asset, (15.16), as

$$d_i^k = A^k \sum_1^n v_{ij}(\alpha_j - r) + H^k \sum_1^n v_{ij}\sigma_{jr} \qquad i = 1,2,\ldots,n \quad (15.21)$$

where $d_i^k \equiv w_i^k W^k$; $H^k \equiv -(\partial c^k/\partial r)/(\partial c^k/\partial W^k)$, and σ_{jr} is the (instantaneous) covariance between the return on the jth asset and changes in the interest rate $(= \rho_{jr}\sigma_j g)$. By inspection of (15.21), the ratio of the demands for risky assets is a function of preferences, and hence the standard separation theorem does not obtain. However, generalized separation (see Cass and Stiglitz, 1970) does obtain. In particular, it will be shown that all investors' optimal portfolios can be represented as a linear combination of three mutual funds (portfolios).

---

31 The reader should not interpret this statement as implying a causal relation between interest rates and yields. All that is questioned is whether there exists an implicit functional relation between the interest rate and other yields.

Although not necessary for the theorem, it will throw light on the analysis to assume there exists an asset (by convention, the nth one) whose return is perfectly negatively correlated with changes in r, i.e. $\rho_{nr} = -1$. One such asset might be riskless (in terms of default) long-term bonds.[32] In this case, we can rewrite the covariance term σ_{jr} as

$$\sigma_{jr} = \rho_{jr}\sigma_j g$$

$$= -\frac{g(\rho_{jn}\sigma_j\sigma_n)}{\sigma_n} \quad \text{because } \rho_{jr} = -\rho_{jn}$$

$$= -g\sigma_{jn}/\sigma_n \tag{15.22}$$

where g is the standard deviation of the change in r. From (15.22), we can write the second term in the demand function (15.21), $\Sigma_1^n v_{ij}\sigma_{jr}$, as $-g(\Sigma_1^n v_{ij}\sigma_{jn})/\sigma_n$ which equals zero for $i \neq n$ and equals $-g/\sigma_n$ for $i = n$, because the v_{ij} are the elements of the inverse of the variance–covariance matrix of returns.[33] Hence, we can rewrite (15.21) in the simplified form

$$d_i^k = A^k \sum_1^n v_{ij}(\alpha_j - r) \quad i = 1,2,...,n - 1 \tag{15.23}$$

$$d_n^k = A^k \sum_1^n v_{nj}(\alpha_j - r) - \frac{gH^k}{\sigma_n}$$

Theorem 15.2 ("Three-Fund" Theorem)

Given n risky assets and a riskless asset satisfying the conditions of this section, then there exist three portfolios ("mutual funds") constructed from these assets such that (a) all risk-averse investors, who behave according to (15.8), will be indifferent between choosing portfolios from among the original $n + 1$ assets or from these three funds; (b) the proportions of each fund's portfolio invested in the individual assets are purely "technological" (i.e. depend only on the variables in the investment opportunity set for individual assets and not on investor preferences); and (c) the investor's demands for the funds do not require knowledge either of the investment opportunity set for the individual assets or of the asset proportions held by the funds.

32 We only interpret this asset as a long-term bond as a conceptual device. Although long-term bonds will be highly correlated with short rate changes, it is quite likely that they are not perfectly correlated.
33 I am indebted to Fischer Black for pointing out this simplification.

PROOF

Let the first fund hold the same proportions as the risky fund in Theorem 15.1: namely, $\delta_k = \Sigma_1^n v_{kj}(\alpha_j - r)/\Sigma_1^n\Sigma_1^n v_{ij}(\alpha_j - r)$, for $k = 1,2,...,n$. Let the second fund hold only the nth asset and the third fund only the riskless asset. Let λ_i^k be the fraction of the kth investor's wealth invested in the ith fund, $i = 1,2,3$ ($\Sigma_1^3\lambda_i^k = 1$). To prove (a), we must show that there exists an allocation (λ_1^k, λ_2^k) which exactly replicates the demand functions (15.23), i.e. that

$$\lambda_1^k\delta_i = \frac{A^k}{W^k} \sum_1^n v_{ij}(\alpha_j - r) \quad i = 1, 2,..., n - 1$$

$$\lambda_1^k\delta_n + \lambda_2^k = \frac{A^k}{W^k} \sum_1^n v_{nj}(\alpha_j - r) - \frac{gH^k}{\sigma_n W^k} \tag{15.24}$$

From the definition of δ_i, the allocation $\lambda_1^k = (A^k/W^k)\Sigma_1^n\Sigma_1^n v_{ij}(\alpha_j - r)$ and $\lambda_2^k = -gH^k/\sigma_n W^k$ satisfies (15.24). Part (b) follows from the choice for the three funds. To prove (c), we must show that investors will select this allocation, given only the knowledge of the (aggregated) investment opportunity set, i.e. given (α, α_n, r, σ, σ_n, ρ, g) where α and σ^2 are the expected return and variance on the first fund's portfolio and ρ is its correlation coefficient with the return on the second fund. From the definition of δ_i, it is straightforward to show that $(\alpha - r)/\sigma^2 = \Sigma_1^n\Sigma_1^n v_{ij}(\alpha_j - r)$ and $\rho = \sigma(\alpha_n - r)/\sigma_n(\alpha - r)$. The demand functions for the funds will be of the same form as (15.23) with $n = 2$, and the proportions derived from these equations are λ_1^k and λ_2^k where λ_1^k can be rewritten as $A^k(\alpha - r)/\sigma^2 W^k$. QED

Theorem 15.2 is a decentralization theorem which states that, if investors believe that professional portfolio managers' estimates of the distribution of returns are at least as good as any the investor might form, then the investment decision can be separated into two parts by the establishment of three financial intermediaries (mutual funds) to hold all individual assets and to issue shares of their own for purchase by individual investors. Funds one and three provide the "service" to investors of an (instantaneously) efficient risk-return frontier while fund two allows investors to hedge against unfavorable intertemporal shifts in the frontier. Note that the demand for the second fund by the kth investor, $\lambda_2^k W^k$, will be greater than, equal to, or less than zero depending on whether $\partial c^k/\partial r$ is greater than, equal to, or less than zero, which is consistent with the hedging behavior discussed in the general case of Section 15.5.

15.8 THE EQUILIBRIUM YIELD RELATION AMONG ASSETS

Given the demand functions (15.23), we now derive the equilibrium market-clearing conditions for the model of Section 15.7, and from these, we derive the equilibrium relation between the expected return on an individual asset and the expected return on the market.

From (15.23), the aggregate demand functions $D_i = \Sigma_1^K d_i^k$ can be written as

$$D_i = A \sum_1^n v_{ij}(\alpha_j - r) \quad i = 1,2,\dots,n-1$$

$$D_n = A \sum_1^n v_{nj}(\alpha_j - r) - \frac{Hg}{\sigma_n} \tag{15.25}$$

where $A \equiv \Sigma_1^K A^k$ and $H \equiv \Sigma_1^K H^k$. If N_i is the number of shares supplied by the ith firm and if it is assumed that the asset market is *always* in equilibrium, then

$$N_i = \sum_1^K N_i^k$$

$$dN_i = \sum_1^K dN_i^k \quad i = 1, 2,\dots, n+1 \tag{15.26}$$

Furthermore, $\Sigma_1^{n+1} N_i P_i = \Sigma_1^{n+1} D_i \equiv M$, where M is the (equilibrium) value of all assets, the market.

The equilibrium dynamics for market value can be written as

$$dM = \sum_1^{n+1} N_i \, dP_i + \sum_1^{n+1} dN_i(P_i + dP_i)$$

$$= \sum_1^K dW^k$$

$$= \sum_1^{n+1} D_i \frac{dP_i}{P_i} + \sum_1^K (y^i - c^i) \, dt \tag{15.27}$$

Hence, changes in the value of the market come about by capital gains on current shares outstanding (the first term) and by expansion of the total number of shares outstanding (the second term). To separate the two effects, we use the same technique employed to solve this problem for the individual firm. Let P_M be the price per "share" of the market portfolio and let N be the number of shares where $NP_M \equiv M$. Then, $dM = N\,dP_M + dN(P_M + dP_M)$, and P_M and N are defined by the stochastic differential equations

$$N\,dP_M \equiv \sum_1^{n+1} N_i\,dP_i$$

$$dN(P_M + dP_M) \equiv \sum_1^{n+1} dN_i(P_i + dP_i) \tag{15.28}$$

where, by construction, dP_M/P_M is the rate of return on the market (portfolio).

Substituting from (15.27) into (15.28) and using (15.11), we have

$$dN(P_M + dP_M) = \sum_1^K (y^i - c^i)\,dt$$

$$N\,dP_M = \sum_1^{n+1} D_i\,\frac{dP_i}{P_i} \tag{15.29}$$

If $w_i \equiv N_i P_i/M = D_i/M$, the fractional contribution of the ith firm to total market value, then, from (15.6) and (15.29), the rate of return on the market can be written as

$$\frac{dP_M}{P_M} = \left[\sum_1^n w_j(\alpha_j - r) + r \right] dt + \sum_1^n w_j \sigma_j\,dz_j \tag{15.30}$$

Substituting $w_i M$ for D_i in (15.25), we can solve for the equilibrium expected returns on the individual assets:

$$\alpha_i - r = \frac{M}{A} \sum_1^n w_j \sigma_{ij} + \frac{Hg}{A\sigma_n} \sigma_{in} \quad i = 1,2,\dots,n \tag{15.31}$$

As with any asset, we can define $\alpha_M \,(\equiv \Sigma_1^n w_j(\alpha_j - r) + r)$, $\sigma_{iM} \,(\equiv \Sigma_1^n w_j \sigma_{ij})$, and $\sigma_M^2 \,(\equiv \Sigma_1^n w_j \sigma_{jM})$ as the (instantaneous) expected return, covariance, and variance of the market portfolio. Then (15.31) can be rewritten as

$$\alpha_i - r = \frac{M}{A} \sigma_{iM} + \frac{Hg}{A\sigma_n} \sigma_{in} \quad i = 1,2,\dots,n \tag{15.32}$$

and multiplying (15.32) by w_i and summing, we have

$$\alpha_M - r = \frac{M}{A}\sigma_M^2 + \frac{Hg}{A\sigma_n}\sigma_{Mn} \tag{15.33}$$

Noting that the nth asset satisfies (15.32), we can use it together with (15.33) to rewrite (15.32) as[34]

$$\alpha_i - r = \frac{\sigma_i(\rho_{iM} - \rho_{in}\rho_{nM})}{\sigma_M(1 - \rho_{nM}^2)}(\alpha_M - r) + \frac{\sigma_i(\rho_{in} - \rho_{iM}\rho_{nM})}{\sigma_n(1 - \rho_{nM}^2)}(\alpha_n - r)$$

$$i = 1,2,\ldots,n - 1 \tag{15.34}$$

Equation (15.34) states that, in equilibrium, investors are compensated in terms of expected return for bearing market (systematic) risk and for bearing the risk of unfavorable (from the point of view of the aggregate) shifts in the investment opportunity set; and it is a natural generalization of the Security Market Line of the static CAPM. Note that if a security has no market risk (i.e. $\beta_i = 0 = \rho_{iM}$), its expected return need not be equal to the riskless rate as forecast by the usual model.

Under what conditions will the Security Market Plane equation (15.34) reduce to the (continuous-time) Security Market Line, equation (15.20)? From inspection of the demand equations (15.21), appropriately aggregated, the conditions are

$$H = \sum_1^K - \frac{\partial c^k/\partial r}{\partial c^k/\partial W^k} \equiv 0 \tag{15.35a}$$

or

$$\sigma_{ir} \equiv 0 \quad i = 1,2,\ldots,n \tag{15.35b}$$

There is no obvious reason to believe that (15.35a) should hold unless $\partial c^k/\partial r \equiv 0$ for each investor, and the only additive utility function for which this is so is the Bernoulli logarithmic function.[35] Condition (15.35b)

34 Provided that $|\rho_{nM}| < 1$. Otherwise, (15.34) reduces to (15.20).
35 Hence (15.20) would be the correct specification for the equilibrium relations among expected returns in the "growth-optimum" model (Roll, 1973; and this volume, Ch. 6) even when the investment opportunity set is not constant through time. As shown in Section 16.6, (15.20) will also obtain if there is only one state variable in the economy. See also Chamberlain (1988).

could obtain in two ways: $g \equiv 0$, i.e. the interest rate is nonstochastic, which is not so; or $\rho_{ir} \equiv 0$, i.e. all assets' returns are uncorrelated with changes in the interest rate. While this condition is possible, it would not be a true equilibrium state.

Suppose that by a quirk of nature, $\rho_{ir} \equiv 0$ for all available real assets. Then, since the nth asset does not exist, (15.34) reduces to (15.20). Consider constructing a "manmade" security (e.g. a long-term bond) which is perfectly negatively correlated with changes in the interest rate, and hence, by assumption, not correlated with any other asset or the market (i.e. $\beta_n = 0$). Since $D_n = 0$, we have, from (15.25), that $\alpha_n - r = Hg\sigma_n/A \neq 0$, if $g \neq 0$ and $H \neq 0$. Thus, even though security h has a zero beta, investors will pay a premium (relative to the riskless rate) to other investors for creating this security.

An implication of this analysis for the theory of the term structure of interest rates is that long-term riskless bonds will not satisfy the Expectations Hypothesis ($\alpha_n = r$), even if they have no market risk. The premium charged is not a liquidity premium, and it will be either positive or negative depending on the sign of H. These results are consistent with the Habitat Theory (see Modigliani and Sutch, 1966), if one interprets "habitat" as a stronger (or weaker) preference to hedge against changes in future investment opportunities.

15.9   EMPIRICAL EVIDENCE

Although the model has not been formally tested, we can do some preliminary analysis using the findings of Black, Jensen, and Scholes (1972) and some later unpublished work of Scholes (1971). As mentioned earlier, they found that portfolios constructed to have zero covariance with the market (i.e. $\beta = 0$) had average returns that significantly exceeded the riskless rate, which suggests that there is (at least) another factor besides the market that systematically affects the returns on securities. They call this second factor the "beta factor" because an individual security's covariance with it is a function of the security's beta. In particular, high-beta ($\beta > 1$) stocks had negative correlation and low-beta ($\beta < 1$) stocks had positive correlation. We can summarize the Black, Jensen, and Scholes specification and empirical findings as follows:

$$\alpha_i - r = \beta_i(\alpha_M - r) + \gamma_i(\alpha_0 - r) \tag{15.36}$$

where α_0 is the expected return on the "zero-beta" portfolio, and

$$\alpha_0 > r \tag{15.37a}$$

$$\gamma_i = \gamma_i(\beta_i) \text{ with } \gamma_i(1) = 0 \text{ and } \partial\gamma_i/\partial\beta_i < 0 \qquad (15.37b)$$

While the finding of a second factor is consistent with the *a priori* specification of our model, it cannot be said that their specific findings are in agreement with the model without some further specification of the effect of a shift in r on the investment opportunity set. However, if a shift in r is an instrumental variable for a shift in capitalization rates generally, then an argument can be made that the two are in agreement.

The plan is to show that qualitative characteristics of the coefficient $\sigma_i(\rho_{in} - \rho_{iM}\rho_{nM})/\sigma_n(1 - \rho_{nM}^2)$ in (15.34) as a function of β_i would be the same as those of γ_i in (15.37b), and that the empirical characteristics of the zero-beta portfolio are similar to those of a portfolio of long-term bonds.

If we take the Security Market Line, $\alpha_i = r + \beta_i\lambda$, where $\lambda \equiv \alpha_M - r$, as a reasonable first approximation to the relation among capitalization rates, α_i, then we can compute the logarithmic elasticity of α_i with respect to r as a function of β_i to be

$$\psi(\beta_i) \equiv \frac{r(1 + \beta_i\lambda')}{r + \beta_i\lambda} \qquad (15.38)$$

where $\lambda' \equiv \partial\lambda/\partial r$ is the change in the slope of the Security Market Line with a change in r. From (15.27), we have that this elasticity is almost certainly a monotone decreasing function of β_i since $\psi'(\beta_i) \equiv \partial\psi/\partial\beta_i < 0$ if $\psi(1) < 1$.[36]

If we write the value of firm i as $V_i \equiv \overline{X}_i/\alpha_i$ where $\overline{X}_i$ is the "long-run" expected earnings and α_i is the rate at which they are capitalized, then the percentage change in firm value due to a change in r can be written as

$$\left(\frac{\mathrm{d}V_i}{V_i}\right)_r \equiv \left(\frac{\partial\overline{X}_i/\partial r}{\overline{X}_i} - \frac{\partial\alpha_i/\partial r}{\alpha_i}\right)\mathrm{d}r \qquad (15.39)$$

If we neglect, as second order, the effect of a shift in r on expected future earnings, then the residual effect on return due to a change in r, after taking out the common market factor, will be a systematic function of β_i:

$$d\epsilon(\beta_i) \equiv \left(\frac{\mathrm{d}V_i}{V_i}\right)_r - \beta_i\left(\frac{\mathrm{d}V_M}{V_M}\right)_r$$

---

36 $\psi(1) \geq 1$ would imply that $\lambda'/\lambda \geq 1/r$ which, for typical values of r, would imply a very large positive increase in the slope of the Security Market Line. It is contended that such a shift would be highly unlikely.

$$= -\psi(\beta_i)\,\frac{dr}{r} + \beta_i\psi(1)\,\frac{dr}{r}$$

$$= -\phi(\beta_i)\,\frac{dr}{r} \tag{15.40}$$

where $\phi(\beta_i) \equiv \psi(\beta_i) - \beta_i\psi(1)$ satisfies $\phi(1) = 0$ and $\phi'(\beta_i) < 0$. From (15.40), the correlation coefficient between $d\epsilon$ and dr, $\rho_{\epsilon r}$, will satisfy

$$\rho_{\epsilon r} \gtreqless 0 \text{ as } \beta_i \lesseqgtr 1 \tag{15.41}$$

From the definition of $d\epsilon$ in (15.40), $\rho_{\epsilon r}$ is the partial correlation coefficient, $\rho_{ir} - \rho_{iM}\rho_{rM}$. By definition the nth asset in (15.34) is perfectly negatively correlated with changes in r. Hence, (15.41) can be rewritten as

$$\rho_{in} - \rho_{iM}\rho_{nM} \lesseqgtr 0 \text{ as } \beta_i \lesseqgtr 1 \tag{15.42}$$

Hence, the coefficient of $\alpha_n - r$ in (15.34) could be expected to have the same properties as γ_i in (15.36) and (15.37b).

It still remains to be determined whether the zero-beta portfolio is a proxy for our long-term bond portfolio. Since there are no strong theoretical grounds for $\alpha_n - r$ to be positive[37] and since the zero-beta portfolio is an empirical construct, we resort to an indirect empirical argument based on the findings of Black, Jensen, and Scholes (1972) and Scholes (1971).

Since Scholes found the correlation between the market portfolio and the bond portfolio, ρ_{Mn}, to be close to zero and the correlation between the zero-beta portfolio and the bond portfolio to be significantly positive, it then follows from (15.36) that one would expect to find $\alpha_n - r$ significantly positive.

While the analysis of this section can only be called preliminary, the model specification of Section 15.7 does seem to be more consistent with the data than the CAPM.[38, 39]

---

37   One could argue that $\alpha_n > r$ on the grounds that current consumption is a normal good and, hence, $\partial c/\partial r < 0$ for most people. Also, the existence of wage income would tend to force $\alpha_n > r$. Finally, in a number of studies of the term structure, investigators have found positive premiums on long-term bonds, implying that $\alpha_n > r$.

38   Scholes is in the process of testing the model of Section 15.7. Rie (1972) has also examined the effect of capitalization rate changes on the CAPM.

*39   The following sections do not appear in the original paper (Merton, 1973b).

15.10   AN $(m + 2)$-FUND THEOREM AND THE SECURITY MARKET HYPERPLANE

In the preceding sections, mutual-fund theorems and the equilibrium structure of expected returns on assets were derived in environments where the dynamics of the investment opportunity set are either nonstochastic or described by a single stochastic state variable. We now extend that analysis to the general model of Section 15.5. As discussed at the end of that section, we adopt the notation $S(t) = [S_1(t),...,S_m(t)]$ to denote the m generic state variables required to describe the dynamics of the investment opportunity set. Thus, the system of equations (15.12) for $X(t)$ can be replaced by a corresponding system for $S(t)$. The model is made slightly more general by also permitting investors' preferences to be state dependent. That is, as in Chapter 6, preference functions in (15.8) are now written as $U = U(c, S, t)$ and $B = B(W, S, T)$.

Without loss of generality,[40] we can assume that $S_i(t) > 0$ for $i = 1,...,m$ and for all t. Adopting a similar notation to (15.12), we can thus write the dynamics for $S(t)$ as

$$dS_i = f_i S_i \, dt + g_i S_i \, dq_i \qquad i = 1,2,...,m \qquad (15.43)$$

where $f_i(S, t)$ and $g_i(S, t)$ are well-behaved functions that have finite values for all $S_i < \infty$, $i = 1,...,m$.

From (15.16) and (15.43), the investor's optimal demand for asset i can be written as[41]

$$d_i = A \sum_1^n v_{ij}(\alpha_j - r) + \sum_1^m \sum_1^n H_k S_k g_k \sigma_j \eta_{kj} v_{ij} \qquad i = 1,2,...,n$$

$$(15.44)$$

where, as in Section 15.5, $A = -J_W/J_{WW}$ and $H_k = -J_{kW}/J_{WW}$. The interpretation of A in terms of the direct utility and optimal-consumption functions given in (15.17) still applies. However, the state dependence of the direct utility function changes the interpretation of H_k so that (15.18) now becomes

---

40   If some state variable S_i has the possibility of negative values, then simply replace it with $S_i' \equiv \exp(S_i)$. Because S_i and S_i' are in one-to-one correspondence, S_i can always be recovered from S_i'. Moreover, by Itô's lemma, if the dynamics of S_i follow an Itô process, then so does S_i'. That is, $dS_i'/S_i' = dS_i + (dS_i)^2/2$.

41   The structure of the first-order conditions (15.14) and (15.15) is not changed by the state dependence of preferences (cf. Chapter 6). The reader will note the change in the definition for f_i and g_i from (15.12): namely, the f_i and g_i in (15.12) correspond here to $f_i S_i$ and $g_i S_i$, respectively. Similarly, the subscript k on J here denotes partial differentiation with respect to S_k instead of x_k.

$$H_k = -\frac{\partial c/\partial S_k}{\partial c/\partial W} - \frac{U_{cS_k}}{U_{cc}(\partial c/\partial W)} \tag{15.45}$$

In the specialized environments of Sections 15.6 and 15.7, Theorems 15.1 and 15.2 provide the prescriptions for a small set of specific portfolios or mutual funds that can be used to construct all optimal portfolios. In the language of Chapter 2, these portfolios span the efficient portfolio set. To derive a general mutual-fund theorem that includes Theorems 15.1 and 15.2 as special cases, we first provide a more detailed description of mutual funds and develop the stochastic properties for the returns on a selected set of such portfolios.

For our purposes, a mutual fund is a financial intermediary with assets represented by a portfolio of traded securities, and the value of its assets is given by the market value of its portfolio. The liabilities of the fund are represented by a single class of shares, and the asset value per share is determined by dividing the value of the fund's assets by the number of shares outstanding. The fund is committed to either issue (sell) new shares or redeem (buy) existing shares at the asset value per share. If $V(t)$ denotes the price per share of the fund at time t, then $V(t)$ will equal the asset value per share. We assume that the fund reinvests all dividends and proceeds from sales of its assets. The fund, therefore, pays no dividends on its own shares. Investors can generate cash by redeeming shares at asset value per share. Under these conditions, $V(t + T)/V(t)$ will equal the total return per dollar of investment in the portfolio of the fund between t and $t + T$.

Let $x_j(t)$ denote the fraction of the fund's portfolio allocated to traded asset k at time t, $j = 1,...,n$, and let $1 - \Sigma_1^n x_j(t)$ be the fraction allocated to the riskless asset. Although borrowing and short-selling are permitted, the investment policy of the fund is restricted to the set of policies that ensures that $V(t) > 0$, almost certainly, for all t. If, moreover, $V(t) = 0$, then $x_j(t) = 0$, $j = 1,...,n$. It follows that the dynamics for the price per share of the fund can be written as

$$\frac{dV}{V} = \left[\sum_1^n x_j(\alpha_j - r) + r \right] dt + \sum_1^n x_j\sigma_j \, dz_j \tag{15.46}$$

Analysis in Section 15.5 of the demand functions for assets (15.16) shows that investors hold assets in part to hedge against "unfavorable" changes in the state variables of their environment. The analysis in Section 15.7 suggests that the extent to which investors can hedge against these changes depends on the degree of correlation between the state variables and the returns on the available securities. If we define $Y_i(t) \equiv S_i(t)/V(t)$, then $Y_i(t)/Y_i(0)$ measures the discrepancy between the growth of state variable S_i and the cumulative total return on the fund's portfolio between dates 0 and t. The probability distribution for $Y_i(t)/Y_i(0)$ thus provides an indicator of the effectiveness of the fund as an instrument to hedge against changes in state variable S_i. By Itô's lemma, we have from (15.43) and (15.46) that

$$d(\log Y_i) = d(\log S_i) - d(\log V)$$
$$= \theta_i(t)\,dt + \phi_i(t)\,d\epsilon_i \qquad (15.47)$$

where

$$\theta_i(t) \equiv f_i - \frac{1}{2}g_i^2 + \frac{1}{2}\sum_1^n\sum_1^n x_j x_k \sigma_{jk} - r - \sum_1^n x_j(\alpha_j - r)$$

$$\phi_i^2(t) \equiv g_i^2 + \sum_1^n\sum_1^n x_j x_k \sigma_{jk} - 2\sum_1^n x_j \sigma_j \eta_{ij} g_i$$

$d\epsilon_i \equiv 0$ if $\phi_i(t) = 0$, and otherwise $d\epsilon_i \equiv (g_i\,dq_i - \Sigma_1^n x_j\sigma_j\,dz_j)/\phi_i(t)$, a standard Wiener process.

Theorem 15.3

If the portfolio policy of the fund $\{x_j\}$ is chosen at each date t so as to minimize the unanticipated difference between the growth of S_i and V, then $x_j = g_i\delta_{ij}$ where $\delta_{ij} \equiv \Sigma_1^n v_{kj}\sigma_k\eta_{ik}$, $j = 1,\ldots,n$.

PROOF

From (15.47), the set $\{x_j\}$ that meets the hypothesized condition is the one that minimizes $\phi_i^2(t)$ for each t. The first-order conditions for a minimum are $\partial\phi_i^2/\partial x_j = 2(\Sigma_1^n x_k\sigma_{jk} - \sigma_j\eta_{ij}g_i) = 0$, $j = 1,\ldots,n$. Solving this linear system by matrix inversion gives the portfolio weights $x_j = g_i\Sigma_1^n v_{kj}\sigma_k\eta_{ik}$, $j = 1,\ldots,n$. \hfill QED

By setting $g_i = 1$ in the proof of Theorem 15.3, it follows immediately that the return on the portfolio with proportions $x_j = \delta_{ij}$, $j = 1,\ldots,n$, has the largest possible correlation with dq_i among all feasible portfolios. But, From Theorem 15.3, we have that $x_j/x_k = \delta_{ij}/\delta_{ik}$, j, $k = 1,\ldots,n$, for every $g_i > 0$. Therefore, the returns on the portfolios with weights $\{g_i\delta_{ij}\}$ and $\{\delta_{ij}\}$, respectively, are perfectly positively correlated. Thus, the returns on the portfolio which satisfies the hypothesized condition of Theorem 15.3 will also have the largest possible correlation with unanticipated changes in S_i. This maximal-feasible correlation coefficient, ρ_i^*, can be written as

$$\rho_i^* = \left(\sum_1^n \delta_{ij} \eta_{ij} \sigma_j \right)^{1/2}$$

$$= \left(\sum_1^n \sum_1^n v_{kj} \sigma_k \sigma_j \eta_{ik} \eta_{ij} \right)^{1/2} \tag{15.48}$$

If, as suggested, degree of correlation measures the effectiveness of an investment instrument for hedging against changes in state variables, then portfolios that satisfy Theorem 15.3 should play an important role in the construction of investors' optimal portfolios. Let $V_i(t)$ denote the price per share of a mutual fund with an investment policy that satisfies Theorem 15.3 with respect to S_i, $i = 1,...,m$. By substitution of $x_j = g_i \delta_{ij}$ into (15.46), the dynamics for V_i can be written as

$$\frac{dV_i}{V_i} = \alpha_i^* \, dt + \sigma_i^* \, dz_i^* \qquad i = 1,2,...,m \tag{15.49}$$

where $\alpha_i^* \equiv r + g_i \Sigma_1^n \delta_{ij}(\alpha_j - r)$; $\sigma_i^* \equiv g_i \rho_i^*$; and $dz_i^* \equiv (\Sigma_1^n \delta_{ij} \sigma_j \, dz_j)/\rho_i^*$ is a standard Wiener process.

If Y_i measures the discrepancy between S_i and V_i, then by substitution of the portfolio weights $x_j = g_i \delta_{ij}$ into (15.47), we have that $\theta_i = f_i - \alpha_i^* - \phi_i^2/2$; $\phi_i^2 = [1 - (\rho_i^*)^2]g_i^2$; and $d\epsilon_i = (dq_i - \rho_i^* \, dz_i^*)/[1 - (\rho_i^*)^2]^{1/2}$ for $\rho_i^* < 1$. By definition of Y_i, $d(\log S_i) = d(\log V_i) + d(\log Y_i)$, and hence, from (15.47), we can rewrite the state-variable dynamics as

$$d(\log S_i) = [\alpha_i^* - \tfrac{1}{2}(\sigma_i^*)^2 + \theta_i] \, dt + \sigma_i^* \, dz_i^* + \phi_i \, d\epsilon_i \qquad i = 1,2,...,m \tag{15.50}$$

From (15.48) and the definition of $d\epsilon_i$, we have that for any traded asset k

$$\frac{dP_k}{P_k} d\epsilon_i = \frac{(g_i \eta_{ik} \sigma_k - \Sigma_1^n x_j \sigma_{jk}) \, dt}{g_i[1 - (\rho_i^*)^2]^{1/2}}$$

$$= 0 \tag{15.51}$$

because, from the proof of Theorem 15.3, $g_i \eta_{ik} \sigma_k - \Sigma_1^n x_j \sigma_{jk} = 0$, $k = 1,...,n$. Thus, for $i = 1,...,m$, $d\epsilon_i$ is uncorrelated with the returns on all traded assets and is therefore uncorrelated with the returns on all portfolios. It follows from (15.50) and (15.51) that

$$\frac{dS_i}{S_i} \frac{dP_k}{P_k} = g_i \sigma_k \eta_{ik} \, dt = \sigma_i^* \sigma_k (dz_i^* dz_k) = \frac{dV_i}{V_i} \frac{dP_k}{P_k}$$

$$i = 1,...,m; \, k = 1,...,n$$

Moreover, because dV_i/V_i is the return on a portfolio of traded assets, we have from (15.50) and (15.51) that $g_i \, dq_i = \sigma_i^* \, dz_i^* + \phi_i \, d\epsilon_i$, and hence that $\eta_{ik}^* \equiv (dq_i \, dz_k^*)/dt$ is given by

$$\eta_{ik}^* = \frac{\sigma_i^*(dz_i^* \, dz_k^*)}{g_i \, dt} \qquad i, k = 1,2,...,m \qquad (15.52)$$

In an environment where the investment opportunity set is nonstochastic and preferences are not state dependent, the investor has no need for hedging portfolios as described in (15.49). As shown in Theorem 15.1 for that case, all investors' optimal portfolios can be generated by two mutual funds: a mean–variance-efficient portfolio of risky assets and the riskless asset. Let $V_{m+1}(t)$ denote the price per share on a mutual fund whose investment policy is to hold a mean–variance-efficient portfolio of risky assets and let $V_{m+2}(t)$ denote the price per share on a fund that holds the riskless asset. $dV_{m+2}/V_{m+2} = r \, dt$, and therefore $V_{m+2}(T)/V_{m+2}(t)$ $= \exp[\int_t^T r(\tau) \, d\tau]$. From Theorem 15.1, the portfolio weights $x_k =$ $[\Sigma_1^n v_{kj}(\alpha_j - r)]/\lambda$, $k = 1,...,n$, will satisfy the mean–variance efficiency condition of fund $m + 1$ for any $\lambda > 0$. In Chapter 6, we showed that the portfolio which maximizes the expected logarithmic rate of return is an instantaneously mean–variance-efficient portfolio with $x_k = \Sigma_1^n v_{kj}(\alpha_j - r)$, $k = 1,...,n$. We can therefore choose fund $m + 1$ to be the growth-optimum portfolio by setting $\lambda = 1$.[42] The dynamics for the return on this fund can be written as

$$\frac{dV_{m+1}}{V_{m+1}} = \alpha_{m+1}^* \, dt + \sigma_{m+1}^* \, dz_{m+1}^* \qquad (15.53)$$

where

$$\alpha_{m+1}^* \equiv r + \sum_1^n \sum_1^n v_{kj}(\alpha_j - r)(\alpha_k - r)$$

$$(\sigma_{m+1}^*)^2 \equiv \sum_1^n \sum_1^n v_{kj}(\alpha_j - r)(\alpha_k - r) = \alpha_{m+1}^* - r > 0$$

42   In Chapter 6, we saw that the growth-optimum portfolio is the optimal portfolio for an investor whose objective is to maximize $E_t\{\log[W(T)]\}$ for $t < T$. For the purposes of this chapter, we could select any mean–variance-efficient portfolio for fund $m + 1$. However, as shown in Chapters 6, 14, and 16, the growth-optimum portfolio has special significance in the continuous-time theory of finance. Thus, to connect the analysis here with these other chapters, we select the growth-optimum portfolio as our mean–variance-efficient portfolio.

and

$$\mathrm{d}z^*_{m+1} \equiv \left[\sum_1^n \sum_1^n v_{kj}(\alpha_j - r)\sigma_k \, \mathrm{d}z_k \right] \bigg/ \sigma^*_{m+1}$$

is a standard Wiener process. A mean–variance-efficient portfolio has the following important property.

Theorem 15.4

Let $\mathrm{d}V/V$ be the return on any feasible portfolio constructed from the n risky assets and the riskless asset. If $\mathrm{d}V_{m+1}/V_{m+1}$ is the return on a mean–variance-efficient portfolio, then $\alpha - r = \beta(\alpha^*_{m+1} - r)$ where α is the expected rate of return on the portfolio and $\beta \equiv (\mathrm{d}V/V)(\mathrm{d}V_{m+1}/V_{m+1})$ $/(\mathrm{d}V_{m+1}/V_{m+1})^2$.

PROOF

From (15.46), (15.53), and the definition of β, $\beta \, \mathrm{d}t = (\Sigma_1^n x_j \sigma_j \, \mathrm{d}z_j \, \mathrm{d}z^*_{m+1})/ \sigma^*_{m+1}$. Moreover, $\sigma_j \, \mathrm{d}z_j \, \mathrm{d}z^*_{m+1} = [\Sigma_1^n \Sigma_1^n v_{ki}(\alpha_i - r)\sigma_{kj}/\lambda\sigma^*_{m+1}] \, \mathrm{d}t$. Therefore, $\beta = \Sigma_1^n \Sigma_1^n x_j(\alpha_i - r)(\Sigma_1^n v_{ki}\sigma_{kj})/\lambda(\sigma^*_{m+1})^2$. But, $\Sigma_1^n v_{ki}\sigma_{kj} = 0$ for $i \neq j$ and $\Sigma_1^n v_{ki}\sigma_{kj} = 1$ for $i = j$ and $\lambda(\sigma^*_{m+1})^2 = \alpha^*_{m+1} - r$. Hence, $\beta = \Sigma_1^n x_j(\alpha_j - r)/(\alpha^*_{m+1} - r)$. By definition of α, $\alpha - r = \Sigma_1^n x_j(\alpha_j - r)$. Thus, $\alpha - r = \beta(\alpha^*_{m+1} - r)$.   QED

In both the Sharpe–Lintner–Mossin CAPM and the special version of our continuous-time model in Section 15.6, equilibrium conditions require that the market portfolio is a mean–variance-efficient portfolio. Thus, Theorem 15.4 provides a formal derivation of the Security Market Line, equation (15.20).

Having established the stochastic properties of the returns on the $m + 2$ mutual funds with prices $[V_1(t),...,V_{m+2}(t)]$, we now show that this set of funds is sufficient to generate optimal portfolios for all risk-averse investors.

Theorem 15.5 An (m + 2)-Fund Theorem

There exist $m + 2$ mutual funds constructed from the n risky traded assets and the riskless asset such that (a) all risk-averse investors will be indifferent between choosing portfolios from among the original $n + 1$ assets or from these $m + 2$ funds; (b) the investors' demands for the funds do not require knowledge either of the investment opportunity set for the individually traded assets or of the asset proportions held by the funds; (c) the investment policy for each fund's portfolio holdings of the individually traded assets does not require knowledge of the preferences or endowments of the fund's shareholders.

PROOF

Let σ_{ij}^* denote the covariance rate between dV_i/V_i and dV_j/V_j, i, $j = 1,\ldots,m + 1$, and v_{ij}^* denote the ijth element of the inverse of the variance–covariance matrix $[\sigma_{ij}^*]$. By the symmetry of $[\sigma_{ij}^*]$ and the definition of an inverse, $\Sigma_1^{m+1} v_{ij}^* \sigma_{kj}^* = \Sigma_1^{m+1} v_{ij}^* \sigma_{jk}^* = 0$ if $i \neq k$ and $\Sigma_1^{m+1} v_{ij}^* \sigma_{kj}^* = 1$ if $i = k$. Consider an investor who selects his portfolio by combining only the $m + 2$ funds with returns dV_i/V_i, $i = 1,\ldots,m + 2$. The investor's optimal demand for fund i has the same structural form as (15.44): namely,

$$d_i^* = A \sum_1^{m+1} v_{ij}^*(\alpha_j^* - r) + \sum_1^m \sum_1^{m+1} H_k S_k \sigma_j^* g_k \eta_{kj}^* v_{ij}^* \qquad i = 1,\ldots,m + 1$$

where, as in (15.52), $\eta_{kj}^* \equiv (dq_k \ dz_j^*)/dt$. From (15.52), $\eta_{kj}^* = \sigma_{kj}^*/g_k \sigma_j^*$. Therefore,

$$\sum_1^m \sum_1^{m+1} H_k S_k \sigma_j^* g_k \eta_{kj}^* v_{ij}^* = \sum_1^m H_k S_k \left(\sum_1^{m+1} \sigma_{kj}^* v_{ij}^* \right) = H_i S_i \qquad i = 1,\ldots,m$$

$$= 0 \qquad i = m + 1$$

From Theorem 15.4, $\alpha_j^* - r = \lambda \sigma_{j\,m+1}^*, j = 1,\ldots,m + 1$, and $\lambda = (\alpha_{m+1}^* - r)/(\sigma_{m+1}^*)^2 = 1$ from (15.53). It follows that

$$\sum_1^{m+1} v_{ij}^*(\alpha_j^* - r) = \sum_1^{m+1} v_{ij}^* \sigma_{j\,m+1}^* = 0 \qquad i = 1,\ldots,m$$

$$= 1 \qquad i = m + 1$$

Hence, $d_i^* = H_i S_i$, $i = 1,\ldots,m$, and $d_{m+1}^* = A$. $d_{m+2}^* = W - \Sigma_1^{m+1} d_i^*$. The investor's (indirect) holdings of asset j from the original n traded risky assets is determined by multiplying the dollar demand for fund i by the fraction of the portfolio of fund i allocated to asset j and summing from $i = 1,\ldots,m + 1$. From Theorem 15.3 and (15.53), the investor's holding of asset j is given by

$$\sum_1^m d_i^* g_i \left(\sum_1^n v_{kj} \sigma_k \eta_{ik} \right) + d_{m+1}^* \sum_1^n v_{jk}(\alpha_k - r)$$

$$= \sum_1^m \sum_1^n H_i S_i g_i v_{kj} \sigma_k \eta_{ik} + A \sum_1^n v_{jk}(\alpha_k - r) = d_j$$

as given in (15.44), $j = 1,...,n$. Hence, the investor who selects his portfolio from the $m + 2$ funds ends up holding the identical portfolio that he would have chosen from among the n individually traded risky assets and the riskless asset. This proves (a).

The optimal demands for the funds $\{d_i^*\}$ require the investor to know only the investment opportunity set $\{\alpha_i^*, \sigma_{ij}^*, r, \eta_{ki}^*\}$ for the $m + 2$ funds. Thus, to form his optimal portfolio, the investor need not know either the composition of the funds' portfolios or the joint probability distributions for the returns on the individual assets held by the funds. This proves (b).

By inspection of Theorem 15.3, the investment policy to construct fund i, $i = 1,...,m$, requires only knowledge of the variance–covariance matrix of returns among the n risky assets $[\sigma_{ij}]$ and their covariances with the unanticipated changes in the state variables $\{\eta_{kj}, g_k, k = 1,...,m; j = 1,...,n\}$. These policies do not require knowledge of either the expected returns on assets, $\alpha_j, j = 1,...,n$, or the expected rate of growth in $S_i, f_i, i = 1,...,m$. From (15.53), the construction of the growth-optimum mean–variance-efficient fund $m + 1$ requires knowledge of the means, variances, and covariances of the returns on the n risky traded assets and the riskless interest rate. It does not, however, require knowledge about the state-variable dynamics. Construction of riskless fund $m + 2$ requires no knowledge. In all cases, the investment policies of the $m + 2$ funds do not require knowledge of the funds' shareholders' preferences or endowments (i.e. $A, W, H_k, k = 1,...,m$). This proves (c).   QED

In the proof of Theorem 15.5, it was assumed that the variance–covariance matrix of the funds' returns $[\sigma_{ij}^*]$ is nonsingular. If it were singular, then one or more of the funds' returns can be exactly replicated by a portfolio combination of the other funds. Such funds are redundant securities, and therefore the number of funds required to generate the optimal portfolio set can be smaller than $m + 2$. Such redundancies must occur if the number of state variables is greater than or equal to the number of traded securities (i.e. $m \geq n$). Redundancies will also occur if none of the returns on the traded securities is correlated with unanticipated changes in one or more of the state variables. In that case, investors cannot hedge against changes in those state variables. If, however, $n \gg m$, then Theorem 15.5 provides a basis for a theory of mutual-fund financial intermediation and information separation in a capital market with a large number of traded securities.

As in the discussion of Theorem 15.1 in footnote 30, the set of funds that generates ("spans") the set of optimal portfolios in Theorem 15.5 is unique only up to a nonsingular linear transformation of those portfolios. That is, let $(V'_1,...,V'_{m+1}, V'_{m+2})$ denote the price vector of any set of $m + 2$ mutual funds that span the set of optimal portfolios where, without loss of generality, $V'_{m+2} = V_{m+2}$, the riskless-asset fund.[43] If $[\sigma^*_{ij}]$ has full rank, then there must exist a nonsingular $(m + 1) \times (m + 1)$ matrix L such that the returns satisfy $[dV'_1/V'_1 - r\ dt,...,dV'_{m+1}/V'_{m+1} - r\ dt] = [dV_1/V_1 - r\ dt,...,dV_{m+1}/V_{m+1} - r\ dt]L$.

In Chapter 2 on the static theory of portfolio selection, Theorem 2.13 describes the relations between the returns on traded securities and the returns on any set of spanning portfolios that must obtain if risk-averse investors' preferences depend only on the distribution of "end-of-period" wealth. The analogous theorem in the dynamical, continuous-time framework with state-dependent investor preferences is as follows.

Theorem 15.6

The set of linearly independent portfolios $(V'_1,...,V'_{m+2})$ generates the set of all optimal portfolios if and only if at each time t, there exist numbers $\{b_{ki}\}$ such that for every traded asset k, $k = 1,...,n$, $dP_k/P_k = r\ dt + \Sigma_1^{m+1} b_{ki}(dV'_i/V'_i - r\ dt) + d\psi_k$ where (a) $E_t\{d\psi_k\} = 0$; (b) $d\psi_k dV'_i/V'_i = 0$ for $i = 1,...,m + 1$; and (c) $d\psi_k\ dS_i/S_i = 0$ for $i = 1,...,m$.

PROOF

See Appendix 15A.

Theorem 15.6 implies that the realized return on any traded asset k (and hence, any portfolio of such assets) can always be decomposed into two parts: the "systematic" part, $r\ dt + \Sigma_1^{m+1}b_{ki}(dV'_i/V'_i - r\ dt)$, that can be exactly replicated by a portfolio combination of the $m + 2$ mutual funds that generate the set of optimal portfolios, and the "nonsystematic" part, $d\psi_k$, that is uncorrelated with the return on the $m + 2$ spanning funds and uncorrelated with unanticipated changes in the state variables of the environment. Because $d\psi_k$ is uncorrelated with the returns on all optimal portfolios, the nonsystematic part is also called the "diversifiable-risk" component of the return on asset k. Moreover, because asset returns and

43   Since all spanning sets must be capable of producing a riskless return if a riskless asset exists, nothing of content is lost by imposing this condition.

state-variable dynamics follow Itô processes, the correlation properties of $\mathrm{d}\psi_k$ imply the generally stronger condition that

$$E_t\{\mathrm{d}\psi_k | \mathrm{d}V_1'/V_1', \ldots, \mathrm{d}V_{m+1}'/V_{m+1}', \mathrm{d}S_1/S_1, \ldots, \mathrm{d}S_m/S_m\} = 0$$

In Section 15.8, market-clearing conditions were imposed to derive the equilibrium structure of expected returns on assets in the special case where a single state variable is sufficient to describe changes in the investment opportunity set. We now undertake that same task for the general model of this section.

From Theorem 15.5, investors' demand for assets can be written as if they all selected their optimal portfolios from $m + 2$ mutual funds. In equilibrium, the market portfolio is equal to the aggregation of all investors' optimal portfolios. Thus, the return on the market portfolio can be expressed as a portfolio combination of the returns on the $m + 2$ funds. If, in a similar fashion to (15.25) in Section 15.8, we define D_i^* as the aggregate demand for fund i, then, from the proof of Theorem 15.5, $D_i^* = H_i'S_i$, $i = 1,\ldots,m$, $D_{m+1}^* = A'$, and $D_{m+2}^* = M - \Sigma_1^{m+1} D_i^*$, where H_i' and A' are the sum over all investors of H_i and A, respectively, and M is aggregate wealth.

If, as in (15.30), $w_i^* \equiv D_i^*/M$ denotes the equilibrium fraction of national wealth invested in fund i, $i = 1,\ldots,m + 2$, then the rate of return on the market portfolio can be written as

$$\frac{\mathrm{d}P_M}{P_M} = \sum_1^{m+1} w_i^* \left(\frac{\mathrm{d}V_i}{V_i} - r\,\mathrm{d}t\right) + r\,\mathrm{d}t$$

$$= \alpha_M\,\mathrm{d}t + \sigma_M\,\mathrm{d}z_M \tag{15.54}$$

where $\alpha_M \equiv \Sigma_1^{m+1} w_i^*(\alpha_i^* - r) + r$; $\sigma_{iM}^* \equiv \Sigma_1^{m+1} w_j^*\sigma_{ij}^*$; $\sigma_M^2 \equiv \Sigma_1^{m+1} w_j^*\sigma_{jM}^*$; and $\mathrm{d}z_M \equiv (\Sigma_1^{m+1} w_j^*\sigma_j^*\,\mathrm{d}z_j^*)/\sigma_M$ is a standard Wiener process.

For risk-averse investors, $w_{m+1}^* = A'/M > 0$. Thus, by rearranging terms in (15.54), we can express the return on fund $m + 1$ as a portfolio combination of the returns on the m "hedging" funds and the market portfolio, namely

$$\frac{\mathrm{d}V_{m+1}}{V_{m+1}} = r\,\mathrm{d}t + \sum_1^m \delta_i^*\left(\frac{\mathrm{d}V_i}{V_i} - r\,\mathrm{d}t\right) + \delta_M^*\left(\frac{\mathrm{d}P_M}{P_M} - r\,\mathrm{d}t\right) \tag{15.55}$$

where $\delta_i^* \equiv -w_i^*/w_{m+1}^*$, $i = 1,\ldots,m$, and $\delta_M^* \equiv 1/w_{m+1}^*$. Thus, we have from (15.55) that the growth-optimum, mean–variance-efficient fund $m + 1$ can be replaced by the market portfolio, and the revised set of $m + 2$ funds spans the set of optimal portfolios.

That Theorem 15.5 still applies if the market portfolio is substituted for the mean–variance-efficient fund has important implications for the theory of financial intermediation and information separation among agents. As noted in the proof of part (c) of Theorem 15.5, construction of the m hedging funds requires only that the fund managers know the variances and covariances among the returns on traded assets and the relevant state variables. The fund managers do not have to know either the expected returns on the assets or the expected changes in the state variables. However, from (15.53), to construct the mean–variance-efficient fund requires the fund manager to know the expected returns on all traded assets as well as the variance–covariance matrix of their returns. In contrast, to construct a market portfolio, the fund manager need only hold assets in relative proportions to their observed market prices and therefore he requires no probability distribution information at all. Thus, to construct the set of $m + 2$ spanning funds consisting of the m hedging funds, the market portfolio, and the riskless fund does not require knowledge of the expected returns on assets.

If, as has been assumed throughout, returns on assets are generated by Itô processes and observed continuously, then because $(dP_k/P_k)(dP_j/P_j) = \sigma_{kj}\, dt$ is nonstochastic, the variances and covariances are observable directly from the time series of asset returns and state-variables changes, a data set common to all investors. In contrast, because dP_k/P_k $(= \alpha_k\, dt + \sigma_k\, dz_k)$ is stochastic, the expected returns $\{\alpha_k\}$ are not directly observable from these time series. Moreover, since our model permits the investment opportunity set to change stochastically over time, even the availability of a long time series of historical, realized asset returns does not ensure that expected returns can be estimated within any specified accuracy.[44] Thus, the information required by financial intermediaries to create a set of spanning mutual funds is considerably less than would seem to be required in the proof of Theorem 15.5. Of course, to create their optimal portfolios from among the $m + 2$ funds, investors do require estimates of $(\alpha_1^*,...,\alpha_m^*,\alpha_M)$, and, indeed, some financial institutions may offer such estimates as a service. However, the analysis shows that the information required to provide this forecast service is "separable" from that required to provide efficient mutual-fund financial intermediation services.[45]

44 Williams (1977, Section 2) and Merton (1980) provide more extensive discussions of the reasons why variances and covariances of returns can be estimated from time series of returns much more accurately than expected returns if returns are described by Itô processes. See also the survey article on continuous-time econometric models by Bergstrom (1988) and the papers by Lo (1986, 1988) and Nelson (1991).

45 Williams (1977), Gennotte (1986), and Dothan and Feldman (1986) solve the combined optimal estimation-and-portfolio-selection problem in continuous time where investors or their agents estimate expected returns using historical data.

Let $(V'_1,...,V'_{m+2})$ denote the prices on the spanning portfolio set with the market portfolio replacing the mean–variance-efficient portfolio, i.e. $V'_i = V_i$, $i = 1,...,m$, and $V'_{m+1} = P_M$. Define $\sigma'_{ij} \equiv \sigma^*_{ij}$; $\sigma'_{i\,m+1} \equiv \sigma^*_{iM}$ for i, $j = 1,...,m$, with $\sigma'_{m+1\,m+1} \equiv \sigma^2_M$; and define $\alpha'_i \equiv \alpha^*_i$, $i = 1,...,m$, with $\alpha'_{m+1} \equiv \alpha_M$. From Theorem 15.6, we have that the expected excess return on traded asset k must satisfy

$$\alpha_k - r = \sum_{1}^{m+1} \beta_{ki}(\alpha'_i - r) \qquad k = 1,2,...,n \qquad (15.56)$$

where $\beta_{ki} \equiv [\Sigma_1^{m+1} v'_{ij}(dP_k/P_k)(dV'_j/V'_j)]/dt$, $i = 1,...,m + 1$, and v'_{ij} is the ijth element of the inverse of the variance–covariance matrix $[\sigma'_{ij}]$.[46] Equation (15.56) relates the equilibrium expected excess returns on all traded assets and portfolios to the $m + 1$ equilibrium expected excess returns on the m hedging portfolios and the market portfolio. If, as in the model of Section 15.6, the state variables are nonstochastic, then (15.56) reduces to the continuous-time version of the Security Market Line, (15.20). It becomes the Security Market Plane, (15.34), in the model of Section 15.7. Thus, we call the general form of (15.56), the *Security Market Hyperplane*.

Techniques of valuation, whether for securities or capital investment projects by firms, almost always begin with the determination of the risk class of the security or project, followed by various procedures that relate its value to prices of traded assets in the same risk class. As shown for the definition of the risk of a security in Section 2.3, two assets in the same risk class will, at equilibrium prices, have the same expected returns.[47] In an environment of complete certainty, for example, all assets are in the same risk class and their equilibrium expected returns are all equal to the interest rate. If equilibrium prices satisfy the Sharpe–Lintner–Mossin CAPM, then the expected excess return on each asset is in direct and positive proportion to its beta, and thus all assets with the same beta are in the same risk class. By inspection of the Security Market Hyperplane (15.56), the $(m + 1)$-vector $(\beta_{k1},...,\beta_{k\,m+1})$ for asset k defines its risk class and all assets with the same vector of betas have the same equilibrium expected returns.[48]

---

46 The reader will note that the formula for the $\{\beta_{ki}\}$ is the same as for the theoretical multiple regression coefficients generated by the regression of the excess returns of asset k on the excess returns of the $m + 2$ mutual funds. Indeed, as noted in the text, $E_t\{d\psi_k|dV'_i/V'_i\}, i = 1,...,m + 1\} = 0$, the conditional expectation requirement for valid application of regression analysis.

47 In capital budgeting applications, the equilibrium expected return common to the risk class is called the "cost of capital" of the project.

48 Unlike the relation between beta and expected return in the CAPM, the correspondence between expected return and the beta vector of an asset is not one-to-one. Two assets with identical beta vectors will have the same expected return.

From Theorem 15.6, it is readily apparent that an equivalent equation to (15.56) can be derived for any collection of portfolios that generates the set of optimal portfolios. The set of spanning portfolios selected depends on the initial information set available and the additional information to be extracted from such equations. For example, if the initial information set includes the joint distribution for $(V_1,...,V_{m+2})$, then there would be little point in using the equation corresponding to (15.56) to determine the risk classes of assets. From Theorem 15.4, the expected excess return on any asset k is directly proportional to $\beta = (dP_k/P_k)(dV_{m+1}/V_{m+1})/(dV_{m+1}/V_{m+1})^2$. Thus, knowledge of the covariance structure between the returns on assets and the return on the growth-optimum portfolio V_{m+1} alone is sufficient information to determine the risk class of every asset.

Although the relation in Theorem 15.4 can always be used to determine an asset's risk class, its application for this purpose will generally be "circular." That is, unless a mean–variance-efficient portfolio can be identified from some other condition of the model,[49] the information required in (15.53) to construct the V_{m+1} portfolio includes knowledge of the expected returns on all traded assets, which is, of course, the very information that is to be extracted. In contrast, variances and covariances are the only statistical data required to determine the portfolio compositions of $(V'_1,...,V'_{m+2})$ and the $(\beta_{k1},...,\beta_{k\ m+1})$ in equation (15.56). Hence, the application of the Security Market Hyperplane to determine risk classes of assets is not inherently circular.

Although $(\beta_{k1},...,\beta_{k\ m+1})$ can be derived from variance–covariance information alone, determination of the expected return on asset k, α_k, from (15.56) requires knowledge of $(\alpha'_1,...,\alpha'_{m+1},r)$. Suppose that the expected returns $\bar{\alpha}_i$, $i = 1,...,m + 1$ are known for some collection of $m + 1$ securities. Let $\{\bar{\beta}_{ki}\}$, $i = 1,...,m + 1$, denote the coefficients in (15.56) for security k in that collection, $k = 1,...,m + 1$. Let B denote the $(m + 1) \times (m + 1)$ matrix, whose kith element is $\bar{\beta}_{ki}$. If B is nonsingular, then from (15.56), we have that

$$\alpha'_i - r = \sum_1^{m+1} B_{ij}^{-1}(\bar{\alpha}_j - r) \qquad i = 1,...,m + 1 \qquad (15.57)$$

where B_{ij}^{-1} is the ijth element of the inverse of B. Thus, if the expected returns are known for any such collection of $m + 1$ securities, then by

For a given set of numbers $\alpha'_i - r, i = 1,...,m + 1$, it is, of course, possible for two assets to have the same expected return and not have the elements of their beta vector match. Thus, in this general model, an asset's expected return is not sufficient to determine its risk class.

49 For example, in the classical CAPM, the market portfolio is a mean–variance-efficient portfolio.

substitution for $\alpha_i' - r$ from (15.57) into (15.56), the expected returns on all traded assets can be determined.

15.11 ˙THE CONSUMPTION-BASED CAPITAL ASSET PRICING MODEL

Because the state variables in Section 15.10 are generic, the model of that section is robust in the sense that it can capture investors' desires to hedge against other economic events in addition to shifts in the investment opportunity set. To either test or apply the model requires, of course, that the relevant state variables of the environment can be identified.

One approach to solving this identification problem is the purely empirical one generally associated with applications of the Ross (1976a) Arbitrage Pricing Theory. From the derived specification of asset-return dynamics in Theorem 5.6, factor analysis can be applied directly to the historical time series of returns to calculate the "implied" state variables of the environment.[50] An alternative approach is to specify the state variables from *a priori* theoretical reasoning. The Consumer-Services Model of Merton (1975b, 1977c) provides a list of potential candidates. Solnik (1973, 1974) and Stulz (1981) apply the model of Section 15.10 in an international context and associate the state variables with country-specific tastes and production technologies. A particularly imaginative and fundamental contribution to this theoretical approach is Breeden's (1979) Consumption-Based Capital Asset Pricing Model.

To develop the Breeden model, we begin by deriving the stochastic properties of the marginal-utility-of-wealth function, $\partial J/\partial W$, for a given investor. From the proof of Theorem 15.5, the investor's accumulation equation can be written in terms of the returns on the $m + 2$ mutual funds $(V_1, \ldots, V_{m+2})$, defined in (15.49) and (15.53), as

$$dW = \left[\sum_1^m H_i S_i (\alpha_i^* - r) + A(\alpha_{m+1}^* - r) + rW - c \right] dt$$

$$+ \sum_1^m H_i S_i \sigma_i^* \, dz_i^* + A\sigma_{m+1}^* \, dz_{m+1}^* \tag{15.58}$$

Define $G(W, S, t) \equiv \partial J/\partial W = J_W$. From (15.43), (15.58) and Itô's lemma, the dynamics for G can be expressed as

---

50   For discussion, pro and con, of this approach, see Brown (1989), Chamberlain and Rothschild (1983), Connor and Korajczyk (1988), Constantinides (1989), Dhrymes, Friend, and Gultekin (1984, 1985), Dybvig and Ross (1985), Lehmann and Modest (1988), Roll and Ross (1980), Rothschild (1986), Shanken (1982, 1985), and Trzcinka (1986).

$$\frac{dG}{G} = \mu \; dt + \frac{J_{WW}}{J_W} \left(\sum_1^m H_i S_i \sigma_i^* \; dz_i^* + A \sigma_{m+1}^* \; dz_{m+1}^* \right)$$

$$+ \sum_1^m \left(\frac{J_{Wi}}{J_W} \right) S_i g_i \; dq_i$$

$$(15.59)$$

where μ is the expected rate of growth of G, and

$$\mu G = J_{WW} \left[\sum_1^m H_i S_i (\alpha_i^* - r) + A(\alpha_{m+1}^* - r) + rW - c \right] + J_{Wt}$$

$$+ \sum_1^m J_{Wk} f_k S_k + \frac{1}{2} J_{WWW} \left[\sum_1^m \sum_1^m H_i H_j S_i S_j \sigma_{ij}^* \right.$$

$$+ 2A \sum_1^m H_i S_i \sigma_{im+1}^* + A^2 (\sigma_{m+1}^*)^2 \left] + \frac{1}{2} \sum_1^m \sum_1^m J_{Wki} g_k g_i S_k S_i \nu_{ki} \right.$$

$$+ \sum_1^m \sum_1^m J_{WWk} H_i S_i S_k \sigma_{ik}^* + A \sum_1^m J_{WWk} \sigma_{km+1}^* S_k$$

Noting that $A \equiv -J_W/J_{WW}$ and that $J_{Wi}/J_W = H_i/A$, we can rewrite (15.59) as

$$\frac{dG}{G} = \mu \; dt - \sigma_{m+1}^* \; dz_{m+1}^* - \sum_1^m \frac{H_i S_i}{A} (\sigma_i^* \; dz_i^* - g_i \; dq_i)$$

$$= \mu \; dt - \sigma_{m+1}^* \; dz_{m+1}^* + \sum_1^m \frac{H_i S_i}{A} \phi_i \; d\epsilon_i \qquad (15.60)$$

where, from (15.50), $\phi_i \; d\epsilon_i = g_i \; dq_i - \sigma_i^* \; dz_i^*$.

From (15.51), we have that, for any traded asset k, $(dP_k/P_k) \; d\epsilon_i = 0$, $i = 1,\ldots,m$. It follows from (15.60) that

$$\frac{dP_k}{P_k} \frac{dG}{G} = - \frac{dP_k}{P_k} \sigma_{m+1}^* \; dz_{m+1}^* = - \frac{dP_k}{P_k} \frac{dV_{m+1}}{V_{m+1}}$$

But $(\alpha_{m+1}^* - r)/(\sigma_{m+1}^*)^2 = 1$, and from Theorem 15.4,

$$\frac{dP_k}{P_k} \frac{dV_{m+1}}{V_{m+1}} = \frac{(\alpha_k - r)(\sigma_{m+1}^*)^2 \; dt}{\alpha_{m+1}^* - r}$$

Hence, we have that

$$\alpha_k - r = - \frac{dP_k}{P_k} \frac{dG}{G} \Big/ dt \qquad k = 1,\ldots,n \qquad (15.61)$$

Thus, the expected excess return on every traded asset (and therefore every portfolio of such assets) is equal to the negative of the instantaneous covariance between the return on the asset and the realized growth rate of the investor's marginal utility of wealth.[51]

If there are K individual investors in the economy and G^q denotes the marginal utility of wealth for investor q, then it follows immediately from (15.61) that

$$\frac{dP_k}{P_k} \frac{dG^i}{G^i} = \frac{dP_k}{P_k} \frac{dG^j}{G^j} \qquad k = 1,\ldots,n \qquad (15.62)$$

for $i, j = 1,\ldots,K$. Moreover, if investors' optimal consumption rules satisfy the first-order condition (15.14), then $U_c = J_W \equiv G$, and (15.61) and (15.62) can be interpreted in terms of covariances between returns on assets and the growth rates of the marginal utilities of consumption.

Like the Security Market Hyperplane (15.56), (15.61) specifies an equilibrium relation among expected returns on assets. But, unlike in (15.56), the application of (15.61) to determine expected returns requires knowledge of investor preferences. Preferences are probably more difficult to estimate from the available data sets than expected returns. Thus, (15.61) will not in general provide a useful empirical specification for the determination of asset risk classes and expected returns. However, Breeden (1979) shows that with certain restrictions on preferences, (15.61) can be transformed into an otherwise preference-free specification.

Suppose that the direct utility function for investor q is not state dependent. That is, $U^q = U^q(c^q, t)$ does not depend explicitly on $[S_1,\ldots,S_m]$. If the optimal consumption rule, c^q, satisfies (15.14), then by Itô's lemma

$$dG^q = U^q_{cc} \, dc^q + U^q_{ct} \, dt + \frac{U^q_{ccc}(dc^q)^2}{2} \qquad (15.63)$$

If $\Delta_q \equiv E_t\{dc^q/c^q\}/dt$ denotes the expected rate of growth of investor q's consumption, then from rearranging (15.60) and (15.63) we have that

---

51   Equation (15.61) is similar to the relation derived between expected returns and the b_p^K risk measure in Theorem 2.4.

$$\frac{dc^q}{c^q} = \Delta_q \, dt - \frac{1}{\delta^q} \left(\frac{dG^q}{G^q} - \mu^q \, dt \right)$$

$$= \Delta_q \, dt + \frac{\sigma^*_{m+1}}{\delta^q} \, dz^*_{m+1} - \sum_1^m \Gamma_i^q S_i \phi_i \, d\epsilon_i \qquad (15.64)$$

where $\delta^q \equiv -U_{cc}^q c^q / U_c^q$, investor q's relative risk aversion for consumption, and $\Gamma_i^q \equiv H_i^q / A^q \delta^q = -J_{Wi}^q / U_{cc}^q c^q$, $i = 1,\dots,m$.

From (15.63) and (15.64),

$$\frac{dP_k}{P_k} \frac{dG^q}{G^q} = -\delta^q \frac{dP_k}{P_k} \frac{dc^q}{c^q}$$

Hence, for any investor q with state-independent preferences, we have from (15.61) and (15.62) that

$$\alpha_k - r = \delta^q \frac{dP_k}{P_k} \frac{dc^q}{c^q} \bigg/ dt \qquad k = 1,\dots,n \qquad (15.65)$$

Thus, for risk-averse investors ($\delta^q > 0$), the expected excess return on any traded asset is directly and positively proportional to the instantaneous covariance of its return with the realized rate of growth of investor q's optimal consumption.

With these stochastic properties of G and c^q established, we now derive Breeden's main result.

Theorem 15.7

Let C denote the aggregate consumption rate. If, for every investor q, $U^q = U^q(c^q, t)$ and $U_c^q = J_W^q$, $q = 1,\dots,K$, then at each date t and for each traded asset k, there exists a number $\beta_{kC} \equiv (dP_k/P_k)(dC/C)/dt$ such that (a) $\alpha_k = r$ if $\beta_{kC} = 0$, and (b) for any asset j with $\beta_{jC} \neq 0$, $\alpha_k - r = \beta_{kC}(\alpha_j - r)/\beta_{jC}$, $k = 1,\dots,n$.

PROOF

By definition, $C = \Sigma_1^K c^q$, and therefore $dC/C = \Sigma_1^K x_q(dc^q/c^q)$ where $x_q \equiv c^q/C$ is investor q's (nonnegative) fraction of aggregate consumption. It follows that

$$\beta_{kC} \equiv \frac{dP_k}{P_k} \frac{dC}{C} \bigg/ dt = \frac{dP_k}{P_k} \left(\sum_1^K x_q \frac{dc^q}{c^q} \right) \bigg/ dt = \sum_1^K x_q \frac{dP_k}{P_k} \frac{dc^q}{c^q} \bigg/ dt$$

By hypothesis, all investors' preferences are state independent and their optimal consumption rules satisfy (15.14). Hence, (15.65) applies for all investors and

$$\frac{dP_k}{P_k}\frac{dc^q}{c^q}\bigg/ dt = \frac{\alpha_k - r}{\delta^q} \qquad q = 1,\dots,K$$

Therefore, $\beta_{kC} = (\alpha_k - r)/\delta$ where $\delta \equiv 1/(\Sigma_1^K x_q/\delta^q)$, the weighted harmonic mean of investors' relative risk aversions. Because $\delta^q > 0$, $x_q \geqslant 0$ and $\Sigma_1^K x_q = 1$, $\delta > 0$. Thus, $\alpha_k = r$ if $\beta_{kC} = 0$, which establishes (a). If, for some asset j, $\beta_{jC} \neq 0$, then $(\alpha_j - r)/\beta_{jC} = \delta$. It follows that for every asset k, $k = 1,\dots,n$, $\alpha_k - r = \delta\beta_{kC} = \beta_{kC}(\alpha_j - r)/\beta_{jC}$ which establishes (b).

QED

Unlike in (15.61), the equilibrium relation among expected returns provided by Theorem 15.7 does not require knowledge of preferences. Moreover, time series data on aggregate consumption are available. From the proof of Theorem 15.7, the equilibrium expected return on any asset k is a strictly increasing function of β_{kC}. Therefore, these "consumption betas" provide a complete ordering of assets' risks. In particular, if an asset's return is procyclical with respect to changes in aggregate consumption (i.e. $\beta_{kC} > 0$), then it must be priced to yield an expected return larger than the riskless interest rate. If an asset's return is countercyclical (i.e. $\beta_{kC} < 0$), then investors will hold the asset in their optimal portfolios even though its expected return is smaller than the interest rate. Hence, the relation in Theorem 15.7 is isomorphic to the Security Market Line of the static CAPM where covariance with changes in aggregate consumption replaces covariance with changes in aggregate wealth as the relevant measure of an asset's risk. The Breeden model of Theorem 15.7 is thus called the *Consumption-Based Capital Asset Pricing Model* (CCAPM).

The CCAPM is a considerably more general model than the classical CAPM.[52] Unlike the CAPM, the CCAPM does not imply that all investors hold perfectly correlated, mean–variance-efficient portfolios. Mean–variance-efficient portfolios do, however, have an important place in the CCAPM. From (15.64) and the proof of Theorem 15.7, the dynamics of aggregate consumption can be written as

---

52   The CCAPM is valid for the general model of Section 15.5 whereas the CAPM will obtain only in the special case of the model in Section 15.6. Moreover, Breeden (1979, Sections 6 and 7) extends the CCAPM to the case of no riskless asset and multiple consumption goods. Duffie and Zame (1989) show that it holds even when the state-variable dynamics are not Markov processes.

$$\frac{dC}{C} = \Delta \, dt + \frac{\sigma^*_{m+1}}{\delta} dz^*_{m+1} - \sum_1^m \Gamma_i S_i \phi_i \, d\epsilon_i \qquad (15.66)$$

where $\Delta \equiv \Sigma_1^K x_q \Delta_q$ is the expected growth rate of aggregate consumption and $\Gamma_i \equiv \Sigma_1^K x_q \Gamma_i^q$, $i = 1,...,m$. From (15.51), the returns on all assets are uncorrelated with $d\epsilon_i$, $i = 1,...,m$. Hence, by inspection of (15.64) and (15.66), the growth-optimum mean–variance-efficient fund V_{m+1} is the portfolio with the maximum possible correlation of its return with changes in either individual or aggregate consumption. If, moreover, there exists a security whose return is perfectly correlated with the change in aggregate consumption, then (a) the security must be a mean–variance-efficient portfolio, and (b) $\Sigma_1^m \Sigma_1^m \Gamma_i \Gamma_j \phi_i \phi_j (d\epsilon_i \, d\epsilon_j) = 0$. In an economy where investor preferences and endowments satisfy the hypothesized conditions of Theorem 15.7, but can otherwise be arbitrary, condition (b) implies almost certainly that $\phi_i \, d\epsilon_i \equiv 0$, $i = 1,...,m$, because the $\{\Gamma_i\}$ can take on almost any values.

Theorem 15.8

Under the hypothesized conditions of Theorem 15.7, if the set of traded assets is such that investors can perfectly hedge all the state-variable changes, dS_j, $j = 1,...,m$, then (a) the change in each investor's optimal consumption is perfectly positively correlated with the change in aggregate consumption; (b) the change in aggregate consumption is perfectly positively correlated with the return on the growth-optimum mean–variance-efficient portfolio V_{m+1}; and (c) the consumption allocation is a Pareto optimum.

PROOF

By hypothesis, the conditions of Theorem 15.7 apply, and hence (15.64) and (15.66) are valid for all investors. By hypothesis, investors can construct perfect hedges against changes in each state variable. That is, in (15.48), $\rho_i^* = 1$, $i = 1,...,m$. Therefore, from (15.47), $\phi_i \, d\epsilon_i \equiv 0$, $i = 1,...,m$. From (15.64), $dc^q/c^q = \Delta_q \, dt + (\sigma^*_{m+1}/\delta^q) \, dz^*_{m+1}$ with $\delta^q > 0$, $q = 1,...,K$, which establishes (a). From (15.66), $dC/C = \Delta \, dt + (\sigma^*_{m+1}/\delta) \times dz^*_{m+1}$ with $\delta > 0$ and $dV_{m+1}/V_{m+1} = \alpha^*_{m+1} \, dt + \sigma^*_{m+1} \, dz^*_{m+1}$, which establishes (b). The proof of Pareto optimality, (c), is given in Chapter 16 and in Breeden (1979, 1984). QED

The perfect-correlation results (a) and (b) of Theorem 15.8 do not imply that investors' optimal portfolios are perfectly correlated. Moreover, (a)

and (b) will not obtain if investor preferences are state dependent. However, as shown in Chapter 16, the allocational-efficiency result (c) will still obtain with state-dependent preferences if perfect-hedging instruments are available.[53]

The consumption betas of Theorem 15.7 provide an attractive alternative to the Security Market Hyperplane for the purpose of determining asset risk classes. Not only does the CCAPM collapse the multiple dimensions of risk $(\beta_{k1},...,\beta_{k\,m+1})$ of an asset to the single β_{kC}, but it also eliminates the requirement that the m state variables $(S_1,...,S_m)$ be identified.

Given its elegant simplicity, the CCAPM is remarkably robust. It is somewhat less general, however, than either the Security Market Hyperplane (15.56) or equation (15.61). For (15.56) and (15.61) to apply requires only that the optimal portfolio demands derived from first-order condition (15.15) are satisfied. The CCAPM requires that both (15.15) and first-order condition (15.14), $U_c = J_W$, be satisfied and that U depends only on current consumption and time. If, as in the Grossman–Laroque (1990) model, there are either indivisibilities or transactions costs in consumer durables, then the CCAPM specification fails because $U_c \neq J_W$. In their model, our equation (15.15) remains valid, and hence the Security Market Hyperplane relation still applies. Equation (15.15) is also unaffected by state-dependent preferences or preferences that exhibit some amount of intertemporal complementarity of consumption.[54]

There is a considerable and growing body of empirical research on testing the CCAPM. As summarized in Breeden, Gibbons, and Litzenberger (1989), the empirical results to date are "mixed." See also Grossman, Melino, and Shiller (1987) and Longstaff (1989). Cornell (1981) suggests that the temporal stability required of the betas makes tests of the CCAPM using time series data no easier a task than the estimation of the Security Market Hyperplane relation. Mankiw and Shapiro (1985) conclude that, despite the theoretical inferiority of the Security Market Line specification, the empirical performance of the CAPM seems to be superior to the CCAPM.

Real-world preferences may not be time additive or temporally independent. There may be significant indivisibilities and transactions costs in

53 The Pareto-optimality result of Theorem 15.8 provides an additional argument for the creation of aggregate-consumption-linked bonds as discussed in Merton (1983b; this volume, Ch. 18).
54 As discussed in Chapter 6, the Markov assumption required for stochastic dynamic programming restricts the class of preference dependence on past consumption to a finite number of "summary" variables. However, Huang and Kreps (1985), Duffie and Epstein (1992), and Hindy and Huang (1992) extend the result to include preferences that depend on the entire past sample path of consumption.

consumption, and especially consumer durables. The mixed empirical performance of the CCAPM could thus be a reflection of the resulting "sluggishness" in the adjustment of real-world consumption in response to changes in the capital-asset component of wealth. The mixed performance could also be the result of measurement errors in the available time series data for aggregate consumption. Real-world asset returns are quite volatile and exhibit little high-frequency correlation with lagged variables of any sort. Hence, lagged or "smoothed" estimates of "true" aggregate consumption can severely influence estimates of covariances between contemporaneous changes in consumption and asset returns. The possibility of measurement errors is enhanced by the specification requirement that the observation interval between measured, successive changes must be of short duration.[55] Resolution of the empirical-performance issue for the CCAPM remains an open question.

15.12   CONCLUSION

An intertemporal model of the capital market has been developed which is consistent with both the limited liability of assets and the expected utility maxim extended to state-dependent preferences. An $m + 2$ mutual-fund theorem was derived, and the stochastic properties of the portfolios that span the set of optimal portfolios were determined. It was shown that the Security Market Line relation of the static CAPM obtains only under very special additional assumptions. In general, an asset's risk is multidimensional as described by the Security Market Hyperplane. If, however, investor preferences are neither state dependent nor dependent on previous consumption and if each investor's consumption rule equates the marginal utilities of wealth and consumption at each time t, then Breeden's

---

55   As with the Security Market Hyperplane, the expected-return relations derived in Theorem 15.7 involve instantaneous covariances which formally implies continuous observations of consumption and asset returns. As discussed in Merton (1980, 1982b (this volume, Ch. 3)), a good approximation to these instantaneous covariances can be estimated from discrete-time observations provided that the interval spacing h is sufficiently small. Accurate asset-return data are available on a daily interval, but no such data are available for aggregate consumption. Hence, estimation of the Security Market Hyperplane relation should not have the potentially serious measurement-error problems of the CCAPM, because the $(\beta_{k1}, ..., \beta_{km+1})$ can be estimated from asset returns alone. A discrete-time version of the CCAPM (where h need not be small) can be derived, which relates an asset's expected return to its covariance with the marginal utility of consumption. However, to test this version requires both a representative investor for the economy and estimation of the preference function for that investor. See Hansen and Singleton (1983).

CCAPM applies, and each asset's risk is completely specified by the covariance of its return with the change in aggregate consumption.

The focus of the study is on the derivation of equilibrium asset prices from the optimal asset-demand behavior of investors. Hence, the analysis treats as exogenous some variables and their associated stochastic processes that would clearly be endogenous in a complete general equilibrium formulation of the model. In particular, no attempt was made to set down the conditions on the underlying information structure of the economy required to ensure the diffusion-process representation posited for asset-price returns and state-variable dynamics. Other than the brief discussion in Section 15.3, there was also no development of the production or supply side of asset formation.

Proof of existence of a general rational expectations equilibrium in the continuous-time model is a subtle and nontrivial matter. Nevertheless, considerable progress has been made in demonstrating the consistency of our assumed dynamics with the conditions for intertemporal general equilibrium. Huang (1985a, b) proves that if information in an economy with continuous trading evolves according to diffusion processes, then intertemporal equilibrium asset prices will also evolve according to diffusion processes. Although the model of this chapter assumes homogeneous beliefs, Duffie and Huang (1985) show that permitting heterogeneous probability assessments among investors causes no important difficulties with the results, provided that all investors' probability measures are uniformly absolutely continuous. Hellwig (1982) and Duffie and Huang (1986) develop rational expectations equilibrium models with continuous trading and differential information among investors. In a dynamic model of insider trading with sequential auctions, Kyle (1985) derives an equilibrium model of continuous trading as the limiting case. He shows that equilibrium prices will follow Brownian motions as the time interval between successive auctions goes to zero.

In a path-breaking paper, Cox, Ingersoll and Ross (1985a) use the assumption of constant-returns-to-scale production technologies with stochastic technical progress and outputs to develop a general equilibrium version of our model that explicitly integrates the production and financial sectors of the economy. The rational expectations equilibrium dynamics derived for asset prices in their model are consistent with the general price dynamics posited here. Indeed, as is shown in Chapter 16, even the simple models of Sections 15.6–15.9 are consistent with general equilibrium pricing in an economy with production. In perhaps the most general analyses to date, Duffie (1986) and Huang (1987) derive conditions for the existence of intertemporally valid asset prices in the continuous-trading setting. In short, the model of this chapter can pass the "model validation" test of consistency with general equilibrium analysis.

Appendix 15A: Proof of Theorem 15.6

To prove the "if" part of the theorem, it must be shown that investors' optimal portfolios, as selected from among the $m + 2$ portfolios $(V'_1,...,V'_{m+2})$ alone, remain optimal if investors are given the additional opportunity to invest in the individually traded assets. For any traded asset with $d\psi_k \equiv 0$, this requirement is trivially satisfied because the $m + 2$ portfolios can be mixed to exactly replicate the return on asset k (i.e. asset k is a redundant security). Therefore, in the following, assume that $(d\psi_k)^2 > 0$, $k = 1,...,n$. Let dV/V denote the return on a portfolio that allocates portfolio fraction x_k to traded asset k, $k = 1,...,n$; $x_{n+i} = -\Sigma_1^n x_k b_{ki}$ to portfolio V'_i, $i = 1,...,m + 1$; and the balance of the portfolio to the riskless asset, V'_{m+2}. By substitution of the hypothesized dynamics for dP_k/P_k, we have that for *any* choice of x_k, $k = 1,...,n$, $dV/V = r\,dt + d\psi$ where $d\psi \equiv \Sigma_1^n x_k\,d\psi_k$. By the definition of $d\psi$, it follows that $d\psi$ satisfies hypothesized conditions (a), (b), and (c) of the theorem.

Giving the investor the opportunity to invest in $(V'_1,...,V'_{m+2})$ and the n traded assets is clearly equivalent to giving the investor the opportunity to invest in $(V'_1,...,V'_{m+2})$ and the portfolio with return dV/V where the investor can also select the $\{x_k\}$. Thus, if we show that the optimal demand for the portfolio is zero for any $\{x_k\}$, then the "if" part of the theorem is proved.

Equation (15.44) provides the investor's optimal demand functions for n risky assets. For notational simplicity, we redefine terms in (15.44): let $n = m + 2$; d_i be the demand for portfolio V'_i, $i = 1,...,n - 1$; d_n be the demand for portfolio V; and $[\sigma_{ij}]$ be the variance–covariance matrix of returns among the portfolios $(V'_1,...,V'_{m+1}, V)$. From (a), $E_t\{d\psi\} = 0$ and therefore $E_t\{dV/V\}/dt = \alpha_n = r$. From (b) $d\psi\,dV'_i/V'_i = 0, i = 1,...,m + 1$, and therefore, $\sigma_{in} = (dV'_i/V'_i)(dV/V)/dt = 0$, $i = 1,...,n - 1$, $\sigma_n^2\,dt = (d\psi)^2$. Thus, $v_{nj} = 0, j = 1,...,n - 1$, and $v_{nn} = 1/\sigma_n^2$. From (15.44),

$$d_n = A \sum_1^n v_{nj}(\alpha_j - r) + \sum_1^m \sum_1^n H_k S_k g_k \sigma_j \eta_{kj} v_{nj}$$

But,

$$A \sum_1^n v_{nj}(\alpha_j - r) = \frac{A(\alpha_n - r)}{\sigma_n^2} = 0$$

because $\alpha_n = r$, and

$$\sum_1^m \sum_1^n H_k S_k g_k \sigma_j \eta_{kj} v_{nj} = \sum_1^m H_k S_k g_k \eta_{kn}/\sigma_n$$

because $v_{nj} = 0$, $j \neq n$. From condition (c), $0 = d\psi \, dS_i/S_i = (dV/V)$ $(dS_i/S_i) = \sigma_n g_i \eta_{in} \, dt$, $i = 1,\ldots,m$. Hence, $d_n = 0$, independently of the choice of $\{x_k\}$ in dV/V. Thus, $(V_1',\ldots,V_{m+1}', V_{m+2}')$ can generate all optimal portfolios.

To prove the "only if" part of the theorem, it is sufficient to do so for the particular $m + 2$ mutual funds $(V_1,\ldots,V_{m+2})$ described in Theorem 15.5. The reason is, as discussed in the text, that the excess returns on any other spanning set of portfolios are just a nonsingular linear transformation of the excess returns on this set. Thus, $d\psi_k dV_i'/V_i' = 0$ for $i = 1,\ldots,m + 1$ if and only if $d\psi_k dV_i/V_i = 0$ for $i = 1,\ldots,m + 1$. Let dV/V now denote the return on a portfolio that allocates, at each time t, $V(t)$ dollars to traded asset k, $-x_i V(t)$ dollars to mutual fund i, $i = 1,\ldots,m + 1$, and $V(t)\Sigma_1^{m+1} x_i$ dollars to the riskless fund, V_{m+2}. For $V(t) > 0$, $dV/V = dP_k/P_k - \Sigma_1^{m+1} x_i(dV_i/V_i - r \, dt)$. Suppose that the $\{x_i\}$ are chosen so as to minimize the variance of the return on the portfolio, i.e. minimize

$$\left(\frac{dV}{V}\right)^2 = \left(\frac{dP_k}{P_k}\right)^2 - 2\sum_1^{m+1} x_i \frac{dP_k}{P_k}\frac{dV_i}{V_i} + \sum_1^{m+1}\sum_1^{m+1} x_i x_j \sigma_{ij}^* \, dt$$

Then we have that

$$x_i = \left[\sum_1^{m+1} v_{ij}^* \frac{dP_k}{P_k}\frac{dV_j}{V_j}\right]\Big/ dt \qquad i = 1,\ldots,m + 1$$

For $q = 1,\ldots,m + 1$, we have that

$$\sum_1^{m+1} x_i \frac{dV_i}{V_i}\frac{dV_q}{V_q} = \sum_1^{m+1}\sum_1^{m+1} v_{ij}^* \frac{dP_k}{P_k}\frac{dV_j}{V_j} \sigma_{iq}^* = \frac{dP_k}{P_k}\frac{dV_q}{V_q}$$

because $\Sigma_1^{m+1} v_{ij}^* \sigma_{iq}^* = 0$ for $j \neq q$ and $\Sigma_1^{m+1} v_{ij}^* \sigma_{iq}^* = 1$ for $j = q$. It follows that

$$\frac{dV}{V}\frac{dV_q}{V_q} = \frac{dP_k}{P_k}\frac{dV_q}{V_q} - \sum_1^{m+1} x_i \frac{dV_i}{V_i}\frac{dV_q}{V_q} = 0 \qquad q = 1,\ldots,m + 1$$

In particular, therefore, $(dV/V)(dV_{m+1}/V_{m+1}) = 0$. From this and Theorem

15.4, it follows that $E_t\{dV/V\} = r\,dt$. Define $d\psi_k \equiv dV/V - r\,dt$. By definition of ψ_k and dV/V,

$$\frac{dP_k}{P_k} = \frac{dV}{V} + \sum_{1}^{m+1} x_i\left(\frac{dV_i}{V_i} - r\,dt\right) = r\,dt + \sum_{1}^{m+1} b_{ki}\left(\frac{dV_i}{V_i} - r\,dt\right) + d\psi_k$$

where $b_{ki} \equiv [\Sigma_1^{m+1} v_{ij}^*(dP_k/P_k)(dV_j/V_j)]/dt$. Thus, to prove the "only if" part of the theorem, we need only show that $d\psi_k$ satisfies conditions (a), (b), and (c). $E_t\{d\psi_k\} = E_t\{dV/V\} - r\,dt = 0$ establishes (a). $d\psi\,dV_i/V_i = (dV/V)(dV_i/V_i) = 0$, $i = 1,\ldots,m + 1$, establishes (b). From (15.50) and (15.51), we have that, for any portfolio of traded assets, $(dV/V)(dS_i/S_i) = (dV/V)(dV_i/V_i)$, $i = 1,\ldots,m$. Therefore, for the specific portfolio constructed here, $d\psi_k\,dS_i/S_i = (dV/V)(dS_i/S_i) = 0$ for $i = 1,\ldots,m$, which establishes (c). QED

16

A Complete-Markets General Equilibrium Theory of Finance in Continuous Time

16.1 INTRODUCTION

Most general equilibrium models in finance have as their genesis either the Sharpe–Lintner–Mossin Capital Asset Pricing Model (CAPM) or the Arrow–Debreu complete-markets model. The development of the intertemporal-equilibrium asset pricing model in Chapter 15 follows the tradition of the CAPM. In this chapter, the continuous-time model is reformulated to fit the framework of Arrow and Debreu. In addition to showing the connection between the models, this reformulation permits direct application to the continuous-time model of the well-known and powerful results on allocational efficiency that obtain in an Arrow–Debreu world.

The Arrow–Debreu model requires a complete set of pure securities for every possible state of the world at every point in time. Because the dynamics of the continuous-time model are described by diffusion processes, there is a continuum of possible states over any finite interval of time. Therefore, complete markets in this model would seem to require an uncountable number of pure Arrow–Debreu securities. However, as we know from the work of Arrow (1953) and Radner (1972), an Arrow–Debreu equilibrium allocation can be achieved without a full set of pure time-state-contingent securities if the menu of available securities is sufficient for agents to use dynamic trading strategies to replicate the payoff structures of the missing pure securities. Under this condition, the markets are said to be "dynamically-complete." The application of continuous-trading portfolio strategies to match the payoff structures of nonexistent securities is a central theme of the partial-equilibrium pricing analyses in Chapters 13 and 14. In this chapter, we shall show that if the dynamical evolution of the economy can be described by a vector of Markov diffusion processes, then a dynamically-complete Radner-type equilibrium can be achieved with a finite number of traded securities.

In an environment more general than the one posited here, Duffie and Huang (1985) analyze the role that continuous trading plays in successfully implementing Arrow–Debreu equilibria with infinite-dimensional commodity spaces. In particular, they derive necessary and sufficient conditions for continuous-trading portfolio strategies with a finite number of securities to effectively complete the markets. By working with martingale representation theorems, Duffie and Huang show that the class of dynamics for which these results obtain extends beyond vector diffusion processes to include some non-Markov path-dependent processes. However, fitting the continuous-time model into the Arrow–Debreu framework does lead to some loss in generality. Specifically, the formulation requires that, at each point in time, the set of traded securities must be rich enough to permit investors to perfectly hedge against instantaneous stochastic changes in each of the relevant state variables of the system. Within the context of the model of Chapter 15 with m state variables, perfect-hedging capability implies that there exist m traded securities or feasible portfolios such that $\rho_i^* = 1$ in (15.48) and $\phi_i \, d\epsilon_i \equiv 0$ in (15.50) for $i = 1,...,m$. With the exception of Theorem 15.8, the mutual-fund theorems, the dynamics of optimal consumption, and the equilibrium structure of asset prices derived in Chapter 15 do not require this perfect-hedging assumption. Thus, the class of market structures that supports the results of Chapter 15 is more general than the one that supports dynamically-complete markets.

In the model of this chapter, we specify an information structure for the economy in which information evolves according to a vector Markov diffusion process. The exogenous uncertainties of the economy are described by a finite-dimensional vector Wiener process $[dq_1,...,dq_m]$ with a nonsingular correlation-coefficient matrix with its kjth element denoted by $\rho_{kj} \equiv (dq_k \, dq_j)/dt$, $k,j = 1,...,m$. We further posit that a finite-dimensional n-vector of positive state variables, $S(t) \equiv [S_1(t),...,S_n(t)]$ ($n \geq m$) provides sufficient information to completely describe the state of the economy at time t. That is, the current values of all economic variables at time t can be expressed as functions of $S(t)$ and t. Following the notation in (15.43), we write the dynamics for $S(t)$ as

$$dS_i = f_i S_i \, dt + g_i S_i \, dq_i \qquad i = 1,...,n \qquad (16.1)$$

where $f_i[S(t), t]$ and $g_i[S(t), t]$ are well-behaved functions with finite values for all $S(t)$, and for each t and $S(t) = S$, there exist numbers $\{\delta_{ij}(S, t)\}$ such that

$$dq_j = \sum_1^m \delta_{ij} \, dq_i \qquad j = m + 1,...,n \qquad (16.2)$$

If, by construction, $g_i > 0$ for $i = 1,...,m$, then $[S_1(t),...,S_m(t)]$ are called the "primal" state variables, because their instantaneous stochastic changes capture all the exogenous unanticipated changes in the economy. $[S_{m+1}(t),...,S_n(t)]$ are called the "supplementary" state variables because their instantaneous stochastic changes are perfectly correlated with some linear combination of the changes in the primal state variables. The reason for including the supplementary state variables is to support the Markov assumption in our general equilibrium analysis. To make optimal decisions, agents will generally require some summary information about the historical time path of the economy. Thus, to maintain the Markov structure of the state-space description, it may be necessary to add more state variables to carry forward that summary information. Although adding these supplementary state variables increases the dimensionality of the state-space description, it does *not* increase the dimensionality of the evolving uncertainties of the economy.

The posited structure for the capital markets is that there are m traded risky assets with prices $[V_1(t),...,V_m(t)]$ and a riskless security with an instantaneously certain return denoted by $r(t)$. Huang (1985a, b, 1987) has proved that, if information evolves according to diffusion processes, then equilibrium asset prices must also. Hence, the dynamics of traded asset prices can be written as

$$dV_i = \alpha_i V_i \, dt + \sigma_i V_i \, dz_i \qquad i = 1,...,m \qquad (16.3)$$

where $\{\alpha_i, \sigma_i, dz_i\}$ are as defined in (15.6). As noted at the outset, a dynamically-complete market structure requires that the set of traded assets permits agents to perfectly hedge against stochastic changes in the state variables (i.e. $\rho_i^* = 1$ in (15.50), $i = 1,...,m$). Therefore, with no further loss in generality, we can assume that the instantaneous return on asset i is perfectly positively correlated with the instantaneous change in S_i, $i = 1,...,m$. That is, we posit that[1]

$$dz_i = dq_i \qquad i = 1,...,m \qquad (16.4)$$

It follows from (16.4) that $dz_i \, dz_j = dq_i \, dq_j = \rho_{ij} \, dt$ and hence that the covariance of the returns between asset i and j, σ_{ij}, equals $\rho_{ij}\sigma_i\sigma_j$, i, $j = 1,...,m$. Note that the inclusion of supplementary state variables in the state-space description (i.e. $n > m$) does not increase the number of traded securities required for investors to perfectly hedge. From (16.2) and (16.4), there always exists a feasible portfolio combination of the m traded

---

1 If individual traded securities did not satisfy this condition, then using the construction rules from Theorems 15.3 and 15.5, a set of mutual funds could be created that do satisfy this condition.

assets and the riskless security which has a return that is instantaneously perfectly correlated with dS_j for $j = m + 1,...,n$.

As in Chapter 15, we assume a single consumption good and that there are N consumer–investors with preferences such that the kth consumer acts so as to

$$\max E_0\left\{ \int_0^{T^k} U^k[c^k(t), S(t), t]\, dt + B^k[W^k(T^k), S(T^k), T^k]\right\} \quad k = 1,...,N$$

$$(16.5)$$

where U^k and B^k are strictly increasing, concave functions of c^k and W^k. Because direct preferences can be state dependent, we have from Section 6.4 that the analysis to follow will also apply to more general environments including multiple consumption goods and preference functions with nonzero intertemporal complementarity of consumption.

With these preference assumptions, we have from Theorem 15.5 that the set of m traded securities in (16.3) and the riskless security spans the set of all investors' optimal portfolios.[2] Thus, from investors' perspectives, any additional securities are redundant. It follows that, at each t, the equilibrium investment opportunity set, $\{\alpha_i(t), r(t), \sigma_{ij}(t)\}$, depends at most on $S(t)$ and t.

The general equilibrium analysis begins in Section 16.2 with the development of the financial intermediation sector of the economy. Building on the production theory for derivative securities in Chapter 14, we derive the manufacturing process and production cost for intermediaries to create a complete set of pure Arrow–Debreu securities. An endogenous correspondence between the quantities of Arrow–Debreu securities produced and the demands for traded assets by intermediaries is derived from these processes. The prices for default-free and noncallable bonds are determined in terms of the pure securities' prices and the equilibrium term structure of interest rates is thus established.

In Section 16.3, the lifetime consumption and portfolio-selection problem examined in Chapters 4–6 and 15 is reformulated in an Arrow–Debreu complete-markets framework. The intertemporal-equilibrium structure of consumption and asset demands is derived. The analysis is also used to provide further economic intuition into the Cox–Huang model of Chapter 6 and to determine conditions under which investors select optimal policies that avoid the possibility of personal bankruptcy.

---

2   In this chapter, the returns on the growth-optimum portfolio are perfectly correlated with a combination of the m traded securities used to hedge against state-variable changes. Hence, the $m + 2$ spanning funds of Theorem 15.5 reduce to $m + 1$ funds.

A general equilibrium solution for prices and allocations is derived in Section 16.4 for the case of pure exchange. In Sections 16.5 and 16.6, production is introduced and an intertemporal general equilibrium model is developed. The chapter closes with a summary discussion of the equilibrium structure and allocational efficiency of the complete-markets version of the continuous-time model.

16.2 FINANCIAL INTERMEDIATION WITH DYNAMICALLY-COMPLETE MARKETS

The theory of intermediation developed in Chapter 14 focuses on the risk-pooling and risk-sharing products created by financial-services institutions. Products examined range from standardized instruments such as a group of mutual funds with characteristics described in Theorem 15.5 to custom products tailored to meet the specific requirements of each investor. Contingent-claims analysis (CCA) is the tool used to derive the production technologies and costs for intermediaries to create these custom derivative securities. As discussed, such financial products and the associated activities of their producers are redundant in a frictionless environment with no information-gathering or transactions costs. Thus, to provide a nontrivial role for intermediaries in our equilibrium analysis here, we assume that some investors and business firms face transactions costs for trading and issuing securities directly in the capital markets. However, to preserve the CCA production theory for intermediaries, we follow the model in Chapter 14 and posit that financial intermediaries, as the lowest-cost transactors, can trade continuously in the capital market at no cost. In applying this model to derive equilibrium prices and allocations, we shall further assume that the financial-services industry is competitive so that financial-product prices equal their marginal production costs.

In the production theory of Chapter 14, a manufacturing technology is developed to create Arrow–Debreu securities that are contingent on traded asset prices. In this section, we generalize that analysis to derive the production technology and cost for intermediaries to create a complete set of Arrow–Debreu securities with payoffs contingent on the state of the economy $S(t)$ at each time t.

From (16.2), we can express $\rho_{ij} \, dt \equiv dq_i \, dq_j, \, i, j = 1,\dots,n$ as functions of ρ_{ki} and δ_{ij}, $k, i = 1,\dots,m$ and $j = m + 1,\dots,n$. Define h_j by

$$h_j \equiv f_j - r - g_j \, \frac{\alpha_j - r}{\sigma_j} \qquad j = 1,\dots,m$$

$$\equiv f_j - r - g_j \sum_1^m \delta_{ij} \frac{\alpha_i - r}{\sigma_i} \qquad j = m+1,\dots,n \qquad (16.6)$$

Let $\Pi(S, t; \bar{S}, \tau)$ denote the solution to the linear partial differential equation

$$0 = \frac{1}{2} \sum_1^n \sum_1^n g_i g_j \rho_{ij} S_i S_j \Pi_{ij} + \sum_1^n (r + h_j) S_j \Pi_j + \Pi_t - r\Pi$$

$$(16.7)$$

subject to the boundary conditions that $\Pi(S, t; \bar{S}, \tau) \geq 0$ and $\int_0^\infty \dots \int_0^\infty \Pi(S, t; \bar{S}, \tau)\, d\bar{S}_1 \dots d\bar{S}_n$ exists for all S and $t < \tau < \infty$; $\Pi(S, \tau; \bar{S}, \tau) = \delta(S_1 - \bar{S}_1)\delta(S_2 - \bar{S}_2)\dots\delta(S_n - \bar{S}_n)$ where $\delta(\cdot)$ is the Dirac delta function and $\bar{S} \equiv [\bar{S}_1,\dots,\bar{S}_n]$ is a vector of specified positive numbers. Subscripts on Π denote partial derivatives with respect to $S_1,\dots,S_n$, and t. $\{h_j, g_j, r, \rho_{ij}\}$ are functions of S and t, and under mild regularity conditions on these functions, a solution to (16.7) exists and is unique.

Consider the continuous-trading portfolio strategy that allocates fraction

$$x_j(t) = \frac{\Pi_j g_j S_j + \Sigma_{m+1}^n \Pi_k g_k S_k \delta_{jk}}{\sigma_j V(t)} \qquad (16.8)$$

to traded asset j, $j = 1,\dots,m$ and fraction $1 - \Sigma_1^m x_j(t)$ to the riskless security at time t, where $V(t)$ denotes the current value of the portfolio. It follows from (16.3), (16.6), and (16.8) that the dynamics of the portfolio value can be written as

$$dV = V\left\{ \left[\sum_1^m x_j(\alpha_j - r) + r \right] dt + \sum_1^m x_j \sigma_j\, dz_j \right\}$$

$$= \left[rV + \sum_1^n \Pi_j S_j(f_j - h_j - r) \right] dt$$

$$+ \sum_1^m \left(\Pi_j g_j S_j + \sum_{m+1}^n \Pi_k g_k S_k \delta_{jk} \right) dz_j$$

$$= \left[rV + \sum_1^n \Pi_j S_j(f_j - h_j - r) \right] dt + \sum_1^n \Pi_j g_j S_j\, dq_j \qquad (16.9)$$

because, from (16.2), $dq_k = \Sigma_1^m \delta_{jk} dq_j$, $k = m+1,\dots,n$, and, from (16.4), $dz_j = dq_j$, $j = 1,\dots,m$.

Π is a solution to (16.7) and is therefore twice-continuously differentiable. Thus, Itô's lemma can be used to describe the stochastic process for $Y(t) \equiv \Pi[S(t), t; \bar{S}, \tau]$ as

$$dY = \left(\frac{1}{2}\sum_1^n \sum_1^n g_i g_j \rho_{ij} S_i S_j \Pi_{ij} + \sum_1^n \Pi_j f_j S_j + \Pi_t\right)dt + \sum_1^n \Pi_j g_j S_j \, dq_j \tag{16.10}$$

where Π and its derivatives are evaluated at $S = S(t)$ at each time t. Because Π satisfies (16.7), (16.10) can be rewritten as[3]

$$dY = \left[r\Pi + \sum_1^n \Pi_j S_j(f_j - h_j - r)\right]dt + \sum_1^n \Pi_j g_j S_j \, dq_j \tag{16.11}$$

From (16.9) and (16.11), $dY - dV = r(\Pi - V)\,dt = r(Y - V)\,dt$, which is an ordinary differential equation with solution $Y(t) - V(t) = [Y(0) - V(0)] \exp[\int_0^t r(u)\,du]$. But, $Y(t) \equiv \Pi[S(t), t; \bar{S}, \tau]$. Therefore, if the initial investment in the portfolio is chosen so that $V(0) = \Pi[S(0), 0; \bar{S}, \tau]$, then we have that

$$V(t) = \Pi[S(t), t; \bar{S}, \tau] \quad 0 \leqslant t \leqslant \tau \tag{16.12}$$

Thus, from (16.12), a feasible dynamic trading strategy using only the m traded risky assets and the riskless security has been constructed that has a payoff at $t = \tau$ of $\delta[S_1(\tau) - \bar{S}_1]...\delta[S_n(\tau) - \bar{S}_n]$.

Because $\Pi(S, t; \bar{S}, \tau)$ is a solution to (16.7) which satisfies $\Pi \geqslant 0$, $V(t) = \Pi[S(t), t; \bar{S}, \tau] \geqslant 0$ for all $S(t)$ and t. Therefore, after an initial investment of $V(0) = \Pi[S(0), 0; \bar{S}, \tau]$, the prescribed trading strategy requires neither additional infusions nor withdrawals of capital. That is, it is a self-financing portfolio. Thus, $\Pi[S(0), 0; \bar{S}, \tau]$ is the total production cost for the intermediary to create an instrument with the specified payoff function. It follows from (16.12) that the production cost to manufacture this instrument at time t is $\Pi[S(t), t; \bar{S}, \tau]$.

Along the lines of analysis in Section 14.3, we now show that the portfolio strategies specified by (16.8) for various values of τ and the vector of parameters $\bar{S}$ replicate the payoff structure of a complete set of Arrow–Debreu pure securities with a continuum of states. Let $d\bar{S}_k > 0$ denote the infinitesimal differential of the parameter $\bar{S}_k$, $k = 1,...,n$ and define $d\bar{S} \equiv d\bar{S}_1 d\bar{S}_2...d\bar{S}_n$. Consider a combined portfolio strategy that at

---

3 From (16.7), $\frac{1}{2}\Sigma_1^n \Sigma_1^n g_i g_j \rho_{ij} S_i S_j \Pi_{ij} + \Pi_t = -\Sigma_1^n (r + h_j) S_j \Pi_j + r\Pi$.

time t invests $Q(\bar{S})\Pi[S(t), t; \bar{S}, \tau]\, d\bar{S}$ in portfolio strategy (16.8) for each of the continuum of parameter values $\bar{S}$, where Q is a specified function. If $I(t; Q)$ denotes the total amount of investment in this combined portfolio at time t, then

$$I(t; Q) = \int_S Q(S)\, \Pi[S(t), t; S, \tau]\, dS \qquad (16.13)$$

where we adopt the shorthand notation, $\int_S dS$, for $\int_0^\infty \dots \int_0^\infty dS_1\, dS_2 \dots dS_n$. If this combined-portfolio strategy is followed until time τ, then the value of the portfolio is given by

$$\int_S Q(S)\, \delta[S_1(\tau) - S_1] \dots \delta[S_n(\tau) - S_n]\, dS = Q[S(\tau)] \qquad (16.14)$$

Consider the particular limiting case in which $Q(S) = 1$ for $\bar{S}_k - d\bar{S}_k/2 \leqslant S_k \leqslant \bar{S}_k + d\bar{S}_k/2$, $k = 1,\dots,n$, and $Q(S) = 0$ otherwise. It follows from (16.14) that the value of the portfolio at $t = \tau$ is equal to \$1 if $S(\tau) = \bar{S}$ and is equal to \$0, otherwise. This payoff structure is identical with that specified for an Arrow–Debreu pure security. By the Mean Value Theorem applied to (16.13), the investment required at time t to produce this payoff is $\Pi[S(t), t; \bar{S}, \tau]\, d\bar{S}$. Therefore, at time t, the production cost for an intermediary to create an Arrow–Debreu security that pays \$1 if $S(\tau) = \bar{S}$ and nothing otherwise is $\Pi[S(t), t; \bar{S}, \tau]\, d\bar{S}$. The production technology is specified by the trading rules in (16.8).

The formal steps taken in the derivation of production costs for Arrow–Debreu securities here parallel those followed in Section 14.3. There is an important substantive difference, however. Because Chapter 14 is focused on derivative-security pricing, the state space for describing the payouts to the pure securities is defined by the prices of traded assets or securities. Here, the state space is defined by a vector of state variables, none of which need be speculative prices. Therefore, the pure securities in Chapter 14 are derivative securities whereas the Arrow–Debreu securities in this chapter are not.

The differences between these two types of pure securities are captured in the differences between the partial differential equations that govern their prices or production costs. As with all true derivative securities, determination of the prices of the pure securities in Chapter 14 does not require knowledge of the expected returns on either the underlying traded securities or their derivatives. This result is confirmed by inspection of (14.9)–(14.11). In contrast, inspection of (16.6) and (16.7) shows that the solution for $\Pi(S, t; \bar{S}, \tau)$ requires, in general, knowledge of the expected returns on all m traded assets.[4] If, however, state variable S_k were itself a speculative price, then $(f_k - r)/g_k = (\alpha_k - r)/\sigma_k$ as a condition to rule out arbitrage between V_k and S_k, two securities with perfectly correlated returns. In that case, from (16.6), $h_k = 0$, and from (16.7), neither α_k nor f_k need be known to compute Π.

In a general equilibrium analysis with the usual convexity conditions on preferences and production technologies to ensure uniqueness of the equilibrium, all asset prices (including $V_1(t),\ldots,V_m(t)$) can be expressed as functions of $S(t)$ and t. In general, this function will not be one-to-one. If, however, it is invertible, then $S(t)$ can be expressed as a function of n selected asset prices. In that case, without further loss of generality, we can choose to describe the state space in terms of these n asset prices. The governing equation for this derivative-security representation of Arrow–Debreu prices is given by (16.7) with $\rho_{ij}g_ig_j$ replaced by σ_{ij} and $h_j = 0$, i, $j = 1,\ldots,n$.

As discussed in Chapter 14, the Arrow–Debreu pure securities can serve as building blocks for the intermediary to create more complex financial products. Suppose for example that a customer wants a security which pays a continuous dividend flow from $t = 0$ to $t = T$ according to the schedule $\{G[S(t),\ t]\}$ with a terminal lump-sum payout at $t = T$ specified by $H[S(T)]$. From (16.14), this payout pattern can be replicated by a portfolio of pure securities that holds for each $t \in (0,\ T]$ and each possible $\bar{S}$, $G(\bar{S}, t)$ dt units of the pure security which pays \$1 if $S(t) = \bar{S}$ and also holds for each possible $\bar{S}$, $H(\bar{S})$ units of the pure security which pays \$1 if $S(T) = \bar{S}$. From (16.13), the investment required to acquire this portfolio of pure securities at time t can be expressed as

$$I(t;\ G,\ H) = \int_t^T \int_S G(S,\ \tau)\Pi[S(t),\ t;\ S,\ \tau]\ dS\ d\tau$$

$$+ \int_S H(S)\Pi[S(t),\ t;\ S,\ T]\ dS$$

$$(16.15)$$

Hence, given the production costs for pure securities and the schedule of payments, we have from (16.15) that the production cost for the intermediary to create this financial product can be computed by mere quadrature as a continuously weighted sum of the production costs for the various

---

4 Note that $(dV_i/V_i)^2 = \sigma_i^2\ dt$, $(dS_i/S_i)^2 = g_i^2\ dt$, and $dV_i/V_i - (\sigma_i/g_i)\ dS_i/S_i = [r - (r + h_i)\sigma_i/g_i]\ dt$, $i = 1,\ldots,m$. Therefore, if V_i, S_i, and r are continuously observable, then investors can observe h_i without error, and hence they must agree on the value of h_i, $i = 1,\ldots,m$. It follows that investors do not have to agree on the unobservable α_i and f_i to agree on the pricing of Π in (16.7).

Arrow–Debreu securities. After issue, (16.15) is the current value of the liability (at reproduction cost).

Because the schedule of payments to the financial product can be replicated by a linear combination of pure securities, the production technology using traded assets to create the product can be expressed as a continuously weighted combination of the production technologies for the associated set of Arrow–Debreu securities. That is, let $d_j(t)$ denote the dollar amount of traded asset j required by an intermediary at time t to perfectly hedge the liability created by issuing the financial product. From (16.8) and (16.12), the replicating portfolio trading rules can be written as, for $j = 1,\ldots,m$,

$$d_j(t) = \int_t^T \int_S x_j(t;\, S,\, \tau) G(S,\, \tau) \Pi[S(t),\, t;\, S,\, \tau]\, dS\, d\tau$$

$$+ \int_S x_j(t;\, S,\, T) H(S) \Pi[S(t),\, t;\, S,\, T]\, dS \qquad (16.16a)$$

and

$$d_{m+1}(t) = I(t;\, G,\, H) - \sum_1^m d_j(t) \qquad (16.16b)$$

where $d_{m+1}(t)$ is the holding of the riskless security.

As an example of the application of (16.15) and (16.16), consider the creation of zero-coupon default-free bonds. These securities are of particular interest because their prices are used to calculate the term structure of interest rates. An intermediary's cost of producing a bond that, with certainty, pays \$1 at time T is given by (16.15) with $G \equiv 0$ and $H = 1$. If a bond with the same terms is traded, then to rule out an arbitrage opportunity for intermediaries, its equilibrium price at time t, $B(t;\, T)$, must satisfy

$$B(t;\, T) = \int_S \Pi[S(t),\, t;\, S,\, T]\, dS \qquad (16.17)$$

If $R(t;\, T)$ denotes the continuously compounded yield to maturity on the bond, then

$$R(t;\, T) = -\frac{\log[B(t;\, T)]}{T - t} \qquad (16.18)$$

Hence, from (16.17) and (16.18), we have a complete description of the equilibrium term structure of interest rates as a function of the state variables of the economy and time. Moreover, by applying Itô's lemma to (16.17) and (16.18), we can describe the dynamics of the term structure and the risk characteristics of default-free bonds in terms of the fundamental uncertainties in the economy. The prices and risk characteristics of noncallable, default-free coupon bonds follow from the no-arbitrage condition that their prices are sums of the prices of zero-coupon bonds. That is, if $B_C(t; \tau)$ denotes the current price of a coupon bond that pays $\bar{C}$ dollars at time t_i ($\geq t$), $i = 1,\dots,n$, and a principal amount of $\bar{P}$ at its maturity date τ, then to rule out arbitrage

$$B_C(t; \tau) = \bar{C}\left[\sum_1^n B(t; t_i)\right] + \bar{P}B(t; \tau) \qquad (16.19)$$

In sum, the production technologies and costs for financial products can be determined by an intermediary in a two-step process.[5] First, from the schedule of payouts that define the financial product, calculate the quantities and maturities of the Arrow–Debreu securities needed to replicate these payouts. Second, by substituting the costs of these pure securities into (16.15) and (16.16), compute the production cost and the positions in the traded assets required to hedge the liability created by issuing the financial product.

Our discussion of intermediation practices has focused on the supply function of financial products. That is, a customer demands a particular financial product and the intermediary supplies it. By issuing the product, the intermediary takes on a liability. To hedge this liability, the intermediary acquires additional assets in the form of traded securities (according to rules (16.16a) and (16.16b)). These assets are financed by charging the customer a price (at least) equal to the production cost given in (16.15). The acquisition of assets by the intermediary is thus induced by customer demands for its liabilities. However, in servicing its customers, the flow of causality for the intermediary's actions can be the reverse. For example, a business firm may want to raise capital by issuing a security to an intermediary as in a private placement. In that case, the purchase of the security by the intermediary adds to its stock of assets, and thereby induces the intermediary to issue additional liabilities to finance it. To determine the (maximum) price to pay for the security, the intermediary calculates the amount it can raise by issuing a collection of liabilities with payouts that

---

5 If, as discussed in footnote 1, the m securities are actually mutual funds containing individual traded securities, then there is a third step of translating the demands for the funds into demands for the individual securities contained within each of the funds.

exactly match the time-state-contingent payments it will receive from the security. This computation is identical in magnitude to equation (16.15) but opposite in sign to reflect that cash flows into the intermediary from the issue of liabilities. Similarly, the intermediary's transactions in traded assets to hedge the acquired security are given by (16.16a) and (16.16b) with reverse signs. Hence, the same two-step process used by the intermediary to evaluate the cost and determine the production technology for financial products that it sells can also be used to evaluate and hedge financial assets that it purchases from its issuer customers.

As is well known, there is a great variety of financial structures for an economy that will support Arrow–Debreu equilibrium allocations. Thus, the formal equilibrium analysis of this chapter does not require a detailed specification of that structure. However, by framing the analysis within a specific institutional arrangement, we can perhaps provide a better understanding of the mechanisms by which these efficient allocations can be achieved. In our economy, individual investors can trade directly in the capital market, buy and sell shares in mutual funds, or purchase custom-designed securities from intermediaries. Business firms can raise capital either by issuing securities directly in the capital market or by selling them to intermediaries. Intermediaries can trade continuously without cost and the financial-services industry is competitive. Under these conditions, those investors and firms that can also transact continuously without cost will be indifferent between using intermediaries or undertaking direct transactions in the capital market to implement their plans. However, agents facing nonzero costs will strictly prefer the intermediation route.

As shown in Section 14.5, efficient and competitive intermediation allows all investors to achieve lifetime consumption–bequest allocations as if they could trade continuously without cost. However, as also discussed there, to be feasible, the contractual payments between the intermediary and the investor must be contingent on observable variables that cannot be controlled by either party. Thus, within the context of this chapter, the feasibility of the state-contingent securities requires that the state variables $S(t)$ be observable and that the dynamics of $S(t)$ cannot be controlled by any agent or organized coalition of agents. This requirement is clearly satisfied if the $S(t)$ represent the "states of nature." Although sufficient, such true exogeneity is not necessary. For example, the aggregate capital stock of the economy is not exogenous because the collective investment and consumption decisions by agents affect the time path along which it evolves. However, provided that neither the intermediary nor its customer can measurably control its dynamics, the aggregate capital stock is an acceptable state variable for the determination of contractual payments between the parties. Similarly, the prices of well-diversified portfolios of traded assets also qualify as proper state variables if intermediaries and investors are "price-takers" in the capital market.

In preparation for the general equilibrium analysis of later sections, we summarize the role and actions of financial intermediaries. Their primary function is to service investors and issuers by selling financial products to them and by purchasing their securities. Using (16.15) and (16.16) to analyze each transaction and aggregating over all customer transactions, each intermediary can determine its net customer liability and risk exposure. This net exposure is hedged by transactions in the $m + 1$ assets traded in the capital market. The net liability of the intermediary can be expressed in terms of units of pure securities. As with $G(S, \tau)$ dτ and $H(S, T)$ in (16.15), the aggregate payments on financial products involve both continuous-flow payments which are infinitesimal at each instant in time and lump-sum ones of noninfinitesimal amounts paid at discrete points in time. To simplify notation but preserve the distinction between stocks and flows, we represent all payments as flows by describing the lump-sum payment schedules as "impulse" functions. So, for example, a payment of $H(S, T)$ at time T is written as $[H(S, \tau) \, \delta(T - \tau)]$ dτ where $\delta(\cdot)$ is the Dirac delta function. It follows that $\int_a^b [H(S, \tau) \, \delta(T - \tau)]$ d$\tau = H(S, T)$ for any a, b such that $a < T < b$, and equals zero otherwise. $H(S, \tau)$ $\delta(T - \tau)$ is called an *impulse function*.

The net customer liability of the intermediary can be expressed in terms of units of pure securities. This net exposure is hedged by transactions in the $m + 1$ assets traded in the capital market. Let $M(t; \bar{S}, \tau)$ dτ denote the (exposure-equivalent) number of units outstanding at time t of the pure security which pays \$1 if $S(\tau) = \bar{S}$ for a specified $\tau > t$. The total value (at reproduction cost) of an intermediary's net customer liabilities at time t is thus given by

$$L(t) = \int_t^\infty \int_S M(t; S, \tau) \Pi[S(t), t; S, \tau] \mathrm{d}S \, \mathrm{d}\tau \qquad (16.20)$$

Let $D_j(t)$ denote the aggregate holdings of traded asset j required by an intermediary to perfectly hedge these net liabilities at time t, where $D_{m+1}(t)$ is the amount of the riskless security held. From (16.8) and (16.12), we can write the hedging-portfolio trading rules as, for $j = 1,\ldots,m$,

$$D_j(t) = \int_t^\infty \int_S x_j(t; S, \tau) \; M(t; S, \tau) \Pi[S(t), t; S, \tau] \, \mathrm{d}S\mathrm{d}\tau$$

$$= \int_t^\infty \int_S \frac{M(t; S, \tau)}{\sigma_j} \left\{ \Pi_j[S(t), t; S, \tau] g_j S_j \right.$$

$$+ \sum_{m+1}^n \Pi_k[S(t), t; S, \tau] g_k S_k \delta_{kj} \bigg\} \, \mathrm{d}S \, \mathrm{d}\tau$$

$$(16.21a)$$

and

$$D_{m+1}(t) = L(t) - \sum_1^m D_j(t) \tag{16.21b}$$

Customers' demands for Arrow–Debreu securities, both directly and indirectly, through their demands for more complex financial products, cause intermediaries to purchase or sell assets traded in the capital market. Taking account of any netting from offsetting customer transactions, (16.21a) and (16.21b) quantify these induced demands of intermediaries for those traded assets. The formulation of the lifetime consumption and portfolio-selection problem in the next section has consumers implementing all their optimal plans by purchasing Arrow–Debreu securities from intermediaries. We shall use (16.21a) and (16.21b) there to translate these derived customer demands for pure securities into demand functions for traded assets.

16.3 OPTIMAL CONSUMPTION AND PORTFOLIO RULES WITH DYNAMICALLY-COMPLETE MARKETS

In this section, individual consumers are assumed to implement their lifetime consumption and bequest allocations entirely by the purchase of pure Arrow–Debreu securities at the outset of their programs. Each investor's optimal portfolio of these securities is determined by the static-optimization method in Arrow and Debreu. It is then shown that this Arrow–Debreu allocation is identical with that derived by the dynamic-optimization methods of Chapters 4–6 and 15, where investors can trade continuously without cost.

We assume throughout this section that the financial-services industry is competitive and that intermediaries offer Arrow–Debreu securities of all maturities with payments contingent on the observable state variables of the economy. It follows from the competitive assumption that prices charged by the intermediaries for the pure securities are equal to their production costs as given in (16.7). In addition to trading directly in the capital market, intermediaries offer and trade units of a group of mutual funds with the properties described by Theorem 15.5. All intermediaries agree on the trading rules required to construct these portfolios and every intermediary can continuously monitor the composition of each of the funds. These mutual-fund assumptions assure the existence of a set of securities (with observable prices) that includes the riskless security, traded assets with the properties of (16.3) and (16.4), and a growth-optimum, mean–variance-efficient portfolio.

Before analyzing the consumer-choice problem, it will be helpful to establish certain properties of the growth-optimum portfolio. As in Section 6.2.1, let $X(t)$ denote the price at time t of one unit of the growth-optimum portfolio constructed from the m traded assets and the riskless security. From (6.2), the dynamics of $X(t)$ can be written as

$$dX = (\mu^2 + r)X \, dt + \mu X \, dz \tag{16.22}$$

where $\mu^2 \equiv \Sigma_1^m \Sigma_1^m v_{kj}(\alpha_k - r)(\alpha_j - r) > 0$ and the Wiener process $dz \equiv [\Sigma_1^m \Sigma_1^m v_{kj}(\alpha_j - r)\sigma_k \, dz_k]/\mu$ with v_{kj} equal to the kjth element of the inverse of the variance–covariance matrix of returns $[\sigma_{ij}]$. Let $\sigma_{xj} \equiv [(dX/X)(dV_j/V_j)]/dt$ denote the instantaneous covariance between the return on the growth-optimum portfolio and the return on traded asset j, $j = 1,\ldots,m$. Because the growth-optimum portfolio is instantaneously mean–variance efficient and because the ratio of its instantaneous expected excess return to its variance equals unity, we have from Theorem 15.4 that for all t and $S(t)$

$$\sigma_{xj} = \alpha_j - r \qquad j = 1,\ldots,m \tag{16.23}$$

Suppose that the price of the growth-optimum portfolio at each t can be expressed as a twice continuously differentiable function of the state variables of the economy and time. That is, $X(t) = F[S(t), t]$. If subscripts on F denote partial derivatives, then it follows from (16.1), (16.2), and Itô's lemma that for $S(t) = S$

$$
\begin{aligned}
\mu \, dz &= \sum_1^n \frac{F_j(S, t)}{F(S, t)} g_j S_j \, dq_j \\
&= \sum_1^m \left[\frac{F_j(S, t)}{F(S, t)} g_j S_j + \sum_{m+1}^n \frac{F_i(S, t)}{F(S, t)} g_i S_i \delta_{ji} \right] dq_j
\end{aligned} \tag{16.24}
$$

and

$$\mu^2(S, t) = \frac{\mathcal{L}[F|S, t] - rF(S, t)}{F(S, t)} \tag{16.25}$$

where $\mathcal{L}[\cdot|S, t]$ is the Dynkin differential operator defined by

$$\mathcal{L}[\cdot|S, t] = \frac{1}{2} \sum_1^n \sum_1^n \rho_{ij} g_i g_j S_i S_j \frac{\partial^2}{\partial S_i \partial S_j} + \sum_1^n f_i S_i \frac{\partial}{\partial S_i} + \frac{\partial}{\partial t} \tag{16.26}$$

Let $P(S, t; \bar{S}, \tau)$ denote the conditional probability density function for the state variables of the economy, i.e. $P(S, t; \bar{S}, \tau) \, d\bar{S}$ is the probability that at time $\tau (\geq t)$, $S(\tau) = \bar{S}$, given that at time t, $S(t) = S$. From (3.42), P is given by the solution to the linear partial differential equation

$$0 = \mathcal{L}[P|S, t] \tag{16.27}$$

subject to the boundary conditions $P(S, t; \bar{S}, \tau) \geq 0$ and $\int_{\bar{S}} P(S, t; \bar{S}, \tau) \, d\bar{S} = 1$ for all S and $t < \tau$; and $P(S, \tau; \bar{S}, \tau) = \delta(S_1 - \bar{S}_1)...\delta(S_n - \bar{S}_n)$ where $\delta(\cdot)$ is the Dirac delta function.

Theorem 16.1

If, for each t, $X(t) = F[S(t), t]$ and if $\Pi(S, t; \bar{S}, T)$ is given by (16.7), then $X(t)P[S(t), t; \bar{S}, T] = F(\bar{S}, T)\Pi[S(t), t; \bar{S}, T]$ for all $\bar{S}$ and all $T \geq t$.

PROOF

Define $\psi(S, t) \equiv F(S, t)P(S, t; \bar{S}, T)/F(\bar{S}, T)$ for $t \leq T$ and all S. By Itô's lemma,

$$\frac{d\psi}{\psi} = \frac{dF}{F} + \frac{dP}{P} + \frac{dP}{P}\frac{dF}{F}$$

$$\frac{dP}{P}\frac{dF}{F} = \sum_1^n \frac{P_i}{P}g_iS_i \, dq_i \frac{dF}{F} = \sum_1^n \frac{\psi_i}{\psi}g_iS_i \, dq_i \frac{dF}{F} - \sum_1^n \frac{F_i}{F}g_iS_i \, dq_i \frac{dF}{F}$$

because $P_i/P = \psi_i/\psi - F_i/F$. But,

$$\sum_1^n \frac{\psi_i}{\psi}g_iS_i \, dq_i \frac{dF}{F} = \sum_1^m \left(\frac{\psi_i}{\psi}g_iS_i + \sum_{m+1}^n \frac{\psi_k}{\psi}g_kS_k\delta_{ik}\right)\frac{\sigma_{xi}}{\sigma_i} \, dt$$

$$= \sum_1^n \frac{\psi_i}{\psi}(f_i - r - h_i)S_i \, dt$$

from (16.2), (16.6), and (16.23). From (16.24), $\sum_1^n (F_i/F)g_iS_i \, dq_i(dF/F) = (dF/F)^2 = \mu^2 \, dt$. Therefore, $(dP/P)(dF/F) = [\sum_1^n(\psi_i/\psi)(f_i - r - h_i)S_i - \mu^2] \, dt$. $E_t\{dP\} = \mathcal{L}[P|S, t] = 0$ for $S = S(t)$ and $E_t\{dF\} = (\mu^2 + r)F \, dt$. Hence, $E_t\{d\psi/\psi\} = [\mathcal{L}[\psi|S, t]/\psi] \, dt = [\mu^2 + r + \sum_1^n(\psi_i/\psi)(f_i - r - h_i)S_i - \mu^2] \, dt$. Therefore, $\mathcal{L}[\psi|S, t] - r\psi + \sum_1^n \psi_i(r + h_i - f_i)S_i = 0$. From (16.26) and inspection of (16.7), ψ satisfies partial differential equation (16.7). By definition of ψ and from (16.27), $\psi(S, T) = \delta(S_1 - \bar{S}_1)...\delta(S_n - $

$\bar{S}_n$). It follows that $\psi(S, t) = \Pi(S, t; \bar{S}, T)$. But, $X(t) = F[S(t), t]$. Therefore, $X(t) P[S(t), t; \bar{S}, T] = F(\bar{S}, T)\Pi[S(t), t; \bar{S}, T]$ for all S and $T \geq t$.   QED

Thus, from Theorem 16.1, if the value of the growth-optimum portfolio can be expressed as a smooth function of the state variables, then knowledge of any two of the three functions X, P, or Π permits immediate computation of the third. As we shall see in the sections to follow, the function F is endogenously determined as part of the intertemporal general equilibrium solution for the economy. However, for the purposes of this section, we can assume that the hypothesized conditions of Theorem 16.1 are satisfied by making $X(t)$ one of the supplementary state variables. That is, by convention, let $X(t) = F[S(t), t] \equiv S_n(t)$. As discussed in the previous section and in Section 14.5, permitting the state-contingent payoffs on the pure securities to depend on the price of a well-diversified portfolio is consistent with feasible, arms-length contracts between intermediaries and investors, provided that none of the parties can influence the time path of the portfolio's price. Having established Theorem 16.1, we now turn to the problem of consumer choice using Arrow–Debreu securities.

Consumer preferences are specified by (16.5). For clarity, we write $c^k(t)$ as $c^k(S, t)$ to denote the kth consumer–investor's consumption at time t if $S(t) = S$. Similarly, let $W^k(S, T^k)$ denote his bequest of wealth at time T^k if $S(T^k) = S$. Dropping the k superscript except where essential, we formulate the lifetime consumption and bequest allocation problem in the complete-markets framework as follows: for initial wealth $W(0)$, select a program so as to

$$\max \left\{ \int_0^T \int_S P(S, t)U[c(S, t), S, t] \, dS \, dt \right.$$

$$\left. + \int_S P(S, T)B[W(S, T), S, T] \, dS \right\} \tag{16.28}$$

subject to the budget constraint

$$W(0) \geq \int_0^T \int_S \Pi(S, t)c(S, t) \, dS \, dt + \int_S \Pi(S, T) \, W(S, T) \, dS \tag{16.29a}$$

and the nonnegativity constraints

$$c(S, t) \geq 0 \text{ and } W(S, T) \geq 0 \text{ for all } S \text{ and } 0 \leq t \leq T \tag{16.29b}$$

where, in (16.28) and (16.29a), $P(S, t)$ and $\Pi(S, t)$ are short for $P[S(0), 0; S, t]$ and $\Pi[S(0), 0; S, t]$, respectively.

Although (16.28) is an intertemporal-choice problem, it can be solved using Kuhn–Tucker methods in a static fashion, because neither $P(S, t)$ nor $\Pi(S, t)$ are affected by the control variables c and W. For all S and t, $0 \leq t \leq T$, such that $P(S, t) > 0$, we have that the first-order conditions derived from (16.28)–(16.29) can be written as

$$P(S, t)U_c[c^*(S, t), S, t] = \lambda_1\Pi(S, t) - \lambda_2(S, t) \qquad (16.30a)$$

$$P(S, t)B_W[W^*(S, T), S, T] = \lambda_1\Pi(S, T) - \lambda_3(S, T) \qquad (16.30b)$$

$$\lambda_1[W(0) - \int_0^T \int_S \Pi(S, t)\, c^*(S, t)\, dS\, dt - \int_S \Pi(S, T)W^*(S, T)\, dS] = 0 \qquad (16.30c)$$

$$\lambda_2(S, t)c^*(S, t) = 0 \text{ and } \lambda_3(S, T)W^*(S, T) = 0 \qquad (16.30d)$$

where λ_1 is the Kuhn–Tucker multiplier reflecting the budget constraint and $\{\lambda_2(S, t), \lambda_3(S, T)\}$ are a continuum of multipliers covering the nonnegativity constraints (16.29b).

By the assumptions that U and B are strictly increasing, we have ruled out investor satiation for either consumption or bequests. Therefore, the shadow price of initial endowment, λ_1, is strictly positive and from (16.30c), the budget constraint applied to the optimal allocation holds with strict equality. From (16.30a) and (16.30d), we have that

$$\lambda_2(S, t) = \max[0, \lambda_1\Pi(S, t) - P(S, t)U_c(0, S, t)] \qquad (16.31)$$

and, from (16.30b) and (16.30d), we have that

$$\lambda_3(S, T) = \max[0, \lambda_1\Pi(S, T) - P(S, T)B_W(0, S, T)] \qquad (16.32)$$

Because $U_{cc} < 0$ and $B_{WW} < 0$ everywhere, both U_c and B_W are globally invertible functions. Hence, define the inverse functions Q and R by $Q(y, S, t) \equiv U_c^{-1}(y)$ and $R(y, S, T) \equiv B_W^{-1}(y)$. It follows that both Q and R are strictly decreasing functions of y. From (16.30a), (16.30b), (16.31), and (16.32), the optimal state-contingent consumption and bequest functions can be expressed as

$$c^*(S, t) = \max\left\{0, Q\left[\frac{\lambda_1\Pi(S, t)}{P(S, t)}, S, t\right]\right\} \qquad 0 \leq t \leq T \qquad (16.33a)$$

and

$$W^*(S, T) = \max\left\{0, R\left[\frac{\lambda_1 \Pi(S, T)}{P(S, T)}, S, T\right]\right\} \tag{16.33b}$$

To complete the solution for the optimal-allocation program requires only the determination of λ_1. Because $\lambda_1 > 0$, we have from (16.30c) that λ_1 is the solution to the transcendental algebraic equation given by

$$0 = W(0) - \left(\int_0^T \int_S \Pi(S, t) \max\left\{0, Q\left[\frac{\lambda_1 \Pi(S, t)}{P(S, t)}, S, t\right]\right\} dS \, dt\right.$$

$$\left. + \int_S \Pi(S, T) \max\left\{0, R\left[\frac{\lambda_1 \Pi(S, T)}{P(S, T)}, S, T\right]\right\} dS\right) \tag{16.34}$$

Because Q and R are strictly decreasing functions of y and $\Pi > 0$, there exists a unique positive solution to (16.34). By inspection, the solution λ_1 depends only on the initial endowment $W(0)$ and the initial state of the economy $S(0)$. Substituting for λ_1 in (16.33a) and (16.33b) completes the solution for the optimal consumption and bequest allocations.

The investor implements his entire allocation at time zero by buying pure securities from intermediaries. Let $\hat{M}(t; \bar{S}, \tau) \, d\tau$ denote the number of units of the pure security (which pays \$1 if $S(\tau) = \bar{S}$) held by the investor at time t. It follows from (16.33) that the investor's purchases of pure securities at $t = 0$ are given by

$$\hat{M}(0; \bar{S}, \tau) = c^*(\bar{S}, \tau) + W^*(\bar{S}, \tau)\delta(T - \tau) \tag{16.35}$$

for all $\bar{S}$ and $\tau \leq T$. Note that because $c^*(S, t) \geq 0$ and $W^*(S, T) \geq 0$, $\hat{M}(0; \bar{S}, t) \geq 0$ for all $\bar{S}$ and t. Thus, to implement his optimal allocation, the investor neither borrows nor short-sells any securities, and therefore his wealth at any time t is always nonnegative. Thus, to meet the optimal demands for securities, the intermediaries do not have to monitor the creditworthiness of their individual-investor customers.

Having derived the optimal allocation rules in the Arrow–Debreu framework, we now show that the sample paths of consumption and wealth generated by following (16.33) are identical with those generated by the optimal dynamic programming solutions presented in Chapters 4–6 and 15. The proof follows directly from the Cox and Huang (1989b) formulation developed in a less general form in Chapter 6.

The Cox–Huang approach can be described as maximizing the objective function (16.28) (with the understanding that $S_n(t) \equiv X(t)$), subject to the nonnegativity constraint (16.29b) and the constraint that

$$W(0) \geq X(0) \left[\int_0^T \int_S P(S, t) \frac{\hat{c}(t)}{X(t)} \, dS \, dt + \int_S P(S, T) \frac{\hat{W}(T)}{X(T)} \, dS \right]$$

(16.36)

As in Theorem 6.1, Cox and Huang (1989b) show that there exists a solution to the dynamic programming formulation of the problem $[c^*(t), W^*(T)]$ if and only if $c^*(t) = \hat{c}^*(t)$ for $t \leq T$ and $W^*(T) = \hat{W}^*(T)$. Hence, to prove that our optimal allocation (16.33) is identical to the dynamic programming solution, we need only show that (16.33) is a solution to the Cox–Huang formulation. But, from Theorem 16.1, $X(0)/X(t) = \Pi[S(0), 0; S, t]/P[S(0), 0; S, t]$ where it is understood that $X(t)$ is the value of the growth-optimum portfolio at time t, contingent on $S(t) = S$. By substitution for $X(0)/X(t)$ into (16.36), (16.36) becomes (16.29a). Therefore, the Cox–Huang solution is identical to our solution (16.33). In Chapter 6, we promised further economic intuition into the meaning of constraint (16.36). As we see, (16.36) of the Cox–Huang formulation is simply the budget constraint (16.29a).

Because the solution to (16.28)–(16.29) is a true intertemporal optimum, it must satisfy the "time-consistency" condition that the optimal state-contingent consumption and bequest quantities specified in (16.33) are also those that would be selected if the investor reexamined his remaining choices at some later date t. It follows that the program given by (16.33) must satisfy the investor's budget constraint at time t. Therefore, if $W^k(t)$ denotes the optimally invested wealth of investor k at time t, then we have that, for $0 \leq t \leq T^k$,

$$W^k(t) = \int_t^{T^k} \int_S \Pi[S(t), t; S, \tau]c^k(S, \tau) \, dS \, d\tau$$

$$+ \int_S \Pi[S(t), t; S, T^k]W^k(S, T^k) \, dS \qquad (16.37)$$

where $c^k(S, \tau)$ and $W^k(S, T^k)$ satisfy (16.33). Hence, $\hat{M}^k(t; \bar{S}, \tau) = \hat{M}^k(0; \bar{S}, \tau)$ in (16.35) for $t \leq \tau \leq T^k$ and all $\bar{S}$. If $\lambda_1^k(t) \equiv \lambda_1^k[S(t), W^k(t), t]$ denotes the shadow cost of the budget constraint at time t, then from Theorem 16.1 and the time-consistency condition applied to (16.33), we have that, for all S and $\tau > t$,

$$\frac{\lambda_1^k(t)}{\lambda_1^k(0)} = \frac{P[S(t), t; S, \tau]\Pi[S(0), 0; S, \tau]}{P[S(0), 0; S, \tau]\Pi[S(t), t; S, \tau]} = \frac{X(0)}{X(t)} \qquad (16.38)$$

It follows from (16.38) that if an investor is not satiated by his initial endowment (i.e. $\lambda_1^k(0) > 0$), then with probability one he never reaches satiation in finite time (i.e. $\lambda_1^k(t) > 0$). From (16.37) and (16.38), given the initial distribution of wealth $\{W^k(0)\}$, the distribution of wealth at any later date t is completely specified by $S(t)$.

After the derivation of the Cox–Huang solution to the lifetime consumption-choice problem in Chapter 6, we promised to provide further economic intuition into the effects of the nonnegativity constraints on consumption and wealth. Consider the unconstrained solution to (16.28) with initial wealth $W^+(0)$ and (16.29b) left out. If $c^{**}(S, t)$ and $W^{**}(S, T)$ denote the unconstrained allocations, then from (16.30a) and (16.30b) with $\lambda_2 \equiv 0$ and $\lambda_3 \equiv 0$, we have that

$$c^{**}(S, t) = Q\left[\frac{\lambda_1'\Pi(S, t)}{P(S, t)}, S, t\right] \qquad 0 \leqslant t \leqslant T \qquad (16.39a)$$

and

$$W^{**}(S, T) = R\left[\frac{\lambda_1'\Pi(S, T)}{P(S, T)}, S, T\right] \qquad (16.39b)$$

where λ_1' is determined so as to satisfy the budget constraint

$$W^+(0) = \int_0^T \int_S \Pi(S, t)Q\left[\frac{\lambda_1'\Pi(S, t)}{P(S, t)}, S, t\right] dS\, dt$$
$$+ \int_S \Pi(S, T)R\left[\frac{\lambda_1'\Pi(S, T)}{P(S, T)}, S, T\right] dS \qquad (16.40)$$

From (16.40), λ_1' is a continuous and strictly decreasing function of $W^+(0)$. Suppose we choose $W^+(0)$ so that $\lambda_1' = \lambda_1$, the solution to (16.34). It follows from (16.33) and (16.39) that for this choice of $W^+(0)$

$$c^*(S, t) = \max[0, c^{**}(S, t)]$$
$$= c^{**}(S, t) + \max[0, -c^{**}(S, t)] \qquad (16.41a)$$

and

$$W^*(S, T) = \max[0, W^{**}(S, T)]$$
$$= W^{**}(S, T) + \max[0, -W^{**}(S, T)] \qquad (16.41b)$$

Formally, $\max[0, -c^{**}(S, t)]\, dt$ is the payoff to a put-option security on unconstrained optimal consumption flow at time t, with a zero exercise price and expiration date t. Similarly, $\max[0, -W^{**}(S, T)]$ is the payoff to a zero-exercise-price put option on unconstrained optimal terminal wealth with expiration date T. The cost of buying a portfolio of such put options to cover all the negative payoffs to the entire unconstrained optimal consumption–bequest program is thus given by

$$f[S(0), W^+(0)] = \int_0^T \int_S \Pi(S, t) \max[0, -c^{**}(S, t)] \, dS \, dt$$

$$+ \int_S \Pi(S, T) \max[0, -W^{**}(S, T)] \, dS \quad (16.42)$$

Substituting for $c^*(S, t)$ and $W^*(S, T)$ from (16.41) into (16.34) and rearranging terms, we have from (16.42) that

$$W(0) - f[S(0), W^+(0)] = \int_0^T \int_S \Pi(S, t) \, c^{**}(S, t) \, dS \, dt$$

$$+ \int_S \Pi(S, T) \, W^{**}(S, T) \, dS \quad (16.43)$$

By inspection of (16.40) with $\lambda'_1 = \lambda_1$, we have from (16.43) that

$$W(0) - f[S(0), W^+(0)] = W^+(0) \quad (16.44)$$

The relation between the constrained and unconstrained solutions to (16.28) can thus be described as follows. The investor solves for his unconstrained optimal consumption–bequest program as a function of some initial wealth $W^+(0)$. Because neither negative consumption nor negative wealth is feasible, to "implement" this program, the investor must purchase a portfolio of put-option securities with payoffs that make up any "shortfall" between $c^{**}(S, t)$ and zero and $W^{**}(S, T)$ and zero. The cost of these shortfall guarantees is $f[S(0), W^+(0)]$. The investor therefore allocates $W^+(0)$ of his wealth to pursue the unconstrained program and the balance, $W(0) - W^+(0)$, to pay for the guarantees. The optimal constrained program is the optimal unconstrained-cum-guarantees one that satisfies his budget constraint $W(0) = W^+(0) + f[S(0), W^+(0)]$. If $c^{**}(S, t) \geq 0$ for all S and t and $W^{**}(S, T) \geq 0$, then from (16.42), $f = 0$ and $W^+(0) = W(0)$. Otherwise, $f > 0$ and $W^+(0) < W(0)$.

Cox and Huang (1989b) were the first to recognize that the cost to the investor of the nonnegativity constraints (16.29b) can be expressed as a reduction in wealth equal to the cost of buying a set of put options that guarantee satisfaction of these constraints, less the benefits of truncating the value of the portfolio at zero.[6] In addition to providing a rather intuitive description of the impact of these constraints on the optimal program, this approach provides a useful computational method for solving the constrained optimization problem in those cases where a closed-form solution to the unconstrained problem is known.

As shown in Chapter 6, if the returns on the growth-optimum portfolio follow a geometric Brownian motion, then infinite-lived investors with state-independent, strictly increasing and concave utility functions choose optimal portfolios that never risk ruin. That is, optimally invested wealth for such investors satisfies prob$\{W(t) > 0\} = 1$ for all t. Under the same conditions, Cox and Huang (1989b, Proposition 3.1) prove the same result for finite-lived investors and $t < T$. By positing two additional regularity conditions, we now extend that result to include state-dependent preferences and more general dynamics for the growth-optimum portfolio.

Regularity Condition 1

For every noninfinitesimal $\delta > 0$ and each t and $\bar{t}$ such that $t \geq \bar{t} + \delta$, the support of the conditional random variable return on the growth-optimum portfolio, $X(t)/X(\bar{t})$, is the entire positive real line. That is, for any finite number M, prob$\{X(t)/X(\bar{t}) > M | X(\bar{t}), S(\bar{t})\} > 0$.

Let $\psi(X, t; \bar{X}, \bar{t})$ denote the set of all S such that for $t > \bar{t}$, prob$\{S(t) = S | X(t) = X, X(\bar{t}) = \bar{X}\} > 0$. Because prob$\{X(\tau) > 0 | X(0) > 0\} = 1$, ψ is empty for $X \leq 0$. For investor k in (16.28), define the function $G^k(X; \bar{X}, S, t) \equiv U_c^k(0, S, t)(X/\bar{X})$ for $t < T^k$. Because $U_c^k > 0$, $G^k > 0$ for $X/\bar{X} > 0$.

Regularity Condition 2

For each t, $0 \leq t < T^k$, there exists a finite number X^+ such that for all $X \geq X^+$ and $S \in \psi(X, t; \bar{X}, \bar{t})$, $G^k(X; \bar{X}, S, t)$ is a strictly increasing, unbounded function of X.

Theorem 16.2

If Regularity Conditions 1 and 2 hold for investor k and $W^k(0) > 0$, then investor k never risks ruin and prob$\{W^k(t) > 0\} = 1$ for $0 \leq t < T^k$.

---

6 For the development of this result in discrete time for both the one-period static model and the Arrow–Debreu model with a finite number of states, see Merton (1990a, Sections 4 and 5).

PROOF

The proof is by contradiction. Suppose that $W^k(\bar{t}) = 0$ for some $\bar{t} < T^k$. Then, from (16.37), $c^k(S, t) = 0$ for all possible S and $\bar{t} < t \leq T^k$. This implies from (16.33a) and Theorem 16.1 that, for $\bar{t} < t < T^k$, $U^k_c(0, S, t) \leq \lambda^k_1 X(0)/X(t)$ for each possible $X(t)$, conditional on $X(\bar{t}) = \overline{X}$ and $S \in \psi[X(t), t; \overline{X}, \bar{t}]$. From the definition of G^k, it follows that $G^k[X(t); \overline{X}, S, t] \leq \lambda^k_1 X(0)/\overline{X}$ for all possible $X(t)$. $X(\bar{t}) = \overline{X}$ is positive with probability one, and λ^k_1 is positive and finite because $W^k(0) > 0$. Hence, with probability one, $\lambda^k_1 X(0)/\overline{X}$ is a positive finite number, independent of $X(t)$, S, and t. Therefore, for $\overline{X} > 0$, we have from Regularity Condition 2 that there exists a finite number M such that, for all $X > \overline{X}M$, $G^k(X; \overline{X}, S, t) > \lambda^k_1 X(0)/\overline{X}$ unless $\psi(X, t; \overline{X}, \bar{t})$ is empty for all such X. But, from Regularity Condition 1, we have that for $\overline{X} > 0$ and $t \geq \bar{t} + \delta$ for any noninfinitesimal $\delta > 0$, $\psi(X, t; \overline{X}, \bar{t})$ is a nonempty set for all $X < \infty$. Hence, by contradiction, $\text{prob}\{W^k(\bar{t}) > 0\} = 1$ for all $\bar{t} < T^k$.   QED

The Regularity Conditions 1 and 2 are rather mild. Regularity Condition 1 holds for the prototypical case of geometric Brownian motion investigated in Chapter 6. From this and (16.22), it follows that Regularity Condition 1 will obtain if, for all S and t, $\mu^2(S, t) \geq \epsilon > 0$ and $\mu^2(S, t) + r(S, t) \geq m > -\infty$. Regularity Condition 2 holds immediately if preferences are smooth and state independent. For state-dependent preferences, it simply rules out those cases where the utility dependence on variables other than consumption completely "swamps" the usual wealth and consumption-substitution effects. Thus, the conclusion of Theorem 16.2 is robust.

The investor can implement his optimal consumption–bequest program by buying from an intermediary either a custom contract with promised state-contingent payments given by (16.33) or a portfolio of pure securities with composition given by (16.35). To ensure performance on the custom contract, the intermediary invests the proceeds from its sale in the m traded assets and riskless security according to rule (16.16) with $G(S, t) = c^*(S, t)$ and $H(S) = W^*(S, T)$. Alternatively, to hedge the sale of pure securities, the intermediary invests the proceeds in traded assets according to rule (16.21) with $\hat{M}(0; S, \tau)$ given by (16.35). Either form of implementation produces the same induced demand by the intermediary for the traded assets.

Given the initial distribution of wealth $\{W^k(0)\}$ and the initial values of the state variables $S(0)$, we have from (16.33a) that aggregate consumption flow at time t for $S(t) = S$ can be written as

$$C(S, t) = \sum_1^N \max\left(0, Q^k\left\{\frac{\lambda^k_1 \Pi[S(0), 0; S, t]}{P[S(0), 0; S, t]}, S, t\right\}\right) \quad (16.45)$$

where it is understood that $Q^k(\cdot, S, t) \equiv 0$ for all $t > T^k$, $k = 1,...,N$. Similarly, from (16.33b), we can express the aggregate flow of bequests at time t as an impulse function given by

$$H(S, t) = \sum_1^N \max\left(0, R^k\left\{\frac{\lambda_1^k\Pi[S(0), 0; S, t]}{P[S(0), 0; S, t]}, S, t\right\}\delta(T^k - t)\right)$$
(16.46)

where $\delta(\cdot)$ is the Dirac delta function. As with individual consumption and bequests, the "time-consistency" condition for an intertemporal optimum implies that the state-contingent aggregate schedules determined at time 0, $C(S, t)$ and $H(S, t)$, do not change over time.

If $M^*(S, t)\,dt$ denotes the optimal aggregate number of units demanded of the pure security that pays \$1 if $S(t) = S$, then it follows from (16.35), (16.45), and (16.46) that

$$M^*(S, t) = C(S, t) + H(S, t) \qquad (16.47)$$

From the "time-consistency" condition, $\{M^*(S, t)\}$, as determined at time zero, does not change over time. Therefore, from (16.21) and (16.47), the aggregate optimal demands for the traded assets at time t with $S(t) = S$ can be written as, for $j = 1,...,m$

$$D_j^*(S, t) = \int_t^\infty \int_{\bar{S}} \frac{M^*(\bar{S}, \tau)}{\sigma_j(S, t)}[\Pi_j(S, t; \bar{S}, \tau)g_j(S, t)S_j$$

$$+ \sum_{m+1}^n \Pi_k(S, t; \bar{S}, \tau)g_k(S, t)S_k\delta_{jk}(S, t)]\,dS\,d\tau \quad (16.48a)$$

$$D_{m+1}^*(S, t) = \sum_1^N W^k(t) - \sum_1^M D_j^*(S, t) \qquad (16.48b)$$

where D_{m+1}^* is the aggregate demand for the riskless security and $W^k(t)$ is given by (16.37). Hence, as a necessary condition for equilibrium, the market values of the traded assets must satisfy

$$V_j(t) = D_j^*(S, t) \qquad j = 1,...,m \qquad (16.49)$$

for $S(t) = S$ and all t. Therefore, given the initial distribution of wealth $\{W^k(0)\}$ and $S(0)$, we have from (16.7), (16.27), and (16.45)–(16.49) that the equilibrium prices of traded assets at time t are determined by the current values of the state variables $S(t)$.

16.4   GENERAL EQUILIBRIUM: THE CASE OF PURE EXCHANGE

In this section, we derive a set of intertemporal equilibrium plans, prices, and rational expectations for an economy in which the output of the consumption good is exogenous. The derivation takes place in two steps. We first show that there exists a unique set of positive and finite prices for the growth-optimum portfolio such that the optimal planned consumption allocations of all investors are fulfilled for every possible $S(t)$ and all t. We then derive a set of rational expectations about asset-price and interest-rate dynamics that support these market-clearing optimal consumption allocations.

We begin by specifying the exogenous relations in the economy. For analytical convenience, the dynamics of the primal state variables $[S_1(t),...,S_m(t)]$ in (16.1) are assumed to follow an exogenous Markov process with $\{f_i, g_i, \rho_{ij}\}$ known functions. Thus, the only supplementary state variable is the price of the growth-optimum portfolio, $X(t)$. The aggregate flow of output at time t is exogenously given by $Y(S_1,...,S_m, t)$ and $Y > 0$ for all t and $S_j(t) = S_j, j = 1,...,m$. All output is perishable and hence there is no physical storage technology. To simplify the proof of existence and uniqueness of equilibrium, we posit that investors' preferences in (16.5) satisfy $U_c^k > 0$ for $c^k < \infty$ and $U_c^k < \infty$ for $c^k > 0$, $k = 1,...,N$. Moreover, any state dependence of direct preferences involves only the exogenous state variables, $[S_1(t),...,S_m(t)]$. To avoid the complexity of accounting for interconsumer transfers from bequests, we assume either that $B^k \equiv 0$ in (16.5) or that $T^k = \infty$, $k = 1,...,N$.[7]

The general equilibrium analysis requires further elaboration on the properties of the traded assets $[V_1,...,V_m]$. For this purpose, it is convenient to choose the mutual-fund interpretation for these assets, as discussed in footnote 1. We assume that there are m firms that collectively own the current and future aggregate output of the economy. The distribution of ownership among the firms is specified by $\{Y_k[S_1(t),...,S_m(t), t]\}$ where Y_k is the nonnegative, state-contingent dividend flow paid by firm k at time t, $k = 1,...,m$, and $Y = \Sigma_1^m Y_k$. To ensure feasibility of dynamically-complete markets, the $\{Y_k\}$ are taken to be linearly independent functions. If $A_k(S, t)$ denotes the market value of firm k at time t, then from (16.15) we have that, for $S(t) = S$

---

7 $T^k = \infty$ is usually justified by assuming that each individual has a bequest function for the next generation in his family and that families continue on indefinitely. We could accommodate the prospect of uncertain lifetimes for individuals or families by introducing life-annuity contracts which close the model by specifying the disposition of assets among the surviving members of the economy.

$$A_k(S, t) = \int_t^\infty \int_{\underline{S}} Y_k(\overline{S}_1,...,\overline{S}_m, \tau)\Pi(S, t; \overline{S}, \tau) \, d\overline{S} \, d\tau \qquad k = 1,...,m$$

$$(16.50)$$

By applying Itô's lemma to (16.50), we can express the conditional means, variances, and covariances of the returns on these m firms as a function of S and t. For $j = 1,...,m$, the manager of fund j trades these firms' shares according to the strategy

$$w_{jk}(S, t) = \frac{\zeta_{jk}}{\Sigma_1^m \zeta_{ji}} \qquad k = 1,...,m \qquad (16.51)$$

where w_{jk} denotes the portfolio fraction of fund j allocated to firm k and $\{\zeta_{jk}\}$ is defined in Theorem 15.3. From that theorem, strategy (16.51) ensures that the returns on each of the funds' portfolios satisfy (16.4). From (16.51), $\Sigma_1^m w_{jk}(S, t) = 1$, $j = 1,..., m$, and therefore none of the funds invests in the riskless security. If $\Gamma_{jk}(S, t)$ denotes the fraction of firm k owned by fund j at time t, then $\Gamma_{jk}(S, t) = w_{jk}(S, t)V_j(t)/A_k(S, t)$ and $V_j(t) = \Sigma_1^m \Gamma_{jk}(S, t)A_k(S, t)$. It follows from (16.50) that the value of fund j at time t with $S(t) = S$ can be written as

$$V_j(t) = \int_t^\infty \int_{\underline{S}} E_j(S, t; \overline{S}, \tau)\Pi(S, t; \overline{S}, \tau) \, d\overline{S} \, d\tau \qquad j = 1,...,m$$

$$(16.52)$$

where $E_j(S, t; \overline{S}, \tau) \equiv \Sigma_1^m \Gamma_{jk}(S, t)Y_k(\overline{S}_1,...,\overline{S}_m, \tau)$.

Because $X(t)$ is an endogenous variable from the perspective of general equilibrium, it is convenient to separate explicitly the dependence of consumer demands on $X(t)$ from the dependence on the exogenous variables $S(t) \equiv [S_1(t),...,S_m(t)]$. Thus, we write the time-state-contingent optimal consumption schedule for investor k as $c^k(X, S, t)$ for $X(t) = X$ and $S(t) = S$. Similarly, state-contingent aggregate consumption as given in (16.45) is expressed as $C(X, S, t)$. Without loss of generality, we adopt the convention that $X(0) = 1$ so that $X(t)$ denotes both the price and the cumulative return on the growth-optimum portfolio between time 0 and time t.

Using Theorem 16.1 to substitute for Π/P, we rewrite (16.45) as

$$C(X, S, t) = \sum_1^N \hat{Q}^k\left(\frac{\lambda_1^k}{X}, S, t\right) \qquad (16.53)$$

where $\hat{Q}^k \equiv \max[0, Q^k(\lambda_1^k/X, S, t)]$. Because $\partial Q^k(y, S, t)/\partial y < 0$, $\partial\hat{Q}^k(y, S, t)/\partial y < 0$ for $Q^k > 0$ and is zero otherwise. Define the state-contingent aggregate excess-demand function $\phi(X, S, t) \equiv C(X, S, t) - Y(S, t)$ for $X(t) = X$ and $S(t) = S$. For the consumption-good market to clear and equilibrium to obtain, there must exist an X, $0 < X < \infty$, for each t and each possible $S(t)$ such that

$$\phi[X, S(t), t] = 0 \qquad (16.54)$$

From (16.30a) and Theorem 16.1, $U_c^k(c^k, S, t) \leq \lambda_1^k/X$ with equality holding if $Q^k \geq 0$. Because $U_c^k > 0$ for $c^k < \infty$, it follows that $X = \infty$ only if $Q^k = \infty$. Hence, for finite output flows, $\phi(\infty, S, t) > 0$. Because $\lambda_1^k > 0$ and $U_c^k < \infty$ for $Q^k > 0$, $X = 0$ only if $\hat{Q}^k = 0$ for $k = 1,...,N$. Hence, $C(0, S, t) = 0$ and therefore $\phi(0, S, t) < 0$ because $Y(S, t) > 0$ for all S and t. Because $\partial Q^k(y, S, t)/\partial y < 0$ and Y does not depend on X, $\partial C/\partial X > 0$ and $\partial\phi/\partial X > 0$ for $C > 0$. From these monotonicity conditions and the continuity of C in X, it follows that for any given set of positive numbers, $\lambda_1 \equiv [\lambda_1^1,...,\lambda_1^N]$, there exists a unique, positive and finite X that satisfies (16.54) for each t and each possible $S(t)$.

For given λ_1, let $X(t) = F[S(t), t; \lambda_1]$ denote the state-contingent price schedule for the growth-optimum portfolio such that F is the solution to $\phi[F, S(t), t] = 0$. We now show that for a specified distribution of initial endowments $\{W^k(0)\}$, the λ_1 which satisfies each investor's budget constraint is positive and unique. From (16.34) and (16.36), we can write the budget constraint of investor k for $X(t) = F$ as

$$W_0^k = \int_0^{T^k} \int_S P(S, t) \frac{\hat{Q}^k[\lambda_1^k/F(S, t; \lambda_1), S, t]}{F(S, t; \lambda_1)} \, dS \, dt \qquad (16.55)$$

where $P(S, t) = P[S(0), 0; S, t]$ is given by the solution to (16.27) with $n = m$. For $F(S, t; \lambda_1)$ positive and finite, $\lambda_1^k = 0$ implies that $\hat{Q}^k = \infty$ because $U_c^k > 0$ for $c^k < \infty$. For $\lambda_1^k = \infty$, $\hat{Q}^k = 0$. Hence, for $W_0^k > 0$, a solution to (16.55) with $0 < \lambda_1^k < \infty$ exists by the continuity of $\hat{Q}^k$ and F. A sufficient condition for a unique solution is that the integrand in (16.55) is a strictly decreasing function of λ_1^k. Because $X(t) = F$ is an explicit function of S and t, $P(S, t)$ is the joint probability density function over the exogenous variables $[S_1(t),...,S_m(t)]$ only. Hence, $P(S, t)$ does not depend on λ_1. Because $P > 0$, it is thus sufficient for uniqueness to show that $\hat{Q}^k/F$ is strictly decreasing in λ_1^k for all S and t where $\hat{Q}^k > 0$. Let $y_k \equiv \lambda_1^k/F(S, t; \lambda_1)$, $k = 1,...,N$. By the Implicit Function Theorem applied to (16.54), we have that for $\hat{Q}^k > 0$

$$\frac{\partial F}{\partial \lambda_1^k} = \frac{\partial \hat{Q}^k/\partial y_k}{\Sigma_1^N y_j \partial \hat{Q}^j/\partial y_j} \qquad k = 1,...,N \qquad (16.56)$$

For S and t such that $\hat{Q}^k > 0$, the derivative of $\hat{Q}^k/F$ in the integrand of (16.55) can be expressed as

$$\frac{\partial(\hat{Q}^k/F)}{\partial\lambda_1^k} = \left[\frac{\partial\hat{Q}^k}{\partial y_k}\left(1 - y_k\frac{\partial F}{\partial\lambda_1^k}\right) - \frac{\hat{Q}^k}{F}\frac{\partial F}{\partial\lambda_1^k}\right]\bigg/ F \qquad (16.57)$$

Because $\partial\hat{Q}^j/\partial y_j < 0$ and $y_j > 0$ for $\hat{Q}^j > 0$, $j = 1,...,N$, we have from (16.56) that $0 < y_k\partial F/\partial\lambda_1^k \leqslant 1$ for $\hat{Q}^k > 0$. It therefore follows from (16.57) that $\partial(\hat{Q}^k/F)/\partial\lambda_1^k < 0$ for $\hat{Q}^k > 0$. Hence, for a given distribution of initial endowments, the λ_1 that satisfies (16.52) for $k = 1,...,N$ is unique, and thus the equilibrium price schedule for the growth-optimum portfolio, $F[S(t), t]$, is also unique.

Having found the price schedule for $X(t)$, which ensures that the optimal planned consumption by all investors is fulfilled for every possible $S(t)$ and all t, we now determine the set of rational beliefs about asset-price and interest-rate dynamics that are consistent with this price schedule. From (16.3) and (16.24) with $n = m$, we have that

$$\sigma_{xi} = \sigma_i(S, t)\sum_1^m \frac{F_j(S, t)}{F(S, t)} g_j(S, t)\rho_{ij}(S, t) S_j \qquad i = 1,...,m$$

It follows from (16.23) that

$$\frac{\alpha_i(S, t) - r(S, t)}{\sigma_i(S, t)} = \sum_1^m \frac{F_j(S, t)}{F(S, t)} g_j(S, t)\rho_{ij}(S, t)S_j \qquad (16.58)$$

for $i = 1,...,m$ and $S(t) = S$. Because $(\mu\,dz)^2 = \mu^2\,dt$, we have from (16.24) that

$$\mu^2(S, t) = \sum_1^m\sum_1^m \frac{F_i(S, t)F_j(S, t)g_i(S, t)g_j(S, t)\rho_{ij}(S, t)S_iS_j}{[F(S, t)]^2} \tag{16.59}$$

Given $\mu^2(S, t)$ from (16.59), we have from (16.25) and (16.26) that the equilibrium interest rate when $S(t) = S$ must satisfy

$$r(S, t) = \frac{\mathscr{L}[F|S, t]}{F(S, t)} - \mu^2(S, t) \qquad (16.60)$$

Note that because the economy in this section has no production or storage technology, it is wholly consistent with equilibrium that $r(S, t) < 0$ for some values of S and t.

Using (16.58)–(16.60) to specify the endogenous expectations functions that appear in (16.7), we can solve (16.7) to determine the rational-expectations equilibrium prices for all Arrow–Debreu securities, $\{\Pi(S, t; \overline{S}, \tau)\}$, as well as the partial-derivative functions $\{\Pi_j(S, t; \overline{S}, \tau)\}$, $j = 1,\ldots,m$. Using these equilibrium pure-security prices, the equilibrium values of the business firms and traded mutual funds, $\{A_k\}$ and $\{V_j\}$, are determined by (16.50) and (16.52), respectively. From (16.47) and (16.54), in equilibrium, $M^*(S, t) = Y(S, t)$ for $S(t) = S$ and all t. From (16.48a), (16.49), and (16.52), we have by rearranging terms that, for $j = 1,\ldots,m$,

$$\sigma_j(S, t) = g_j(S, t) \frac{S_j \int_t^\infty \int_{\overline{S}} Y(\overline{S}, \tau) \Pi_j(S, t; \overline{S},\tau)\, d\overline{S}\, d\tau}{\int_t^\infty \int_{\overline{S}} E_j(S, t; \overline{S}, \tau) \Pi(S, t; \overline{S}, \tau)\, d\overline{S}\, d\tau} \qquad (16.61)$$

Substituting for $\sigma_j(S, t)$ and $r(S, t)$ from (16.60) and (16.61) into (16.58) and rearranging terms, we have the specification for the equilibrium $\alpha_j(S, t), j = 1,\ldots,m$. This completes the general equilibrium description for the economy.

In closing this section, we show that the equilibrium allocations, prices, and expectations can be derived from a "representative consumer" characterization. That is, the equilibrium solution is as if there were a single, utility-maximizing consumer whose endowment equals national wealth.

From (16.53), aggregate optimal consumption $C(X, S, t)$ satisfies the condition that $\partial C/\partial X > 0$ for $C > 0$ and all S and t. It follows that $C(X, S, t)$ is an invertible function for all $C > 0$. If Q^{-1} denotes the inverse function such that $Q^{-1}[C(X, S, t)] = X$, then define the aggregate marginal-utility-of-consumption function U_C, for each $C > 0$, by

$$U_C(C, S, t) \equiv 1/Q^{-1}(C, S, t) \qquad (16.62)$$

where, by inspection of (16.53), Q^{-1} depends parametrically on the distribution of initial endowments among the N consumers in the economy. If $X^+(S, t)$ denotes the largest value of $X(t)$ such that $C(X, S, t) = 0$ for $X \le X^+(S, t)$, then we complete the specification of U_C by the condition that

$$U_C(0, S, t) \equiv 1/X^+(S, t) \qquad (16.63)$$

By partial integration of (16.62) with respect to C, $U(C, S, t)$ is determined up to a positive affine transformation. $U_C > 0$ and for $C > 0$, $U_{CC} = -(\partial Q^{-1}/\partial C)/(Q^{-1})^2 = -1/(X^2 \partial C/\partial X) < 0$. Hence, U is a strictly increasing and strictly concave function of C, properties which are shared by the preference orderings of each of the N consumers. From (16.62), it follows that, for $C > 0$,

$$\frac{-U_C(C, S, t)}{U_{CC}(C, S, t)} = X \frac{\partial C}{\partial X} \qquad (16.64)$$

From Theorem 16.1 with $X(0) = 1$, $X(t) = P(S, t)/\Pi(S, t)$ for all S and t. Substituting for $P(S, t)/\Pi(S, t)$ in (16.30a), we have that for $c^k > 0$, $U_c^k(c^k, S, t) = \lambda_1^k/X(t)$. It therefore follows that, for $c^k > 0$ and $k = 1,...,N$,

$$\frac{-U_c^k(c^k, S, t)}{U_{cc}^k} = X \frac{\partial c^k}{\partial X} \qquad (16.65)$$

But, $\partial C/\partial X = \Sigma_1^N \partial c^k/\partial X$. Hence, from (16.64) and (16.65), we have that

$$\frac{-U_C(C, S, t)}{U_{CC}(C, S, t)} = \sum_1^N \frac{-U_c^k(c^k, S, t)}{U_{cc}^k(c^k, S, t)} \qquad (16.66)$$

for C equal to aggregate optimal consumption. Therefore, absolute risk aversion for the aggregate utility function is at each point in time equal to the harmonic mean of the absolute risk aversions of the N consumers in the economy.

For C equal to aggregate optimal consumption, $Q^{-1} = X(t) = P(S, t)/\Pi(S, t)$. It follows from (16.62) that for $C > 0$

$$U_C(C, S, t) = \frac{\Pi(S, t)}{P(S, t)} \qquad (16.67)$$

for all S and t. By inspection, (16.67) is identical to the first-order condition (16.30a) for an interior optimum, with $\lambda_1 = 1$. Moreover, because aggregate initial wealth, $W(0)$, equals $\Sigma_1^N W^k(0)$ and because $C(X, S, t) = \Sigma_1^N c^k(X, S, t)$, $W(0)$ and $C(X, S, t)$ satisfy the budget constraint (16.30c) with $\lambda_1 = 1$. Therefore, equilibrium allocations, prices, and expectations for the economy are the same as for a single-person economy with preferences given by $U(C, S, t)$ and initial endowment $W(0)$.

16.5 GENERAL EQUILIBRIUM: THE CASE OF PRODUCTION

In this section, we extend the pure-exchange model to include production in a "putty-putty" economy in which all investment is reversible. Capital as well as output can thus be consumed, and therefore the price of a unit of capital equals the price of the consumption good which is numeraire. In line with the model of the preceding section, we posit production flows that are instantaneously certain. This assumption is relaxed in the analysis in Section 16.6.

In addition to the m exogenous state variables, $S(t) \equiv [S_1(t),...,S_m(t)]$, there are two supplementary state variables: the aggregate capital stock, $K(t)$, and the price of the growth-optimum portfolio, $X(t)$. As in (16.50), we posit m business firms with firm j owning $K_j(t)$ units of capital at time t and $\Sigma_1^m K_j(t) = K(t)$. Each firm also owns a production technology with state-contingent output flow for firm j denoted by $Y_j(S, t; I_j)$ where I_j is the amount of capital employed in this technology at time t, $j = 1,...,m$. Each of these production technologies satisfies the regularity conditions that, for $j = 1,...,m$,

$$Y_j = 0 \text{ and } \frac{\partial Y_j}{\partial I_j} = \infty \qquad \text{for } I_j = 0 \qquad (16.68a)$$

and

$$\frac{\partial Y_j}{\partial I_j} > 0 \text{ and } \frac{\partial^2 Y_j}{\partial I_j^2} < 0 \quad \text{for } 0 < I_j < \infty \qquad (16.68b)$$

Each firm can either use its capital in its own technology or rent (or sell) it to other firms. If capital does not physically depreciate, then the instantaneous rental rate on capital equals the riskless interest rate, because all production flows are instantaneously certain. Hence, the state-contingent profit flow at time t for production by firm j is $Y_j[S(t), t; I_j] - r(t)I_j$. It follows from (16.50) that the value of firm j at time t is given by

$$A_j(S, K, t; K_j) = K_j + \int_t^\infty \int_{\underline{K}} \int_{\underline{S}} [Y_j(\overline{S}, \tau; I_j) - r(\tau)I_j]$$

$$\times \Pi(S, K, t; \overline{S}, \overline{K}, \tau) \, d\overline{S} \, d\overline{K} \, d\tau \qquad (16.69)$$

for $S(t) = S$, $K(t) = K$, $K_j(t) = K_j$, and $j = 1,...,m$.

Each firm is a price-taker in the capital markets and chooses its state-contingent production plans so as to maximize its market value. If $I_j^*(t)$ denotes the value-maximizing quantity of capital employed by firm j for production at time t, then, from (16.69), $\partial A_j/\partial I_j = 0$ at $I_j = I_j^*$ which implies the first-order condition

$$0 = \frac{\partial Y_j(S, t; I_j^*)}{\partial I_j} - r \quad j = 1,...,m \qquad (16.70)$$

for $S(t) = S$, $K(t) = K$, $r(t) = r$, and all t. From the continuity and strict concavity of Y_j as posited in (16.68b), there exists a unique solution to (16.70), $I_j^* = I_j^*(S, r, t)$, for any positive r, and from (6.68a), $I_j^* > 0$ for all finite r.[8] Although K_j affects the value of firm j, with the posited perfect rental market for capital, it is readily apparent from (16.70) that the distribution of ownership of the capital stock among firms does not affect equilibrium production decisions.

Define the excess-demand function in the rental market for capital at time t by $\psi(S, K, r, t) \equiv \Sigma_1^m[I_j^*(S, r, t) - K_j(t)] = \Sigma_1^m I_j^*(S, r, t) - K$ for $S(t) = S$ and $K(t) = K$. If equilibrium is to obtain, then there must exist a number r for each t and each possible $S(t)$ and $K(t)$ such that

$$0 = \psi[S(t), K(t), r, t] \qquad (16.71)$$

From (16.68b) and (16.70), $r = 0$ only if $I_j^* = \infty$. Hence, for $K(t)$ finite, $\psi[S(t), K(t), 0, t] > 0$. From (16.68a) and (16.70), $I_j^* = 0$ if $r = \infty$, and thus $\psi[S(t), K(t), \infty, t] < 0$ for $K(t) > 0$. By the Implicit Function Theorem applied to (16.70), $\partial I_j^*/\partial r = 1/(\partial^2 Y_j/\partial I_j^2)$. From the strict concavity of output in (16.68b), it follows that equilibrium investment in each of the production processes is a decreasing function of the interest rate and hence $\partial \psi/\partial r = \Sigma_1^m \partial I_j^*/\partial r < 0$. Therefore, by these monotonicity and continuity properties of ψ, we have that there exists a unique, positive and finite solution to (16.71) for all $S(t)$, $K(t)$, and t. Define $r(S, K, t)$ to be the solution to $0 = \psi(S, K, r, t)$. Then, for $S(t) = S$ and $K(t) = K$, $r(S, K, t)$ is the unique state-contingent schedule of equilibrium interest rates.

In equilibrium, $K = \Sigma_1^m I_j^*$, and hence we have that

$$\frac{\partial r(S, K, t)}{\partial K} = \frac{1}{\Sigma_1^m \partial I_j^*/\partial r} < 0 \qquad (16.72)$$

By substitution of the equilibrium interest rate schedule for r into (16.70), the equilibrium schedule of investment plans can be expressed as $I_j^*(S, K, t)$ for $S(t) = S$, $K(t) = K$, and $j = 1,...,m$. Along the equilibrium path, $1 = \Sigma_1^m \partial I_j^*/\partial K$, and therefore, from (16.70) and (16.72), it follows that

$$0 < \frac{\partial I_j^*(S, K, t)}{\partial K} < 1 \qquad j = 1,...,m \qquad (16.73)$$

---

8   If the technologies were linear so that $\partial Y_j/\partial I_j = a_j \geq 0$ and $\partial^2 Y_j/\partial I_j^2 = 0$, then either $a_j = r$ or $a_j < r$ with $I_j^* = 0$. We analyze a more general case of linear technologies in Section 16.6.

$\partial Y_j/\partial r = r\partial I_j^*/\partial r < 0$, $j = 1,...,m$, and from (16.70) and (16.73), we have that in equilibrium

$$0 < \frac{\partial Y_j}{\partial K} < r(S, K, t) \qquad j = 1,...,m \qquad (16.74)$$

In sum, the equilibrium interest rate is a decreasing function of the aggregate capital stock. Equilibrium investment and production output for each technology are decreasing functions of the interest rate and increasing functions of the aggregate capital stock.

Let $Y(S, K, t) \equiv \Sigma_1^m Y_j[S, t; I_j^*(S, K, t)]$ denote equilibrium aggregate output at time t. As in Section 16.4, define the state-contingent excess-demand function for aggregate output at time t by $\phi(S, K, X, \dot{K}, t) \equiv \dot{K} + C(X, S, t) - Y(S, K, t)$ where $\dot{K}$ denotes the change in the aggregate capital stock at time t. Note that just as Y does not depend directly on X, so C does not depend directly on K. For the output market to clear and equilibrium to obtain, aggregate net new investment, $\dot{K}$, and the price of the growth-optimum portfolio, X, must be such that $\phi[S(t), K(t), X, \dot{K}, t] = 0$ for all possible $S(t)$ and $K(t)$ and all t. Therefore, for a given X, the equilibrium state-contingent schedule for capital accumulation is given by

$$\dot{K}(S, K, t; X) = Y(S, K, t) - C(X, S, t) \qquad (16.75)$$

for $S(t) = S$ and $K(t) = K$. Because investment is reversible and capital can be consumed, there are no restrictions on the sign of $\dot{K}$. $\partial \dot{K}/\partial K = \partial Y/\partial K = r(S, K, t) > 0$ and $\partial \dot{K}/\partial X = -\partial C/\partial X < 0$. Moreover, because Y and C are instantaneously deterministic, it follows from (16.75) that equilibrium aggregate changes in capital are also instantaneously nonstochastic.

To complete the general equilibrium description of the economy, we need only determine the equilibrium state-contingent schedule for the price of the growth-optimum portfolio. As in Section 16.4, let $X(t) = F(S, K, t)$ denote the equilibrium price of the growth-optimum portfolio at time t when $S(t) = S$ and $K(t) = K$. To determine F, we note that, by Itô's lemma and (16.22), $d(1/X) = -(r\,dt + \mu\,dz)/X$, and therefore the instantaneous expected change in $1/X$ equals $-(r/X)\,dt$. Define $L(S, K, t) \equiv 1/F(S, K, t)$. From Itô's lemma, it follows that L satisfies

$$0 = \frac{1}{2}\sum_1^m \sum_1^m g_i g_j \rho_{ij} S_i S_j L_{ij} + \sum_1^m f_i S_i L_i + \dot{K} L_K + L_t + rL$$

$$(16.76)$$

558   Continuous-Time Finance

where subscripts on L denote partial derivatives, $\dot{K} = Y(S, K, t) - C(1/L,$ $S, t)$ from (16.75), and $r = r(S, K, t)$ from (16.71). The solution to (16.76) with $0 < L < \infty$ and $L(S, K, 0) = 1/X(0) = 1$ provides the equilibrium price for the growth-optimum portfolio, $F(S, K, t) = 1/L(S, K, t)$ for $S(t) = S$ and $K(t) = K$. Moreover, it can be shown that $\partial F/\partial K > 0$. In the case of pure exchange (i.e. $\dot{K} \equiv 0$), the equilibrium F was determined by simply solving the algebraic transcendental equation (16.54). Exemplifying the increased analytical complexity caused by including production, the determination of F from (16.76) requires the solution of a nonlinear partial differential equation.

The balance of the equilibrium analysis follows the pure-exchange case. With $F(S, K, t)$ determined, μ^2 and $(\alpha_i - r)/\sigma_i$, $i = 1,...,m$, are derived from (16.58) and (16.59). Together with $r(S, K, t)$ from (16.71), these specify the endogenous expectations functions in (16.7). The solution of (16.7) provides the rational-expectations equilibrium prices for all Arrow–Debreu securities, $\{\Pi(S, K, t; \bar{S}, \bar{K}, \tau)\}$. With $\{I_j^*\}$ from (16.70) and $r(S, K, t)$ from (16.71), the pure-security prices are used to determine the equilibrium values of the m business firms as given by (16.69).

16.6 A GENERAL EQUILIBRIUM MODEL IN WHICH THE CAPITAL ASSET PRICING MODEL OBTAINS

In this section, a general equilibrium model with production is derived in which the continuous-time version of the Sharpe–Lintner–Mossin CAPM obtains. Consider an economy similar to the one just analyzed, but with the production technologies now given by

$$dG_j = I_j(a_j \, dt + b_j \, dq_j) \qquad j = 1,...,m + 1 \qquad (16.77)$$

where the technological coefficients $\{a_j, b_j\}$ are exogenously specified constants with $b_j > 0$, $j = 1,...,m$, and $b_{m+1} = 0$, so that there is a riskless technology.[9] The technologies exhibit constant-returns-to-scale in investment, I_j, and unlike $\{Y_j dt\}$ in the preceding section, the instantaneous outputs on the m risky production processes $\{dG_j\}$ are stochastic. To provide economic intuition into the processes, we use an agrarian interpretation for the economy. If I_j bushels of wheat are planted in technology j at time t, then the quantity of wheat produced at time $t + dt$ is $I_j + dG_j$.

---

9 The analysis in this section generalizes in a straightforward fashion to include production technologies of the form $dG_j = I_j(a_j \, dt + \Sigma_1^m b_{jk} dq_k)$ where the $\{b_{jk}\}$ are constants over time. See also Chamberlain (1988) for other conditions under which the CAPM obtains in the continuous-time model.

Because dG_j can be negative, a poor harvest can cause a reduction in the capital stock that depends on the deployment of capital among the technologies. Although each a_j is assumed to be finite, there are no restrictions on its sign. If, for instance, $a_{m+1} = 0$, then there is riskless physical storage with no cost. If $a_{m+1} < 0$, then such storage is costly with depreciation rate $|a_{m+1}|$.

To simplify the analysis and ensure that the CAPM result obtains, we further posit that preferences in (16.5) are state independent with $U^k = U^k(c^k, t)$ and $T^k = \infty$, $k = 1,\dots,N$. We also assume that the dynamics for the m exogenous state variables, $\{dS_i\}$ in (16.1), are such that $\{f_i, g_i, \rho_{ij}\}$ are constants, $i, j = 1,\dots,m$. As before, there are two supplementary state variables: $X(t)$, the price of the growth-optimum portfolio; and $K(t)$, the aggregate capital stock, where $X(0) = 1$ and $K(0) > 0$. As defined in (16.3) and (16.4), there are m traded risky securities and a riskless security which earns the interest rate $r(t)$.

There are $m + 1$ business firms with firm j owning technology j and $K_j(t)$ units of capital at time t with $\Sigma_1^{m+1} K_j(t) = K(t)$. At each time t, each firm chooses the quantity of capital to employ in its own technology and rents (or sells) any of its excess capital to other firms. All rental arrangements for capital are demand contracts that require the renter firm to provide adequate assurances that the rent will be paid and the borrowed capital returned. With such assurances, it follows that the spot rental rate for capital equals the riskless interest rate.

Because production outputs are instantaneously stochastic, each firm assures its rental payments by hedging its production risks with short-sales of the appropriate amounts of traded securities. The proceeds from these short-sales are invested in the riskless security. In our agrarian setting, these hedging transactions are similar to the sale of forward contracts by farmers to hedge the value of their future harvests. If $\hat{I}_j(t)$ denotes the amount of traded security j held short by firm j to hedge its production at time t, then the net operating cash flow or profit to firm j between t and $t + dt$, $d\hat{G}_j$, is given by, for $j = 1,\dots,m$,

$$d\hat{G}_j = dG_j - \hat{I}_j \frac{dV_j}{V_j} + r(\hat{I}_j - I_j)\, dt \qquad (16.78)$$

where operating profit is measured by treating all capital employed in production as rented. Of course, firm j also receives rental payments of $rK_j\, dt$ on the capital it owns. Substituting from (16.3) and (16.77) into (16.78) and rearranging terms, we can rewrite (16.78) as

$$d\hat{G}_j = [(a_j - r)I_j - (\alpha_j - r)\hat{I}_j]\, dt + (b_j I_j - \sigma_j \hat{I}_j)\, dq_j \qquad j = 1,\dots,m$$

$$(16.79)$$

By inspection of (16.79), firm j can perfectly hedge its profit by choosing $\hat{I}_j = b_j I_j / \sigma_j$. With this selection for $\hat{I}_j$, the operating profits to firm j are instantaneously certain as in the model of the preceding section. Thus we adopt the notation that $[Y_j(I_j) - rI_j] \, dt \equiv d\hat{G}_j$ when $\hat{I}_j = b_j I_j / \sigma_j$. It follows by substitution for $\hat{I}_j$ into (16.79) that the perfectly hedged profit flow to firm j is given by

$$Y_j(I_j) - rI_j = \left(a_j - r - b_j \frac{\alpha_j - r}{\sigma_j} \right) I_j \qquad j = 1,\ldots,m \quad (16.80)$$

From (16.80) and (16.69), we can thus write the value of firm j at time t as

$$A_j(S, K, t; K_j) = K_j + \int_t^\infty \int_{\underline{K}} \int_{\underline{S}} \left(a_j - r(\tau) - \frac{b_j[\alpha_j(\tau) - r(\tau)]}{\sigma_j(\tau)} \right)$$

$$\times I_j(\tau) \Pi(S, K, t; \bar{S}, \bar{K}, \tau) \, d\bar{S} \, d\bar{K} \, d\tau$$

$$(16.81)$$

for $S(t) = S$, $K(t) = K$, $K_j(t) = K_j$, and $j = 1,\ldots,m$. For firm $m + 1$ with the riskless technology, there is no need to hedge. However, for notational symmetry, we choose the convention that $b_{m+1}/\sigma_{m+1} \equiv 1$ and firm $m + 1$ thus short-sells $\hat{I}_{m+1} = I_{m+1}$ of the riskless security. Hence, with $\alpha_{m+1} \equiv r$, $Y_{m+1}(I_{m+1}) - rI_{m+1} = (a_{m+1} - r)I_{m+1}$.

If, as assumed throughout, firms are price-takers in the financial markets, then each firm perceives its actions as not affecting either r or $(\alpha_j - r)/\sigma_j$, $j = 1,\ldots,m$. These competitive firms choose their optimal investments $\{I_j^*\}$ so as to maximize their market values. From (16.70), (16.81), and the physical feasibility condition that $I_j^* \geq 0$, it follows that the optimal investment schedule for firm j satisfies $I_j^* = 0$ for $a_j - r - b_j(\alpha_j - r)/\sigma_j < 0$; indifference among all nonnegative and finite values of I_j^* for $a_j - r - b_j(\alpha_j - r)/\sigma_j = 0$; and $I_j^* = \infty$ for $a_j - r - b_j(\alpha_j - r)/\sigma_j > 0$, $j = 1,\ldots,m + 1$. As is usual for economies with competitive firms and constant-returns-to-scale technologies, the equilibrium quantity of investment in each technology is determined by the aggregate demands for traded assets. However, because equilibrium requires that $0 \leq I_j^* < \infty$, it follows that $I_j^*[a_j - r - b_j(\alpha_j - r)/\sigma_j] = 0$ always, with $I_j^* = 0$ if $a_j - r - b_j(\alpha_j - r)/\sigma_j < 0$, $j = 1,\ldots,m + 1$. By substitution of this condition into (16.81), we have that the equilibrium value of firm j is thus given by

$$A_j(S, K, t; K_j) = K_j \qquad j = 1,\ldots,m + 1 \quad (16.82)$$

for $K_j(t) = K_j$, and the equilibrium value of each technology is zero. As in Section 16.5, with a perfect rental market for capital, the distribution of ownership of the capital stock among firms does not affect their production decisions.

As we saw in (16.58) and (16.61), without explicitly specifying the terms of the m traded risky securities, only the ratios $\{(\alpha_j - r)/\sigma_j\}$ are determined in equilibrium. Hence, for convenience and without loss of generality,[10] we posit that the terms of these traded securities are such that

$$\sigma_j = b_j \qquad j = 1,\ldots,m \qquad (16.83)$$

It follows that the variances and covariances of the returns on the m traded risky securities are given by

$$\sigma_{ij} = b_i b_j \rho_{ij} \qquad j = 1,\ldots,m \qquad (16.84)$$

and each σ_{ij} is constant over time because b_i, b_j, and ρ_{ij} are constants, i, $j = 1,\ldots,m$.

Using (16.83), we can rewrite the conditions for equilibrium as $I_j^*(a_j - \alpha_j) = 0$, with $I_j^* = 0$ if $a_j < \alpha_j$, $j = 1,\ldots,m + 1$. Define the functions $\{e_j(t)\}$ so that the equilibrium expected rates of return on the $m + 1$ traded securities can be expressed as

$$\alpha_j(t) = a_j + e_j(t) \qquad j = 1,\ldots,m + 1 \qquad (16.85)$$

$e_j(t)$ is the equilibrium expected excess return that can be earned by investing in traded security j instead of production technology j. It follows that if the rental market for capital is to clear, then the $\{e_j(t)\}$ must satisfy

$$e_j(t)I_j^*(t) = 0 \text{ and } e_j(t) \geq 0 \qquad j = 1,\ldots,m + 1 \qquad (16.86)$$

That is, if $e_j(t) > 0$, then investing in financial security j dominates investing in production technology j, and hence technology j will not be used at time t.

From (16.86), equilibrium quantities of investment in production are determined by the investment opportunity set $\{\alpha_j, r, \sigma_{ij}, i, j = 1,\ldots,m\}$ in the financial markets. We therefore turn to the analysis of portfolio demands for financial assets. By assumption, none of the state variables of the economy enters into the direct utility functions of investors as specified in (16.5). Hence, from the analysis in Chapter 15, the only state variables

---

10 To see this, we can always substitute a portfolio containing the traded security j and the riskless security for traded security j in the analysis where $dV_j'/V_j' = [w_j(\alpha_j - r) + r] \, dt + w_j\sigma_j \, dq_j$ and w_j is selected so that $w_j = b_j/\sigma_j$, $j = 1,\ldots,m$.

to enter investors' indirect utility functions, $\{J^k\}$, are those required to describe stochastic changes in the investment opportunity set. Because $\{a_j, b_j, \rho_{ij}\}$ in (16.77) are constants, the production-possibility set does not depend on the exogenous state variables $\{S(t)\}$. Hence, the only state variables that influence the investment opportunity set are $X(t)$ and $K(t)$. As will be shown, the equilibrium values of $X(t)$ and $K(t)$ have a one-to-one correspondence. It is therefore only necessary to use one of them. Although, in a reduced-form description of the equilibrium, the quantity of the capital stock is more fundamental than the price of the growth-optimum portfolio, $X(t)$ is the more natural state variable for the structural analysis of investors' optimal portfolio demands. That is, in an information structure sense, $X(t)$, as a speculative price, is a more directly observable variable than is $K(t)$.

If investors believe that a single state variable is sufficient to describe the investment opportunity set, then investors' optimal portfolio demands are as in the model of Section 15.7. If $J^k(W^k, X, t)$ denotes investor k's indirect utility function, then from (15.44) the investor's optimal demand for traded asset i can be written as

$$d_i^k = A^k \sum_1^m v_{ij}(\alpha_j - r) + H_X^k X \sum_1^m \sigma_{xj} v_{ij} \qquad i = 1,\ldots,m \quad (16.87)$$

where $A^k \equiv -J_W^k/J_{WW}^k$ and $H_X^k \equiv -J_{XW}^k/J_{WW}^k$. But, from (16.23), $\sigma_{xj} = \alpha_j - r$. Therefore, (16.87) can be rewritten as

$$d_i^k = (A^k + H_X^k X) \sum_1^m v_{ij}(\alpha_j - r)$$

$$= (A^k + H_X^k X) w_i^g \qquad i = 1,\ldots,m \qquad (16.88)$$

where, from (6.1), $w_i^g \equiv \sum_1^m v_{ij}(\alpha_j - r)$ is the fraction of the growth-optimum portfolio invested in risky security i. From (16.88), $d_i^k/d_j^k = w_i^g/w_j^g$ for $i, j = 1,\ldots,m$ and $k = 1,\ldots,N$. Therefore, all investors hold all risky assets in the same relative proportions and these relative proportions are the same as in the growth-optimum portfolio. It follows that two-fund spanning of the efficient portfolio set applies and Theorem 15.1 obtains. Hence, in equilibrium, the relative proportions of risky securities in the market portfolio are the same as in the growth-optimum portfolio. But, the growth-optimum portfolio is instantaneously mean–variance efficient. Therefore, the market portfolio is also instantaneously mean–variance efficient, and from (15.20), the Security Market Line of the CAPM obtains. That is, equilibrium expected returns will satisfy

$$\alpha_j - r = \beta_j(\alpha_M - r) \qquad j = 1,\dots,m \qquad (16.89)$$

where $\beta_j \equiv \sigma_{jM}/\sigma_M^2$ and $\alpha_M - r$ is the expected excess return on the market portfolio.

As in the model of Section 15.7, $H_X^k X \sum_1^m \sigma_{xj} v_{ij}$ in (16.87) represents investor k's "differential" demand for security i induced by the desire to hedge against stochastic changes in the investment opportunity set. As proved in Theorem 15.2, these hedging demands generally lead to three-fund spanning of the efficient portfolio set and to the corresponding equilibrium condition of the Security Market Plane as given in (15.34). The reason that the three funds reduce to two and the Security Market Plane reduces to the Security Market Line in the model here is that changes in the opportunity set are instantaneously perfectly correlated with the returns on the market portfolio.[11]

To derive the equilibrium dynamics of the investment opportunity set, it is convenient to transform the functions A^k and H_X^k, which depend on W^k, X, and t, into functions that depend on X and t only. From (6.10) and (6.14), we have that for state-independent direct utility, the optimal consumption of investor k can be written as $c^k(t) = c^k[X(t), t; W^k(0)]$. If $W^k = W^k[X(t), t]$ denotes investor k's optimally invested wealth at time t, then from Theorem 6.3, W^k satisfies the linear partial differential equation

$$0 = \tfrac{1}{2}\mu^2 X^2 W_{XX}^k + rXW_X^k + W_t^k - rW^k + c^k \qquad (16.90)$$

subject to the boundary conditions $W^k(0, t) = 0$ and $\log(W^k)/\log(X)$ bounded for all X, where subscripts on W^k denote partial derivatives. As noted in Chapter 6, Cox and Huang (1989b, Proposition 2.2) prove that $W_X^k > 0$ if $W^k > 0$. From Theorem 16.2, $W^k = 0$ if and only if $X = 0$, and therefore $W_X^k > 0$, if $X > 0$. From Theorem 6.2, the optimal demand of investor k for traded security i must satisfy

$$d_i^k = [W_X^k(X, t)X]w_i^g \qquad i = 1,\dots,m \qquad (16.91)$$

for $X(t) = X$. From (16.88) and (16.91), it follows by substituting $W^k(X, t)$ for W^k in J^k, that $A^k + H_X^k X = W_X^k(X, t)X$, $k = 1,\dots,N$.

If $W \equiv \sum_1^N W^k$ denotes aggregate wealth, then from $C \equiv \sum_1^N c^k$ and the linearity of (16.90), it follows that W satisfies the partial differential equation

$$0 = \tfrac{1}{2}\mu^2 X^2 W_{XX} + rXW_X + W_t - rW + C \qquad (16.92)$$

---

11   In the context of the Security Market Plane, (15.34), $\rho_{nM} = 1$ and therefore, to rule out arbitrage, $(\alpha_n - r)/\sigma_n = (\alpha_M - r)/\sigma_M$. Noting that $\rho_{iM} = \rho_{in}$, $i = 1,\dots,n$, we have that (15.34) reduces to (16.89).

If $D_i \equiv \Sigma_1^N d_i^k$ denotes aggregate demand by investors for security i, then because $W_X = \Sigma_1^N W_X^k$, we have from (16.91) that

$$D_i = [W_X(X, t)X]w_i^g \qquad i = 1,\ldots,m \qquad (16.93)$$

for $X(t) = X$. From the adding-up condition, $W = \Sigma_1^{m+1}D_i$, we have that aggregate demand by investors for the riskless security can be written as

$$D_{m+1} = W(X, t) - [W_X(X, t)X]w \qquad (16.94)$$

for $X(t) = X$, where $w \equiv \Sigma_1^m\Sigma_1^m v_{ij}(\alpha_j - r)$ is the fraction of the growth-optimum portfolio that is invested in risky traded securities.

The supply function of securities comes from the hedging transactions by firms in connection with their optimal production decisions and from the issuing of equity shares to finance their ownership of the capital stock. From (16.80) and (16.83), we have that, for $j = 1,\ldots,m + 1$, firm j holds a short position of I_j^* in traded security j. The proceeds from these short-sales are invested in the riskless security and thereby firms, in the aggregate, demand $\Sigma_1^{m+1}I_j^*$ of the riskless security. Because firms hedge their production risks, their equity shares are perfect substitutes for the riskless security. Hence, by issuing shares, firms, in the aggregate, supply $\Sigma_1^{m+1}A_j$ of the riskless security. Therefore, for the traded securities market to clear, it follows that in equilibrium

$$D_j = I_j^* \qquad j = 1,\ldots,m \qquad (16.95a)$$

and

$$D_{m+1} = I_{m+1}^* + \sum_1^{m+1} A_j - \sum_1^{m+1} I_j^* \qquad (16.95b)$$

From (16.82), $\Sigma_1^{m+1}A_j = \Sigma_1^{m+1}K_j = K$ because firms own the entire capital stock. For the rental market to clear, $\Sigma_1^{m+1}I_j^* = K$, and therefore $\Sigma_1^{m+1}A_j - \Sigma_1^{m+1}I_j^* = 0$. Hence, we can rewrite (16.95a) and (16.95b) as

$$D_j = I_j^* \qquad j = 1,\ldots,m + 1$$
$$(16.96)$$

Because $\Sigma_1^{m+1}D_j = W(X, t)$ and $\Sigma_1^{m+1}I_j^* = K$, it follows from the summation of (16.96) that in equilibrium

$$W(X, t) = K \qquad (16.97)$$

for $X(t) = X$ and $K(t) = K$. As already noted, $W_X(X, t)X > 0$ for $X > 0$ and $W(0, t) = 0$. Therefore, in equilibrium, $X(t) = 0$ if and only if $K(t) = 0$. Moreover, because $W_X > 0$, W is an invertible function for all $X > 0$. Thus, X and K are in one-to-one correspondence, and the equilibrium price of the growth-optimum portfolio is given by

$$X(t) = W^{-1}[K(t)] \qquad (16.98)$$

Because C is a known function of X and t from (16.53), the determination of $W(X, t)$ from (16.92) requires only that μ^2 and r be specified. Hence, we need only determine α_j, r, σ_{ij}, $i, j = 1,...,m$ to complete the equilibrium description of the economy.

From (16.84), the variances and covariances of security returns are constants determined by the exogenously specified production technologies. Therefore, the only endogenous components of the equilibrium investment opportunity set are r and α_j, $j = 1,...,m$. From (16.93), (16.94), and (16.96), $I_j^* = (W_X X)w_j^g$, $j = 1,...,m$, and $I_{m+1}^* = (W - W_X X w)$. Because $I_j^* \geq 0$, $w_j^g > 0, j = 1,...,m$, and $0 \leq \Sigma_1^m w_j^g = w \leq W/W_X X$. From (16.86), the equilibrium investment opportunity set at time t must satisfy, for $i = 1,...,m$,

$$e_i(t) = \alpha_i(t) - a_i \geq 0$$
$$w_i^g = \Sigma_1^m v_{ij}[e_j(t) + a_j - r(t)] \geq 0 \qquad (16.99)$$
$$e_i(t)w_i^g = 0$$

and

$$e_{m+1}(t) = r(t) - a_{m+1} \geq 0$$

$$w = \sum_1^m \sum_1^m v_{ij}[e_j(t) + a_j - r(t)] \leq W/(W_X X) \qquad (16.100)$$

$$e_{m+1}(t)[W/(W_X X) - w] = 0$$

The α_j and r are derived in a two-step process by first finding a solution to (16.99) for a given r and then applying (16.100) to determine the equilibrium r.

As the first step, consider the quadratic programming problem[12]

---

12 I thank A. Perold of Harvard University for suggesting this method for solving (16.99).

$$\max B(u_1,\ldots,u_m) \tag{16.101}$$

subject to the linear constraints $u_i \geq a_i - r$, $i = 1,\ldots,m$, where $B \equiv -(\Sigma_1^m \Sigma_1^m v_{ij} u_i u_j)/2$ with $\{v_{ij}\}$, $\{a_i\}$ the same constants as in (16.99) and r treated as a parameter. The first-order conditions for an optimum $\{u_k^*\}$ are given by, for $k = 1,\ldots,m$,

$$0 = \gamma_k - \Sigma_1^m v_{kj} u_j^* \tag{16.102a}$$

and

$$u_k^* + r - a_k \geq 0 \quad \gamma_k \geq 0 \tag{16.102b}$$

and

$$\gamma_k(u_k^* + r - a_k) = 0 \tag{16.102c}$$

where $(\gamma_1,\ldots,\gamma_m)$ are the Kuhn–Tucker multipliers representing the shadow costs of the inequality constraints. The matrix $[v_{ij}]$ is nonsingular, symmetric, and positive definite. Under these conditions, it is well known that there exists a unique solution $[u_1^*,\ldots,u_m^*]$ to (16.102).[13] Moreover, the $\{u_k^*\}$ are continuous and piecewise linear functions of the parameter r. Except at a finite number of points, $r = r_i$, $i = 1,\ldots,M$, the $\{u_k^*\}$ are differentiable functions of r. By inspection of (16.102a), γ_k is also a continuous and piecewise linear function of r, $k = 1,\ldots,m$.

Let $B^*(r) \equiv -\Sigma_1^m \Sigma_1^m v_{ij} u_i^* u_j^*/2$ denote the optimized value of the objective function in (16.101). If $r \geq \bar{r} \equiv \max\{a_j\}$, then by inspection of (16.102), $u_j^* = 0$, $\gamma_j = 0$, $j = 1,\ldots,m$ and $B^*(r) = 0$. If $r < \bar{r}$, then from (16.102b), at least one $u_k^* > 0$, and from (16.102a) and (16.102b), at least one $\gamma_k > 0$. Because $[v_{ij}]$ is a positive definite matrix, $B^*(r) < 0$ for all $r < \bar{r}$ and, in particular, $B^*(-\infty) = -\infty$. Further, because the $\{v_{ij}\}$ do not depend on r and the constraints are linear in r, it is straightforward to show that $B^*(r)$ is a strictly concave function of r for all $r < \bar{r}$.

We now show that the solution to equation system (16.102) provides the solution to system (16.99). As a trial solution to (16.99) let $e_j^*(t) \equiv u_j^* + r - a_j$, $j = 1,\ldots,m$. From (16.102b), $e_j^*(t) \geq 0$, $j = 1,\ldots,m$, which satisfies the first requirement of a solution to (16.99). From (16.102a) and (16.102b) we have that $\gamma_k = \Sigma_1^m v_{kj}[e_j^*(t) + a_j - r] \geq 0$, $k = 1,\ldots,m$, which satisfies the second requirement of a solution to

---

13   Although for general $\{v_{ij}\}$ and $\{a_j\}$, no analytical solution to (16.102) can be found, numerical computation of the solution is no more difficult than solving a standard linear programming problem.

(16.99). From (16.102a) and (16.102c) it follows that $\gamma_k e_k^*(t) = e_k^*(t)\Sigma_1^m v_{kj}[e_j^*(t) + a_j - r] = 0$, $k = 1,\ldots,m$, which satisfies the third and final requirement of a solution to (16.99). Hence, for a given r, there exists a unique solution to (16.99) for both the equilibrium expected returns on the risky traded assets and the equilibrium portfolio fractions in the growth-optimum portfolio, and the solution is given by, for $k = 1,\ldots,m$,

$$\alpha_k(r) = u_k^*(r) + r \qquad (16.103a)$$

and

$$w_k^g(r) = \gamma_k(r) \qquad (16.103b)$$

where $\{u_k^*, \gamma_k\}$ are the solutions to (16.102). It follows from (16.103) that both $\alpha_k(r)$ and $w_k^g(r)$ are continuous and piecewise linear functions of r, $k = 1,\ldots,m$. Moreover, except at a finite number of points, $r = r_i$, $i = 1,\ldots,M$, they are differentiable functions of r.

From (16.102), if $r \geq \bar{r}$, then $u_k^*(r) = 0$ and $\gamma_k(r) = 0$, and $\alpha_k(r) = r > a_k$ and $w_k^g(r) = 0$, $k = 1,\ldots,m$. Hence, for $r \geq \bar{r}$, the expected returns on all securities are the same and the growth-optimum portfolio contains only the riskless security. Otherwise, for $r < \bar{r}$, there is at least one k such that $w_k^g(r) > 0$ and $\alpha_k(r) = a_k$, and the growth-optimum portfolio is nondegenerate. Note that (16.103) provides a general equilibrium example of the posited structure in Section 15.7, in which the entire investment opportunity set can be expressed as a function of the riskless interest rate alone.

As defined in (16.22), the expected excess return and variance rate on the growth-optimum portfolio is given by $\mu^2 = \Sigma_1^m \Sigma_1^m v_{kj}(\alpha_k - r)(\alpha_j - r)$. It follows from (16.103a) and (16.101) that, for a given r, $\mu^2 = -2B^*(r)$. Therefore, we have that

$$\begin{aligned} \mu^2(r) &= \infty && \text{for } r = -\infty \\ &> 0 && \text{for } -\infty < r < \bar{r} \qquad (16.104) \\ &= 0 && \text{for } r \geq \bar{r} \end{aligned}$$

Furthermore, μ^2 is a continuous and piecewise quadratic function of r. Because $B^*(r)$ is a strictly concave function of r for $r < \bar{r}$, $\mu^2(r)$ is a strictly convex funtion of r for $r < \bar{r}$. From (16.102c), $\gamma_k > 0$ only if $u_k^* = a_k - r$, and $\gamma_k = 0$, otherwise. Therefore, for $r \neq r_i$, $i = 1,\ldots,M$, we have that

$$\gamma_k \frac{du_k^*}{dr} = -\gamma_k \qquad k = 1,\ldots,m \qquad (16.105)$$

For $r < \bar{r}$, $r \neq r_i$, $i = 1,...,M$, we have from (16.102a) and (16.105) that

$$
\begin{aligned}
\frac{d\mu^2}{dr} &= 2 \sum_1^m \sum_1^m v_{kj} u_j^* \frac{du_k^*}{dr} \\
&= 2 \sum_1^m \gamma_k \frac{du_k^*}{dr} \\
&= -2 \sum_1^m \gamma_k < 0
\end{aligned}
\tag{16.106}
$$

because $\gamma_k \geq 0$ with at least one $\gamma_k > 0$ for $r < \bar{r}$. From (16.106) and the continuity of $\mu^2(r)$, it follows that μ^2 is a strictly decreasing function of r for $-\infty < r < \bar{r}$. Because μ^2 is strictly convex for $r < \bar{r}$, we have from (16.106) that, for $r < \bar{r}$ and $r \neq r_i$, $i = 1,...,M$,

$$
\frac{d^2\mu^2}{dr^2} = -2 \sum_1^m \frac{d\gamma_k}{dr} > 0
\tag{16.107}
$$

Because γ_k is a continuous function of r, $k = 1,...,m$, it follows from (16.107) that $\Sigma_1^m \gamma_k$ is a strictly decreasing function of r for $-\infty < r < \bar{r}$.

To determine the equilibrium interest rate, turn now to the solution of (16.100). $w = \Sigma_1^m w_k^g$ is the fraction of the growth-optimum portfolio allocated to risky securities. From (16.103b), we have that

$$
w(r) = \sum_1^m \gamma_k(r)
\tag{16.108}
$$

It follows from (16.108) that $w(r)$ is a continuous, piecewise linear function of r and that

$$
\begin{aligned}
w(r) &= \infty \quad &\text{for } r = -\infty \\
&> 0 \quad &\text{for } -\infty < r < \bar{r} \\
&= 0 \quad &\text{for } r \geq \bar{r}
\end{aligned}
\tag{16.109}
$$

From (16.106), $d\mu^2/dr = -2w(r)$ and, from (16.107), $w(r)$ is a strictly decreasing function of r for $-\infty < r < \bar{r}$. Thus, in equilibrium, the fraction of the growth-optimum portfolio allocated to the riskless security, $1 - w(r)$, is a strictly increasing function of r for $r < \bar{r}$.

Since $K(t) = 0$ implies that $K(t + \tau) = 0$ for all $\tau \geq 0$ and that all economic activities cease, we assume that $K(t) > 0$ in the analysis to follow. Hence, from (16.98), $W/(W_X X) > 0$ for $X = X(t)$ because $X(t) > 0$. From (16.100), the equilibrium interest rate must satisfy $r(t) \geq a_{m+1}$ for all t. In the case in which $a_{m+1} > a_k$, $k = 1,\ldots,m$, we thus have that $r(t) \geq \bar{r}$, and, from (16.109), $W/(W_X X) > w[r(t)] = 0$ for all X and t. It follows from (16.100) that $e_{m+1}(t) = 0$ for all X and t. Therefore, if $a_{m+1} \geq \bar{r}$, equilibrium investment and security returns satisfy

$$r(t) = a_{m+1}$$

$$\mu^2(a_{m+1}) = 0$$

$$I^*_{m+1}(t) = K(t)$$

$$I^*_j(t) = 0$$

$$\alpha_j(t) = a_{m+1} \qquad j = 1,\ldots,m \qquad (16.110)$$

for all $K(t)$ and t. Hence, for $a_{m+1} \geq \bar{r}$, the economy never makes any risky investments and the investment opportunity set is constant over time.

Having determined the equilibrium in this degenerate case, we assume for the balance of the analysis that $a_{m+1} < \bar{r}$. If, for some t, $r(t) \geq \bar{r}$, then $w[r(t)] = 0$ which implies that $e_{m+1}(t) = 0$ in (16.100). But $e_{m+1}(t) = 0$ implies that $r(t) = a_{m+1} < \bar{r}$, a contradiction. Therefore, we have that

$$a_{m+1} \leq r(t) < \bar{r} \qquad (16.111)$$

for all t. Because $w(r)$ is a strictly decreasing function of r for $r < \bar{r}$, we have from (16.109) and (16.111) that

$$w(a_{m+1}) \geq w[r(t)] > 0 \qquad (16.112)$$

for all t, with $w(a_{m+1}) > w[r(t)]$ for $r(t) > a_{m+1}$.

Consider the case in which the values of X and t are such that $W/(W_X X) \geq w(a_{m+1})$. If $r(t) > a_{m+1}$, then $W/(W_X X) > w[r(t)]$, which implies from (16.100) that $e_{m+1}(t) = 0$. But, $e_{m+1}(t) = 0$ implies that $r(t) = a_{m+1}$, a contradiction. Therefore, the equilibrium interest rate satisfies

$$r(t) = a_{m+1} \quad \text{for } \frac{W[X(t),\, t]}{W_X[X(t),\, t]X(t)} \geq w(a_{m+1}) \qquad (16.113)$$

Note that (16.113) includes (16.110) as a special case.

Consider now the case in which the values of X and t are such that $w(a_{m+1}) > W/(W_X X)$. From (16.100), $w[r(t)] \leq W/(W_X X)$, and therefore $r(t) > a_{m+1}$. But this implies that $e_{m+1}(t) > 0$. Hence, from (16.100), we have that the equilibrium interest rate must satisfy

$$w[r(t)] = \frac{W[X(t), t]}{W_X[X(t), t]X(t)} \tag{16.114}$$

Because $r(t) > a_{m+1}$, we have that $I^*_{m+1}(t) = 0$ and $\Sigma^m_1 I^*_j(t) = K(t)$.

From (16.109), $w(r)$ is a continuous function that takes on all values on the positive real line for $-\infty \leq r < \bar{r}$. Hence, for any $y > 0$, there always exists an r such that $w(r) = y$. Further, because $w(r)$ is strictly decreasing for $r < \bar{r}$, $w(r)$ is invertible and the solution to $0 = w(r) - y$ is unique for any $y > 0$. Therefore, if w^{-1} denotes this inverse function, then from (16.113) and (16.114) we have that, for each possible $X(t)$ and t, the equilibrium interest rate is unique and given by

$$r(t) = \max \left\{ a_{m+1}, \ w^{-1}\left(\frac{W[X(t), t]}{W_X[X(t), t]X(t)} \right) \right\} \tag{16.115}$$

From (16.84), (16.103a), and (16.115), the equilibrium investment opportunity set at time t is unique and given by[14]

$$\alpha_k(t) = u^*_k[r(t)] + r(t) \quad k = 1,\ldots,m$$
$$\sigma_{ij} = b_i b_j \rho_{ij} \qquad\qquad i, j = 1,\ldots,m \tag{16.116}$$

$$\mu^2(t) = \sum_1^m \sum_1^m v_{ij} u^*_i[r(t)] u^*_j[r(t)] \tag{16.117}$$

As derived from (16.88), the market portfolio is a combination of the growth-optimum portfolio and the riskless security. From (16.93) and (16.94), the equilibrium fractional allocation to $X(t)$ in the market portfolio at time t is $W_X[X(t), t]X(t)/W[X(t), t]$. For $X(t) = X$ and $W_X X/W \leq 1/w(a_{m+1})$, it follows from (16.113) that

$$\alpha_M(t) = a_{m+1} + \frac{W_X X}{W} \mu^2(a_{m+1})$$

---

14 For a more general analysis of the relation between changes in equilibrium investment and the investment opportunity set, see Sundaresan (1984), Breeden (1986), and Dumas (1989).

$$\sigma_M^2(t) = \left(\frac{W_X X}{W}\right)^2 \mu^2(a_{m+1}) \tag{16.118}$$

In this region of X and t, the investment opportunity set remains constant and $\alpha_M(r) - r(t)$ and $\sigma_M(t)$ change in direct proportion to the change in $W_X X/W$. The Market Price of Risk, $[\alpha_M(t) - r(t)]/\sigma_M(t) = \mu(a_{m+1})$, is constant.

For $X(t) = X$ and $W_X X/W > 1/w(a_{m+1})$, we have from (16.114) that

$$\alpha_M(t) = r(t) + \frac{\mu^2[r(t)]}{w[r(t)]}$$

$$\sigma_M^2(t) = \frac{\mu^2[r(t)]}{w^2[r(t)]} \tag{16.119}$$

with $r(t) > a_{m+1}$. In this region of X and t, the investment opportunity set changes with changes in X and t, and we can analyze the effect of a change in the interest rate on the risk-return characteristics of the market portfolio.

From (16.102), (16.103), and (16.108), $w(r)$ is a linear function of r for $a_{m+1} \leqslant r_i < r < r_{i+1}, i = 1,..., M$. It is straightforward to show that in this region

$$w(r) = \delta_2 - \delta_1 r$$

$$\mu^2(r) = \delta_3 + \frac{w^2(r)}{\delta_1} \tag{16.120}$$

where $\delta_1 \equiv \Sigma\Sigma \, v_{ij} > 0$; $\delta_2 \equiv \Sigma\Sigma \, v_{ij} a_j$; $\delta_3 \equiv \Sigma\Sigma \, v_{ij} a_i a_j - \delta_2^2/\delta_1 \geqslant 0$; and Σ denotes summation over the set $\{j | w_j^g > 0, \, \alpha_j = a_j \text{ for } r_i < r < r_{i+1}\}$. This set is not empty for $r < \bar{r}$ and its composition is the same for all $r \in (r_i, r_{i+1})$. Further, $\delta_3 = 0$ only if all the a_j in the set are equal. For $r(t) = r$ and $r_i < r < r_{i+1}$, we have from (16.119) and (16.120) that

$$\alpha_M(t) = r + \frac{w(r)}{\delta_1} + \frac{\delta_3}{w(r)}$$

$$\sigma_M^2(t) = \frac{1}{\delta_1} + \frac{\delta_3}{w^2(r)} \tag{16.121}$$

Because $dw(r)/dr = -\delta_1 < 0$, it follows from differentiation of (16.121) that

$$\frac{d\alpha_M}{dr} = \frac{\delta_1 \delta_3}{w^2(r)} \geq 0$$

$$\frac{d\sigma_M^2}{dr} = \frac{2\delta_1 \delta_3}{w^3(r)} \geq 0$$

$$\frac{d[(\alpha_M - r)/\sigma_M]}{dr} = -\frac{w(r)}{\mu(r)} < 0 \qquad (16.122)$$

Hence, the Market Price of Risk is a decreasing function of the interest rate, and unless all the a_j are equal, the expected return and variance of return on the market portfolio increase as the interest rate increases.

To complete the general equilibrium description of the economy, we substitute for r and μ^2 from (16.115) and (16.116) into (16.92). The solution of (16.92) provides $W(X, t)$ and $W(X, t)/[W_X(X, t)X]$, which by substitution into (16.115) and (16.116) determines the equilibrium investment opportunity set as a function of X and t. From (16.98), the equilibrium price of the growth-optimum portfolio at time t is given by $X(t) = W^{-1}[K(t)]$. The equilibrium distribution of investment among the production technologies at time t is specified by

$$I_k^*(t) = W_X[X(t), t]X(t) \sum_1^m v_{kj}[\alpha_j(t) - r(t)] \qquad k = 1,\ldots,m$$

$$I_{m+1}^*(t) = K(t) - \sum_1^m I_k^*(t) \qquad (16.123)$$

Because $X(t) = W^{-1}[K(t)]$, equilibrium aggregate consumption, investment, and the interest rate can all be expressed as functions of $K(t)$ and t. Noting that $I_j^* > 0$ only if $\alpha_j = a_j$, $j = 1,\ldots,m$, we can write the accumulation equation for the equilibrium aggregate capital stock as

$$dK = \left\{ \sum_1^m I_j^*(K, t)[a_j - r(K, t)] + r(K, t)K - C(K, t) \right\} dt$$

$$+ \sum_1^m I_j^*(K, t)b_j \, dq_j \qquad (16.124)$$

for $K(t) = K$. By inspection of (16.123) and (16.124), the equilibrium dynamics for the capital stock follow a Markov process.

Given the functions $r = r(X, t)$ and $\mu^2 = \mu^2(X, t)$, (16.92) is a linear partial differential equation. However, because $r(t)$ and $\mu^2(t)$ in (16.115) and (16.117) depend on W and W_X, their substitution into (16.92) to simultaneously determine W, r, and μ^2 causes (16.92) to become non-linear. Thus, as in Section 16.5, the introduction of production significantly complicates the computational requirements for determining the general equilibrium solution for the economy. The analysis, however, is greatly simplified in the case where the equilibrium investment opportunity set is constant over time.

From (16.113) and (16.114), the means, variances, and covariances of the returns on the traded securities will be constant if, for all X and t, either (a) $W(X, t)/[W_X(X, t)X] \geq w(a_{m+1})$ or (b) $W(X, t)/[W_X(X, t)X] = \beta$, a positive constant. To determine whether (a) applies for a particular aggregate consumption function, simply solve (16.92) with $r = a_{m+1}$ and $\mu^2 = \mu^2(a_{m+1})$, which is linear, and check whether the solution satisfies (a). If (b) applies, then W must have the form

$$W(X, t) = g(t)X^{1/\beta} \tag{16.125}$$

where $\beta > 0$, $g(t) > 0$ and $g(0) = K(0)$ because $X(0) = 1$. It follows from (16.115) and (16.120) that $r(t) = r$ and $\mu^2(t) = \mu^2$ are constants given by

$$r = \max\left(a_{m+1}, \frac{\delta_2 - \beta}{\delta_1}\right)$$

$$\mu^2 = \delta_3 + \frac{w^2(r)}{\delta_1} \tag{16.126}$$

where $w^2(r) = \min[w^2(a_{m+1}), \beta^2]$. By substitution for W and its derivatives from (16.125) into (16.92), we have that, for all X and t,

$$[\dot{g}(t) + \eta g(t)]X^{1/\beta} + C(X, t) = 0 \tag{16.127}$$

where $\eta \equiv -[r\beta^2 + (\mu^2/2 - r)\beta - \mu^2/2]/\beta^2$. Therefore, for (b) to obtain, the aggregate consumption function must have the form

$$C(X, t) = h(t)X^{1/\beta} \tag{16.128}$$

where $h(t) > 0$ and $\dot{g}(t) + \eta g(t) + h(t) = 0$ for all t.

To determine the set of preferences that produces (16.128) as an optimal aggregate consumption function, we substitute from (16.128) into (16.62) to obtain

$$U_C(C, t) = \left[\frac{C}{h(t)}\right]^{-\beta} \tag{16.129}$$

From (16.129), it follows that, up to a positive affine transformation, U must have the form

$$U(C, t) = \frac{[h(t)]^{\beta} C^{\gamma}}{\gamma} \tag{16.130}$$

where $\gamma \equiv 1 - \beta < 1$ because $\beta > 0$. Hence, by inspection of (16.130), if the utility function for the representative investor is an isoelastic member of the Hyperbolic Absolute Risk Aversion (HARA) family of preference functions, then the equilibrium investment opportunity set is constant over time. Moreover, the returns on traded securities, the growth-optimum portfolio, and, from (16.118) and (16.119), the market portfolio are all jointly log-normally distributed. Thus, there exists an intertemporal general equilibrium model of an economy with production that is consistent with the return dynamics posited in the model of Section 15.6.[15]

16.7 CONCLUSION

Under the condition that there exist traded securities with returns that are instantaneously perfectly correlated with the changes in all state variables in the economy, we have shown that the continuous-time model is equivalent to the Arrow–Debreu complete-markets model. From Debreu's classic proof that with complete markets, a competitive equilibrium is a Pareto optimum, it follows that the equilibrium allocations derived for the continuous-time model in this chapter are Pareto optimal. The continuous-time model provides a concrete demonstration of the Arrow and Radner observation that dynamic trading in securities can be a substitute for a full set of markets for pure securities. Furthermore, from (16.7), we have a computational method for determining the prices of the continuum of possible Arrow–Debreu securities in terms of the distributional parameters of a finite number of traded securities.

Although our analysis assumes homogeneous beliefs among agents, it can easily be extended to include heterogeneous beliefs with the same generality as in the standard Arrow–Debreu model. As given in (16.27), let $P^k(S, t; \bar{S}, \tau)$ denote investor k's assessment of the conditional probability that $S(\tau) = \bar{S}$, given $S(t) = S$, $k = 1,...,N$. From (16.30a), investor k's optimal allocations will satisfy

---

15 This special case of the general equilibrium model provides a counter-example to the claim by Rosenberg and Ohlson (1976) that the assumption of joint log-normality for security returns, and the resulting constant proportions of risky assets in the market portfolio, is inconsistent with equilibrium pricing unless the returns on all assets are perfectly correlated.

$$P^k(S, t; \overline{S}, \tau) \, U_c^k[c^*(\overline{S}, t), \overline{S}, \tau] = \lambda_1^k \Pi(S, t; \overline{S}, \tau) - \lambda_2^k(\overline{S}, \tau)$$

$$(16.131)$$

As in the standard model, to rule out the perception of possible arbitrage, beliefs must satisfy $P^k(S, t; \overline{S}, \tau) = 0$ if and only if $P^j(S, t; \overline{S}, \tau) = 0$ for k, $j = 1,...,N$.[16] Let $P(S, t; \overline{S}, \tau)$ be any "consensus" probability function satisfying $P(S, t; \overline{S}, \tau) = 0$ if and only if $P^k(S, t; \overline{S}, \tau) = 0$ for $k = 1,...,N$. Define the "pseudo" preference function for investor k, $\overline{U}^k$, by

$$\overline{U}^k(c, \overline{S}, \tau) \equiv U^k(c, \overline{S}, \tau) \, \frac{P^k(S, t; \overline{S}, \tau)}{P(S, t; \overline{S}, \tau)}$$

Note that for $P^k > 0$, $P^k/P > 0$, and that $\overline{U}^k$ exhibits the same monotonicity and concavity conditions with respect to c that were psited for U^k. It follows that (16.131) can be rewritten as

$$P(S, t; \overline{S}, \tau) \overline{U}_c^k[c^*(\overline{S}, t), \overline{S}, \tau] = \lambda_1^k \Pi(S, t; \overline{S}, \tau) - \lambda_2^k(\overline{S}, \tau)$$

$$(16.132)$$

for $P > 0$, which is the same as (16.30a). Thus, the optimal behavior of investor k with heterogeneous beliefs cannot be distinguished from that of an investor with different preferences and consensus beliefs.[17]

As it provides new insights into economic behavior under uncertainty, the continuous-time analysis also provides a synthesizing structure that reaffirms old ones. As we have seen, those classic models of finance – the Markowitz–Tobin mean–variance model, the Sharpe–Lintner–Mossin CAPM, the Modigliani–Miller theorems as well as the Arrow–Debreu model – are all far more robust than had been believed. There is still much to be done, however. Research is just under way to determine to what extent the analysis in this chapter, including the powerful Cox–Huang technique, can be applied in the incomplete-markets context of Chapter 15, where $|\rho_i^*| < 1$ in (15.50).[18] Because human capital represents such a large part of wealth, it is essential that future research focus on the effects of nontraded assets on individual behavior and on the role of institutions in

---

16   The probability measures supporting P^k and P^j respectively are called "equivalent" measures (cf. Harrison, 1985, p. 9).

17   Of course, with heterogeneous beliefs, the equilibrium allocations are Pareto optimal in the weak sense that beliefs are treated like preferences. That is, superior allocations could be achieved by a pooling of the information that gives rise to the differences in probability beliefs.

18   Breeden (1984), Föllmer and Sonderman (1986), Pagès (1987, 1989), He and Pearson (1991), and He (1989, Ch. 1) provide some promising results. See Duffie (1987, 1988) and Duffie and Shafer (1985, 1986) for general discussion of equilibrium with incomplete markets.

minimizing the efficiency losses from nontradeability.[19] Along the lines of Williams (1977), Detemple (1986), Dothan and Feldman (1986), Gennotte (1986), Detemple and Kihlstrom (1987), and Feldman (1989), more work is needed in making endogenous the learning process and analyzing the effects of information asymmetries among agents. See also the applications of adaptive control in Duncan and Pasik-Duncan (1989a, c). Although the models in Sections 16.5 and 16.6 included production, they are far from satisfactory because they do not allow sufficient path dependence to reflect the more realistic conditions of long lead-times for implementing investments as well as their irreversibility.

19 See Williams (1979), Grossman and Shiller (1982), Adler and Detemple (1988), Brown (1988), Svensson (1988), Bodie and Samuelson (1989), Samuelson (1989), He and Pagès (1990), Svensson and Werner (1990), and Bodie, Merton, and Samuelson (1992) for some results on the effects of nontradeable assets in the continuous-time model. See also Section 21.4.

Part VI

Applications of the Continuous-Time Model to Selected Issues in Public Finance:

Long-Run Economic Growth,
Public Pension Plans, Deposit Insurance,
and Loan Guarantees

17

An Asymptotic Theory of Growth Under Uncertainty

17.1 INTRODUCTION

The neoclassical theory of capital accumulation and growth under certainty for both positive and optimal savings functions has received extensive study in the literature for almost two decades. However, the study of capital accumulation under uncertainty began much later and these analyses for the most part confine themselves to linear technologies. In his pioneering work, Phelps (1962), and later Levhari and Srinivasan (1969), Hahn (1970), Stigum (1972), and Leland (1974), examine the optimal consumption–saving decision under uncertainty with a given linear production technology. Hakansson (1970), Leland (1968) and Samuelson (1969) in discrete time and Merton (1969a, 1971; this volume, Chs 4 and 5) in continuous time, along with a host of other authors, have studied the combined consumption–saving-portfolio problem where the production functions are linear but where there is a choice among alternative technologies.

There have been a few notable exceptions to this concentration on linear technologies. In a seminal paper, Mirrlees (1965) tackled the stochastic Ramsey problem in a continuous-time neoclassical one-sector model subject to uncertainty about technical progress. Later (Mirrlees, 1971, 1974), he expanded his analysis to other types of technologies. Mirman (1973) for positive savings functions and Brock and Mirman (1972) for optimal savings functions, using a discrete-time neoclassical one-sector model, proved the existence, uniqueness, and stability of a steady-state (or asymptotic) distribution for the capital-to-labor ratio. These steady-state

Reproduced from *Review of Economic Studies*, 42, July 1975, 375–93. The contents of this paper were presented in various forms at the NBER Conference on Growth Theory (Yale, December 1971); Mathematical Economics Seminar (Rochester, March 1973); Mathematical Economics Seminar (Columbia, April 1973). My appreciation to the participants for their helpful comments. My special thanks to R. M. Solow for many discussions. Aid from the National Science Foundation is gratefully acknowledged. F. Bourguignon (1974) has independently derived a number of the results in this paper.

distributions are the natural generalizations under uncertainty to the golden-age/golden-rule levels of the capital-to-labor ratio as deduced in the certainty case. While these papers are important contributions with respect to existence and uniqueness, they have little to say about the specific structure of these asymptotic distributions or about the biases (in an expected-value sense) induced by assuming a certainty model when, in fact, outcomes are uncertain.

The basic model used in this chapter is a one-sector neoclassical growth model of the Solow type where the dynamics of the capital-to-labor ratio can be described by a diffusion-type stochastic process. The particular source of uncertainty chosen is the population size although the analysis would be equally applicable to technological or other sources of uncertainties. The first part of the chapter analyzes the stochastic processes and asymptotic distributions for various economic variables, for an exogenously given savings function, and deduces a number of first-moment relations which will obtain in the steady state. In addition, the special case of a Cobb–Douglas production function with a constant savings function is examined in detail and the steady-state distributions for the capital-to-labor ratio, interest rate, etc. are derived. The second part of the chapter investigates the stochastic Ramsey problem and a correspondence between this problem and an auxiliary problem involving the steady-state distribution only is derived which generalizes the notion of minimizing divergence from bliss to the stochastic case.

17.2 THE MODEL

We assume a one-sector neoclassical model with a constant-returns-to-scale, strictly concave production function $F(K, L)$, where $K(t)$ denotes the capital stock and $L(t)$ denotes the labor force which is assumed to be proportional to the population size. The capital accumulation equation can be written as

$$\dot{K}(t) = F[K(t), L(t)] - \lambda K(t) - C(t) \tag{17.1}$$

where λ is the rate of depreciation (assumed to be nonnegative and constant) and $C(t)$ is aggregate consumption.

The source of uncertainty in the model is the population size $L(t)$. A reasonable stochastic process for the population dynamics can be deduced from a simple branching process for population growth.[1] Let h denote the length of time between "generations" and $X_i(t + h)$ denote the random

---

1 See Cox and Miller (1968, p. 235) and Feller (1966, p. 325). However, as will be shown, we use a modified version of the processes presented there.

variable number of offspring (net of deaths) for the ith person alive at time t. It is assumed that the expected number of offspring (net of deaths) per person per unit time, n, is a constant and the same for all individuals in every generation. It is also assumed that the random variable deviation from the mean can be written as the sum of two independent components: (a) a "systematic" component, $\sigma\eta(t; h)$, reflecting random effects common to all individuals at a given point in time t such as changes in social mores and tastes with respect to child-bearing, natural disaster, widespread disease, discovery of a "wonder" drug, national economic conditions, etc.[2] (this component is assumed to be independently and identically distributed over time);[3] and (b) a "nonsystematic" component, $v_i\epsilon_i(t; h)$, reflecting random effects specific to the ith person alive at time t.[4]

This assumed process can be formally described by a conditional stochastic equation for $X_i(t + h)$, conditional on $L(t) = L$:

$$X_i(t + h) = nh + \sigma\eta(t; h) + v_i\epsilon_i(t; h) \quad i = 1,2,...,L \quad (17.2)$$

where n, σ, and v_i are constants; $E_t\{\eta\}=E_t\{\epsilon_i\} = 0$; $E_t\{\eta^2\} = E_t\{\epsilon_i^2\} = h$; $E_t\{\eta\epsilon_i\} = 0 = E_t\{\epsilon_i\epsilon_j\}$, $i \neq j$; $E_t\{\eta(t; h)\eta(t + kh; h)\} = 0$, $k = 1,2,...$, and E_t is the conditional expectation operator, conditional on knowledge of all (relevant) events which have occurred as of time t.

To obtain a stochastic difference equation for the population size, note that

$$L(t + h) - L(t) = \Sigma X_i(t + h)$$

and hence, by summing equation (17.2) from $i = 1$ to L, we have that

---

2   One might reasonably question the assumption that the distribution for η be exogenous and independent of L since per capita wealth K/L may affect both birth and death rates, and for finite amounts of land, L may also be influenced through "crowding." However, since endogenously determined population growth is not central to the discussion and its inclusion would follow the same lines of analysis, we exclude it for brevity and simplicity. For a discussion of endogenous population growth in the certainty case, see Merton (1969b).

3   In an extension to the discussion in footnote 2, one might question the assumption of serial independence for η. The analysis could be modified to allow for serial dependence by introducing Ornstein–Uhlenbeck type processes (Cox and Miller, 1968, p. 225). However, the cost of introducing these processes would be a more complex multidimensional dynamic structure, and it is not clear that the asymptotic distributions would be greatly affected by such serial dependencies.

4   The terms "individual," "family," and "group" are used interchangeably in much the same way as "population size" and "labor force" are in the standard analysis. Provided that the number of families is roughly proportional to the number of people and the number of people per family is not large, none of the analysis is materially affected by this interchange of interpretation.

$$L(t + h) - L(t) = nLh + \sigma L\eta(t; h) + \Sigma v_i \epsilon_i(t; h) \qquad (17.3)$$

conditional on $L(t) = L$. From (17.3), the conditional expected change in population can be written as

$$E_t\{L(t + h) - L(t)|L(t) = L\} = nLh \qquad (17.4)$$

and the conditional variance as

$$\text{var}[L(t + h) - L(t)|L(t) = L] = \left[\sigma^2 L^2 + \left(\frac{1}{L} \Sigma v_i^2 \right) L \right] h$$
$$(17.5)$$

If the v_i are bounded and approximately the same size, then $\Sigma v_i^2/L = O(1)$ (e.g. if $v_i = v$, then $\Sigma v_i^2/L = v^2$). Hence, for large populations ($L \gg 1$) and $\sigma^2 > 0$, one can reasonably neglect the contribution of the "nonsystematic" components to total population variance, and simplify the analysis by approximating (17.5) with

$$\text{var}[L(t + h) - L(t)|L(t) = L] \approx \sigma^2 L^2 h \qquad (17.6)$$

Because the major goal of the chapter is to develop additional properties of the steady-state distribution beyond those of existence and uniqueness, we choose to work in continuous time and restructure the discrete-time stochastic process for population size as a diffusion process.[5] The "surrogate" random variable for population size generated by the diffusion process approximation to (17.3) has a continuous density function on the nonnegative real line, and its sample path over time will be continuous with probability one. Hence, for it to be a reasonable description of the population dynamics, the population size must be large enough to ignore the inherent discreteness of the birth–death process and large enough to justify the continuity assumption for changes over time. In addition, the approximation becomes more accurate for large values of the time variable t when compared with the interval between successive transitions, h. This is particularly important because we are primarily interested in the steady-state distribution where $t = \infty$.

The procedure of approximating discrete-time processes by diffusion processes is useful because the mathematical methods associated with a

5   This combination provided enormous simplifications in the study of the consumption-portfolio problem. For examples, see Merton (1969a, 1971, 1973b; this volume, Chs 4, 5, and 15). For further discussion of the diffusion approximation to the branching process, see Cox and Miller (1968, p. 237) or Feller (1966, p. 326). Note that they analyze the case where birth rates across individuals are independent (i.e. $\sigma^2 = 0$), and hence the variance of their process is proportional to L instead of L^2 as in our case.

continuum generally lend themselves more easily to analytical treatment than those associated with discrete processes. In addition, a large body of theory has been developed for the analysis of diffusion processes.

Apart from boundary conditions, the transition probabilities for a diffusion process are completely determined by a functional description of its instantaneous (infinitesimal) conditional mean and variance,[6] and hence (17.4) and (17.6) are sufficient specifications to determine the appropriate "surrogate" diffusion process.

Although the diffusion sample path is continuous, it is not differentiable. Therefore, differential equations with standard time derivatives cannot be used to describe the dynamics. However, there is a generalized theory of stochastic differential equations developed by Itô and McKean[7] which is applicable to diffusion processes. In particular, the surrogate population dynamics corresponding to the discrete model described in (17.3) can be written as

$$dL = nL \, dt + \sigma L \, dz \qquad (17.7)$$

where dz stands for a Wiener process and nL and $\sigma^2 L^2$ are the instantaneous mean and variance per unit time, respectively. Using Itô's lemma,[8] (17.7) can be integrated, and by inspection the random variable $L(t)/L(0)$ will have a log-normal distribution with

$$E_0\{\log[L(t)/L(0)]\} = (n - \tfrac{1}{2}\sigma^2)t$$

$$\equiv \mu t \qquad (17.8a)$$

and

$$\text{var}\{\log[L(t)/L(0)]\} = \sigma^2 t \qquad (17.8b)$$

Having established a valid continuous-time formulation for the population dynamics, we now determine the dynamics for capital accumulation. As in the certainty model, the dynamics can be reduced to a one-dimensional process by working in intensive (per capita) variables. Define

$k(t) \equiv K(t)/L(t)$, capital-to-labor ratio
$c(t) \equiv C(t)/L(t)$, per capita consumption
$f(k) \equiv F(K, L)/L = F(K/L, 1)$, per capita (gross) output
$s(k) \equiv 1 - c/f(k)$, (gross) savings per unit output

---

6 See Feller (1966, p. 321).
7 See Itô and McKean (1964) and McKean (1969).
8 See Appendix 17A. For the particular integration of (17.7), see McKean (1969, p. 33).

Because smooth functional transformations of diffusion processes are diffusion processes, the dynamics for k will be a diffusion process whose stochastic differential equation representation can be written as[9]

$$dk = b(k) \ dt - [a(k)]^{1/2} \ dz \qquad (17.9)$$

where $b(k) \equiv s(k)f(k) - (n + \lambda - \sigma^2)k$ is the instantaneous expected change in k per unit time and $a(k) \equiv \sigma^2 k^2$ is the instantaneous variance. Hence, the accumulation equation in per capita units follows a diffusion process and the transition probabilities for $k(t)$ are completely determined by the functions $b(k)$ and $a(k)$.

Before going on to analyze the distributional characteristics of k, it is important to distinguish between the stochastic process for k and the one for K. While the sample path for k is not differentiable, the sample path for K is. Since at a point in time, t, both $K(t)$ and $L(t)$ are known, output at that time, $F(K, L)$, is known, and from (17.1), K has a well-defined time derivative which is locally certain. Hence, competitive factor shares are well defined and the same as in the certainty model; namely, the interest rate r and the wage rate w satisfy

$$r = f'(k) \qquad (17.10a)$$

and

$$w = f(k) - kf'(k) \qquad (17.10b)$$

Thus, unlike in the portfolio models, there is no "current" uncertainty, but only "future" uncertainty, and the returns to capital (and labor) over the next "period" (instant) are known with certainty. The returns to capital would be viewed by an investor as more like those obtained by continually reinvesting in (very) short-term bonds (i.e. "rolling-over shorts") when the future interest rates are stochastic than those obtained by investing in common stocks with end-of-period price uncertainty.[10]

17.3   THE STEADY-STATE DISTRIBUTION FOR k

Just as in the certainty model the existence and quantitative properties of the steady-state economy can be examined, so can they be for the

---

9   For a derivation of (17.9) using Itô's lemma, see Appendix 17A.
10   See Merton (1973b; this volume, Ch. 15) for a discussion of the distinction between the two types of uncertainty with respect to interest rates and common stocks.

uncertainty model. However, instead of there being a unique point k^* in the steady state, there is a unique distribution for k which is time and initial-condition independent and toward which the stochastic process for k tends. As such it is the natural generalization of the certainty case which is included as a limiting case when dispersion tends to zero.

Since existence and uniqueness properties are not the major goals of this chapter, we assume throughout that the following set of sufficient conditions for existence are satisfied: (a) $f(k)$ is concave and satisfies the Inada conditions; (b) $s(k) > 0$ for all $k < \bar{k}$, for some positive $\bar{k}$; and (c) $n + \lambda - \sigma^2 > 0$.[11]

As discussed in the previous section, the stochastic process for k is completely determined by the functions $b(k)$ and $a(k)$ which in turn depend upon the particular production function and saving rule. However, it is possible to deduce a general functional representation for the steady-state probability distribution. Let $\pi_k(\cdot)$ be the steady-state density function for the capital-to-labor ratio. As is deduced in Appendix 17B, $\pi_k(\cdot)$ will satisfy

$$\pi_k(k) = \frac{m}{a(k)} \exp\left[\int^k \frac{2b(x)}{a(x)} \, dx \right] \tag{17.11}$$

where m is a constant chosen so that $\int_0^\infty \pi_k(x) \, dx = 1$. Substituting for $b(k)$ and $a(k)$ from (17.9), we can rewrite (17.11) as

$$\pi_k(k) = mk^{-2(n + \lambda)/\sigma^2} \exp\left[\frac{2}{\sigma^2} \int^k \frac{s(x)f(x)}{x^2} \, dx \right] \tag{17.12}$$

While (17.12) does show that the determination of the steady-state distribution reduces to one of "mere" quadrature, little more can be said about $\pi_k(\cdot)$ directly without further specifying the function $s(\cdot)f(\cdot)$. However, without further specification of this function, one can deduce certain moment relations which must obtain in the steady state.

If $g(k)$ is a "well-behaved" function[12] of k and E is the expectation

---

11   The sufficiency of these conditions for existence is shown in Appendix 17B. Actually, a weaker condition than (17.3) would be $n - \frac{1}{2}\sigma^2 + \lambda = \mu + \lambda > 0$. However, in that case, certain first-moment relations in the steady state would not exist including $E\{k\}$ which would diverge. Since (17.3) is not much stronger than $\mu + \lambda > 0$, we prefer it. Also, if $n > \sigma^2$, then $\mu > 0$ which implies that, with probability one, $L(t) \to \infty$ as $t \to \infty$. Hence, the $L \gg 1$ assumption of the approximation in (17.6) and the conditions under which the diffusion approximation is accurate will be satisfied for any positive initial population and sufficiently large t.
12   Sufficiently "well behaved" would be that g is a C^2 function on the interval $(0, \infty)$ and that $\lim_{k \to 0} g'k^2\pi = \lim_{k \to \infty} g'k^2\pi = 0$.

operator over the steady-state distribution for k, then

$$E\left\{g'(k)[s(k)f(k) - (n + \lambda - \sigma^2)k] + \frac{\sigma^2}{2} g''(k)k^2\right\} = 0 \quad (17.13)$$

The proof for (17.13) can be found in Appendix 17C.

Armed with (17.13), one can deduce a number of steady-state moment equalities among a variety of interesting economic relations by simply choosing the appropriate function for $g(\cdot)$. For example, for $g(k) = k$, we have that

$$E\{s(k)f(k)\} = (n + \lambda - \sigma^2)E\{k\} \quad (17.14)$$

and if $s(k) = s$, a positive constant, then

$$E\{f(k)\} = \frac{n + \lambda - \sigma^2}{s} E\{k\} \quad (17.14a)$$

For $g(k) = \log(k)$, we have that

$$E\left\{\frac{s(k)f(k)}{k}\right\} = n + \lambda - \tfrac{1}{2}\sigma^2$$

$$= \mu + \lambda \quad (17.15)$$

and, if $s(k) = s$, then

$$E\left\{\frac{f(k)}{k}\right\} = \frac{\mu + \lambda}{s} \quad (17.15a)$$

The reader can try other forms for $g(\cdot)$ and deduce still more relations.

17.4 THE COBB–DOUGLAS/ CONSTANT-SAVINGS-FUNCTION ECONOMY

There is a specific functional form for $s(\cdot)f(\cdot)$ of no little interest where the steady-state distributions for all economic variables can be solved for in closed form. If it is assumed that the production function is Cobb–Douglas, $f(k) = k^\alpha$, $0 < \alpha < 1$, and that gross savings is a constant fraction of output[13] (s is a constant, $0 < s \leqslant 1$), then by substituting the particular functional form in (17.12) and integrating, we have that π_k will satisfy

$$\pi_k(k) = mk^{-2(n + \lambda)/\sigma^2} \exp\left[-\frac{2s}{(1 - \alpha)\sigma^2} k^{-(1 - \alpha)} \right] \qquad (17.16)$$

While the constant, m, could be determined by direct integration, it will throw light on the whole analysis to compute it in an indirect way. If $R = k^{\alpha-1}$, the output-to-capital ratio, and $\pi_R(R)$ is its steady-state density function, then, from (17.16),

$$\pi_R(R) = \pi_k(k) \Big/ \left| \frac{dR}{dk} \right|$$

$$= \frac{m}{1 - \alpha} R^{\gamma-1} \exp(-bR) \qquad (17.17)$$

where $\gamma \equiv 2(\mu + \lambda)/(1 - \alpha)\sigma^2 > 0$ and $b \equiv 2s/(1 - \alpha)\sigma^2 > 0$. By inspection, R has a gamma distribution,[14] and therefore, m must satisfy

$$m = \frac{(1 - \alpha)b^\gamma}{\Gamma(\gamma)} \qquad (17.18)$$

where $\Gamma(\cdot)$ is the gamma function. Because R has a gamma distribution, we have that the moment-generating function for R is

$$\phi(\theta) \equiv E\{\exp(\theta R)\}$$

$$= \left(1 - \frac{\theta}{b}\right)^{-\gamma} \qquad (17.19)$$

and for nonintegral or negative moments we have that

$$\Phi(\theta) \equiv E\{R^\theta\}$$

$$= \frac{\Gamma(\theta + \gamma)}{\Gamma(\gamma)} b^{-\theta} \qquad (17.20)$$

13 Therefore, $c = (1 - s)f(k)$. The analysis of this section would be identical for a Modigliani–Pigou type consumption function where $c = (1 - s)f(k) + \delta k$ with δ a positive constant. The formulas would be the same with $\lambda + \delta$ substituted wherever λ appears.
14 For a description of the gamma distribution, see Feller (1966, p. 46).

for $\theta > -\gamma$. The density functions and moments of the distributions for all the economic variables can be deduced from (17.17)–(17.20), and the more important ones are summarized in Table 17.1.

Since most of the literature on growth models has neglected uncertainty, it is useful to know whether the steady-state solutions obtained in these analyses are unbiased estimates of the first-moments of the corresponding steady-state distributions. Unfortunately, the certainty estimates are biased as is illustrated in Table 17.2 using the closed-form solutions of this section. In particular, the certainty estimates for expected per capita consumption, output, and capital are too small while the estimates for the output-to-capital ratio and the interest rate are too large. These results suggest that care must be taken in using the certainty analysis even as a first-moment approximation theory.[15]

Table 17.1 Steady-State Probability Distributions

$$b \equiv \frac{2s}{(1 - \alpha)\sigma^2}$$

$$\gamma \equiv \frac{2(n + \lambda - \frac{1}{2}\sigma^2)}{(1 - \alpha)\sigma^2} = \frac{2(\mu + \lambda)}{(1 - \alpha)\sigma^2}$$

$$\eta \equiv \frac{1 - \alpha}{\alpha}$$

Capital-to-labor ratio ($k \equiv K/L$)
  Density function

$$\pi_k(k) = 0 \qquad\qquad\qquad\qquad\qquad\qquad k \leq 0$$

$$= \frac{(1 - \alpha)b^\gamma}{\Gamma(\gamma)} \, k^{-2(n+\lambda)/\sigma^2} \exp(-bk^{\alpha-1}) \quad k > 0$$

  Moment-generating function

$$\Phi_k(\theta) = E\{k^\theta\} = \frac{\Gamma[\gamma - \theta/(1 - \alpha)]}{\Gamma(\gamma)} b^{\theta/(1-\alpha)} \qquad \theta < (1 - \alpha)\gamma$$

15 It should be pointed out that, although the first moment of the steady-state distribution does not equal the certainty estimate, the mode of the steady-state distribution for k is the same as the certainty steady-state value for k. By differentiating $\pi_k(k)$ in (17.12) and setting it equal to zero, we have that $s(M)f(M) = (n + \lambda)M$ where M is the mode of the steady-state distribution for k, independent of σ^2. Hence, k and all other variables in Tables 17.1 and 17.2 converge in distribution to a spike at the certainty value. I am indebted to an editor for pointing this out.

Per capita output ($y \equiv f(k) = k^\alpha$)
  Density function

$$\pi_y(y) = 0 \qquad\qquad\qquad y \le 0$$

$$= \frac{\eta b^\gamma}{\Gamma(\gamma)} y^{-(\eta\gamma+1)} \exp(-by^{-\eta}) \quad y > 0$$

Moment-generating function

$$\Phi_y(\theta) = E\{y^\theta\} = \frac{\Gamma(\gamma - \theta/\eta)}{\Gamma(\gamma)} b^{\theta/\eta} \quad \theta < \eta\gamma$$

Output-to-capital ratio ($R = f(k)/k = k^{\alpha-1}$)
  Density function

$$\pi_R(R) = 0 \qquad\qquad\qquad R \le 0$$

$$= \frac{b^\gamma}{\Gamma(\gamma)} R^{\gamma-1} \exp(-bR) \quad R > 0$$

Moment-generating function

$$\Phi_R(\theta) = E\{R^\theta\} = \frac{\Gamma(\gamma + \theta)}{\Gamma(\gamma)} b^{-\theta}$$

$$\phi_R(\theta) = E\{\exp(\theta R)\} = \left(1 - \frac{\theta}{b}\right)^{-\gamma}$$

Interest rate ($r = f'(k) = \alpha k^{\alpha-1}$)
  Density function

$$\pi_r(r) = 0 \qquad\qquad\qquad r \le 0$$

$$= \frac{(b/\alpha)^\gamma}{\Gamma(\gamma)} r^{\gamma-1} \exp\left(-\frac{br}{\alpha}\right) \quad r > 0$$

Moment-generating function

$$\Phi_r(\theta) = E\{r^\theta\} = \frac{\Gamma(\gamma + \theta)}{\Gamma(\gamma)} \left(\frac{b}{\alpha}\right)^{-\theta}$$

$$\phi_r(\theta) = E\{\exp(r\theta)\} = \left(1 - \frac{\alpha\theta}{b}\right)^{-\gamma}$$

Table 17.2 A Comparison of Steady-State Expected Values with Steady-State Certainty Estimates

Variable	Expected Value	Certainty Estimate
Capital-to-labor ratio	$$E\{k\} = \frac{\Gamma\left[\dfrac{2(n+\lambda-\sigma^2)}{(1-\alpha)\sigma^2}\right]}{\Gamma\left[\dfrac{2(n+\lambda-\frac{1}{2}\sigma^2)}{(1-\alpha)\sigma^2}\right]}\left[\dfrac{2s}{(1-\alpha)\sigma^2}\right]^{1/(1-\alpha)}$$	$$> \left(\frac{s}{n+\lambda}\right)^{1/(1-\alpha)}$$
Per capita output	$$E\{f(k)\} = \frac{n+\lambda-\sigma^2}{s}E\{k\}$$	$$> \left(\frac{s}{n+\lambda}\right)^{\alpha/(1-\alpha)}$$
Per capita consumption	$$E\{c\} = \frac{(1-s)(n+\lambda-\sigma^2)}{s}E\{k\}$$	$$> (1-s)\left(\frac{s}{n+\lambda}\right)^{\alpha/(1-\alpha)}$$
Capital-to-output ratio	$$E\{k/f(k)\} = \frac{s}{n+\lambda-\frac{1}{2}(2-\alpha)\sigma^2}$$	$$> \frac{s}{n+\lambda}$$
Output-to-capital ratio	$$E\{f(k)/k\} = \frac{n+\lambda-\frac{1}{2}\sigma^2}{s}$$	$$< \frac{n+\lambda}{s}$$
Interest rate	$$E\{f'(k)\} = \frac{\alpha(n+\lambda-\frac{1}{2}\sigma^2)}{s}$$	$$< \frac{\alpha(n+\lambda)}{s}$$

In this and previous sections it has been shown that by working in continuous time and modeling the stochastic dynamics with diffusion processes, a number of important properties of the steady-state distributions in addition to existence and uniqueness can be determined. In the special case of this section, a complete analytical description was possible. Even in those cases where closed-form solutions are not deducible, powerful numerical integration techniques are available for solution of the parabolic partial differential equations satisfied by the transition probabilities and moment-generating functions. Hence, both simulation and estimation of the model are feasible. While the analysis presented assumed uncertain population size, the approach extends itself in a straightforward fashion to a variety of other specifications. For example, Mirrlees (1965) has labor-augmenting technical progress as the source of uncertainty in his model where the (future) level of technical progress is log-normally distributed. The analysis presented here would be identical for his model where the intensive variables are in *efficiency* rather than per capita units.

There are partial differential equations for multidimensional diffusion processes corresponding to the ones for the one-dimensional process examined here. Hence, multisector models with more than one source of uncertainty can be studied with the same mode of analysis used here.

In addition, these analyses often provide "throw-offs" useful in other areas of research. For example, in developing a theory for the term structure of interest rates, it is usually necessary to postulate some process for the basic short-rate over time.[16] Using the model of this section, we can derive an analytical description for the interest rate process.[17] Since $r \ (\equiv \alpha k^{\alpha - 1})$ is a smooth monotone function of k, the interest rate dynamics will be generated by a diffusion process. From (17.9) and Itô's lemma, we can deduce the form for the stochastic differential equation for r to be

$$dr = (Ar - Br^2)\,dt + vr\,dz \qquad (17.21)$$

where

$$A \equiv (1 - \alpha)\left(n + \lambda - \frac{\alpha}{2}\sigma^2\right) > 0$$

$$B \equiv (1 - \alpha)\frac{s}{\alpha} \qquad (17.22)$$

$$v^2 \equiv (1 - \alpha)^2 \sigma^2$$

---

16 Cf. Merton (1970b; this volume, Section 11.7).

*17 For further developments along these lines, see Sundaresan (1984, pp. 81–7).

Using Itô's lemma again, we can stochastically integrate (17.21) to obtain an expression for the random variable $r(t)$, conditional on $r(0) = r_0$, in terms of random variables with known distributions: namely,

$$r(t) = \frac{r_0 \exp[(A - \tfrac{1}{2}v^2)t + vZ(t)]}{1 + r_0 B \int_0^t \exp[(A - \tfrac{1}{2}v^2)s + vZ(s)] \, ds} \tag{17.23}$$

where $Z(t) \equiv \int_0^t dz$ is a Gaussian-distributed random variable with a zero mean and $E\{Z(s)Z(s')\} = \min(s, s')$. By inspection of (17.23), $1/r(t)$ is equal to a weighted integral of log-normally-distributed random variables. Since it has already been shown that $r(t)$ has a gamma distribution as $t \to \infty$, we have as a curious side-result that the distribution of an infinite integral of log-normal variates is inverse gamma.

17.5   THE STOCHASTIC RAMSEY PROBLEM

In the previous sections, an expression for the steady-state distribution of the capital-to-labor ratio was determined for an arbitrary savings function. We now turn to the problem of determining the optimal savings policy under uncertainty.[18] Formally, the finite-horizon problem is to find a savings policy, $s^*(k, T - t)$, so as to

$$\max E_0 \left\{ \int_0^T U[(1 - s)f(k)] \, dt \right\} \tag{17.24}$$

subject to $k(T) \geq 0$ with probability one and where $U(\cdot)$ is a strictly concave von Neumann–Morgenstern utility function of per capita consumption for the representative person or central planner. The technique used to solve the problem is stochastic dynamic programming. Let

$$J[k(t), t; T] \equiv \max E_t \left\{ \int_t^T U[(1 - s)f(k)] \, d\tau \right\} \tag{17.25}$$

$J(\cdot)$ is called the Bellman function and, by the principle of optimality,[19] J

---

*18   For later work, see Foldes (1978) and Malliaris and Brock (1982).
19   Sufficient differentiability of the Bellman function J is assumed in the dynamic programming formulation. However, provided that an optimal solution with bounded controls exists, the strict concavity of U and the smoothness of the dynamics for k are sufficient to ensure differentiability for $k > 0$. For a rigorous development of the optimality equation (17.26), see Kushner (1967), and for a less formal discussion, see Merton (1969a, 1971; this volume, Chs 4 and 5).

must satisfy

$$0 = \max_{\{s\}} \left\{ U[(1 - s)f] + \frac{\partial J}{\partial t} + \frac{\partial J}{\partial k}(sf - \beta k) + \frac{1}{2}\frac{\partial^2 J}{\partial k^2}\sigma^2 k^2 \right\} \quad (17.26)$$

where the stochastic process for k satisfies (17.9) and $\beta \equiv n + \lambda - \sigma^2 > 0$. The first-order condition to be satisfied by the optimal policy s^* is

$$U'[(1 - s^*)f] = \frac{\partial J}{\partial k} \quad (17.27)$$

where $U'(c) \equiv dU/dc$. To solve for s^* (in principle), one solves (17.27) for s^* as a function of k, $T - t$ and $\partial J/\partial k$, and substitutes into (17.26) which becomes a partial differential equation for J. Having solved this equation, one substitutes back into (17.27) to determine s^* as a function of k and $T - t$.[20]

Because of the nonlinearity of the Bellman partial differential equation, closed-form solutions are rare. However, in the limiting infinite-horizon ($T \rightarrow \infty$) case of Ramsey (1928), the analysis is substantially simplified because this partial differential equation reduces to an ordinary differential equation. Since the stochastic process for k is time-homogeneous and $U(\cdot)$ is not a function of t, we have from (17.25) that

$$\frac{\partial J}{\partial t} = -E_t\{U([1 - s^*(k, T - t)]f[k(T - t)])\} \quad (17.28)$$

If an optimal policy exists,[21] $f(\cdot)$ satisfies the Inada conditions, and $\beta > 0$, then

$$\lim_{T \rightarrow \infty} s^*(k, T - t) = s^*(k, \infty) = s^*(k)$$

and from the analysis in the previous sections, there will exist a steady-state distribution for k, π_k^*, associated with the optimal policy $s^*(k)$. Taking the limit in (17.28) we have that

$$\lim_{T \rightarrow \infty} \frac{\partial J}{\partial t} = -E^*\{U[(1 - s^*)f(k)]\} \equiv -B \quad (17.29)$$

20   This is the standard procedure for solving continuous-time, dynamic programming problems. See Merton (1969a, 1971; this volume, Chs 4 and 5) for explicit examples of solution.
21   There is an extensive literature on the existence of an optimal policy for the Ramsey problem under certainty. For a discussion of existence under uncertainty, see Mirrlees (1965, 1971).

where E^* is the expectation operator over the steady-state distribution π_k^* and B is the level of expected utility of per capita consumption in the Ramsey-optimal steady state which is independent of the initial condition $k(t)$.

From the Bellman equation, (17.26), and (17.29), we have that, as $T \to \infty$, J must satisfy the ordinary differential equation

$$0 = U[(1 - s^*)f] - B + J'(s^*f - \beta k) + \tfrac{1}{2}J''\sigma^2 k^2 \qquad (17.30)$$

where primes denote derivatives with respect to k.[22] By differentiating the first-order condition (17.27) with respect to k, we have that

$$J'' = U''[(1 - s^*)f(k)]\left[(1 - s^*)f'(k) - \frac{ds^*}{dk}f(k)\right] \qquad (17.31)$$

Substituting for J'' and J' from (17.27) and (17.31) into (17.30) and rearranging terms, we can rewrite (17.30) as

$$0 = -\tfrac{1}{2}\sigma^2 k^2 f U'' \frac{ds^*}{dk} + (fU' - \tfrac{1}{2}\sigma^2 k^2 U'' f')s^* + \tfrac{1}{2}\sigma^2 k^2 U'' f' - U'\beta k + U - B$$

$$(17.32)$$

which is a first-order differential equation for s^*. Note that for the (degenerate) case of certainty ($\sigma^2 = 0$), (17.32) reduces to

$$s^*f - \beta k = \frac{B - U}{U'} \qquad (17.32a)$$

which is "Ramsey's Rule," where B is the "bliss level" of utility associated with maximum steady-state consumption and $\dot{k} = s^*f - \beta k$ along the optimal certainty path.

In the certainty case and without regard to the time-optimal path associated with max $\int_0^\infty U(c)\,dt$, the optimal steady-state capital-to-labor ratio can be determined by the static maximization of $U[c(k)]$ in the steady state (i.e. with $\dot{k} = 0$ and $c(k) = f(k) - \beta k$). The solution for all strictly concave utility functions is the well-known Golden Rule, $f'(k^*) = \beta$.

---

22 The boundary condition for (17.30) is a transversality-type condition that, as $t \to \infty$, $\lim E_0\{J[k(t), t]\} = 0$. Note that because (17.30) does not contain J explicitly, any candidate solution $\hat{J}$ which satisfies $E_0\{\hat{J}[k(t), t]\} = H$, a constant, can be made to satisfy the transversality condition by setting $J[k(t), t] = \hat{J}[k(t), t] - H$.

Hence, it is natural to ask whether there exists a corresponding method using only the steady-state distribution for determining the optimal savings policy under uncertainty.

To answer this question, we consider the problem of finding the savings policy, $s^{**}(k)$, that maximizes the expected utility of per capita consumption over the steady-state distribution, i.e.

$$\max_{\{s\}} E\{U[(1 - s)f(k)]\} = \max_{\{s\}} \int_0^\infty U[(1 - s)f(k)]\pi_k(k) \, dk$$

$$(17.33)$$

which is the natural generalization to uncertainty of the static maximization under certainty.[23]

From (17.12), we can rewrite the steady-state density function for k as

$$\pi_k(k) = mk^{-\delta} \exp\left[\frac{2}{\sigma^2} h(k)\right] \qquad (17.34)$$

where

$$\delta \equiv 2 + \frac{2\beta}{\sigma^2}$$

$$h(k) \equiv \int^k s(x)f(x)x^{-2} \, dx$$

$$\dot{h}(k) \equiv \frac{dh}{dk} = s(k)f(k)k^{-2}$$

$$\ddot{h}(k) \equiv \frac{d^2h}{dk^2} = \frac{ds}{dk} fk^{-2} + sf'k^{-2} - 2sfk^{-3} \qquad (17.35)$$

and m is a constant chosen such that $m \int_0^\infty k^{-\delta} \exp[2h(k)/\sigma^2] \, dk = 1$. Substituting from (17.34) for π_k and noting that, from (17.35), $(1 - s)f = f - k^2\ddot{h}$, we can rewrite (17.33) as the constrained maximization problem

---

23   Unlike in the certainty case where a single k^* is chosen, we must choose a steady-state distribution, π^*, which is completely determined by the policy variable $s(k)$. In the certainty case, $\pi^* = \delta(k - k^*)$ where $\delta(\cdot)$ is the Dirac delta function and k^* depends on s^* through the steady-state constraint that $s^* = \beta k^*/f(k^*)$. Hence, from the monotonicity of $\beta k/f(k)$, (17.33) reduces to $\max\{U[f(k) - \beta k]\}$, where the choice variable is k.

$$\max\left\{\left[m\int_0^\infty U(f - k^2\dot{h})k^{-\delta}\exp\left(\frac{2h}{\sigma^2}\right)dk\right]\right.$$

$$\left. + \lambda\left[1 - m\int_0^\infty k^{-\delta}\exp\left(\frac{2h}{\sigma^2}\right)dk\right]\right\} \qquad (17.36)$$

where λ is the usual multiplier for the constraint. Inspection of (17.36) shows that, formally, it is identical to a standard intertemporal maximization problem under certainty where the independent variable is k instead of time. Hence, either the classical calculus of variations or the maximum principle can be employed to solve it. The Euler equations for (17.36) can be written as

$$0 = \frac{d}{dk}\left[U'k^{2-\delta}\exp\left(\frac{2h}{\sigma^2}\right)\right] + \frac{2}{\sigma^2}k^{-\delta}\exp\left(\frac{2h}{\sigma^2}\right)(U - \lambda) \quad (17.37a)$$

$$0 = \int_0^\infty U\pi_k(k)\,dk - \lambda\int_0^\infty \pi_k(k)\,dk \qquad (17.37b)$$

$$0 = 1 - m\int_0^\infty k^{-\delta}\exp\left(\frac{2h}{\sigma^2}\right)dk \qquad (17.37c)$$

Carrying out the differentiation in (17.37a), substituting for $\ddot{h}$, $\dot{h}$, and δ from (17.35), and rearranging terms, we can rewrite (17.37a) as

$$0 = -U''k^2f\frac{ds^{**}}{dk} + \left(-U''k^2f' + \frac{2}{\sigma^2}fU'\right)s^{**} + k^2f'U'' - \frac{2\beta}{\sigma^2}kU'$$

$$+ \frac{2}{\sigma^2}(U - \lambda) \qquad (17.38)$$

where $s^{**}(k)$ is the optimal policy associated with (17.36) and (17.37).

A comparison of (17.38) and (17.32) shows that the two differential equations are identical except for the constant terms λ and B. However, from (17.37b), we see that

$$\lambda = \int_0^\infty U[(1 - s^{**})f]\pi^{**}(k)\,dk$$

$$= \max E\{U(c)\}$$

$$= B$$

by its definition in (17.29). Hence, the optimal policy associated with (17.36) and the one associated with (17.24) for $T = \infty$ are identical, i.e. $s^{**}(k) = s^*(k)$. Just as in the certainty case, the criterion

$$\max E_0 \left\{ \int_0^\infty (U - \lambda)\, dt \right\}$$

has the interpretation of minimizing the (expected) divergence from bliss and clearly, in the certainty case, λ is the utility of maximum sustainable consumption. One major difference in the uncertainty case is that the steady-state maximization gives the optimal savings policy for all time and not just the asymptotically optimal savings policy. Further, while we have demonstrated the correspondence between the two problems only for the special case of continuous-time diffusion processes, it is probably not a difficult task to prove it for general time-homogeneous Markov processes and time-independent utility functions.

Unfortunately, inspection of (17.38) shows that there is no unique optimal steady-state distribution for k for all concave utilities corresponding to the Golden Rule under certainty. However, there is a special case where unanimity obtains.

Suppose $f(k)$ is Cobb–Douglas and we ask the question, "what *constant* savings function is optimal?" From the correspondence between (17.24) with $T = \infty$ and (17.36), the problem can be formulated as choose the constant s^* so as to

$$\max_{\{s\}} \int_0^\infty U[(1 - s)k^\alpha]\pi(k; s)\, dk \qquad (17.40)$$

where from (17.16) and (17.18)

$$\pi(k; s) = \frac{1 - \alpha}{\Gamma(\gamma)} b^\gamma k^{-\delta} \exp(-bk^{\alpha-1})$$

and δ is as defined in (17.35); $\gamma \equiv (\delta - 1)/(1 - \alpha)$ and $b \equiv 2s/(1 - \alpha)\sigma^2$. The first-order condition for a maximum in (17.40) is

$$0 = \int_0^\infty \left(\frac{\partial \pi}{\partial s} U - k^\alpha U' \pi \right) dk \qquad (17.41)$$

Define $V(k; s) \equiv U[(1 - s)k^\alpha]$. Noting that

$$V' \equiv dV/dk = \alpha(1 - s)k^{\alpha-1}U'$$

and

$$\frac{\partial \pi}{\partial s} = \left[\frac{\gamma}{s} - \frac{2k^{\alpha-1}}{(1-\alpha)\sigma^2}\right]\pi$$

we can rewrite (17.41) as

$$0 = \left(\int_0^\infty \left\{\alpha(1-s^*)\left[\frac{\gamma}{s^*} - \frac{2k^{\alpha-1}}{(1-\alpha)\sigma^2}\right]V\pi - k\pi V'\right\} dk\right)\bigg/ \alpha(1-s^*)$$

$$(17.41a)$$

Using integration by parts, we have that

$$\int_0^\infty (k\pi)V' \, dk = Vk\pi \, \bigg|_0^\infty - \int_0^\infty V\frac{d}{dk}(k\pi) \, dk$$

$$= 0 - \int_0^\infty V\frac{d}{dk}(k\pi) \, dk \qquad (17.42)$$

by the definition of π and the concavity of V. Using $d(k\pi)/dk = [1 + b^*(1-\alpha)k^{\alpha-1} - \delta]\pi$ in (17.42) and substituting (17.42) into (17.41a), we can rewrite (17.41a) as

$$0 = \int_0^\infty V\pi\left\{\left[b^*(1-\alpha) - \frac{2\alpha(1-s^*)}{(1-\alpha)\sigma^2}\right]k^{\alpha-1} + \left[\frac{\alpha(1-s^*)\gamma}{s^*} + 1 - \delta\right]\right\} dk$$

$$(17.43)$$

By inspection, the integrand of (17.43) will be identically zero for all V, π, and k if $s^* = \alpha$. Hence, in the class of constant savings rules with a Cobb–Douglas production function, the optimal rule is $s^* = \alpha$ for all concave utility maximizers.

Appendix 17A: Itô's Lemma

While the sample paths of diffusion-type stochastic processes are continuous with probability one, they are not differentiable. Hence, standard differential equation representations cannot be used to describe the dynamics of such processes. However, a complete theory of stochastic differential equations for processes of this type has been developed (cf. Itô and McKean, 1964; and McKean, 1969) which allows for (stochastic) integration and differentiation in a manner similar to that of the ordinary calculus. The stochastic analog to the Fundamental Theorem of the

Calculus is called Itô's lemma, which for one-dimensional, time-dependent diffusion processes can be stated as follows (McKean, 1969, p. 32).

Itô's lemma

Let $F(x, t)$ be a C^2 function defined on $R^2 \times [0, \infty)$ and take the stochastic integral

$$x(t) = x(0) + \int_0^t b(x, s) \, ds + \int_0^t [a(x, s)]^{1/2} \, dz$$

Then the time-dependent random variable $y \equiv F$ is a stochastic integral and its stochastic differential is

$$dy = \frac{\partial F}{\partial x} \, dx + \frac{\partial F}{\partial t} \, dt + \frac{1}{2} \frac{\partial^2 F}{\partial x^2} (dx)^2$$

where

$$dx = b(x, t) \, dt + [a(x, t)]^{1/2} \, dz$$

and the product of the differentials $(dx)^2$ is defined by the multiplication rule

$$dz \, dz = 1 \, dt$$

$$dz \, dt = 0$$

Itô's lemma is a particularly powerful practical tool for the analysis of stochastic dynamics. For examples of its application to some economic problems, see Merton (1969a, 1971, 1973b; this volume, Chs 4, 5, and 15). The lemma shows exactly how to differentiate and hence integrate functions of Wiener processes. Since diffusion processes can be written as functional transformations of Wiener processes, the lemma allows one to immediately deduce the dynamics for any well-behaved function of a diffusion-process random variable. Thus, by inspection of the resulting Itô equation, one can determine the instantaneous mean and variance for the transformed process and hence all the information necessary to determine the transition probabilities and moments of the transformed process. Further, as is illustrated in the text by deducing the distribution for future interest rates in the Cobb–Douglas example, it is sometimes possible to use Itô's lemma to integrate the differential equation directly to obtain a representation for the random variable as a function of the initial value, time, and a random variable whose distribution is well known (e.g. Gaussian), even when no closed-form solution exists for the transition probabilities.

To determine the stochastic differential for the capital-to-labor ratio, $k \equiv K/L$, we apply Itô's lemma as follows:

$$k = \frac{K}{L} \equiv G(L, t)$$

$$\frac{\partial G}{\partial L} = -\frac{K}{L^2} = -\frac{k}{L}$$

$$\frac{\partial^2 G}{\partial L^2} = \frac{2K}{L^3} = \frac{2k}{L^2}$$

$$\frac{\partial G}{\partial t} = \frac{\dot{K}}{L} = sf(k) - \lambda k \tag{17A.1}$$

from (17.1). From Itô's lemma,

$$dk = \frac{\partial G}{\partial L} dL + \frac{\partial G}{\partial t} dt + \frac{1}{2} \frac{\partial^2 G}{\partial L^2} (dL)^2 \tag{17A.2}$$

From (17.7) and Itô's lemma, we have that

$$dL = nL \, dt + \sigma L \, dz$$
$$(dL)^2 = \sigma^2 L^2 \, dt \tag{17A.3}$$

Substituting from (17A.1) and (17A.3) into (17A.2), we have that

$$dk = -\frac{k}{L} (nL \, dt + \sigma L \, dz) + [sf(k) - \lambda k] \, dt + \frac{1}{2} \frac{2k}{L^2} \sigma^2 L^2 \, dt$$

$$= [sf(k) - (\lambda + n - \sigma^2)k] \, dt - \sigma k \, dz \tag{17A.4}$$

which is equation (17.9).

Finally, there is a multidimensional version of Itô's lemma for vector-valued diffusion processes (cf. McKean, 1969, p. 32).

Appendix 17B: The Steady-State Distribution for a Diffusion Process

Let $X(t)$ be the solution to the Itô equation

$$dx = b(x)\, dt + [a(x)]^{1/2}\, dz \tag{17B.1}$$

where $a(\cdot)$ and $b(\cdot)$ are C^2 functions on $[0, \infty)$ and independent of t with $a(x) > 0$ on $(0, \infty]$ and $a(0) = b(0) = 0$. Then $X(t)$ describes a diffusion process taking on values in the interval $[0, \infty]$ with $X = 0$ and $X = \infty$ natural absorbing states, i.e. if $X(t) = 0$, then $X(\tau) = 0$ for $\tau > t$ and similarly for $X(t) = \infty$.

Let $p(X, t; X_0)$ be the conditional probability density for X at time t, given $X(0) = X_0$. Because $X(t)$ is a diffusion process, its transition density function will satisfy the Kolmogorov–Fokker–Planck "forward" equation (Feller, 1966, p. 326; Cox and Miller, 1968, p. 215):

$$\frac{1}{2}\frac{\partial^2}{\partial x^2}[a(x)p(x, t; X_0)] - \frac{\partial}{\partial x}[b(x)p(x, t; X_0)] = \frac{\partial p(x, t; X_0)}{\partial t} \tag{17B.2}$$

Suppose that X has a steady-state distribution, independent of X_0, i.e.

$$\lim_{t \to \infty} p(X, t; X_0) = \pi(x)$$

Then, $\lim_{t \to \infty} (\partial p/\partial t) = 0$, and π will satisfy

$$\frac{1}{2}\frac{d^2}{dx^2}[a(x)\pi(x)] - \frac{d}{dx}[b(x)\pi(x)] = 0 \tag{17B.3}$$

By standard methods, one can integrate (17B.3) twice to obtain a formal solution for $\pi(x)$: namely,

$$\pi(x) = m_1 I_1(x) + m_2 I_2(x) \tag{17B.4}$$

where

$$I_1(x) \equiv \frac{1}{a(x)} \exp\left[2\int^x \frac{b(y)}{a(y)}\, dy\right]$$

and

$$I_2(x) \equiv \frac{1}{a(x)} \int^x \exp\left[2\int_y^x \frac{b(s)}{a(s)}\, ds\right] dy$$

and m_1 and m_2 are constants to be chosen such that

$$\int_0^\infty \pi(x)\, dx = 1$$

While the formal solution is straightforward, the proof of existence and the determination of the constants is more difficult. Formally, a steady-state distribution will always exist in the sense that either (a) x will be absorbed at one of the natural boundaries (i.e. a degenerate distribution with a Dirac function for a density), or (b) it will have a finite density function on the interval $(0, \infty)$, or (c) it will have a discrete probability mix of (a) and (b). However, we are interested in the conditions under which a strictly nontrivial steady-state distribution exists (possibility (b)). Under such conditions, the boundaries are said to be *inaccessible*, i.e. $\text{prob}\{X(t) \le \epsilon\} \to 0$ and $\text{prob}\{X(t) \ge 1/\epsilon\} \to 0$ as $\epsilon \to 0$. Further, it can be shown that the boundaries are inaccessible if and only if $\int_0^x I_2(y)\, dy$ and $\int_x^\infty I_2(y)\, dy$ both diverge and $\int_0^\infty I_1(y)\, dy$ is bounded. Hence, under these conditions, we can conclude that $m_2 = 0$.

We now prove that the boundaries are inaccessible for the stochastic process (17.9) described in the text. From (17.9) and the assumptions of Section 17.3, we have that

$$b(k) \equiv s(k)f(k) - (n + \lambda - \sigma^2)k \qquad (17B.5)$$

and

$$a(k) \equiv \sigma^2 k^2 \qquad (17B.6)$$

where $f(k)$ is a concave function satisfying $\lim_{k\to 0} f'(k) = \infty$ and $\lim_{k\to\infty} f'(k) = 0$; $0 < \epsilon \le s(k) \le 1$; $n + \lambda - \sigma^2 > 0$.

The method of proof is to compare the stochastic process generated by (17.9) with another stochastic process which is known to have inaccessible boundaries and then to show that the probability that k reaches its boundaries is no larger than the probability that the comparison process reaches its boundaries.

Using Itô's lemma (Appendix 17A), we can write the stochastic differential equation for $x \equiv \log(k)$ as

$$dx = h(x)\, dt - \sigma\, dz \qquad (17B.7)$$

where

$$h(x) \equiv \exp(-x)s[\exp(x)]f[\exp(x)] - (n + \lambda - \tfrac{1}{2}\sigma^2) \qquad (17B.8)$$

Using the assumptions that $0 < \epsilon \leq s[\exp(x)]$ and $f'(0) = \infty$ along with L'Hospital's rule, we have that

$$\lim_{x \to -\infty} h(x) = \infty$$

and similarly, using the assumptions that $s[\exp(x)] \leq 1$ and $f'(\infty) = 0$, we have that

$$\lim_{x \to \infty} h(x) = -(n + \lambda - \tfrac{1}{2}\sigma^2) < 0 \tag{17B.9}$$

By continuity, there exists an $\underline{x} > -\infty$ such that, for all $x \in [-\infty, \underline{x}]$, there exists a $\delta_1 > 0$ such that

$$h(x) \geq h(\underline{x}) \geq \delta_1 > 0 \tag{17B.10}$$

Similarly, there exists an $\bar{x} < \infty$ such that, for all $x \in [\bar{x}, \infty]$, there exists a $\delta_2 < 0$ such that

$$h(x) \leq h(\bar{x}) \leq \delta_2 < 0 \tag{17B.11}$$

Consider a Wiener process $W_1(t)$ with drift δ_1 and variance σ^2 defined on the interval $[-\infty, \underline{x}]$ where $\underline{x}$ is a reflecting barrier, i.e.

$$dW_1 = \delta_1 \, dt - \sigma \, dz \tag{17B.12}$$

for $W_1 \in [-\infty, \underline{x}]$. Cox and Miller (1968, p. 223–5) have shown that such a process with $\delta_1 > 0$ has a nondegenerate steady state, and hence $-\infty$ is an inaccessible boundary. Comparing (17B.12) and (17B.7), we see that the two processes differ only by the drift term. Further, from (17B.10), the drift on x is always at least as large as the drift on W_1 in the interval $[-\infty, \underline{x}]$. Therefore, the probability that x will be absorbed at $-\infty$ is no greater than for W_1, and hence $-\infty$ is an inaccessible boundary for x. But $x \equiv \log(k)$. Thus, zero is an inaccessible boundary for the k process.

Consider a Wiener process $W_2(t)$ with drift δ_2 and variance σ^2 defined on the interval $[\bar{x}, \infty]$ where $\bar{x}$ is a reflecting barrier. Again, using the Cox and Miller analysis, W_2 will have a nondegenerate steady state provided that $\delta_2 < 0$. But from (17B.11), the drift on x will be at least as negative as δ_2 on the interval $[\bar{x}, \infty]$, and hence ∞ is an inaccessible boundary for x. Therefore, ∞ is an inaccessible boundary for k. Hence, we have proved that under the assumptions of the text, both boundaries of the k process are inaccessible and that a nontrivial steady-state distribution for k exists. Note that, as mentioned in footnote 11, we only require the weaker assumption that $n + \lambda - \tfrac{1}{2}\sigma^2 > 0$ used in (17B.9) to prove existence.

Because the boundaries are inaccessible, we also have that $m_2 = 0$ in (17B.4). A first integral of (17B.3) gives

$$\frac{1}{2}\frac{d}{dx}[a(x)\pi(x)] - b(x)\pi(x) = \tfrac{1}{2}m_2 = 0 \tag{17B.13}$$

for a nondegenerate steady state. We use this result in Appendix 17C.

Finally, the solution for the nondegenerate steady state distribution can be written as

$$\pi(x) = \frac{m}{a(x)}\exp\left[2\int^x \frac{b(y)}{a(y)}\,dy\right] \tag{17B.14}$$

where m is chosen so that $\int_0^\infty \pi(x)\,dx = 1$.

Appendix 17C: More Steady-State Properties

Let $X(t)$ be a random variable whose dynamics can be written as the Itô stochastic differential equation

$$dx = b(x)\,dt + [a(x)]^{1/2}\,dz \tag{17C.1}$$

where $a(x)$ and $b(x)$ are such that x has a steady-state distribution $\pi(x)$ which satisfies (17B.14).

Let $g = g(x)$ be a time-independent function of x. Provided that g is a sufficiently well-behaved function, the stochastic process generating g will also be a diffusion process with a stochastic differential equation representation

$$dg(x) = b_g(x)\,dt + [a_g(x)]^{1/2}\,dz \tag{17C.2}$$

where by Itô's lemma (Appendix 17A),

$$b_g(x) \equiv g'(x)b(x) + \tfrac{1}{2}g''(x)a(x)$$
$$a_g(x) \equiv [g'(x)]^2 a(x) \tag{17C.3}$$

If $g(\cdot)$ is twice-continuously differentiable and $g'(\cdot)$ satisfies the conditions

$$\lim_{x\to 0}[g'(x)a(x)\pi(x)] = \lim_{x\to\infty}[g'(x)a(x)\pi(x)] = 0$$

then

$$E\{b_g(x)\} \equiv E\{g'(x)b(x) + \tfrac{1}{2}g''(x)a(x)\} = 0 \tag{17C.4}$$

where E is the expectation operator over the $\pi(\cdot)$ distribution.

Proof of (17C.4) follows directly from integration by parts of

$$E\{b_g(x)\} = \int_0^\infty [g'(x)b(x) + \tfrac{1}{2}g''(x)a(x)]\pi(x)\,dx \qquad (17C.5)$$

Integrating by parts,

$$\int_0^\infty g''(x)a(x)\pi(x)\,dx = [g'(x)a(x)\pi(x)]\Big|_0^\infty - \int_0^\infty g'(x)\frac{d}{dx}[a(x)\pi(x)]\,dx$$

$$= -\int_0^\infty g'(x)\frac{d}{dx}[a(x)\pi(x)]\,dx \qquad (17C.6)$$

from the limit conditions imposed on $g'(x)$. Substituting from (17C.6) into (17C.5) and rearranging terms, we have that

$$E\{b_g(x)\} = \int_0^\infty g'(x)\left\{b(x)\pi(x) - \frac{1}{2}\frac{d}{dx}[a(x)\pi(x)]\right\}\,dx$$

$$= 0 \qquad (17C.7)$$

because $\pi(\cdot)$ satisfies (17B.13), and hence the term in curly brackets is identically zero. QED

18

On Consumption-Indexed
Public Pension Plans

18.1 INTRODUCTION

Most economists using a standard life-cycle analysis would probably agree
that the primary objective of a pension system is to provide a standard of
living in retirement comparable with that enjoyed during the working
years. Nevertheless, there is considerable disagreement on how that
objective can best be achieved. Broadly, the disagreements are on the
appropriate roles for private pension plans and a public pension plan in the
pension system and on whether or not the pension system should also be
used for redistribution or transfers. The most elegant approach to the
problem would undoubtedly be to solve for the optimal overall pension
system with a simultaneous determination of the optimal forms for both
public and private parts. However, the analysis here is more limited in its
scope because its focus is principally on the public part of the system and
because it examines only one of the many possible functions that such a
system might serve in any real-world implementation. That is, the sole
intent of the system is assumed to be the retirement objective and not, for
example, also to redistribute wealth. This chapter should thus be viewed as
only a prologue to a more complete functional analysis of the overall
pension system, including the important issue of the degree of integration
between private and public pension plans.

Analysis of the public part of the system is a natural starting place
because, whatever form the overall pension system takes, it will surely
include a significant public pension plan component. As I shall discuss,
there are a number of theoretical arguments to support such a component
as part of an optimal system. Moreover, as a practical matter independent

Reproduced from *Financial Aspects of the U.S. Pension System*, Z. Bodie and
J. Shoven, eds, 1983, Chicago: University of Chicago Press, 259–76. Aid from the
National Bureau of Economic Research and the National Science Foundation is
gratefully acknowledged. My thanks to F. Black, S. Fischer, D. Holland,
L. Summers, and L. Thurow for many helpful discussions and to L. Summers for
providing me with the data for Table 18.1. Any opinions expressed are mine and
are not necessarily those of my helpful colleagues, NBER, or NSF.

of any theoretical welfare arguments that economists might provide to the contrary, the public pension system in the United States, after almost half a century of operating experience, is not going to be eliminated, especially when a significant fraction of the population is not covered by any private pension plan. The current problems with Social Security do, however, present the possibility for major changes in the structure of the public pension system. It would therefore seem to be somewhat difficult to analyze the optimal design of private pension plans and the associated issue of integration until the structure of the public system is more firmly established.

In theory, the characteristic differences between a public and a private pension system are that participation in a public system is mandatory and that the public system cannot be "custom tailored" to meet the specific preferences of each individual participant. Such a clear distinction is valid if the private system were solely *laissez-faire* individual saving. However, as the private system has evolved, the operational significance of this distinction, at least at the level of analysis presented here, is less clear. Participation in most existing private pension plans is virtually mandatory. In a typical defined-contribution plan, individual choice of amounts contributed and where the funds are invested is quite limited, and in defined-benefit plans there is typically no choice at all. Therefore, the analysis presented here in the context of a public system is readily adaptable to an organized private pension system.

The arguments for a public pension system with mandatory participation fall into two basic categories: externalities and private market failure. An important example of the former is the utility externality that other people's welfare is one of the arguments of individual utility functions. That is, people care about others and, among other things, will not let them starve in retirement. From this, we get a classical example of the free-rider problem, which cannot be solved by the private markets but can be solved by an appropriately designed mandatory public pension system. A second example is the possibility of economies of scale in information costs. Virtually everyone faces the decision of how much to save for retirement and where to invest those savings during the working years. The marginal cost of obtaining the education and gathering the necessary data to make informed decisions, as well as the time spent implementing these decisions, will vary substantially across individuals as a function of their prior education and their wealth. (Presumably, a professor of finance by virtue of his training would have a lower marginal cost than a professor of physics.) The cost of buying the service of informed decisions will be lower (as a percentage of wealth) for those who are wealthy than for those of modest means. While such costs could be reduced by pooling, this solution almost assumes away the problem because pooling requires adequate information and opportunity to form a cohesive group.

If, therefore, a pension plan were designed which reasonably approximated the plan which most individuals would choose if they were informed, then by making participation in the plan mandatory the resources used in individual education and data gathering would be saved and the maximum benefits of pooling to reduce operating costs could be achieved. The benefits of such mandatory participation must, of course, be compared with the cost in terms of loss in individual freedom of choice. As already noted, existing private pension plans permit little choice. Although this data point favors the hypothesis that the benefits outweigh the costs, it is hardly a sufficient basis for a policy decision.

The second basic category of arguments for a public pension plan is that the efficiency of risk bearing can be improved. That is, the government can provide diversification possibilities that are not available in the private markets and thereby issue financial instruments, which the private sector cannot. One example would be intergenerational risk sharing, which cannot be covered by private markets (see Fischer, 1983). Another would be to use either taxes and transfers (see Merton, 1983c) or taxes and the issue of securities within the pension system to provide diversification of some of the risks of assets which are not tradeable (as is the case for much of human capital).

With these general reasons for a public pension plan as background, I shall summarize briefly the consumption-indexed plan to be studied before turning to a formal analysis in the context of a simple intertemporal equilibrium model in Section 18.2. In Section 18.3, I discuss the merits and feasibility of such plans.

The plan is a mandatory fully funded savings plan of the defined-contribution type wherein required contributions by each member of the plan are a fixed proportion of that member's consumption. As with current private defined-contribution plans, each member has an individual account which is credited with his contributions (less any deduction for operating expenses of the plan).

Contributions and earnings in each member's account are invested in aggregate per capita consumption-indexed life annuities, defined to be an instrument that pays a constant fraction of aggregate per capita consumption to its holder (the member) each period, such payments beginning at a prespecified date (the date at which the member begins to receive his benefits) and continuing until the member dies. If the member dies before the commencement date, the annuity is worthless. Benefits, therefore, are in the form of a life annuity indexed to aggregate per capita consumption.

The commencement date for benefits is at a specified age (e.g. age 60), whether or not the recipient has retired. This provision is to avoid possibly undesirable distortions of the decision to retire. However, provision could be made for delaying the receipt of benefits to a later age. Contributions are mandatory from some statutory beginning age (e.g. age 21) until the commencement date.

One way to administer such a plan would be to create a public corporation which would be responsible for issuing the indexed life annuities to plan members where these annuities would constitute its senior liabilities. The US government would be the residual liability or equityholder of the corporation and would have unlimited liability. The assets of the corporation would come from member contributions and be invested in the broadest available portfolio of marketable securities.

The number of units of life annuities issued to an account is on a "mark-to-market" basis at the time each contribution is received. That is, the value of a unit of a life annuity issued is determined by current market prices and mortality tables. To make this possible, it would be necessary for the government to issue aggregate per capita consumption-indexed bonds of various maturities.

To prevent attempts to circumvent mandatory participation in the plan, retirement benefits are assumed to be neither assignable nor attachable. For similar reasons, integration of private pension plans with the public plan are permitted, but only to the extent that the combined benefits received by the individual are no less than he would have received from the public plan alone.

18.2   A SIMPLE INTERTEMPORAL EQUILIBRIUM MODEL

In this section, a continuous-time consumption-choice model of the type presented by Merton (1971, 1973b; this volume, Chs 5 and 15) is used to analyze the system of mandatory saving and consumption-linked retirement benefits.

Consider an economy where all people have the same lifetime utility of consumption which is given for a person born at time t_0 by

$$E_{t_0}\left\{ \int_{t_0}^{t_0+t} \frac{[c(s; s - t_0)]^{\gamma}}{\gamma} \exp[-\rho(s - t_0)] \, ds \right\} \qquad \gamma < 1 \quad (18.1)$$

where $c(t; \tau)$ is consumption at time t of a person of age τ and E_t is the conditional expectation operator, conditional on knowing all relevant information available at time t. Each person has an uncertain lifetime where $\tilde{t}$ denotes the random variable age of death, and the probability that the person will die between τ and $\tau + d\tau$, conditional on being alive at age τ, is given by $\lambda(\tau) \, d\tau$ where $\dot{\lambda}(\tau) > 0$. Each individual acts so as to maximize (18.1) subject to his initial wealth w_0.

If the event of death is independent of other economic variables, then, along the lines of the proof of Theorem VI of Merton (1971; this volume, Theorem 5.6), we can rewrite (18.1) as

$$E_{t_0}\left\{ \int_{t_0}^{\infty} f(s - t_0; 0) \exp[-\rho(s - t_0)] \frac{[c(s; s - t_0)]^{\gamma}}{\gamma} \, ds \right\} \tag{18.2}$$

where $f(\tau; \tau')$ is the probability that the person will be alive at age τ conditional on being alive at age τ'. By the definition of $\lambda(\tau)$, f satisfies

$$f(\tau; \tau') = \exp\left[- \int_{\tau'}^{\tau} \lambda(s) \, ds \right] \tag{18.3}$$

By assumption, individuals have no bequest function. Hence it will be optimal for each person to enter into a life annuity contract wherein his wealth goes to the issuer if he dies and he receives a payment if he lives. One such arrangement would be a series of short-term contracts wherein at age τ the individual agrees to bequeath his wealth, $w(t; \tau)$, to the issuer if he dies between time t and $t + dt$ and the issuer agrees to pay him a dividend $D \, dt$ if he lives. If there are enough people in the economy to diversify away completely the risk of individual deaths, and if the contracts (like futures contracts) require no side-payments between issuer and purchaser, then the competitive equilibrium dividend will be $\lambda(\tau)w(t; \tau) \, dt$.

In addition to the annuity contract, the person will choose an optimal portfolio allocation of his wealth. As shown, for example, by Merton (1971; this volume, Ch. 5), the fractions of his optimal portfolio allocated to the available investments are independent of his wealth or age because his utility function is of the isoelastic form. Therefore, all investors in the economy will hold identical portfolios (except for scale). Hence, without loss of generality, I assume that all people invest in a single security. The rate of return on this security, dM/M, is assumed to follow an Itô process given by

$$\frac{dM}{M} = \alpha \, dt + \sigma \, dz \tag{18.4}$$

where the instantaneous expected rate of return α and the instantaneous variance of the return σ^2 are constants over time. It follows from (18.4) that the return on this security is log-normally distributed. Moreover, as a necessary condition for equilibrium, this security must be a market portfolio (i.e. a portfolio which contains all available investments and holds them in proportion to their market values).

The accumulation equation for the wealth of a person of age τ at time t can therefore be written as

$$dw(t; \tau) = \{[\lambda(\tau) + \alpha]w(t; \tau) - c(t; \tau)\} \, dt + \sigma w(t; \tau) \, dz \quad (18.5a)$$

if he does not die between t and $t + dt$ and as

$$dw(t; \tau) = -w(t; \tau) \quad (18.5b)$$

if he dies between t and $t + dt$.

Along the lines of the derivation by Merton (1971; this volume, equation (5.48)), the optimal consumption demand for a person of age τ at time t can be written as

$$c(t; \tau) = a(\tau)w(t; \tau) \quad (18.6a)$$

where $a(\tau)$ is a solution to the differential equation

$$0 = \frac{\dot{a}(\tau)}{a(\tau)} - a(\tau) + \lambda(\tau) + \mu \quad (18.6b)$$

with $\mu \equiv (\rho - \gamma\alpha)/(1 - \gamma) + \gamma\sigma^2/2$. By inspection, optimal consumption is a function of both wealth and age, and the marginal propensity to consume (out of wealth) will be an increasing function of age if $\dot{\lambda}(\tau) \geq 0$. Similarly, the distribution of the wealth of a person who is alive at time $t + s$, given his wealth at time t, will depend, not only on his wealth at time t and the return experience on his portfolio between t and $t + s$, but also on his age at time t.

Using Itô's lemma, we have from (18.6) that

$$\frac{dc(t; \tau)}{c(t; \tau)} = \frac{dw(t; \tau)}{w(t; \tau)} + \frac{\dot{a}(\tau)}{a(\tau)} \, dt \quad (18.7)$$

Conditional on the person not dying between t and dt, we have by substitution from (18.5) and (18.6) that (18.7) can be rewritten as

$$\frac{dc(t; \tau)}{c(t; \tau)} = (\alpha - \mu) \, dt + \sigma \, dz \quad (18.8)$$

and, of course, if he dies then $dc(t; \tau)/c(t; \tau) = -1$. By inspection of (18.8), the dynamic path of a person's optimal lifetime consumption follows a Markov process independent of either his wealth or his age (except for the "stopping point"). That is, given his consumption at time t, $c(t; \tau)$, his consumption (if alive) at time $t + s$ has a log-normal distribution which can be represented by

$$c(t + s; \tau + s) = c(t; \tau) \exp[(\alpha - \mu)s + \sigma s^{1/2}\epsilon] \qquad (18.9)$$

where ϵ is a standard normal random variable. Thus, unlike the percentage change in wealth, which is age dependent, the percentage change in consumption is the same for all people alive. It follows, therefore, that

$$\frac{c(t + s; \tau + s)}{c(t; \tau)} = \frac{c(t + s; \tau' + s)}{c(t; \tau')} \qquad (18.10)$$

for all people alive at time $t + s$ and $\tau, \tau' \geq 0$.

Armed with (18.8) and (18.10), we can now proceed to derive the dynamic properties of aggregate per capita consumption $C(t)$. If $L(t; \tau)$ denotes the number of people of age τ in the economy at time t, then the total population size $L(t)$ equals $\int_0^\infty L(t; \tau) \, d\tau$. Therefore, aggregate per capita consumption is equal to

$$C(t) = \int_0^\infty \frac{L(t; \tau)c(t; \tau)}{L(t)} \, d\tau$$

If the birthrate at time t is given by $b(t)$, then the change in aggregate per capita consumption is given by

$$dC(t) = \int_0^\infty \frac{L(t; \tau) \, dc(t; \tau)}{L(t)} \, d\tau - H(t)C(t) \, dt \qquad (18.12)$$

where

$$H(t) \equiv \frac{b(t)[C(t) - c(t; 0)] - \int_0^\infty \lambda(\tau)L(t; \tau)[C(t) - c(t; \tau)] \, d\tau/L(t)}{C(t)}$$

The properties of $H(t)$ are, of course, dependent on demographic assumptions. However, they also depend on the distribution of consumption per capita. If, for example, the distribution of per capita consumption were uniform—i.e. $c(t; \tau) = C(t)$, for all τ—then $H(t) = 0$, independent of demographics. In a stable population $(b(t) = \int_0^\infty \lambda(\tau)L(t; \tau) \, d\tau/L(t))$,

$$H(t) = \frac{-\int_0^\infty \lambda(\tau)L(t; \tau) \, [c(t; 0) - c(t; \tau)] \, d\tau}{L(t)C(t)}$$

and the sign of H will depend primarily on the distribution of per capita consumption between the very young and the very old, where the marginal death rate $\lambda(\tau)$ is largest. If that distribution is approximately equal—$c(t; 0) \approx c(t; \tau)$ for large τ—and the population is growing, then the sign of $H(t)$ will equal the sign of $C(t) - c(t; 0)$, the difference between the general population per capita consumption and per capita consumption of the very young.

Even without taking into account the interaction between population growth and economic conditions, the analysis of stochastic demographic models is formidable. And, while the deathrate (at least in the short run) may be exogenous, the birthrate is surely affected by economic conditions. Therefore, although explicit consideration of the process for $H(t)$ is important for many issues in this chapter, no such analysis will be undertaken here. Instead, I simply postulate that $H(t) = 0$.[1]

If $H(t) = 0$, then we have by substitution from (18.8) that (18.12) can be rewritten as

$$dC(t) = \frac{\int_0^\infty L(t; \tau)c(t; \tau)\,d\tau}{L(t)}[(\alpha - \mu)\,dt + \sigma\,dz]$$

$$= (\alpha - \mu)C(t)\,dt + \sigma C(t)\,dz \qquad (18.13)$$

A comparison of (18.8) with (18.13) shows that, except for scale, each person's optimal consumption follows a stochastic process identical with the one for aggregate per capita consumption. That is, conditional on being alive at time $t + dt$, $dc(t; \tau)/c(t; \tau) = dC(t)/C(t)$, independent of the person's age τ. Therefore, we have for person j that his consumption (if he is alive) at time t can be written as

$$c_j(t) = \beta_j C(t) \qquad (18.14)$$

where $\beta_j \equiv c(t_j; 0)/C(t_j)$ and t_j is his birthdate.

Consider now a mandatory savings and retirement plan where, beginning at age T_0, each person must contribute at rate δ times his consumption until, at age T_1, the person begins to receive his life annuity retirement benefits. During the accumulation period of length $\tau_a \equiv T_1 - T_0$, each person's contribution is invested in a per capita aggregate consumption-linked life annuity contract matched to his age at the time of the contribution.

---

1 On the matter of the assumed stability of $H(t)$, I note that because $c(t; 0)$ depends strongly on the initial endowments of the very young, $c(t; 0)/C(t)$ is likely to be larger when the value of human capital relative to other factors of wealth is larger. It also seems reasonable that the birthrate will be higher when the relative economic value of children is high. However, if $c(t; 0)/C(t) < 1$, then comparative statics reveal that these two effects work in opposite directions on $H(t)$ in a stabilizing fashion.

Let $A(t, \tau; T_1)$ denote the equilibrium price at time t of a life annuity contract which begins its payments at age T_1 and the purchaser is currently age τ. The promised stream of payments is equal to $C(s)$ per unit of time from time $s = t + T_1 - \tau$ until the purchaser dies. Let $P(t; \tau)$ denote the equilibrium price at time t of a consumption-linked pure discount bond of maturity τ which pays $C(t + \tau)$ dollars at time $t + \tau$. If, as I have assumed, individual death risk can be diversified away, then the competitive equilibrium price for A can be written as

$$A(t, \tau; T_1) = \int_0^\infty f(s + T_1; \tau) P(t; s + T_1 - \tau) \, ds \qquad (18.15)$$

where, as previously defined, $f(\tau; \tau')$ is the probability of being alive at age τ conditional on being alive at age τ'.

For the economy of this section, an explicit formula for the $P(t; \tau)$ can be derived by competitive arbitrage. From (18.13),

$$C(t + \tau) = C(t) \exp\left[(\alpha - \mu - \tfrac{1}{2}\sigma^2)\tau + \sigma \int_t^{t+\tau} dz(s) \right]$$

Therefore, the realized return on the discount bond between t and $t + \tau$ is

$$\frac{C(t + \tau)}{P(t; \tau)} = \left[\frac{C(t)}{P(t; \tau)} \exp(-\mu\tau) \right] \times \exp\left[\left(\alpha - \frac{1}{2}\sigma^2\right)\tau + \sigma \int_t^{t+\tau} dz(s) \right]$$

However, from (18.4), the return per dollar from investing in the market portfolio between t and $t + \tau$ is $\exp[(\alpha - \tfrac{1}{2}\sigma^2)\tau + \sigma \int_t^{t+\tau} dz(s)]$. Therefore, to avoid arbitrage, $P(t; \tau)$ must satisfy

$$P(t; \tau) = C(t) \exp(-\mu\tau) \qquad (18.16)$$

It follows from (18.16) that the instantaneous rate of return on the bond, $dP/P = \alpha dt + \sigma dz$, is the same as on the market. Substituting for P from (18.16), we can rewrite (18.15) as

$$A(t, \tau; T_1) = C(t) \exp[-\mu(T_1 - \tau)] \int_0^\infty \exp(-\mu s) \, f(s + T_1; \tau) \, ds \qquad (18.17)$$

Moreover, it is straightforward to show that, for $\tau < T_1$,

$$\frac{dA}{A} = [\alpha + \lambda(\tau)] \, dt + \sigma \, dz \qquad (18.18)$$

if the owner of the contract is alive at $t + dt$ and $dA/A = -1$ if the owner dies between t and $t + dt$.

Let $V(t; \tau)$ denote the value of the accumulated retirement account for a person of age τ at time t. Under this retirement plan, with accumulations in units of a consumption-linked life annuity, the value can be expressed as

$$V(t; \tau) = N(\tau)A(t, \tau; T_1) \tag{18.19}$$

where $N(\tau)$ equals the number of units accumulated at age τ. By Itô's lemma, $dV = N(\tau)\, dA + \dot{N}(\tau)A\, dt$ if the person lives to time $t + dt$ and $dV = -V$ if he dies between t and $t + dt$. Under the mandatory saving plan, $\dot{N}(\tau)A(t,\tau;T_1) = \delta c(t;\tau)$ and $N(T_0) = 0$. From (18.14), $c(t;\tau) = \beta C(t)$, and if the retirement plan is designed to provide fraction η ($0 < \eta \leq 1$) of the person's optimal retirement-period consumption, then δ should be chosen so that at retirement the number of units accumulated, $N(T_1)$, equals $\eta\beta$.

If the retirement plan is fully funded and actuarially fair, then at age T_0 the present value of the person's future contributions should be equal to the present value of the annuity payments to be received during retirement. Under the terms of the mandatory saving plan, the person will contribute at the rate $\delta c(t;\tau) = \delta\beta C(t)$ (as long as he is alive) until he reaches T_1. Therefore, at age T_0, the present value of his future contributions, $F(t; T_0)$, is given by

$$F(t; T_0) = \int_0^{T_1-T_0} f(s + T_0; T_0)\delta\beta P(t; s)\, ds$$

$$= \delta\beta \int_0^{\tau_a} f(s + T_0; T_0)P(t; s)\, ds \tag{18.20}$$

If the plan is to provide $N(T_1) = \eta\beta$ units in retirement, then the present value of these retirement benefits at age T_0 is $\eta\beta A(t, T_0; T_1)$. Therefore δ must be chosen such that $F(t; T_0) = \eta\beta A(t, T_0; T_1)$, and from (18.15) and (18.20) we have that

$$\delta = \frac{\eta \int_0^\infty f(s + T_1; T_0)P(t; s + \tau_a)\, ds}{\int_0^{\tau_a} f(s + T_0; T_0)P(t; s)\, ds} \tag{18.21}$$

Substituting for P from (18.16), we can rewrite (18.21) as

$$\delta = \frac{\eta \exp(-\mu\tau_a)\int_0^\infty f(s + T_1; T_0) \exp(-\mu s)\, ds}{\int_0^{\tau_a} f(s + T_0; T_0) \exp(-\mu s)\, ds} \tag{18.22}$$

By inspection of (18.22), the required contribution fraction does not depend on endowments or the individual contributor's age. It does, of course, depend on the statutory retirement age, T_1; the accumulation period, τ_a; and the target fraction of retirement period consumption provided by the plan, η. Therefore, δ can be kept constant over time and still meet the objectives of the plan. The only changes required would be in response to large cumulative changes in the mortality tables, f or μ, and these would probably be infrequent. Moreover, because the plan is fully funded and accumulations earn a fair market return, such changes in f or μ as might occur will cause no significant distortions even if δ were not adjusted over time.

To provide a crude estimate of the magnitude of δ, I assume (a) that the accumulation period $\tau_a = 45$ years; (b) that during the accumulation period the mortality rate is a constant, λ, equal to 0.0138 per year; and (c) that during the retirement period the mortality rate is a constant, λ, equal to 0.0666 per year and in no event will anyone live longer than 30 years after retirement. The average rate of growth of aggregate per capita real consumption from 1947 to 1981 is approximately 2 percent per year. If the expected real rate of return on all wealth in the economy, α, is taken to be 4 percent, then from (18.13) we derive an estimate for μ of 2 percent. Substituting these numbers into (18.22), we have that

$$\delta = 0.10\eta \qquad\qquad (18.23)$$

That is, to provide for all retirement consumption ($\eta = 1$) would require a contribution rate of about 10 percent. While such a rate may seem large (requiring contributions of the order of $200 billion in 1981), 10 percent is a common contribution rate (on income) in many existing private defined-contribution plans, and the current maximum contribution rate for Keogh plans is 15 percent. To provide further perspective, I would also note that the combined employee–employer contributions to Social Security in the fourth quarter of 1981 were at an annual rate of $245 billion. It is, of course, unlikely that a public pension plan would be expected to provide for all retirement consumption, and therefore the necessary contribution rate would be considerably less than 10 percent.

18.3   ON THE MERITS AND FEASIBILITY OF A CONSUMPTION-INDEXED PUBLIC PLAN

While the analysis in the previous section demonstrates a consumption-indexed public retirement plan, it is presented within the context of a model where such plans are redundant. That is, with perfect markets for both assets and annuities, no utility externalities, and rational and informed people, there is no need for such public intervention. From this base, however, imperfections can be introduced to provide at least a qualitative analysis of the benefits of the plan for comparison with alternative plans if, and when, such intervention were deemed appropriate.

For example, a significant feature of this plan is that contributions be invested in aggregate-consumption-linked life annuities. If important assets within the economy, such as human capital and real estate, are either nontradeable or not available in divisible lots, then even a broad-based portfolio of tradeable assets will not provide a fully efficient diversified portfolio. However, an individual's consumption is likely to be strongly correlated with his wealth (or permanent income) whether that wealth is tradeable or not, and therefore a security whose return is perfectly correlated with aggregate per capita consumption is likely to represent a better diversified holding than a portfolio containing only marketable securities.

If there are systematic differences among large segments of the population as to the types of nontradeable assets they hold, then it is possible to improve diversification efficiency still further. For example, the young in the economy may be forced to hold too large a fraction of their wealth in human capital because it is not tradeable while the old hold too small a fraction in human capital because they cannot buy it. As I have shown elsewhere (Merton, 1983c), risk bearing can be improved by a system that taxes wages and pays wage-linked retirement benefits. However, as that analysis amply demonstrates, such further diversification gains are earned at the expense of having a pay-as-you-go retirement system with a risk of significant distortions from the associated taxes and transfers.

Diamond (1977) has suggested that one reason for a social security system is the absence in the private markets of "real" or "indexed" investments by which people of normal means can accumulate savings for retirement. However, "real" fixed-income bonds would only protect such savers against the uncertainties of inflation. They would not protect the saver against the risk of real increases in the standard of living. As shown in Table 18.1, real per capita consumption in the United States has increased at an average rate of 1.96 percent per year from 1947 to 1981. Moreover, the annual standard deviation of that growth rate is 1.68 percent. Hence, if a person's sense of economic well-being depends not only on the absolute level of his consumption but also on its level relative to those around him, then the risk in utility terms of a price-level-linked investment can be considerable, especially over a long accumulation period. A consumption-linked investment protects against both inflation and real changes in the standard of living. It has the further practical advantage of avoiding the index problem because it is not necessary to distinguish between nominal and real changes.

Table 18.1 Levels and Growth Rates of US Aggregate Real Consumption and Over-Age-16 Population, 1947–1981

Year	Aggregate Consumption (Billion 1972 $)		Population (Millions)		Per Capita Consumption (Thousand 1972 $)	
	Level	Percentage Change	Level	Percentage Change	Level	Percentage Change
1947	305.8	–	103.4	–	2.957	–
1948	312.2	2.1	104.5	1.1	2.987	1.0
1949	319.3	2.3	105.6	1.0	3.023	1.2
1950	337.3	5.6	106.6	1.0	3.163	4.6
1951	341.6	1.3	107.7	1.0	3.171	0.3
1952	350.1	2.5	108.8	1.0	3.217	1.5
1953	363.4	3.8	110.6	1.6	3.286	2.1
1954	370.0	1.8	111.7	1.0	3.313	0.8
1955	394.1	6.5	112.7	1.0	3.496	5.5
1956	405.4	2.9	113.8	1.0	3.562	1.9
1957	413.8	2.1	115.1	1.1	3.596	1.0
1958	418.0	1.0	116.4	1.1	3.592	−0.1
1959	440.4	5.4	117.9	1.3	3.736	4.0
1960	452.0	2.6	119.8	1.6	3.774	1.0
1961	461.4	2.1	121.3	1.3	3.802	0.7
1962	482.0	4.5	123.0	1.3	3.919	3.1
1963	500.5	3.8	125.2	1.8	3.999	2.0
1964	528.0	5.5	127.2	1.7	4.150	3.8
1965	557.5	5.6	129.2	1.6	4.314	3.9
1966	585.7	5.1	131.2	1.5	4.465	3.5
1967	602.7	2.9	133.3	1.6	4.521	1.3
1968	634.4	5.3	135.6	1.7	4.680	3.5
1969	657.9	3.7	137.8	1.7	4.773	2.0
1970	672.1	2.2	140.2	1.7	4.794	0.5
1971	696.8	3.7	142.6	1.7	4.887	1.9
1972	737.1	5.8	145.8	2.2	5.056	3.5
1973	768.5	4.3	148.2	1.7	5.183	2.5
1974	763.6	−0.6	150.8	1.7	5.063	−2.3
1975	780.2	2.2	153.4	1.7	5.084	0.4
1976	823.7	5.6	156.0	1.7	5.279	3.8
1977	863.9	4.9	158.6	1.6	5.448	3.2
1978	904.8	4.7	161.1	1.6	5.618	3.1
1979	930.9	2.9	163.6	1.6	5.689	1.3

1980	935.1	0.5	166.2	1.6	5.625	−1.1
1981	958.9	2.5	168.6	1.4	5.688	1.1
Average growth rate	3.44			1.45		1.96
Standard deviation	1.75			0.32		1.68

Source: consumption data are taken from US Department of Commerce, Bureau
  of Economic Analysis, *National Income and Product Accounts of the United
  States*, Table 1.2; noninstitutional population 16 and over data are from US
  Department of Labor, Bureau of Labor Statistics

In another context, Fischer (1983) argues that the government should issue bonds linked to wage income. While it is likely that such bonds would be superior to price-level-linked bonds for most saving plans, at least in theory, they may not be as efficient as consumption-linked bonds. One reason is that changes in wage income capture the returns to only one segment (albeit an important one) of national wealth, while consumption changes depend on all segments. A second reason is that wage income is more likely to have a significant transient component than is consumption since, by the Life-Cycle Hypothesis, consumption depends on permanent income or wealth. How important the difference would be between wage-income- and consumption-linked bonds is, of course, an empirical matter, and one that warrants further study.

There are relatively limited opportunities in existing private markets to accumulate savings in life annuities, and none where those savings are invested in consumption-linked investments. In the absence of such instruments, the individual may be forced to save too much relative to his bequest motive. By investing contributions in life annuities, the proposed plan permits a person to accumulate adequate amounts for retirement with smaller contributions. The additional available funds from this reduced contribution rate can be used either for more current consumption or to purchase life insurance or other saving instruments to meet bequest motives. This feature is especially important in a *mandatory* saving plan because, for the *same* target level of retirement benefits, it reduces the welfare loss of the plan to those in poor health or those who have no bequest motive.

A second significant feature of the plan is that retirement benefits are linked to aggregate per capita consumption. The arguments in favor of consumption-linked benefits are essentially the same as those given for consumption-linked accumulations. So, for example, while a number of people, including Diamond (1977), have argued for real or price-indexed fixed annuities for retirement benefits, per capita consumption-linked benefits are likely to dominate such annuities because they protect the retiree against both uncertainties in the inflation rate and changes in the standard of living.

The success of a consumption-indexed plan (whether public or private) depends critically on the existence of per capita aggregate-consumption-linked bonds. In their absence, administrators of the plan would be required to estimate the fair market value of such bonds in order to determine how many units to credit to each account during the accumulation period and to determine how much to pay in benefits during retirement. I need hardly mention the extreme difficulties associated with making these appraisals, especially when such instruments have never traded. Moreover, for a public plan, there would likely be times when strong political pressure would be brought to bear on the administrators to "adjust" their appraisals. Even if such pressure were in fact resisted, the mere prospect of a potential conflict of interest could taint the entire system.

In theory, the private sector could create a market for per capita aggregate-consumption-linked bonds and provide consumption-linked life annuities through financial intermediaries. Indeed, some might argue that the fact that such instruments have not been created is strong evidence in favor of the hypothesis that there is no need for them. However, if this hypothesis is correct, then close surrogates for these instruments must already exist in the market, since – as suggested, for example, by Breeden's (1979) analysis – there is a strong theoretical foundation for the belief that an aggregate-consumption-linked security would be widely demanded. I know of no such combination of available securities.

There is, of course, the alternative hypothesis that the nonexistence of such instruments is an example of private market "failure." That is, even though there would be a demand for these instruments, there is insufficient incentive for investment bankers, for example, to undertake the costs of educating both purchasers and issuers, especially when the latter have no assets that are naturally matched to this type of liability. Similarly, in the absence of a "thick" market for consumption-linked bonds, financial intermediaries probably would be reluctant to issue such annuity liabilities because there is no asset which can be purchased to hedge these liabilities. Of course, some intermediaries might be induced to take some limited amount of risk without being hedged, but this limited amount would surely be inadequate for the scale required for pension plans. On the other hand, it appears that the government is a "natural" intermediary to issue consumption-linked bonds because it has the power to tax expenditures. That is, the government could institute a consumption tax proportional to the number of consumption-linked bonds outstanding and the revenues from the tax would exactly match the required liability payments. Moreover, there appears to be no significant social cost to the government's issuing consumption-linked bonds, and there may be social benefits from the government's financing the deficit in this form.[2] While the principal reason for discussing the creation of such bonds here is their essential role in pension plans, I believe that, independent of pension plans, consumption-linked bonds would be an ideal investment instrument for private saving generally. If this belief is correct, and if the government did issue such bonds, then it is likely that private financial intermediaries would introduce consumption-linked annuities and corporations would issue consumption-linked liabilities. The existence of such private sector financial instruments would serve to make consumption-indexed pension plans more efficient by providing better pricing information for the plans' annuities and a broader base of securities in which to invest the plans' assets.

Even if the private sector could efficiently provide consumption-linked bonds and life annuities, as I noted in Section 18.1, private pension plans alone cannot handle either information cost or utility externalities. While it is difficult to measure how other people's welfare enters into an individual's utility function, I believe that it is likely to do so in a relative fashion. That is, we are less inclined to worry about or make transfers to those who have a relatively high standard of living. Among those with the same current standard of living, we are more sympathetic toward those who have fallen on "hard times" and experienced a decline from their past standard. If this assessment is correct, then a public plan along the lines discussed here appears to efficiently handle this utility externality for people in retirement. By requiring individuals to make contributions proportional to their consumption during their working years and investing these contributions in per capita consumption-linked life annuities, the plan ensures an accumulated amount sufficient to support a retirement consumption path for individuals at a level (relative to aggregate per capita consumption) similar to that which they enjoyed during the working phase of their life. Linking benefits to per capita aggregate consumption provides for a continuation of their standard of living throughout the retirement years. Thus, a plan with these features meets the objective of ensuring an appropriate relative standard of living in retirement for everyone and it also handles the free-rider problem.

These features do not, of course, solve the redistribution problem for those whose relative standard of living is too low during their working years. However, a reasonable argument can be made that it is more efficient to make the necessary transfers by other, more direct means at the

---

2 Fischer (1983) discusses a number of social benefits from the government's issuing wage-income-linked bonds, including possible intergenerational risk sharing that private markets cannot provide. Many of the same benefits would come from consumption-linked bonds, and indeed, if a consumption tax is less distorting than a wage tax, then the consumption-linked bonds may be superior.

time when they are needed (during the working years) instead of attempting to do so indirectly by redistributing future benefits within the retirement plan. There are other good economic arguments for keeping the transfer system and the retirement system separate, but that is not the focus of this chapter. I would note, however, that the plan analyzed here would automatically handle much of the redistribution problem for people in their retirement years if a proper transfer system were devised for people during their working years. Transfers received and consumed during the working years will increase future retirement benefits proportionately because the required contributions to the plan are proportional to consumption. Transfers in the form of a total or partial credit for the individual's required contribution to his retirement account would work in a similar fashion, provided that the cost of this transfer is not borne by the retirement plan itself.

Having reviewed the merits of a consumption-indexed pension plan, I now turn to the issue of its feasibility. Although the idea of investing accumulations in consumption-linked life annuities is new, the basic structure of the plan is simple and is essentially the same as a standard defined-contribution pension plan. It is therefore a relatively easy plan to explain and understand. Its format also has the attraction of stability in the sense that neither its basic structure nor the parameters of the structure (such as the contribution rate or the period of accumulation) would require much change over time, even in the face of significant variations in economic conditions. It does, however, require that an appropriate measure for aggregate per capita consumption be chosen.[3] To select the proper measure would require further study to determine how consumer durable purchases should be treated and whether or not to include items such as leisure time which are not normally included in measures of consumption. There is also the issue of what population measure to use. While investigation of these issues is beyond the scope of this chapter, their resolution is not an insurmountable problem. With this measurement problem solved, there does not appear to be any major difficulty with the government's issuing consumption-linked bonds and using their prices to determine the value of consumption-linked life annuities.

The main feasibility problems with a public plan as described here are likely to be associated with the method of collecting the required contributions and the maintenance of the individual accumulation accounts. Though I have not investigated in detail the amount of computation and record keeping required in the current Social Security system, it appears

---

3 It is not, of course, true that every model of lifetime consumption choice will lead to an efficient allocation of retirement consumption which depends only on aggregate per capita consumption. For example, Breeden's (1979) important theorems on this matter will not apply if utility of consumption is state dependent.

likely that the amount required for individual account maintenance would not be significantly larger for a consumption-linked plan. However, the collection in such a plan would probably be more difficult than for current Social Security because the base is consumption rather than income. As outlined, the plan requires that the amount of each contribution be identifiable in the same way that individual federal income tax payments are identified. Therefore, the method of collection necessary for its implementation would probably be like that of the income tax, with consumption determined as the residual from a cash flow analysis. The feasibility of such a collection system is currently a topic of considerable discussion among economists, principally in the context of the feasibility of an individual expenditure tax (see Aaron and Boskin, eds, 1980; Pechman, ed., 1980). Although I will not undertake a serious analysis of feasibility here, I would note that there is an important difference between an expenditure tax and the mandatory contribution part of a fully funded retirement plan. Because it is a defined-contribution plan and accumulations earn a competitive rate, cheating is less of a problem to the extent that people treat contributions as saving and not as a tax. Indeed, the rich, high-income, and well-informed people who might be thought to have the greatest incentive and opportunity to cheat on a tax are probably the most likely to view such contributions as saving, since these are the people who now voluntarily enter into deferred compensation and Keogh plans. In general, those who cheat on contributions are primarily cheating themselves. However, one slight modification which might make the collection part of the plan more effective would be to have withholding of the required contribution based on income, as is currently the practice for Social Security, and then to have refunds or additional contributions based on the computation of consumption made in conjunction with the filing of federal income tax returns.

A more radical modification of the plan described here was suggested to me by Lester Thurow. The collections for the plan would be done at the aggregate level by a value-added tax. The aggregate amount collected would then be distributed as contributions to individual accumulation accounts in proportion to the amount of income reported on the individual's federal tax return. The administrative benefits of this modification depend on the relative costs of collection for a value-added tax versus a residual cash flow computation on the income tax return. It does have the attractive feature that those who cheat by under-reporting income on their federal tax will lose some of their retirement benefits (which they presumably paid for through the value-added tax). The principal disadvantage of this modification is that the aggregate contributions will now be treated as a consumption tax, which can distort the labor–leisure decision. However, the credit to individual retirement accounts based on income will act as a subsidy to wage income, which may offset this distortion at least in part.[4] This modification would become considerably more attractive if the government chooses to use a value-added tax to finance general government expenditures.

In summary, although the method of collecting contributions poses the principal feasibility problem for such a public plan, a number of different methods would seem to serve as close substitutes provided that it remains essentially a defined-contribution plan which earns a fair rate of return on accumulations and pays benefits indexed to consumption.

If a policy decision were made to adopt a public pension plan with a basic structure like the one analyzed here, there would still be the further critical policy decision of what fraction of retirement period consumption should be the target for the plan. Presumably, those who are most concerned about the plan's success in dealing with information cost and utility externalities would advocate a high fraction and those who are most concerned about preserving individual choice would advocate a low fraction. The correct policy decision will surely depend on the amount of other retirement saving that people are likely to make, especially in housing and private pension plans. The resolution of this policy issue, therefore, requires an analysis of the overall pension system. Since that was the note on which I began, it seems an appropriate place for me to end.

---

4   As I have shown elsewhere (Merton, 1983c), the distortion of the labor–leisure decision of a consumption tax can be offset by linking future retirement benefits to current wage income.

An Analytic Derivation
of the Cost of Deposit
Insurance and Loan
Guarantees:

An Application of Modern Option
Pricing Theory

It is not uncommon in the arrangement of a loan to include as part of the financial package a guarantee of the loan by a third party. Examples are guarantees by a parent company of loans made to its subsidiaries or government guarantees of loans made to private corporations. Also included would be guarantees of bank deposits by the Federal Deposit Insurance Corporation. As with other forms of insurance, the issuing of a guarantee imposes a liability or cost on the guarantor. In this chapter, a formula is derived to evaluate this cost. The method used is to demonstrate an isomorphic correspondence between loan guarantees and common-stock put options, and then to use the well-developed theory of option pricing to derive the formula.

19.1 INTRODUCTION

The essential functions of a bank are to lend money to firms and individuals and to serve as a riskless repository for the short-term funds of firms and individuals. The bank charges interest on the loans and pays interest or provides noncash services to depositors for the use of their funds.

The traditional advantages to depositors of using a bank rather than making direct market purchases of fixed-income securities are economies of scale, smaller transactions costs, liquidity, and convenience. However,

Reproduced from *Journal of Banking and Finance*, 1, June 1977, 3–11. Aid from the National Science Foundation is gratefully acknowledged.

these are important advantages only if deposits can be treated as riskless. Otherwise, to determine which bank to use, the depositor must assume the role of a security analyst and analyze the balance sheets of the bank, its management, and overall market conditions to determine the risks. Even if such analyses are performed, it would be prudent for the depositor to diversify his holdings across many banks. Moreover, these analyses and holdings would have to be revised as conditions changed.

Hence, for the small depositor particularly, there are large information and surveillance costs to be saved if the institutional structure of the bank were such that the safety of the deposits was assured without requiring these analyses. While this could be accomplished by requiring that banks invest only in short-term government securities, such a requirement would not allow banks to perform their other function, which is to lend money to firms and individuals. Moreover, such a restriction would require surveillance to ensure compliance. While such surveillance could be carried out in a centralized fashion (e.g. by a government regulatory agency), the financial burden from noncompliance would still be borne by the depositor.

A sensible alternative choice would be to have third-party guarantees where the capability and willingness of that party to meet its obligations are beyond question. For the scale of the banking system, this almost certainly means that the third party would be the government or one of its agencies. While these guarantees could take the form of guarantees on the loans made by banks, a less expensive and more efficient alternative form is to guarantee the deposits. Indeed, one observes widespread use of such deposit guarantees although their institutional forms differ. In the United States, there is the separately funded Federal Deposit Insurance Corporation (FDIC) for commercial banks and the Federal Savings and Loan Insurance Corporation (FSLIC) for savings and loan associations. In other countries the government may own the banks or there may simply be a widespread belief that the government will act to, in effect, guarantee deposits. Indeed, it is probably fair to say that, although the FDIC is separately funded, there is a further belief that the US government would take the necessary actions to protect depositors in the event of a major default by banks that bankrupted the FDIC. To the extent that such implicit guarantees are politically binding, they impose a cost on the guarantor which is essentially the same as for explicit guarantees.

In this chapter, a systematic theory for determining these costs is presented.[1] As will be shown, techniques for solving this problem can be found in the seemingly unrelated area of finance called option pricing theory. Indeed, the properties of deposit insurance viewed as a security are

---

*1 For later research along the lines here, see Merton (1978 (this volume, Ch. 20), 1990b), Jones and Mason (1980), Sosin (1980), Ronn and Verma (1986), Pennacchi (1987a, b), Selby, Franks, and Karki (1988), and Fries and Perraudin (1991).

isomorphic to those of a put option.[2] This is fortunate because recent research has led to a major "breakthrough" in the development of an option pricing theory.

In a seminal paper, Black and Scholes (1973) developed an explicit formula for pricing call options[3] on common stocks. While there had been a number of earlier efforts dating back at least to 1900, the Black–Scholes analysis is a major advance for two reasons. First, the important assumptions required to derive the formula are substantially weaker than in the earlier efforts. Second, the inputs required by the formula are either directly observable variables or variables that can be readily estimated. Hence, the formula can be empirically tested, and if proved satisfactory, it can then be used as a practical tool.

Such tests have been made in at least two studies with generally favorable outcomes.[4] Moreover, the Black–Scholes formula is probably the analytical tool most widely used by investors and market-makers in the rapidly growing organized option-exchange markets.

While call options are a very specialized type of financial instrument, it is straightforward to see that the Black–Scholes techniques can be applied to the pricing of corporate liabilities in general. Hence their original analysis has led to a unified theory for the pricing of virtually any financial claim on the firm.[5] Further, because the formulas derived do not require a history of market prices for the type of security being evaluated, it shows great promise as an appraisal tool for evaluating nontradeable securities such as insurance contracts, which is the substantive subject of this chapter.[6]

19.2   A MODEL FOR PRICING DEPOSIT INSURANCE

As discussed in Section 19.1, the development of the deposit-insurance pricing model has as its foundation the isomorphic relation between deposit insurance and common-stock put options. Hence, before develop-

---

2   The essential terms of the contract are defined later in the chapter. For further discussion of put options, see Black and Scholes (1973), Merton (1973a (this volume, Ch. 8); 1973c), Brennan and Schwartz (1977a), and Parkinson (1977).

3   A call option gives its owner the right to buy a specified number of shares of a given stock at a specified price per share on or before a specified date. For an alternative derivation of the Black–Scholes model, see Merton (1973a; this volume, Ch. 8). Smith (1976) provides an excellent survey article of the research on option pricing theory.

4   See Black and Scholes (1972) and Galai (1975).

5   See Merton (1974; this volume, Ch. 12) and Smith (1976).

6   Brennan and Schwartz (1976) have used a similar model to evaluate the cost of certain insurance company guarantees of equity-based life insurance plans.

ing the model, I make a brief digression to summarize the relevant findings in option pricing theory.

The essential terms of a "European"[7] put option on a common stock are that its owner has the right to sell a specified number of shares of a given stock at a specified price per share (the "exercise price") on a specified date (the "expiration date"). A put option purchase is different from the sale of a futures contract because the put owner has a choice whether or not to "exercise his option" to sell at the specified price. Indeed, if this option is not exercised on the expiration date, the contract expires and is worthless. Hence, if on the expiration date the stock price per share, S, is higher than the exercise price per share, E, the put owner would clearly not exercise his right to sell the stock at the exercise price when he could sell it on the open market at a higher price. In this case, the owner would allow the put to expire worthless. However, if on the expiration date the stock price was lower than the exercise price, then the put owner would exercise his right, and the value of the put option would be the difference between the exercise price and the stock price, $E - S$, times the number of shares specified in the put contract.

Thus, the value of a put on one share of stock at the expiration date can be written as

$$P(0) = \max(0, E - S) \tag{19.1}$$

where $P(T)$ is the price of a put with length of time T to go before expiration.

Since the value of the put at expiration depends on the stock price, its value prior to expiration will depend on the probability distribution for the range of stock prices on the expiration date.

Using the standard "frictionless" market asumptions and the additional assumption that the stochastic process generating the stock's returns can be described by a diffusion process with a constant variance per unit time,[8] Black and Scholes impose the condition of "no arbitrage opportunities" to derive a formula for the value of a put option. The formula can be written as

$$P(T) = E \exp(-rT)\Phi(y_2) - S\Phi(y_1) \tag{19.2}$$

7 The term "European" is applied to options that can only be exercised on the expiration date. An "American" type of option can be exercised on or before the expiration date.

8 The model can be derived in various modified forms to allow for relaxation of most of the "frictionless" market assumptions. Also, the constant variance rate assumption is not necessary. See Smith (1976) for a discussion of these modifications. For expositional convenience, the original Black–Scholes assumptions are retained throughout the chapter.

where

$$y_1 \equiv \frac{\log(E/S) - (r + \sigma^2/2)T}{\sigma T^{1/2}}$$

$$y_2 \equiv y_1 + \sigma T^{1/2}$$

$\Phi(\cdot)$ is the cumulative standard normal density function, S is the current price per share for the stock, r is the market rate of interest per unit time on riskless securities, and σ^2 is the variance rate per unit time for the (logarithmic) rate of the return on the stock. While (19.2) may appear formidable, it only requires as inputs the interest rate, the exercise price, the current stock price, the length of time until expiration, and the variance rate. Of these, only the variance rate on the stock is not directly observable, and it can be reasonably estimated. Note, more importantly, that neither the expected return on the stock nor investor's preferences are required as inputs. Hence the formula is robust with respect to both these nonobservable variables. This completes the digression.

With this as background, consider the following simple model of a firm that borrows money by issuing a single homogeneous debt issue. The terms of the debt are that the firm promises to pay a total of B dollars on a specified date (the "maturity" date) and, in the event that the promised payment is not made, the firm defaults to the bondholders all the assets of the firm. There are no interim or coupon payments required on the debt, and so the debt is a term discount issue.

On the maturity date, if the value of the firm's assets, V, is larger than the promised payment on the bond issue, B, then it is in the interests of the equityholders for the management to make the payment (by selling assets if necessary). Hence, the value of the debt issue at this point will be B, and the value of equity will be $V - B$. However, if on the maturity date the value of the firm's assets is less than the promised payment, then the management will be unable to make the payment even by selling assets. Hence, the firm is defaulted to the bondholders and the value of the debt issue will be V. The value of the equity will be zero.

In an abbreviated form, at the maturity date, the value of the debt can be written as $\min(V, B)$ and the value of the equity as $\max(0, V - B)$. As long as there is a positive probability that the value of the assets on the maturity date can be less than the promised payment, then there is a positive probability of bankruptcy, and the debt is risky. In another paper (Merton, 1974; this volume, Ch. 12), I have analyzed the evaluation of such risky debt along Black–Scholes lines.

Consider the impact of a third-party guarantee of the payment to the bondholders where there is no uncertainty about the obligations of the guarantee being met. The terms of the guarantee are that, in the event that the management does not make the promised payment to the bondholders, the guarantor will meet these payments. However, if such an event occurs, the firm will default its assets to the guarantor. In effect, the guarantor has ensured that the value of the firm's assets on the maturity date will be at least B dollars. Like a traditional insurance policy, the guarantee has value to the insured and imposes a cost on the insurer. Hence, the firm would normally be expected to pay for the guarantee an amount at least equal to its actuarial cost.

To determine this cost, I begin by reexamining the payoffs to the various claims on the maturity date. If the value of the firm's assets exceeds the promised payment, then, as without the guarantee, the bondholders receive B and the equityholders receive $V - B$. However, if the value of the assets is less than the promised payment, then the bondholders receive B, the equityholders receive nothing, and the third-party guarantor has a net payout or loss of $B - V$, the discrepancy between the promised payment and the value of assets.

In an abbreviated form, at the maturity date, the value of equity is the same with or without the guarantee, $\max(0, V - B)$; the value of the debt is always B and therefore riskless; and the value of the guarantor's "claim" is $\min(0, V - B)$ which is nonpositive. In effect, the result of the guarantee is to create an additional cash inflow to the firm of $-\min(0, V - B)$ dollars. But $-\min(0, V - B)$ can be rewritten as $\max(0, B - V)$. Hence, if $G(T)$ is the value to the firm of the guarantee when the length of time until the maturity date of the bond is T, then

$$G(0) = \max(0, B - V) \qquad (19.3)$$

By comparing (19.3) with (19.1), we see that the payoff structure of the loan guarantee is identical with that of a put option, where in (19.3) the promised payment B corresponds to the exercise price E, and the value of the firm's assets V corresponds to the common stock's price S. Essentially, by guaranteeing the debt issue, the guarantor has issued a put option on the assets of the firm which gives management the right to sell those assets for B dollars on the maturity date of the debt.

Hence, using the identical arguments used by Black and Scholes to derive the value of a put option written in (19.2), we can derive a formula for the value of the guarantee, and it can be written as

$$G(T) = B\exp(-rT)\,\Phi(x_2) - V\Phi(x_1) \qquad (19.4)$$

where

$$x_1 \equiv \frac{\log(B/V) - (r + \sigma^2/2)T}{\sigma T^{1/2}}$$

$$x_2 \equiv x_1 + \sigma T^{1/2}$$

V is the current value of the assets of the firm, and σ^2 is now the variance rate per unit time for the logarithmic changes in the value of the assets.

Equation (19.4) can be used to evaluate the cost to the guarantor of guaranteeing a discount debt issue with a face value of B dollars and maturity T.

Let $B \exp[-R(T)T]$ be the market value of the debt when there is no guarantee, where $R(T)$ is the promised yield. Clearly, the market value of the debt with a guarantee is $B \exp(-rT)$ and therefore

$$G(T) + B \exp[-R(T)T] = B \exp(-rT)$$

or

$$\frac{G(T)}{B \exp(-rT)} = 1 - \exp\{-[R(T) - r]T\} \qquad (19.4a)$$

Equation (19.4a) gives the cost of the loan guarantee as a fraction of the amount of money raised. I have computed (Merton, 1974; this volume, Table 12.1) values of $R(T) - r$ for a variety of maturity dates, variance rates, and firm values. Inspection of these values will demonstrate that the cost of loan guarantees can be substantial.

Now, suppose that the firm is a bank and the debt issue corresponds to deposits. Because most deposits are of the demand type, the model assumption of a term-debt issue is not strictly applicable. However, if one reinterprets the length of time until maturity as the length of time until the next audit of the bank's assets, then from the point of view of the guarantor the model's structure is reasonable even for demand deposits. Therefore, from the point of view of the guarantor, deposits can be treated as if they were term and interest bearing.

For deposit insurance where both principal and interest are guaranteed, the insured deposits will be riskless and their current value can be written as

$$D = B \exp(-rT) \qquad (19.5)$$

If g is the cost of the guarantee per dollar of insured deposits, i.e. $G(T)/D$, then from (19.4) the formula for g can be written as a function of two variables:

$$g(d, \tau) = \Phi(h_2) - \frac{1}{d}\Phi(h_1) \qquad (19.6)$$

where

$$h_1 \equiv \frac{\log(d) - \tau/2}{\tau^{1/2}}$$

$$h_2 \equiv h_1 + \tau^{1/2}$$

$d \equiv D/V$ is the current deposit-to-asset value ratio, and $\tau \equiv \sigma^2 T$ is the variance of the logarithmic change in the value of the assets during the term of the deposits. Hence, as long as the deposit-to-asset value ratio and the volatility of the underlying assets remain fixed, the cost of deposit insurance per dollar of deposits is constant. As one would expect, the change in the cost with respect to an increase in the deposit-to-asset value ratio is positive and is given by

$$\frac{\partial g}{\partial d} = \frac{\Phi(h_1)}{d^2}$$

The change in the cost with respect to an increase in τ is also positive and is given by

$$\frac{\partial g}{\partial \tau} = \frac{\Phi'(h_1)}{2d\tau^{1/2}}$$

where the prime denotes the first derivative. Hence, an increase in either the variance rate of the assets or the length of time that the insurance is in force will increase the cost per dollar of deposits.

From (19.6), we have that changes in the market rate of interest will have no effect on the cost of deposit insurance unless such changes affect the deposit-to-asset value ratio. To develop some sense of the magnitudes implied by (19.6), Table 19.1 displays the cost per dollar of deposits for different values of d and τ. It is typical for banks to have relatively low volatility assets and high deposit-to-asset ratios. The reader is reminded that V is something like the "fair" or "market" value of the assets and not the book value. To put the various τ values in Table 19.1 in perspective, the $\tau = 0.003$ would correspond to a one-year term where the volatility of the assets is similar to those historically observed from holding long-term US government bonds.[9] Lower values of τ correspond to either less volatile assets or a shorter term. The table includes values where the cost exceeded \$0.0001 per dollar of deposits. The $d = 1$ case is included as the theoretically limiting case where asset value equals deposits.

---

*9 In the decade following the original publication of the paper, bond prices have been far more volatile than this historical number indicates. At times, the measured τ has been as high as 0.040.

Table 19.1 **Cost of Deposit Insurance per Dollar of Insured Deposits**

Cost of Deposit Insurance ($)	Deposit-to-Asset Value Ratio	τ
0.00055	0.85	0.00600
0.00040	0.85	0.00550
0.00028	0.85	0.00500
0.00018	0.85	0.00450
0.00011	0.85	0.00400
0.00326	0.90	0.00600
0.00274	0.90	0.00550
0.00223	0.90	0.00500
0.00176	0.90	0.00450
0.00132	0.90	0.00400
0.00093	0.90	0.00350
0.00060	0.90	0.00300
0.00015	0.90	0.00200
0.01209	0.95	0.00600
0.01102	0.95	0.00550
0.00992	0.95	0.00500
0.00880	0.95	0.00450
0.00765	0.95	0.00400
0.00647	0.95	0.00350
0.00528	0.95	0.00300
0.00287	0.95	0.00200
0.00172	0.95	0.00150
0.00072	0.95	0.00100
0.00033	0.95	0.00075
0.03089	1.00	0.00600
0.02958	1.00	0.00550
0.02820	1.00	0.00500
0.02676	1.00	0.00450
0.02523	1.00	0.00400
0.02360	1.00	0.00350
0.02185	1.00	0.00300
0.01784	1.00	0.00200
0.01545	1.00	0.00150
0.01262	1.00	0.00100
0.01093	1.00	0.00075
0.00892	1.00	0.00050
0.00631	1.00	0.00025
0.00564	1.00	0.00020
0.00489	1.00	0.00015
0.00399	1.00	0.00010
0.00282	1.00	0.00005
0.00126	1.00	0.00001

20

On the Cost of Deposit Insurance When There are Surveillance Costs

A model for evaluating the cost of deposit insurance is derived that explicitly takes into account surveillance or auditing costs and provides for random auditing times. The method used to derive this evaluation formula exploits the isomorphic correspondence between loan guarantees and common-stock put options. Because of these auditing costs, the equilibrium rate of return on deposits will be below the market interest rate even in a competitive banking industry with no transactions costs. Further, it is shown that the auditing cost component of the deposit insurance premium is, in effect, paid for by the depositors, and the put option component is paid for by the equityholders of the bank.

20.1 INTRODUCTION

In an earlier paper on the cost of deposit insurance and loan guarantees (Merton, 1977a; this volume, Ch. 19), I demonstrated an isomorphic correspondence between loan guarantees and common-stock put options. Using this correspondence and the well-developed theory of option pricing, a formula was derived to evaluate these liabilities. If the guarantor chooses to audit only at the end of a finite, specified period, then the same analysis applies to the evaluation of demand-deposit guarantees. While the reason given for the finite time between audits was the cost to the guarantor of "continuous surveillance," no explicit recognition of these costs was presented in the model.

Although based on the same structure, the model developed in this chapter extends the earlier development to take into account explicitly

Reproduced from *Journal of Business*, 51, July 1978, 439–52. I thank Fischer Black for many helpful discussions. This paper was presented at the Joint Stanford–Berkeley Seminar in Finance, February 1977. I thank the participants for their comments. Aid from the National Science Foundation is gratefully acknowledged.

surveillance or auditing costs and to provide for random auditing times. Under the assumption of free entry into the banking industry, the equilibrium interest rate on deposits is derived. Further, it is shown that, in effect, depositors "pay" for the surveillance costs and the equityholders of the bank "pay" for the put option component of the deposit guarantee.

20.2   ASSUMPTIONS OF THE MODEL

In this chapter, a bank is defined to be an institution that holds financial assets and finances their purchase by equity and by issuing deposits that are fully insured. From the point of view of depositors, each bank is a perfect substitute for every other bank, and therefore $R + s$ must be the same for all banks where R is the interest rate on deposits and s is the rate paid in the form of services. The banking industry is assumed competitive in the sense that there are no barriers to entry.

It is assumed that the deposits are guaranteed by the government or one of its agencies (e.g. the Federal Deposit Insurance Corporation, FDIC). While the formal analysis does not require that the guarantor be the government, it does require that the capability and willingness of the guarantor to meet its obligations are essentially beyond question. Otherwise, a second guarantor might be required for the first one; and a third for the second; and so on. The resulting "layering" of surveillance costs would probably be inefficient. Moreover, in the absence of detailed information and analysis, depositors might well use the size of the guarantor as a selector for greater safety, and this tendency could make it difficult for the "guarantor industry" to the banking system to have a competitive structure.

To develop the model, the following additional assumptions are made.

1   Trading in securities takes place continuously in time.
2   The securities and exchange markets are "sufficiently perfect," and asset-return dynamics are such that securities are priced so as to satisfy the Security Market Line equation in the (continuous-time version of the) Capital Asset Pricing Model (CAPM).[1]
3   There exists an exchange market where some investors and institutions (including the banks and the FDIC) can borrow or lend at the same rate

---

1   The Security Market Line equation states that the equilibrium expected excess return on a security is proportional to the expected excess return on the market where the proportionality factor, called "beta," is equal to the ratio of the security's return covariance with the market to the variance of the return on the market. The CAPM is thoroughly discussed in Jensen (1972b). See Merton (1973b; this volume, Ch. 15) for the continuous-time version used in this chapter.

of interest r, which is taken to be constant through time. Therefore, to avoid arbitrage by these investors, $r \geq R + s$.

4   At least some investors face a transactions cost for lending in the exchange market that can be measured for the jth investor as tc_j per unit time per dollar. So, the return per unit time for lending by the jth investor is $r_j = r - tc_j$. Hence, if $R + s > r_j$, then the jth investor will lend indirectly through deposits, and if $R + s < r_j$, then the jth investor will lend directly through the exchange market.

5   Although individual deposits are of the demand type, it is assumed that the dynamics for aggregate deposits for a given bank, D, are nonstochastic and described by $dD/dt = gD$ where the percentage growth in deposits, g, is a known constant.[2] The dynamics for the value of a given bank's assets, V, can be described by a diffusion-type stochastic process with stochastic differential equation

$$dV = [\alpha V - (R + s)D]\, dt + dD + \sigma V\, dz$$
$$= [\alpha V - (R + s - g)D]\, dt + \sigma V\, dz \qquad V > 0$$
$$= 0 \qquad\qquad\qquad\qquad\qquad\qquad\qquad\quad V = 0$$

where α is the instantaneous expected rate of return on the assets per unit time; σ^2 is the instantaneous variance of the return per unit time and is assumed constant; dz is a standard Gauss–Wiener process.

6   The FDIC charges the bank a one-time premium to insure all the deposits of the bank in perpetuity provided that the bank is solvent (i.e. $V > D$). For purposes of this provision, solvency of the bank is determined by audit.[3] If, at the time of an audit, the bank is found to be solvent, then the bank continues operations unaffected. If, at the time of an audit, the bank is insolvent (i.e. $V < D$), then the FDIC liquidates the bank and pays off the depositors. It uses a random-time audit procedure where the event of an audit is Poisson distributed with characteristic parameter λ, and successive audit times are independently and identically distributed. There is a cost per audit to the FDIC which can be described by a first-degree homogeneous function $C(V, D)$. Therefore, the audit cost per dollar of deposits, C/D, can be written as $c(x)$ where $x \equiv V/D$. It is assumed that $c(x)$ is a continuous and bounded function for all $x \geq 0$.

2   To keep the bank's treatment of deposits from becoming a "Ponzi game," the exogenous growth rate of aggregate deposits, g, is assumed to be less than or equal to the total return on deposits, $R + s$.

3   The one exception is when $V = 0$ and $g < R + s$. In this case, the bank will be unable to pay the promised return, $R + s$, on deposits. This "default" is assumed to cause an immediate audit by the FDIC. This exception can be formally handled in the framework of the text by having λ "jump" to infinity when $V = 0$ and $g < R + s$.

20.3 THE EVALUATION OF FEDERAL DEPOSIT INSURANCE CORPORATION LIABILITIES

When the FDIC insures a bank's deposits, it receives a premium and assumes a liability of actual and potential future cash outflows for surveillance costs and for any "shortfall" between assets and deposits in the event of the bank's liquidation. In this section, a formula for the value of these liabilities is derived using the methods pioneered by Black and Scholes in the evaluation of options and corporate liabilities.[4] For convenience, the values will be derived treating the cash outflows as positive inflows, and therefore the derived values will be positive. As with standard cost function analysis, these values will be the "cost" to the FDIC.

Assume that the value of the liability can be written as a twice-differentiable function $P(V, D)$ with continuous first derivatives.[5] The return on the liability and its change in price over a short time interval will depend not only on the changes in V and D, but also on whether an audit takes place during that interval. If an audit takes place, then there is a cash flow of $C(V, D)$. In addition, if the bank is insolvent, then there is a second cash flow of $D - V$ and the liability of the FDIC ceases (i.e. $P = 0$). If dR_P is the rate of return on the liability, then, using Itô's lemma,[6] we can write dR_P (conditional on $P(V, D) = P$) as

$$P\, dR_P = L[P(V, D)]\, dt + \sigma V \frac{\partial P}{\partial V}\, dz \qquad \text{if no audit occurs}$$

$$= L[P(V, D)]\, dt + \sigma V \frac{\partial P}{\partial V}\, dz + C(V, D)$$
$$\text{if an audit occurs and } V > D$$

$$(20.1)$$

$$= L[P(V, D)]\, dt + \sigma V \frac{\partial P}{\partial V}\, dz + C(V, D) + D - V - P$$

$$\text{if an audit occurs and } V < D$$

4   See Black and Scholes (1973). Smith (1976) is an excellent review article that covers many applications of this method to the pricing of financial instruments. In particular, Brennan and Schwartz (1976) have used the method to evaluate the cost of certain insurance company guarantees of equity-based life insurance plans.

5   While this is stated as an assumption, I have proved elsewhere (Merton, 1977b; this volume, Ch. 13) that if such a "smooth" solution exists, then it is the equilibrium valuation function; i.e. other "candidate" solutions that are either discontinuous or have discontinuous first derivatives at any interior point cannot be the equilibrium solution.

6   For references on Itô's lemma and extensions and for a treatment of stochastic differential equations that combine "mixed" Wiener and Poisson processes, see Merton (1976a; this volume, Ch. 9, especially footnote 8).

where L is an operator defined by

$$L \equiv \frac{1}{2}\sigma^2 V^2 \frac{\partial^2}{\partial V^2} + [\alpha V - (R + s - g)D]\frac{\partial}{\partial V} + gD\frac{\partial}{\partial D}$$

and, with probability one, no more than one audit occurs in an instant.

If the event of an audit is independent of the return on the stock market, then from (20.1) the only source of systematic risk in the return on P is through its dependence on V (i.e. the dz term in (20.1)). Therefore, the beta of the return on P, β_P, can be written in terms of the beta of the return on V, β_V, as

$$\beta_P = \frac{\sigma V(\partial P/\partial V)}{P}\frac{\beta_V}{\sigma} \tag{20.2}$$

From Assumption 2 and (20.2), the equilibrium expected return per unit time on P, α_P, must satisfy

$$\alpha_P - r = \frac{V(\partial P/\partial V)(\alpha - r)}{P} \tag{20.3}$$

Because the event of audit is Poisson distributed, the probability of an audit over the next instant is $\lambda\, dt$ and the probability of no audit is $1 - \lambda\, dt$. Taking expectations in (20.1), we have

$$P\alpha_P = L[P(V, D)] + \lambda C(V, D) \qquad \text{for } V > D$$
$$= L[P(V, D)] + \lambda[C(V, D) + D - V - P] \quad \text{for } V < D \tag{20.4}$$

Combining (20.3) and (20.4) and simplifying terms, we have that P must satisfy the partial differential equations

$$\frac{1}{2}\sigma^2 V^2 \frac{\partial^2 P}{\partial V^2} + [rV - (R + s - g)D]\frac{\partial P}{\partial V} + gD\frac{\partial P}{\partial D} - rP + \lambda C(V, D) = 0$$

$$\text{for } V > D \qquad (20.5\text{a})$$

and

$$\frac{1}{2}\sigma^2 V^2 \frac{\partial^2 P}{\partial V^2} + [rV - (R + s - g)D]\frac{\partial P}{\partial V} + gD\frac{\partial P}{\partial D} - (r + \lambda)P$$

$$+ \lambda[C(V, D) + D - V] = 0 \qquad \text{for } V < D \qquad (20.5\text{b})$$

Equations (20.5) can be converted to ordinary differential equations by the change in variables $x \equiv V/D$ and $p \equiv P/D$ where x is the asset-to-deposit ratio and p is the FDIC liability per dollar of deposits. If $p_1 \equiv p(x)$ for $x \geq 1$ and $p_2 \equiv p(x)$ for $0 \leq x \leq 1$, then from (20.5) we have

$$\tfrac{1}{2}\sigma^2 x^2 p_1'' + [(r - g)x - (R + s - g)]p_1' - (r - g)p_1 + \lambda c(x) = 0 \qquad x \geq 1$$
$$\tag{20.6a}$$

and

$$\tfrac{1}{2}\sigma^2 x^2 p_2'' + [(r - g)x - (R + s - g)]p_2' - (r + \lambda - g)p_2 + \lambda[c(x) + 1 - x]$$

$$= 0 \qquad x \leq 1 \tag{20.6b}$$

where primes denote derivatives.

The boundary conditions for (20.6) are as follows:

$$p_1(1) = p_2(1) \quad \text{(continuity of } p(x)) \tag{20.7a}$$

$$p_1'(1) = p_2'(1) \quad \text{(continuity of } p'(x)) \tag{20.7b}$$

$$p_2(0) = \frac{\lambda[1 + c(0)]}{r + \lambda - g} \tag{20.7c}$$

$$p_1(x) \text{ is bounded as } x \to \infty \tag{20.7d}$$

Boundary conditions (20.7a) and (20.7b) are required by continuity, and (20.7c) and (20.7d) are proved in Appendix 20A.

The general homogeneous solutions to (20.6) will be confluent hypergeometric functions. However, in the particular case where the growth rate in aggregate deposits equals the total return on deposits (i.e. $g = R + s$), the homogeneous solutions are simple polynomials. In light of the substantial simplification in the solutions and because it appears to do little violence to the general substantive properties of the results, I adopt this additional assumption for the balance of the chapter.

With this assumption, the complete solution to (20.6) can be written as

$$p_1(x) = a_1 x + a_2 x^{-\delta} + Q_1(x) \qquad x \geq 1 \tag{20.8a}$$

$$p_2(x) = b_1 x^k + b_2 x^\xi + \frac{\lambda}{\mu + \lambda} - x + Q_2(x) \qquad x \leq 1 \tag{20.8b}$$

where the various parameters and functions are defined as follows:

$$Q_1(x) \equiv \frac{\lambda \delta}{\mu(1 + \delta)} \left[x^{-\delta} \int^x y^{\delta - 1} c(y)\, dy - x \int^x y^{-2} c(y)\, dy \right]$$

$$Q_2(x) \equiv \frac{\lambda\delta}{\mu(k - \zeta)}\left[x^\zeta \int^x y^{-\zeta-1}c(y) \, dy - x^k \int^x y^{-k-1}c(y) \, dy\right]$$

$$k \equiv \tfrac{1}{2}\{1 - \delta + [(1 + \delta)^2 + \gamma]^{1/2}\} > 1 \qquad (20.9)$$

$$\zeta \equiv 1 - \delta - k < 0$$

$$\mu \equiv r - g = r - (R + s) > 0$$

$$\gamma \equiv 8\lambda/\sigma^2 > 0$$

$$\delta \equiv 2\mu/\sigma^2 > 0$$

and a_1, a_2, b_1, and b_2 are constants to be chosen so as to satisfy the boundary conditions (20.7).

The solutions in (20.8) depend on the form of the cost function $c(x)$. However, for a variety of functions, the integrations for the $Q_i(x)$ in (20.9) can be performed to yield a closed-form solution. For example, if c is a polynomial, then the Q_i are also polynomials, or if c is exponential, then the Q_i are incomplete gamma functions. While the interested reader can try these various forms, I will assume in further exposition the special case where the audit cost per dollar of deposits is constant (i.e. $c(x) = K$).

In that special case, the solution to (20.8), including boundary conditions (20.7), can be written as

$$p_1(x) = \frac{\lambda K}{\mu} - \frac{1}{\mu(\mu + \lambda)(\delta + k)}[\mu^2(k - 1) + \lambda(\lambda K k - \mu)]x^{-\delta} \qquad x \geq 1$$

$$(20.10a)$$

$$p_2(x) = \frac{\lambda(K + 1)}{\mu + \lambda} - x + \frac{1}{\delta + k}\left[1 + \frac{\delta}{\mu(\mu + \lambda)}(\mu^2 + \lambda^2 K)\right]x^k \qquad x \leq 1$$

$$(20.10b)$$

Inspection of (20.10) shows that, unlike the analysis in Merton (1977a; this volume, Ch. 19), the FDIC liability per dollar of deposits is not a monotonically decreasing function of the asset-to-deposit ratio. The reason is that there are two sources of the FDIC liability: (a) the guarantee of deposits (i.e. the "put option part") which is a monotonically decreasing function, and (b) the surveillance or audit cost which is a monotonically increasing function. The latter increases even though the cost per audit is constant because the expected number of audits prior to a "successful" audit where the bank is found to be insolvent is an increasing function of the asset-to-deposit ratio. Clearly, for a very small asset-to-deposit ratio ($x \ll 1$), an increase in that ratio will cause a tiny increase in the probability of more than one audit prior to liquidation, and it will cause almost a dollar-for-dollar reduction in the liability of the FDIC to the depositors when the bank is (almost certainly) found to be insolvent. Hence, in this

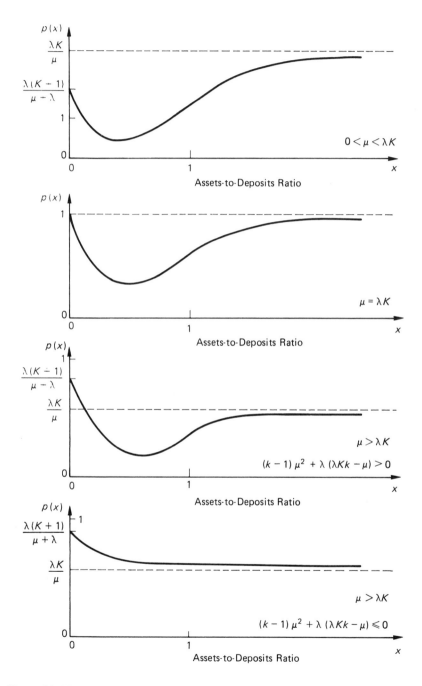

Figure 20.1 Federal Deposit Insurance Corporation Liability per Dollar of Deposits, $p(x)$.

region, the liability would be expected to decline in response to an increase in x. However, for larger values of x, the tradeoff generally shifts more in the other direction until for $x \gg 1$ the increase in audit costs completely swamps the small reduction in deposit liability. Figure 20.1 plots some typical patterns.

The reader is reminded that the FDIC never "observes" itself as having the liability given by $p_2(x)$ because, if it audits a bank and finds it insolvent, the bank is liquidated and the FDIC liability per dollar of deposits at that point is $1 - x + K$. However, to determine the correct solution in the "observed" region $(x > 1)$, it is necessary to solve for $p_2(x)$.

A comparative statics analysis of the impact on the FDIC liability, $p_1(x)$, of changes in the parameter values will generally show a lack of monotonicity for the same reason that a change in the asset-to-deposit ratio did. Hence, any such formal analysis is postponed until equilibrium conditions are derived.

20.4 THE EVALUATION OF BANK EQUITY

To determine the equilibrium deposit rate, it is first necessary to determine the value of bank equityholder's shares. The procedure used follows along the same lines used to derive the value of FDIC liabilities.

Consider a bank that has paid the necessary premium to the FDIC and currently has assets with value V and deposits in the amount of D. Assume that the value of the bank's shares can be written as a twice-differentiable function $F(V, D)$ with continuous first derivatives. As was true for the FDIC liability evaluation, the return on the shares over a short time interval will depend on whether an audit takes place during that interval as well as on changes in V and D. If an audit takes place and the bank is solvent (i.e. $V > D$), then there will be no impact on the shares' return. However, if there is an audit and the bank is insolvent, then the shares become worthless. As was implicitly assumed in the asset-dynamics description in Assumption 5, the equityholders receive no dividend payouts. Hence, using the identical procedure used to derive equations (20.5a) and (20.5b), we have that F must satisfy

$$\tfrac{1}{2}\sigma^2 V^2 \frac{\partial^2 F}{\partial V^2} + [rV - (R + s - g)D]\frac{\partial F}{\partial V} + gD\frac{\partial F}{\partial D} - rF = 0$$

$$\text{for } V > D \qquad (20.11a)$$

$$\tfrac{1}{2}\sigma^2 V^2 \frac{\partial^2 F}{\partial V^2} + [rV - (R + s - g)D]\frac{\partial F}{\partial V} + gD\frac{\partial F}{\partial D} - (r + \lambda)F = 0$$

$$\text{for } V < D \qquad (20.11b)$$

If we define $f(x) \equiv F/D$, the value of equity per dollar of deposits, then (20.11) can be rewritten as a system of ordinary differential equations:

$$\tfrac{1}{2}\sigma^2 x^2 f_1'' + \mu x f_1' - \mu f_1 = 0 \qquad \text{for } x \geq 1 \qquad (20.12a)$$

$$\tfrac{1}{2}\sigma^2 x^2 f_2'' + \mu x f_2' - (\mu + \lambda)f_2 = 0 \qquad \text{for } x \leq 1 \qquad (20.12b)$$

where $f(x) = f_1(x)$ when $x \geq 1$ and $f(x) = f_2(x)$ when $x \leq 1$ and the simplifying assumption that $g = R + s$ has been used.

The boundary conditions to be applied to (20.12), are

$$f_1(1) = f_2(1) \qquad (20.13a)$$

$$f_1'(1) = f_2'(1) \qquad (20.13b)$$

$$f_2(0) = 0 \qquad (20.13c)$$

$$\lim_{x \to \infty}[f_1(x)/x] = 1 \qquad (20.13d)$$

Boundary conditions (20.13a) and (20.13b) are continuity requirements; (20.13c) follows because with probability one the bank will be liquidated and the shares will be worthless; (20.13d) follows because the only liability of the bank, deposits, expressed in units of per dollar of deposits, is bounded.

The complete solution to (20.12) with boundary conditions (20.13) can be written as

$$f_1(x) = x - \frac{k-1}{\delta + k}x^{-\delta} \qquad x \geq 1 \qquad (20.14a)$$

$$f_2(x) = \frac{1 + \delta}{\delta + k}x^k \qquad x \leq 1 \qquad (20.14b)$$

Inspection of (20.14) shows that the equity per dollar of deposits is a monotonically increasing function of the asset-to-deposit ratio. As is usually the case for limited-liability, levered equity, $f(x)$ is a strictly convex function for $x < 1$. However, unlike the standard case, it is strictly concave for $x > 1$.

In the usual limited-liability, levered-equity case (see Merton, 1974; this volume, Ch. 12), the equity position can be viewed as ownership of the assets levered by an unlimited-liability riskless debt issue combined with an implicit put option on the value of the assets. In the case of the bank equity, the position is the same except that the rate paid on the "riskless debt part" is not r but $R + s$. It is the positive spread, $\mu = r - (R + s)$, that induces the concavity. However, the equity is still "levered" in the sense that the percentage change in $f(x)$ for a given percentage change in x is always greater than one.

Not only does the positive spread induce concavity but it also causes many of the usual comparative statics results, such as "an increase in the volatility of the underlying assets will increase the value of levered equity," not to obtain. The common-sense of this departure is that the bank, in addition to its tangible assets as measured by V, has a valuable "intangible" asset: as long as it is solvent the bank pays less than the riskless rate on its deposits. By increasing the volatility of its assets when currently solvent, it increases the likelihood of becoming insolvent and thereby increases the likelihood of losing this intangible asset. Indeed, this effect is strong enough to obtain even when the bank is moderately insolvent. However, if it is already substantially below the solvency level, then by increasing the volatility of its assets the bank will increase the likelihood of becoming solvent by the time of the next audit.

20.5   ON THE EQUILIBRIUM DEPOSIT RATE

Consider an investor or firm that is deciding whether or not to enter the banking industry. If the proposed investment is to have initial financial assets of V and initial deposits of D, then the initial equity investment required, I_e, is $I_e = V + H(V, D) - D$ where $H(V, D)$ is the one-time premium charged by the FDIC for insuring the bank's deposits. To be willing to enter the banking industry, the value of bank equity after entering must be greater than or equal to the initial equity investment required. That is, from (20.14a),

$$Df_1(x) - I_e = D\left(1 - \frac{k-1}{\delta + k} x^{-\delta} - h\right) \geq 0 \qquad (20.15)$$

where $h \equiv H/D$ is the premium per dollar of deposits and (20.14a) is the relevant formula because initially V must exceed D.

If the FDIC is operated on a "no-subsidy"–"no-excess-profits" basis then the premium h must be chosen to cover costs (i.e. $h = p_1(x)$). Substituting for h from (20.10a) into (20.15), we have as a necessary condition for entry

$$\left(1 - \frac{\lambda K}{\mu}\right)\left[1 - \frac{\lambda k x^{-\delta}}{(\mu + \lambda)(\delta + k)}\right] \geq 0 \qquad (20.16)$$

Moreover, for $\mu > 0$ and $x \geq 1$, a necessary and sufficient condition for

(20.16) to obtain is that $\mu \geq \lambda K$, with the equality in (20.16) holding if and only if $\mu = \lambda K$.

If there are no barriers to entry into banking, then a necessary condition for equilibrium is $\mu \leq \lambda K$, and, for an "interior" and sustaining equilibrium, $\mu = \lambda K$. Therefore, the equilibrium deposit rate R^* is given by

$$R^* = r - s - \lambda K \qquad (20.17)$$

As is the usual case for a constant-returns-to-scale industry, the scale of each bank is indeterminate, but the industry size as measured by deposits is determined from the aggregate demand for deposits by investors according to the schedule implied by Assumption 4.

The equilibrium spread between the market interest rate and the total rate of return on deposits exactly equals the expected auditing costs per deposit per unit time. So, in effect, depositors pay for the cost of surveillance, and the bank's equityholders pay for the deposit guarantee which is, in fact, an asset-value guarantee.

The equilibrium premium charged by the FDIC per dollar of deposits can be written as

$$p_1^*(x) = 1 - \frac{k^* - 1}{\delta^* + k^*} x^{-\delta^*} \qquad (20.18)$$

where $k^* = \frac{1}{2}\{1 - \delta^* + [(1 + \delta^*)^2 + \gamma]^{1/2}\}$ and $\delta^* = 2\lambda K/\sigma^2$. The equilibrium value of equity per dollar of deposits can be written as

$$f_1^*(x) = x - \frac{k^* - 1}{\delta^* + k^*} x^{-\delta^*} \qquad (20.19)$$

To derive the formulas, it was assumed that once a bank selected a volatility rate for its assets it could not change it. However, comparative statics applied to (20.19) will show that if a bank "cheats" on the variance rate, then it will do so in the direction of choosing *less volatile* assets rather than more volatile assets, provided the bank is solvent and there is a positive spread on the deposit rate. This finding is in sharp contrast with the usual result for levered equity as was discussed in Section 20.4 and provides an attractive "stabilizing" side-effect to this structure. However, this result will no longer obtain once the bank is sufficiently insolvent (i.e. once x is sufficiently smaller than unity).

A final note on this point. If the FDIC chose to completely subsidize depositors by charging a premium that produced an equilibrium spread of zero (i.e. $\mu = 0$ and $R^* = r - s$), then the equilibrium value of equity would be

$$f_1^*(x) = x - 1 + 1/k^* \tag{20.20}$$

with $\delta^* = 0$, and in this case, if the banks cheated, they would choose more volatile assets.

20.6 CONCLUSION

Although the model presented in this chapter is simple, it does allow for audit costs and random auditing. By explicit recognition of these costs, it leads to an equilibrium rate of return on deposits which is below the market interest rate even in a competitive banking industry with no transactions costs.

There are many directions in which the model could be extended. For example, the introduction of stochastic deposits and finite-time guarantees with intermittent payments to the FDIC would be important steps in improving the realism of the model. Further improvements would be to make the audit rate parameter λ state dependent based on the information learned by the FDIC at the last audit and to choose the λ function to minimize FDIC costs.

Finally, the same type of model can be applied to the "other side" of bank operations, namely, demand loans. Because banks have surveillance costs of their loans, they face, with respect to their customers, a surveillance problem similar to those of the FDIC in this chapter. Hence, using a similar analysis, a positive spread between bank demand-loan rates and the exchange market rate can be derived.

Appendix 20A

In this appendix, the boundary conditions (20.7c) and (20.7d) used to solve for the FDIC liability per dollar of deposits, $p(x)$, are shown to be the appropriate ones.

For boundary condition (20.7d) to be valid, it is sufficient to show that $p(x)$ is a bounded function. To prove it is bounded, consider the worst situation. Let D_0 be the level of deposits at time zero. The FDIC can guarantee its ability to pay off all deposits at any time if it invests D_0 dollars in the riskless-asset-earning interest rate r because $g < r$. To cover the audit costs, suppose it was known for certain that the bank would never be insolvent and therefore that the FDIC would have to pay the audit costs forever. By assumption, the cost per audit per dollar of deposits, $c(x)$, is a bounded function. Let M be chosen such that $c(x) \leq M$ for all x. Clearly, the current value of the cost of auditing using M as the cost per audit per dollar of deposits and assuming that auditing will go on forever is an upper bound to the actual liability to the FDIC created by auditing costs. Under these conditions, the only uncertainty about the stream of audit costs is the timing of the audits. However, by assumption, the event of an audit is independent of the return on the market. Therefore, the current value of the cost of auditing using M for the cost per audit per dollar of deposits is equal to the present value of the expected auditing costs discounted at the riskless rate of interest.

If an audit takes place at time t, then the cost of the audit will be $D(t)M = D_0 \exp(gt) M$. Because the event of an audit is Poisson distributed, the probability of an audit during the time interval $(t, t + dt)$ is λdt. Therefore, the expected audit costs for the time interval $(t, t + dt)$ is $\lambda D(t)M \, dt = \lambda D_0 \exp(gt)M \, dt$, and the present value of the expected audit costs is $\exp(-rt) [\lambda D_0 \exp(gt)M] \, dt = \lambda D_0 M \exp(-\mu t) \, dt$ where $\mu = r - g > 0$. To compute the current value of all audit costs, we simply integrate over t from zero to infinity, i.e.

$$\int_0^\infty \lambda D_0 M \exp(-\mu t) \, dt = \frac{D_0 \lambda M}{\mu}$$

Therefore, the total FDIC liability at time zero, $D_0 p(x)$, is less than or equal to $D_0 + D_0 \lambda M/\mu$, or $p(x) \le 1 + \lambda M/\mu$. Hence, for $\mu > 0$, $p(x)$ is a bounded function.

Boundary condition (20.7c) gives the value of $p(x)$ for $x = 0$. From the posited dynamics for V and $g = R + s$, $V = 0$ is a natural absorbing barrier. Hence, given that $V = 0$, it is a certainty that at the time of the next audit, the FDIC will have to pay the full amount of the deposits and the audit cost. However, once these are paid, there will be no further liability for the FDIC. Hence, the only source of uncertainty is the time of the audit.

Therefore, as in the previous analysis, the current value of the liability will equal the present value of the expected cost discounted at the riskless rate of interest. If the next audit takes place at time t, then the payout will be $D(t) + c(0)D(t) = [1 + c(0)]D_0 \exp(gt)$. Because the event of an audit is Poisson distributed, the probability that the next audit takes place in time interval $(t, t + dt)$ is given by the exponential distribution, $\lambda \exp(-\lambda t) \, dt$. Consequently, the current value of the FDIC liability $D_0 p(0)$ is given by

$$D_0 p(0) = \int_0^\infty [1 + c(0)]D_0 \exp(gt) \exp(-rt) \lambda \exp(-\lambda t) \, dt$$

$$= \frac{\lambda [1 + c(0)]D_0}{\mu + \lambda}$$

and $p(0) = \lambda[1 + c(0)]/(\mu + \lambda)$, which is boundary condition (20.7c). As discussed in footnote 3, in the case where $g < R + s$ the depositors cannot be paid by the bank, and therefore an audit takes place immediately. This condition can be treated formally by letting λ go to infinity when $V = 0$. Taking this limit in the above expression gives $p(0) = 1 + c(0)$.

21

Optimal Investment Strategies for University Endowment Funds

21.1   INTRODUCTION

To examine the question of optimal investment strategies for university endowment funds, one must, of course, address the issue of the objective function by which optimality is to be measured. My impression is that practicing money managers essentially side-step the issue by focusing on generically efficient risk-return objective functions for investment which are just as applicable to individuals or non-academic institutions as they are to universities. Perhaps the most common objective of this type is mean-variance efficiency for the portfolio's allocations. Black (1976b) provides a deeper approach along those lines that takes account of tax and other institutional factors including certain types of non-endowment assets held by institutions. The Ford Foundation study of 1969 gave some early practical (if ex-post, somewhat untimely) guidance for investment allocations.

Much of the academic literature (which is not copious) seems to focus on appropriate spending policy for endowment, taking as given that the objective for endowment is to provide a perpetual level flow of expected real income (cf. Eisner, 1974; Litvack, Malkiel, and Quandt, 1974; Nichols, 1974; and Tobin, 1974). Ennis and Williamson (1976) present a history of spending patterns by universities and a discussion of various spending rules adopted. They also discuss the interaction between spending and investment policies. Fama and Jensen (1985) discuss the role of non-profit institutions as part of a general analysis of organizational forms and investment objective functions, but they do not address the functions of endowment in such institutions.

In contrast, Hansmann (1990) provides a focused and comprehensive review of the various possible roles for a university's endowment. Despite the broad coverage of possibilities ranging from tax incentives to promot-

Reproduced from *Studies of Supply and Demand in Higher Education*, C. T. Clotfelter and M. Rothschild, eds., 1993, Chicago: University of Chicago Press. © 1993 by the National Bureau of Economic Research. All rights reserved. My thanks to M. Rothschild for his many helpful comments on an earlier draft.

ing intergenerational equity, he is unable to find compelling empirical evidence to support any particular combination of objectives. Indeed, he concludes that "...prevailing endowment spending rules seem inconsistent with most of these objectives" (p. 39). Hansmann goes on to assert (pp. 39–40): "It appears, however, that surprisingly little thought has been devoted to the purposes for which endowments are maintained and that, as a consequence, their rate of accumulation and the pattern of spending from their income have been managed without much attention to the ultimate objectives of the institutions that hold them."

The course taken here to address this question is in the middle range: it does not attempt to specify in detail the objective function for the university, but it does derive optimal investment and expenditure policy for endowment in a context which takes account of overall university objectives and the availability of other sources of revenue besides endowment. In that respect, it follows along lines similar to the discussion in Black (1976b, pp. 26–8). In addition, our model takes explicit account of the uncertainties surrounding the costs of university activities. As a result, the analysis reveals another (perhaps somewhat latent) purpose for endowment: namely, hedging against unanticipated changes in those costs. Formal trading rules for implementing this hedging function are derived in Sections 21.3 and 21.4. However, the chapter neither assesses which costs, as an empirical matter, are more important to hedge nor does it examine the feasibility of hedging those costs using available traded securities. The interested reader should see Brinkman (1981, 1990), Brovender (1974), Nordhaus (1989), and Snyder (1988) where the various costs of universities are described and modeled, both historically and prospectively.

Grinold, Hopkins, and Massy (1978) develop a budget-planning model which also integrates endowment returns with other revenue and expense flows of the university. However, their model differs significantly from the one presented here, perhaps because their focus is on developing policy guidelines for expenditures instead of optimal intertemporal management of endowment.

In the section to follow, we describe the basic insights provided by our analysis and discuss in a qualitative fashion the prescriptions for endowment policy. The formal mathematical model for optimal expenditures and investment that supports those prescriptions is developed in Sections 21.3 and 21.4. It is based on a standard intertemporal consumption and portfolio-selection model. Hence, the formal structure of the optimal demand functions is already widely studied in the literature. It is the application of this model to the management of university endowment which is new. For analytical simplicity and clarity, the model is formulated in continuous time. However, it is evident from the work of Constantinides (1989), Long (1974b), and Merton (1977c) that a discrete-time version of the model would produce similar results.

21.2 OVERVIEW OF BASIC INSIGHTS AND PRESCRIPTIONS FOR POLICY

As indicated at the outset, a standard approach to the management of endowment is to treat it as if it were the only asset of the university. A consequence of this approach is that optimal portfolio strategies are focused exclusively on providing an efficient tradeoff between risk and expected return. The most commonly used measure of endowment portfolio risk is the variance (or equivalently, standard deviation) of the portfolio's return. As is well known, the returns on all mean-variance efficient portfolios are perfectly correlated. Thus, a further consequence of treating endowment as the only asset is that the optimal endowment portfolios of different universities should have quite similar risky investment allocations, at least as measured by the correlations of the portfolio returns.

Universities, as we all know, do have other assets, both tangible and intangible, many of which are important sources of cash flow. Examples of such sources are gifts, bequests, university business income, and public and private-sector grants. Taking explicit account of those assets in the determination of the endowment portfolio can cause the optimal composition of that portfolio to deviate significantly from mean-variance efficiency. That is, two universities with similar objectives and endowments of the same size can nevertheless have very different optimal endowment portfolios if their non-endowment sources of cash flow are different.

A procedure for selecting the investments for the endowment portfolio that takes account of non-endowment assets is as follows:

Step 1: Estimate the market value that each of the cash flow sources would have if it were a traded asset. Also determine the investment risk characteristics that each of those assets would have as a traded asset.

Step 2: Compute the *total wealth* or net worth of the university by adding the capitalized values of all the cash flow sources to the value of the endowment.

Step 3: Determine the optimal portfolio allocation among traded assets using the university's *total* wealth as a base. That is, treat both endowment and cash-flow-source assets as if they could be traded.

Step 4: Using the risk characteristics determined in Step 1, estimate the "implicit" investment in each traded asset category that the university has as the result of owning the non-endowment (cash-flow-source) assets. Subtract those implicit investment amounts from the optimal portfolio allocations in Step 3 to determine the optimal "explicit" investment in each traded asset, which is the actual optimal investment allocation for the endowment portfolio.

As a simple illustration, consider a university with $400 million in endowment assets and a single non-endowment cash-flow source. Suppose that the only traded assets are stocks and cash. Suppose further that the university estimates in Step 1 that the capitalized value of the cash-flow source is \$200 million with risk characteristics equivalent to holding \$100 million in stock and \$100 million in cash. Thus, the total wealth of the university in Step 2 is (\$400 + 200 =) \$600 million. Suppose that from standard portfolio selection techniques, the optimal fractional allocation in Step 3 is .6 in stocks and .4 in cash or \$360 million and \$240 million, respectively. From the hypothesized risk characteristics in Step 1, the university already has an (implicit) investment of \$100 million in stocks from its non-endowment cash-flow source. Therefore, we have in Step 4 that the optimal amount for the endowment portfolio to invest in stocks is \$260 million, the difference between the \$360 million optimal total investment in stocks and the \$100 million implicit part. Similarly, the optimal amount of endowment invested in cash equals (\$240 − 100 =) \$140 million.

The effect on the composition of the optimal endowment portfolio induced by differences in the size of non-endowment assets can be decomposed into two parts: the wealth effect and the substitution effect. To illustrate the wealth effect, consider two universities with identical preference functions and the same size endowments, but one has non-endowment assets and the other does not. If, as is perhaps reasonable to suppose, the preference function common to each exhibits decreasing absolute risk aversion, then the university with the non-endowment assets (and hence larger net worth) will prefer to have a larger total investment in risky assets. So, a university with a \$400 million endowment as its only asset would be expected to choose a dollar exposure to stocks that is smaller than the \$360 million chosen in our simple example by a university with the same size endowment and a non-endowment asset valued at \$200 million. Such behavior is consistent with the belief that wealthier universities can "afford" to take larger risks with their investments. Thus, if the average risk of the non-endowment assets is the same as the risk of the endowment-only-university's portfolio, then the university with those assets will optimally invest more of its endowment in risky assets.

The substitution effect on the endowment portfolio is caused by the substitution of non-endowment asset holdings for endowment asset holdings. To illustrate, consider again our simple example of a university with a \$400 million endowment and a \$200 million non-endowment asset. However, suppose that the risk characteristics of the asset are changed so that it is equivalent to holding \$200 million in stocks and no cash. Now in Step 4, the optimal amount for the endowment portfolio to invest in stocks is \$160 million, the difference between the \$360 million optimal total investment in stocks and the \$200 implicit part represented by the non-endowment asset. The optimal amount of endowment invested in cash rises to ($240 − 0 =) $240 million. If instead the risk characteristics of the asset had changed in the other direction to an equivalent holding of $0 in stocks and $200 million in cash, the optimal composition of the endowment portfolio would be ($360 − 0 =) $360 million in stocks and ($240 − 200 =) $40 million in cash.

Note that the changes in risk characteristics do not change the optimal deployment of *total* net worth ($360 million in stocks and $240 million in cash). However, the non-endowment assets are not carried in the endowment portfolio. Hence, different risk characteristics for those assets do change the amount of substitution they provide for stocks and cash in the endowment portfolio. Thus, the composition of the endowment portfolio will be affected in both the scale and fractional allocations among assets.

With the basic concept of the substitution effect established, we now apply it in some examples to illustrate its implications for endowment investment policy. Consider a university that on a regular basis receives donations from alums. Clearly, the cash flows from future contributions are an asset of the university, albeit an intangible one. Suppose that the actual amount of gift-giving is known to be quite sensitive to the performance of the general stock market. That is, when the market does well, gifts are high and when it does poorly, gifts are low. Through this gift-giving process, the university thus has a "shadow" investment in the stock market. Hence, all else the same, it should hold a smaller portion of its endowment in stocks than another university with smaller amounts of such market-sensitive gift-giving.

The same principle applies to more specific asset classes. If an important part of gifts to a school that specializes in science and engineering comes from entrepreneur alums, then the school *de facto* has a large investment in venture capital and hi-tech companies and it should therefore invest less of its endowment funds in those areas. Indeed, if a donor is expected to give a large block of a particular stock, then the optimal explicit holding of that stock in the endowment can be negative. Of course, an actual short position may not be truly optimal if such short sales offend the donor. That the school should optimally invest less of its endowment in the science and technology areas where its faculty and students have special expertise may seem a bit paradoxical. But, the paradox is resolved by the principle of diversification once the endowment is recognized as representing only a part of the assets of the university.

The same analysis and conclusion applies if alum wealth concentrations are in a different class of assets, such as real estate instead of shares of stock. Moreover, much the same story also applies if we were to change the example by substituting government and corporate grants for donations and gift-giving as the sources of cash flows. That is, the magnitudes of such grant support for engineering and applied science may well be positively correlated with the financial performance of companies in hi-tech indus-tries. If so, then the prospect of future cash flows to the university from the grants creates a shadow investment in those companies.

The focus of our analysis is on optimal asset allocation for the endow-ment portfolio. However, the nature and size of a university's non-endowment assets significantly influence optimal policy for spending endowment. As shown in Section 21.4, for a given overall expenditure rate as a fraction of the university's total net worth, the optimal spending rate out of endowment will vary, depending on the fraction of net worth represented by non-endowment assets, the expected growth rate of cash flows generated by those assets, and capitalization rates. Hence, neglecting those other assets will generally bias the optimal expenditure policy for endowment.

In addition to taking account of non-endowment assets, our analysis differs from the norm because it takes account of the uncertainty surround-ing the costs of the various activities such as education, research, and knowledge storage that define the purpose of the university. The break-down of activities can of course be considerably more refined. For instance, one activity could be the education of a full-tuition-paying undergraduate and a second could be the education of an undergraduate who receives financial aid. The unit (net) cost of the former is the unit cost of providing the education less the tuition received and the unit cost of the latter is this cost plus the financial aid given. As formally demonstrated in Section 21.3, an important function of endowment investments is to hedge against unanticipated changes in the costs of university activities.

As an example, consider the decision as to how much (if any) of the university's endowment to invest in local residential real estate. From a standard mean-variance-efficiency analysis, it is unlikely that any material portion of the endowment should be invested in this asset class. However, consider the cost structure faced by the university for providing teaching and research. Perhaps the single largest component is faculty salaries. Universities of the same type and quality compete for faculty from the same pools. To be competitive, they must offer a similar standard of living. Probably the largest part of the differences among universities in the cost of providing this same standard of living is local housing costs. By investing in local residential housing, the university hedges itself against this future cost uncertainty by acquiring an asset whose value is higher than expected when the differential cost of faculty salaries is higher than expected. This same asset may also provide a hedge against unanticipated higher costs of off-campus housing for students which would in turn require more financial aid if the university is to compete for the best students. Note: this prescription of targeted investment in very specific real estate assets to hedge against an unanticipated rise in a particular university's costs of faculty salaries and student aid should not be confused with the often-stated (but empirically questionable) assertion that investments in real estate generally are a good hedge against inflation. See Bodie (1976, 1982) for empirical analysis of the optimal assets for hedging against general inflation.

Similar arguments could be used to justify targeted investment of endowment in various commodities such as oil as hedges against unanticipated changes in energy costs. Uncertainty about those costs is especially significant for universities located in extreme climates and for universities with major laboratories and medical facilities that consume large quantities of energy.

The hedging role for endowment can cause optimal investment positions that are in the opposite direction from the position dictated by the substitution effects of non-endowment assets. For example, consider a specialized institute of biology that receives grants from bio-tech companies and gifts from financially successful alums. As already explained, such an institute has a large shadow investment in bio-tech stocks and it should therefore underweight (perhaps to zero) its endowment investments in such stocks. Suppose however that the institute believes that the cost of keeping top faculty will rise by considerably more than tuition or grants in the event that there is a strong demand for such scientists outside academe. Then it may be optimal to invest a portion of its endowment in bio-tech stocks to hedge this cost even though those stocks' returns are highly correlated with alum gifts and industry grants.

As demonstrated in Section 21.3, the hedging role for endowment derived here is formally valid as long as there are traded securities with returns that have non-zero correlations with unanticipated changes in the activity costs. However, the practical significance for this role turns on the magnitude of the correlations. As illustrated in Bodie's (1976, 1982) work on hedging against inflation, it is often difficult to construct portfolios (using only standard types of traded securities) that are highly correlated with changes in the prices of specific goods and services. Nevertheless, the enormous strides in financial engineering over the last decade have greatly expanded the opportunities for custom financial contracting at reasonable costs. As we move into the twenty-first century, it will become increasingly more common for the financial services industry to offer to its customers private contracts or securities that allow efficient hedging when the return properties of publicly-traded securities are inadequate. That is, implementation of the quantitative strategies prescribed in Sections 21.3 and 21.4 will become increasingly more practical for universities and other endowment institutions. See the discussions in Chapter 14 and in Merton (1990b, pp. 264–9) for a prospective view on financial innovation and the development of custom financial contracting.

There are of course a variety of issues involving endowment management that have not been addressed but could be within the context of our model. One such issue is the decision whether to invest endowment in specific-purpose real assets such as dormitories and laboratories instead of financial (or general-purpose physical) assets. The returns on those real assets are likely to be strongly correlated with the costs of particular university activities and thereby the assets form a good hedge against unexpected rises in those costs. However, because the real asset investments are specialized and largely irreversible, shifting the asset mix toward such investments reduces flexibility for the university. That is, with financial assets, the university has more options as to what it can do in the future. In future research, I plan to analyze this choice problem more formally by using contingent-claims analysis to value the tradeoff between greater flexibility in selecting future activities and lower costs in producing a given set of activities.

Another issue not explicitly examined is the impact of long-term, fixed liabilities such as faculty tenure contracts on the management of endowment. Our formal model of Sections 21.3 and 21.4 that uses contingent-claims analysis (CCA) can handle this extension. See McDonald (1974) and Merton (1985) for CCA-type models for valuing tenure and other wage guarantee contracts.

In summary, the chapter explores two classes of reasons why optimal endowment investment policy and expenditure policy can vary significantly among universities. The analysis suggests that trustees and others who judge the prudence and performance of policies by comparisons across institutions should take account of differences in both the mix of activities of the institutions and the capitalized values of their non-endowment sources of cash flows. With this, the overview is completed and we now turn to the development of the mathematical model for the process and the derivation of the quantitative rules for implementation.

21.3 THE MODEL

The functions or purposes of the university are assumed to be a collection of activities or outputs such as education, training, research, and storage of knowledge. We further assume that the intensities of those activities can be quantified and there exists a preference ordering for ranking alternative intertemporal programs. In particular, the criterion function for this ranking can be written as

$$\max E_0 \left[\int_0^\infty \overline{U}[Q_1, \ldots, Q_m, t] \, dt \right] \tag{21.1}$$

where $Q_j(t)$ denotes the quantity of activity j per unit time undertaken at time t, $j = 1, \ldots, m$; the preference function $\overline{U}$ is assumed to be strictly concave in $(Q_1,...,Q_m)$; and E_t denotes the expectation operator, conditional on knowing all relevant information as of time t. This preference ordering satisfies the classic von Neumann-Morgenstern axioms of choice, exhibits positive risk aversion, and includes "survival" (of the institution) as a possible objective. The infinite time horizon structure in (21.1) implies only that there need not be a definite date when the university will liquidate. As shown in Sections 5.8 and 18.2, $\overline{U}$ can reflect the mortality characteristics of an uncertain liquidation date.

The intertemporally additive and independent preference structure in (21.1) can be generalized to include non-additivity, habit-formation and other path-dependent effects on preferences, along the lines of Bergman (1985), Constantinides (1990), Detemple and Zapatero (1989), Duffie and Epstein (1989), Hindy and Huang (1989), Sundaresan (1989), and Svensson (1989). However, as shown in Section 6.4, those more-realistic preference functions do not materially affect the optimal portfolio demand functions. Moreover, just as Grossman and Laroque (1990) show for transactions costs in consumption, so it can be shown here that imposing adjustment costs for changing the levels of university activities does not alter the structure of the portfolio demand functions. Hence, because the focus of the chapter is on optimal investment (rather than optimal expenditure) strategies, we assume no adjustment costs for activities and retain the additive independent preference specification to provide analytical simplicity.

Let $S_j(t)$ denote the (net) cost to the university of providing one unit of activity j at time t, $j = 1,...,m$. For example, if $j = 1$ denotes the activity of having full-tuition-paying undergraduates, then S_1 would be the unit cost of providing the education minus the tuition received. If $j = 2$ denotes the activity of having undergraduates who receive financial aid, the unit cost S_2 would equal S_1 plus the financial aid given. In general, all costs and receipts such as tuition that are directly linked to the quantities of specific activities undertaken are put into the activity costs or prices, $\{S_j\}$. As will be described, fixed costs and sources of positive cash flows to the university that do not depend directly on the activity quantities are handled separately. As in equations (6.65b) and (15.43), we assume that the dynamics for these costs are described by the stochastic differential equations, for $S \equiv (S_1,...,S_m)$,

$$dS_j = f_j(S, t)S_j \, dt + g_j(S, t)S_j \, dq_j, \qquad j = 1,...,m \qquad (21.2)$$

where f_j is the instantaneous expected rate of growth in S_j, g_j is the instantaneous standard deviation of the growth rate, and dq_j is a Wiener process with the instantaneous correlation coefficient between dq_i and dq_j given by v_{ij}, $i, j = 1,...,m$. f_j and g_j are such that $dS_j \geq 0$ for $S_j = 0$ which ensures that $S_j(t) \geq 0$. Especially since $\{S\}$ has components that depend on tuition, financial aid and other variables over which the university has some control, one would expect that the dynamic path for those costs would be at least partially endogenous and controllable by the university, even though competition among universities would limit the degree of controllability. However, as specified, (21.2) is an exogenous process, not controlled by the university. Alternatively, it can be viewed as the "reduced-form" process for S after optimization over non-portfolio choice variables.

The university is assumed to have N non-endowment sources of cash flows which we denote by $Y_k(t)$ dt for the kth source at time t. As noted in Section 21.2, examples of such sources are gifts, bequests, university business income, and public and private-sector grants. It can also be used to capture transfer-pricing for the use of buildings and other university-specific assets where Y_k is the rental rate and this rental fee appears as an offsetting charge in the $\{S_j\}$ for the appropriate university activities. The dynamics for these cash flows are modeled by, for $Y \equiv (Y_1,...,Y_N)$,

$$dY_k = \mu_k(Y, S, t)Y_k \, dt + \delta_k(Y, S, t)Y_k \, d\epsilon_k \qquad (21.3)$$

where μ_k and δ_k depend at most on the current levels of the cash flows and the unit costs of university activities and $d\epsilon_k$ is a Wiener process, $k = 1,...,N$. Equation (21.3) can also be used to take account of fixed costs or liabilities of the university such as faculty tenure commitments, by letting $Y_k < 0$ to reflect a cash outflow. However, the focus here is on assets only and therefore, we assume that μ_k and δ_k are such that $dY_k \geq 0$ for $Y_k = 0$ which implies that $Y_k(t) \geq 0$ for all t.

By inspection of (21.2) and (21.3), the dynamics for $\{Y, S\}$ are jointly Markov. A more realistic model would have μ_k and δ_k depend on both current and historical values of $Q_1,...,Q_m$. For example, if a university has undertaken large amounts of research activities in the past, it may attract more grants and gifts in the future. The university may also affect the future expected cash flows from non-endowment sources by investing now in building up those sources. Thus, the dynamic process for Y should be in part controllable by the university. However, again for analytical simplicity, the Y process is taken as exogenous, because that abstraction does not significantly alter the optimal portfolio demand functions.

If for $k = 1,...,N$, $V_k(t)$ denotes the capitalized value at time t of the stream of future cash flows, $Y_k(\tau)$ for $\tau \geq t$, and if $K(t)$ denotes the value of the endowment at time t, then the net worth or wealth of the university, $W(t)$ is given by

$$W(t) = K(t) + \sum_{1}^{N} V_k(t) \qquad (21.4)$$

A model for determining the $V_k(t)$ from the posited cash flow dynamics in (21.3) is developed in Section 21.4.

The endowment of the university is assumed to be invested in traded assets. There are n risky assets and a riskless asset. If $P_j(t)$ denotes the price of the jth risky asset at time t, then the return dynamics for the risky assets are given by, for $j = 1,\ldots,n$,

$$dP_j = \alpha_j P_j \, dt + \sigma_j P_j \, dZ_j \qquad (21.5a)$$

where α_j is the instantaneous expected return on asset j; σ_j is the instantaneous standard deviation of the return; and dZ_j is a Wiener process. The instantaneous correlation coefficients $\{\rho_{ij}, \eta_{kj}, \zeta_{lj}\}$ are defined by, for $j = 1,\ldots,n$,

$$
\begin{aligned}
dZ_i \, dZ_j &= \rho_{ij} \, dt, & i &= 1,\ldots,n \\
dq_k \, dZ_j &= \eta_{kj} \, dt, & k &= 1,\ldots,m \qquad (21.5b) \\
d\epsilon_l \, dZ_j &= \zeta_{lj} \, dt, & l &= 1,\ldots,N
\end{aligned}
$$

For computational simplicity and to better isolate the special characteristics of endowment management from general portfolio management, we simplify the return dynamics specification and assume that $\{\alpha_j, \sigma_j, \rho_{ij}\}$ are constants over time, $i, j = 1,\ldots,n$. As shown in Sections 5.5 and 6.2.1, this assumption of a constant investment opportunity set implies that $\{P_j(t + \tau)/P_j(t)\}, j = 1,\ldots,n$, for $\tau > 0$ are jointly lognormally distributed. The riskless asset earns the interest rate r which is also constant over time. Optimal portfolio selection for general return dynamics would follow along the lines of Chapters 5, 15, and 16.

To analyze the optimal intertemporal expenditure and portfolio-selection problem for the university, we begin with a further simplified version of the model in which the university's entire net worth is endowment [i.e., $Y_k(t) = V_k(t) = 0, k = 1,\ldots,N$ and $W(t) = K(t)$]. The budget-equation dynamics for $W(t)$ are then given by,

$$dW = \left[\left(\sum_1^n w_j(t)(\alpha_j - r) + r \right) W - \sum_1^m Q_k S_k \right] dt + \sum_1^n w_j(t) W \sigma_j \, dZ_j$$

$$(21.6)$$

where $w_j(t)$ = the fraction of the university's wealth allocated to risky asset j at time t, $j = 1,\ldots,n$; the fraction allocated to the riskless asset is thus $1 - \Sigma_1^n w_j(t)$. Trustees, donors, and the government are assumed not to impose explicit limitations on investment policy for the endowment, other than general considerations of prudence. In particular, borrowing and short-selling are permitted and so the choice for $\{w_j\}$ is unrestricted. We further posit that spending out of endowment is not restricted, either with respect to overall expenditure or with respect to the specific activities on which it is spent. However, we do impose the feasibility restrictions that total expenditure at time t, $\Sigma_1^m Q_k S_k$, must be nonnegative and zero wealth is an absorbing state (i.e., $W(t) = 0$ implies $W(t + \tau) = 0$ for $\tau > 0$).

At each time t, the university chooses a quantity of activities $(Q_1,...,Q_m)$ and a portfolio allocation of its wealth so as to maximize lifetime utility of the university as specified in (21.1). Just as for the case of multiple consumption goods analyzed in Section 6.4, so the solution for the optimal program here can be decomposed into two parts. First, at each t, solve for the utility-maximizing quantities of individual activities, $\{Q_1,...,Q_m\}$, subject to an overall expenditure constraint, $C(t) = \Sigma_1^m Q_k(t) S_k(t)$. Second, solve for the optimal level of overall expenditures at time t and the optimal portfolio allocation of endowment.

The first part is essentially the static activity-choice problem under uncertainty

$$\max_{\{Q_1,...,Q_m\}} \overline{U}[Q_1,...,Q_m, t] \tag{21.7}$$

subject to $C(t) = \Sigma_1^m Q_k S_k(t)$. As in equation (6.74), the first-order conditions for the optimal activity bundle $(Q_1^*,...,Q_m^*)$ are given by, for $S_k(t) = S_k$,

$$\overline{U}_k[Q_1^*,...,Q_m^*, t]/S_k = \overline{U}_j[Q_1^*,...,Q_m^*, t]/S_j \quad k, j = 1,...,m \tag{21.8}$$

with $C(t) = \Sigma_1^m Q_k^* S_k$, where subscripts on $\overline{U}$ denote partial derivatives (i.e., $\overline{U}_k \equiv \partial \overline{U}/\partial Q_k$). It follows from (21.8) that the optimal quantities can be written as $Q_k^* = Q_k^*[C(t), S(t), t]$, $k = 1,...,m$.

Define the indirect utility function U by $U[C(t), S(t), t] \equiv \overline{U}[Q_1^*,...,Q_m^*, t]$. By substituting U for $\overline{U}$, we can rewrite (21.1) as

$$\max E_0 \left[\int_0^\infty U[C(t), S(t), t]\, dt \right] \tag{21.9}$$

where the "max" in (21.9) is over the intertemporal expenditure path $\{C(t)\}$ and portfolio allocations $\{w_j(t)\}$. Thus, as in equation (6.75), the original optimization problem is transformed into a single-expenditure choice problem with "state-dependent" utility (where the "states" are the relative costs or prices of the various activities). Once the optimal total expenditure rules, $\{C^*(t)\}$, are determined, the optimal expenditures on individual activities are determined by (21.8) with $C^*(t) = \Sigma_1^m Q_k^* S_k$.

The solution of (21.9) follows by applying stochastic dynamic programming as in Chapters 4, 5, and 6. Define the Bellman or derived-utility function J by:

$$J[W, S, t] \equiv \max E_t\{\textstyle\int_t^\infty U[C(\tau), S(\tau), \tau]\, d\tau\}$$

conditional on $W(t) = W$ and $S(t) = S$. From equation (6.66), J will satisfy

$$\begin{aligned}
0 = \max_{\{C, w\}} &\left(U[C, S, t] + \lambda C + J_t + J_W\left[\left(\sum_1^n w_j(\alpha_j - r) + r \right)W - C \right] \right.\\
&+ \sum_1^m J_i f_i S_i + \frac{1}{2} J_{WW} \sum_1^n \sum_1^n w_i w_j \sigma_{ij} W^2 \\
&\left. + \sum_1^m \sum_1^n J_{iW} w_j W g_i S_i \sigma_j \eta_{ij} + \frac{1}{2} \sum_1^m \sum_1^m J_{ij} g_i S_i g_j S_j v_{ij} \right)
\end{aligned} \qquad (21.10)$$

subject to $J(0, S, t) = \int_t^\infty \overline{U}[0,\ldots,0,\tau]\, d\tau$, where subscripts on J denote partial derivatives with respect to W, t, and S_i, $i = 1,\ldots,m$ and $\sigma_{ij} \equiv \rho_{ij}\sigma_i\sigma_j$, the instantaneous covariance between the return on security i and j. λ is a Kuhn-Tucker multiplier reflecting the non-negativity constraint on C and at the optimum, it will satisfy $\lambda^* C^* = 0$. The first-order conditions derived from (21.10) are

$$0 = U_C[C^*, S, t] + \lambda^* - J_W(W, S, t) \qquad (21.11a)$$

and

$$0 = J_W(\alpha_i - r) + J_{WW} \sum_1^n w_j^* W \sigma_{ij} + \sum_1^m J_{kW} g_k S_k \sigma_i \eta_{ki}, \quad i = 1,\ldots,n \qquad (21.11b)$$

where $C^* = C^*(W, S, t)$ and $w_i^* = w_i^*(W, S, t)$ are the optimal expenditure and portfolio rules expressed as functions of the state variables and subscripts on U denote partial derivatives.

From (21.11a), the optimal expenditure rule is given by

$$U_C[C^*, S, t] = J_W(W, S, t) \quad \text{for} \quad C^* > 0$$
$$\lambda^* = \max\{0, J_W(W, S, t) - U_C[0, S, t]\} \qquad (21.12)$$

As in equation (6.69), from (21.11b), the optimal portfolio allocation can be written as

$$w_i^* W = Ab_i + \sum_1^m H_k h_{ki}, \qquad i = 1,\ldots,n \qquad (21.13)$$

where $b_i \equiv \Sigma_1^n v_{ij}(\alpha_j - r)$; $h_{ki} \equiv \Sigma_1^n \sigma_j g_k S_k \eta_{kj} v_{ij}$; v_{ij} is the ij-element of the inverse of the instantaneous variance-covariance matrix of returns $[\sigma_{ij}]$; $A \equiv -J_W/J_{WW}$ (the reciprocal of absolute risk aversion of the derived-utility function); and $H_k \equiv -J_{kW}/J_{WW}$, $k = 1,\ldots,m$. A and H_k depend on the individual university's intertemporal preferences for expenditures and its current net worth. However, b_i and h_{ki} are determined entirely by the dynamic structures for the asset price returns and the unit costs of the various activities undertaken by universities. Hence, those parameters are the same for all universities, independent of their preferences or endowment size.

To provide some economic intuition about the optimal allocation of endowment in (21.13), consider as a frame of reference the "standard" intertemporal portfolio-selection problem with state-independent utility, $U = U[C(t), t]$. As shown in Section 5.5, given the posited return dynamics in (21.5a), all such investors will hold instantaneously mean-variance efficient portfolios as their optimal portfolios. For $\partial U/\partial S_k \equiv U_k \equiv 0$, $H_k \equiv 0$, $k = 1,\ldots,m$. Hence, in this case, (21.13) becomes $w_i^* W = Ab_i$, and $w_i^* W/w_j^* W = b_i/b_j$, the same for all investors. This is the well-known result that the relative holdings of risky assets are the same for all mean-variance efficient portfolios. However, the state-dependent preferences for universities induced by the uncertainty surrounding the relative costs of undertaking different desired activities causes the more complex demand structure in (21.13).

To better understand this differential demand, $w_i^* W - Ab_i = \Sigma_1^m H_k h_{ki}$, it is useful to examine the special case where, for each cost S_k, there exists an asset whose instantaneous return is perfectly correlated with changes in S_k. By renumbering securities if necessary, choose the convention that $\eta_{kk} = 1$ in (21.5b), $k = 1,\ldots,m$ ($m < n$). As shown in equations (6.70) and (6.71), it follows that in this case, $h_{kk} = g_k S_k/\sigma_k$ for $k = 1,\ldots,m$ and $h_{kj} = 0$ for $k \neq j$. Hence, we can rewrite (21.13) as

$$\begin{aligned} w_i^* W &= Ab_i + H_i g_i S_i/\sigma_i & i &= 1,\ldots,m \\ &= Ab_i & i &= m+1,\ldots,n \end{aligned} \qquad (21.14)$$

By the strict concavity of U with respect to C, J is strictly concave in W. Hence, $J_{WW} < 0$ and $H_i = -J_{iW}/J_{WW}$ is positively proportional to J_{iW}. Thus, relative to a "normal" investor with state-independent preferences (i.e., $H_i \equiv 0$, $i = 1,\ldots,m$), but the same current level of absolute risk aversion (i.e., $-J_{WW}/J_W$), the university will optimally hold more of asset i if $J_{iW} > 0$ and less if $J_{iW} < 0$, $i = 1,\ldots,m$.

The intuition for this behavior is as discussed in Section 6.4. If $J_{iW} > 0$, then, at least locally, the university's marginal utility (or "need") for wealth or endowment becomes larger if the cost of undertaking activity i increases and it becomes smaller if this cost decreases. Because the return on asset i is perfectly positively correlated with the cost of activity i, a greater-than-expected increase in S_i will coincide with a greater-than-expected return on asset i. By holding more of asset i than a "normal" investor, the university thus assures itself of a relatively larger endowment in the event that S_i increases and the need for wealth becomes more important. The university, of course, pays for this by accepting a relatively smaller endowment in the event that S_i decreases and wealth is less important. The behavioral description for $J_{iW} < 0$ is just the reverse, because the need for endowment decreases if the cost of activity i increases.

To perhaps help in developing further insights, we use (21.12) to interpret the differential demand component in (21.14) in terms of the indirect utility and optimal expenditure functions. By differentiating (21.12), we have that for $C^*(W, S, t) > 0$,

$$J_{WW} = U_{CC}[C^*, S, t]\frac{\partial C^*}{\partial W}$$

$$J_{kW} = U_{CC}[C^*, S, t]\frac{\partial C^*}{\partial S_k} + U_{Ck}[C^*, S, t]$$

$$A = -U_C[C^*, S, t]/\left(U_{CC}[C^*, S, t]\frac{\partial C^*}{\partial W}\right) \tag{21.15}$$

$$H_k = -\left\{\frac{\partial C^*}{\partial S_k} \middle/ \frac{\partial C^*}{\partial W}\right\} + U_{Ck}[C^*, S, t]/\left(-U_{CC}[C^*, S, t]\frac{\partial C^*}{\partial W}\right)$$

for $k = 1,...,m$. Because $U_{CC} < 0$ and $\partial C^*/\partial W > 0$ for $C^* > 0$, we see that the sign of H_k is determined by the impact of a change in the cost of activity k on two items: the optimal level of total current expenditure and the marginal utility of expenditure. So, for example, if an increase in S_k would cause both a decrease in optimal expenditure ($\partial C^*/\partial S_k < 0$) and an increase in the marginal utility of expenditure ($U_{Ck} > 0$), then from (21.15), $H_k > 0$ and the university will optimally hold more of asset k than the corresponding investor with a mean-variance efficient portfolio.

Following the portfolio rule in (21.14) causes the university's optimal portfolio to be mean-variance inefficient and therefore, the return on the endowment will have greater volatility than other feasible portfolios with the same expected return. However, the value of the endowment or net worth of the university is not the "end" objective. Instead, it is the "means" by which the ends of a preferred expenditure policy can be implemented. Viewed in terms of the volatility of the time path of *expenditure* (or more precisely, the *marginal utility of expenditure*), the optimal strategy given in (21.14) is mean-variance efficient [cf. Breeden (1979) and Sections 15.5 and 15.11]. That is, because $\partial C^*/\partial W > 0$, the additional increment in wealth that, by portfolio construction, occurs precisely when S_k increases will tend to offset the negative impact on C^* caused by that increase. There is thus a dampening of the unanticipated fluctuations in expenditure over time. In sum, we see that in addition to investing in assets to achieve an efficient risk-return tradeoff in wealth, universities should optimally use their endowment to hedge against unanticipated and unfavorable changes in the costs of the various activities that enter into their direct utility functions.

In closing this section, we note that the interpretation of the demand functions in the general case of (21.13) follows along the same lines as for the special case of perfect correlation leading to (21.14). As shown for the general case in Section 15.10, the differential demands for assets reflect attempts to create portfolios with the maximal feasible correlations between their returns and unanticipated changes in the S_k, $k = 1,...,m$. These maximally-correlated portfolios perform the same hedging function as assets $1,...,m$ in the limiting case of perfect correlation analyzed in (21.14). Furthermore, if other state variables besides the various activities' costs (e.g., changes in the investment opportunity set) enter a university's derived utility function, then a similar structure of differential asset demands to hedge against the unanticipated changes in these variables will also obtain.

21.4 OPTIMAL ENDOWMENT MANAGEMENT WITH OTHER SOURCES OF INCOME

In the previous section, we identified hedging of the costs of university activities as a reason for optimally deviating from "efficient" portfolio allocations when endowment is the only means for financing those activities. In this section, we extend the analysis to allow other sources of cash flow to support the activities. To simplify the analysis, we make two additional assumptions: first, we posit that μ_k and δ_k in (21.3) are constants, which implies that $Y_k(t)/Y_k(0)$ is log-normally distributed, $k = 1,...,N$. Second, we assume that for each k, there exists a traded security whose return is instantaneously perfectly correlated with the unanticipated change in Y_k, $k = 1,...,N$. By renumbering if necessary, we use the convention that traded security k is instantaneously perfectly correlated with Y_k. Hence, it follows that $\zeta_{kk} = 1$ in (21.5b) and,

$$d\epsilon_k = dZ_k, \qquad k = 1,...,N \qquad (21.16)$$

These two assumptions permit us to derive a closed-form solution for the capitalized values of the cash flows, $\{V_k(t)\}$, using contingent-claims analysis. As will be shown, those valuation functions are independent of the university's preferences or wealth level.

From (21.3), (21.5), and (21.16) with μ_k and δ_k constant, we have that the cash flows can be written as a function of the traded asset prices as follows, for $k = 1,...,N$

$$Y_k(t) = Y_k(0) \exp[-\phi_k t] [P_k(t)/P_k(0)]^{\beta_k} \tag{21.17}$$

where $\phi_k \equiv \beta_k(\alpha_k - \sigma_k^2/2) - (\mu_k - \delta_k^2/2)$ and $\beta_k \equiv \delta_k/\sigma_k$. That (21.17) obtains can be checked by applying Itô's lemma. We now derive the capitalized value for Y_k along the lines of Sections 13.2 and 16.2.

Let $F^k[P_k, t]$ be the solution to the partial differential equation, for $0 \leqslant t \leqslant T_k$

$$0 = \tfrac{1}{2} \sigma_k^2 P_k^2 F_{11}^k + rP_k F_1^k - rF^k + F_2^k + Y_k \tag{21.18}$$

subject to the boundary conditions:

$$F^k[0, t] = 0 \tag{21.19a}$$

$$F^k/(P_k)^{\beta_k} \text{ bounded as } P_k \to \infty \tag{21.19b}$$

$$F^k[P_k, T_k] = 0 \tag{21.19c}$$

where subscripts on F^k in (21.18) denote partial derivatives with respect to its arguments P_k and t; Y_k is given by (21.17); and T_k is the last date at which the university receives the cash flows from source k, $k = 1,...,N$. It is a mathematical result that a solution exists to (21.18)−(21.19) and that it is unique. Moreover, for $Y_k \geqslant 0$, $F^k \geqslant 0$ for all P_k and t.

Consider a dynamic portfolio strategy in which $F_1^k[P_k(t), t]P_k(t)$ is allocated to traded asset k at time t and $V(t) - F_1^k[P_k(t), t]P_k(t)$ is allocated to the riskless asset, where $V(t)$ is the value of the portfolio at time t. Furthermore, let the portfolio distribute cash (by selling securities if necessary) according to the flow-rate rule

$$D_2[P_k, t] = Y_k(t) \tag{21.20}$$

as given by (21.17). Then the dynamics of the portfolio can be written as, for $P_k(t) = P_k$ and $V(t) = V$,

$$dV = F_1^k[P_k, t] \, dP_k + ([V - F_1^k[P_k, t]P_k]r - D_2[P_k, t]) \, dt \tag{21.21}$$

Since F^k satisfies (21.18), it is a twice continuously differentiable function and therefore, by Itô's lemma, we can write the dynamics for F^k as

$$dF^k = [\tfrac{1}{2} \sigma_k^2 P_k^2 F_{11}^k + F_2^k] \, dt + F_1^k \, dP_k \qquad (21.22)$$

But, F^k satisfies (21.18) and hence, $\tfrac{1}{2} \sigma_k^2 P_k^2 F_{11}^k + F_2^k = rF^k - rP_kF_1^k - Y_k$. Substituting into (21.22), we can rewrite (21.22) as

$$dF^k = F_1^k \, dP_k + [rF^k - rP_kF_1^k - Y_k] \, dt \qquad (21.23)$$

From (21.21) and (21.23), we have that

$$dV - dF^k = [rV - rP_kF_1^k - D_2 - rF^k + rP_kF_1^k + Y_k] \, dt$$
$$= r[V - F^k] \, dt \qquad (21.24)$$

because $D_2 = Y_k$. By inspection, (21.24) is an ordinary differential equation with solution

$$V(t) - F^k[P_k(t), t] = (V(0) - F^k[P_k(0), 0]) \exp[rt] \qquad (21.25)$$

Thus, if the initial investment in the portfolio is chosen so that $V(0) = F^k[P_k(0), 0]$, then for all t and $P_k(t)$, we have that

$$V(t) = F^k[P_k(t), t] \qquad (21.26)$$

To ensure that the proposed portfolio strategy is feasible, we must show that its value is always nonnegative for every possible sample path for the price P_k and all t, $0 \leq t \leq T_k$. Because F^k is the solution to (21.18) and $Y_k \geq 0$, $F^k \geq 0$ for all P_k and t. It follows from (21.26) that $V(t) \geq 0$ for all P_k and t. We have therefore constructed a feasible dynamic portfolio strategy in traded asset k and the riskless asset that produces the stream of cash flows $Y_k(t) \, dt$ for $0 \leq t \leq T_k$ and has zero residual value ($V(T_k) = 0$) at T_k.

Because the derived strategy exactly replicates the stream of cash flows generated by source k, it is economically equivalent to owning the cash flows $Y_k(t)$ for $t \leq T_k$. It follows that the capitalized value of these cash flows satisfies

$$V_k(t) = F^k[P_k(t), t] \qquad (21.27)$$

for $k = 1,\dots,N$. Note that by inspection of (21.18)–(21.19), F^k, and hence $V_k(t)$, does not depend on either the university's preferences or its net worth. The valuation for source k is thus the same for all universities.

Armed with (21.27), we now turn to the optimal policy for managing endowment when the university has N non-endowment sources of cash flows. The procedure is the one outlined in Section 21.2. To derive the optimal policy, note first that even if those non-endowment sources cannot actually be sold by the university for legal, ethical, moral hazard, or asymmetric information reasons, the university can achieve the *economic* equivalent of a sale by following the "mirror-image" or reverse of the replicating strategy. That is, by (short-selling or) taking a $-F_1^k[P_k(t), t]P_k$ position in asset k and borrowing $[F^k - F_1^k P_k]$ of the riskless asset at each t, the portfolio will generate a positive amount of cash, $F^k[P_k, t]$, available for investment in other assets at time t. The entire liability generated by shorting this portfolio is exactly the negative cash flows, $\{-Y_k \, dt\}$, for $t \leqslant T_k$, because $V_k(T_k) = F^k[P_k, T_k] = 0$. But, since the university receives $Y_k \, dt$ for $t \leqslant T_k$ from source k, this short-portfolio liability is entirely offset. Hence, to undertake this strategy beginning at time t is the economic equivalent of selling cash-flow source k for a price of $V_k(t) = F^k[P_k(t), t]$.

As discussed more generally in Section 14.5, the optimal portfolio strategy will be as if all N non-endowment assets were sold and the proceeds, together with endowment, invested in the n risky traded assets and the riskless asset. This result obtains because it is feasible to sell (in the economic sense) the non-endowment assets and because all the economic benefits from those assets can be replicated by dynamic trading strategies in the traded assets. Hence, there is neither an economic advantage nor a disadvantage to retaining the non-endowment assets. It follows that the optimal demand for the traded risky assets is given by (21.13) and the demand for the riskless asset is given by $(1 - \Sigma_1^n w_i^*)W(t)$, where from (21.4) and (21.27),

$$W(t) = K(t) + \sum_1^N F^k[P_k(t), t] \qquad (21.28)$$

Because, however, the university has not actually sold the non-endowment assets, the optimal demands given by (21.13) and (21.28) include both *implicit* and *explicit* holdings of the traded assets. That is, the university's ownership of non-endowment cash-flow source k at time t is equivalent to having an additional net worth of $F^k[P_k(t), t]$ (as reflected in (21.28)) *and* to having $F_1^k[P_k(t), t]P_k(t)$ invested in traded asset k and $[F^k[P_k(t), t] - F_1^k[P_k(t), t]P_k(t)]$ invested in the riskless asset. Thus, ownership of source k causes implicit investments in traded asset k and the riskless asset. Optimal explicit investment in each traded asset is the position actually observed in the endowment portfolio and it is equal to the optimal demand given by (21.13) and (21.28) minus the implicit investment in that asset resulting from ownership of non-endowment assets. Let $D_i^*(t)$ denote the optimal *explicit* investment in traded asset i by the university at time t. It follows from (21.13) that

$$D_i^*(t) = Ab_i + \sum_1^m H_k h_{ki} - F_1^i[P_i(t), t]P_i(t), \qquad i = 1,...,N$$

$$= Ab_i + \sum_1^m H_k h_{ki}, \qquad i = N + 1,...,n \qquad (21.29)$$

where $W(t)$ used in the evaluation of A and H_k is given by (21.28). If we number the riskless asset by "$n + 1$," then explicit investment in the riskless asset can be written as

$$D_{n+1}^*(t) = [1 - \sum_1^n w_j^*(t)]W(t) - \sum_1^N [F^i[P_i(t), t] - F_1^i[P_i(t), t]P_i(t)]$$

$$= K(t) - \sum_1^n D_j^*(t) \qquad (21.30)$$

By inspection of (21.29), it is apparent that in addition to the hedging of activity costs, the existence of non-endowment sources of cash flow will cause further differences between the observed holdings of assets in the optimal endowment portfolio and the mean-variance-efficient portfolio of a "standard" investor. Similarly, from (21.30), the observed mix between risky assets and the riskless asset will differ from the true economic mix.

To explore further the effects of those non-endowment sources of cash flows, we solve the optimal expenditure and portfolio-selection problem for a specific utility function, $\overline{U}$. However, in preparation for that analysis, we first derive explicit formulas for the capitalized values of those sources when $Y_k(t)$ is given by (21.17). As already noted, there exists a unique solution to (21.18) and (21.19). Hence, it is sufficient to simply find a solution. As can be verified by direct substitution into (21.18), the value of cash flow source k is given by, for $k = 1,...,N$,

$$F^k[P_k(t), t] = Y_k(0) \exp[-\phi_k t](1 - \exp[-\theta_k(T_k - t)])[P_k(t)/P_k(0)]^{\beta_k}/\theta_k \qquad (21.31)$$

where β_k, ϕ_k are as defined in (21.17) and

$$\theta_k \equiv r + \beta_k(\alpha_k - r) - \mu_k \qquad (21.31a)$$

It follows from (21.31) that, for $k = 1,...,N$

$$F_1^k[P_k(t),\ t]P_k(t) = \beta_k F^k[P_k(t),\ t] \qquad (21.32)$$

which implies that the capitalized value of source k has a constant elasticity with respect to the price of traded asset k. Equation (21.32) also implies that the replicating portfolio strategy is a constant-proportion or rebalancing strategy which allocates fraction β_k of the portfolio to traded asset k and fraction $(1 - \beta_k)$ to the riskless asset. In the case when positive fractions are allocated to both assets (i.e., $(1 - \beta_k) > 0$ and $\beta_k > 0$), then F^k is a strictly concave function of P_k. If $\beta_k > 1$, then F^k is a strictly convex function of P_k and the replicating portfolio holds traded asset k leveraged by borrowing. In the watershed case of $\beta_k = 1$, F^k is a linear function of P_k and the replicating portfolio holds traded asset k only.

Using (21.17) and (21.27), we can rewrite (21.31) to express the capitalized value of source k in terms of the current cash flow it generates: namely

$$V_k(t) = Y_k(t)(1 - \exp[-\theta_k(T_k - t)])/\theta_k, \qquad k = 1,...,N \quad (21.33)$$

From (21.17), (21.31a), and (21.32), it is a straightforward application of Itô's lemma to show that the total expected rate of return for holding source k from t to $t + dt$ is given by

$$E_t[Y_k(t)\ dt + dV_k]/V_k(t) = (\mu_k + \theta_k)\ dt$$

$$= [r + \beta_k(\alpha_k - r)]\ dt \qquad (21.34)$$

Thus, if the rights to the cash flows Y_k between t and T_k were sold in the market place, the expected rate of return that would be required by investors to bear the risk of these flows is $r + \beta_k(\alpha_k - r)$. Therefore, θ_k equals the required expected rate of return ("the capitalization rate") minus the expected rate of growth of the cash flows, μ_k. By inspection of (21.33), $V_k(t)$ can be expressed by the classic present-value formula for assets with exponentially growing cash flows. For $\theta_k > 0$, the perpetual $(T_k = \infty)$ value is $Y_k(t)/\theta_k$ and the limiting "earnings-to-price" ratio, $Y_k(t)/V_k(t)$, is θ_k, a constant. Applying the closed-form solution for F^k, we can by substitution from (21.27) and (21.32) into (21.29) and (21.30) rewrite the optimal demand functions as

$$D_i^*(t) = Ab_i + \sum_1^m H_k h_{ki} - \beta_i V_i(t), \qquad i = 1,...,N$$

$$= Ab_i + \sum_1^m H_k h_{ki}, \qquad i = N + 1,...,n$$
$$(21.35a)$$

and

$$D_{n+1}^*(t) = [1 - \sum_{1}^{n} w_j^*(t)]W(t) - \sum_{1}^{N} (1 - \beta_i)V_i(t)$$

$$= K(t) - A\sum_{1}^{n} b_j - \sum_{1}^{m}\sum_{1}^{n} H_k h_{kj} + \sum_{1}^{N} \beta_i V_i(t)$$

$$(21.35b)$$

Having derived explicit formulas for the values of non-endowment assets, we turn now to the solution of the optimal portfolio and expenditure problem in the special case where the university's objective function is given by

$$\overline{U}[Q_1,...,Q_m, t] = \exp[-\rho t]\sum_{1}^{m} \Gamma_j \log Q_j \qquad (21.36)$$

with $\rho > 0$ and $\Gamma_j \geq 0, j = 1,...,m$. Without loss of generality, we assume that $\Sigma_1^m \Gamma_i = 1$. From (21.8), the optimal Q_j satisfy

$$Q_j^*(t) = [\Gamma_j C(t)]/S_j(t), \quad j = 1,...,m \qquad (21.37)$$

From (21.36) and (21.37), the indirect utility function can be written as

$$U[C, S, t] = \exp[-\rho t]\{\log C - \sum_{1}^{m} \Gamma_j[\log S_j - \log(\Gamma_j)]\} \quad (21.38)$$

It follows from (21.11a) that the optimal expenditure rule is

$$C^*(t) = \exp[-\rho t](1/J_W[W, S, t]) \qquad (21.39)$$

It is straightforward to verify by substitution into (21.10), (21.11a), and (21.11b) that

$$J[W, S, t] = \frac{1}{\rho} \exp[-\rho t]\log W + I[S, t] \qquad (21.40)$$

for some function $I[S, t]$. By the verification theorem of dynamic programming, satisfaction of (21.10), (21.11a), and (21.11b) is sufficient to ensure that J in (21.40) is the optimum.

It follows from (21.40) that $J_{kW} = 0$ and hence that $H_k = 0$ in (21.13) and (21.35), $k = 1,...,m$. Therefore, for the log utility specified in (21.36), there are no differential hedging demands for assets to protect against unanticipated changes in the costs of university activities. The optimal allocation of the university's total net worth is thus instantaneously mean-variance efficient. Noting that $A = -J_W/J_{WW} = W$, we have that (21.35) can be written in this special case as

$$D_i^*(t) = b_i W - \beta_i V_i(t), \qquad i = 1,\ldots,N$$
$$= b_i W, \qquad i = N + 1,\ldots,n \qquad (21.41a)$$

and

$$D_{n+1}^*(t) = \left(1 - \sum_1^n b_j\right) W - \sum_1^N (1 - \beta_i) V_i(t) \qquad (21.41b)$$

By inspection of (21.41), in the absence of non-endowment assets, the fraction of endowment allocated to risky asset i in the university's optimal portfolio is b_i, $i = 1,\ldots,n$ and the fraction allocated to the riskless asset is $(1 - \Sigma_1^n b_j)$, independent of the level of endowment. If $\chi_i^* \equiv D_i^*(t)/K(t)$ is the optimal fraction of endowment invested in asset i, then from (21.41), the difference in fractional allocations caused by the non-endowment assets is

$$\chi_i^*(t) - b_i = R[b_i - \beta_i \lambda_i], \qquad i = 1,\ldots,N$$
$$= Rb_i, \qquad i = N + 1,\ldots,n \qquad (21.42a)$$

and

$$\chi_{n+1}^*(t) - \left(1 - \sum_1^n b_j\right) = -R\left[\sum_1^n b_k - \sum_1^N \beta_k \lambda_k\right] \qquad (21.42b)$$

where $\lambda_k \equiv V_k(t)/\Sigma_1^N V_i(t)$ is the fraction of the capitalized value of the university's total non-endowment assets contributed by cash flow source k at time t, $k = 1,\ldots,N$ and $R \equiv \Sigma_1^N V_i(t)/K(t)$ is the ratio of the values of the university's non-endowment assets to its endowment assets at time t.

As discussed in Section 21.2, the differences in (21.42) are the result of two effects: (i) the "wealth" effect caused by the difference between the net worth and the endowment of the university and (ii) the "substitution" effect caused by the substitution of non-endowment asset holdings for traded asset holdings. Suppose, for concreteness, that the expected returns, variances, and covariances are such that a positive amount of each traded risky asset is held in mean-variance-efficient portfolios. Then, $b_i > 0$, $i = 1,\ldots,n$. It follows that the impact of the wealth effect in (21.42), $\{Rb_i\}$, is unambiguous: it causes a larger fraction of the optimal endowment portfolio to be allocated to each risky asset and therefore, a smaller percentage allocation to the riskless asset. Because $\beta_i \geq 0$ and $\lambda_i > 0$, $i = 1,...,N$, we have that the impact of the substitution effect in (21.42), $\{R\beta_i\lambda_i\}$, is also unambiguous: for those traded assets $1,...,N$ for which the non-endowment assets are substitutes, the fractional allocation is smaller; for the traded assets $N + 1,...,n$, the fractional allocation is unchanged; and the allocation to the riskless asset thus increases.

Because the wealth and substitution effects are in opposite directions for $b_k > 0$, whether the optimal endowment portfolio allocates an incrementally larger or smaller fraction to traded asset k depends on whether $b_k > \beta_k\lambda_k$ or $b_k < \beta_k\lambda_k$. $\beta_k\lambda_k$ is the fraction of the total increment to net worth (from non-endowment assets) that is implicitly invested in asset k as the result of owning cash flow source k. If that fraction exceeds the optimal one for total wealth, b_k, then the optimal endowment portfolio will hold less than the mean-variance-efficient allocation. Indeed, if $\lambda_k > (1 + R)b_k/(R\beta_k)$, then $\chi_k^*(t) < 0$ and the university would optimally short-sell traded asset k in its portfolio. This is more likely to occur when R is large (i.e., non-endowment assets are a large part of university net worth) and λ_k is large (i.e., cash flow source k is a large part of the value of non-endowment assets).

The implications of (21.42) for optimal endowment fit the intuitions discussed at length in Section 21.2. For instance, if a significant amount of gift-giving to a particular university depends on the performance of the general stock market, then in effect that university has a "shadow" investment in that market. Hence, all else the same, it should hold a smaller portion of its endowment in stocks than another university with smaller amounts of such market-sensitive gift-giving. As noted in Section 21.2, much the same substitution-effect story applies to concentrations in other assets, including real estate. The same analysis also follows where grants from firms or the government are likely to be strongly correlated with the financial performance of stocks in the related industries. However, the underweightings in those assets for substitution-effect reasons can be offset by sufficiently strong demands to hedge against costs, as is illustrated by the bio-tech example in Section 21.2.

The analysis leading to (21.29) and (21.30) requires that there exist traded securities which are instantaneously perfectly correlated with the changes in $Y_1,...,Y_N$. If this "complete market" assumption is relaxed, then the capitalized values of those non-endowment cash flow sources will no longer be independent of the university's preferences and endowment. However, the impact on endowment investments will be qualitatively similar. This more general case of non-replicable assets can be analyzed along the lines of Svensson (1988).

We can use our model to examine the impact of non-endowment cash flow sources on optimal expenditure policy. From (21.39) and (21.40), we have that the optimal expenditure rule is the constant-proportion-of-net-worth policy

$$C^*(t) = \rho W(t) \tag{21.43}$$

However, current expenditure *from endowment* will not follow a constant proportion strategy. Optimal expenditure from endowment at time t is $[C^*(t) - \Sigma_1^N Y_k(t)]\, dt$, which can be either positive or negative (implying net saving from non-endowment cash flow sources). If $s^*(t)$ denotes the optimal expenditure rate as a fraction of endowment ($\equiv [C^*(t) - \Sigma_1^N Y_k(t)]/K(t)$), then from (21.4) and (21.43)

$$s^*(t) = \rho + R(t)[\rho - y(t)] \tag{21.44}$$

where $R(t)$ is as defined in (21.42) and $y(t) \equiv [\Sigma_1^N Y_k(t)]/[\Sigma_1^N V_k(t)]$ is the current yield on the capitalized value of the non-endowment sources of cash flow. In the special case of (21.33) where the cash flows are all perpetuities (i.e., $T_k = \infty$ and $\theta_k > 0$, $k = 1,...,N$), $V_k(t) = Y_k(t)/\theta_k$, and the current yield on source k is constant and equal to θ_k. In that case, $y(t) = \Sigma_1^N \lambda_k \theta_k$, the value-weighted current yield. From (21.31a), θ_k will tend to be smaller for assets with higher expected growth rates of cash flow, $\{\mu_k\}$. If on average, the current yield on non-endowment assets is less than ρ, then the current spending rate out of endowment will exceed ρ. If the current yield is high so that $y(t) > \rho$, then $s^*(t) < \rho$. Indeed, if $y(t) > \rho(1 + R)/R$, then $s^*(t) < 0$ and optimal total expenditure is less than current cash flow generated by non-endowment sources. Because both $R(t)$ and $\lambda_k(t)$ change over time, we have from (21.44) that the optimal current expenditure rate from endowment is not a constant, even when expected returns on assets, the interest rate, and the expected rate of growth of non-endowment cash flows are constants.

We can also analyze the dynamics of the mix of the university's net worth between endowment and non-endowment assets. If $\alpha \equiv r + \Sigma_1^n b_i(\alpha_i - r)$ denotes the instantaneous expected rate of return on the growth-optimum, mean-variance-efficient portfolio, then as shown in Section 6.2.1, the resulting distribution for that portfolio is log-normal with instantaneous expected return $\alpha(> r)$ and instantaneous variance rate equal to $(\alpha - r)$. It follows from (21.6), (21.41), and (21.43) that the dynamics for the university's net worth are such that $W(t)/W(0)$ is log-normally distributed with

$$E_0[W(t)] = W(0)\exp[(\alpha - \rho)t]$$
$$E_0(\log[W(t)/W(0)]) = [(\alpha + r)/2 - \rho]t$$
$$\mathrm{Var}(\log[W(t)/W(0)]) = (\alpha - r)t \tag{21.45}$$

If $X_k(t) \equiv V_k(t)/W(t)$ denotes the fraction of net worth represented by non-endowment cash flow source k, then because V_k and W are each log-normally distributed, $X_k(t)$ is log-normally distributed and from (21.33) and (21.45)

$$E_0[X_k(t)] = X_k(0)\exp[(\rho - \theta_k)t]$$

$$E_0(\log[X_k(t)/X_k(0)]) = [\mu_k + \rho - (\alpha + r + \delta_k^2)/2]t$$

$$\text{Var}(\log[X_k(t)/X_k(0)]) = [\delta_k^2 + \alpha + r - 2(\mu_k + \theta_k)]t \qquad (21.46)$$

for $k = 1,...,N$.

From (21.46), the fraction of total net worth represented by all sources of non-endowment cash flow, $X(t) \equiv \Sigma_1^N X_k(t) = R(t)/[1 + R(t)]$, is expected to grow or decline depending on whether $\rho > \theta_{\min}$ or $\rho < \theta_{\min}$ where $\theta_{\min} \equiv \min[\theta_k]$, $k = 1,...,N$. In effect, a university with either a high rate of time preference or at least one (perpetual) high-growth non-endowment asset (i.e., with $\rho > \theta_{\min}$) is expected to "eat" its endowment. Indeed, it may even go to a "negative" endowment by borrowing against the future cash flows of its non-endowment assets. Whether this expected growth in $X(t)$ is the result of declining expected net worth or rising asset values can be determined from (21.45). Because $\alpha > r$, if $\rho \leq r$, then both the arithmetic and geometric expected rates of growth for net worth are positive. For $\rho < \theta_{\min}$, it follows that $E_0[X(t)] \to 0$ as $t \to \infty$. Hence, in the long run of this case, endowment is expected to become the dominant component of the university's net worth. Of course, these "razor's edge" results on growth or decline reflect the perpetual, constant-growth assumptions embedded in non-endowment cash flow behavior. However, this special case does capture the essential elements affecting optimal portfolio allocation and expenditure policies. [cf. Tobin (1974).]

The formal analysis here assumes that endowment is fungible for other assets and that neither spending nor investment policy are restricted. Such restrictions on endowment could be incorporated using the same Kuhn-Tucker type analysis used in Section 21.3 to take account of the constraint that total expenditure at each point in time is nonnegative. The magnitudes of the Kuhn-Tucker multipliers at the optimum would provide a quantitative assessment of the cost of each such restriction. However, including those restrictions is not likely to materially change the basic insights about hedging and diversification derived in the unrestricted case. The model can also be integrated into a broader one for overall university financial planning. Such integration would permit the evaluation of other non-endowment financial policies such as whether the university should sell forward contracts for tuition.

Bibliography

Aaron, H.J. and M.M. Boskin, eds (1980), *The Economics of Taxation*, Studies in Government Finance, Washington, DC: Brookings Institution.

Aase, K. (1984), "Optimum Portfolio Diversification in a General Continuous-Time Model," *Stochastic Processes and Their Applications*, 18: 81–98.

Aase, K. (1988), "Contingent Claims Valuation When the Security Price is a Combination of an Itô Process and a Random Point Process," *Stochastic Processes and Their Applications*, 28: 185–220.

Adler, M. and J. Detemple (1988), "On the Optimal Hedge of a Nontraded Cash Position," *Journal of Finance*, 43 (March): 143–53.

Adler, M. and B. Dumas (1983), "International Portfolio Choice and Corporation Finance: A Synthesis," *Journal of Finance*, 38 (June): 925–84.

Ahn, C. and H. Thompson (1988), "Jump-Diffusion Processes and the Term Structure of Interest Rates," *Journal of Finance*, 43 (March): 155–74.

Ames, W. (1977), *Numerical Methods for Partial Differential Equations*, New York: Academic Press.

Arditti, F. and K. John (1980), "Spanning by Options," *Journal of Financial and Quantitative Analysis*, 15 (March): 1–19.

Arnold, L. (1974), *Stochastic Differential Equations: Theory and Applications*, New York: Wiley.

Arrow, K.J. (1953), "Le Rôle des Valeurs Boursières pour la Répartition la Meilleure des Risques," *Econometrie*, Colloques Internationaux du Centre National de la Recherche Scientifique, Vol. XI, Paris, 41–7.

Arrow, K.J. (1964), "The Role of Securities in the Optimal Allocation of Risk Bearing," *Review of Economic Studies*, 31 (April): 91–6.

Arrow, K.J. (1965), *Aspects of the Theory of Risk Bearing*, Helsinki: Yrjö Jahanssonin Säätio.

Bachelier, L. (1900), "Théorie de la Spéculation," *Annales de l'Ecole Normale Supérieure*, 3, Paris: Gauthier-Villars. English translation in Cootner, ed. (1964).

675

Baldwin, C. (1972), "Pricing Convertible Preferred Stock According to the Rational Option Pricing Theory," B.S. dissertation, Massachusetts Institute of Technology, Cambridge, MA.

Baldwin, C., D. Lessard, and S. Mason (1983), "Budgetary Time Bombs: Controlling Government Loan Guarantees," *Canadian Public Policy*, 9: 338–46.

Baldwin, C. and K. Clark (1991), "Modularity, Real Options and Industry Structure," unpublished paper, Graduate School of Business Administration, Harvard University, Boston, MA (September).

Ball, C.B. and W.N. Torous (1983), "Bond Price Dynamics and Options," *Journal of Financial and Quantitative Analysis*, 19 (December): 517–31.

Ball, C.B. and W.N. Torous (1985), "On Jumps in Common Stock Prices and Their Impact on Call Option Pricing," *Journal of Finance*, 40 (March): 155–73.

Banz, R.W. and M.H. Miller (1978), "Prices for State-Contingent Claims: Some Estimates and Applications," *Journal of Business*, 51 (October): 653–72.

Barone-Adesi, G. and R. Whaley (1987), "Efficient Analytic Approximations of American Option Values," *Journal of Finance*, 42 (June): 301–20.

Barron, E. and R. Jensen (1990), "A Stochastic Control Approach to the Pricing of Options," *Mathematics of Operations Research*, 15 (February): 49–79.

Bawa, V.S. (1975), "Optimal Rules for Ordering Uncertain Prospects," *Journal of Financial Economics*, 2 (March): 95–121.

Beckers, S. (1981), "Standard Deviations Implied in Option Prices as Predictors of Future Stock Price Variability," *Journal of Banking and Finance*, 5 (September): 363–82.

Bensaid, B., J. Lesne, H. Pagès, and J. Scheinkman (1991), "Derivative Asset Pricing With Transactions Costs," Working Paper, Banque de France, Centre de Recherche, Paris, France.

Bensoussan, A. (1982), *Stochastic Control by Functional Analysis Methods*, Amsterdam: North-Holland.

Bensoussan, A. (1983), "Maximum Principle and Dynamic Programming Approaches of the Optimal Control of Partially Observed Diffusions," *Stochastics*, 9: 169–222.

Bensoussan, A. (1984), "On the Theory of Option Pricing," ACTA *Applicandae Mathematicae*, 2 (June): 139–58.

Bergman, Y. (1985), "Time Preference and Capital Asset Pricing Models," *Journal of Financial Economics*, 14 (March): 145–59.

Bergman, Y. (1991), "Option Pricing With Divergent Borrowing and Lending Rates," Working Paper, Department of Economics, Brown University, Providence, RI (April).

Bergstrom, A.R. (1988), "The History of Continuous-Time Econometric

Models," *Econometric Theory*, 4 (December): 365–83.

Bernstein, P.L. (1992), *Capital Ideas: The Improbable Origins of Modern Wall Street*, New York: Free Press.

Bertsekas, D.P. (1974), "Necessary and Sufficient Conditions for Existence of an Optimal Portfolio," *Journal of Economic Theory*, 8 (June): 235–47.

Bhattacharya, S. and G. Constantinides, eds (1989), *Frontiers of Modern Financial Theory*: *Theory of Valuation*, Totowa, NJ: Rowman & Littlefield.

Bick, A. (1982), "Comments on the Valuation of Derivative Assets," *Journal of Financial Economics*, 10 (November): 331–45.

Bismut, J.M. (1975), "Growth and Optimal Intertemporal Allocation of Risks," *Journal of Economic Theory*, 10 (April): 239–57.

Black, F. (1972), "Capital Market Equilibrium with Restricted Borrowing," *Journal of Business*, 45 (July): 444–55.

Black, F. (1976a), "The Pricing of Commodity Contracts," *Journal of Financial Economics*, 3 (January–March): 167–79.

Black, F. (1976b), "The Investment Policy Spectrum: Individuals, Endowment Funds and Pension Funds," *Financial Analysts Journal*, 32 (January–February): 23–31.

Black, F. (1987), "This Week's Citation Classic," *Current Contents/Social and Behavioral Science*, 19, No. 33 (August 17), Philadelphia, PA: Institute for Scientific Information.

Black, F. (1989), "How We Came Up With the Option Formula," *Journal of Portfolio Management*, 15 (Winter): 4–8.

Black F. and J.C. Cox (1976), "Valuing Corporate Securities: Some Effects of Bond Indenture Provisions," *Journal of Finance*, 31 (May): 351–68.

Black, F., E. Derman, and W. Toy (1990), "A One-Factor Model of Interest Rates and Its Application to Treasury Bond Options," *Financial Analysts Journal*, 46 (January–February): 33–9.

Black, F., M.C. Jensen, and M. Scholes (1972), "The Capital Asset Pricing Model: Some Empirical Tests," in M.C. Jensen, ed. (1972a).

Black, F. and A. Perold (1992), "Theory of Constant Proportion Portfolio Insurance," *Journal of Economic Dynamics and Control*, 16, No. 4.

Black, F. and M. Scholes (1972), "The Valuation of Option Contracts and a Test of Market Efficiency," *Journal of Finance*, 27 (May): 399–418.

Black, F. and M. Scholes (1973), "The Pricing of Options and Corporate Liabilities," *Journal of Political Economy*, 81 (May–June): 637–54.

Blomeyer, E. (1986), "An Analytic Approximation for the American Put Price for Options on Stocks with Dividends," *Journal of Financial and Quantitative Analysis*, 21 (June): 229–33.

Bodie, Z. (1976), "Common Stock as a Hedge Against Inflation," *Journal of Finance*, 31 (May): 459–70.

Bodie, Z. (1990), "Inflation Insurance," *Journal of Risk and Insurance*, 57 (December): 634–45.

Bodie, Z., R.C. Merton, and W. Samuelson (1992), "Labor Supply Flexibility and Portfolio Choice in a Life-Cycle Model," *Journal of Economic Dynamics and Control*.

Bodie, Z. and W. Samuelson (1989), "Labor Supply Flexibility and Portfolio Choice," Working Paper No. 3043, National Bureau of Economic Research, Cambridge, MA (July).

Bookstaber, R.M. (1981), *Option Pricing and Strategies in Investing*, Reading, MA: Addison-Wesley.

Borch, K. (1969), "A Note on Uncertainty and Indifference Curves," *Review of Economic Studies*, 36 (January): 1–4.

Bourguignon, F. (1974), "A Particular Class of Continuous-Time Stochastic Growth Models," *Journal of Economic Theory*, 9 (October): 141–58.

Boyle, P.P. (1977), "Options: A Monte Carlo Approach," *Journal of Financial Economics*, 4 (May): 323–38.

Boyle, P.P. (1988), "A Lattice Framework for Option Pricing with Two State Variables," *Journal of Financial and Quantitative Analysis*, 23 (March): 1–12.

Boyle, P.P., J. Evnine, and S. Gibbs (1989), "Numerical Evaluation of Multivariate Contingent Claims," *Review of Financial Studies*, 2: 241–50.

Boyle, P.P. and E. Kirzner (1985), "Pricing Complex Options: Echo-Bay Ltd. Gold Purchase Warrants," *Canadian Journal of Administrative Sciences*, 2 (December): 294–306.

Boyle, P.P. and E. Schwartz (1977), "Equilibrium Prices of Guarantees Under Equity-Linked Contracts," *Journal of Risk and Insurance*, 44 (December): 639–80.

Boyle, P.P. and T. Vorst (1992), "Option Replication in Discrete Time With Transactions Costs," *Journal of Finance*, 47 (March).

Branson, W. and D. Henderson (1984), "The Specification and Influence of Asset Markets," in R. Jones and P. Kenen, eds, *Handbook of International Economics*, Amsterdam: North-Holland.

Breeden, D.T. (1979), "An Intertemporal Asset Pricing Model with Stochastic Consumption and Investment Opportunities," *Journal of Financial Economics*, 7 (September): 265–96. Reprinted in Bhattacharya and Constantinides, eds (1989).

Breeden, D.T. (1984), "Futures Markets and Commodity Options: Hedging and Optimality in Incomplete Markets," *Journal of Economic Theory*, 32 (April): 275–300.

Breeden, D.T. (1986), "Consumption, Production, Inflation and Interest Rates: A Synthesis," *Journal of Financial Economics*, 16 (May): 3–39.

Breeden, D.T., M. Gibbons, and R. Litzenberger (1989), "Empirical Tests of the Consumption-Oriented CAPM," *Journal of Finance*, 44 (June): 231–62.

Breeden, D.T. and R. Litzenberger (1978), "Prices of State-Contingent Claims Implicit in Option Prices," *Journal of Business*, 51 (October): 621–51.

Brennan, M. and E. Schwartz (1976), "The Pricing of Equity-Linked Life Insurance Policies with an Asset Value Guarantee," *Journal of Financial Economics*, 3 (June): 195–214.

Brennan, M. and E. Schwartz (1977a), "The Valuation of American Put Options," *Journal of Finance*, 32 (May): 449–62.

Brennan, M. and E. Schwartz (1977b), "Savings Bonds, Retractable Bonds and Callable Bonds," *Journal of Financial Economics*, 5 (August): 67–88.

Brennan, M. and E. Schwartz (1977c), "Convertible Bonds: Valuation and Optimal Strategies for Call and Conversion," *Journal of Finance*, 32 (December): 1699–716.

Brennan, M. and E. Schwartz (1978), "Corporate Income Taxes, Valuation and the Problem of Optimal Capital Structure," *Journal of Business*, 51 (January): 103–14.

Brennan, M. and E. Schwartz (1979), "A Continuous Time Approach to the Pricing of Bonds," *Journal of Banking and Finance*, 3 (July): 133–55.

Brennan, M. and E. Schwartz (1980), "Analyzing Convertible Bonds," *Journal of Financial and Quantitative Analysis*, 15 (November): 907–29.

Brennan, M. and E. Schwartz (1983), "Alternative Methods for Valuing Debt Options," *Finance*, 4 (October): 119–37.

Brennan, M. and E. Schwartz (1985a), "Evaluating Natural Resource Investments," *Journal of Business*, 58 (April): 135–57.

Brennan, M. and E. Schwartz (1985b), "Determinants of GNMA Mortgage Prices," *Journal of the American Real Estate & Urban Economics Association*, 13 (Fall): 209–28.

Brennan, M. and E. Schwartz (1988), "Time-Invariant Portfolio Insurance Strategies," *Journal of Finance*, 43 (June): 283–300.

Brennan, M. and E. Schwartz (1989), "Portfolio Insurance and Financial Market Equilibrium," *Journal of Business*, 62 (October): 455–72.

Brennan, M. and R. Solanki (1981), "Optimal Portfolio Insurance," *Journal of Financial and Quantitative Analysis*, 16 (September): 279–300.

Brenner, M., ed. (1983), *Option Pricing*, Lexington, MA: D.C. Heath.

Brenner, M., G. Courtadon, and M. Subrahmanyam (1985), "Options on the Spot and Options on Futures," *Journal of Finance*, 60 (December): 1303–17.

Brinkman, P.T. (1981), "Factors Affecting Instructional Costs at Major

Research Universities," *Journal of Higher Education*, 59 (May–June): 265–79.

Brinkman, P.T. (1990), "Higher Education Cost Functions," in S. Hoenack and E. Collins, eds., *The Economics of American Universities*, Albany: State University of New York Press.

Briys, E. (1988), "Demande d'Assurance, Décisions de Consommation et de Portefeuille: Une Analyse en Temps Continu," Working Paper, Centre Hautes Etudes Commerciales–Institut Supérieur des Affaires, Jouy-en-Josas, France.

Briys, E., M. Crouhy, and H. Schlesinger (1988), "Optimal Hedging Under Non Separable Preferences," unpublished paper, Centre Hautes Etudes Commerciales–Institut Supérieur des Affaires, Jouy-en-Josas, France.

Brock, W. (1982), "Asset Prices in a Production Economy," in J. McCall, ed., *The Economics of Information and Uncertainty*, Chicago, IL: University of Chicago Press.

Brock, W. and L. Mirman (1972), "Optimal Economic Growth and Uncertainty: The Discounted Case," *Journal of Economic Theory*, 4 (June): 479–513.

Brovender, S. (1974), "On the Economics of a University: Toward the Determination of Marginal Cost of Teaching Services," *Journal of Political Economy*, 82 (May–June): 657–64.

Brown, D.P. (1988), "The Implications of Nonmarketable Income for Consumption-Based Models of Asset Pricing," *Journal of Finance*, 43 (September): 867–80.

Brown, S.J. (1989), "The Number of Factors in Security Returns," *Journal of Finance*, 44 (December): 1247–62.

Buser, S., P. Hendershott, and A. Sanders (1985), "Pricing Life-of-Loan Rate Caps on Default-Free Adjustable-Rate Mortgages," *Journal of the American Real Estate & Urban Economics Association*, 13 (Fall): 248–60.

Capozza, D. and R. Helsley (1990), "The Stochastic City," *Journal of Urban Economics*, 28 (September): 187–203.

Capozza, D. and G. Schwann (1990), "The Value of Risk in Real Estate Markets," *Journal of Real Estate Finance and Economics*, 3 (June): 117–40.

Carlton, D. (1984), "Futures Markets: Their Purpose, Their History, Their Growth, Their Successes and Failures," *Journal of Futures Markets*, 4 (Fall): 237–71.

Cass, D. and J.E. Stiglitz (1970), "The Structure of Investor Preferences and Asset Returns, and Separability in Portfolio Allocation: A Contribution to the Pure Theory of Mutual Funds," *Journal of Economic Theory*, 2 (June): 122–60.

Cass, D. and M.E. Yaari (1967), "Individual Savings, Aggregate Capital Accumulation, and Efficient Growth," in K. Shell, ed., *Essays on the Theory of Optimal Economic Growth*, Cambridge, MA: MIT Press.

Chamberlain, G. (1983), "A Characterization of the Distributions that Imply Mean–Variance Utility Functions," *Journal of Economic Theory*, 29 (February): 185–201.

Chamberlain, G. (1988), "Asset Pricing in Multiperiod Securities Markets," *Econometrica*, 56 (November): 1283–300.

Chamberlain, G. and M. Rothschild (1983), "Arbitrage and Mean–Variance Analysis on Large Asset Markets," *Econometrica*, 51 (September): 1281–301.

Chen, A.H.Y. (1970), "A Model of Warrant Pricing in a Dynamic Market," *Journal of Finance*, 25 (December): 1041–60.

Chen, N. and J.E. Ingersoll (1983), "Exact Pricing in Linear Factor Models with Finitely-Many Assets: A Note," *Journal of Finance*, 38 (June): 985–8.

Chiang, R., T. Lai, and D. Ling (1986), "Retail Leasehold Interests: A Contingent Claim Analysis," *Journal of the American Real Estate & Urban Economics Association*, 14 (Summer): 216–29.

Chung, K. and R. Williams (1983), *An Introduction to Stochastic Integration*, Boston, MA: Birkhauser.

Churchill, R.V. (1963), *Fourier Series and Boundary Value Problems*, 2nd Edition, New York: McGraw-Hill.

Clark, P.K. (1973), "A Subordinated Stochastic Process with Finite Variance for Speculative Prices," *Econometrica*, 41 (January): 135–55.

Connor, G. and R. Korajczyk (1988), "Risk and Return in an Equilibrium APT: Application of a New Test Methodology," *Journal of Financial Economics*, 21 (September): 255–89.

Constantinides, G. (1983), "Capital Market Equilibrium With Personal Tax," *Econometrica*, 51 (May): 611–37.

Constantinides, G. (1984), "Warrant Exercise and Bond Conversion in Competitive Markets," *Journal of Financial Economics*, 13 (September): 371–97.

Constantinides, G. (1986), "Capital Market Equilibrium with Transactions Costs," *Journal of Political Economy*, 94 (August): 842–62. Reprinted in Bhattacharya and Constantinides, eds (1989).

Constantinides, G. (1989), "Theory of Valuation: Overview and Recent Developments," in Bhattacharya and Constantinides, eds (1989).

Constantinides, G. (1990), "Habit Formation: A Resolution of the Equity Premium Puzzle," *Journal of Political Economy*, 98 (June): 519–43.

Constantinides, G. and J.E. Ingersoll (1984), "Optimal Bond Trading with Personal Taxes," *Journal of Financial Economics*, 13 (September): 299–336. Reprinted in Bhattacharya and Constantinides, eds (1989).

Constantinides, G. and R. Rosenthal (1984), "Strategic Analysis of the Competitive Exercise of Certain Financial Options," *Journal of Economic Theory*, 32 (February): 128–38.

Constantinides, G. and M. Scholes (1980), "Optimal Liquidation of Assets in the Presence of Personal Taxes: Implications for Asset Pricing," *Journal of Finance*, 35 (May): 439–43.

Cooper, I.A. and A.S. Mello (1991), "The Default Risk of Swaps," *Journal of Finance*, 46 (June): 597–620.

Cootner, P.H., ed. (1964), *The Random Character of Stock Market Prices*, Cambridge, MA: MIT Press.

Cootner, P.H. (1966), "The Stochastic Theory of Bond Prices," unpublished paper, Massachusetts Institute of Technology, Cambridge, MA (December).

Cornell, B. (1981), "The Consumption Based Asset Pricing Model: A Note on Potential Tests and Applications," *Journal of Financial Economics*, 9 (March): 103–8.

Courtadon, G. (1982), "A More Accurate Finite Difference Approximation for the Valuation of Options," *Journal of Financial and Quantitative Analysis*, 17 (December): 697–703.

Cox, D.A. and H.D. Miller (1968), *The Theory of Stochastic Processes*, New York: Wiley.

Cox, J. C. and C. Huang (1989a), "Option Pricing Theory and Its Applications," in Bhattacharya and Constantinides, eds (1989).

Cox, J.C. and C. Huang (1989b), "Optimum Consumption and Portfolio Policies When Asset Prices Follow a Diffusion Process," *Journal of Economic Theory*, 49 (October): 33–83.

Cox, J.C. and C. Huang (1991), "A Variational Problem Arising in Financial Economics," *Journal of Mathematical Economics*, 20: 465–87.

Cox, J.C., J.E. Ingersoll, and S. A. Ross (1979), "Duration and the Measurement of Basis Risk," *Journal of Business*, 52 (January): 51–61.

Cox, J.C., J.E. Ingersoll, and S.A. Ross (1980), "An Analysis of Variable Rate Loan Contracts," *Journal of Finance*, 35 (May): 389–404.

Cox, J.C., J.E. Ingersoll, and S.A. Ross (1981), "The Relation between Forward Prices and Futures Prices," *Journal of Financial Economics*, 9 (December): 321–46.

Cox, J.C., J.E. Ingersoll, and S.A. Ross (1985a), "An Intertemporal General Equilibrium Model of Asset Prices," *Econometrica*, 53 (March): 363–84.

Cox, J.C., J.E. Ingersoll, and S.A. Ross (1985b), "A Theory of the Term Structure of Interest Rates," *Econometrica*, 53 (March): 385–408.

Cox, J.C. and S.A. Ross (1976), "The Valuation of Options for Alternative Stochastic Processes," *Journal of Financial Economics*, 3 (January–March): 145–66.

Cox, J.C., S.A. Ross, and M. Rubinstein (1979), "Option Pricing: A

Simplified Approach," *Journal of Financial Economics*, 7 (September): 229–63.

Cox, J.C. and M. Rubinstein (1983), "A Survey of Alternative Option Pricing Models," in M. Brenner, ed. (1983).

Cox, J.C. and M. Rubinstein (1985), *Options Markets*, Englewood Cliffs, NJ: Prentice-Hall.

Crouhy, M. and D. Galai (1991), "Warrant Valuation and Equity Volatility," in F. Fabozzi, ed., *Advances in Futures and Options Research*, Vol. 5, Greenwich, CT: JAI Press.

Cummins, J.D. (1988), "Risk-Based Premiums for Insurance Guarantee Funds," *Journal of Finance*, 43 (September): 823–39.

Davis, M.H.A. and A.R. Norman (1990), "Portfolio Selection with Transactions Costs," *Mathematics of Operations Research*, 15 (November): 676–713.

Debreu, G. (1959), *Theory of Value*, New York: Wiley.

Dellacherie, C. and P. Meyer (1982), *Probabilities and Potential B: Theory of Martingales*, Amsterdam: North-Holland.

Denny, J. and G. Suchanek (1986), "On the Use of Semimartingales and Stochastic Integrals to Model Continuous Trading," *Journal of Mathematical Economics*, 15: 255–66.

Detemple, J. (1986), "Asset Pricing in a Production Economy With Incomplete Information," *Journal of Finance*, 41 (June): 383–91.

Detemple, J. and R. Kihlstrom (1987), "Information Acquisition and Valuation in a Continuous-Time Model," Working Paper No. 47, Kellogg Graduate School of Management, Northwestern University, Evanston, IL (December).

Detemple, J. and F. Zapatero (1989), "Optimal Consumption-Portfolio Policies with Habit Formation," unpublished paper, Graduate School of Business, Columbia University, New York, NY.

Dettman, J.W. (1969), *Mathematical Methods in Physics and Engineering*, 2nd Edition, New York: McGraw-Hill.

Dewing, A.S. (1934), *A Study of Corporation Securities: Their Nature and Uses in Finance*, New York: Ronald Press Co.

Dhrymes, P., I. Friend, and N. Gultekin (1984), "A Critical Examination of the Empirical Evidence on the Arbitrage Pricing Theory," *Journal of Finance*, 39 (June): 323–47.

Dhrymes, P., I. Friend, and N. Gultekin (1985), "New Tests of the APT and their Implications," *Journal of Finance*, 40 (July): 659–74.

Diamond, P.A. (1977), "A Framework for Social Security Analysis," *Journal of Public Economics*, 8: 275–98.

Dixit, A. (1989a), "Hysteresis, Import Penetration, and Exchange Rate Pass-Through," *Quarterly Journal of Economics*, 104 (May): 205–28.

Dixit, A. (1989b), "Entry and Exit Decisions Under Uncertainty," *Journal of Political Economy*, 97 (June): 620–38.

Dothan, M.U. (1978), "On the Term Structure of Interest Rates," *Journal of Financial Economics*, 6 (March): 59–69.

Dothan, M.U. and D. Feldman (1986), "Equilibrium Interest Rates and Multiperiod Bonds in a Partially Observable Economy," *Journal of Finance*, 41 (June): 369–82.

Dothan, M.U. and J.T. Williams (1981), "Education as an Option," *Journal of Business*, 54 (January): 117–39.

Dreyfus, S.E. (1965), *Dynamic Programming and the Calculus of Variations*, New York: Academic Press.

Duffie, D. (1986), "Stochastic Equilibria: Existence, Spanning Number, and the 'No Expected Financial Gain from Trade' Hypothesis," *Econometrica*, 54 (September): 1161–84.

Duffie, D. (1987), "Stochastic Equilibria with Incomplete Financial Markets," *Journal of Economic Theory*, 41 (April): 405–16.

Duffie, D. (1988), *Security Markets: Stochastic Models*, New York: Academic Press.

Duffie, D. and L. Epstein (1989), "Stochastic Differential Utility and Asset Pricing," unpublished manuscript, Graduate School of Business, Stanford University, Stanford, CA (September).

Duffie, D. and C. Huang (1985), "Implementing Arrow–Debreu Equilibria by Continuous Trading of Few Long-lived Securities," *Econometrica*, 53 (November): 1337–56.

Duffie, D. and C. Huang (1986), "Multiperiod Securities Markets with Differential Information: Martingales and Resolution Times," *Journal of Mathematical Economics*, 15: 283–303.

Duffie, D. and W. Shafer (1985), "Equilibrium in Incomplete Markets I: A Basic Model of Generic Existence," *Journal of Mathematical Economics*, 14: 285–300.

Duffie, D. and W. Shafer (1986), "Equilibrium in Incomplete Markets II: Generic Existence in Stochastic Economies," *Journal of Mathematical Economics*, 15: 199–216.

Duffie, D. and W. Zame (1989), "The Consumption-Based Capital Asset Pricing Model," *Econometrica*, 57 (November): 1279–97.

Dumas, B. (1988), "Pricing Physical Assets Internationally," Working Paper No. 12–88, Rodney L. White Center for Financial Research, Wharton School of Finance and Commerce, University of Pennsylvania, Philadelphia, PA.

Dumas, B. (1989), "Two-Person Dynamic Equilibrium in the Capital Market," *Review of Financial Studies*, 2: 157–88.

Dumas, B. and E. Luciano (1991), "An Exact Solution to a Dynamic Portfolio Choice Problem Under Transactions Costs," *Journal of Finance*, 46 (June): 577–95.

Duncan, T. and B. Pasik-Duncan (1989a), "Adaptive-Control of a Continuous-Time Portfolio and Consumption Model," *Journal of*

Optimization Theory and Applications, 61 (April): 47–52.

Duncan, T. and B. Pasik-Duncan (1989b), "Rate of Convergence for an Estimator in a Portfolio and Consumption Model," *Journal of Optimization Theory and Applications*, 61 (April): 53–9.

Duncan, T. and B. Pasik-Duncan (1989c), "Adaptive-Control of Three Continuous-Time Portfolio and Consumption Models," *Journal of Optimization Theory and Applications*, 61 (April): 61–71.

Dunn, K. and J. McConnell (1981), "Valuation of GNMA Mortgage-Backed Securities," *Journal of Finance*, 36 (June): 599–616.

Dybvig, P. and S.A. Ross (1982), "Portfolio Efficient Sets," *Econometrica*, 50 (November): 1525–46.

Dybvig, P. and S.A. Ross (1985), "Yes, the APT is Testable," *Journal of Finance*, 40 (September): 1173–88.

Eastham, J. and K. Hastings (1988) "Optimal Impulse Control of Portfolios," *Mathematics of Operations Research*, 13 (November): 588–605.

Eisner, R. (1974), "Endowment Income, Capital Gains and Inflation Accounting: Discussion," *American Economic Review*, 64 (May): 438–41.

Emanuel, D. (1983a), "Warrant Valuation and Exercise Strategy," *Journal of Financial Economics*, 12 (August): 211–36.

Emanuel, D. (1983b), "A Theoretical Model for Valuing Preferred Stock," *Journal of Finance*, 38 (September): 1133–55.

Ennis, R. and J.P. Williamson (1976), "Spending Policy for Educational Endowments," Research and Publication Project, The Common Fund (January).

Eun, C. (1985), "A Model of International Asset Pricing Under Imperfect Commodity Arbitrage," *Journal of Economic Dynamics and Control*, 9 (November): 273–89.

Eytan, T. and G. Harpaz (1986), "The Pricing of Futures and Options Contracts on the Value Line Index," *Journal of Finance*, 41 (September): 843–55.

Fama, E.F. (1963), "Mandelbrot and the Stable Paretian Hypothesis," *Journal of Business*, 36 (October): 420–9.

Fama, E.F. (1965a), "The Behavior of Stock Market Prices," *Journal of Business*, 38 (January): 34–105.

Fama, E.F. (1965b), "Portfolio Analysis in a Stable Paretian Market," *Management Science*, 11 (January): 404–19.

Fama, E.F. (1970a), "Efficient Capital Markets: A Review of Theory and Empirical Work," *Journal of Finance*, 25 (May): 383–417.

Fama, E.F. (1970b), "Multiperiod Consumption–Investment Decisions," *American Economic Review*, 60 (March): 163–74.

Fama, E.F. (1978), "The Effects of a Firm's Investment and Financing Decisions on the Welfare of its Securityholders," *American Economic*

Review, 68 (June): 272–84.

Fama, E.F. (1991), "Efficient Capital Markets: II," *Journal of Finance*, 46 (December): 1575–1617.

Fama, E.F. and M.C. Jensen (1985), "Organizational Forms and Investment Decisions," *Journal of Financial Economics*, 14 (March): 101–19.

Fama, E.F. and M.H. Miller (1972), *The Theory of Finance*, New York: Holt, Rinehart & Winston.

Farrar, D.E. (1962), *The Investment Decision Under Uncertainty*, Englewood Cliffs, NJ: Prentice-Hall.

Farrell, J.L. (1974), "Analyzing Covariation of Returns to Determine Homogeneous Stock Groupings," *Journal of Business*, 47 (April): 186–207.

Feeney, G.J. and D. Hester (1967), "Stock Market Indices: A Principal Components Analysis," in D. Hester and J. Tobin, eds, *Risk Aversion and Portfolio Choice*, New York: Wiley.

Feldman, D. (1989), "The Term Structure of Interest Rates in a Partially Observable Economy," *Journal of Finance*, 44 (July): 789–812.

Feldstein, M.S. (1969), "Mean-Variance Analysis in the Theory of Liquidity Preference and Portfolio Selection," *Review of Economic Studies*, 36 (January): 5–12.

Feller, W. (1966), *An Introduction to Probability Theory and Its Applications*, Vol. 2, New York: Wiley.

Figlewski, S. (1989), "Options Arbitrage in Imperfect Markets," *Journal of Finance*, 44 (December): 1289–1311.

Finnerty, J.D. (1988), "Financial Engineering in Corporate Finance: An Overview," *Financial Management*, 17 (Winter): 14–33.

Fischer, S. (1969), *Essays on Assets and Contingent Commodities*, Ph.D. dissertation, Department of Economics, Massachusetts Institute of Technology, Cambridge, MA.

Fischer, S. (1972), "Assets, Contingent Commodities, and the Slutsky Equations," *Econometrica*, 40 (March): 371–85.

Fischer, S. (1975), "The Demand for Index Bonds," *Journal of Political Economy*, 83 (June): 509–34.

Fischer, S. (1978), "Call Option Pricing When the Exercise Price is Uncertain, and the Valuation of Index Bonds," *Journal of Finance*, 33 (March): 169–76.

Fischer, S. (1983), "Welfare Aspects of Government Issue of Indexed Bonds," in R. Dornbusch and M.H. Simonsen, eds, *Inflation, Debt, and Indexation*, Cambridge, MA: MIT Press.

Fischer, S. and R.C. Merton (1984), "Macroeconomics and Finance: The Role of the Stock Market," in K. Brunner and A. H. Melzer, eds, *Essays on Macroeconomic Implications of Financial and Labor Markets and Political Processes*, Vol. 21, Amsterdam: North-Holland.

Fleming, W. and R. Rishel (1975), *Deterministic and Stochastic Optimal*

Control, New York: Springer-Verlag.

Foldes, L. (1978), "Optimal Saving and Risk in Continuous Time," *Review of Economic Studies*, 45 (February): 39–65.

Föllmer, H. and D. Sonderman (1986), "Hedging of Non-Redundant Contingent-Claims," in W. Hildenbrand and A. Mas-Colell, eds, *Contributions to Mathematical Economics, in Honor of Gérard Debreu*, Amsterdam: North-Holland.

Ford Foundation Advisory Committee on Endowment Management (1969), Managing Educational Endowments: Report to the Ford Foundation, New York: Ford Foundation.

Friedman, A. (1975), *Stochastic Differential Equations and Applications*, Vol. 1, New York: Academic Press.

Friend, I. and J. Bicksler, eds (1977), *Risk and Return in Finance*, Vols I and II, Cambridge, MA: Ballinger.

Friend, I. and M. Blume (1970), "Measurement of Portfolio Performance Under Uncertainty," *American Economic Review*, 60 (September): 561–75.

Fries, S.M. and W.R.M. Perraudin (1991), "Banking Policy and the Pricing of Deposit Guarantees: A New Approach," unpublished paper, International Monetary Fund, Washington, DC (September).

Galai, D. (1975), *Pricing of Options and the Efficiency of the Chicago Board Options Exchange*, Ph.D. dissertation, Graduate School of Business, University of Chicago, Chicago, IL.

Galai, D. (1983), "A Survey of Empirical Tests of Option Pricing Models," in M. Brenner, ed. (1983).

Galai, D. (1988), "Corporate Income Taxes and the Valuation of the Claims on the Corporation," *Research in Finance*, Vol. 7, Greenwich, CT: JAI Press: 75–90.

Galai, D. and R. Masulis (1976), "The Option Pricing Model and the Risk Factor of Stock," *Journal of Financial Economics*, 3 (January–March): 53–81.

Galai, D. and M. Schneller (1978), "Pricing of Warrants and the Value of the Firm," *Journal of Finance*, 33 (December): 1333–42.

Garman, M. and S. Kohlhagen (1983), "Foreign Currency Option Values," *Journal of International Money and Finance*, 2 (December): 231–8.

Garman, M. and J.A. Ohlson (1981), "Valuation of Risky Assets in Arbitrage-Free Economies with Transactions Costs," *Journal of Financial Economics*, 9 (September): 271–80.

Gastineau, G.L. (1979), *The Stock Options Manual*, 2nd Edition, New York: McGraw-Hill.

Gatto, M., R. Geske, R. Litzenberger, and H. Sosin (1980), "Mutual Fund Insurance," *Journal of Financial Economics*, 8 (September): 283–317.

Geltner, D. (1989), "On the Use of the Financial Option Price Model to

Value and Explain Vacant Urban Land," *Journal of the American Real Estate & Urban Economics Association*, 17 (Summer): 142–58.

Gennotte, G. (1986), "Optimal Portfolio Choice Under Incomplete Information," *Journal of Finance*, 41 (July): 733–46.

Geske, R. (1977), "The Valuation of Corporate Liabilities as Compound Options," *Journal of Financial and Quantitative Analysis*, 12 (November): 541–52.

Geske, R. (1978), "Pricing of Options With Stochastic Dividend Yield," *Journal of Finance*, 33 (May): 617–25.

Geske, R. (1979), "The Valuation of Compound Options," *Journal of Financial Economics*, 7 (March): 63–81.

Geske, R. and H. Johnson (1984), "The American Put Option Valued Analytically," *Journal of Finance*, 39 (December): 1511–24.

Geske, R. and R. Roll (1984), "On Valuing American Call Options With the Black–Scholes European Formula," *Journal of Finance*, 39 (June): 443–55.

Geske, R. and K. Shastri (1985), "Valuation by Approximation: A Comparison of Alternative Option Valuation Techniques," *Journal of Financial and Quantitative Analysis*, 20 (March): 45–72.

Gihman, I. and A. Skorohod (1972), *Stochastic Differential Equations*, New York: Springer-Verlag.

Gilster, J.E., Jr. and W. Lee (1984), "The Effect of Transaction Costs and Different Borrowing and Lending Rates on the Option Pricing Model: A Note," *Journal of Finance*, 43 (September): 1215–21.

Girsanov, I.V. (1960), "On Transforming a Certain Class of Stochastic Processes by Absolutely Continuous Substitution Measures," *Theory of Probability and Its Applications*, 5: 285–301.

Goldenberg, D. (1991), "A Unified Method for Pricing Options on Diffusion Processes," *Journal of Financial Economics*, 29 (March): 3–34.

Goldman, M.B. (1974), "A Negative Report on the 'Near Optimality' of the Max-Expected-Log Policy as Applied to Bounded Utilities for Long Lived Programs," *Journal of Financial Economics*, 1 (May): 97–103.

Goldman, M.B., H.B. Sosin, and L.A. Shepp (1979), "On Contingent Claims that Insure Ex-Post Optimal Stock Market Timing," *Journal of Finance*, 34 (May): 401–13.

Graaff, J. De V. (1950), "Mr Harrod on Hump Saving," *Economica*, 17 (February): 81–90.

Grabbe, J. (1983), "The Pricing of Call and Put Options on Foreign Exchange," *Journal of International Money and Finance*, 2 (December): 239–53.

Green, R.C. and R.A. Jarrow (1987), "Spanning and Completeness in Markets With Contingent Claims," *Journal of Economic Theory*, 41 (February): 202–10.

Grinold, R., D. Hopkins, and W. Massy (1978), "A Model for

Long-Range University Budget Planning Under Uncertainty," *Bell Journal of Economics*, 9 (Autumn): 396–420.

Grinols, E. (1984), "Production and Risk Leveling in the Intertemporal Capital Asset Pricing Model," *Journal of Finance*, 39 (December): 1571–95.

Grossman, S. and G. Laroque (1990), "Asset Pricing and Optimal Portfolio Choice in the Presence of Illiquid Durable Consumption Goods," *Econometrica*, 58 (January): 25–51.

Grossman, S., A. Melino and R. Shiller (1987), "Estimating the Continuous-Time Consumption-Based Asset Pricing Model," *Journal of Business and Economic Statistics*, 5 (July): 315–27.

Grossman, S. and R. Shiller (1982), "Consumption Correlatedness and Risk Measurement in Economies With Non-Traded Assets and Heterogeneous Information," *Journal of Financial Economics*, 10 (July): 195–210.

Grundy, B. (1991), "Option Prices and the Underlying Asset's Return Distribution," *Journal of Finance*, 46 (July): 1045–69.

Hadar, J. and W.R. Russell (1969), "Rules for Ordering Uncertain Prospects," *American Economic Review*, 59 (March): 25–34.

Hadar, J. and W.R. Russell (1971), "Stochastic Dominance and Diversification," *Journal of Economic Theory*, 3 (September): 288–305.

Hahn, F.H. (1970), "Savings and Uncertainty," *Review of Economic Studies*, 37 (January): 21–4.

Hakansson, N.H. (1970), "Optimal Investment and Consumption Strategies under Risk for a Class of Utility Functions," *Econometrica*, 38 (September): 587–607.

Hakansson, N.H. (1971), "Capital Growth and the Mean–Variance Approach to Portfolio Selection," *Journal of Financial and Quantitative Analysis*, 6 (January): 517–57.

Hakansson, N.H. (1976), "The Purchasing Power Fund: A New Kind of Financial Intermediary," *Financial Analysts Journal*, 32 (November–December): 49–59.

Hakansson, N.H. (1979), "The Fantastic World of Finance: Progress and the Free Lunch," *Journal of Financial and Quantitative Analysis*, 14 (Proceedings Issue): 717–34.

Hamilton, J. H. (1987), "Taxation, Savings, and Portfolio Choice in a Continuous-Time Model," *Finances Publiques/Public Finance*, 42: 264–82.

Hanoch, G. and H. Levy (1969), "The Efficiency Analysis of Choices Involving Risk," *Review of Economic Studies*, 36 (July): 335–46.

Hansen, L. and K.J. Singleton (1983), "Stochastic Consumption, Risk Aversion and the Temporal Behavior of Stock Returns," *Journal of Political Economy*, 91 (April): 249–65.

Hansmann, H. (1990), "Why Do Universities Have Endowments?" *Journal of Legal Studies*, 19 (January): 3–42.

Hardy, G.H., J.E. Littlewood, and G. Pölya (1959), *Inequalities*, Cambridge: Cambridge University Press.

Harrison, J.M. (1985), *Brownian Motion and Stochastic Flow Systems*, New York: Wiley.

Harrison, J.M. and D. Kreps (1979), "Martingales and Arbitrage in Multiperiod Securities Markets," *Journal of Economic Theory*, 20 (July): 381–408.

Harrison, J.M. and S. Pliska (1981), "Martingales and Stochastic Integrals in the Theory of Continuous Trading," *Stochastic Processes and Their Applications*, 11: 215–60.

Harrison, J.M. and S. Pliska (1983), "A Stochastic Calculus Model of Continuous Trading: Complete Markets," *Stochastic Processes and Their Applications*, 15: 313–16.

Harrison, J.M. and A. Taylor (1978), "Optimal Control of a Brownian Motion Storage System," *Stochastic Processes and Their Applications*, 6 (January): 179–94.

Hawkins, G. (1982), "An Analysis of Revolving Credit Agreements," *Journal of Financial Economics*, 10 (March): 59–82.

He, H. (1989), *Essays in Dynamic Portfolio Optimization and Diffusion Estimations*, Ph.D. dissertation, A.P. Sloan School of Management, Massachusetts Institute of Technology, Cambridge, MA.

He, H. (1990), "Convergence From Discrete- to Continuous-Time Contingent Claims Prices," *Review of Financial Studies*, 3: 523–46.

He, H. (forthcoming), "Optimal Consumption-Portfolio Policies: A Convergence From Discrete to Continuous-Time Models, *Journal of Economic Theory*.

He, H. and H. Pagès (1990), "Consumption and Portfolio Decisions With Labor Income and Borrowing Constraints," Working Paper No. 200, Walter A. Haas School of Business, University of California at Berkeley, Berkeley, CA (August).

He, H. and N.D. Pearson (1991), "Consumption and Portfolio Policies with Incomplete Markets and Short-Sale Constraints: The Infinite Dimensional Case," *Journal of Economic Theory*, 54 (August): 259–304.

Heath, D.C. and R.A. Jarrow (1987), "Arbitrage, Continuous Trading, and Margin Requirements," *Journal of Finance*, 42 (December): 1129–42.

Heath, D.C., R.A. Jarrow, and A. Morton (forthcoming), "Bond Pricing and the Term Structure of Interest Rates: A New Methodology for Contingent Claims Valuation," *Econometrica*.

Hellwig, M.F. (1982), "Rational Expectations Equilibrium with Conditioning on Past Prices," *Journal of Economic Theory*, 26 (April): 279–312.

Henriksson, R. and R.C. Merton (1981), "On Market Timing and Investment Performance Part II: Statistical Procedures for Evaluating Forecasting Skills," *Journal of Business*, 54 (October): 513–34.

Herstein, I. and J. Milnor (1953), "An Axiomatic Approach to Measurable Utility," *Econometrica*, 21 (April): 291–7.

Hindy, A. and C. Huang (1989), "On Intertemporal Preferences With a Continuous Time Dimension II: The Case of Uncertainty," Working Paper No. 2105–89, A.P. Sloan School of Management, Massachusetts Institute of Technology, Cambridge, MA (March).

Ho, T. and S. Lee (1986), "Term Structure Movements and Pricing Interest Rate Contingent Claims," *Journal of Finance*, 42 (December): 1129–42.

Ho, T. and R.F. Singer (1982), "Bond Indenture Provisions and the Risk of Corporate Debt," *Journal of Financial Economics*, 10 (December): 375–406.

Ho, T. and R.F. Singer (1984), "The Value of Corporate Debt With a Sinking Fund Provision," *Journal of Business*, 57 (July): 315–36.

Hodges, S. and A. Neuberger (1989), "Optimal Replication of Contingent Claims Under Transactions Costs," unpublished paper, Financial Options Research Centre, University of Warwick, Coventry (September).

Huang, C. (1985a), "Information Structure and Equilibrium Asset Prices," *Journal of Economic Theory*, 53 (February): 33–71.

Huang, C. (1985b), "Information Structures and Viable Price Systems," *Journal of Mathematical Economics*, 14: 215–40.

Huang, C. (1987), "An Intertemporal General Equilibrium Asset Pricing Model: The Case of Diffusion Information," *Econometrica*, 55 (January): 117–42.

Huang, C. and K. Kreps (1985), "Intertemporal Preferences with a Continuous Time Dimension: An Exploratory Study," unpublished paper, Massachusetts Institute of Technology, Cambridge, MA (December).

Hull, J. (1989), *Options, Futures and Other Derivative Securities*, Englewood Cliffs, NJ: Prentice-Hall.

Hull, J. and A. White (1987), "The Pricing of Options on Assets With Stochastic Volatilities," *Journal of Finance*, 42 (June): 281–300.

Hull, J. and A. White (1988), "The Use of the Control Variate Technique in Option Pricing," *Journal of Financial and Quantitative Analysis*, 23 (September): 237–51.

Hull, J. and A. White (1990a), "Valuing Derivative Securities Using the Explicit Finite Difference Method," *Journal of Financial and Quantitative Analysis*, 25 (March): 87–100.

Hull, J. and A. White (1990b), "Pricing Interest-Rate-Derivative Securities," *Review of Financial Studies*, 3: 573–92.

Ingersoll, Jr, J.E. (1976), "A Theoretical Model and Empirical Investigation of the Dual Purpose Funds: An Application of Contingent-Claims Analysis," *Journal of Financial Economics*, 3 (January–March): 82–123.

Ingersoll, Jr, J.E. (1977), "A Contingent-Claims Valuation of Convertible Securities," *Journal of Financial Economics*, 4 (May): 289–322.

Ingersoll, Jr, J.E. (1987), *Theory of Financial Decision Making*, Totowa, NJ: Rowman & Littlefield.

Itô, K. (1951), "On Stochastic Differential Equations," *Memoirs of American Mathematical Society*, 4: 1–51.

Itô, K. (1974), "Stochastic Differentials," *Applied Mathematics and Optimization*, 1: 374–81.

Itô, K. (1987), *Kiyoshi Itô Selected Papers*, New York: Springer-Verlag.

Itô, K. and H.P. McKean, Jr (1964), *Diffusion Processes and Their Sample Paths*, New York: Academic Press.

Jagannathan, R. (1984), "Call Options and the Risk of Underlying Securities," *Journal of Financial Economics*, 13 (September): 425–34.

Jamshidian, F. (1991), "Forward Induction and Construction of Yield Curve Diffusion Models," *Journal of Fixed Income*, 1 (June): 62–74.

Jarrow, R.A. (1987), "The Pricing of Commodity Options with Stochastic Interest Rates," in F. Fabozzi, ed., *Advances in Futures and Options Research*, Vol. 2, Greenwich, CT: JAI Press.

Jarrow, R.A. and D. Madan (1991), "Option Pricing Using the Term Structure of Interest Rates to Hedge Systematic Discontinuities in Asset Returns," unpublished paper, Johnson Graduate School of Management, Cornell University, Ithaca, NY (February).

Jarrow, R.A. and M. O'Hara (1989), "Primes and Scores: An Essay on Market Imperfections," *Journal of Finance*, 44 (December): 1263–87.

Jarrow, R.A. and J.B. Wiggins (1989), "Option Pricing and Implicit Volatilities," *Journal of Economic Surveys*, 3: 59–81.

Jarrow, R.A. and E. Rosenfeld (1984), "Jump Risks and the Intertemporal Capital Asset Pricing Model," *Journal of Business*, 57 (July): 337–52.

Jarrow, R.A. and A.T. Rudd (1983), *Option Pricing*, Homewood, IL: Richard D. Irwin.

Jensen, M.C. (1969), "Risk, the Pricing of Capital Assets and the Evaluation of Investment Portfolios," *Journal of Business*, 42 (April): 167–247.

Jensen, M.C., ed. (1972a), *Studies in the Theory of Capital Markets,* New York: Praeger.

Jensen, M.C. (1972b), "Capital Markets: Theory and Evidence," *Bell Journal of Economics and Management Science*, 2 (Autumn): 357–98.

Jensen, M.C. and W. Meckling (1976), "Theory of the Firm: Managerial Behavior, Agency Costs and Ownership Structure," *Journal of Financial Economics*, 3 (October): 305–60.

Johnson, H. (1983), "An Analytic Approximation for the American Put Price," *Journal of Financial and Quantitative Analysis*, 18 (March): 141–8.

Johnson, H. (1987), "Options on the Maximum or the Minimum of Several Assets," *Journal of Financial and Quantitative Analysis*, 22 (September): 277–83.

Johnson, H. and D. Shanno (1987), "Option Pricing When the Variance is Changing," *Journal of Financial and Quantitative Analysis*, 22 (June): 143–51.

Johnson, H. and R.M. Stulz (1987), "The Pricing of Options with Default Risk," *Journal of Finance*, 42 (June): 267–80.

Jones, E.P. (1984), "Option Arbitrage and Strategy with Large Price Changes," *Journal of Financial Economics*, 13 (March): 91–113.

Jones, E.P. and S. Mason (1980), "Valuation of Loan Guarantees," *Journal of Banking and Finance*, 4 (March): 89–107.

Jorion, P. (1988), "On Jump Processes in the Foreign Exchange and Stock Markets," *Review of Financial Studies*, 1 (Winter): 427–45.

Kandel, S. and S.A. Ross (1983), "Some Intertemporal Models of Portfolio Selection With Transactions Costs," Working Paper No. 107, CRSP, University of Chicago, Chicago, IL (September).

Karatzas, I. (1988), "On the Pricing of American Options," *Applied Mathematics and Optimization*, 17 (January): 37–60.

Karatzas, I. (1989), "Optimization Problems in the Theory of Continuous Trading," *SIAM Journal of Control and Optimization*, 27 (November): 1221–59.

Karatzas, I., J. Lehoczky, S. Sethi, and S. Shreve (1986), "Explicit Solutions of a General Consumption/Investment Problem," *Mathematics of Operations Research*, 11 (May): 261–94.

Karlin, S. and H.M. Taylor (1981), *A Second Course in Stochastic Processes*, New York: Academic Press.

Kassouf, S.T. (1968), "Stock Price Random Walks: Some Supporting Evidence," *Review of Economics and Statistics*, 50 (May): 275–8.

Kester, C. (1984), "Growth Options and Investment: Reducing the Guesswork in Strategic Capital Budgeting," *Harvard Business Review*, (March–April): 153–60.

Kim, I.J. (1990), "The Analytic Valuation of American Options," *Review of Financial Studies*, 3: 547–72.

King, B.R. (1966), "Market and Industry Factors in Stock Price Behavior," *Journal of Business*, 39 (January): 139–90.

Kouri, P. (1976), "The Determinants of the Forward Premium," IIES Seminar Paper No. 62, University of Stockholm, Stockholm (August).

Kouri, P. (1977), "International Investment and Interest Rate Linkages Under Flexible Exchange Rates," in R.Z. Aliber, ed., *The Political Economy of Monetary Reform*, London: Macmillan.

Kouri, P. and J. de Macedo (1978), "Exchange Rates and the International Adjustment Process," *Brookings Papers in Economic Activity*, 1: Washington, DC: Brookings Institution.

Kraus, A. and S.A. Ross (1982), "The Determination of Fair Profits for the Property–Liability Insurance Firm," *Journal of Finance*, 37 (September): 1015–28.

Kreps, D. (1981), "Arbitrage and Equilibrium in Economies with Infinitely Many Commodities," *Journal of Mathematical Economics*, 8 (March): 15–35.

Krylov, N. (1980), *Controlled Diffusion Processes*, New York: Springer-Verlag.

Kuhn, H.W. and A.W. Tucker (1951), "Nonlinear Programming," in J. Neyman, ed., *Proceedings of the Second Berkeley Symposium of Mathematical Statistics and Probability*, Berkeley, CA: University of California Press.

Kunita, H. and S. Watanabe (1967), "On Square-Integrable Martingales," *Nagoya Mathematics Journal*, 30: 209–45.

Kushner, H.J. (1967), *Stochastic Stability and Control*, New York: Academic Press.

Kyle, A.S. (1985), "Continuous Auctions and Insider Trading," *Econometrica*, 53 (November): 1315–35.

Latané, H. and R. Rendleman (1976), "Standard Deviations of Stock Price Ratios Implied in Option Prices," *Journal of Finance*, 31 (May): 369–82.

Lehmann, B. and D. Modest (1988), "The Empirical Foundations of the Arbitrage Pricing Theory," *Journal of Financial Economics*, 21 (September): 213–54.

Leland, H. (1968), *Dynamic Portfolio Theory*, Ph.D. dissertation, Department of Economics, Harvard University, Cambridge, MA.

Leland, H. (1972), "On the Existence of Optimal Policies under Uncertainty," *Journal of Economic Theory,* 4 (February): 35–44.

Leland, H. (1974), "Optimal Growth in a Stochastic Environment: The Labor-Surplus Economy," *Review of Economic Studies*, 41 (January): 75–86.

Leland, H. (1980), "Who Should Buy Portfolio Insurance?" *Journal of Finance*, 35 (May): 581–94.

Leland, H. (1985), "Option Pricing and Replication With Transactions Costs," *Journal of Finance*, 40 (December): 1283–301.

Leonard, R.J. (1971), *An Empirical Examination of a New General Equilibrium Model for Warrant Pricing*, M.S. dissertation, A.P. Sloan School of Management, Massachusetts Institute of Technology, Cambridge, MA.

Levhari, D. and T.N. Srinivasan (1969), "Optimal Savings Under Uncertainty," *Review of Economic Studies*, 36 (April): 153–63.

Levy, H. (1985), "Upper and Lower Bounds on Put and Call Option Value: Stochastic Dominance Approach," *Journal of Finance*, 40 (September): 1197–217.

Lintner, J. (1965a), "The Valuation of Risk Assets and the Selection of Risky Investments in Stock Portfolios and Capital Budgets," *Review of Economics and Statistics*, 47 (February): 13–37.

Lintner, J. (1965b), "Security Prices, Risk and Maximal Gains From Diversification," *Journal of Finance*, 20 (December): 587–615.

Litvack, J., B. Malkiel, and R. Quandt (1974), "A Plan for the Definition of Endowment Income," *American Economic Review*, 64 (May): 433–42.

Livingston, M. (1977), "Industry Movements of Common Stocks," *Journal of Finance*, 32 (June): 861–74.

Lo, A. (1986), "Statistical Tests of Contingent Claims Asset-Pricing Models: A New Methodology," *Journal of Financial Economics*, 17 (September): 143–74.

Lo, A. (1987), "Semi-Parametric Upper Bounds for Option Prices and Expected Payoffs," *Journal of Financial Economics*, 19 (December): 373–87.

Lo, A. (1988), "Maximum Likelihood Estimation of Generalized Itô Processes with Discretely Sampled Data," *Econometric Theory*, 4 (August): 231–47.

Long, J.B. (1974a), "Discussion," *Journal of Finance*, 29 (May): 485–8.

Long, J.B. (1974b), "Stock Prices, Inflation, and the Term Structure of Interest Rates," *Journal of Financial Economics*, 1 (July): 131–70.

Longstaff, F. (1989), "Temporal Aggregation and the Continuous-Time Capital Asset Pricing Model," *Journal of Finance*, 44 (September): 871–88.

Longstaff, F. and E. Schwartz (1991), "Interest-Rate Volatility and the Term Structure: A Two-Factor General Equilibrium Model," unpublished paper, Anderson Graduate School of Management, University of California at Los Angeles, Los Angeles, CA (June).

Lopez, A. (1961), *Problems in Stable Population Theory*, Office of Population Research, Princeton University, Princeton, NJ.

Luskin, D., ed. (1988), *Portfolio Insurance: A Guide to Dynamic Hedging*, New York: John Wiley & Sons.

de Macedo, J., J.A. Goldstein, and D.M. Meerschwam (1984), "International Portfolio Diversification: Short-Term Financial Assets and Gold," in J.F. Bilson and R.C. Martson, eds, *Exchange Rate Theory and Practice*, Chicago, IL: University of Chicago Press.

Machina, M. (1982), " 'Expected Utility' Analysis without the Independence Axiom," *Econometrica*, 50 (March): 277–323.

MacMillan, L. (1986), "Analytic Approximation for the American Put Option," in F. Fabozzi, ed., *Advances in Futures and Options Research*, Vol. 1, Greenwich, CT: JAI Press.

Madan, D., F. Milne, and H. Shefrin (1989), "The Multinomial Option Pricing Model and Its Brownian and Poisson Limits," *Review of*

Financial Studies, 2: 251–65.

Magill, M. and G. Constantinides (1976), "Portfolio Selection With Transactions Costs," *Journal of Economic Theory*, 13 (October): 245–63.

Majd, S. and S.C. Myers (1985), "Valuing the Government's Tax Claim on Risky Corporate Assets," Working Paper No. 1553, National Bureau of Economic Research, Cambridge, MA.

Majd, S. and S.C. Myers (1987), "Tax Asymmetries and Corporate Income Tax Reform," in M. Feldstein, ed., *Effects of Taxation on Capital Accumulation*, Chicago, IL: University of Chicago Press.

Majd, S. and R. Pindyck (1987), "Time to Build, Option Value, and Investment Decisions," *Journal of Financial Economics*, 18 (March): 7–28.

Malliaris, A.G. and W.A. Brock (1982), *Stochastic Methods in Economics and Finance*, Amsterdam: North-Holland.

Manaster, S. and G. Koehler (1982), "The Calculation of Implied Variances from the Black–Scholes Model: A Note," *Journal of Finance*, 37 (March): 227–30.

Mandelbrot, B. (1963a), "New Methods in Statistical Economics," *Journal of Political Economy*, 61 (October): 421–40.

Mandelbrot, B. (1963b), "The Variation of Certain Speculative Prices," *Journal of Business*, 36 (October): 394–419.

Mandl, P. (1968), *Analytical Treatment of One-Dimensional Markov Processes*, New York: Springer-Verlag.

Mankiw, N.G. and M.D. Shapiro (1985), "Risk and Return: Consumption Beta versus Market Beta," *Review of Economics and Statistics*, 68 (August): 452–9.

Marcus, A.J. (1987), "Corporate Pension Policy and the Value of PBGC Insurance," in Z. Bodie, J.B. Shoven, and D.A. Wise, eds, *Issues in Pension Economics*, Chicago, IL: University of Chicago Press.

Margrabe, W. (1978), "The Value of an Option to Exchange One Asset for Another," *Journal of Finance*, 33 (March): 177–86.

Markowitz, H. (1952), "Portfolio Selection," *Journal of Finance*, 7 (March): 77–91.

Markowitz, H. (1959), *Portfolio Selection: Efficient Diversification of Investment*, New York: Wiley.

Marsh, T. and E. Rosenfeld (1983), "Stochastic Processes for Interest Rates and Equilibrium Bond Prices," *Journal of Finance*, 38 (May): 635–46.

Mason, S. (1981), "Consumption and Investment Incentives Associated with Welfare Programs," Working Paper No. 79–34, Graduate School of Business Administration, Harvard University, Boston, MA (December).

Mason, S. and S. Bhattacharya (1981), "Risky Debt, Jump Processes, and Safety Covenants," *Journal of Financial Economics*, 9 (September): 281–307.

Mason, S. and R.C. Merton (1985), "The Role of Contingent Claims Analysis in Corporate Finance," in E. Altman and M. Subrahmanyan, eds, *Recent Advances in Corporate Finance*, Homewood, IL: Richard D. Irwin.

McConnell, J. and E. Schwartz (1986), "LYON Taming," *Journal of Finance*, 41 (July): 561–76.

McDonald, J. (1974), "Faculty Tenure as a Put Option: An Economic Interpretation," *Social Science Quarterly*, 55 (September): 362–71.

McDonald, R. and D. Siegel (1985), "Investment and the Valuation of Firms When There is an Option to Shut Down," *International Economic Review*, 26 (June): 331–49.

McDonald, R. and D. Siegel (1986), "The Value of Waiting to Invest," *Quarterly Journal of Economics*, 101 (November): 707–27.

McKean, Jr, H.P. (1965), "Appendix: A Free Boundary Problem for the Heat Equation Arising From a Problem in Mathematical Economics," *Industrial Management Review*, 6 (Spring): 32–9. Reprinted in Samuelson (1972a).

McKean, Jr, H.P. (1969), *Stochastic Integrals*, New York: Academic Press.

McShane, E.J. (1974), *Stochastic Calculus and Stochastic Models*, New York: Academic Press.

Melino, A. and S. Turnbull (1990), "Pricing Foreign Currency Options With Stochastic Volatility," *Journal of Econometrics*, 45 (July/August): 239–65.

Merton, R.C. (1969a), "Lifetime Portfolio Selection Under Uncertainty: The Continuous-Time Case," *Review of Economics and Statistics*, 51 (August): 247–57. Reprinted here as Chapter 4.

Merton, R.C. (1969b), "A Golden Golden-Rule for Welfare-Maximization in an Economy with a Varying Population Growth Rate," *Western Economic Journal*, 4 (December): 307–18.

Merton, R.C. (1970a), "An Empirical Investigation of the Samuelson Rational Warrant Pricing Theory," Chapter 5 in *Analytical Optimal Control Theory as Applied to Stochastic and Nonstochastic Economics*, Ph.D. dissertation, Department of Economics, Massachusetts Institute of Technology, Cambridge, MA.

Merton, R.C. (1970b), "A Dynamic General Equilibrium Model of the Asset Market and Its Application to the Pricing of the Capital Structure of the Firm," Working Paper No. 497–70, A.P. Sloan School of Management, Massachusetts Institute of Technology, Cambridge, MA. Reprinted here as Chapter 11.

Merton, R.C. (1971), "Optimum Consumption and Portfolio Rules in a Continuous-Time Model," *Journal of Economic Theory*, 3 (December): 373–413. Reprinted here as Chapter 5.

Merton, R.C. (1972a), "An Analytic Derivation of the Efficient Portfolio Frontier," *Journal of Financial and Quantitative Analysis*, 7 (September): 1851–72.

Merton, R.C. (1972b), "Appendix: Continuous-Time Speculative Processes," in R.H. Day and S.M. Robinson, eds, *Mathematical Topics in Economic Theory and Computation*, Philadelphia, PA: Society for Industrial and Applied Mathematics. Reprinted in *SIAM Review*, 15 (January 1973): 34–8.

Merton, R.C. (1973a), "Theory of Rational Option Pricing," *Bell Journal of Economics and Management Science*, 4 (Spring): 141–83. Reprinted here as Chapter 8.

Merton, R.C. (1973b), "An Intertemporal Capital Asset Pricing Model," *Econometrica*, 41 (September): 867–87. Reprinted here as Chapter 15.

Merton, R.C. (1973c), "The Relationship Between Put and Call Option Prices: Comment," *Journal of Finance*, 28 (March): 183–4.

Merton, R.C. (1974), "On the Pricing of Corporate Debt: The Risk Structure of Interest Rates," *Journal of Finance*, 29 (May): 449–70. Reprinted here as Chapter 12.

Merton, R.C. (1975a), "An Asymptotic Theory of Growth Under Uncertainty," *Review of Economic Studies*, 42 (July): 375–93. Reprinted here as Chapter 17.

Merton, R.C. (1975b), "Theory of Finance from the Perspective of Continuous Time," *Journal of Financial and Quantitative Analysis*, 10 (November): 659–74.

Merton, R.C. (1976a), "Option Pricing When Underlying Stock Returns are Discontinuous," *Journal of Financial Economics*, 3 (January–March): 125–44. Reprinted here as Chapter 9.

Merton, R.C. (1976b), "The Impact on Option Pricing of Specification Error in the Underlying Stock Price Returns," *Journal of Finance*, 31 (May): 333–50.

Merton, R.C. (1976c), "Continuous-Time Portfolio Theory and the Pricing of Contingent Claims," Working Paper No. 881–76, A.P. Sloan School of Management, Massachusetts Institute of Technology, Cambridge, MA.

Merton, R.C. (1977a), "An Analytic Derivation of the Cost of Deposit Insurance and Loan Guarantees: An Application of Modern Option Pricing Theory," *Journal of Banking and Finance*, 1 (June): 3–11. Reprinted here as Chapter 19.

Merton, R.C. (1977b), "On the Pricing of Contingent Claims and the Modigliani–Miller Theorem," *Journal of Financial Economics*, 5 (November): 241–9. Reprinted here as Chapter 13.

Merton, R.C. (1977c), "A Reexamination of the Capital Asset Pricing Model," in Friend and Bicksler, eds (1977).

Merton, R.C. (1978), "On the Cost of Deposit Insurance When There are Surveillance Costs," *Journal of Business*, 51 (July): 439–52. Reprinted here as Chapter 20.

Merton, R.C. (1980), "On Estimating the Expected Return on the Market:

An Exploratory Investigation," *Journal of Financial Economics*, 8 (December): 323–61.

Merton, R.C. (1981), "On Market Timing and Investment Performance Part I: An Equilibrium Theory of Value for Market Forecasts," *Journal of Business*, 54 (July): 363–406.

Merton, R.C. (1982a), "On the Microeconomic Theory of Investment Under Uncertainty," in K.J. Arrow and M. Intriligator, eds, *Handbook of Mathematical Economics*, Vol. II, Amsterdam: North-Holland.

Merton, R.C. (1982b), "On the Mathematics and Economics Assumptions of Continuous-Time Models," in W.F. Sharpe and C.M. Cootner, eds, *Financial Economics: Essays in Honor of Paul Cootner*, Englewood Cliffs, NJ: Prentice-Hall. Reprinted here as Chapter 3.

Merton, R.C. (1983a), "Financial Economics," in E.C. Brown and R.M. Solow, eds, *Paul Samuelson and Modern Economic Theory*, New York: McGraw-Hill.

Merton, R.C. (1983b), "On Consumption-Indexed Public Pension Plans," in Z. Bodie and J. Shoven, eds, *Financial Aspects of the U.S. Pension System*, Chicago, IL: University of Chicago Press. Reprinted here as Chapter 18.

Merton, R.C. (1983c), "On the Role of Social Security as a Means for Efficient Risk-Bearing in an Economy Where Human Capital is Not Tradeable," in Z. Bodie and J. Shoven, eds, *Financial Aspects of the U.S. Pension System*, Chicago, IL: University of Chicago Press.

Merton, R.C. (1985), "Comment: Insurance Aspects of Pensions," in D.A. Wise, ed., *Pensions, Labor and Individual Choice*, Chicago, IL: University of Chicago Press.

Merton, R.C. (1987a), "A Simple Model of Capital Market Equilibrium with Incomplete Information," *Journal of Finance*, 42 (July): 483–510.

Merton, R.C. (1987b), "On the Current State of the Stock Market Rationality Hypothesis," in R. Dornbusch, S. Fischer, and J. Bossons, eds, *Macroeconomics and Finance: Essays in Honor of Franco Modigliani*, Cambridge, MA: MIT Press.

Merton, R.C. (1989), "On the Application of the Continuous-Time Theory of Finance to Financial Intermediation and Insurance," Twelfth Annual Lecture of the Geneva Association, *The Geneva Papers on Risk and Insurance*, 14 (July): 225–62.

Merton, R.C. (1990a), "Capital Market Theory and the Pricing of Financial Securities," in B. Friedman and F. Hahn, eds, *Handbook of Monetary Economics*, Amsterdam: North-Holland.

Merton, R.C. (1990b), "The Financial System and Economic Performance," *Journal of Financial Services Research*, 4 (December): 263–300.

Merton, R.C. (1992), "Optimal Investment Strategies for University Endowment Funds," in C.T. Clotfelter and M. Rothschild, eds, *The*

Economics of Higher Education, Chicago, IL: University of Chicago Press. Reprinted here as Chapter 21.

Merton, R.C., Z. Bodie, and A.J. Marcus (1987), "Pension Plan Integration as Insurance Against Social Security Risk," in Z. Bodie, J.B. Shoven, and D.A. Wise, eds, *Issues in Pension Economics*, Chicago, IL: University of Chicago Press.

Merton, R.C. and P.A. Samuelson (1974), "Fallacy of the Log-Normal Approximation to Optimal Portfolio Decision Making Over Many Periods," *Journal of Financial Economics*, 1 (May): 67–94. Reprinted in Friend and Bicksler, eds (1977).

Merton, R.C., M. Scholes, and M. Gladstein (1978), "The Returns and Risk of Alternative Call Option Portfolio Investment Strategies," *Journal of Business*, 51 (April): 183–242.

Merton, R.C., M. Scholes, and M. Gladstein (1982), "The Returns and Risks of Alternative Put-Option Portfolio Investment Strategies," *Journal of Business*, 55 (January): 1–55.

Merton, R.C. and M. Subrahmanyam (1974), "The Optimality of a Competitive Stock Market," *Bell Journal of Economics and Management Science*, 5 (Spring): 145–70.

Merton, R.K. (1948), "The Self-Fulfilling Prophecy," *Antioch Review* (Summer): 193–210.

Merton, R.K. (1957), *Social Theory and Social Structure*, Revised and Enlarged Edition, Glencoe, IL: The Free Press.

Meyer, R.F. (1970), "On the Relationship among the Utility of Assets, the Utility of Consumption, and Investment Strategy in an Uncertain, but Time-Invariant World," in J. Lawrence, ed., *OR69: Proceedings of the Fifth International Conference on Operational Research*, London: Tavistock Publications.

Miller, M.H. (1977), "Debt and Taxes," *Journal of Finance*, 32 (May): 261–76.

Miller, M.H. (1986), "Financial Innovation: The Last Twenty Years and The Next," *Journal of Financial and Quantitative Analysis*, 21 (December): 459–71.

Miller, M.H. and F. Modigliani (1961), "Dividend Policy, Growth, and the Valuation of Shares," *Journal of Business*, 34 (October): 411–33.

Mirman, L. (1973), "Steady State Behavior of One Class of One-Sector Growth Models with Uncertain Technology," *Journal of Economic Theory*, 6 (June): 219–42.

Mirrlees, J.A. (1965), "Optimal Accumulation Under Uncertainty," unpublished paper (December).

Mirrlees, J.A. (1971), "Optimum Growth and Uncertainty," IEA Workshop in Economic Theory, Bergen (July).

Mirrlees, J.A. (1974), "Optimal Accumulation Under Uncertainty: The Case of Stationary Returns to Investment" in J. Drèze, ed., *Allocation*

Under Uncertainty: Equilibrium and Optimality, New York, NY: John Wiley & Sons.

Modigliani, F. and R. Brumberg (1954), "Utility Analysis and the Consumption Function: An Interpretation of Cross-Section Data," in K. Kurihara, ed., *Post Keynesian Economics*, New Brunswick, NJ: Rutgers University Press.

Modigliani, F. and M.H. Miller (1958), "The Cost of Capital, Corporation Finance, and the Theory of Investment," *American Economic Review*, 48 (June): 261–97.

Modigliani, F. and C.R. Sutch (1966), "Innovations in Interest Rate Policy," *American Economic Review*, 56 (May): 178–97.

Mossin, J. (1966), "Equilibrium in a Capital Asset Market," *Econometrica*, 35 (October): 768–83.

Myers, S.C. (1977), "Determinants of Corporate Borrowing," *Journal of Financial Economics*, 5 (November): 147–75.

Myers, S.C. (1984), "Finance Theory and Financial Strategy," *Interfaces*, 14 (January–February): 126–37.

Myers, S.C. and S. Majd (1983), "Calculating Abandonment Value Using Option Pricing Theory," Working Paper No. 1462–83, A.P. Sloan School of Management, Massachusetts Institute of Technology, Cambridge, MA.

Nachman, D. (1988), "Spanning and Completeness With Options," *Review of Financial Studies*, 1 (Fall): 311–28.

Naik, V. and M. Lee (1990), "General Equilibrium Pricing of Options on the Market Portfolio With Discontinuous Returns," *Review of Financial Studies*, 3: 493–521.

Nelson, D. (1991), "Conditional Heteroskedasticity in Asset Returns: A New Approach," *Econometrica*, 59 (March): 347–70.

Nelson, D. and K. Ramaswamy (1990), "Simple Binomial Processes as Diffusion Approximations in Financial Models," *Review of Financial Studies*, 3: 393–430.

von Neumann, J. and O. Morgenstern (1947), *Theory of Games and Economic Behavior*, 2nd Edition, Princeton, NJ: Princeton University Press.

Nichols, D. (1974), "The Investment Income Formula of the American Economic Association," *American Economic Review*, 64 (May): 420–6.

Nielsen, L.T. (1986), "Mutual Fund Separation: Factor Structure and Robustness," Working Paper 86/87-2-3, Graduate School of Business, University of Texas at Austin, Austin, TX (September).

Nordhaus, W. (1989), "Risk Analysis in Economics: An Application to University Finances," unpublished paper, Cowles Foundation, Yale University, New Haven, CT (May).

Overdahl, J.A. (1988), "The Early Exercise of Options on Treasury Bond Futures," *Journal of Financial and Quantitative Analysis*, 23

(December): 437–49.

Paddock, J., D. Siegel, and J. Smith (1988), "Option Valuation of Claims on Real Assets: The Case of Offshore Petroleum Leases," *Quarterly Journal of Economics*, 103 (August): 479–508.

Pagès, H. (1987), "Optimal Consumption and Portfolio Policies When Markets are Incomplete," unpublished paper, Department of Economics, Massachusetts Institute of Technology, Cambridge, MA (February).

Pagès, H. (1989), *Three Essays in Optimum Consumption*, Ph.D. dissertation, Department of Economics, Massachusetts Institute of Technology, Cambridge, MA.

Parkinson, M. (1977), "Option Pricing: The American Put," *Journal of Business*, 50 (January): 21–36.

Pechman, J.A., ed. (1980), *What Should be Taxed: Income or Expenditure?* Studies of Government Finance, Washington, DC: Brookings Institution.

Penati, A. and G. Pennacchi (1989), "Optimal Portfolio Choice and the Collapse of a Fixed-Exchange Rate Regime," *Journal of International Economics*, 27 (August): 1–24.

Pennacchi, G. (1987a), "Alternative Forms of Deposit Insurance: Pricing and Bank Incentive Issues," *Journal of Banking and Finance*, 11 (June): 291–312.

Pennacchi, G. (1987b), "A Reexamination of the Over- (or Under-) Pricing of Deposit Insurance," *Journal of Money, Credit and Banking*, 19 (August): 340–60.

Perrakis, S. (1986), "Option Bounds in Discrete Time: Extensions and the Pricing of the American Put," *Journal of Business*, 59 (January): 119–41.

Perrakis, S. and P. Ryan (1984), "Option Pricing Bounds in Discrete Time," *Journal of Finance*, 39 (June): 519–27.

Phelps, E.S. (1962), "The Accumulation of Risky Capital: A Sequential Utility Analysis," *Econometrica*, 30 (October): 729–43.

Pindyck, R. (1988), "Irreversible Investment, Capacity Choice, and the Value of the Firm," *American Economic Review*, 78 (December): 969–85.

Pliska, S. (1986), "A Stochastic Calculus Model of Continuous Trading: Optimal Portfolios," *Mathematics of Operations Research*, 11 (May): 371–82.

Pratt, J.W. (1964), "Risk Aversion in the Small and in the Large," *Econometrica*, 32 (January): 122–36.

Press, J.S. (1967), "A Compound Events Model for Security Prices," *Journal of Business*, 40 (July): 317–35.

Radner, R. (1972), "Existence of Plans, Prices, and Price Expectations in a Sequence of Markets," *Econometrica*, 40 (March): 289–303.

Ramaswamy, K. and S. Sundaresan (1985), "The Valuation of Options on

Futures," *Journal of Finance*, 60 (December): 1319–39.

Ramaswamy, K. and S. Sundaresan (1986), "The Valuation of Floating Rate Instruments: Theory and Evidence," *Journal of Financial Economics*, 17 (December): 251–72.

Ramsey, F.P. (1928), "A Mathematical Theory of Saving," *Economic Journal*, 38 (December): 543–59.

Rendleman, R. and B. Bartter (1979), "Two-State Option Pricing," *Journal of Finance*, 34 (December): 1093–110.

Richard, S. (1975), "Optimal Consumption, Portfolio, and Life Insurance Rules for an Uncertain Lived Individual in a Continuous-Time Model," *Journal of Financial Economics*, 2 (June): 187–204.

Richard, S. (1977), "Optimal Impulse Control of a Diffusion Process with Both Fixed and Proportional Costs of Control," *SIAM Journal of Control and Optimization*, 15 (January): 79–91.

Richard, S. (1978), "An Arbitrage Model of the Term Structure of Interest Rates," *Journal of Financial Economics*, 6 (March): 33–57.

Richard, S. and M. Sundaresan (1981), "A Continuous-Time Equilibrium Model of Forward Prices and Futures Prices in a Multigood Economy," *Journal of Financial Economics*, 9 (December): 347–72.

Rie, D. (1972), "Single Parameter Risk Measures and Multiple Sources of Risk: A Re-Examination of the Data Based on Changes in Determinants of Price Over Time," Working Paper No. 14-72, Rodney L. White Center for Financial Research, Wharton School of Finance and Commerce, University of Pennsylvania, Philadelphia, PA.

Ritchken, P. (1985), "On Option Bounds," *Journal of Finance*, 40 (September): 1197–217.

Ritchken, P. (1987), *Options: Theory, Strategy, and Applications*, Glenview, IL: Scott, Foresman and Company.

Rogers, L. and D. Williams (1987), *Diffusions, Markov Processes, and Martingales*, Vol. 2, *Itô Processes*, New York: John Wiley & Sons.

Roll, R. (1973), "Evidence on the 'Growth-Optimum' Model," *Journal of Finance*, 28 (June): 551–66.

Roll, R. (1977), "An Analytic Valuation Formula for Unprotected American Call Options on Stocks With Known Dividends," *Journal of Financial Economics*, 5 (November): 251–8.

Roll, R. and S.A. Ross (1980), "An Empirical Investigation of the Arbitrage Pricing Theory," *Journal of Finance*, 35 (December): 1073–103.

Ronn, E.I. and A.K. Verma (1986), "Pricing Risk-Adjusted Deposit Insurance: An Option-Based Model," *Journal of Finance*, 41 (September): 871–95.

Rosenberg, B. (1972), "The Behavior of Random Variables With Nonstationary Variance and the Distribution of Security Prices," Working Paper No. 11, Graduate School of Business Administration,

University of California, Berkeley, CA (December).

Rosenberg, B. and J.A. Ohlson (1976), "The Stationary Distribution of Returns and Portfolio Separation in Capital Markets: A Fundamental Contradiction," *Journal of Financial and Quantitative Analysis*, 11 (September): 393–402.

Rosenfeld, E. (1980), *Stochastic Processes of Common Stock Returns: An Empirical Examination*, Ph.D. dissertation, A.P. Sloan School of Management, Massachusetts Institute of Technology, Cambridge, MA.

Ross, S.A. (1976a), "Arbitrage Theory of Capital Asset Pricing," *Journal of Economic Theory*, 13 (December): 341–60.

Ross, S.A. (1976b), "Options and Efficiency," *Quarterly Journal of Economics*, 90 (February): 75–89.

Ross, S.A. (1978), "Mutual Fund Separation in Financial Theory: The Separating Distributions," *Journal of Economic Theory*, 17 (April): 254–86.

Rothschild, M. (1986), "Asset Pricing Theories," in W.P. Heller, R.M. Starr, and D.A. Starrett, eds, *Uncertainty, Information and Communication: Essays in Honor of Kenneth J. Arrow*, Vol. III, Cambridge: Cambridge University Press.

Rothschild, M. and J.E. Stiglitz (1970), "Increasing Risk I: A Definition," *Journal of Economic Theory*, 2 (September): 225–43.

Rothschild, M. and J.E. Stiglitz (1971), "Increasing Risk II: Its Economic Consequences," *Journal of Economic Theory*, 3 (March): 66–84.

Rubinstein, M. (1985), "Alternative Paths to Portfolio Insurance," *Financial Analysts Journal*, 41 (July–August): 42–52.

Ryder, H.E. and G.M. Heal (1973), "Optimal Growth with Intertemporally Dependent Preferences," *Review of Economic Studies*, 40 (January): 1–31.

Sachdeva, K. (1986), "On the Equality of Two Lower Bounds on the Call Price: A Note," *Journal of Financial and Quantitative Analysis*, 21 (June): 235–7.

Samuelson, P.A. (1965a), "Rational Theory of Warrant Pricing," *Industrial Management Review*, 6 (Spring): 13–31. Reprinted in Samuelson (1972a).

Samuelson, P.A. (1965b), "Proof That Properly Anticipated Prices Fluctuate Randomly," *Industrial Management Review*, 6 (Spring): 41–9. Reprinted in Samuelson (1972a).

Samuelson, P.A. (1967a), "General Proof That Diversification Pays," *Journal of Financial and Quantitative Analysis*, 2 (March): 1–13. Reprinted in Samuelson (1972a).

Samuelson, P.A. (1967b), "Efficient Portfolio Selection for Pareto–Levy Investments," *Journal of Financial and Quantitative Analysis*, 2 (June): 107–22. Reprinted in Samuelson (1972a).

Samuelson, P.A. (1968), "Review of *Beat the Market*," *Journal of*

American Statistical Association, 63 (September): 1049–51.

Samuelson, P.A. (1969), "Lifetime Portfolio Selection by Dynamic Stochastic Programming," *Review of Economics and Statistics*, 51 (August): 239–46. Reprinted in Samuelson (1972a).

Samuelson, P.A. (1970), "The Fundamental Approximation Theory of Portfolio Analysis in Terms of Means, Variances, and Higher Moments," *Review of Economic Studies*, 37 (October): 537–42. Reprinted in Samuelson (1972a).

Samuelson, P.A. (1971), "The 'Fallacy' of Maximizing the Geometric Mean in Long Sequences of Investing or Gambling," *Proceedings of the National Academy of Sciences*, 68 (October): 2493–6. Reprinted in Samuelson (1972a).

Samuelson, P.A. (1972a), in R.C. Merton, ed., *The Collected Scientific Papers of Paul A. Samuelson*, Vol. III, Cambridge, MA: MIT Press.

Samuelson, P.A. (1972b), "Mathematics of Speculative Price," in R.H. Day and S.M. Robinson, eds, *Mathematical Topics in Economic Theory and Computation*, Philadelphia, PA: Society for Industrial and Applied Mathematics. Reprinted in *SIAM Review*, 15 (January 1973): 1–42.

Samuelson, P.A. (1973), "Proof That Properly Discounted Present Values of Assets Vibrate Randomly," *Bell Journal of Economics and Management Science*, 4 (Autumn): 369–74.

Samuelson, P.A. (1977), "St. Petersburg Paradoxes: Defanged, Dissected, and Historically Described," *Journal of Economic Literature*, 15 (March): 24–55.

Samuelson, P.A. (1989), "A Case at Last for Age-Phased Reduction in Equity," *Proceedings of the National Academy of Sciences*, 86 (November): 9048–51.

Samuelson, P.A. and R.C. Merton (1969), "A Complete Model of Warrant Pricing that Maximizes Utility," *Industrial Management Review*, 10 (Winter): 17–46. Reprinted in Samuelson (1972a) and here as Chapter 7.

Samuelson, P.A. and R.C. Merton (1974), "Generalized Mean-Variance Tradeoffs for Best Perturbation Corrections to Approximate Portfolio Decisions," *Journal of Finance*, 29 (March): 27–40.

Schaede, U. (1988), "Forwards and Futures in Tokugawa-Period Japan: A New Perspective on the Dōjima Rice Market," unpublished paper, Universitaet Marburg, Marburg, Germany (May).

Schaefer, S. and E. Schwartz (1987), "Time-Dependent Variance and the Pricing of Bond Options," *Journal of Finance*, 42 (December): 1113–28.

Schmalensee, R. and R. Trippi (1978), "Common Stock Volatility Expectations Implied by Option Premia," *Journal of Finance*, 33 (March): 129–47.

Scholes, M. (1971), "The Relationship between the Returns on Bonds and the Returns on Stocks," unpublished paper, Massachusetts Institute of

Technology, Cambridge, MA (November).

Scholes, M. (1976), "Taxes and the Pricing of Options," *Journal of Finance*, 31 (May): 319–32.

Schwartz, E. (1977), "The Valuation of Warrants: Implementing a New Approach," *Journal of Financial Economics*, 4 (January): 79–93.

Schwartz, E. (1982), "The Pricing of Commodity-Linked Bonds," *Journal of Finance*, 37 (May): 525–39.

Schwartz, E. and W.N. Torous (1989), "Prepayment and the Valuation of Mortgage-Backed Securities," *Journal of Finance*, 44 (June): 375–92.

Scott, L. (1987), "Option Pricing When the Variance Changes Randomly: Theory, Estimation, and Application," *Journal of Financial and Quantitative Analysis*, 22 (December): 419–38.

Selby, M.J.P., J.R. Franks, and J.P. Karki (1988), "Loan Guarantees, Wealth Transfers and Incentives to Invest," *Journal of Industrial Economics*, 37 (September): 47–65.

Selby, M.J.P. and S. Hodges (1987), "On the Evaluation of Compound Options," *Management Science*, 33 (March): 347–55.

Sethi, S.P. and J. Lehoczky (1981), "A Comparison of the Itô and Stratonovich Formulation of Problems in Finance," *Journal of Economic Dynamics and Control*, 3 (November): 343–56.

Sethi, S.P. and M. Taksar (1988), "A Note on Merton's 'Optimum Consumption and Portfolio Rules in a Continuous-Time Model,' " *Journal of Economic Theory*, 46 (December): 395–401.

Shanken, J. (1982), "The Arbitrage Pricing Theory: Is it Testable?" *Journal of Finance*, 37 (December): 1129–40.

Shanken, J. (1985), "Multi-Beta CAPM or Equilibrium APT? A Reply," *Journal of Finance*, 40 (September): 1189–96.

Sharpe, W.F. (1964), "Capital Asset Prices: A Theory of Market Equilibrium Under Conditions of Risk," *Journal of Finance*, 19 (September): 425–42.

Sharpe, W.F. (1970), *Portfolio Theory and Capital Markets*, New York: McGraw-Hill.

Sharpe, W.F. (1976), "Corporate Pension Funding Policy," *Journal of Financial Economics*, 3 (June): 183–93.

Sharpe, W.F. (1978), *Investments*, Englewood Cliffs, NJ: Prentice-Hall.

Shastri, K. and K. Tandon (1987), "Valuation of American Options on Foreign Currency," *Journal of Banking and Finance*, 11 (June): 245–69.

Slater, L.J. (1966), "Confluent Hypergeometric Functions," Chapter 13 in *Handbook of Mathematical Functions*, Applied Mathematics Series 55, National Bureau of Standards (August).

Smith, Jr, C.W. (1976), "Option Pricing: A Review," *Journal of Financial Economics*, 3 (January–March): 3–52.

Smith, Jr, C.W. (1979), "Applications of Option Pricing Analysis," in J.L. Bicksler, ed., *Handbook of Financial Economics*, Amsterdam: North-Holland.

Smith, G.D. (1978), *Numerical Solution of Partial Differential Equations: Finite Difference Methods*, Oxford: Clarendon Press.

Snyder, G.L. (1969), "Alternative Forms of Options," *Financial Analysts Journal*, 25 (September–October): 93–9.

Snyder, T. (1988), "Recent Trends in Higher Education Finance: 1976–77 to 1985–86," in T. Snyder and E. Galambos, eds., *Higher Education Administrative Costs: Continuing the Study*, Office of Educational Research and Improvement, Department of Education, Washington, D.C.

Solnik, B.H. (1973), *European Capital Markets*, Lexington, MA: Lexington Books.

Solnik, B.H. (1974), "An Equilibrium Model of the International Capital Market," *Journal of Economic Theory*, 8 (August): 500–24.

Solnik, B.H. (1989), "The Application of the Continuous-Time Theory of Finance to Swap Valuation," *Geneva Papers on Risk and Insurance*, 14 (July): 275–8.

Sosin, H. (1980), "On the Valuation of Federal Loan Guarantees to Corporations," *Journal of Finance*, 35 (December): 1209–21.

Spatt, C. and F. Sterbenz (1988), "Warrant Exercise, Dividends, and Reinvestment Policy," *Journal of Finance*, 43 (June): 493–506.

Sprenkle, C.M. (1961), "Warrant Prices as Indicators of Expectations and Preferences," *Yale Economic Essays*, 1: 172–231. Reprinted in Cootner, ed. (1964).

Stiglitz, J.E. (1969), "A Re-Examination of the Modigliani–Miller Theorem," *American Economic Review*, 59 (December): 78–93.

Stiglitz, J.E. (1970), "A Consumption-Oriented Theory of the Demand for Financial Assets and the Term Structure of Interest Rates," *Review of Economic Studies*, 37 (July): 321–51.

Stiglitz, J.E. (1972), "On Some Aspects of the Pure Theory of Corporate Finance: Bankruptcies and Take-overs," *Bell Journal of Economics and Management Science*, 2 (Autumn): 458–82.

Stiglitz, J.E. (1974), "On the Irrelevance of Corporate Financial Policy," *American Economic Review*, 64 (December): 851–86.

Stigum, B. (1972), "Balanced Growth Under Uncertainty," *Journal of Economic Theory*, 5 (August): 42–68.

Stoll, H.R. (1969), "The Relationship between Put and Call Option Prices," *Journal of Finance*, 24 (December): 802–24.

Stratonovich, R.L. (1968), *Conditional Markov Processes and Their Application to the Theory of Optimal Control*, New York: American Elsevier.

Stulz, R.M. (1981), "A Model of International Asset Pricing," *Journal of Financial Economics*, 9 (December): 382–406.

Stulz, R.M. (1982), "Options on the Minimum or the Maximum of Two Risky Assets: Analysis and Applications," *Journal of Financial Economics*, 10 (July): 161–85.

Stulz, R.M. (1984), "Currency Preferences, Purchasing Power Risk, and the Determination of Exchange Rates in an Optimizing Model," *Journal of Money, Credit, and Banking*, 16 (August): 302–16.

Stulz, R.M. and H. Johnson (1985), "An Analysis of Secured Debt," *Journal of Financial Economics*, 14 (December): 501–21.

Sun, T. (1987), "Transactions Costs and Intervals in a Discrete–Continuous Time Setting for Consumption and Portfolio Choice," Chapter 1 in *Connections Between Discrete-Time and Continuous-Time Financial Models*, Ph.D. dissertation, Graduate School of Business, Stanford University, Stanford, CA.

Sundaresan, S. (1984), "Consumption and Equilibrium Interest Rates in Stochastic Production Economies," *Journal of Finance*, 39 (March): 77–92.

Sundaresan, S. (1985), "Intertemporally Dependent Preferences in the Theories of Consumption, Portfolio Choice, and Equilibrium Asset Pricing," Working Paper, Graduate School of Business, Columbia University, New York.

Sundaresan, S. (1989), "Intertemporally Dependent Preferences and the Volatility of Consumption and Wealth," *Review of Financial Studies*, 2: 73–89.

Sundaresan, S. (1991), "Valuation of Swaps," in S. Khoury, ed., *Recent Developments in International Banking and Finance*, Amsterdam: North-Holland.

Svensson, L.E.O. (1988), "Portfolio Choice and Asset Pricing With Non-Traded Assets," Working Paper No. 2774, National Bureau of Economic Research, Cambridge, MA (November).

Svensson, L.E.O. (1989), "Portfolio Choice with Non-Expected Utility in Continuous Time," *Economics Letters*, 30 (October): 313–17.

Svensson, L.E.O. and I. Werner (1990), "Nontraded Assets in Incomplete Markets: Pricing and Portfolio Choice," Working Paper, Graduate School of Business, Stanford University, Stanford, CA.

Taksar, M., M.J. Klass, and D. Assaf (1988), "A Diffusion Model for Optimal Portfolio Selection in the Presence of Brokerage Fees," *Mathematics of Operations Research*, 13 (May): 277–94.

Thorp, E.O. (1973), "Extensions of the Black–Scholes Option Model," 39th Session of the International Statistical Institute, Vienna (August): 1029–36.

Thorp, E.O. and S.T. Kassouf (1967), *Beat the Market*, New York: Random House.

Tobin, J. (1958), "Liquidity Preference as Behavior Towards Risk," *Review of Economic Studies*, 25 (February): 68–85.

Tobin, J. (1965), "The Theory of Portfolio Selection," in F.B.R. Brechling and F.H. Hahn, eds, *The Theory of Interest Rates*, London: Macmillan.

Tobin, J. (1969), "Comment on Borch and Feldstein," *Review of*

Economic Studies, 36 (January): 13–14.

Tobin, J. (1974), "What is Permanent Endowment Income?" *American Economic Review*, 64 (May): 427–32.

Torous, W.N. (1985), "Differential Taxation and the Structure of Interest Rates," *Journal of Banking and Finance*, 9 (August): 363–85.

Triantis, A. and J. Hodder (1990), "Valuing Flexibility as a Complex Option," *Journal of Finance*, 45 (June): 549–65.

Trzcinka, C. (1986), "On the Number of Factors in the Arbitrage Pricing Model," *Journal of Finance*, 41 (June): 347–68.

Tufano, P. (1989), *Three Essays on Financial Innovation*, Ph.D. dissertation, Business Economics, Harvard University, Cambridge, MA.

Van Horne, J.C. (1969), "Warrant Valuation in Relation to Volatility and Opportunity Costs," *Industrial Management Review*, 10 (Spring): 17–32.

Vasicek, O. (1977), "An Equilibrium Characterization of the Term Structure," *Journal of Financial Economics*, 5 (November): 177–88.

de la Vega, J.P. (1688), *Confusión de Confusiones*, English translation by H. Kallenbenz (1957), No. 13, The Kress Library Series of Publications, The Kress Library of Business and Economics, Harvard University, Cambridge, MA.

Wallace, N. (1981), "A Modigliani–Miller Theorem for Open-Market Operations," *American Economic Review*, 71 (June): 267–74.

Welles, C. (1971), "The Beta Revolution: Learning to Live With Risk," *Institutional Investor*.

Whaley, R. (1979), "A Note on an Analytical Formula for Unprotected American Call Options on Stocks with Known Dividends," *Journal of Financial Economics*, 7 (October): 375–80.

Whaley, R. (1981), "On the Valuation of American Call Options on Stocks with Known Dividends," *Journal of Financial Economics*, 9 (June): 207–12.

Whaley, R. (1986), "Valuation of American Futures Options: Theory and Empirical Tests," *Journal of Finance*, 41 (March): 127–50.

Wiggins, J.B. (1987), "Option Values Under Stochastic Volatility: Theory and Empirical Estimates," *Journal of Financial Economics*, 19 (December): 351–72.

Williams, J.T. (1977), "Capital Asset Prices with Heterogeneous Beliefs," *Journal of Financial Economics*, 5 (November): 219–39.

Williams, J.T. (1979), "Uncertainty and the Accumulation of Human Capital Over the Life Cycle," *Journal of Business*, 52 (October): 521–48.

Williamson, O.E. (1988), "Corporate Finance and Corporate Governance," *Journal of Finance*, 43 (July): 567–91.

Willinger, W. and M. Taqqu (1991), "Toward a Convergence Theory for Continuous Stochastic Securities Market Models," *Mathematical Finance*, 1 (January): 55–99.

Author Index

Subject Index